T5-CPZ-146

ANTARCTIC ECOLOGY
VOLUME 1

ANTARCTIC ECOLOGY

Edited by

M. W. HOLDGATE

The Nature Conservancy
London, England

VOLUME 1

Published for THE SCIENTIFIC COMMITTEE ON ANTARCTIC RESEARCH *by*

1970 ACADEMIC PRESS
LONDON AND NEW YORK

ACADEMIC PRESS INC. (LONDON) LTD
BERKELEY SQUARE HOUSE
BERKELEY SQUARE
LONDON, W1X 6BA

U.S. Edition published by
ACADEMIC PRESS INC.
111 FIFTH AVENUE
NEW YORK, NEW YORK 10003

Library of Congress Catalog Card Number: 70-92399
SBN 12-352101-7

PRINTED IN GREAT BRITAIN BY
W & J MACKAY & CO LTD, CHATHAM, KENT

List of Contributors

R. J. ADIE, *Department of Geology, The University, Edgbaston, Birmingham, England.*

ANELIO AGUAYO L., *Marine Biological Station, University of Chile, Vina del Mar, Chile.*

VERNON AHMADJIAN, *Department of Botany, University of Massachusetts, Amherst, Massachusetts, U.S.A.*

S. E. ALLEN, *The Nature Conservancy, Merlewood Research Station, Grange-over-Sands, Lancashire, England.*

A. P. ANDRIASHEV, *Zoological Institute, U.S.S.R. Academy of Sciences, Leningrad, U.S.S.R.*

P. M. ARNAUD, *Station Marine d'Endome, Marseille, France.*

D. H. ASHTON, *Antarctic Division, Department of External Affairs and Botany School, University of Melbourne, Melbourne, Australia.*

J. H. BAKER, *Department of Botany, University College, London, England.*

E. BALECH, *Estación Hidrobiológica de Puerto Quequén, Necochea, Argentina.*

J. R. BECK, *British Antarctic Survey Biological Unit, Monks Wood Experimental Station, Abbots Ripton, Huntingdon, England.*

N. V. BELYAEVA, *Institute of Oceanology, U.S.S.R. Academy of Sciences, Moscow, U.S.S.R.*

R. E. BENOIT, *Department of Biology, Virginia Polytechnic Institute, Blacksburg, Virginia, U.S.A.*

L. BRUNDIN, *Swedish Museum of Natural History, Stockholm, Sweden.*

R. W. BURTON, *Weston House, Albury, Surrey, England.*

R. E. CAMERON, *Bioscience Section, Jet Propulsion Laboratory, California Institute of Technology, Pasadena, California, U.S.A.*

ROBERT CARRICK, *Mawson Institute for Antarctic Research, University of Adelaide, South Australia.*

J. CASTILLO, *Departmento de Zoology, Universidad de Concepcion, Concepcion, Chile.*

D. R. CLINE, *Department of Ecology and Behavioral Biology, University of Minnesota, Minneapolis, Minnesota, U.S.A.*

A. C. CUELLO, *Instituto de Neurobiologia and Instituto Antartico Argentino, Buenos Aires, Argentina.*

C. N. DAVID, *Bioscience Section, Jet Propulsion Laboratory, California Institute of Technology, Pasadena, California, U.S.A.*

P. K. DAYTON, *Department of Zoology, University of Washington, Seattle, Washington U.S.A.*

R. DELEPINE, *Laboratoire de Biologie Végétale Marine, Paris 5, France.*
A. L. DEVRIES, *Department of Food Science and Technology, University of California at Davis, Davis, California, U.S.A.*
H. H. DEWITT, *Darling Center for Research, University of Maine, Walpole, Maine, U.S.A.*
C. M. DRABEK, *Department of Zoology, University of Arizona, Tucson, Arizona, U.S.A.*
M. J. DUNBAR, *McGill University, Montreal, Canada.*
S. Z. EL-SAYED, *Department of Oceanography, Texas A & M University, College Station, Texas, U.S.A.*
R. ELSNER, *Department of Human Physiology, University of Adelaide, South Australia.*
A. W. ERICKSON, *Department of Ecology and Behavioral Biology, University of Minnesota, Minneapolis, Minnesota, U.S.A.*
INIGO EVERSON, *British Antarctic Survey Biological Unit, Monks Wood Experimental Station, Abbots Ripton, Huntingdon, England.*
R. E. FEENEY, *College of Agricultural and Environmental Sciences, University of California, Davis, California, U.S.A.*
G. E. FOGG, *Department of Botany, Westfield College, London, England.*
HIROSHI FUKUSHIMA, *Biological Institute, Yokohama City University, Yokohama, Japan.*
V. A. GALLARDO, *Departmento de Zoology, Universidad de Concepcion, Concepcion, Chile.*
C. H. GIMINGHAM, *Department of Botany, University of Aberdeen, Aberdeen, Scotland.*
CHARLES R. GOLDMAN, *Institute of Ecology, University of California, Davis, California, U.S.A.*
S. W. GREENE, *Department of Botany, University of Birmingham, Birmingham, England.*
E. N. GRUZOV, *Zoological Institute, Academy of Sciences, Leningrad, U.S.S.R.*
J. A. GULLAND, *Fisheries Department, F.A.O., Rome, Italy.*
ERNEST T. HAJEK, *Universidad de Chile, Santiago, Chile.*
C. L. HALL, JR., *Virginia Polytechnic Institute, Blacksburg, Virginia, U.S.A.*
J. D. HAYS, *Lamont-Doherty Geological Observatory of Columbia University, Palisades, New York, U.S.A.*
O. W. HEAL, *The Nature Conservancy, Merlewood Research Station, Grange-over-Sands, Lancashire, England.*
JOEL W. HEDGPETH, *Department of Oceanography, Oregon State University, Corvallis, Oregon, U.S.A.*
WLADIMIR HERMOSILLA, *Universidad de Chile, Santiago, Chile.*
R. B. HEYWOOD, *British Antarctic Survey Biological Unit, Monks Wood Experimental Station, Abbots Ripton, Huntingdon, England.*

M. W. HOLDGATE, *The Nature Conservancy, London, England.*

J. T. HOLLIN, *The Royal Geographical Society, London, England.*

A. J. HORNE, *Department of Biological Sciences, University of Dundee, Dundee, Scotland.*

SUSAN E. INGHAM, *Mawson Institute for Antarctic Research, University of Adelaide, South Australia.*

L. IRVING, *Institute of Arctic Biology, University of Alaska, College, Alaska.*

HEINZ JANETSCHEK, *Institut für Zoologie, Universität, Innsbruck, Austria.*

J. F. JENKIN, *Antarctic Division, Department of External Affairs and Botany School, University of Melbourne, Melbourne, Australia.*

J. KALFF, *Department of Zoology, McGill University, Montreal, Canada.*

J. KING, *Bioscience Section, Jet Propulsion Laboratory, California Institute of Technology, Pasadena, California, U.S.A.*

G. A. KNOX, *Zoology Department, University of Canterbury, Christchurch, New Zealand.*

G. L. KOOYMAN, *Scripps Institution of Oceanography, University of California, La Jolla, California, U.S.A.*

O. G. KOZLOVA, *Institute of Oceanology, Academy of Sciences, Moscow, U.S.S.R.*

C. LENFANT, *Department of Medicine, University of Washington, Seattle, Washington, U.S.A.*

ROBERT E. LERESCHE, *Department of Pathobiology, JohnsHopkins University, Baltimore, Maryland, U.S.A.*

M. C. LEWIS, *Department of Botany, University of Birmingham, Birmingham, England.*

R. I. LEWIS SMITH, *British Antarctic Survey, Department of Botany, University of Aberdeen, Aberdeen, Scotland.*

R. E. LONGTON, *Department of Botany, University of Winnipeg, Winnipeg, Manitoba, Canada.*

I. MACKENZIE LAMB, *Farlow Herbanium, Harvard University, Cambridge, Massachusetts, U.S.A.*

N. A. MACKINTOSH, *Natural Environment Research Council, Whale Research Unit, British Museum (Natural History), London, England.*

R. R. MAKAROV, *Department of Fisheries and Oceanography, Moscow, U.S.S.R.*

A. W. MANSFIELD, *Fisheries Research Board of Canada, Arctic Biological Station, St. Anne De Bellevue, Quebec, Canada.*

P. A. MOISEEV, *Institute of Fisheries and Oceanography, Moscow, U.S.S.R.*

R. W. MORRIS, *University of Oregon, Eugene, Oregon, U.S.A.*

A. G. NAUMOV, *Department of Fisheries and Oceanography, Moscow, U.S.S.R.*

MAGNAR NORDERHAUG, *Norsk Polarinstitutt, Oslo, Norway.*

NILS ARE ØRITSLAND, *Institute of Zoophysiology, University of Oslo, Oslo, Norway.*

TORGER ØRITSLAND, *Institute of Marine Research, Directorate of Fisheries, Bergen, Norway.*

R. T. PAINE, *Department of Zoology, University of Washington, Seattle, Washington, 98105, U.S.A.*

YU. E. PERMITIN, *V.N.I.R.O. All-Union Research Institute of Marine Fisheries and Oceanography, Moscow, U.S.S.R.*

M. V. PROPP, *Murmansk Marine Biological Institute, U.S.S.R. Academy of Sciences, Moscow, U.S.S.R.*

A. F. PUSHKIN, *Murmansk Marine Biological Institute, Academy of Sciences, Murmansk, U.S.S.R.*

R. RALPH, *Department of Zoology, University of Aberdeen, Aberdeen, Scotland.*

CARLTON RAY, *Department of Pathobiology, School of Hygiene and Public Health, Johns Hopkins University, Baltimore, Maryland, U.S.A.*

G. A. ROBILLIARD, *Department of Zoology, University of Washington, Seattle, Washington, 98105, U.S.A.*

EMANUEL D. RUDOLPH, *College of Biological Sciences and Institute of Polar Studies, The Ohio State University, Columbus, Ohio, U.S.A.*

F. SAIZ, *Universidad de Chile, Santiago, Chile.*

V. V. SHEVTSOV, *Department of Fisheries and Oceanography, Moscow, U.S.S.R.*

J. SHIMOIZUMI, *Society of Biological Science Education, Tokyo, Japan.*

D. B. SINIFF, *Department of Ecology and Behavioral Biology, University of Minnesota, Minneapolis, Minnesota, U.S.A.*

WILLIAM J. L. SLADEN, *Department of Pathobiology, Johns Hopkins University, Baltimore, Maryland, U.S.A.*

E. A. SMITH, *British Antarctic Survey Biological Unit, Monks Wood Experimental Station, Abbots Ripton, Huntingdon, England.*

R. N. SMITH, *British Antarctic Survey Biological Unit, Monks Wood Experimental Station, Abbots Ripton, Huntingdon, England.*

B. STONEHOUSE, *Department of Zoology, The University of British Columbia, Vancouver, B.C., Canada.*

M. H. THURSTON, *National Institute of Oceanography, Wormley, Surrey, England.*

W. L. N. TICKELL, *Department of Zoology, Makerere University College, Kampala, Uganda.*

P. J. TILBROOK, *British Antarctic Survey Biological Unit, Monks Wood Experimental Station, Abbots Ripton, Huntingdon, England.*

F. C. UGOLINI, *University of Washington, Seattle, Washington, U.S.A.*

E. M. van Zinderen Bakker, *Department of Botany, University of the Orange Free State, Bloemfontein, South Africa.*

N. M. Voronina, *Shivshov Institute of Oceanology, Academy of Sciences, Moscow, U.S.S.R.*

M. G. White, *British Antarctic Survey Biological Unit, Monks Wood Experimental Station, Abbots Ripton, Huntingdon, England.*

A. T. Wilson, *Victoria University of Wellington, Wellington, New Zealand.*

G. S. Wilson, *British Antarctic Survey Biological Unit, Monks Wood Experimental Station, Abbots Ripton, Huntingdon, England.*

E. C. Young, *Department of Zoology, University of Canterbury, Christchurch, New Zealand.*

B. A. Zenkovich, *V.N.I.R.O. All-Union Research Institute of Marine Fisheries and Oceanography, Moscow, U.S.S.R.*

V. V. Zernova, *Institute of Oceanology, Academy of Sciences, Moscow, U.S.S.R.*

Preface

The Scientific Committee on Antarctic Research (SCAR) is a Scientific Committee of ICSU charged with furthering the co-ordination of scientific activity in Antarctica, with a view to framing a scientific programme of circumpolar scope and significance. As such, it is concerned with the exchange of scientific information about research plans and results among the nations who have worked actively in Antarctica in recent years. SCAR conducts much of its business through Working Groups, which suggest priorities for research in their special disciplines and organize symposia to discuss recent progress. This volume arises from the second Symposium organized by the Working Group on Biology.

At the first Symposium, held in Paris in 1962, scientists delivered papers that spanned almost the whole field of biology, from microbiology through plant and animal biogeography, ecology and physiology to human physiology and psychology. The resulting volume, while rich in information, lacked any clearly defined theme. Moreover, in 1962, many biological disciplines had had a short history in Antarctica and preliminary descriptive survey work was still going on. Generalizations about the flora and fauna of the region and their adaptive physiology were hardly possible. In the six years that elapsed between that symposium and the second, held in Cambridge in 1968, there was both a broadening and deepening of the research effort. Increasingly sophisticated laboratory facilities were provided, and more specialized ecological, ethological and physiological research became possible. Overland traverses and airborne reconnaissance yielded a picture of the topography of the continent and of the disposition of its ice mantle which, if not fully complete, contained no major gaps. Conservation measures, drafted in the first instance by the SCAR Working Group on Biology, gained international acceptance among the signatory powers of the Antarctic Treaty. The Working Group itself grew in cohesion and effectiveness.

When the time came to plan the second symposium, therefore, the Working Group decided that there should be a major theme, and Antarctic Ecology was chosen. This choice recognized that, now that the species of plant and animal present in Antarctica were broadly known, the greatest interest among biologists was becoming concentrated on the relationships between this biota and the rigorous polar environment. The adaptations of species and ecosystems to an area of extreme cold, and to the long polar winter darkness which imposes a seasonal regime upon photosynthesis, were becoming central in Antarctic biological research. At the same time, influenced by the International Biological Programme, many biologists had turned to the study of productivity: of the rates and methods by which living organisms fix and use solar energy, and transfer this energy from one to another along food chains. Finally, mounting demands for protein food were turning the attention of both scientists and technologists to the productive Antarctic seas, with their high standing crops of krill, and potential economic importance. All these developments made "ecology" the proper theme for the occasion.

Between 29 July and 3 August 1968, twenty-five review papers and fifty-eight supporting papers were delivered by scientists from eleven of the twelve SCAR nations and from Canada and Sweden. The review papers were by acknowledged authorities selected by the Symposium Organizing Committee: the supporting papers were chosen from those offered by National Committees. It is a commentary on the healthy state of Antarctic biological research that the number of papers could readily have been doubled: many National Committees had a difficult task of screening before they made any nominations at all, and the international organizing committee then had the thankless task of reducing the number still further. Not all the papers delivered have been included in these volumes. The initial session of the symposium was devoted to a review of the history of Antarctic biological research and of the efforts of the SCAR nations in recent years. These are, to a considerable degree, matters of domestic interest and the papers delivered have consequently been reprinted in SCAR's own information sheet, the SCAR Bulletin. No attempt was made to repeat the admirable historical summaries provided to the first symposium by N. A. Mackintosh and by R. Garrick and S. E. Ingham, which may be found in the proceedings of that meeting. Similarly, a session of the Symposium devoted to the discussion of new techniques, attracted papers of great value, but it is in the nature of things that the new techniques of today are the commonplace methods of tomorrow and for this reason this more transient material has been excluded from the volumes. What is left is a series of reviews and research papers on scientific themes within, or relevant to, the broad field of ecology.

In several sessions, papers on Arctic ecological situations have been included for comparison, and they provide a salutary reminder that the Southern Hemisphere has no monopoly of high-polar situations. Indeed, because of the contrasts as well as the similarities between the two extremes of the world which support floras and faunas very different in composition and history, comparative research may be of increasing value to the interpretation of results.

The order of presentation of the papers has also been changed. At the Symposium, attention was first devoted to the land ecosystem, and then successively to freshwater and sea. In these volumes the order is reversed. After a brief consideration of past environments and biotas, the sequence runs through marine plankton and its pelagic consumers, marine benthos, fishes, seals and sea-birds. Broadly, this sequence parallels the major food chains in the Antarctic Ocean, and emphasizes the place of phytoplankton and krill at the heart of the total ecosystem. In the Antarctic, the productive ocean rings a cold desert, and much of the nutrients available to the land and freshwater ecosystems are derived from the sea via seabirds and seals which resort to the land to breed or moult. The discussion of freshwaters, and of terrestrial soils, vegetation and fauna thus follows logically in Volume II, which concludes with a review of conservation.

One of the major aims of a Symposium is the exchange of ideas in free discussion, and this is particularly valuable when, as in the present case, much of the information is new and participants come from widely separated lands and rarely meet. Not all the comments made in these discussions have been published in this book, but an attempt has been made to record those that contain new information or modify the conclusions of the main papers. For convenience (it is hoped!) these discussion records have been collected at the end of each series of papers treating a particular theme, and they have been further subdivided by subject. As a further aid to the reader not familiar with literature on Antarctic biology, brief introductory notes have been placed at the start of each main group of papers, referring in particular to major sources of further information or summarizing fields not fully treated in the contributions that follow.

As organizer of the Symposium, Editor of these volumes, and Secretary of the SCAR Working Group on Biology between 1964 and 1968, I have drawn heavily on the support of many colleagues. I would like to take this opportunity of thanking the Secretary of SCAR, Dr G. de Q. Robin, my fellow members of the Working Group and the Symposium Planning Committee, and all those specialists I have consulted from time to time, for their very great assistance. The Symposium was successful because of the hard work and help of the staff of the Scott Polar Research Institute, where the Secretariat of SCAR is based. In particular, I would like to record my debt, and that of all other participants, to Mrs Maralyn Calder, who made most of the day-to-day arrangements for the meeting, and has undertaken the typing and correspondence during the preparation of these volumes.

M. W. Holdgate

October 1969

Contents

List of Contributors v

Preface xi

Part I. Past Environments

INTRODUCTION 3
PAST ENVIRONMENTS AND CLIMATES OF ANTARCTICA 7
Raymond J. Adie
ANTARCTIC GLACIOLOGY, GLACIAL HISTORY AND ECOLOGY 15
John T. Hollin
THE CLIMATIC RECORD OF ANTARCTIC OCEAN SEDIMENTS 20
James D. Hays
THE MCMURDO DRY VALLEYS 21
A. T. Wilson
QUATERNARY CLIMATES AND ANTARCTIC BIOGEOGRAPHY 31
E. M. Van Zinderen Bakker
ANTARCTIC LAND FAUNAS AND THEIR HISTORY 41
Lars Brundin
DISCUSSION 54

Part II. Marine Ecosystems

INTRODUCTION 67
ANTARCTIC MARINE ECOSYSTEMS 69
G. A. Knox
MARINE BIOGEOGRAPHY OF THE ANTARCTIC REGIONS 97
Joel W. Hedgpeth
ECOSYSTEM ADAPTATION IN MARINE POLAR ENVIRONMENTS 105
M. J. Dunbar
DISCUSSION 112

Part III. Plankton and its Pelagic Consumers

INTRODUCTION 117
ON THE PRODUCTIVITY OF THE SOUTHERN OCEAN 119
Sayed Z. El-Sayed . .
PHYTOPLANKTON OF THE SOUTHERN OCEAN 136
V. V. Zernova
THE DISTRIBUTION AND ENDEMISM OF SOME ANTARCTIC MICROPLANKTERS . 143
E. Balech
DIATOMS IN SUSPENSION AND IN BOTTOM SEDIMENTS IN THE SOUTHERN INDIAN AND PACIFIC OCEANS 148
O. G. Kozlova
REGULARITIES IN THE DISTRIBUTION OF PLANKTONIC FORAMINIFERA IN THE WATER AND SEDIMENTS OF THE SOUTHERN OCEAN 154
N. V. Belyaeva

Seasonal Cycles of Some Common Antarctic Copepod Species . . . 162
N. M. Voronina
The Biology and the Distribution of the Antarctic Krill . . . 173
R. R. Makarov, A. G. Naumov and V. V. Shevtsov
The Consumption of Krill by Antarctic Fishes 177
Yu. E. Permitin
Whales and Plankton in Antarctic Waters 183
B. A. Zenkovich
Discussion 186

Part IV. The Pelagic Resources of the Southern Ocean

Introduction 193
Whales and Krill in the Twentieth Century 195
N. A. Mackintosh
Some Aspects of the Commercial use of the Krill Resources of the Antarctic Seas 213
P. A. Moiseev
The Development of the Resources of the Antarctic Seas . . . 217
J. A. Gulland
Discussion 224

Part V. Marine Benthos

Introduction 233
Bottom Communities of the Upper Sublittoral of Enderby Land and the South Shetland Islands 235
E. N. Gruzov and A. F. Pushkin
The Study of Bottom Fauna at Haswell Islands by SCUBA Diving . 239
M. V. Propp
Quantitative Observations on the Benthic Macrofauna of Port Foster (Deception Island) and Chile Bay (Greenwich Island) 242
V. A. Gallardo and J. Castillo
Benthic Faunal Zonation as a Result of Anchor Ice at McMurdo Sound, Antarctica 244
Paul K. Dayton, Gordon A. Robilliard and R. T. Paine
Frequency and Ecological Significance of Necrophagy among the Benthic Species of Antarctic Coastal Waters 259
Patrick M. Arnaud
Vertical Zonation of Marine Vegetation in the Antarctic . . . 268
R. Delepine, I. Mackenzie Lamb and M. H. Zimmerman
Growth in *Bovallia gigantea* Pfeffer (Crustacea: Amphipoda) . . . 269
Michael H. Thurston
Aspects of the Breeding Biology of *Glyptonotus antarcticus* (Eights) (Crustacea, Isopoda) at Signy Island, South Orkney Islands . 279
Martin G. White
Discussion 286

Part VI. Fishes

Introduction 295

CRYOPELAGIC FISHES OF THE ARCTIC AND ANTARCTIC AND THEIR SIGNIFICANCE IN POLAR ECOSYSTEMS 297
A. P. Andriashev
THE CHARACTER OF THE MIDWATER FISH FAUNA OF THE ROSS SEA, ANTARCTICA 305
Hugh H. Dewitt
RESPIRATORY METABOLISM OF *Chaenocephalus aceratus* 315
Inigo Everson and R. Ralph
FREEZING RESISTANCE IN ANTARCTIC FISHES 320
Arthur L. Devries
THE BIOCHEMISTRY OF FREEZING RESISTANCE OF SOME ANTARCTIC FISH . 329
R. N. Smith
THERMOGENESIS AND ITS POSSIBLE SURVIVAL VALUE IN FISHES 337
Robert W. Morris
BIOCHEMISTRY OF PROTEINS AND ENZYMES OF ANTARCTIC FISH . . . 344
Robert E. Feeney
DISCUSSION 352

Part VII. The Biology of Seals

INTRODUCTION 359
BIOLOGY AND POPULATION DYNAMICS OF ANTARCTIC SEALS 361
Torger Øritsland
SEALING AND SEAL RESEARCH IN THE SOUTH-WEST ATLANTIC PACK ICE, SEPT.-OCT. 1964 367
T. Øritsland
POPULATION DENSITIES OF SEALS IN THE WEDDELL SEA, ANTARCTICA, IN 1968 377
D. B. Siniff, D. R. Cline and A. W. Erickson
CENSUS OF PINNIPEDIA IN THE SOUTH SHETLAND ISLANDS 395
Anelio Aguayo L.
POPULATION ECOLOGY OF ANTARCTIC SEALS 398
Carleton Ray
WEDDELL SEALS OF SIGNY ISLAND 415
E. A. Smith and R. W. Burton
POPULATION DYNAMICS AND EXPLOITATION OF SOME ARCTIC SEALS . . 429
A. W. Mansfield
DISCUSSION 447

Part VIII. Adaptation in Seals

INTRODUCTION 453
MORPHO-PHYSIOLOGICAL ADAPTATIONS IN MARINE MAMMALS FOR LIFE IN POLAR AREAS 455
Laurence Irving
ENERGETIC SIGNIFICANCE OF ABSORPTION OF SOLAR RADIATION IN POLAR HOMEOTHERMS 464
Nils Are Øritsland
TOLERANCE TO SUSTAINED HYPOXIA IN THE WEDDELL SEAL, *Leptonychotes Weddelli* 471
C. Lenfant, R. Elsner, G. L. Kooyman and C. M. Drabek
DIVING DURATION IN PREGNANT WEDDELL SEALS 477
Robert Elsner, Gerald L. Kooyman and Charles M. Drabek

THE GLANDULAR PATTERN OF THE EPIPHYSIS CEREBRI OF THE WEDDELL SEAL 483
Augusto Claudio Cuello
VISION OF THE WEDDELL SEAL (*Leptonychotes Weddelli*) 490
G. S. Wilson
DISCUSSION 495

Part IX. Ecology of Antarctic Birds

INTRODUCTION 503
ECOLOGY AND POPULATION DYNAMICS OF ANTARCTIC SEA BIRDS . . 505
Robert Carrick and Susan E. Ingham
ADAPTATION IN POLAR AND SUBPOLAR PENGUINS (*Spheniscidae*) . . 526
B. Stonehouse
BREEDING SEASONS AND MOULT IN SOME SMALLER ANTARCTIC PETRELS . 542
J. R. Beck
BIENNIAL BREEDING IN ALBATROSSES 551
W. L. N. Tickell
THE ROLE OF THE LITTLE AUK, *Plautus alle* (L.), IN ARCTIC ECOSYSTEMS . 558
Magnar Norderhaug
BIOLOGY OF THE GREAT SKUA 561
R. W. Burton
THE TECHNIQUES OF A SKUA—PENGUIN STUDY 568
E. C. Young
NEW AND DEVELOPING TECHNIQUES IN ANTARCTIC ORNITHOLOGY . . 585
William J. L. Sladen and Robert E. Leresche
DISCUSSION 597

Contents of Volume 2

Part X. Freshwater Ecosystems

INTRODUCTION 607
ANTARCTIC FRESHWATER ECOSYSTEMS 609
Charles R. Goldman
NOTES ON THE DIATOM FLORA OF ANTARCTIC INLAND WATERS 628
Hiroshi Fukushima
THE PHYSIOLOGY OF ANTARCTIC FRESHWATER ALGAE 632
G. E. Fogg and A. J. Horne
THE MOUTHPARTS AND FEEDING HABITS OF *Parabroteas sarsi* (DADAY) AND *Pseudoboeckella silvestri*, DADAY (COPEPODA, CALANOIDA) 639
Ronald B. Heywood
ARCTIC LAKE ECOSYSTEMS 651
J. Kalff
DISCUSSION 664

Part XI. Soils

INTRODUCTION 671
ANTARCTIC SOILS AND THEIR ECOLOGY 673
F. C. Ugolini
SOILS OF THE MARITIME ANTARCTIC ZONE 693
S. E. Allen and O. W. Heal
THE MICROBIOLOGY OF SOME DRY VALLEY SOILS OF VICTORIA LAND, ANTARCTICA 697
R. E. Benoit and C. L. Hall, Jr.
MICROBIOLOGY, ECOLOGY AND MICROCLIMATOLOGY OF SOIL SITES IN DRY VALLEYS OF SOUTHERN VICTORIA LAND, ANTARCTICA 702
R. E. Cameron, J. King and C. N. David
YEASTS, MOULDS AND BACTERIA FROM AN ACID PEAT ON SIGNY ISLAND . 717
J. H. Baker
DISCUSSION 723

Part XII. Vegetation

INTRODUCTION 729
ANTARCTIC TERRESTRIAL PLANTS AND THEIR ECOLOGY 733
I. Mackenzie Lamb
BRYOPHYTE AND LICHEN COMMUNITIES IN THE MARITIME ANTARCTIC . 752
C. H. Gimingham and R. I. Lewis Smith
THE EFFECTS OF CLIMATE ON ANTARCTIC PLANTS 786
S. W. Greene and R. E. Longton
ADAPTATIONS OF ANTARCTIC TERRESTRIAL PLANTS 801
Vernon Ahmadjian
LOCAL DISSEMINATION OF PLANT PROPAGULES IN ANTARCTICA 812
E. D. Rudolph

GROWTH AND PRODUCTIVITY OF THE MOSS *Polytrichum alpestre* HOPPE IN ANTARCTIC REGIONS 818
R. E. Longton
A COMPARISON OF PLANT GROWTH AT AN ARCTIC AND ANTARCTIC STATION . 838
M. C. Lewis and S. W. Greene
PRODUCTIVITY STUDIES ON MACQUARIE ISLAND VEGETATION 851
J. F. Jenkin and D. H. Ashton
DISCUSSION 864

Part XIII. Terrestrial Fauna

INTRODUCTION 869
ENVIRONMENTS AND ECOLOGY OF TERRESTRIAL ARTHROPODS IN THE HIGH ANTARCTIC 871
Heinz Janetschek
THE TERRESTRIAL ENVIRONMENT AND INVERTEBRATE FAUNA OF THE MARITIME ANTARCTIC 886
P. J. Tilbrook
THE COLONIZATION OF INTRODUCED LITTER BY SUBANTARCTIC SOIL AND MOSS ARTHROPODS 897
Francisco Sáiz, Ernst T. Hajek and Wladimir Hermosilla
THE BIOLOGY OF *Cryptopygus antarcticus* 908
P. J. Tilbrook
DISCUSSION 919

Part XIV. Conservation

INTRODUCTION 923
CONSERVATION IN THE ANTARCTIC 924
M. W. Holdgate
CONSERVATION AROUND SHOWA BASE 946
J. Shimoizumi
DISCUSSION 949

Author Index 955

Subject Index 969

Part I

PAST ENVIRONMENTS

Past Environments

There are senses in which Antarctica resembles an oceanic island. The present continent is a land mass lying at the hub of the Southern Hemisphere and isolated by a band of ocean nowhere less than 500 miles (800 km) wide. If, therefore, the ice sheets at the maximum of the Quaternary glaciation overrode the entire land surface and eliminated the terrestrial flora and fauna from the continent and its fringing archipelagos the present terrestrial Antarctic biota would of necessity have had to be derived from postglacial transoceanic dispersal. Conversely, if refugia persisted throughout the Quaternary, the present scanty fauna and flora of the continent could contain species with a far longer Antarctic history and, hypothetically, more perfected adaptive systems. Reaching back further in time, the environmental conditions that prevailed in Antarctica through the Tertiary and earlier periods, and the past spatial relationships between Antarctica and the other continents must clearly be considered if the origins of the present biota are to be interpreted properly. The study of past environments in Antarctica is thus of evident significance for the ecologist and biogeographer.

In the first paper in this section, R. J. Adie summarizes present knowledge of the geological history of Antarctica. There is now good evidence for believing that the two areas now known as East Antarctica and West Antarctica have had different geological histories, the former being the older, and that they have not always lain in the same position relative to each other or to the other southern continents. Modern geophysical evidence, especially from palaeomagnetic studies, and from the use of radio-isotope techniques to determine the absolute ages of rocks, have contributed significantly to the interpretation of this complex history. There is good evidence, also, to show that the climate has varied cyclically from intense glaciation to desert, and that for much of its geological history Antarctica has been subject at least to temperate conditions. The present ice sheet appears to have had its origin in a cooling that began in Miocene times, perhaps 5–7 million years ago. Much detailed information can be found in the Proceedings of the first SCAR Symposium on Antarctic Geology (Adie, 1964).

The sediments in the oceans about Antarctica preserve a record of different climatic periods, and the paper presented to the Symposium by Dr J. D. Hays reviewed the evidence they provide for changes in marine circulation over the past 4·5 million years, and that at its maximum extent the northernmost margin of the pack zone was one about 2° north of its present limit. It has not, unfortunately, proved possible to publish this paper in full in the present volume, but there is considerable relevant information both in the Antarctic Geology Symposium and in papers by Znachko-Yakorvsky and Ravich, Ewing, Houtz and Leyden, Heenen, Tharp and Hollister, and Hays, in the Proceedings of the SCAR Symposium on Antarctic Oceanography (SCAR, 1968).

The synthesis of geology, geophysics and the study of ocean sediments thus provides a consistent picture of a pre-Miocene Antarctica with a substantial biota.

The history and maximal extent of the Pleistocene ice sheet is considered by Hollin in this section, and the question of survival of at least some species of cryptogams and invertebrates through the ice maximum by Brundin, Van Zinderen Bakker, Janetschek, and others in discussion. The presence of species with a high degree of endemism, especially among the arthropod fauna of Antarctica, strongly hints that these may be the survivors of a fauna which developed in the high mountains of the continent before the main ice sheet extended, and the glaciological evidence does not appear to contradict such a view. Antarctic glaciology has been reviewed in several recent papers (e.g. in Odishaw, 1964, and Hatherton, 1965), and in 1969 was discussed at a SCAR Symposium held at Hanover, New Hampshire, the proceedings of which are likely to appear in 1970.

The history, especially in postglacial times, of the Antarctic and Subantarctic flora, and the former role of Antarctica as a dispersal route and evolutionary centre for animal groups are considered respectively by Van Zinderen Bakker and by Brundin in this section. The former paper formed one only of a series delivered at a three-day meeting of the Subcommittee on Quaternary Studies of the SCAR Working Group on Biology, held before the main Symposium. All the papers read at this meeting are to appear in a special volume (Van Zinderen Bakker, 1969). Brundin's contribution, in so far as it discusses the present fauna of Antarctica, should be considered in relation to the recent monograph by Gressitt (1967), while the evaluation of Chironomid relationships is developed in full detail by Brundin (1966). Much information on the biogeography of the southern temperate zone as a whole and the history of its biota, is summarized in the discussion led by Pantin (1960).

No review of Antarctic Climatology has been included in this section. That by Phillpot delivered to the first SCAR Symposium on Antarctic Biology, (Carrick, Holdgate and Prevost, 1964) remains useful, while fuller information is available in two symposium volumes by Van Rooy (1957) and the Australian Bureau of Meteorology (1960). The paper by Rubin in Odishaw (1964) and the Soviet Antarctic Atlas (Tolstikov, 1966) also provide valuable sources. In recent years increasing attention has been devoted to microclimatology and reference to some of the results is made by Greene and Longton, in a later section of the present volume, and by Greene and Holtom, Longton and Holdgate, and Longton in the proceedings of a recent Royal Society discussion (Smith, 1967).

References

Adie, R. J. (ed.) (1964). *Antarctic Geology, Proceedings of the first international symposium on Antarctic geology*. Amsterdam: North Holland Pub. Co.

Australian Bureau of Meteorology (1960). *Antarctic Meteorology*. Melbourne: Pergamon.

Brundin, L. (1966). Transantarctic relationships and their significance, as evidenced by Chironomid Midges. *Kungl. Svenska. Vetenskapsakad. Handl.*, 11, No. 1.

Carrick, R., Holdgate, M. W. and Prevost, J. (eds) (1964). *Biologie Antarctique: Antarctic Biology*. Paris: Hermann.

Gressitt, J. L. (ed.) (1967). *Entomology of Antarctica*. Antarctic Research Series, Vol. 10. American Geophysical Union.

Hatherton, T. (ed.) (1965). *Antarctica*. New York: Frederick A. Praeger.

Odishaw, H. (ed.) (1964). *Research in Geophysics*. Vol. 1. *Solid earth and interface phenomena*. Cambridge, Mass.: M.I.T. Press.

Pantin, C. F. A. (Leader) (1960). A discussion on the biology of the Southern cold temperate Zone. *Proc. R. Soc.* (B), **152**, No. 949, pp. 429–682.

SCAR (1968). *Antarctic Oceanography*. Ed. R. I. Currie. Cambridge: Scott Polar Research Institute.

Smith, T. E. (organizer) (1967). A discussion on the Terrestrial Antarctic ecosystem. *Phil. Trans. R. Soc.* (B), **252**, No. 777, pp. 167–392.

Van Rooy, M. P. (ed.) (1957). *Meteorology of the Antarctic*. Pretoria: Weather Bureau.

Tolstikov, Ye. I. (ed.) (1966). *Atlas Antarktiki*. Moscow, Leningrad: Glavnoye Upravleniye Geodeziii Kartografiio.

Van Zinderen Bakker, E. M. (ed.) (1969). *Palaeoecology of Africa*, Vol. V. (in the press).

Past Environments and Climates of Antarctica

RAYMOND J. ADIE
British Antarctic Survey, Department of Geology, University of Birmingham, England

I. Introduction

For some time it has been generally accepted that Antarctica is composed of *two* main geological provinces (Adie, 1962), each characterized by its specific history and evolution throughout time. The geological record of east Antarctica ceased abruptly in the Jurassic, whereas that of west Antarctica continued uninterrupted from that time until the Recent (Adie, 1965).

The *Gondwana Province* of east Antarctica is essentially the crystalline continental shield, which has had a complex history of sedimentation and intrusive activity, and on which almost flat-lying Upper Palaeozoic–Lower Mesozoic terrestrial sediments capped by basic volcanic rocks were deposited. Most of its complex Palaeozoic history is recorded in the Transantarctic Mountains, but in the coastal regions the complicated zones of basement gneisses, charnockites, migmatites and "Riphean rocks" are exposed. Post-Palaeozoic tectonism appears to have been relatively simple and is reflected in a broad pattern of late Tertiary block-faulting.

In marked contrast to this, the *Andean Province* of west Antarctica is characteristically a young mountain-range region folded on to the core of the continent. Apart from the early Palaeozoic igneous basement, which was affected by several phases of intrusive activity and late Palaeozoic geosynclinal sedimentation, the record is mainly Mesozoic and Tertiary. This province is the southerly extension of the South American Andes, and as such it reveals the complex mountain-building and folding of the late Triassic (180–200 m. yr. ago), and also the end-Tertiary block-faulting which is typical of the Antarctic Peninsula.

If the respective stratigraphic records of the two provinces (Adie, 1964*a*, *c*; Grindley and Warren, 1964) are compared, even superficially, it is clear that these diametrically opposite regions of Antarctica have had totally different geological histories over the past 600 million years. Even so, the environmental and climatic conditions prevailing during that period of time are firmly recorded in the respective stratigraphic records.

In a review such as this, it is wholly impractical to divorce Antarctica from its rightful geological relationship with the other southern continents (including India) as they are geographically known today. Indeed, to reject the concept of the former southern supercontinent of Gondwanaland and hypotheses of continental drifting would be tantamount to disestablishing many of the fundamental principles upon which stratigraphy and palaeogeography have been built. However, as a cautionary note, it should be made clear that it is necessary to assume the uniformitarian principle that the Earth's climatic zones were the same in the past as at present, if any progress in either palaeogeographical or palaeoclimatological interpretation is to be made.

II. Palaeogeographical Principles

In themselves, geological field observations are merely a means to an end. Though interpretative by-products such as the stratigraphical column can be achieved directly, the ultimate goal is to determine as precisely as possible the past geographical, environmental and climatic conditions prevailing at different stages of time, and the courses of different geological processes under these conditions. The principles of palaeogeography are well established, and the degree and accuracy of interpretation must depend ultimately on the quality of field observation.

Such diverse climates as glacial and desert conditions are readily interpreted from characteristic deposits such as tillites or varves and red beds. But in many cases recording of less obvious features as rain prints and mud cracks may be necessary to supplement main observations, and often recourse to evaluating even the degree of weathering of feldspars in sediments may prove important in the final assessment of environment. Prevailing wind directions of the past can usually be inferred from bedded dune-sand deposits and even from ventifacts buried *in situ*.

III. Palaeontology and Palaeotemperatures

In the past, careful studies on marine molluscan populations, particularly on those of long-ranging species, have yielded valuable information relating growth-rates, shell thicknesses and ageing to variations in climatic environment. These results have been used empirically in conjunction with sedimentological, lithological and even mineralogical observations to detect both widespread and local changes in environmental conditions.

The recent development of techniques to determine the environmental temperatures of marine organisms has reinforced earlier "guesses" based solely upon the shell size and shell thickness of lamellibranchs and gastropods.

The use of $^{18}O/^{16}O$ ratios estimated on calcareous molluscan species, and especially on belemnites, has added greatly to the existing knowledge of marine conditions during the Cretaceous and Tertiary.

IV. Palaeobotany

Fossil plant assemblages, which are usually associated with a terrestrial environment, can be used with a degree of caution as a guide to the general climatic and growth conditions. However, due account should be taken of the "altitudinal climatic factor" which could have considerable bearing on the comparison of floral assemblages at the same latitude. The occurrence of coniferous woods in sediments is indicative of a cool-temperate climate, whereas leaves of deciduous trees in a similar deposit would mean a temperate climate.

In parts of east Antarctica the presence of the well-known *Gangamopteris-Glossopteris* flora in the lowermost Permian glacial deposits is the key to the growth environment, and similarly the association of the lowermost Middle Jurassic giant ferns with lacustrine black shales at Hope Bay is typical of an inland subtropical climate. Certain horizons in the Lower-Middle Campanian marine sediments of the Snow Hill Island area of west Antarctica are characterized by coniferous woods indicative of a cool-temperate climate. Some of these have been bored by marine molluscs, which again provides a clue to their final depositional environment. In contrast, the early Tertiary volcanic sediments and ashes of the South Shetland Islands contain a strange association of *Nothofagus* and *Araucaria*, both of which are typical members of the present-day southern cool-temperate zone of South America.

As in other southern continents, the early Mesozoic terrestrial sediments of east Antarctica contain the *Dicroidium–Otozamites* flora in association with *Antarcticoxylon* woods which characterize a subtropical to even tropical environment. However, in the South Shetland Islands the Triassic is represented by an allied heat-loving genus, *Thinnfeldia*.

V. Coals

Since one of the world's greatest coalfields is located in east Antarctica, the environmental relevance of coals should perhaps be considered here. In contrast to a *Carboniferous* age for the main Upper Palaeozoic coals of the Northern Hemisphere, those of the Southern Hemisphere are *Lower Permian*. In the geological column, coals are known to have formed under widely varying climatic conditions and in many different environments.

It is clear that the Lower Permian coals of Southern Africa, India and Antarctica, with which the *Glossopteris* flora is associated, formed in dank swampy conditions when the climate was cold and wet, and loess from adjacent periglacial areas was being blown into the deposits. Further proof of these conditions is the occurrence of fireclays forming the substratum on which the coals rest. However, the stratigraphically higher Triassic coals of the Transantarctic Mountains formed under totally different conditions. The irregular and thinning coals of the Falla Formation and the Dominion Coal Measures of the Beardmore Glacier area represent deposition in a deltaic environment under a subtropical climate. No doubt the sparse Triassic coals found at Livingston Island, South Shetland Islands, were formed under similar conditions.

Irregular and rare, thin coal seams occur in both the Lower Cretaceous of Alexander Island and in the Upper Cretaceous of the James Ross Island area. Their frequent association with coniferous woods is indicative of a cool-temperate environment of formation. Rare coaly seams, often poorly preserved and definitely immature, have been recorded from the early Tertiary sediments that are interbedded with volcanic ashes at King George Island, South Shetland Islands. There can be no doubt that these coals are also representative of a very cool-temperate climate.

VI. Permo-Carboniferous Glaciation

Although continental or local glaciations have occurred many times throughout geological time, even in the Precambrian, perhaps the most important was the one that overtook and refrigerated the southern continents during the Permo-Carboniferous. At first, evidence for this glaciation in Antarctica could not be found, but detailed field-work has revealed tillites and now it is almost as well known as in the other southern continents. It is conceivable that Antarctica was less severely affected than adjacent landmasses. During the late Carboniferous, east Antarctica was covered by an erosive ice carapace which deposited the ground moraines now recognized as tillites. However, on the site of west Antarctica (including the Antarctic Peninsula) there existed a marginal depositional trough, or geosyncline, into which sedimentary debris that had been stripped from east Antarctica was deposited during the greater part of the Carboniferous. The marine equivalents of the terrestrial tillites have now been recognized in the form of "pebbly mudstones" intercalated with the geosynclinal Trinity Peninsula Series of the Antarctic Peninsula. These sediments were resurrected and folded during the late Triassic orogeny, forming the earliest true Antarctic Peninsula. The importance of such a correlation between east and west Antarctica is indeed one of the few overlaps yet discovered between these two provinces.

VII. Multiple Glaciation

Recent studies on the Pleistocene of Victoria Land (Péwé, 1960; Nichols, 1965) have revealed a complex history of multiple glaciation, which extended back in time far longer than hitherto anticipated. Though there is limited evidence, it is quite probable that multiple glaciation also occurred during the great Permo-Carboniferous glaciation of the Southern Hemisphere, but it is far more difficult to decipher and interpret than for the Pleistocene. Reliance has to be placed on the careful observations of striation directions on multiply-glaciated pavements, such as in the Horlick Mountains (Long, 1964, 1965). It is still a matter for conjecture whether these pavements resulted from the activity of local glaciers, small ice caps or even a vast continental ice sheet.

Subfossil patterned ground, such as that recorded in Victoria Land (Black and Berg, 1964), is a good indicator of interglacial conditions. Whether true fossil patterned ground will be discovered in association with the Permo-Carboniferous tillites is a matter for future field-work, but it would confirm multiple glaciation in Antarctica at that time.

VIII. Sea-level Fluctuations

From the earliest Palaeozoic until the Recent, Antarctica together with the other southern continents has been subjected to sea-level changes, varying in magnitude from continental-scale marine transgressions to minor fluctuations. During the early Cambrian, the sea gradually invaded the continent in the vicinity of Victoria Land, and by the Lower Devonian this transgression had extended almost to the position of the South Pole. However, with the onset of the Permo-Carboniferous refrigeration the marine incursion was abruptly terminated.

There is no remaining evidence for either eustatic or isostatic fluctuations in Antarctica during the late Palaeozoic or Mesozoic, but end-Tertiary sea-level changes of at least 275–305 m are well known in west Antarctica, e.g. Cockburn Island and King George Island (Adie, 1964*b*). Pleistocene and Recent sea-level changes in west and east Antarctica are well known and they have been reviewed by Adie (1964*b*) and Nichols (1968).

IX. Local Climatic Influences

In the history of any great continent there are bound to have been local and temporary influences on the overall climate existing at any particular time. Even today, in the higher equatorial regions, there are active glaciers such as those on Kilimanjaro which are vigorously depositing till and moraine.

The Pleistocene tills at the summit of Mauna Kea, Hawaii, are in a similar category.

Local warming, due primarily to volcanic activity as in present-day Iceland, has undoubtedly played an important part in the geological history of Antarctica. In the Upper Jurassic, both in east and west Antarctica, volcanism was widespread and it was responsible for destroying much of the flora. At this time, activity in the Antarctic Peninsula region was so fierce that great thicknesses of lava and ashes accumulated not only on land but also vast ash showers were blown into the adjacent sea, exterminating the fauna.

During geological time the distribution of landmasses and oceans has not remained constant and therefore there could have been marked changes in sea currents in the past. The respective tracks of warm and cold currents, especially in the Southern Hemisphere, could have had an important influence on the marine fauna. Therefore, interpretative studies over long periods of time could be meaningless in the present context.

X. Palaeomagnetism

Studies on the fossil magnetism—palaeomagnetism—of Antarctic rocks of all ages have provided important information on the former latitudes at which magnetic properties were imparted to these rocks. Striking latitudinal differences from their present positions have been recorded for the southern continents during the past 150 million years. For example, it is believed that India migrated at least 60° of latitude from the Southern to the Northern Hemisphere in this time.

During the Jurassic (about 165 m. yr. ago), east Antarctica occupied a mean latitude of 40°S. At the same time the northern tip of the Antarctic Peninsula reached a subtropical climatic zone in latitude 25–30°S, but in the late Cretaceous to early Tertiary its latitude was only 50–55°S.

XI. Environmental History

A preliminary interpretation of the palaeogeography of Antarctica has been given by Adie (1962), who has discussed briefly climatic fluctuations in relation to environmental, structural and tectonic considerations. To review in detail the past 600 million years of environmental history of a continent so geologically complex as Antarctica at this early stage of exploration is no mean task, and therefore it is preferable to point to the main palaeogeographic features on the basis of what has been stated above.

The early Palaeozoic environment of east Antarctica appears to have been primarily marine, as a result of fluctuating transgressions prior to the Carboniferous. At the onset of glacial conditions in the late Carboniferous, most of east Antarctica suffered refrigeration under an ice-sheet environment. The deposition of tillites on land and the transportation of quantities of detritus to the adjacent Andean geosyncline of west Antarctica characterized this period. With the amelioration of the climate during the lowermost Permian, the *Gangamopteris-Glossopteris* flora gained a foothold on the continent, and in the more suitable swampy environments in east Antarctica thick coals formed. At this time a great depositional basin (analogous to the terrestrial Karroo Basin of Southern Africa) had formed over most of central east Antarctica. As the climate gradually warmed, the vegetation cover became more luxuriant, and rapid erosion of the higher parts of the continental block proceeded in subtropical conditions.

By the Triassic, complete desiccation had imposed itself upon the "Beacon Group Basin", as borne out by the occurrence of red beds and wind-blown deposits, and the diminution of the floral assemblages. In contrast, it was during the late Triassic that the Antarctic Peninsula was first formed by the most important mountain-building movements recorded in Antarctica. However, by the Middle Jurassic the climate in the Antarctic Peninsula region had become subtropical and giant ferns comprised the main flora. Fresh-water lakes, with an abundant gastropod and fish fauna (and even aquatic beetles), were common over the northern part of the peninsula, but in the Alexander Island area offshore deposition was active.

Perhaps the most important volcanic activity in the history of Antarctica terminated the Jurassic. In east Antarctica the major terrestrial basin was flooded by lavas and its sediments were injected by thick basic sheets, whereas in west Antarctica (especially in the Antarctic Peninsula region) lava eruptions were punctuated by explosive ash phases. Such volcanism completed the pre-Pliocene history of east Antarctica and, apart from tectonic activity, records of environment are lacking for the late Mesozoic and Tertiary.

Nevertheless, for west Antarctica there is an exceptionally clear history for this period. With a slightly cooler marine environment, the Mollusca flourished to provide one of the richest Cretaceous marine faunas known from the Southern Hemisphere. Towards the end of the Cretaceous, coinciding with the intrusion of the vast Andean batholiths of the Antarctic Peninsula and Byrd Land, there was a depositional hiatus, but the commencement of the Tertiary saw renewed volcanism in the South Shetland Islands, where thick sequences of basic lavas and ashes were intercalated with local fresh-water sediments bearing the *Nothofagus-Araucaria* flora which is typical of a temperate to cool-temperate climate.

In the Lower Miocene, especially in the James Ross Island area, rejuvenated but short-lived marine deposition under far cooler conditions than in the Cretaceous began. These beds, which contain a "cool" molluscan fauna (according to some authors), have also yielded fossil penguins which could possibly confirm the environmental interpretation of the Mollusca. Volcanic activity that had continued uninterrupted in the South Shetland Islands since the early Tertiary, was renewed with vigour in the Middle Miocene not only in the north of the Antarctic Peninsula but throughout much of west Antarctica. Apparently related to these eruptions were numerous changes in sea-level which were due primarily to increasing tectonism and block-faulting over the whole of Antarctica. By the commencement of the Pliocene, glacial conditions had already been established with a consequent lowering of sea-level.

The stratigraphic records of east and west Antarctica have been interpreted from environmental and climatic viewpoints, and it appears that the continent has undergone a distinctly cyclic history, ranging from extreme refrigeration to desert conditions, and returning to glaciation in the course of 300 million years. Such climatic fluctuations cannot be realistically related to the present geographical position of Antarctica and other explanations outside the scope of the present paper must be sought.

References

Adie, R. J. (1962). The geology of Antarctica. *In* "Antarctic Research: the Matthew Fontaine Maury Memorial Symposium" (H. Wexler, M. J. Rubin and J. E. Caskey, eds) (Geophysical monograph No. 7), American Geophysical Union, Washington, D.C., pp. 26–39.

Adie, R. J. (1964*a*). Geological history. *In* "Antarctic Research" (R. E. Priestley, R. J. Adie and G. de Q. Robin, eds), Butterworth and Co. (Publishers) Ltd, London, pp. 118–62.

Adie, R. J. (1964*b*). Sea-level changes in the Scotia arc and Graham Land. *In* "Antarctic Geology" (R. J. Adie, ed.), North-Holland Publishing Company, Amsterdam, pp. 27–32.

Adie, R. J. (1964*c*). Stratigraphic correlation in west Antarctica. *In* "Antarctic Geology" (R. J. Adie, ed.), North-Holland Publishing Company, Amsterdam, pp. 307–13.

Adie, R. J. (1965). Antarctic geology and continental drift. *Sci. J., Lond.* 1, No. 6, 65–73.

Black, R. F. and Berg, T. E. (1964). Glacier fluctuations recorded by patterned ground, Victoria Land. *In* "Antarctic Geology" (R. J. Adie, ed.), North-Holland Publishing Company, Amsterdam, pp. 107–22.

Grindley, G. W. and Warren, G. (1964). Stratigraphic nomenclature and correlation in the western Ross Sea region. *In* "Antarctic Geology" (R. J. Adie, ed.), North-Holland Publishing Company, Amsterdam, pp. 314–33.

Long, W. E. (1964). The stratigraphy of the Horlick Mountains. *In* "Antarctic Geology" (R. J. Adie, ed.), North-Holland Publishing Company, Amsterdam, pp. 352–63.

Long, W. E. (1965). Stratigraphy of the Ohio Range, Antarctica. *In* "Geology and Paleontology of the Antarctic" (J. B. Hadley, ed.), (Antarctic Research Series, Vol. 6), American Geophysical Union, Washington, D.C., pp. 71–116.

Nichols, R. L. (1965). Antarctic interglacial features. *J. Glaciol.* **5**, No. 40, 433–49.

Nichols, R. L. (1968). Coastal geomorphology, McMurdo Sound, Antarctica. *J. Glaciol.* 7, No. 51, 449–78.

Péwé, T. L. (1960). Multiple glaciation in the McMurdo Sound region, Antarctica—a progress report. *J. Geol.* **68**, No. 5, 498–514.

Antarctic Glaciology, Glacial History and Ecology

JOHN T. HOLLIN
Department of Geological and Geophysical Sciences,
Princeton University, Princeton, New Jersey, U.S.A.

I. Introduction

The aim of this paper is to set out the chief facts about the Antarctic ice sheet in the present and past, especially as they bear on ecology, and to suggest some ways in which ecologists may be able to help in elucidating the past of the ice sheet.

II. The Ice Sheet at the Present Day

Before the IGY, little was known about the main mass of the Antarctic ice sheet, but by now a great deal is known. Useful reviews of this new knowledge have been presented by Robin (1962) and Gow (1965). In brief, the Antarctic ice falls into three geographical divisions: the main, grounded ice sheet, with an area of 12·5 million km^2, the peripheral, floating ice shelves, with an area of 1·5 million km^2, and the ephemeral sea ice, with an area of roughly 12·0 million km^2 in summer and 25·5 million km^2 in winter. The sea-ice areas, which are from Nazarov (1963), will probably be refined in due course from satellite observations.

The main, grounded ice sheet shows a fairly uniform profile. For the outer, coastwise few hundred km this fits very well the parabolic equation $h = 4{\cdot}5\, d^{1/2}$, where h is the elevation of the ice surface in metres and d is the distance inland in metres. Further inland, the profile become flatter, chiefly because the ice there is more sluggish. The profile is not strongly affected by local variations of temperature, accumulation rate or subglacial relief, and this gives empirical support to the theoretical conclusions of Hollin (1962) that Pleistocene changes of temperature and accumulation did not by themselves cause any great changes in the Antarctic ice sheet.

Below the uppermost 10 m or so, which are subject to the annual warming and cooling cycle, the temperature of the ice surface ranges from only a few degrees centigrade below zero at some coastal stations to −58°C in the centre of the continent. The average thickness of the ice sheet, determined chiefly by seismic and radio sounding, must be within 300 m of 2000 m, but the maximum thickness in the centre and a few other areas is over 4000 m. Because the geothermal heat flux should on average be able to sustain a gradient of 1°C/50 m through the ice sheet, if the latter were static one might expect that the base in the centre would be at the melting-point. In practice, the ice sheet is not static, and the downward and outward movement of cold ice has the effect of cooling the base, particularly towards the edges. Even so, parts of the base in the centre might be at the melting-point, and this has now been confirmed at Byrd Station, where recent electro-mechanical drilling met water at the base at 2300 m. A question of current interest is what happens to this water: does it form rivers or a film? In the latter case, it must tend to detach the ice from its bed, and may be a cause of the catastrophic "surges" which have been observed in ice caps and valley glaciers. A. T. Wilson has suggested that vast surges of the Antarctic ice sheet are the triggers for the Pleistocene ice ages: his theory and possible tests for it are discussed by Hollin (1965).

The ice sheet is nourished by snow which at the surface has a density of about 0·35 gm/cm^3 and which compacts to ice at depths up to 100 m or thereabouts. The nourishment or net accumulation is easily measured by stakes, and over the whole continent averages about 15 gm/cm^2 yr. Wastage or ablation is difficult to measure: the amounts involved in melting at the surface and base of the ice sheet are relatively unimportant, and the only significant ablation must be by the calving of icebergs and by melting at the bottom of ice shelves. Measuring the first would involve knowing the ice thickness and velocity all round Antarctica, and the second extensive work beneath the shelves. At present one can only extrapolate from the few observations that have been made. So far, the highest estimates suggest that only 75% of the accumulation can be balanced by calving and 15% by bottom-melting, and many workers have suggested that the ice sheet must be growing. If it is, this could be because it is building up for a surge as in Wilson's theory, or because it is still adjusting to an accumulation increase accompanying the warmer air and more vigorous atmospheric circulation since the last major retreat (Gow, 1965).

It follows from the above that, for both mechanical and budgetary reasons, the boundary of the ice sheet is formed by the sea: if sufficient ice reaches the sea it spreads out as a floating ice shelf, and eventually this breaks and melts away. For this reason, during the Pleistocene ice ages, when the growth of the northern ice sheets abstracted over 100 m of water from the oceans, the lowering of sea-level must have allowed the ice sheet to advance. After concluding, as noted, that temperature and accumulation fluctuations were not very important in Antarctica, Hollin (1962) suggested that the above-sea-level effect would account for most of the evidence of fluctuations of the edge of the ice sheet in phase with those of the northern ice ages. Of course, if Wilson is correct, the latter themselves are caused by surges from the centre of the ice sheet.

III. The Ice Sheet in the Past

Most of the evidence concerning the beginning of the ice sheet comes from the surrounding ocean, and is reviewed by Hays (1970). Potassium-argon dates from volcanics in the "oases" confirm that glaciation began many millions of years ago. The oases, incidentally, are not formed by volcanic heat: they form because they are relatively high, so that the ice flowing towards them from the interior finds it easier to escape through the relatively low, deep valleys on either side of the oases.

There is evidence from both oceanic and terrestrial deposits that once the ice sheet had been established it never disappeared again. However, it occasionally expanded, probably in phase with the northern hemisphere glacial expansions, via the sea-level mechanism mentioned above. The distribution of erratics suggests that during the expansions some of the higher nunataks were always ice free, but that the present coastal oases were completely ice covered. However, perhaps the lowering of sea-level exposed new oases. For example, although the peninsulas and islands at Wilkes Station cover an area 25 by 50 km, their highest point is only just over 100 m, so that their existence would hardly have been suspected if the sea had been 100 m higher.

Following the latest expansion, the last major retreat of the ice-sheet edge appears to have taken place several thousand years ago. This is suggested by radio-carbon dates on algae, foraminifera, mollusca, penguins and seals. The radio-carbon ages have to be corrected for the fact that much of the marine radio-carbon in Antarctica is hundreds of years old to begin with. Most of the dates obtained come from material embedded in the raised beaches around Antarctica. These beaches usually climb to a "marine limit" of some tens of metres, above which the angular material left by deglaciation remains unsorted by the sea. The retreat of the ice edge appears to have slowed down or ended now and, as was noted, the ice-sheet centre may actually be growing.

IV. Implications for Ecologists

During the expansions of the ice sheet Antarctica may have been some degrees colder than it is today. However, perhaps this was not too important for plant and animal life. Thinking of Wilkes Station again, if we want to know if the life forms there could survive such a cooling we can presumably look at present-day places such as McMurdo Sound, where the temperature is already 13°C colder than at Wilkes. More importantly, the Wilkes archipelago and all the other coastal oases in East Antarctica were probably completely ice covered during the last expansion, and this raises the question of what happened to their flora and fauna. As was noted above, perhaps the withdrawal of the sea exposed new oases for colonization: unfortunately any evidence of such colonization is unlikely to have survived the return of the sea. If there were no such colonies, could the Adelie penguins, for example, have "wintered over" in the Subantarctic islands? At Wilkes Station, Adelie colonies that have been abandoned for probably hundreds or thousands of years develop, presumably by frost action, into distinctive mounds of uniformly sized nest pebbles. These mounds show up very strikingly in aerial photographs. It might be worth while keeping an eye open for any such mounds in the Subantarctic islands.

As far as the last major ice retreat is concerned, the radio-carbon evidence from the present coastal areas obviously documents only its later stages. From a glacial geological point of view, it would be useful to know when the retreat actually began, to see if it was truly in phase with the northern retreat that began 18,000 years ago. As the climate improved, some of the earliest immigrants must have been petrels that flew to nest on some of the high nunataks at places such as Cape Hallett. Arnold Heine (personal communication) has pointed out that the oily substance which these birds spit at their enemies builds up to considerable thicknesses in some colonies, and it would be useful if ecologists visiting such areas were able to obtain vertical sections through any such material, with a view in particular to the radiocarbon dating of the lowest layers. To obtain a maximum date, the area concerned would have to be above the moraines and erratics of the last expansion.

In summary, our increasing knowledge of the ice sheet at the present day enables us to suggest how it may have fluctuated in the past. Determining how it actually did fluctuate frequently involves the discovery and dating of fossils. This discovery is something in which both glacial geologists and ecologists can co-operate for their mutual benefit.

Acknowledgements

This paper was written whilst the author was employed by Princeton University under National Science Foundation grant GA-3920.

References

Gow, A. J. (1965). The ice sheet. "Antarctica." (T. Hatherton, ed.), Methuen, London; Frederick A. Praeger, New York, pp. 221–58.

Hays, J. D. (1970). The climatic record of Antarctic Ocean sediments. (This volume.)
Hollin, J. T. (1962). On the glacial history of Antarctica. *J. Glaciol.* **4**, No. 32, 173–95.
Hollin, J. T. (1965). Wilson's theory of ice ages. *Nature, Lond.* **208**, No. 5005, 12–16.
Nazarov, V. S. (1963). Summarized in *Polar Rec.* **12**, No. 77, 205.
Robin, G. de Q. (1962). The ice of the Antarctic. *Scient. Am.* **207**, No. 3, 132–46.

The Climatic Record of Antarctic Ocean Sediments

JAMES D. HAYS
Lamont-Doherty Geological Observatory of Columbia University, Palisades, New York, U.S.A.

The distribution of sediment types around Antarctica is controlled by the outflow of terrigenous material from the continent and the productivity of the Antarctic Ocean surface water. These factors produce a belt of primarily terrigenous sediments, with few microfossils, extending outward from Antarctica to about the northern limit of pack ice; beyond this, a belt of diatom-radiolarian ooze extends to the Antarctic Convergence.

Study of palaeomagnetically dated deep-sea cores spanning 4·5 million years indicates: (1) that the northern boundaries at both of these zones have shifted north repeatedly during the last 400,000 years; (2) the initiation of diatom ooze deposition in the outer zone began about 2 million years ago; (3) glaciation on Antarctica began at least 4·5 million years ago as evidenced by ice-rafted debris in the cores, and (4) during this time two intervals of rapid cooling occurred, one about 2·5 million years ago, the other about 700,000 years ago. The former may be correlative with the first evidence of glaciation on Iceland and New Zealand. The latter correlates with evidence of cooling in low and high northern latitude deep-sea cores.

The McMurdo Dry Valleys

A. T. WILSON
Victoria University of Wellington, New Zealand

I. The Causes of Dry Valleys and Dry Valley Lakes

Although much of the Antarctic continent is covered with ice and snow, there are some small areas which are ice free. One of the largest of these is the McMurdo oasis area.

The first question that might be asked is why are these areas not ice covered like the rest of the continent. To answer this question it is necessary to consider the precipitation/evaporation balance. In this cold and arid region (mean annual temperature of McMurdo oasis region is approximately −20°C) only a very small fraction of the snow that falls ever melts and almost all of it is lost directly by sublimation. The best way of understanding the precipitation/evaporation balance is to consider it in terms of the single parameter, net precipitation. This is defined as being equal to the total precipitation less the total evaporation. If this value is positive for any area in this region, the land surface will be covered with ice and snow. If this value is negative (i.e. sublimation is greater than precipitation), the area will be ice free (a so called "dry area"); that is, unless ice can flow into the area from a region of positive net precipitation. The imaginary line which divides these two regions is called the "snowline" and is the point at which precipitation equals sublimation. Thus the dry areas are those areas which lie below the snowline and into which ice from above the snowline cannot flow. For a given region the net precipitation increases as altitude is increased. As one moves from the sea inland the snowline rises; presumably because total precipitation decreases. As one descends below the snow line the environment becomes drier and drier. Parts of the McMurdo oasis area are the driest on our planet, so dry that $CaCl_2 . 6H_2O$ crystallizes from ice-free saline ponds (e.g. Lake Don Juan). This implies that the mean relative humidity of this area is below 45% RH. Thus one could map the relative aridity of this region by drawing lines parallel to the snowline corresponding to say 80%, 70%, 60%, 50%, 40% relative humidities. These lines will not only be related to such physical phenomena as the presence or absence of permafrost, depth to permafrost, or the length of time the ice in an ice-cored moraine will survive, but also have important ecological implications in this region so inhospitable to living things. An example is the growth of lichen. As is well known from the food and fibre storage industries, fungi can only grow at relative humidities above 80%; thus lichens can only inhabit a strip between the 80% relative humidity line and the snowline.

The McMurdo oasis includes a number of Dry Valleys with enclosed drainage basins. The lowest part of each is occupied by a saline lake. If we consider the evaporation/precipitation balance of the entire drainage system it can be seen that the net excess precipitation of a snowfield will flow below the snowline as a glacier. If the surface area of the glacier is insufficient to balance the sublimation/precipitation budget, the glacier will advance further and further below the snowline toward a situation where the total positive net precipitation above the snowline is balanced by the total negative net precipitation below the snowline. Usually the glacier has pushed sufficiently far below the snowline so that some summer melting takes place. In such cases for a few days during the hottest part of the summer a stream flows away from the glacier snout and feeds a lake which occupies the lowest point of that particular enclosed drainage basin, or that rather special saline lake called the sea. The size of the lake is determined by that area needed to balance the evaporation/precipitation equation for that particular drainage basin. If there is a net precipitation increase to the area the lake level will rise, and if there is a decrease in precipitation the lake level will fall.

II. Relationship Between Lake Levels and Climatic Changes

The susceptibility of the lake level to change depends on what fraction of the total evaporation of the system is accounted for by the lake surface. If this is small a very small increase in net precipitation to the area will lead to an increase in lake area. Thus some lakes are much more susceptible to fluctuation of surface area than others. What is usually measured is lake level. This is not only a function of lake area but also depends on the shape of the depression occupied by the lake. For a flat basin like that occupied by Lake Fryxell a large increase in area can be achieved with little increase in depth, whereas in a steep U-shaped trough, such as occupied by Lake Bonney, the reverse is true.

Thus these Antarctic lakes are very sensitive indicators of changes in net precipitation and hence of glacial advances and retreats.

The above treatment is an oversimplification of the situation and deals with climatic changes only in terms of net precipitation. Let us consider the effect of temperature changes. If the net precipitation were to remain constant but the temperature were to decrease, there would be less summer melting of the glacier, so that it would advance and produce a larger area for evaporation below the snowline. This means that a smaller lake area than before would be needed to balance the system and the lake levels would drop. Conversely if the climate were too warm, more of the glacier would melt and the glacier would retreat, leaving less area below the snowline, so that a larger lake area would be needed to balance the system and the lakes would rise. In such systems it is always difficult to separate the temperature and net precipitation effects, and the lake areas (levels) really only tell us the amount needed to balance the system. However, the effect of temperature is limited for a number of reasons. The whole temperature range between glacial and interglacial periods is only about 6°C. Also to consider the effects of temperature alone we should hold the precipitation (rather than net precipitation) constant. If the temperature is raised, the rate of evaporation would rise, since the vapour pressure of ice is very temperature dependent. This would lead to a rise in the snowline, which would tend to negate the effect of the ice retreat, since it would increase the evaporation per unit area per unit time from the stream and lake surface, which would lead to less lake area being needed to balance the system.

A further effect is that the retreating glacier is replaced by a stream which can contribute almost as much evaporation as the glacier it replaces. Chemical analysis of the water of the Onyx River flowing into Lake Vanda shows that the 18-mile length of the Onyx River provides as much evaporation as the whole surface of Lake Vanda (4 miles by 1 mile).

It is therefore concluded that in this area lake-level fluctuations are controlled largely by fluctuations in the net precipitation.

III. The Evidence for Past Climatic Changes

There is abundant evidence of past changes in lake levels. This evidence takes the form of lake shorelines higher than at present and the presence of chemical concentration gradients in the lakes.

These changes in lake levels must be a record of past climatic change. The question that immediately arises is when was this climate change and what was its cause. Let us consider some examples: Lake Vanda receded from its upper levels (shown very well in Fig. 1) some 3000 years before present. This was determined by the ^{14}C dating of algae found in these upper levels by Professor Wellman. While Lake Vanda stood at its upper level its surface area would have been approximately twice that at present. This suggests, as will be discussed below, that the net precipitation to the snowfields which feed Lake Vanda (i.e. the eastern end of the Wright Valley) would have been 20–40% greater than at present.

In most areas of the world precipitation to a given area is controlled by

FIG. 1. Lake Vanda, Antarctica. Note high lake levels. (U.S. Navy Photo.)

its position relative to the open sea. A very attractive hypothesis is that the Ross Ice Shelf was much further to the south than its present position prior to 3000 years ago. This would mean that there would have been more open sea closer to the snowfields supplying Lake Vanda. The hypothesis that the local alpine glaciers, as distinct from those fed from the polar plateau, are controlled by mean distance to the sea (i.e. the position of the Ross Ice Shelf) is further supported by evidence that the coastal regions to the south of the McMurdo oasis area appear to have been more heavily glaciated up until a few thousand years ago.

All the lakes that occupy the lowest part of the various enclosed drainage basins are chemically stratified and these chemical concentration gradients contain palaeoclimatic information, if we can understand the system sufficiently well to interpret them.

The palaeoclimatic data in the lakes are particularly welcome in the Antarctic, because the more usual methods of dating climatic events, for example ^{14}C dating, are not often applicable in this region. This is because carbonaceous remains are rarely found and when found the "carbon-14 age" of biological material is frequently difficult to interpret. For example, algae may incorporate bicarbonate from melting ice which may have been isolated from the atmosphere for thousands of years.

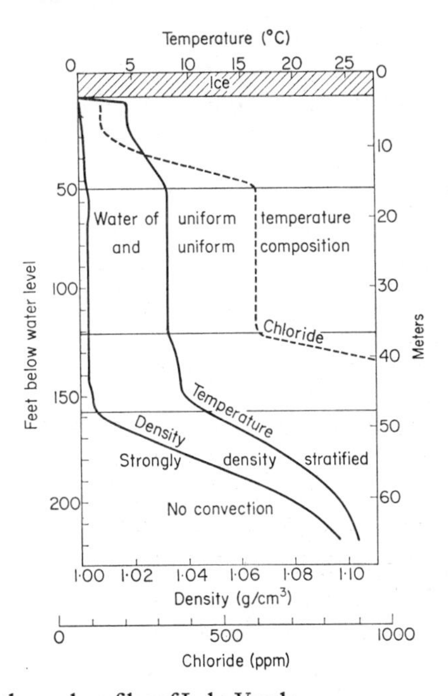

FIG. 2. Chemical and thermal profiles of Lake Vanda.

There are two ways in which the chemistry of the lakes helps us to estimate the dates of past climatic and glacial events—firstly the total amount of salt in the lake and secondly salt gradients that may be present.

Before we can understand the chemistry of the lakes we must understand the chemistry of the whole drainage system. When snow falls on to the snowfields it contains small quantities of salts, the principal cations being sodium and calcium, and the principal anion being chloride. The chemical composition of atmospheric precipitation has been the subject of much study (see, for example, Junge, 1963; Wilson, 1959; Wilson and House, 1965). It is well established that as far as the above cations and anions are concerned the chemical composition of rainfall (and snowfall) depends on the position of the collecting position with respect to the sea. If two areas have atmospheric precipitation of the same chemical composition, the total salt deposited will be directly proportional to the precipitation.

The snow that falls on the snowfields that feed the glaciers of the McMurdo region contains a fraction of a part per million of inorganic salts. It can be seen that if we measure, say, the sodium or chloride content of the snow in the *névé* of a glacier and also the sodium or chloride content of the stream leaving the snout of the glacier it is a simple calculation to determine how much water has been lost from the glacier by sublimation. Such measurements indicate that only a fraction of 1% of the water that falls as snow in *névé* survives to flow as a stream from the snout of the glacier.

These salts then are carried down the stream and eventually end in the lake. Since chloride is a very minor constituent of the rocks of this area, and since the glaciers do almost no cutting and carry very little moraine, it is concluded that the chloride in the lakes is the result of the concentration of large quantities of snow. It is interesting in this connection to mention the effect of permafrost on the streams of the McMurdo Dry Valleys. Because of the extremely low mean annual temperature (*c.* —20°C), any water that percolates into the ground immediately freezes, so that the streams all flow on ice bottoms and the percolation of ground water through sediments, which in the temperate regions can contribute large quantities of soluble salts, is quite impossible.

Thus it is reasonable to conclude that the total chloride in a lake represents the total chloride which has fallen in the drainage area feeding the lake since the lake first formed. Since the lakes in this area have a permanent ice cover many feet thick, chloride can only be removed from the lake in one of two ways. Either the lake will rise until it overflows into another drainage basin (or the sea), or a large glacier can advance through the valley and push the lake contents into the sea. Thus every lake can be considered to have a chloride age which is obtained by dividing the yearly mean chloride inflow rate into the total amount of chloride in the lake. This age is really a minimum age, since it is possible to conceive periods in the past when the total precipitation was much lower than at present. For example, the edge of the Ross Ice Barrier might have been further to the north.

It is difficult to imagine a situation when the precipitation was as much as twice that at present. This is because such an increase would itself lower the snowline converting part of the glacier which now has a negative net precipitation into a region of positive net precipitation. The glaciers would, of course advance and offset this effect, but the real problem is that of rising lake levels that would result. Consider Lake Vanda, for example. At present for every 100 parts of water that are deposited on the snowfields less than 20% is evaporated from the lake surface. This value is deduced from determining the chemical composition of inflow waters and snow on snowfields feeding the lakes and calculating the water lost during the movement from the snowfield to the lake. If the net precipitation for the area were to double, we would be faced with disposing of 200 parts of water and the lake area would have to increase its area at least tenfold. It would have to increase much more than tenfold, in fact, because its surface would be much closer to the snowline and evaporation would not be efficient. It follows from this line of reasoning that any increase in precipitation by, say, a factor of two or more would lead to the filling of the whole valley with lake and expanded glacier and there is no evidence for these very high lake levels.

Thus some picture of past glacial events emerges. Perhaps the most startling result is that some of these lakes, for example Lake Vanda, have chloride ages in excess of 60,000 years. It has generally been assumed by most workers in the Antarctic that these areas had been extensively glaciated during the last ice age (i.e. up until about 10,000 years ago). The salt ages for some of the lakes in this area makes this appear very unlikely. Since the salt in Lake Vanda is largely calcium chloride, whose freezing-point is approximately −50°C, it is almost certain that any through glacier would have pushed the salts in Lake Vanda into the sea.

Turning to the problem of the origin of chemical gradients in the saline lakes of the McMurdo oasis—an extreme example is Lake Vanda.

A brief summary of the physical chemical structure of the lake is given in Fig. 2. The top is covered by 12 ft of ice. The region 11–55 ft and 125–60 ft has a salt gradient and must be weakly density-stratified. The region 55–125 ft has a uniform temperature and uniform chemical composition, and is believed, from heat-transfer considerations, to be a layer of strong convection. The lower region of the lake below 160 ft is strongly density-stratified saline water which is considered, from heat-flow considerations, to be non-convective. Detailed chemical analysis of the water in this region showed that it was principally a solution of calcium chloride.

It is interesting to speculate on the origin of the salt-concentration gradient in the lake. The only reasonable explanation seems to be that at some period in the past the climate was such that the Onyx River did not supply appreciable water to Lake Vanda. Under these conditions the lake level would have dropped until only a few feet of concentrated calcium chloride remained. When the climate changed the Onyx would flow during the summer and fresh water would have flowed on top of this strong salt solution. Since that time the calcium chloride has been diffusing upwards. If such a model is assumed, it is possible to calculate the time in the past when this climatic change occurred (Wilson, 1964).

If it is assumed that Lake Vanda has a flat bottom and vertical sides and that at zero time all the calcium chloride is concentrated in a layer of negligible thickness on the bottom, then the concentration profile at time t is given by:

$$C = \frac{M}{(Dt)^{\frac{1}{2}}} \cdot e^{-\frac{h^2}{4Dt}}$$

where C is the concentration of calcium at distance h from bottom after an elapsed time t; $h =$ distance above bottom; D = diffusion coefficient of calcium chloride = 0·68 cm^2/day at 10°C; M = total mass of calcium chloride per unit area. The calculated profiles for t = 500, 1000, 1500, and 2000 years are given in Fig. 3, together with the experimental data. No corrections have been made for bathymetry. The bottom of the lake is remarkably flat, and the depression which the lake occupies has very steep sides. Bathymetric corrections would raise the values in the upper part of the lake. It is quite

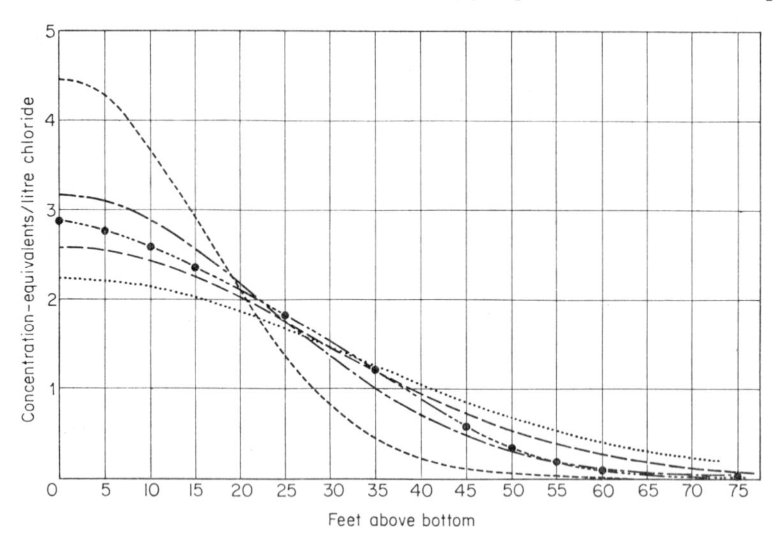

FIG. 3. Age of Lake Vanda from chemical diffusion. ●—···—···—● Experimental Data; ------ 500 years; —··—··—··— 1000 years; ———— 1500 years; ········· 2000 years.

clear that the climatic change occurred about 1200 years ago. Accurate bathymetric data could increase the precision of this calculation.

In the calculation the initial depth before the inflow is taken as being negligible. If this had been taken as any significant depth the gradient near the bottom of the lake would have been flatter. The experimental results suggest that the lake was indeed of small depth at the time of change in climate and also that this change was relatively sharp and definite.

The result for Lake Vanda is of particular interest because it allows an independent calculation on the rate of inflow of salt during the last 1200 years (i.e. the amount of salt not involved in the diffusion cell) and the value so obtained agrees with that computed from the present rate of inflow of water and the chemical composition of that water.

IV. Conclusions

To summarize the results for the glacial history of the Ross Dependency area of the Antarctic, it has been concluded that events should be divided into three separate glacial sequences.

1. Glaciers whose extent are controlled by the height of the Polar Plateau. As has been pointed out above, these have not been of much greater extent than at present for at least the last 20,000 years and may be advancing at present.
2. Alpine glaciers fed from local snowfall. These depend on local precipitation, which depends on the distance to the open sea, which can be strongly influenced by the position of the front of the Ross Ice Shelf. At present these glaciers are vigorous in the northern half of the Ross Dependency and in a state of recession in the southern half of the Ross Dependency. In the central McMurdo oasis area they were advanced much more than at present in the period for 3000–6000 years immediately prior to 3000 years BP, and it is concluded that the front of the Ross Ice Shelf was much further to the south during this period. There is evidence for this glaciation at least as far south as the Darwin Glacier. This glaciation lasted a few thousand years, as evidenced by the limited amount of salt that accumulated in enclosed drainage basins that are now ice free, but which were fed by glacial melt water from this advance, e.g. the south fork of the western end of Wright Valley. This view is also supported by the distribution of salts between the present and higher lake levels of Lake Vanda. For example, there is a dry basin to the west of Vanda which would be flooded if the lake were only a few feet higher than at present. The basin contains negligible salt. This implies that Lake Vanda could not have been higher than at present for more than 6000 years, otherwise the salt from the bottom of the lake would have diffused up into the upper levels and entered

this basin. The period from 3000 years BP to 1200 years BP was a period of glacial recession of alpine glaciers in the McMurdo oasis region. Another advance took place 1200 years ago and a further very minor advance 100 years ago.

3. Glaciers from the sea: due to the grounding of the Ross Ice Shelf and the adoption of an Ice Sheet Profile [cf. Hollin (1962); Penck (1928)], McMurdo Sound was filled with an ice sheet which penetrated a short distance into the Taylor Valley and produced a large lake. This receded 6000 years BP and was replaced by open water.

References

Hollin, J. T. (1962). On the glacial history of the Antarctic. *J. Glaciol.* 4, No. 32, 173–95.

Junge, C. E. (1963). "Air Chemistry and Radioactivity". International Geophysics Series, 4, Academic Press, New York.

Penck, A. (1928). Die Ursachen der Eiszeit. *Sber. preuss. Akad. Wiss.* Phys.-Math. Kl. **6**, 76–85.

Wilson, A. T. (1959). Surface of the ocean as a source of air-borne nitrogenous material and other plant nutrients. *Nature, Lond.* **184**, 99–101.

Wilson, A. T. (1964). Evidence from chemical diffusion of a climatic change in the McMurdo Dry Valleys 1,200 Years Ago. *Nature, Lond.* **201**, 176 7.

Wilson, A. T. and House, D. A. (1965). Chemical composition of South Polar snow. *J. geophys. Res.* **70**, 5515–17.

Quaternary Climates and Antarctic Biogeography

E. M. VAN ZINDEREN BAKKER
University of the Orange Free State, Bloemfontein, South Africa

I. Introduction

The Quaternary ice ages have had a major influence on the distribution of the floras and faunas of the southern end of the world. Since the beginning of the last century science has been speculating about the causes of the most extensive glaciation on earth and its consequences—some of them catastrophic—for plant and animal life.

During the well-known discussion between Darwin and Hooker about the means by which the floras and faunas of the southern region could have reached their present positions, knowledge of the physical environment was still very limited. The important scientific questions were, however, posed by these famous biogeographers with much clarity but many of these problems have not yet been solved. Since then the literature on the biogeography of the circum-Antarctic zone has grown extensively and the efforts of the SCAR nations have contributed much to our present understanding.

At the opening of the discussion organized in 1959 by the Royal Society on the "Biology of the Southern Cold Temperate Zone" Professor C. F. A. Pantin said: "The clear-cut geography of the land masses and their wide separation by the southern ocean, with its intervening islands, throw the paradoxical relations of their faunas and floras into sharp relief" (Pantin, 1960, p. 443). South America, which extends south as far as 55°S, probably had contact with the Antarctic continent via the Scotia Arc until early Tertiary times, while Southern Africa, which only reaches 35°S, has a very isolated position. Australia and New Zealand lie between these two extremes. The picture is made even more diverse by the many small islands which lie scattered in the immense ocean between the four southern land masses.

In recent times our knowledge of Antarctica and the Southern Ocean has expanded in many fields and the geological study of this vast region is well on its way. The ages and origins of most of the southern islands are well known and it appears that only the Falkland Islands, Kerguelen, the South Orkney Islands and South Georgia are of pre-Tertiary age, while the isolated smaller islands are all volcanic in origin and stem from the Tertiary and even Quaternary. The island groups of the New Zealand shelf resemble the Kerguelen archipelago in having "continental" affinities, but owing much of their present composition to Tertiary volcanism. The volcanic history of the southern end of the world is being studied in more detail, since this volcanic activity had a direct influence on southern biogeography by creating and devastating land areas and may have had a more debatable indirect influence on the climate.

The study of ocean sediments has proved to be of considerable value in providing data about the changes which occurred in former environments. Pollen analysis can provide terrestrial evidence which can be cross-checked with oceanic micropalaeontology, ocean current, and climatological studies. It is very encouraging that new radiometric and palaeomagnetic dating techniques can assist us in correlating all these results, but many more quantitative data are desperately needed. Palaeotemperatures, age determinations, and the assessment of zonal limits are essential for any further progress in our knowledge of the south.

The picture of the physical background of the evolutionary process in the southern regions is gradually becoming clearer and more detailed and it appears to be much more complex than was originally thought. To understand the ecological significance of this complex history we have also to study in great detail the present-day flora and fauna of the circum-Antarctic region, their genetical pattern, their autecology and, especially, their means of dispersal. Much more detailed knowledge about the ecology of many different localities is still needed.

II. Climatic Changes in Antarctica and the Southern Hemisphere

The picture which emerges at present is, in general outline, the following. The gradual cooling of Antarctica which set in in mid-Tertiary times at last reached the stage when glaciers expanded and covered the entire continent. The large and varied floras and faunas which had evolved from Palaeozoic times onward were eliminated from the continent and only a small proportion were able to survive in more northern regions. After the commencement of this glaciation the floras and faunas never regained their former range, because, as is known with fair certainty, the Antarctic was never free from ice during the Quaternary. The southern glaciation changed in extent, but the number of pulsations, and their amplitudes, is not yet certain.

Although the cause of the ice ages is still not understood, we know from oceanographic and geological evidence that the glaciations of the Northern Hemisphere were of a secondary nature and started much later than the Antarctic ice cap. The correlation between the variations of these two glacial sequences is still uncertain, but new evidence indicates that, at least during the late upper Pleistocene and the Holocene, the climatic variations in the Southern Hemisphere were, in broad outline, synchronous with the much better-known fluctuations in the Northern Hemisphere. Recent data for the southern land masses, the Argentine Basin and some of the Subantarctic islands considered by the SCAR Subcommittee on Quaternary Studies, will be published elsewhere.

Fossil pollen evidence (van Zinderen Bakker, 1969), supported by many radio-carbon dates, indicates the following correlations.

First, the last severe maximum of the last glaciation or its final stages occurred broadly at the same time at such widely separated sites as Marion Island, the Argentine Basin, southern and tropical South America, Central and East Africa, and Europe.

Second, the definite amelioration of the climate, which marked the end of the postglacial in Europe, set in in the Southern Hemisphere at about 10,000 BP (but at ± 12,000 BP in the Argentine Basin, ± 12,500 BP at Marion Island, and ± 14,000 BP in New Zealand).

It is also interesting that a synchronous cold climatic phase has been described during part of the Atlantic period in Kenya, Colombia, Fuego Patagonia, Southern Chile, Groenvlei (South Africa), the tropical Atlantic and Europe.

The correlations which have been given here do not establish any complete north-south synchrony for all the climatic oscillations which have occurred. There seems, however, to have been a fairly close correspondence between the climatic sequences of both hemispheres, especially as far as temperature changes are concerned.

Once the Antarctic ice cap was formed it radically changed the climatological and oceanographic pattern of the Southern Hemisphere. The climatic zones were pushed Equatorward and the enormous production of cold Antarctic Bottom Water had at the same time a far-reaching effect in low latitudes and even in the Northern Hemisphere. Of more direct importance for the circumpolar area was the Antarctic Surface Current which spread cold water north to 50°S or further and so created a wide zone with glacial and cryonival conditions. All the southern land masses and islands were affected by these major environmental changes. Glaciers descending from the southern Andes covered Tierra del Fuego and northern Patagonia and the middle part of the South Island of New Zealand was ice covered although the glaciers in the Snowy Mountains of south-eastern Australia never reached a great extent (Galloway, 1963). South Africa, being situated further to the north, was affected to a lesser degree, although cryonival phenomena of two different glacial stages have been discovered recently in the Lesotho Mountains (Alexandre, 1962; Sparrow, 1967; Harper, 1969). At the conference of the

Subcommittee on Quaternary Studies (van Zinderen Bakker, 1969) D. L. Linton described very important evidence of colder climates in South Africa.

The decrease in temperature on the larger southern land masses during the last glaciation has been estimated to have been:

in southern Chile 3°C	(Heusser, 1966);
in Lesotho (Southern Africa) 5·5°C	(Harper, 1969);
in south-eastern Australia 4–9°C	(Galloway, 1965);
in Tasmania 5°C	(Galloway, 1965);
in New Zealand (S. Island) 6°C	(Willett, 1950).

During the last glaciation important changes took place in the Southern Ocean. The northward movement of cold Antarctic water with accompanying icebergs changed the oceanic ecosystem in a catastrophic manner. New units of ocean circulation developed and their limits are at present well known as the Antarctic and Subtropical Convergences. There is good reason to believe that the production of cold Antarctic Bottom Water is greater in the South Atlantic section than in the other oceans (Deacon, 1964), and the sectors can even show clear differences in their surface features, as has been indicated by Lamb (1960). The oceanic influence must have reached much further along the west coast of the continents into the equatorial regions. The cold currents accompanied by upwelling of cold water must have been activated during Antarctic glacial maxima. Good evidence is available for a northward shift along the Chilean coast (Heusser, 1960, 1961, 1964, 1966; J. J. and C. R. Groot, 1966). These displacements spread the drying influence of these systems to lower latitudes. A northward shift of the Benguela Current along the west coast of southern Africa could have caused dry conditions in the Stanley-Pool area (de Ploey, 1963). The drying influence of this current could reach far inland in Africa, as there are no barriers comparable with the Andes of South America (van Zinderen Bakker, 1967). The distribution and redistribution of the Kalahari sands as far north as the Congo Basin may well be explained by Antarctic influence in this way. Interesting evidence for a similar displacement along the west Australian coast has recently been obtained from pollen analytical and geological studies in the Timor Sea area which indicate severe aridity and cool water (Andel *et al.*, 1967).

Oceanic changes also had an important influence on palaeoecology during Antarctic glacial maxima because the low sea-level during these periods created extensive new habitats, for instance, along the east coast of Patagonia, where land connections developed between the Falkland Islands and South America, and in the New Zealand area. These land connections made it possible for the flora and fauna to migrate from the glaciated mainland to the present off-lying islands, where they could, at least in part, survive the ice ages.

III. Biogeographical Changes following Antarctic Glaciations

On the basis of his micropalaeontological sediment studies Hays (1965) concluded that the Antarctic Convergence could have shifted northward by about 5° of latitude during Antarctic glacial maxima. It should be realized that these shifts need not have been uniform throughout the circumpolar region. The actual position of the Convergence is influenced by the activation of the wind system, by the production of cold surface water and also by the topography of the ocean bottom (Deacon, 1964; Orren, 1966; van Zinderen Bakker, 1969). In this context we will not discuss the origin of the so-called "Antarctic" flora and fauna of the various southern continents, but it should be noted that a considerable number of these "Antarctic" elements have found their way into Southern Chile and New Zealand.

Pollen analytical studies in southern South America and in the eastern Pacific (Groot and Groot, 1966) and south-western Atlantic (Groot *et al.*, 1967) have shown that a number of glaciations are registered in the fossil records. The southern part of Chile at present receives heavy rainfall from the west winds. This wind-belt has apparently moved in meridional direction, Equatorward during glaciation and southwards during interglacials. During the last glaciation the greater part of Tierra del Fuego was invaded by land ice. The pollen diagrams from the Argentine basin studied by Groot *et al.* (1967) suggest that during this glaciation extensive areas of central and northern Argentina, probably enlarged by an emerged wide coastal plain, were covered by a dry halophytic vegetation. After Tierra del Fuego was deglaciated it was invaded by a succession of different *Nothofagus* species (Auer, 1958), while the vegetational changes in Patagonia were not as spectacular. South America is one of the most interesting areas for the study of Quaternary plant migrations under the influence of changes in temperature and rainfall, since it extends from the Subantarctic into the tropics. These processes, which have been repeated several times, have impoverished the flora, as has been recorded by Auer (1958), who studied interglacial deposits with a flora much richer than the present one. A similar phenomenon has been shown on Macquarie Island by Bunt (1956), while the Antarctic Peninsula and South Georgia lost their biota almost completely during the last glaciation. The latitudinal and climatological position of these areas is of primary importance in this connection.

The African continent probably did not suffer losses from its flora and fauna during the glacial maxima, because there were no glaciations of great extent. On the other hand, the south coast area offered many varied habitats for survival and plants and animals could migrate northward without obstruction as far as the Limpopo valley. The southern part of the African continent which receives summer rain at present will, during Antarctic glacial maxima, have come under the influence of the west winds and cyclonic rain will have penetrated far into the interior. These rains can at present only reach the south-western African coast in winter.

The islands, such as the Tristan da Cunha-Gough Island group, which is situated in the temperate zone, had a fairly stable environment during the last glaciation because of their hyperoceanic climate and their position near the Subtropical Convergence (Wace and Dickson, 1965). This is shown by pollen analytical studies. Important new pollen-bearing material has recently been collected on these islands by N. M. Wace. This stability may also apply to the other islands situated in the temperate zone, such as Île Amsterdam and Île St Paul.

Most of the other southern islands, including New Zealand, have, however, experienced tremendous changes in their biota during the Quaternary. On New Zealand evidence has been found for four glaciations (Suggate, 1965). The glaciers developed mainly on the Southern Alps in the middle part of the South Island. The temperature decrease of 5–7°C (Willett, 1950) was not enough to cause continuous severe frost and permanently frozen ground (Gage, 1965), so the climate must have been cool and humid. The northern part of the North Island and the offlying islands formed the refugia where the warmth-demanding and temperate species could survive during glacial maxima, as the oceanic climate protected them there against extreme conditions. Wardle (1963) has published an interesting map of the probable distribution of the vegetation during the Otira glaciation and concluded that many of these Pleistocene survivors never regained the mainland habitats in postglacial time. The pattern of the present distribution of the many endemic species indicates the areas where no extinction occurred during the glaciation. The extremities of the South Island and especially its northern end are rich in endemic survivors of the temperate and southern elements. It is generally accepted that the postglacial in New Zealand began about 14,000 years ago, but the vegetation has apparently not yet regained its equilibrium since the retreat of the glaciers.

The degree of glaciation of the islands in the Southern Ocean depends largely on their climatic position and their topography. It appears that the "Grande Terre" of the Archipel de Kerguelen, which straddles the Antarctic Convergence, had an aberrant type of glaciation. Bellair (1965) studied the glacial and periglacial phenomena on "Grande Terre" and came to the conclusion that the glaciers could not have been fed by extensive snow reservoirs and were apparently short-lived. He, therefore, postulated big fluctuations in the extent of the glaciers. Certain sheltered areas (including extensive tracts below present sea-level) may well have served as refugia for the flora and fauna during these glaciations, so it is very probable that the greater part of the flora and fauna could have survived, as is also borne out by the fact that ancient plants like *Pringlea antiscorbutica* and insects like the weevil *Canonopis sericea*, which lives on this Crucifer, still occur here. The oceanographic position of the islands makes their environment very sensitive to changes in the position of the Antarctic Convergence, as may be inferred from the pollen-analytical studies of Mlle N. Bellair (N. Bellair and Delebrias, 1967).

Marion and Prince Edward Islands are good examples of relatively young Subantarctic islands. The two islands are both part of a single volcano which has an age of about 300,000 years. Striated platforms have been found not much above sea-level on the old lava flows of Marion Island, demonstrating that these islands have certainly been partially glaciated. Much younger, very uneven, lava flows with an age of less than 20,000 years do not show glacial influence. Pollen analyses of cores from Marion and Prince Edward Islands show that between about 16,000 and 14,000 BP the climate was cold at sea-level. It improved after this time, so that more sensitive plants could grow on an open unprotected site after 14,000 BP. According to the pollen diagrams the climate must have been about the same during the last 11,000–12,000 years as it is at present. It is important to note that the pollen and spores of practically all the plant species which grow on the island at present are to be found in deposits 16,000 years old. This indicates that the components of the present vegetation must have survived the cool period on the islands in favourable sheltered habitats. It is not very likely that the plants migrated to these islands while they were partly glaciated, so we must accept that they gained the islands during a warm interglacial period. The age of the striated platforms has not been determined and it is therefore not known whether they originated during the last or the penultimate glaciation.

If we go further south we come to the islands of the High and Low Antarctic zones, which can never have emerged from their ice cover during the Quaternary, except for a few exposed rock surfaces and some protected beaches. Bouvetøya is a typical example of these glaciated Antarctic islands on which the vegetation consists only of some scattered mosses, lichens and algae (Muller *et al.*, 1967; Holdgate, *et al.*, 1968). The Subantarctic islands may have been wholly or partially ice covered during glaciations. Those that are of Quaternary age and those which lost their entire flora and fauna during a glaciation must have received their new biota by long-distance dispersal, generally from areas to the west. Only seeds with hooks and spines which could adhere to bird feathers, or those which can withstand transport by ocean currents and also light spores or invertebrates could gain these islands. The plants belonging to this category of new immigrants have been classified as "insular" elements by Wace and Dickson (1965) in contrast with the "continental" elements which are not able to cross the vast expanses of water. This comparatively recent migration to these Subantarctic islands explains the low incidence of endemism. These islands are inhabited by the southern cold flora and fauna.

Further north similar processes have occurred on the islands of the temperate zone. Holdgate (1960, 1965) explains the origin of the fauna of the Tristan da Cunha-Gough Island group by long-distance transport from South America. Latitudinal shifts in the West Wind Belt will have favoured the migration to the islands in certain times. Their flora is, however, not of the cold southern type, but temperate in nature, though their marine fauna is related to that of the cold Subantarctic region.

In retrospect it is evident that the Quaternary climates had a profound influence on the biogeography of the entire Antarctic and the surrounding oceans and continents. The ice ages have practically eliminated the complete flora and fauna of the Antarctic continent and have exterminated many species, as the continental elements had very limited means of escaping the rigour of the polar climate. This has led to great impoverishment of many habitats. The small isolated islands are extremely interesting, as they are field laboratories of nature where the influence of different degrees of isolation of small populations can be studied. Evolution is at work here under the pressure of changing climatic conditions and its steps should be followed very closely. We have only begun to appreciate the endless possibilities of biological research in this immense region.

References

Alexandre, J. (1962). Phénomènes Périglaciares dans le Basutoland et le Drakensberg du Natal. *Biul. Peryglac.* **11**, 11–13.

Andel, Tj. H., Ross Heath, G., Moore, T. C. and McGeary, D. F. R. (1967). Late Quaternary History, Climate, and Oceanography of the Timor Sea, Northwestern Australia. *Am. J. Sci.* **265**, 737–58.

Auer, V. (1958). The History of the Flora and Vegetation. Part II of: The Pleistocene of Fuego-Patagonia. *Suomal. Tiedeakat. Toim.* A, III, No. 50, 239 pp., 10 tables.

Bellair, N. (1967). Sédimentologie et Palynologie d'une Tourbière des Kerguelen (Port Christmas—Péninsule Loranchet). Thesis, Fac. des Sci. Paris, 43 pp., 16 plates.

Bellair, N. and Delebrias, G. (1967). Variations climatiques durant le dernier millénaire aux Iles Kerguelen. *C. r. hebd. Séanc. Acad. Sci. Paris* **264**, 2085–8.

Bellair, P. (1965). Un example de glaciation aberrante: Les Îles Kerguelen. *Com. natn. fr. Rech. Antarct.* **11**, 1–27.

Bunt, J. (1956). Living and fossil Pollen from Macquarie Island. *Nature, Lond.* **117**, 339.

Deacon, G. E. R. (1964). The Southern Ocean. In "Antarctic Research" (R. Priestley, R. J. Adie, G. de Q. Robin, eds). p. 301. Butterworths, London.

de Ploey J. (1963). Quelques indices sur l'évolution morphologique et paléoclimatique des environs du Stanley-Pool (Congo). *Lovanium. Fac. Sci.* **17**, 16.

Gage W. (1965). Some characteristics of Pleistocene Cold Climates in New Zealand. *Trans. R. Soc. N.Z. Geol.* 3, No. 2, 11–21.

Galloway, R. W. (1963). Glaciation in the Snowy Mountains: A re-appraisal. *Proc. Linn. Soc. N.S.W.* 88, No. 2., 180–98.

Galloway, R. W. (1965). Late Quaternary Climates in Australia. *J. Geol.* 73, No. 4, 603–18.

Groot, J. J. and Groot, C. R. (1966). Pollen spectra from deepsea sediments as indicators of climatic changes in southern South America. *Mar. Geol.* 4, 525–37.

Groot, J. J., Groot, C. R., Ewing, M., Burckle, L. and Conolly, J. R. (1967). Spores, pollen, diatoms and provenance of the Argentine Basin sediments. *In* "Progress in Oceanography", Vol. 4, Pergamon Press, Oxford, pp. 179–217.

Harper, G. (1969). Periglacial Evidence in Southern Africa during the Pleistocene Epoch. *In* "Palaeoecology of Africa" (E. M. van Zinderen Bakker Sr., ed.), Vol. IV (in the press).

Hays, J. D. (1965), Radiolaria and late Tertiary and Quaternary History of Antarctic Seas. *In* "Biology of the Antarctic Seas II", Antarctic Research Series. 5, pp. 125–84.

Heusser, C. J. (1960). Late-Pleistocene environments of the Laguna de San Rafael area, Chile. *Geogrl Rev.* 50, No. 4, 555–77.

Heusser, C. J. (1960). Late-Pleistocene environments of the Laguna de San Rafael area, American and Patagonia. *Ann. N.Y. Acad. Sci.* 95, No. 1, 642–57.

Heusser, C. J. (1964). Some pollen profiles from the Laguna de San Rafael area, Chile. *In* "Ancient Pacific Floras", (L. M. Cranwell, ed.), Univ. Hawaii Press, Honolulu, pp. 95–114, 1 table.

Heusser, C. J. (1966). Late-Pleistocene pollen diagrams from the Province of Llanquihue, Southern Chile. *Proc. Am. phil. Soc.* 110, No. 4, pp. 269–305.

Holdgate, M. W. (1960). The Fauna of the mid-Atlantic Islands. *Proc. R. Soc.* B **152**, 550–67.

Holdgate, M. W. (1965). The Fauna of the Tristan da Cunha Islands. *Phil. Trans. R. Soc.* B **249**, No. 759, 361–402.

Holdgate, M. W., Tilbrook, P. J. and Vaughan, R. W. (1968). The biology of Bouvetøya. *Br. Ant. Surv. Bull.* **15**, 1–7.

Lamb, H. H. (1960). Discussion in: A Discussion on the Biology of the Southern Cold Temperate Zone. *Proc. R. Soc. Lond.* B **125**, 534–6.

Muller, D. B., Schoeman, F. R. and van Zinderen Bakker Sr, E. M. (1967). Some notes on a biological reconnaissance of Bouvetøya (Antarctic). *S. Afr. J. Sci.* **63**, No. 6, 260–3.

Orren, M. J. (1966). Hydrology of the South West Indian Ocean. *Invest. Rep. Div. Sea Fisheries, Dept. Comm. & Indus.*, Rep. of S. Africa, No. 55, 20 pp., 45 fig.

Pantin, C. F. A. (1960). Introduction to "A discussion on the Biology of the Southern Cold Temperate Zone". *Proc. R. Soc.* B **152**, 431–3.

Sparrow, G. W. A. (1967). Pleistocene Periglacial Topography in Southern Africa. *J. Glaciol.* **6**, No. 46, 551–9.

Suggate, R. P. (1965). Late Pleistocene Geology of the northern part of the South Island. *Bull. geol. Surv. N.Z.* **77**, Govt. printer, Wellington.

van Zinderen Bakker, E. M. (1967). Upper Pleistocene and Holocene stratigraphy and ecology on the basis of vegetation changes in sub-Saharan Africa. *In* "Background to Evolution in Africa" (W. W. Bishop and J. D. Clark, eds), Univ. Chicago Press, Chicago, pp. 125–47.

van Zinderen Bakker, E. M. (1969). Quaternary pollen analytical studies in the Southern Hemisphere with special reference to the sub-Antarctic. *In* "Palaeoecology of Africa" Vol. V (E. M. van Zinderen Bakker Sr, ed.), (in the press).

Wace, N. M. and Dickson, J. H. (1965). The terrestrial botany of the Tristan da Cunha Islands. *Phil. Trans. R. Soc.* B **249**, No. 759, 273–360.

Wardle, P. (1963). Evolution and distribution of the New Zealand Flora, as affected by Quaternary climates. *N.Z. Jl Bot.* **1**, No. 1, 3–17.

Willett, R. W. (1950). The New Zealand Pleistocene snowline, climatic conditions and suggested biological effects. *N.Z. Jl Sci. Technol.* B **32**, No. 1, 18–48.

Antarctic Land Faunas and their History

LARS BRUNDIN
Swedish Museum of Natural History, Stockholm, Sweden

I. Introduction

Thanks to the foundation in 1957 of the Special Committee on Antarctic Research (SCAR) and the consequential scientific collaboration of twelve nations, the last ten years have seen a remarkable increase in our knowledge of the largely ice-covered Antarctic continent and its biota. The reason for this striking and unique scientific activity has been not only a general endeavour to gain information about the least-known continent but also the realization that additional information on past and present Antarctic conditions is of vital importance for our interpretation of many biotic and abiotic phenomena of global extent and significance.

II. The Recent Land Fauna

The free-living true land fauna in Antarctica today is confined to very limited ice-free areas situated mainly in the Peninsular region of West Antarctica and in the Ross sector of East Antarctica. Considering, moreover, the severe climatic and edaphic conditions, it is not surprising that we are dealing here solely with a very poorly developed soil fauna composed of such small animals as protozoa, rotifers, nematodes, tardigrades, mites and springtails.

Main representatives of the simple ecosystems existing under prevailing cold-desert conditions are, according to Janetschek (1963, 1967), the Chalikosystem, comprising barren gravel with microphytes, and the ecologically more pretentious Bryosystem, which is a system of more or less open, rarely closed macrophytic vegetation composed by mosses, lichens, and, more exceptionally, algal cover. Though our knowledge of the connection between the soil fauna and the high-Antarctic environment is still only superficial, it seems clear that humidity rather than temperature is mostly the minimum factor and thus the limiting one (cf. Janetschek, 1967).

The study of the balances of the Antarctic ecosystems at the limits of life, in the face of extreme cold and extreme drought, is a fascinating task, the more so since the relative simplicity of the situation may lead to a full understanding of general ecological principles.

Another important and fascinating task is to try to solve the problem of the history of the Antarctic land fauna and the biogeographical role of Antarctica. What, first and foremost, is the history behind the recent terrestrial fauna? Are its components a random assemblage of late immigrants carried by winds from the surrounding continents and Subantarctic islands after the maximum glaciation during the Pleistocene, or do they represent the most tolerant survivors of a once much richer preglacial Antarctic biota?

Discussing the historical aspect, we have to leave out of consideration the poorly known protozoa, rotifers, nematodes and tardigrades and keep to the arthropod groups Acarina and Collembola. The latest survey of Antarctic arthropod distribution was given by Gressitt in 1967. We learn from him that no less than about 90% of the known species and about 12% of the genera are endemic. If this high endemism is real, it would be good evidence that major parts of the recent mite and springtail faunas are the most tolerant remnants of the old preglacial fauna of Antarctica. In the history of such comparatively primitive groups as those here discussed the maximum glaciation of the Pleistocene is only yesterday, and it would be unrealistic to account for this endemism in terms of long-distance dispersal from somewhere outside Antarctica after glacial maximum, followed by speciation.

In this connection it is interesting that Janetschek (1963) has been able to show that the springtail *Gomphiocephalus hodgsoni* of East Antarctica has such a high-temperature preference as +11°C. According to Janetschek, the species seems not to be in harmony with the severe climate of Antarctica and may therefore have immigrated to Antarctica in relatively recent times. Gressitt (1965) and Wise (1967) are of the same opinion. At the present stage of our knowledge this reasoning does not appear convincing. *Gomphiocephalus* is so far an endemic genus, only known from the coastal areas of South Victoria Land; and we are dealing here with a common species that has been collected in many localities and thus cannot suffer too much under prevailing conditions. The present soil temperatures in the microhabitats of the species must be high enough to permit feeding and reproduction. There is hardly reason to suppose that the present climatic conditions are optimal to any survivors of a preglacial fauna.

On the other hand, if it is agreed that true endemics of East Antarctica are preglacial relicts, it seems necessary to assume the preglacial existence of high mountains, local glaciers, and a cold-adapted high-mountain fauna. Such a situation, which geologists and climatologists are certainly ready to accept, is in no way contradictory to the established existence in preglacial time of a generally much better Antarctic climate than that of today. The difficulties felt here by Wise (1967) as regards the possible relict nature of endemic Collembola of East Antarctica are, therefore, hardly existent.

Janetschek (1963) stresses the remarkable circumstance that in the Ross sector the arthropods are represented by larger populations and larger numbers of species on mountains and nunataks near the coast, at elevations of 1000–1200 m, than along the coast near sea-level, where climate, soil, and food resources seem to be decidedly better. He concludes that historical factors must play an important role and finds it necessary to assume that different arthropods, if future research confirms their endemism and restricted distribution, have survived the glaciation within their present areas in the Transantarctic Mountains. There is good reason to agree with this and with the following statement by him (l.c.): "The fact that under the harshest conditions of the High Antarctic, near the ice plateau, there still exists a chalikosystem belt with microphytes and some species of arthropods, confirms irrefutably that a similarly composed community must have found support for life during the maximum glaciations of the Pleistocene in these mountains at elevations above the ice-level."

However, for a realistic interpretation of the Pleistocene conditions and endurance of life in Antarctica it is important to realize that a somewhat milder and more humid climate than that of today probably was a prerequisite for the formation and maximum development of the Antarctic ice cover. There is reason to ask whether the climate of Antarctica was ever more severe than now. Another important point is the duration of the Antarctic glaciation. There is increasing evidence that the Northern Hemisphere glaciation was primarily a consequence of that in Antarctica, meaning that the latter started in the Pliocene or possibly as early as in the Miocene (cf. Harrington, 1965, and papers of the present symposium). If that be true, the populations of primary high-mountain species of Antarctica must have been exposed to severe selection pressures for a comparatively long time, a process resulting in extinction or increased ability to persist rather than success by evolutionary stability. In this perspective, successful late dispersal into East Antarctica of extra-Antarctic elements by means of single pregnant females appears highly improbable.

It is an interesting fact that, with exception of the dipteran genus *Belgica*, all endemic Antarctic arthropod genera are known only from East Antarctica. Moreover, the faunas of East and West Antarctica appear to have only two species of mites in common (cf. Gressitt, 1967). What is the reason for these striking differences?

We have to admit that a clear-cut answer cannot be given at present. But if the differences are real, it seems sound to suppose that the peculiar genera and species of East Antarctica are the last remnants of a mountain fauna that evolved in relative isolation, perhaps since the mid-Cretaceous. The richer fauna of the Peninsular region (including the South Shetland and South Orkney Islands), enjoying a milder and more humid climate, may be quite as old, but stands out as less peculiar because of long-persisting connections with the fauna of the Southern Andes via the Scotia Arc and now sunken forelands (Holtedahl, 1929). The break in continuity (probably during the Lower to mid-Tertiary) was still more marked by the partial submergence of southern South America and Antarctica as a consequence of the glaciation.

However, when drawing these provisional conclusions it is important to note that we are comparing the immense area of East Antarctica solely with a fraction of West Antarctica, namely the peripheral Antarctic Peninsula; and there are still no arthropods known from the rest of West Antarctica. The searches made in the Jones Mountains and Ellsworth Mountains were negative. These areas were too dry (Gressitt, 1967). If future investigations in West Antarctica beyond latitude 70°S prove positive, these new findings will be of very great interest. The problem is whether they will show relationships with the fauna of the Antarctic Peninsula or with that of East Antarctica.

Surveying the matter, we have to state that our knowledge of the recent Antarctic land fauna is quite insufficient for a full discussion of its history and bearing upon the problem of the former biogeographical role of Antarctica. What we need is first and foremost a detailed investigation of the mite and springtail faunas of the southern temperate zone, especially at high altitudes in the southern Andes, South Africa, South-East Australia, Tasmania and New Zealand. High priority should be given to studies of the practically unknown soil fauna living in the vicinity of the two vast ice-fields of the southern Andes, extending (with a narrow break) over 530 km in a north-south direction. Such investigations would be inexpensive and easy compared with those carried out in Antarctica, but hardly less important, because they stand out as a prerequisite for a proper interpretation of the results reached in Antarctica. This is valid for patterns of adaptation as well as for patterns of relationship and distribution.

But accumulation of new field material, however representative, would only lead to continued speculation if not exploited according to the principles of phylogenetic biogeography.

III. The Nature of Transantarctic Relationships

We have to realize that the species and monophyletic groups of the recent fauna of the globe are largely the results of successive splitting of ancestral species into allopatric daughter species, through the development of new characters in isolated peripheral populations. It is thus clear that the history of a group can be properly understood only if we know the sister group and where and how it is living. The common posession of unique specialization is always decisive for the establishment of sister-group relationships and the consideration of the actual world fauna is a general prerequisite. The relative primitiveness of a group (or species) is also important, since the more primitive group (species) can be supposed normally to be closer to the area occupied by the ancestral species than the specialized sister group (or sister species) (cf. Hennig, 1966; Brundin, 1966).

All groups are, however, not equally accessible to analysis according to the phylogenetic principles touched upon above. Best are those offering numerous structural systems where the direction of evolutionary change is properly understood. Among the Antarctic arthropod fauna, neither the mites nor the springtails seem to meet these conditions. This is a deplorable circumstance jeopardizing our chances of reconstructing their history. It may be significant that no serious attempts to work out the phylogenetic relationships of the Antarctic mites and springtails have as yet been made.

However, facing this dilemma it is gratifying to realize that we have other possibilities at our disposal. Very useful are some old insect groups with disjunct circum-Antarctic distribution belonging to the family *Chironomidae* (Diptera). In the possession of a developmental cycle comprising larva, pupa, and imago, these insects offer three quite different types of organization and adaptation within the limits of a species, which means that many structural systems and evolutionary trends are available for phylogenetic analysis.

With basic experience from Europe and North America the present author has studied the chironomid midges of the southern temperate zone during field-work in South America, South Africa, Australia, Tasmania and New Zealand. The work has been concentrated on three major groups (subfamilies Podonominae, Aphroteniinae, and Diamesinae) confined to cold mountain streams, where large-scale collecting is easy by means of series of net traps. The comprehensive material thus brought together during specialized field-work around the Antarctic continent has undergone a detailed phylogenetic analysis from the species level to the subfamily level (Brundin, 1966).

The three subfamilies display no less than twenty-five cases of transantarctic relationship. The occurrence of multiple transantarctic relationship within each of these strictly monophyletic groups of southern origin shows that there must have been a major evolutionary centre in the south and that a formerly ice-free Antarctica has played an important biogeographical role. The establishment that the twenty-five cases of transantarctic relationship all conform to a rigid pattern in the connection between phylogenetic relationship, relative age, and geographical distribution (replacement of sister groups) is essential to the argument and must be conceived as a proof of the reliability of the results.

The established Southern Hemisphere pattern can be demonstrated by a simple diagram (Fig. 1). We see from this that a group in New Zealand is the sister group of a group occurring in South America, or in South America + Australia. In some cases the New Zealand group is the primitive one, in others the more specialized. A group in Australia–Tasmania, on the other hand, is always a specialized sister group of a subgroup of a South American group. Circles with attached arrows indicate multiple occurrence of accordant trans-antarctic connections within a monophyletic group. In the subfamily Podo-nominae, for example, there seems to be no less than nine such accordant connections.

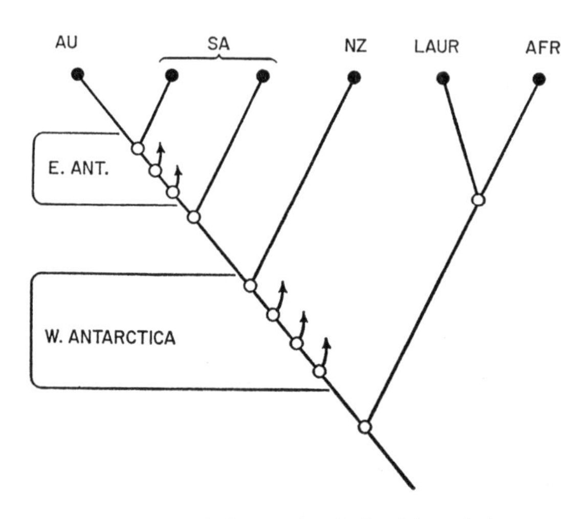

FIG. 1. The connection between phylogenetic relationship, relative age, and geographical distribution in cold-adapted chironomid groups of austral origin. Circles with attached arrows indicate the multiple occurrence of accordant transantarctic connections within a monophyletic group. The different evolutionary and biogeographical role played by East and West Antarctica after the separation of South Africa from the other southern lands in the Upper Jurassic is also indicated.

Compared with the groups just treated, the related group in South Africa takes a more isolated position, giving it a higher rank. We see (Fig. 1) that it forms the sister group of all the other southern groups together; and here amphitropical (bipolar) distribution comes in, since the South African group clearly stands out as the primitive sister group of a major group in the northern continents, Laurasia.

The intimate connection between transantarctic relationships and amphi-tropical distribution demonstrates that proper understanding of southern biogeography is a prerequisite for a realistic general reconstruction of the history of terrestrial life on the globe.

The remarkable circumstance that all groups in Australia and New

Zealand are more closely related to South American groups than to each other stresses not only the negligible influence of chance dispersal over wide expanses of sea on the development of the great patterns, but is also very strong evidence that Antarctica has offered *separate* connections between the two Australasian realms and South America. There can hardly be any uncertainty as to the character of these transantarctic connections. The geologists agree that East and West Antarctica are two distinct geological provinces with a different history. Hence there is good reason to suppose that the amphi-Antarctic elements of South America have been connected with those of Australia–Tasmania via East Antarctica and with those of New Zealand via West Antarctica. The present concentration in New Zealand and southern South America of comparatively primitive groups connected by relationship on the sister-group level is strong evidence that the great arc formed by Andean South America, the Scotia Arc, West Antarctica, and New Zealand has functioned as a vital part of a southern centre of evolution. The evolutionary role thus assigned to that arc agrees well with its dynamic geological nature, since it forms a segment of the old circum-Pacific belt of orogenesis and volcanism.

The general position of the Australian groups as specialized offshoots of major South American groups demonstrates, on the other hand, the subordinate evolutionary importance of Australia in the history of the cold-adapted southern elements treated here. To them Australia has functioned as a receiver.

Like Patagonia, East Antarctica and Australia, the African continent is, geologically speaking, a shield. But its southern margin is formed by the old Cape fold belt, which has obviously been a part of an important southern centre of evolution. The great age of this South African subcentre is proven by the structure of the phylogenetic connections displayed by the rheophil insect groups referred to above.

The biological documentation thus brought forward implies that the southern continents once must have been closely connected according to a certain pattern, and also that the connections were broken according to a certain sequence. The process started with the separation of South Africa. The next event was the break in the connections between New Zealand and West Antarctica, which latter could well have been more clearly separated from East Antarctica than now. The following separation between Australia and East Antarctica antedates quite considerably the break between southern South America and Antarctica.

As to the question of what, if any, geological theory accounts for the inferred palaeogeographical pattern, the answer is that only the modern theory of continental displacement is able to meet all demands raised by the structure of the transantarctic relationships. A consequence of this acknowledgement is acceptance of the time-table set out by proponents of the displacement theory. There is good evidence (cf. the discussion in Brundin, 1966) that the main events of the continental fragmentation occurred during the Upper Jurassic to the Upper Cretaceous. Many groups in the biota of the world would accordingly be much older than generally assumed.

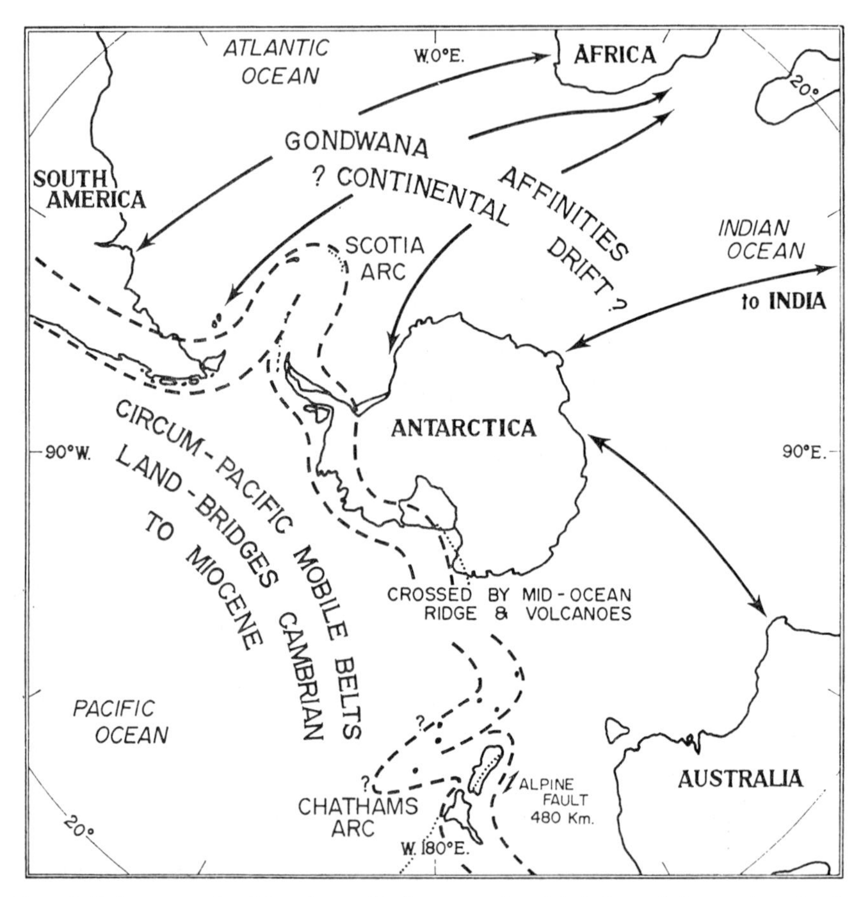

FIG. 2. Paleogeography. The circum-Pacific zone of mobile belts and the southern lands with Gondwana affinities. (From Harrington, 1965, Fig. 7.)

In his paper on the geology of Antarctica, Harrington (1965) presents, as an advice to biogeographers, a hypothetical palaeogeographic map of the southern hemisphere (Fig. 2 of the present paper) that is based on the theory of continental displacement and shows a zone of "circum-Pacific mobile belts" extending from the Andean Cordillera through West

Antarctica to Campbell Island and New Zealand. With regard to the nature of the chironomid transantarctic relationships the palaeogeography outlined by Harrison leaves very little to be desired.

The chironomid midges are still the only major animal group whose transantarctic relationships have been analysed in detail according to strict phylogenetic principles. It would hence be unwise to suppose that future analyses of other groups of animals and plants will always reveal exactly the same pattern. Among factors biasing the history of a group, and not least the routes of dispersal, may be mentioned absolute age, adaptedness and adaptability, and the centre of origin. There is, for example, no trace of southern beeches (*Nothofagus*), living or fossil, in South Africa, probably because the former connections between South Africa and the other southern lands were broken before the origin or diversification of *Nothofagus* during the Cretaceous. Palaeoclimatic conditions and stenotopy may be the reason why a group of high age is restricted, for example, to South Africa and Australia. The orogenic belt extending from the Andes through West Antarctica to New Zealand may always have offered too severe climatic conditions for successful dispersal of less cold-tolerant groups.

To groups of *northern origin* the New Guinea sector may have served as a forking-point for further dispersal southwards, partly along East Australian highlands, partly along the Inner Melanesian Arc to land areas now represented by New Caledonia and New Zealand. Dispersal of that kind would give rise to direct sister-group relationships across the Tasman Sea. Given sufficient time and further progression of the group via West or East Antarctica (or both), the end result of the presupposed transtropic dispersal would be a case of *secondary* transantarctic relationship, in contrast to the *primary* transantarctic relationship displayed by groups of southern origin with amphi-Antarctic distribution. Different cases of the former type, preceded by southward dispersal along the orogenic belts on both sides of the Pacific, or along East African highlands, have been discussed by Du Rietz (1940).

Lacking the firm background of proper phylogenetic argument the different possibilities touched upon above still stand out as vaguely founded hypotheses. Nevertheless the pattern shown by the chironomid midges analysed is most probably only one, though a widely relevant, aspect of a grand austral biogeographic pattern. The main characteristic of the latter is the occurrence of austral disjunctions within strictly monophyletic groups of comparatively great age, demonstrating the former existence of a unitary evolutionary centre in the south that must have been intermittently connected with a corresponding extratropical centre in the northern continents. Series of cases from different chironomid groups illustrate in a conclusive way the successive fractioning of the austral evolutionary centre and reflect at the same time certain palaeogeographic events and conditions. The fact that the inferred nature of the latter is in full agreement with the modern theory of continental displacement provides a strong biological confirmation of the soundness of a far-reaching theory founded on data furnished by geologic, geophysic, and palaeomagnetic research.

The disjunct fractions of monophyletic groups now restricted to southern South America, South Africa, Australia and New Zealand have thus to be conceived as remnants of a former, mainly temperate biota inhabiting the southern parts of the super-continent Gondwana and the adherent sections of the circum-Pacific belt of orogenesis and volcanism. The cold-adapted circum-Antarctic groups among animals and plants simply stand out as the most palpable and striking expressions of former Gondwanic evolution and unity. The geographical position of Antarctica within the Gondwanic assemblage indicates a former biogeographical role the importance of which is well confirmed by the nature of transantarctic relationship.

The question has often been raised and discussed as to whether Antarctica has been a centre of evolution or whether it has functioned only as a part of a more or less continuous land-migration route between South America and Australia–New Zealand. In the light of present knowledge some remarks seem justified.

Harrington (1965) writes: "Considering the small percentage of exposed rock, and the incomplete geological work, the palaeontological record is surprisingly full, and surprisingly normal. Antarctica seems to have had a normal biota of cold-temperate and temperate type for nearly the whole of Phanerozoic (Cambrian and later) time."

But if Antarctica has been inhabited by a normal temperate biota from the end of the Permo-Carboniferous glaciations until the start of the last glaciation in the Mio-Pliocene, there has indeed been ample time for development of numerous local endemisms at different taxonomic levels. There is no reason whatever to suppose that a biota, with about 250 million years at its disposal and inhabiting a great continent with highly diversified topography, would behave in another way. Antarctica cannot have served solely as a dispersal route.

While the position of Antarctica as an active subcentre of a former great austral centre of evolution seems obvious, there are no data supporting the view sometimes expressed that Antarctica has functioned as the very main node of austral evolution and diversification.

IV. Antarctic Fossils and their Significance

Many biologists hold the view that attempts to reconstruct the history of a group in time and space are of little value as long as there are no fossil data available. Such a general statement, however, reveals a deep misunderstanding of the situation. It overlooks the fact that proper knowledge of the phylogenetic relationships of the recent groups is a prerequisite for an interpretation of the fossils. We cannot maintain that a certain fossil group *A* is the sister group of a recent group *B* before we know the recent sister group of *B*. In other words, through the construction of the sister-group system formed by the recent groups we are getting at those unique specialized characters which alone are able to show the phylogenetic position of a fossil group (see Brundin, 1966, Fig. 9, 1968, Fig. 2). But even such a knowledge is, of course, no guarantee, since fossil remnants are rarely so well preserved or so complete that a proper judgement is possible. The crucial characters may belong, for example, to the soft parts of the anatomy of a vertebrate, or to one of the three stages of a holometabolous insect.

It is also important to recognize that if we have properly studied the sister-group system of a recent group (with disjunct distribution around Antarctica, for example), then we have at the same time obtained an insight into the main trends in the history of the group, as demonstrated above. Well-preserved fossils can, of course, greatly enrich the picture and prove the minimum age of a group, but it is fairly pointless to ask for fossils as long as careful phylogenetic studies of the recent groups are still lacking.

However, even if fossils cannot give any direct, precise information about their phylogenetic connections with the recent groups and the history of the latter as monophyletic units, they are at least giving direct and important evidence of the general aspect of the biota of different ages. As to Antarctica, we know some main trends in the floral successions from the Permain to the Lower Tertiary. During the Permian, the Triassic and the Jurassic periods the floral relationships between Antarctica and other parts of the Southern Hemisphere and India were so close as to be almost identical; "this places them all without question within a single Gondwana floral province" (Plumstead, 1964). The rapidly increasing knowledge of the fossil floras of Antarctica and the other southern continents stresses still further the reality of the emerging general picture of former Gondwanic unity.

The Antarctic fossil layers have as yet yielded very few and fragmentary remains of land animals. The Permian insect wings from *Glossopteris* layers of the Theron Mountains are certainly insufficient for a strict discussion of relationships, as are the beetle elytra from Middle Jurassic beds of the Antarctic Peninsula described by Zeuner (1959). The recent find of a jawbone fragment of a labyrinthodont amphibian in Triassic layers at the Beardmore Glacier has attracted great attention in the world press and may turn out eventually to be a further indication of former direct connections between Antarctica and other southern lands.

V. Subantarctic Island Faunas

During the last few years there has been a considerable increase in our knowledge of the Subantarctic island faunas, especially through the efforts of Linsley Gressitt. We are, however, still far from a proper insight into the age and history of these faunas, chiefly because the phylogenetic relationships of the different components are very poorly known. While waiting for adequate analyses all discussions of Subantarctic island biogeography remain more or less in the air. As to such significant island faunas as those of Îles Crozet and Archipel de Kerguelen, the general opinion seems to be that they are on the whole comparatively young and mainly result from wind dispersal. Such general assumptions are of little value. Let me give a relevant example of the importance of the phylogenetic approach.

In chironomid material from Île de la Possession, Îles Crozet, collected in 1968 by Dr Lewis Davies, of Durham University, the dominant species is a member of the subfamily Podonominae. The species, obviously identical with *Microzetia mirabilis* Seg. described recently from Crozet by Séguy (1965), is represented by numerous imagos, pupae, and larvae. *Microzetia* does not belong to the tribe Boreochlini, confined to South Africa and Laurasia, but to the sister tribe, Podonomini, that comprises all podonomine species occurring in South America, Australia–Tasmania and New Zealand. The Crozet genus stands out as a peculiar endemie and is most closely related to the genera *Podonomus* and *Parochlus*, which are both well represented by subgroups in the southern lands just mentioned (cf. Brundin, 1966). The large genus *Podonomus* is probably the sister group of *Microzetia*. The circumstance that *Podonomus* (like *Parochlus*) is involved in multiple transantarctic relationships shows that *Microzetia* cuts deep into podonomid phylogeny and represents a group of very high age. Indeed, if my still provisional analysis of the phylogenetic connections of *Microzetia* is right, we are able to draw the following conclusions.

Microzetia stands out as survivor of a group whose ancestral species existed approximately at the transition between the Jurassic and the Cretaceous, i.e. not very long after the separation of South Africa. The isolation of the Crozet area must have come into existence well before the break in the connections between Antarctica and Australia–New Zealand, a break that gave rise to the endemic *Podonomus* subgroups of New Zealand, Australia and South America. This would imply that the Crozet Archipelago or corresponding, more basic parts of the Crozet Rise have been above sea surface since the Lower Cretaceous. The phylogenetic relationships also indicate that Antarctica was the cradle of *Microzetia*.

References

Brundin, L. (1966). Transantarctic relationships and their significance, as evidenced by chironomid midges; with a monograph of the subfamilies Podonominae, Aphroteniinae and the austral Heptagyiae. *K. svenska VetenskAkad. Handl.* (4) **11**, 1–472.

Brundin, L. (1968). Application of phylogenetic principles in systematics and evolutionary theory. *In* "Current Problems of Lower Vertebrate Phylogeny" (T. Ørvig, ed.), Nobel Symposium 4, 473–95. Stockholm.

Du Rietz, C. E. (1940). Problems of bipolar plant distribution. *Acta phytogeogr. suec.* **13**, 215–82.

Gressitt, J. Linsley (1965). Biogeography and ecology of land arthropods in Antarctica. *In* "Biogeography and Ecology in Antarctica" (P. van Oye and J. van Mieghem, eds), Monogr. Biol. Vol. **15**, pp. 431–90.

Gressitt, J. Linsley (1967). Introduction. *In* Gressitt (ed.), Entomology of Antarctica. *Antarctic Research Series* Vol. **10**, pp. 1–33.

Harrington, H. J. (1965). Geology and morphology of Antarctica. *In* "Biogeography and Ecology in Antarctica" (P. van Oye and J. van Mieghem, eds.), Monogr. Biol. Vol. **15**, pp. 1–71.

Hennig, W. (1966). Phylogenetic systematics. Urbana: University of Illinois Press. 263 pp.

Holtedahl, O. (1929). On the geology and physiography of some antarctic and subantarctic islands. *Scient. Results Norw. Antarct. Exped.* **3**, 1–172.

Janetschek, H. (1963). On the terrestrial fauna of the Ross-Sea area, Antarctica (Preliminary report). *Pacif. Insects.* **5** (1), 305–11.

Janetschek, H. (1967). Arthropod ecology of South Victoria Land. *In* J. L. Gressit (ed.), Entomology of Antarctica. *Antarctic Research Series* **10**, 205–293.

Plumstead, Edna P. (1964). Palaeobotany of Antarctica. *In* "Antarctic Geology" (R. J. Adie, ed.), 637–54. Proc. First Int. Sympos. Antarctic Geology; SCAR Proceedings, 1963: Amsterdam. 758 pp.

Séguy, E. (1965). Deux noveaux Tendipédides des Îles Crozet (Insectes Diptères Nématocères). *Bull. Mus. Hist. nat., Paris* **37** (2), 285–9.

Wise, K. A. J. (1967). Collembola (Springtails). *In* J. L. Gressitt (ed.), Entomology of Antarctica. *Antarctic Research Series* **10**, 123–48.

Zeuner, F. E. (1959). Jurassic beetles from Graham Land, Antarctica. *Palaeontology* **1**, 407–9.

Discussion

THE EARLY HISTORY OF ANTARCTICA

R. J. ADIE

The development of palaeotemperature determination using the oxygen 16/18 method has been an especially important recent advance. Belemnites from the Antarctic are now being studied in the United States, and we hope to learn the temperature régime under which they lived. The study of palaeowinds is also becoming rewarding: work has been done in the U.S.A. and South America and is now starting in the Antarctic.

E. M. VAN ZINDEREN BAKKER

Would Dr Adie explain how the *Glossopteris* flora fits into the scheme he has displayed?

R. J. ADIE

The *Glossopteris* flora became established in the Upper Carboniferous. It was a very important and widespread flora in the Southern Hemisphere, but is quite unrepresented in Northern Hemisphere rocks. It is present throughout the Permian of South Africa and India and persists until the early Triassic. In South America and South Africa it was associated with the *Thinfeldia* flora. In Antarctica the *Glossopteris* flora only occurred in East Antarctica, and is absent from the west. But the *Thinfeldia* flora of Triassic age is found both in East and West Antarctica, and this suggests a floral migration from east to west at this period, perhaps when the continental masses came together at the end of their movement.

E. D. RUDOLPH

What is the evidence for the southern coal deposits having been laid down under cold conditions? How cold? What was the temperature?

R. J. ADIE

Some Antarctic and South African coals interbed with tillites, proving the coldness of the climate. Dark unoxidized shales associated with them are also characteristic of cold conditions.

V. GALLARDO

The diversity of benthic faunas tends to be related to climate. In the Antarctic sublittoral there is a diverse fauna, probably of considerable age. The Arctic benthic communities are more impoverished, perhaps because conditions there have been changing more rapidly. In the temperate periods in the Antarctic were the yearly oscillations of the climate as great as are now found in the temperate zones or was the range narrower?

R. J. ADIE

This important question cannot be answered yet, but it is one field in which work is now beginning.

N. M. WACE

To what extent did Antarctica serve as a land link for the dispersal of animals? One labyrinthodont has now been found: is there other evidence of the presence in Antarctica of land animals that must have walked there?

R. J. ADIE

The phrase "animals that must have walked there" is the key to this question. Antarctica may always have been an area of low faunal abundance. We could expect the red beds of Antarctica to have dinosaur fossils like those present in profusion in these rocks in South Africa, but none has been found. Some may come to light if we have specialists to look for them, but at present this is a real puzzle.

L. BRUNDIN

There are several recent insect groups with a circum-Antarctic distribution. Analysis of their phylogeny and relative ages shows the palaeogeographic pattern clearly and fits with the time-table of probable continental displacement. The biogeographical role of Antarctica cannot be interpreted solely from fossils.

R. J. ADIE

There are many fossil insects in the Antarctic. Well-preserved Coleoptera, some still retaining an iridescent sheen on the elytra, are found in the mid-Jurassic at Hope Bay. But their relationships are obscure and arbitrary new generic names have had to be given to them.

L. BRUNDIN

To interpret the history of Antarctica it is important to make a parallel study of the invertebrates of the circum-Antarctic land areas.

PHYLOGENETIC STUDIES AND THEIR INTERPRETATION

N. M. WACE

I would like to discuss the assumption underlying Dr Brundin's argument. His phylogeny seems to be based solely on a consideration of living organisms, but is it legitimate thus to exclude fossils? I am not clear about Hennig's concept of sister groups: would Dr Brundin please explain?

L. BRUNDIN

Only living organisms can be investigated in all their structural details. Fossils preserve only a selection of characters which may not be those most useful for phylogenetic study. Moreover, all living species ultimately connect with one another and can be traced back to the start of life. If you consider a diagram of their descent, it must link all organisms and fossils can be fitted into the branchings of the system. (Dr Brundin drew Fig. 1 on the blackboard)
If this is assumed to be part of the system of descent, every fossil must have a sister group in the recent fauna, and all extinct species must be able to be fitted in if they are well enough preserved for the essential characteristics to be studied. Most, however, have to be discarded because of their imperfect preservation. If you reconstruct a phylogeny of living groups, however, at least you get a skeleton of the derivation and relationships of all the animals and plants with which the biologist is really concerned.

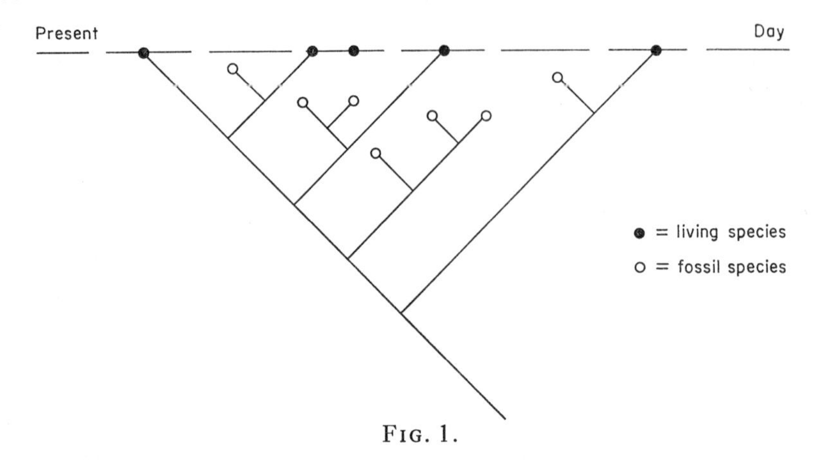

Fig. 1.

K. G. McKenzie

Although animal zoogeography may not be *essential* to the Hennig rationale, it is certainly of great importance for understanding the evolution of species. Winds and oceans influence, and have influenced, animal dispersal. Thus, the West Wind Drift must have played a significant role in the distribution of southern marine animals after the break-up of Gondwanaland. Freshwater organisms, notably Entomostraca, can be transported passively via winds or birds, while winged insects may fly or be blown, even intercontinentally.

I consider that the Hennig diagram can be fitted to any taxa once the basic philosophy is accepted. For example, a Hennig-type phylogenetic pattern is consistent with the evidence available on a group of freshwater cytherid Ostracoda with many living representatives and a fossil history as far back as the mid-Mesozoic.

L. Brundin

Hennig formulated a principle—the search for the sister group—as a fundamental tool in phylogeny. Ernst Mayr and other students of population genetics reiterated the principles on which Hennig's deductions are based. Speciation generally occurs through the spatial and reproductive isolation of peripheral populations: it is thus allopatric. It is very important to remember that the process of speciation is one of splitting, and that the peripheral, new, species will have new characters while the sister group will be a more primitive species more similar in features, distribution, and habitat to the common ancestor. Long-range dispersal may well have happened, but the important thing in deciphering the history of a group is to decide what is the main pattern and what is secondary and the relationships of species must be studied for this. Information about relative ages and geographical displacements are needed as a phylogenetic background to studies of dispersal.

THE AGE OF THE ANTARCTIC ICE CAP

F. Ugolini

How old is the present glaciation in Antarctica?

R. J. ADIE

Until recently it was thought to be only a Pleistocene glaciation—that is, about 1 million years old. But there have been suggestions of an older ice sheet in West Antarctica. Lavas interbedded with moraines have now been found at Deception Island and King George Island, and this may allow us to date an early stage. Lavas interbedded with moraine in Victoria Land prove there was ice there 3·4–3·8 million years ago. Some people guess the ice cap may be as old as 5 million years. The commencement of glaciation could well be much earlier than any dated morainic material, and marine sediment sequences do support this view. Palaeotemperature studies should help clarify the problem, and the establishment of a firm chronology may also allow us to answer the question of whether the southern glaciations set off the northern or vice versa.

L. M. GOULD

It is quite clear that the Pleistocene period cannot be regarded as synonymous with the glacial period. Miocene tillites have been found in the Jones Mountains in Antarctica, and Miocene foraminifera off Mexico demonstrate the influence of cold water pouring out from the Antarctic.

M. J. DUNBAR

How do you define the Pleistocene if it is no longer regarded as contemporaneous with the last cool period?

R. J. ADIE

The Pleistocene is the period from 1 million years ago to the present. We have simply to agree that southern glaciations began in the Miocene. Fossil penguins in three areas, New Zealand, Patagonia, and Seymour Island, would agree with this pattern. We must still, however, resolve the question of whether the Miocene ice sheet was local or a general one, and date the formation of the great continental ice cover.

B. STONEHOUSE

Caution is needed in interpreting evidence provided by fossil penguins. Today penguins live in seas as warm as 23° C. Oxygen isotope palaeotemperatures show that large penguins of the New Zealand Eocene, Oligocene, and Miocene existed in temperatures of 15–23°C, like those now encountered off Peru, Chile, and Australia.

R. J. ADIE

The molluscan faunas associated with fossil penguins at Seymour Island seem from their growth curves and diminutive forms to be cold-water faunas.

K. G. MCKENZIE

Recent work on corals, Mollusca and Foraminifera, shows that Australasia also became cooler in the Miocene.

E. A. SMITH

Biologists look to geologists for help in explaining the conditions under which seals originated. Probably the group evolved in the Northern Hemisphere and moved south, reaching the Antarctic by late Pliocene. Probably this movement followed cold waters; were they following the ice or retreating from it? Were temperatures cold or cooling in the late Eocene to early Pliocene?

R. J. ADIE

There is not enough information to answer this question. It is clear, however, at least that there was access to the Antarctic seas from the north at this time: the continents had split and there were open sea lanes. Unfortunately we have very few seals as fossils.

L. M. CRANWELL

It now appears, from recovery of large, distinctive pollen grains of *Sesame*-type (Pedaliaceae) in lower to middle Campanian deposits of Seymour and Snow Hill Islands, that part of the terrestrial component was derived from plants of very dry environments, comparable with those favoured by the family in its present range (Africa to northern Australia). Association with *Nothofagus* pollen suggests mosaic conditions with desert in the lowlands or in the rain-shadow of montane beech forests.

G. A. KNOX

Has Dr Hays any estimates of the maximum extent of sea ice (pack ice or fast ice) around Antarctica?

J. D. HAYS

Results from three traverses suggest that ice cover during the past 1–1½ million years has not extended more than two degrees further north than now.

M. J. DUNBAR

How much earlier did glaciation begin in the Antarctic than in the Arctic?

E. M. VAN ZINDEREN BAKKER

The first main cooling in some records appears 2½ million years ago and may reflect Antarctic glaciation, while a second cooling 750,000 years ago may be due to the Arctic.

J. D. HAYS

Antarctic deep-ocean cores reveal ice-rafted debris as old as 4½ million years, so glaciers must have reached the sea by then. The oldest tills in Iceland have a date of 3 million years. But one would expect the Arctic glaciation to have begun earlier in Greenland than in Iceland. At the present we can only say we think the Antarctic ice sheets came first.

K. G. MCKENZIE

Was the core from which Dr Hays obtained ice-rafted pebbles on the transect he illustrated? If not, what was its position, and could it possibly indicate ice-rafting of debris from South America?

J. D. HAYS

It was at 62°S, 165°W. Ice-rafting westwards into the Pacific, against the current, seems highly improbable.

G. DE Q. ROBIN

Do the sediments provide any evidence of ice surges?

J. D. HAYS

No, but I could not rule them out without a more careful scrutiny of the cores.

N. A. MACKINTOSH

Dr Hollin stressed the problems involved in the measurement of the rate of calving of icebergs from the ice shelves. Would he say the Ross and Filchner shelves were the main calving areas? About 1925–30 there was a vast number of bergs in the Atlantic sector, and this was thought to be due to a really big break-up in the western Weddell Sea. Such events must complicate measurement of the mean rate of calving.

J. HOLLIN

Rough calculations suggest that the Ross and Filchner Ice Shelves may account for very roughly one-fifth of the ice calving from Antarctica. As you say, the calving process may vary considerably with time. Tsunamis and local ice surges are two factors which have been advanced as a possible cause of increased calving. Satellite observations should be very useful now for determining the origin and movement of large bergs. From a strictly glaciological point of view, however, the rate of ice loss is often most easily and usefully measured some kilometres inland from the calving areas.

SEA-LEVEL CHANGES

L. BRUNDIN

It is said that the Antarctic continental shelf, because of isostatic depression, is lower than the shelf about any other continent. It has been stated that this ice-loading has depressed Antarctica by as much as 1000 m. Does the surface of East Antarctica form a concavity?

J. HOLLIN

If isostatic compensation is complete, as the gravity data are usually held to imply, the centre of Antarctica should be depressed by very roughly 1000 m.

V. GALLARDO

If Antarctica has been depressed isostatically by the weight of the ice, what was the rate of sinking? This must have affected the benthos.

R. J. ADIE

I do not know. But now that the ice is receding, the coastal areas are rising and flights of raised beaches—in the South Shetlands up to twelve or fourteen in number—are present locally. The rate of change must have been fairly rapid here.

A. T. WILSON

These raised beaches could result simply from marginal adjustment following recession of ice from the coastlands, and need not imply an isostatic recovery of the whole continent. The central ice cap may indeed be getting thicker.

T. J. HART

Surely rise and fall in sea-level due to the glacial abstraction of ice could be demonstrated elsewhere than in the Antarctic—for example, there is evidence that the continental shelf of South West Africa has been more deeply submerged recently following a eustatic rise in sea-level following ice melt.

J. HOLLIN

Yes, changes of sea-level are best studied outside Antarctica, where most of the evidence is covered by ice, and where such evidence as there is probably illustrates only local isostatic movement of the land. As you say, the evidence from South West Africa probably illustrates a general eustatic effect.

CHANGES IN MARINE PRODUCTIVITY

L. BRUNDIN

Dr Hays said that the productivity of the circum-Antarctic ocean changed when the ice sheet was formed. In 1956, following work on the highest lake in Jotunheimen, Norway, I came to the conclusion that the grinding of minute rock particles by moving ice liberated much phosphorus in a form available to the phytoplankton. The lake I was studying, although very high, had a well-developed biota in contrast to other high Alpine lakes more remote from a glacier inflow. Could this have been a direct factor increasing Antarctic productivity?

J. D. HAYS

Dr Brundin's suggestion about nutrients is a very good one. Much nutrient very likely did come into the marine ecosystem as "rock flour" from the continent. However, the change in the diatom abundance in the marine cores is a sudden one: were the build-up of nutrients from glacial material the principal cause you would expect a more gradual change.

G. A. KNOX

It was reported that the diatomaceous deposits were replaced by glacial silts south of the Divergence. Surely diatom production in the surface layers is maximal south of the Divergence? Are diatom remains carried by currents north of the Divergence or are they all consumed by benthic filter-feeding organisms?

J. D. HAYS

Productivity is certainly maximal about the Divergence. Some diatoms do appear in the bottom silts there, but glacial material predominates. Remains possibly could be carried north.

D. ASHTON

What is the effect of the sea ice on primary production through the cutting down of light intensity? Would not light starvation depress the phytoplankton and thus lower productivity?

M. J. DUNBAR

By analogy with the Arctic this would be of small importance: enough light penetrates the Arctic ice to allow the phytoplankton to use up the available phosphate.

T. J. HART

But in the Antarctic the phosphate is never exhausted, even though it does get reduced to quite low levels. There is continual replenishment by upwelling from the warm deep layer. Phytoplankton are unlikely to be limited by phosphate levels.

S. Z. EL SAYED

It seems to me that the role of nutrients has been overemphasized by some speakers. Our investigations have clearly demonstrated that it is most unlikely that the productivity of Antarctic waters is limited by nutrient concentrations. Further, although the concentrations of these nutrients are lower north of the Convergence than in Antarctic waters proper, these low values are higher than encountered during winter in temperate regions. As to the productivity of the Antarctic waters, our investigations have shown that it is in the coastal rather than the oceanic areas that these waters are extremely productive.

SURVIVAL THROUGH THE PERIOD OF MAXIMUM GLACIATION

P. J. TILBROOK

Professor van Zinderen Bakker suggested that the Antarctic land fauna and flora were wiped out at ice maximum, but it has been suggested that the present distribution of the oribatid mite *Alaskozetes antarcticus* may be a direct result of survival during the glaciation. This species is found in the Antarctic peninsula—South Orkney area and has two subspecies, one from the South Sandwich Islands and Bouvetøya and the other from eastern Subantarctic islands. J. A. Wallwork has stated that this eastern form is the primitive one and the others are derivatives. He postulates initial dispersal and subspeciation in the pre-drift period and subsequent survival during glaciation due to an intertidal habitat.

E. M. VAN ZINDEREN BAKKER

Could it not have survived in Tierra del Fuego and recolonized West Antarctica by wind dispersal? If it is able to reach Bouvetøya it must be capable of transoceanic dispersal.

P. J. TILBROOK

Alaskozetes has no known close relative in South America.

H. JANETSCHEK

Is it seriously thought that former ice levels were so high that there was no possibility of faunal survival even near the coast? If you examine a transect from Victoria Land coast to the polar plateau, you will find the peaks of arthropod abundance and diversity not at the coasts but on nunataks about 1000 m high. Some species are endemic to these areas. Why should there not have been survival on nunataks in the transantarctic mountains? I understand there are glacial benches on those mountains, so we should be able to determine maximum ice elevation. Certainly in the Himalayas a distinctly different fauna occurs at altitudes of about 5000 m and above: different from that of the valleys which have been overrun by the glaciations. The organisms involved are well able to withstand a glaciation.

E. M. VAN ZINDEREN BAKKER

I am quite happy to accept periglacial survival of cryptogams and arthropods on nunataks.

J. HOLLIN

Many mountain peaks stood out from the ice cap at maximum. It is more difficult to decide whether there were coastal oases, but there probably were. Sea-level was lower and the coastline would be further out from the present land.

G. de Q. Robin

Because of the profile of the ice sheet you would expect the relative rise of the ice to be several times greater near the coast. A small extension of the sheet might cause an elevation of the ice surface by 600–700 m near the coast, but only 100–200 m inland.

L. Brundin

Dr Janetschek has made an important point about the concentration of invertebrates on nunataks at the 1000 m level and not near coasts. We must, of course, be certain about the true level of endemism in the Antarctic before reaching final judgements, but if there are many endemic genera this would be strong evidence for preglacial survival.

CHANGES IN THE DRY VALLEYS

E. D. Rudolph

Professor Wilson referred to lichens ceasing to grow in the dry valleys at the line of 80% Relative Humidity. But many lichens can grow in drier conditions and some fungi down to at least 20%.

A. T. Wilson

My figures were based on the general food-storage literature. Do you actually find fungi in the bottoms of the McMurdo dry valleys?

E. D. Rudolph

No.

F. Ugolini

What caused the replenishment of Lake Vanda 1200 years ago?

A. T. Wilson

Increasing precipitation over the Wilson Piedmont Glacier and increased flow of the Onyx River.

F. Ugolini

Was the Victoria dry valley affected?

A. T. Wilson

Yes. The alpine valley glaciers all have 3000-year-old terminal moraines and then there was a recession with a probable readvance 1200 years ago. Lakes are more sensitive indicators of precipitation fluctuations than glaciers, since they balance the whole precipitation/evaporation system of the catchment. An increase in precipitation by 20% would double the size of Lake Vanda.

ISLAND FLORAS AND FAUNAS

E. M. van Zinderen Bakker

Because the Îles Crozet support a Chironomid of Mesozoic age must we assume that the islands themselves are of such great antiquity?

L. Brundin

In a sense we must. But the Îles Crozet themselves need not be so old, so long as some land area in this region has persisted, for example on the Crozet-Kerguelen ridge.

N. M. WACE

Are Îles Crozet the only Subantarctic station for this midge?

L. BRUNDIN

Yes. However the limnic insect fauna of Kerguelen is very little known, and there are certainly many appropriate habitats there.

M. W. HOLDGATE

Îles Crozet are also peculiar in supporting a Phalangid of the genus *Nuncia* which is otherwise represented in Tasmania, New Zealand, and South America, but nowhere else in the Subantarctic island belt.

L. BRUNDIN

Jeannel also suggested that some relationships of the beetle fauna of Îles Crozet lay with South Africa.

M. W. HOLDGATE

Pringlea antiscorbutica, which appears an ancient and peculiar plant, is also restricted to Îles Crozet, Kerguelen, and the Prince Edward group.

L. M. CRANWELL

Why should the glaciation on Marion Island appear to have ended before that on the South Orkneys or New Zealand?

E. M. VAN ZINDEREN BAKKER

The climatic oscillations may have been smoothed by the oceanic conditions. In New Zealand an Allerød oscillation has been recorded more recently than 14,000 BP and this, and perhaps later cold periods in the postglacial period, may not be recorded on the islands.

S. W. GREENE

It was said that pollen of plants of the present flora had been found on Marion Island since ice retreat 16,000 years ago. To what extent could long-range pollen transport account for their presence in the early horizons? In the Antarctic Peninsula today we find *Nothofagus* grains. How do you discriminate between local and distant sources of pollen?

E. M. VAN ZINDEREN BAKKER

The pollen on Marion is plentiful even in the oldest deposits, and this confirms local origin. Snow samples have yielded stray *Nothofagus* grains, but their concentration is much lower than in the peats.

L. DAVIES

What is the evidence for 16,000 BP as the start of the present vegetation on Marion Island?

E. M. VAN ZINDEREN BAKKER

The oldest lava series on the island is from 270,000 to 76,000 years old. The oldest pollen-bearing deposits we have are 15,000 years old, but we believe the vegetation to have been there much longer than that.

N. M. WACE

We are still debating the relative role of biogeographical and ecological factors in determining distributions in the Southern Hemisphere. More fossil and genetic data are needed, and the kind of trapping Linsley Gressitt is doing, actually catching the organisms in the act of dispersal is most valuable. We should press for an increased programme of aerobiology.

W. S. BENNINGHOFF

Last week [late July, 1968.—Ed.] Dr E. B. Worthington, Mr Hugh Southon, and I began the organization of an international programme of aerobiology under SCIBP. This will seek to obtain direct evidence of the atmosphere transport of organisms and genes.

Part II

MARINE ECOSYSTEMS

Marine Ecosystems

This section brings together three general reviews covering different aspects of the Antarctic marine system. They introduce themes dealt with in greater detail in later sections, and summarize a broad field of literature. G. A. Knox's general ecological treatment can usefully be read in conjunction with the same author's (1960) account of water masses, biogeographic patterns and littoral zonation around the Southern Ocean and with the tentative ecological syntheses by Currie (1964) and Holdgate (1967). Much detailed information, both about ecology and biogeography, summarized here by J. Hedgpeth, is to be found in the proceedings of the first SCAR Symposium on Antarctic Biology (Carrick *et al.*, 1964) (especially biogeography), the proceedings of the SCAR Symposium on Antarctic Oceanography (SCAR, 1968), the long series of *Discovery* reports, and the volumes of the United States Antarctic Research series entitled *Biology of the Antarctic Seas* (American Geophysical Union).

The third review, by M. J. Dunbar, brings to the notice of Antarctic biologists ideas developed in the Arctic concerning the evolution of polar marine ecosystems, and emphasizes (as the physiological papers later in the volume confirm) that the marked seasonal changes in the polar zones, with the short period available for plant growth, may be of more significance in determing the species poverty of these areas than the low temperatures to which most groups seem fairly readily to adapt.

References

American Geophysical Union (1964–7). "Biology of the Antarctic Seas", Vols I–III.

Carrick, R., Holdgate, M. W. and Prevost, J. (1964). "Biologie Antarctique—Antarctic Biology". Hermann, Paris.

Currie, R. I. Environmental features in the ecology of the Antarctic seas. (1964). *In* "Biologie Antarctique—Antarctic Biology" (R. Carrick, M. W. Holdgate and J. Prevost, eds). Hermann, Paris.

Holdgate, M. W. (1967). The Antarctic Ecosystem. *Phil. Trans R. Soc.* B **252**, 363–89.

Knox, G. A. (1960). Littoral Ecology and Biogeography of the Southern Oceans. *Proc. R. Soc.* B **152**, 577–624.

SCAR (1968). "Symposium on Antarctic Oceanography". Scott Polar Research Institute, Cambridge.

Antarctic Marine Ecosystems

G. A. KNOX
Zoology Department, University of Canterbury, Christchurch, New Zealand

I. Introduction

In a recent review Holdgate (1967) has given an excellent account of the Antarctic marine ecosystem, and this is taken as the starting-point for this paper. Since Holdgate's paper was written over two years ago a considerable body of new information reporting the results of recent work in Antarctic seas has become available. This new information is used to extend and modify Holdgate's review. The aim will be to summarize the salient features of the Antartic marine environment, to discuss the factors affecting productivity, to consider the principal feeding relationships, and to point out the requirements for future work.

II. Features of the Antarctic Marine Environment

There have been a number of recent reviews of the circulation patterns and physical characteristics of Antarctic seas (Deacon, 1963, 1964; Brodie, 1965; Herdman, 1966; Kort, 1962), while the environmental features as biological and ecological factors have been considered by Currie (1964) and El Sayed (1966*a*). For the purposes of this discussion the Antarctic Convergence is considered to be the northern boundary of the Antarctic region. Many workers (Kort, 1962; Kort *et al.*, 1965) consider that the Antarctic Convergence cannot be used to designate the northern boundary of the Southern Ocean, since part of the West Wind Drift would be excluded, and would place the northern limit at the Subtropical Convergence: furthermore these Convergences are primarily surface features and the deeper layers of the ocean are in fact continuous with the deep circulation of the major ocean basins to the north.

The almost circular outline of the continent, the continuous ring of water, and the prevailing westerly winds lead to the development over the greater part of the Antarctic Ocean of easterly current systems (Deacon, 1963;

Maksimov and Vorobyev, 1965; Wyrtki, 1960) forming the great West Wind Drift (Fig. 1). Detailed deep observations of temperature and salinity and of the distribution of oxygen and other elements have demonstrated that these waters of the West Wind Drift move eastwards throughout the whole body of the ocean, although the structure of the current is complicated and the flow lines are strongly influenced by the bottom topography.

Near the Antarctic continent there is a narrow zone in which easterly winds prevail and in which the water flow is westward. When the East Wind Drift (Western Coastal Current according to Kort, 1962) meets the east

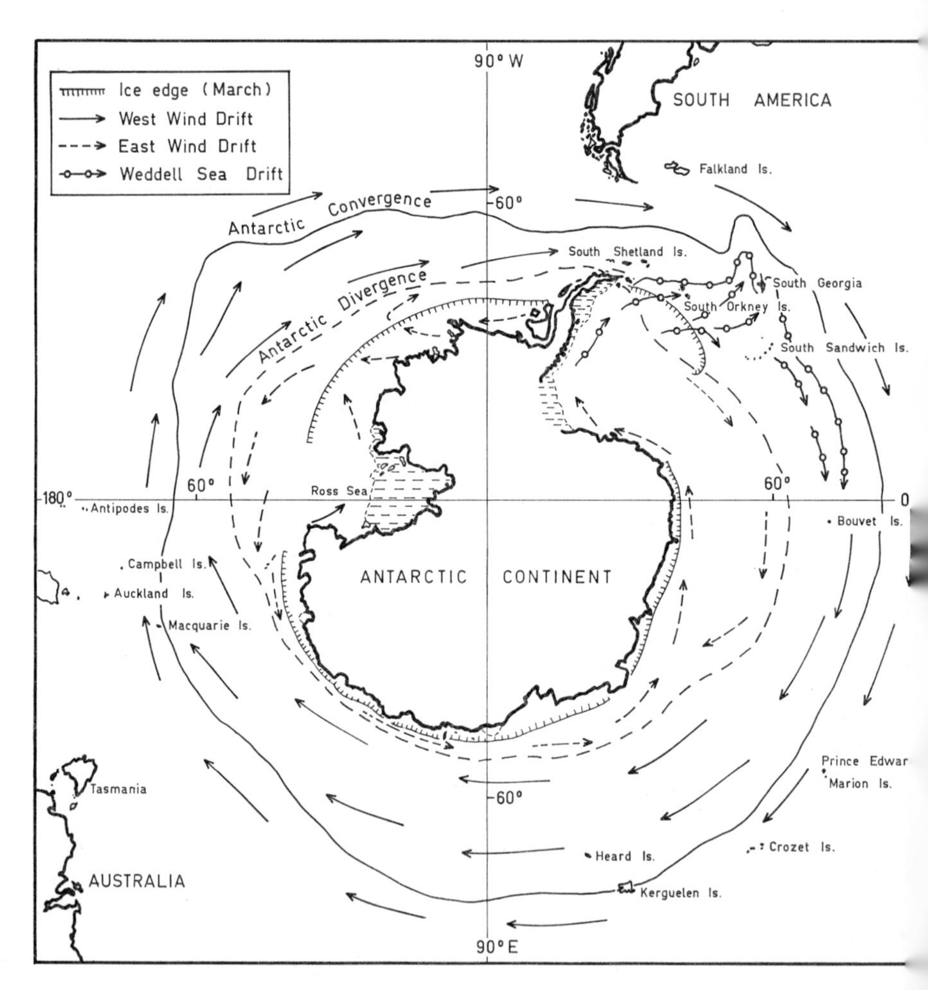

FIG. 1. Antarctica showing the position of the Antarctic Convergence and Divergence and surface currents.

coast of the Antarctic Peninsula it is deflected northwards by the Scotia Ridge to flow eastwards across the Atlantic as the Weddell Drift. The boundary between the eastward and westward current systems marks the position of the Antarctic Divergence, which is characterized by the upwelling of subsurface water. The position of this divergence and the occurrence and strength of the divergent motion are both variable, being strongly dependent on the prevailing meteorological conditions (Ivanov, 1961).

In winter the surface water near the continent (Antarctic Upper Water) is cooled and its salinity reduced as a result of ice formation. As summer progresses this water becomes overlain by warmer less saline water due to the melting of ice and snow. According to Kort (1962) there are a number of distinctive water masses south of the Antarctic Convergence; while Bunt (1968) notes that the physico-chemical characteristics of coastal waters reported by various investigators are, in several important respects, dissimilar

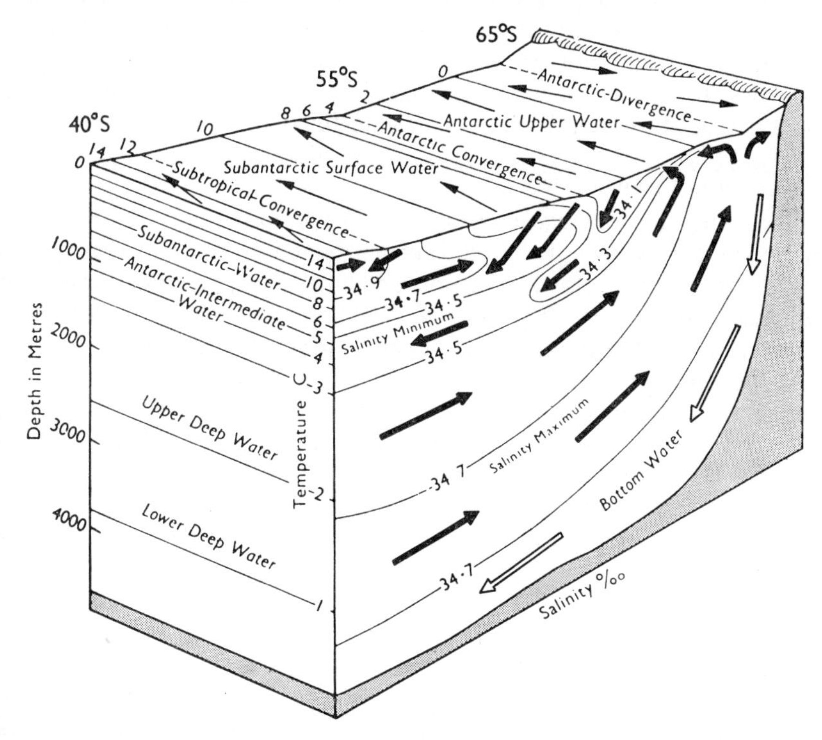

FIG. 2. Schematic diagram of the meridional and zonal flow in the Southern Ocean. (Adapted from Sverdrup *et al.*, 1942). The diagram represents the summer conditions; average positions of Convergence and Divergence shown. The Upper Deep Water is best developed in the Atlantic sector. The south-going component in the Lower Deep Water is weak or reversed in the Pacific. (From Brodie, 1965; Fig. 33, p. 122.)

(Bunt, 1960, for Mawson; Tressler and Ommundsen, 1962, Littlepage, 1965, and Thomas, 1966, for McMurdo Sound; and Filippov, 1965, for the coast between 45° and 95°E), the surface low saline layer varying considerably in thickness, with the degree of vertical stratification showing marked seasonal and geographic differences.

In certain areas, especially in the Weddell Sea, circumstances lead to the formation of very cold high-density water that sinks at the continental margin to form the Antarctic Bottom Water with temperatures less than 0·5°C, and then spreads northwards and eastwards to occupy levels below 4000 m (Fig. 2). Above this is a layer up to 2000 m thick of southward-moving warmer water, the Warm Deep Current or "Deep Water" that is formed in the North Atlantic and perhaps in the Indian and Pacific Oceans. This Deep Water wells up to take the place of the divergent surface waters, thus continuously bringing nutrient salts to the surface waters round the continent. As the Antarctic Upper Water moves north it meets the warmer, lighter, Sub-antarctic Surface Water at the Antarctic Convergence, where it sinks beneath the surface, mixing with the waters above and below to acquire a set of properties that enable Antarctic Intermediate Water to be recognized over a wide extent of the world's oceans (Brodie, 1965).

A. Surface Temperatures

The Antarctic Convergence which marks the northern boundary of the Antarctic Ocean is one of the fundamental boundary zones of the world's oceans (Brodie, 1965). Its position is marked by steep temperature and salinity gradients at the surface (Mackintosh, 1946). Across the Convergence the temperature range in the summer is from 4° to 8°C and in the winter from 1° to 3°C. Surface waters immediately south of the Convergence have an average temperature of about 1–2°C in the winter and 3–5°C in the summer, while further south near the continent temperatures vary only about −1·0° to −1·9°C. Temperature differences between the cold surface and bottom layers and the intermediate warmer layers is less than 5°C; thus the total annual range throughout the area does not exceed 4–5°C and throughout the greater part of the area it is considerably less.

B. Ice

The development of surface ice has a profound effect on the Antarctic ecosystem. There are marked season to season as well as yearly variations in the total area of Antarctic waters subject to surface freezing. Figure 3 shows the approximate mean positions of the ice edge around Antarctica at its maximum winter extent and summer minimum extent (Phillpott, 1964). It has been calculated (Mackintosh and Brown, 1953) that the limits probably lie between a maximum of about 10 million sq. miles ($26 \times 10^6 km^2$) towards the end of the winter and 1–2 million sq. miles (2·6–3·2 × 10^6km^2) in the late summer. Between those limits lie the pack-ice zone within which the nature and distribution of the sea ice is highly variable, and the distribution and proportion of open water equally irregular (Bunt, 1968). This pack-ice zone generally has a well-defined northern boundary, its edge lying approximately in the same position from July to October. The southern limit after

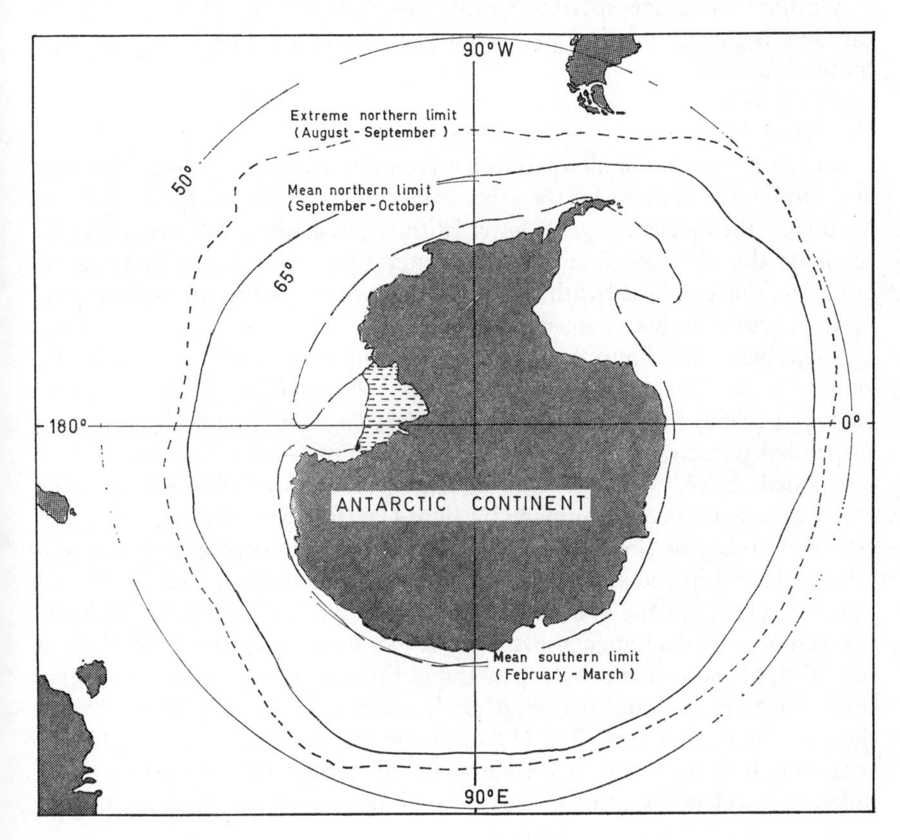

FIG. 3. Antarctica and surrounding seas showing the limits of pack ice. (After Phillpot, 1964; Fig. 1, p. 74.)

late summer melting and break-up is usually reached in February or March. Round the margins of the continent large areas of unbroken fast ice may persist for many years. Ice thickness is affected by the geographic location as well as climatic fluctuations from year to year. Bunt (1968) has estimated that the range of annual development is usually between 1 and 4 metres at inshore stations.

Ice formation affects many of the physical processes which determine primary productivity. As ice forms it extracts fresh water from the sea surface, leaving the water more saline and when it melts it dilutes the surface waters. It undoubtedly reduces the amount of turbulence due to wind action and also must restrict gaseous exchange with the atmosphere. Above all it decreases the amount of light penetration into the sea.

On the basis of ice distribution three concentric zones of variable width can be recognized: (*a*) the open ocean (ice free), (*b*) the pack-ice zone, and (*c*) the fast-ice zone.

C. Solar Radiation

In the far south the alternation between total darkness for half the year and continuous daylight for the other half imposes a seasonal light régime in contrast to the diurnal cycles of lower latitudes. According to Kopanev (1962) sunshine duration in Antarctica is greater than in corresponding Arctic latitudes; this combined with the high transparency of the atmosphere promotes a greater influx of solar radiation.

Light penetration into the waters is determined not only by its intensity, angle of incidence, surface reflection (up to 50% according to data given by El Sayed (1966) for Marguerite Bay in February 1965), and absorption of suspended particles, but also by the presence of fast ice and pack ice as mentioned above. Measurements of light penetration within the pack-ice and sea-ice zone have been made by Bunt (1960) at Mawson, by Littlepage (1965) in McMurdo Sound, by Meguro (1912) and Burckholder and Mandelli (1965*a*, 1965*b*) in the vicinity of the Antarctic Peninsula, by El Sayed and Mandelli (1965) in the Weddell Sea, and El Sayed (1966*b*) in the Bellingshausen Sea. Measurements in the latter locality in February 1965 showed that 21% of the incident light penetrated through a layer of ice one metre thick. There is no doubt that large gradients in light intensity exist beneath the ice. Furthermore, as Bunt (1968) points out, ice crystals are capable of polarizing light and there is certain to be differential absorption of light of different wavelengths although next to nothing is known concerning this.

D. Nutrients

Observations on the distribution of nitrates, phosphates and silicate (Deacon, 1937; Clowes, 1938; El Sayed and Mandelli, 1965) show that levels rarely fall below the maxima of temperate regions and are unlikely to be limiting to phytoplankton growth and development. The mechanism which ensures this abundant supply of nutrients lies in the water movements described above.

Holdgate (1967) has summarized these general features in the following words:

The Antarctic marine environment is thus a deep oceanic system with a strongly marked circulation. Upwelling brings nutrients into the surface waters in considerable quantity. The light régime is seasonal, with abundant light for photosynthesis in summer but very low illumination in water. The temperatures are consistently low throughout the zone. As with many productive oceans, there is considerable turbulence in summer, but stability in winter under the protective ice cover. Granted tolerance of, or physiological adaptation to, the low temperatures, habitat conditions are favourable for life in summer, but owing to the low light intensities, become markedly less so in winter especially in the most southerly areas.

III. Primary Productivity

In any discussion of production and productivity it is necessary to define precisely the meaning of the terms used. The following definitions as used in this paper are based on Dunbar (1968).

Standing crop or *biomass:* The total amount of living substance in an ecosystem at any given time.

Production: The standing crop per unit area or volume averaged per shorter time unit over the year.

Productivity: The rate at which living substance is formed. This is a measure of the energy flow through the ecosystem (i.e. the turnover). According to Dunbar large biomass and high production, since they reflect high energy capital, lead to community stability by making possible specific diversification and the sharing of resources by many species.

We now have a reasonably wide range of measurements of phytoplanton standing crop and primary productivity around the Antarctic continent from the fast ice to across the Antarctic Convergence. The majority of these measurements have, however, been carried out during the summer months and have been largely concerned with phytoplankton determinations in the water column and only a few investigators have been concerned with the contribution made by the ice or *epontic* algae. In addition, we do not yet have published accounts of studies that have followed the yearly cycle of events at any one locality.

In any discussion of phytoplankton production in Antarctic waters it is essential to distinguish between the contributions made by the algae in the water column and that of the epontic algae. Bunt was the first to recognize the importance of the microalgal flora of the ice (Bunt, 1963, 1964, 1968; Bunt and Wood, 1963) in a series of investigations carried out at Mawson and in McMurdo Sound. This flora has also been investigated by Russian workers at Mirny (Haswell Islands) and at Molodiozhnaya (Enderby Land) (Andriashev, 1968).

Bunt distinguishes two microfloral habitats in sea ice, the "snow" communities described by Meguro (1962) and Burckholder and Mandelli (1965*a*) from the Antarctic Peninsula and the "ice" communities which he first described from Mawson. These ice communities form an extensive layer extending through the lower layer of "fluffy" ice to a thickness of 50–100 cm. The groups represented include diatoms, chrysophyceans, dinoflagellates, and green flagellates, of which the former are the most ubiquitous and generally dominant. Bunt (1964) found this ice flora to be markedly shade adapted, photosynthesizing in McMurdo Sound in light intensities that were only 0·01–0·02% of those at the surface of the ice. Bunt and Wood (1963) point out that the epontic communities may exert a significant limiting influence on the planktonic algae by substantially reducing the level of illumination.

A. Standing Crop

Holdgate (1967) and El Sayed (1968) have summarized the available data on phytoplankton standing crop in Antarctic waters. Tables 1 and 2 are based on the available data of phytoplankton standing crop (in terms of chlorophyll *a*) and primary production (in terms of ^{14}C uptake) in the Antarctic Ocean. As El Sayed (1968) points out, except for the relatively better studied areas such as the Drake Passage, the waters west of the Antarctic Peninsula and McMurdo Sound, these productivity data are the results of sporadic and spotty observations.

Table 3 from Holdgate's (1967) account summarizes the data given by Hart (1942) in his examination of the phytoplankton standing crop south of the Antarctic Convergence. The results given in this table together with the more recent data in Tables 2 and 3 indicate that Antarctic waters are comparatively rich in phytoplankton, especially the waters around South Georgia.

B. Primary Production

Basing his assessment on Hart's (1942) data, the only information then published, Ryther (1963) estimated the mean annual primary production to be in the order of 100 g C/m^2 for the Antarctic Ocean as a whole. Currie (1964) gave a figure of 43 g C/m^2 for the annual primary production and more recently Bunt (1968) has estimated that the annual production over the entire region could exceed 70 g C/m^2 of which the direct contribution within the ice layer would be less than 2%.

Perhaps the most striking characteristics of the data presented in Tables 2 and 3 are the extreme seasonal and geographic variability of the productivity of the areas investigated, e.g. the Bransfield and Gerlache Straits are exceedingly productive, when compared to the Drake Passage and the Weddell Sea. Klyashtorin (1964) on the basis of data collected around the Antarctic continent by the *Ob*, gave an average production of 9 mg C/m^3 day. On the other hand, Saijo and Kawashima (1964) in investigations between 40°W and 100°E and Ichimura and Fukushima (1963) in the Indian Ocean Section give

TABLE 1

Organic Carbon and Chlorophyll *a* in Antarctic waters (Summer Mean Values)

Area	*Chlorophyll a (mg/m³)*	*Organic carbon (g/m³/day)*	*Author*
Bellingshausen Sea	0·36	0·24	El Sayed (1968)
Drake Passage	0·73	0·036	El Sayed *et al.* (1964)
Drake Passage	0·78	0·77	El Sayed (1968)
Gerlache Strait	11·6		Burkholder and Sieburth (1961)
Gerlache Strait		0·86	Mandelli and Burkholder (1966)
Gerlache Strait	6·27	1·31	El Sayed (1968)
Bransfield Strait	3·6		Burkholder and Sieburth (1961)
Bransfield Strait	2·4	0·120	El Sayed, Mandelli and Sugimura (1964)
Bransfield Strait		0·70	Mandelli and Burkholder (1966)
Bransfield Strait	0·86	2·76	El Sayed (1968)
NE of S Orkney Is.	4·3	0·215	El Sayed and Mandelli (1965)
Deception Island	14·2	0·710	Burkholder and Sieburth (1961)
Marguerite Bay	2·73	0·46	El Sayed (1968)
Weddell Sea	0·61	0·68	El Sayed (1968)
Africa-Antarctica	0·17	0·03	Saijo and Kawashima (1964)
Antarctic-Indian Sector	0·15–0·6		Ichimura and Fukushima (1963)
Australia-Antarctica	0·28	0·10	Saijo and Kawashima (1964)
Antarctic-Atlantic Sector		0·145	Volkovinsky (1966)
McMurdo Sound	37·5	1·875	Bunt (1964)

TABLE 2

Variations in Chlorophyll *a* Concentrations in Antarctic Waters (After Bunt, 1968, Table II)

Investigator	*Locality*	*Date*	*mg chlorophyll a/m³*
Hart	Ross Sea	Feb. 1934	0·02— 3·60*
Hart	Bellingshausen Sea	Mar. 1934	0·20— 0·50*
Hart	Bellingshausen Sea	Mar. 1938	0·01— 0.37*
C.S.I.R.O.	134–158°E	Feb. 1959	0·05— 1·45
El Sayed and Kawashima	33–72°E	Dec. 1961	0·04— 0·36
El Sayed and Mandelli	Weddell Sea 0–60 m	Jan. 1964	0·14— 0.86
Burkholder and Sieburth	Antarctic Peninsula	Jan. 1959	0·30—26·80
Bunt	Mawson 0–25 m	Dec. 1955	0·14— 3·92
Bunt	McMurdo Sound 3 m	Dec. 1961	up to 55
Bunt	McMurdo Sound	Dec. 1962	up to 2·5

* Data converted from Harvey units using the rough approximation: 1 Harvey unit = 0·3 mg chlorophyll *a* (Strickland, 1965).

TABLE 3

Calculated Minimum and Average Standing Crops in Antarctic Seas
(From Holdgate, 1967, after Hart, 1942)

	Calculated minimum crop (g/m^3)		*Average standing crop (g/m^3)*	
	Maximum	*Minimum*	*Maximum*	*Minimum*
English Channel	20·1	1·06	0·48	0·025
South Georgia	61·5	15·5	1·10	0·28
North Region–Indian Ocean	28·9	16·7	0·23	0·13
North Region–Atlantic Ocean	36·2	10·1	0·14	0·04

very low values for both chlorophyll *a* and ^{14}C uptake. High values, on the other hand, have been recorded by Burckholder and Sieburth (1961), Mandelli and Burckholder (1966), and El Sayed (1966*b*) for the waters west of the Antarctic Peninsula, and Bunt (1963, 1964) has recorded even higher values for McMurdo Sound. In particular, there appear to be wide variations between inshore and offshore waters in the same region. Klyashtorin (1964) recorded mean values in the nearshore regions of Mirny Station and Peter I Island of 120 mg C/m^3 and 61 mg C/m^3.

As Foxton (1964) points out, production is concentrated into approximately six months of the year, with two periods of increase, the first in the spring being greater than the second in the autumn. Recent diving studies by United States investigators under the ice at McMurdo Sound (Anonymous, 1968) indicate that diatoms, which had been conspicuously rare in the water in winter months, had reached maximum bloom capacity in November. Volkovinskiy and Fedosov (1965) point out that intensive photosynthesis occurs at the edge of melting ice and that maximum photosynthesis in Antarctic waters occurs in the surface layers, whereas in Northern Hemisphere waters it occurs at the 25 m depth. Foxton (1964) considers that the physical factors of the environment are the most important in determining the scale and course of events in the Antarctic production cycle while El Sayed and Mandelli (1965) and El Sayed (1968) have considered the possible importance of factors such as nutrient levels, temperature, light, stabilization of the surface waters, and grazing in order to explain the variations which occur.

Bunt (1968) has advanced another factor as possibly being of even greater significance than those mentioned above, a factor unique to polar regions, namely the ice layers at the surface. The ice layer with its epontic algae severely limits the available light for photosynthesis in the water column, hence the date of ice break-up and melting, and thus the period of time for which the seas are ice free is of critical importance in controlling the rate of build-up of the standing crop and hence the total annual production. A short season may only permit a partial build-up of the standing crop. In addition, the break-up of the ice layer probably releases an inoculum of algae into the water column, without which a much longer period would be required in order to build up the maximum standing crop.

IV. Zooplankton

As a result of the pioneer studies of the *Discovery* expeditions we now have a very thorough knowledge of the taxonomy, general distribution, and life cycles of the dominant zooplankton species. However, we do not as yet have an adequate understanding of the quantitative and food web relationships.

A. Zooplankton Standing Crop

Foxton (1956) has summarized the then available information on the zooplankton standing crop in the various latitudinal zones of the Southern Hemisphere (Table 4). It can be seen that Antarctic waters have a significantly greater standing crop than tropical and temperate regions. Voronina (1966) has given details of estimates of the standing crop made on the first and

Table 4

Standing Crop of Zooplankton in the Southern Ocean
(After Foxton, 1956)

(Data expressed as (mg/m³))

	Antarctic	*Subantarctic*	*Tropical*	*Subtropical*
0–50 m	55·2	55·8	33·1	40·5
0–1000 m	25·6	20·9	9·8	9·0

second cruises of the Soviet Antarctic Expedition. In a profile along 20°E from 69°46′S to 36°30′S taken from February 21 to March 11, 1957, it was found that copepods constituted the greater part of the biomass in Antarctic waters. Below 100–200 m the mean amount of zooplankton was 10–50 mg/m^3 along most of the length of the profile, with the exception of stations on the Antarctic Convergence (300 mg/m^3) and the Antarctic Divergence (80 mg/m^3). In the upper levels there were a number of clearly defined maxima with a biomass of more than 100 mg/m^3. The averaged results from all the profiles give estimates of a similar order to those of Foxton. It was found that localities with a high biomass formed zones encircling the continent, their number and position being related to the time of collection of the material. The major components of the zooplankton were the Anarctic copepod species *Rhincalanus gigas*, *Calanus propinquus* and *Calanoides acutus*, contributing 72·8% of the total biomass. It was found that the age composition of the population of the three main species at any one time differ, since they pass through the stages of the life cycle at different times. Because the different stages undergo seasonal vertical migrations they play an important part in determining the biomass at different levels at different times of the year.

The above estimates of standing crop, however, do not take into account the larger zooplankton, especially adult *Euphausia superba* ("krill"), as these are not caught in the sampling nets used. Estimates of the average biomass of *E. superba* are very difficult due to the fact that they are usually found in dense swarms or aggregations. For these swarms Marr (1962) has given figures that range from 2·5 to 29·3 g/m^3; Holdgate (1967) has suggested that the average biomass could be of the order of 50 mg/m^3 concentrated in the top 50 m. This would imply that this species alone has a biomass equal to that of the rest of the zooplankton. According to provisional calculations made by Klumov (1963) the total stocks of Antarctic euphausiids are five billion tons. Holdgate gives a figure of 55 mg/m^3 for the marine zooplankton other than *Euphausia*, including 5 mg/m^3 of carnivores. As he points out, there is very little quantitative information as to the proportion of carnivorous species, although some are known to be abundant (Littlepage, 1964) and the figure of 5 mg is likely to be an underestimate.

B. Phytoplankton-zooplankton Relationships

An inverse correlation between phytoplankton densities and the numbers of zooplankton herbivores in Antarctic waters was demonstrated by Hardy and Gunther (1935). Table 5 from Hardy (1967) illustrates such a relationship between phytoplankton densities and those of three species of euphausiids, an amphipod, and a tunicate. On the whole, it can be seen that there tend to be smaller numbers of animals at the stations with the sparsest phytoplankton (perhaps because of the shortage of food), but also small numbers at the stations with the highest phytoplankton values. Hart (1942) considered that zooplankton grazing was the main factor controlling Antarctic phytoplankton, while Hardy and Gunther (1935) had earlier advanced the hypothesis of animal exclusion to explain the inverse distributional relationship between the phytoplankton and zooplankton. Hardy (1967) has discussed two alternative explanations of this relationship.

One suggested by Steeman-Nielsen is that upwelling water poor in zooplankton but rich in nutrients pushes aside the surface water with its contained plankton. This upwelled water quickly develops abundant phytoplankton in the absence of grazing animals. Such a rich phytoplankton

TABLE 5

Phytoplankton-zooplankton Relationships in Antarctic Waters to the North of South Georgia

Phytoplankton values averaged	*Euphausia superba*	*E. frigida*	*Thysanoessa*	*Parathemisto*	*Salpa fusiformis*
57,500	289	3	17	48	38
290,000	**1913**	**44**	57	**266**	**1781**
483,000	**951**	**47**	94	44	**1051**
2,064,000	**369**	**76**	**136**	**87**	**675**
50,936,500	31	15	**138**	53	246
315,125,000	41	2	69	45	49

The figures are for average numbers in six groups of stations (forty-three in all) arranged in ascending order of phytoplankton values. The figures in bold type indicate values that are above the average for the whole column.

patch will be subject to grazing at the edges outside the immediate upwelling region. Hardy (1967) believes that this is the explanation of the dense phytoplankton patches found off South Georgia. Here low phosphate values were associated with such patches due to its utilization by the plants. Areas of high phosphate were associated with low phytoplankton and high densities of krill and the whales which fed upon it (Hardy and Gunther, 1935; Hardy, 1967).

Hardy (1967) also discusses another explanation of the dense phytoplankton patches which was first put forward by Bogorov (1938). The effect of the ice and its epontic algae in reducing the light available for photosynthesis has been discussed above. The melting of ice as hypothesized by Bunt (1968) would release the epontic algae to seed the water column and the increased light and abundant nutrients would bring about an outburst of diatoms in advance of the increase in zooplankton. The pack ice does not melt evenly and the patches of water most recently covered by ice will have the densest phytoplankton. These will later become the rich feeding-grounds of the krill which will graze them down, and subsequently of the whales.

C. The Characteristics of the Antarctic Zooplankton

There are a number of characteristics which serve to distinguish the Antarctic zooplankton. These are:

1. Almost complete absence of the larval forms of bottom-living animals.
2. The surface layers are poor in species but rich in individuals, the number of species increasing with depth. This relationship is well illustrated by Fig. 4, which shows the increase in copepod species with depth off South Georgia.

3. In addition to the diurnal vertical migration exhibited by many species, the dominant species confined to the Antarctic zone perform an annual vertical migration (Mackintosh, 1960). Species such as *Rhincalanus gigas*, *Eukronia hamata* and *Calanus acutus* drift north in the summer in surface waters descending in the winter to the deeper southward flowing water (Fig. 2). Thus by means of a seasonal vertical migration of between 400 and 600 m they maintain themselves in Antarctic water by means of a circular drift. Since there is a main eastward component in the water movement of both the surface and deep water masses, there is also a constant longitudinal shift (Dell, 1965).

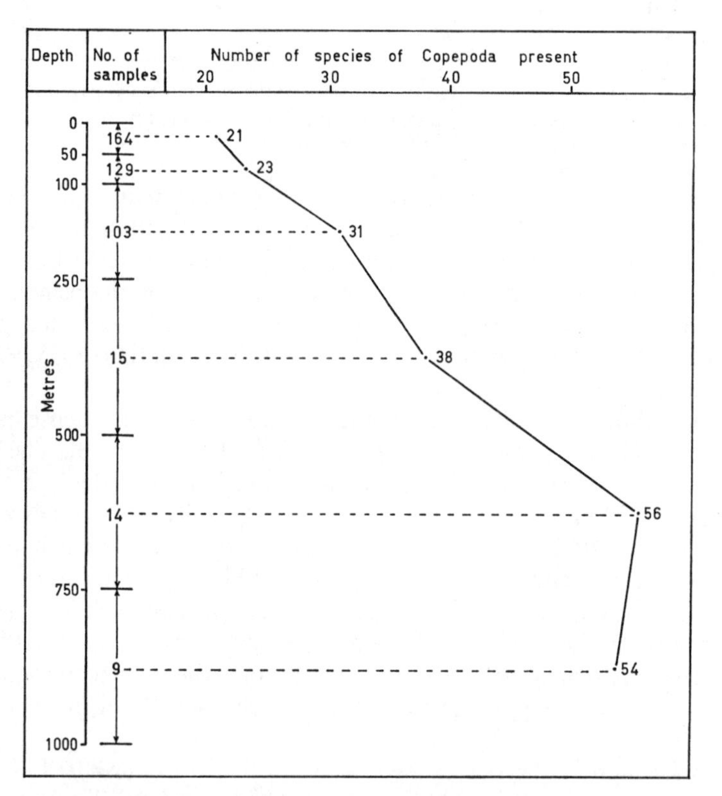

FIG. 4. Graph showing the number of species of Copepoda with increasing depth in Antarctic waters off South Georgia. (After Hardy, 1967; p. 331.)

V. The Benthos

While the scouring motion of ice along the shoreline effectively limits an intertidal flora and fauna to crevice-dwelling species and to seasonal growth of diatoms and filamentous green algae (Knox, 1968), benthic regions below the limit of ice abrasion support astonishingly rich faunas. Benthic faunas under the fast ice have recently been studied in McMurdo Sound by Dearborn (1963, 1967), Littlepage and Pearse (1962) and Tressler (1964), at Mirny and Molodiohnaya by Propp *et al.* (1966), and by Arnaud (1965) and Delepine and Hureau (1963) off the Adelie Coast, while shelf faunas have recently been investiaged in the Ross Sea Sector by Bullivant (1959, 1967), in the Indian Ocean and Pacific Sectors by Belyaev (1964) and off the Sabrina coast by Ushakov (1962, 1963). A general picture of a rich and varied benthic fauna with a considerable degree of uniformity around the continent emerges.

A. The Benthic Environment

The Antarctic shelf is narrow with an average width of 40–150 miles (64–240 km), and generally has a complex structure with the outer edge at a depth of 400–500 m in contrast to the more usual depth of 200 m. Large areas of this shelf are covered with coarse, poorly sorted deposits interspersed with boulders of various sizes and gravel transported by icebergs (Ushakov, 1963). Because the surface of the continent is almost entirely covered by ice, there are no river or wind-borne organic, or inorganic, sediments added to the shelf deposits.

In the McMurdo Sound–Ross Sea region the shallower waters under 200 m have a substrate of volcanic rock, gravel or mixed volcanic gravel and sand (Dearborn, 1967), while the deeper undulating shelf from 200–500 m is typically covered with glacial sediments of silts, sand, gravel, and scattered erratic boulders (Bullivant, 1967). These deposits generally have large amounts of material of organic origin such as foraminiferan tests, sponge spinules, bryozoan skeletons, worm tubes, molluscan shell fragments and calcareous detritus. In deeper waters sandy mud deposits occur.

The physical characteristics of the environment are relatively critical. Tressler's (1964) data for a complete year at McMurdo Sound indicate a yearly mean water temperature of $-1{\cdot}83$°C at 100 m with an extreme range of 0·56°C, and for the bottom waters (585 m) $-1{\cdot}89$°C with an extreme range of only 0·07°C. The salinity of the bottom waters averages 34·85‰ with a range of 0·24‰. The percentage of saturation of dissolved oxygen averages 69% with a range of only 6%. Thus the physical environment is a very uniform one.

Recent investigations have enabled the following generalizations to be made concerning the characteristics of the Antarctic benthic fauna.

1. *There is a great variety in species composition*

Up to 500 different invertebrate species probably occur on the rocky bottom at Haswell Islands according to Andriashev (1968). At McMurdo Sound in volcanic gravel and debris in depths less than 50–60 m, the most conspicuous benthic invertebrates include the anemone *Urticinopsis antarctica;* a large nementine, *Lineus corrigatus;* a large sluggish isopod, *Glyptonotus antarcticus;* a large pycnogonid, *Colossendeis megalonyx;* a bivalve mollusc, *Limatula hodgsoni;* the ophiuroids, *Ophiurolepis gelida* and *Ophicantha antarctica;* and the asteroids *Odonaster validus* and *Diplasterias brucei* (Dearborn, 1967).

On the more rocky substrates down to 200 m both in the Ross Sea (Dearborn, 1967; Bullivant, 1967) and at the Haswell Islands (Andriashev, 1968), there are complex growths of various horny and glass sponges, numerous encrusting and branching bushy colonies of bryozoans, hydroids, alcyonarians, and tubiculous polychaetes. Numerous species live in and on these growths, especially echinoderms and polynoid, serpulid, and terebellid worms. There are also large numbers of foraminifera, their numbers in the shelf deposits being approximately twenty times (agglutinated forms) and sixty times (calcareous forms) greater than on the shelf in the north-west part of the Pacific Ocean (Saidova, 1961). In the deeper waters of the Ross Sea, Bullivant (1967) recognizes a number of major and minor assemblages:

(i) *Deep shelf mixed assemblages.* Found on a coarse sediment with scattered erratic boulders in depths between 256 and 523m.

(ii) *Deep shelf mixed bottom assemblage.* On sandy mud away from the coast in depths between 415 and 752 m. Tubiculous polychaetes are abundant and a sipunculid and an arenaceous foraminiferan (*Rhabdammina* sp.) are common.

(iii) *Pennell bank assemblage.* On a substrate of cobbles with patches of muddy sand, in depths between 201 and 384 m. Bryozoans, gorgonaceans, sponges, tunicates, stylasterine corals, and echinoderms are common.

This picture is similar to that reported for the Indian Ocean sector by Propp *et al.* (1966) and Ushakov (1962). Pasternak and Gruzov (1960) present a table which shows a reduction in the number of sponges, bryozonas and ascidians below 500 m with a relative increase in the number of polychaetes, crustaceans, molluscs, and echinoderms.

2. *Dominance of sessile animals*

The bulk of the organisms are sessile plankton- and detritus-feeding species concentrated in areas where hard substrates are exposed, especially above 500 m. The abundance of ice-rafted boulders and exposed rock favours such growths, which are frequently multi-storied (Bullivant, 1967).

3. *Large size of many species*

Many species reach a size much greater than that attained by similar species in other seas (Andriashev, 1967). Among the sponges a huge bowl-like *Rossella* sp. attains a height of about 130 cm and width of 750 cm. Very large size is also attained by some alcyonarians, pycnogonids, amphipods (*Eusirus*, *Paramphithoe*), ispods (*Glyptonotus*, Serolids), polychaetes (*Eulagisca gigantea*, *Laetmotonice producta*) and nemertine worms (*Lineus*, up to 2 m long).

4. *High standing crop*

So far only Russian workers have published quantitative information on the standing crop of benthic organisms. In shallow waters off the Haswell Islands, Davis Sea in waters less than 50 m deep, the following standing crops of benthic animals have been estimated (Andriashev, 1968):

(*a*) Alcyonarian thickets with abundant accompanying fauna 1–2 kg/m²;
(*b*) thickets of hydroids and sedendary polychaetes 2 + kg/m²;
(*c*) growths of sponges, hydroids and bryozoans, up to 6 kg/m².

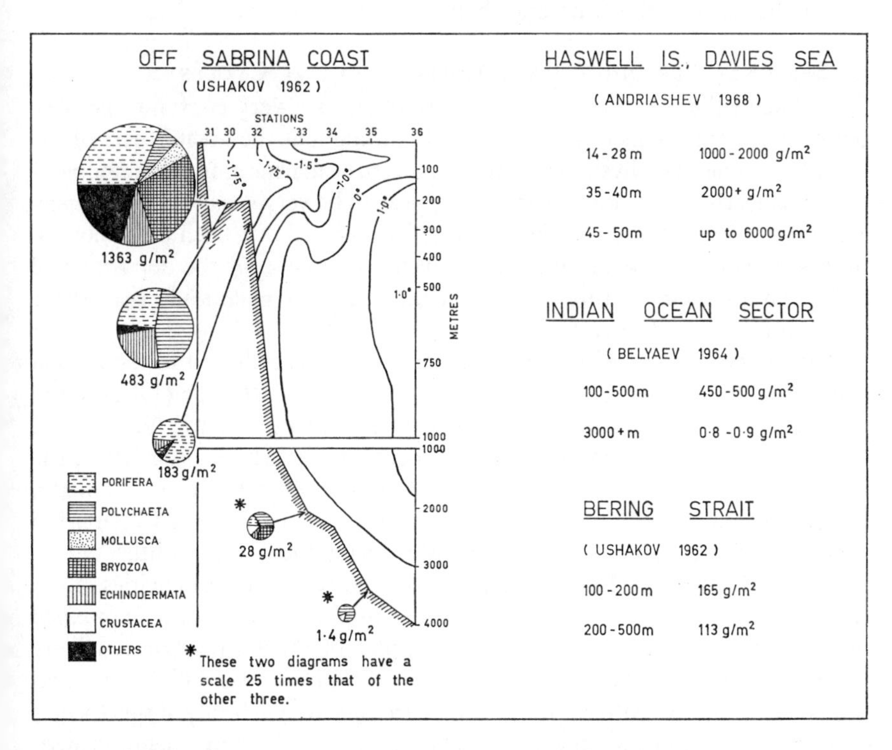

FIG. 5. Benthic standing crop in Antarctica compared with the Northern Hemisphere.

In the Indian Ocean Sector Belyaev and Ushakov (1962) indicated standing crops in the 200–300 m depth range from 183 to 1383 g/m² and average values near the 100–500 m levels of 400–500 g/m² (Fig. 5). These values fell to 28 g/m² at 2000 m and 1·4 g/m² at 3500 m. Average values at depths greater than 3000 m were 0·8–0·9 g/m². These values far exceed the average standing crop at comparable depths in other very productive regions of the ocean. In the western part of the Bering Sea, for example, the average standing crop at depths of 100–200 m is 115 g/m² and at depths of 200–500 m, 113 g/m².

B. Comparisons with the Arctic Benthos

The benthic fauna of the Arctic Ocean is poor by comparison. Whereas Antarctic assemblages are characterized by a large species diversity with considerable variation from station to station in the one region; Arctic assemblages have a lower species diversity with a relatively few dominant species (Ushakov, 1962). Arctic communities (MacGinitie, 1955) are more or less regularly arranged on parallel narrow belts or zones in contrast to the mozaic patterns of the Antarctic shelf.

C. Seasonal Periodicities and Reproductive Cycles

Although the Antarctic marine environment is a very constant one with temperature variations of less than 1·0°C throughout the greater part of the Antarctic Zone, the physiological responses of the marine animals to temperature in a nearly constant environment appear to be very sensitive. In temperate and tropical seas, as Dearborn (1967) has pointed out, such physiological processes as the initiation of gametogenesis, spawning, or the deposition of lipids requires temperature changes of much greater magnitude than those apparently required in Antarctic waters.

The marked periodicity of primary production is reflected in the annual changes in lipid content of Antarctic invertebrates. Littlepage (1964) found that the euphausiid, *Euphausia crystallorophias*, a phytoplankton filter feeder, stored lipids over the summer and these decreased as winter progressed; the carnivorous copepod, *Euchaeta antarctica*, on the other hand, maintained a high lipid content at all times, since the small zooplankton upon which it fed was found in great abundance at all depths during the winter months.

Pearse (1963, 1965, 1966) has studied the reproductive periodicities of the common asteroid *Odonaster validus* and the amphipod *Orchomenella proxima* in McMurdo Sound. He found that samples of the former from Balleny Islands (67°S), Robertson Bay (71°S), and McMurdo Sound (77°S) showed similar reproductive patterns indicating reproductive synchrony of this species over much or all of its Antarctic distribution. *O. validus* ova begin growth primarily during August through February and reach maturity in about eighteen months. The embryos need about two months to reach a dermersal bipinnarian stage. Spawning is in winter from July to November, with the larvae developed in time to take advantage of the summer phytoplankton growth. *O. proxima* is also a winter breeder. Pearse considers that "the reproductive periodicities of *O. validus* are both adapted to and synchronized by the summer period of phytoreproduction and that neither light nor temperature changes have any direct synchronizing role".

It is a striking characteristic of Antarctic invertebrates that a relatively large percentage of the species are ovoviviparous or brood their young (Dell, 1965). As in the Arctic, large-yolked eggs and abbreviated life histories are common.

VI. Food-chain Relationships

Figure 6 shows the principal food-chain relationships in Antarctic seas.

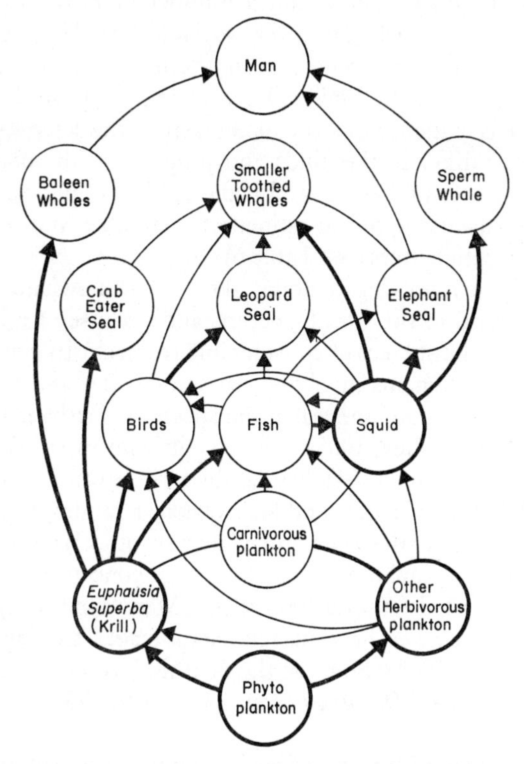

FIG. 6. Food chains in the Antarctica, based on a diagram by Hart (1942). Heavy arrows indicate the probable main diet of the groups to which they point. (After Mackintosh, 1964; Fig. 4, p. 36.)

It illustrates the central position occupied by *Euphausia superba* (Mackintosh, 1964). As pointed out above, it is probable that this species has a biomass equal to that of all the rest of the zooplankton combined. It is characteristically concentrated in dense swarms in the surface waters, in depths of less than 100 m (Mackintosh, 1960), with its zone of greatest concentration confined to the south of the Antarctic Divergence and the Weddell Sea Drift (Marr, 1962). At its maximum northern extent in late winter the ice almost entirely covers the krill. In the summer its northern boundary tends to follow the ice edge southwards.

Of the eight baleen whales in Antarctic waters the blue, fin, and humpback species are the great consumers of *E. superba*, but their population, estimated at 300,000 in 1933–39, has now been reduced by 80–90%. The larger whales are considered to consume more than a ton of krill per day (Nemoto, 1968). What effect the reduction in whale numbers has had on the stocks of *Euphausia* is not known.

Crabeater seals, many fishes, and a number of bird species, especially penguins, also feed on krill. However, as Holdgate (1967) points out, the complexities of feeding preferences in southern seabirds have only recently been explored (see Tickell, 1965). Different species have different feeding ranges and there is evidence that the food taken by the same species in different localities may differ in the kinds and proportions of zooplankton taken (Adelie penguins at Cape Crozier and Hallett; Sladen, personal communication). Holdgate has attempted to estimate the number and biomass of seals and birds in Antarctic waters (see Table 6).

The food chain involving diatoms—krill—baleen whales is one of the shortest to be found in the world's oceans and because of its economic importance has been the subject of considerable research. In contrast very little is known of the food chains involving Antarctic fishes and cephalopods. Of the former there are some ninety benthic species (Marshall, 1964) and sixty pelagic species (Andriashev, 1965). There is little information on the feeding of these fishes. Hureau (1964) has studied the nototheniid, *Trematomus bernacchii*, and found that the food was varied, including algae, Crustacea, molluscs, annelids, and the eggs and young of other species. The pelagic species are doubtless plankton feeders and large concentrations of Antarctic cod have been reported (Andriashev, 1964). Many benthic species, such as *Pleurogramma antarcticum*, have pelagic larval stages feeding under the ice surface (Andriashev, 1968). Some of the benthic carnivorous species attain a large size; specimens of *Dissostichus mawsoni* up to 175 cm long have been recorded.

Even less is known of the role of cephalopods in the Antarctic ecosystem. According to Dell (1965) squids probably feed on krill and other Crustacea. Unfortunately, in spite of their great abundance, they are difficult to catch,

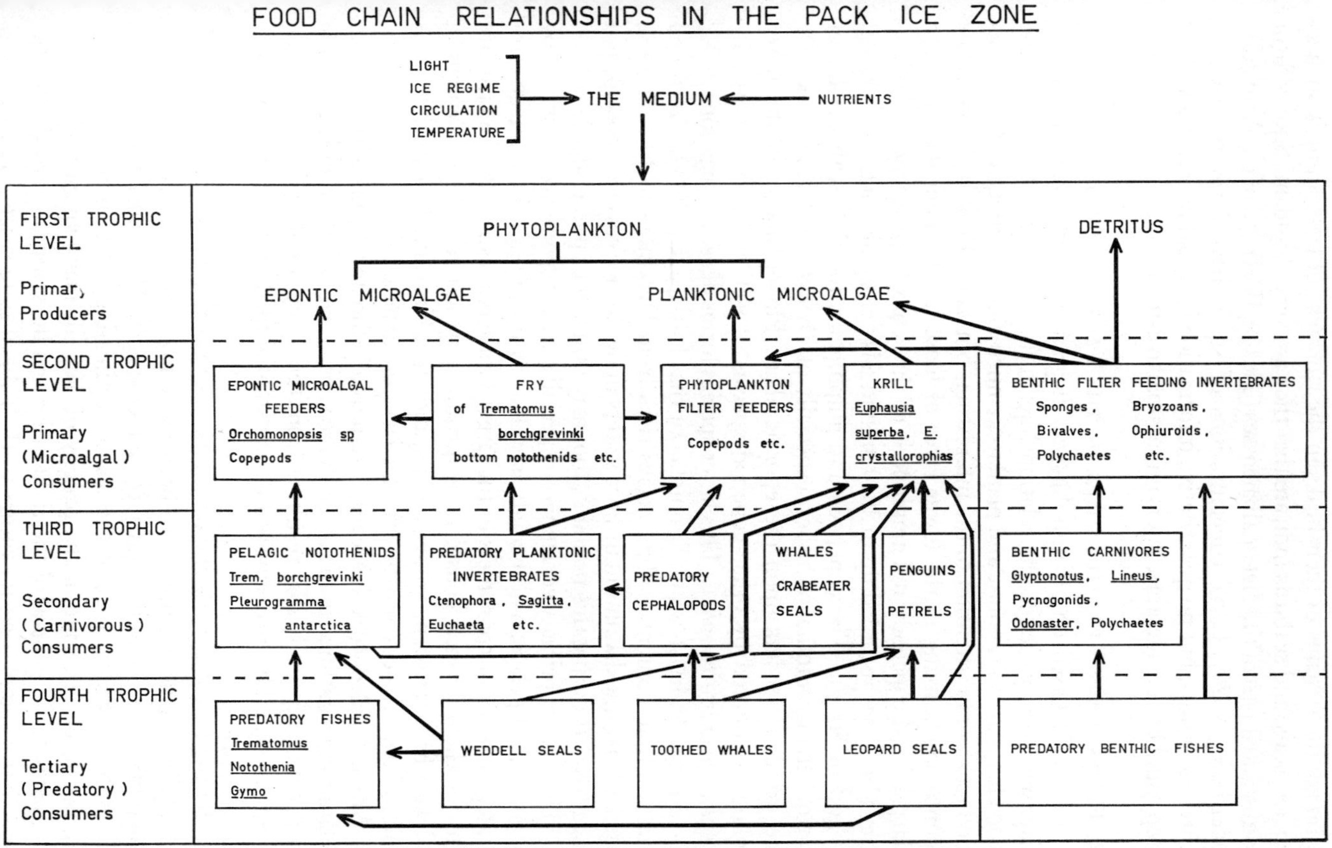

FOOD CHAIN RELATIONSHIPS IN THE PACK ICE ZONE

FIG. 7. Food-chain relationships in the pack-ice zone. Based on an unpublished figure by Andriashev.

although the remains of their beaks in the stomachs of large animals such as whales, seals, and seabirds indicate that they are very abundant. Squids form a substantial part of the diet of albatrosses (Tickell, 1964) and of elephant seals (Matthews, 1929). Large concentrations of squid have been reported in Antarctic waters, but no quantitative information is available. Their standing crop could be considerable, but is impossible to estimate at present.

A. Food-chain Relationships in the Pack-ice Zone

Figure 7, based on an unpublished diagram by Andriashev, illustrates diagrammatically the feeding relationships in the pack ice. At the base of the food chains are the epontic and planktonic microalgae. Andriashev (1967) was the first to draw attention to the interesting, but as yet little explored, ice or epontic fauna living in the lower layer of loose ice. Prominent species are Harpacticoid copepods and amphipods of the genus *Orchomonopsis*. Andriashev (1967) has recorded up to 3040 individuals per square metre with a total weight of 86 gm. The copepods and amphipods, together with the fry of bottom-living nototheniid fishes, especially of *Trematomus borchgrevinki*, are the principal feeders upon the epontic algae. Phytoplankton in the water column is filtered by other copepod species as well as by krill, especially *Euphausia crystallorophias*. This latter species forms dense aggregations under the sea ice. Andriashev (1968) points out that Littlepage (1964) has recorded that the lipid content of this species rises from December to June or July, when planktonic diatoms in inshore waters under the ice cover are absent, and suggests that during this period it, too, may utilize the epontic algae.

The smaller primary consumers, especially the copepods, are consumed by fingerlings of pelagic nototheniids as well as by predatory planktonic invertebrates. The major consumers of the larger Crustacea, especially the krill, are the nototheniid fishes; considerable quantities are also taken by cephalopods, minke whales, seals, penguins, petrels, and other birds. Predatory fishes, seals and toothed whales constitute the tertiary consumer level.

Much detailed work, however, is required before the details of the feeding relationships outlined in the diagram are substantiated. In particular, the role of detritus, especially that resulting from the dying off of the epontic algae, is not known. This may constitute a substantial food resource in the winter.

B. Standing Crop Estimates for Antarctic Seas

While various attempts have been made to estimate the standing crop of phytoplankton and of individual consumer species, Holdgate (1967) has been the only worker to attempt the task of estimating the standing crop at all trophic levels. In spite of the paucity of data for many species, Holdgate's estimates are in general of the right order and his synthesis provides for the first time a sound basis for future work. Table 6 summarizes these estimates

and the following comments are made in the light of more recent information.
1. *Phytoplankton.* These estimates are in line with those of recent workers (El Sayed, 1968).

TABLE 6
Standing-crop Estimates for Antarctic Seas
(After Holdgate, 1967)

PHYTOPLANKTON	320·0 mg/m³
ZOOPLANKTON	
Euphausia ("krill")	50·0 mg/m³
Other species including carnivores	55·0 mg/m³
Total	105·0 mg/m³
CONSUMERS OF ZOOPLANKTON	
Baleen whales	12·8 mg/m³
Lobodon	1·6 mg/m³
Birds	0·12 mg/m³
Fish	no data
Cephalopods	no data
Total less fish and cephalopods	14·52 mg/m³
HIGHER TROPHIC LEVELS	
Toothed whales	0·5 mg/m³
Hydrurga	0·026 mg/m³
Other seals	0·15 mg/m³
Birds	0·1 mg/m³
Total	0·776 mg/m³
BENTHOS	
Invertebrates	400–500 × 10³ mg/m² sea floor
Unavailable to food chains approx.	320 × 10³ mg/m²
Available to food chains approx.	160 × 10³ mg/m²
Vertebrates (bottom feeding fishes)	no data

2. *Zooplankton—Euphausia*

If we can accept the standing-crop estimate for baleen whales the ratio between whales: krill is approximately 1:4. However, the usual order of relationship between secondary and primary consumers is 1:8 to 1:10. This could indicate a standing crop of 100–130 mg/m³ of krill consumed by the whales. To this must be added the amount consumed by seals, fish and cephalopods. We unfortunately do not have adequate data for the standing crop of the latter two groups. Recent Russian work indicates that the stocks of fishes are very much higher than formerly estimated. Thus the amount consumed by these two groups of predators could be at least of the same order as that formerly consumed by the whales, giving a total of 200—260 mg/m^3.

3. *Benthic invertebrates*

The high-standing crop of the shallow Antarctic benthic regions has been commented on earlier in this paper. As indicated in the table, it had been believed that approximately 60% of this standing crop was not available to higher trophic levels. However, recent work (Dayton, personal communication) does not substantiate this. Dayton has found that the large sponges characteristic of these benthic communities are consumed by a number of predators, especially starfish.

It can thus be seen that there are many gaps and that a large amount of quantitative data is needed before the picture is anything like complete.

VI. Future Work

Antarctic marine biology is now moving beyond the purely descriptive phase and the stage is now set for more detailed quantitative estimates and for experimental investigations. This does not mean, however, that there is no further need for descriptive work. The taxonomy of many groups is far from settled and we have detailed information on distributions from a few small areas only.

Areas that spring to mind as requiring urgent investigation are:

1. The role of bacteria. Very little information is available concerning the role of bacteria both as a source of food and in the breakdown of organic material.
2. Organic detritus as a source of food. We need to know the proportion of the brief summer phytoplankton that is directly consumed and to what extent it contributes detrital material to be utilized later by both the plankton and the benthic invertebrates.
3. The interrelationships of the epontic and planktonic communities. The differences in the annual cycles in the fast ice and the pack ice need investigation.
4. Detailed investigations of food-chain relationships on a quantitative and energetic basis.
5. The estimation of turnover rates.
6. Physiological investigations of key species. The Antarctic offers unique opportunities for investigations of this kind.

In spite of the difficulties of working in Antarctic seas, considerable progress has been made since the last Antarctic Biology Symposium. I am confident that the next Symposium will report even greater progress.

Acknowledgements

I would like to thank the many colleagues working in Antarctica for the discussions which have helped to clarify the ideas expressed in this paper. My thanks are also due to Mr D. Cameron for assistance in the preparation of the figures for this paper.

References

Andriashev, A. P. (1965). A general review of the Antarctic fish fauna. *In* "Biogeography and Ecology of Antarctica" (P. van Oye and J. van Mieghem, eds). Junk, The Hague.

Andriashev, A. P. (1968). The problem of life community associated with the lower layers of Antarctic fast ice. *In* "Symposium on Antarctic Oceanography", Scott Polar Research Institute, Cambridge, pp. 147–57.

Anonymous (1968). Summary of field research August–December 1967. *Antarctic J. U.S.* **3**, No. 2, 38–46.

Arnaud, P. (1965). Nature de l'etagement du benthos marin algal et animaldans l'Antartique. *C. r. hebd Seanc. Acad. Sci., Paris*, **26**, No. 1, 265–6.

Belyaev, G. M. (1964). Some patterns in the quantitative distribution of the bottom fauna in the Antarctica. *Soviet Antarct. Exped. Inform. Bull.* **1**, 119–21.

Bogorov, B. G. (1938). Biological seasons in the Arctic Sea. *Dokl. Acad. Nauk. SSSR.* **1918**, 641–4.

Brodie, J. (1965). Oceanography. *In* "Antarctica" (T. Hatherton, ed.) Methuen, London; A. H. and A. W. Reed, Wellington; Frederick A. Praeger, New York.

Bullivant. J. S. (1959). Photography of the bottom fauna of the Ross Sea. *N.Z. Jl Sci.* **2**, No. 4, 485–97.

Bullivant, J. S. (1967). Ecology of the Ross Sea benthos. *In* The Fauna of the Ross Sea. Part 5. General Account, Station Lists and Benthic Ecology. *Bull. N.Z. Dep. scient. ind. Res.* **176**, 76 pp.

Bunt, J. S. (1960). Introductory studies: hydrology and plankton Mawson, June 1956–February 1957. *ANARE Reps*, B **3**, 1–125.

Bunt, J. S. (1963). Diatoms of Antarctic sea-ice as agents of primary production. *Nature, Lond.* **199**, 1255–7.

Bunt, J. S. (1964*a*). The phytoplankton and marine productivity in some inshore waters in Antarctica. *In* "Biologie Antarctique" (R. Carrick, M. Holdgate, and J. Prevost, eds). Hermann, Paris.

Bunt, J. S. (1964*b*). Primary production under the sea ice in Antarctic waters. *In* "Biology of the Antarctic Seas" (M. O. Lee, ed.) Antarctic Research Series **1**, 13–31.

Bunt, J. S. (1968). Microalgae of the Antarctic pack-ice zone. *In* "Symposium on Antarctic Oceanography", Scott Polar Research Institute, Cambridge, pp. 198–219.

Bunt, J. S. and Wood, E. J. F. (1963). Microalgae and sea-ice. *Nature, Lond.* **199**, 1254–5.

Burckholder, P. R. and Mandelli, E. F. (1965*a*). Productivity of microalgae in Antarctic sea-ice. *Science, N.Y.* **149**, No. 3686, 872–4.

Burckholder, P. R. and Sieburth, J. McN. (1961). Phytoplankton and chlorophyll in the Gerlache and Bransfield Straits of Antarctica. *Limnol. Oceanogr.* **6**, 45–52.

Clowes, A. J. (1938). Phosphate and silicate in the Southern Ocean. *"Discovery" Rep.* **19**, 1–20.

Currie, R. I. (1964). Environmental features in the ecology of Antarctic seas. *In* "Biologie Antartique" (R. Carrick, M. Holdgate and J. Prevost, eds). Hermann, Paris.

Deacon, G. E. R. (1937). The hydrology of the Southern Ocean. *"Discovery" Rep.* **15**, 1–123.

Deacon, G. E. R. (1963). The Southern Ocean. *In* "The Sea", Vol. 2 (N. M. Hill, ed.). Interscience Publishers, New York.

Deacon, G. E. R. (1964). Antarctic oceanography. *In* "Biologie Antartique" (R. Carrick, M. Holdgate and J. Prevost, eds). Hermann, Paris.

Dearborn, J. H. (1963). Marine benthos at McMurdo Sound, Antarctica. *Bull. ecol. Soc. Am.* **42**, No. 2, 41–42.

Dearborn, J. H. (1967). Stanford University invertebrate studies on the Ross Sea 1958–61: General account and station list. *In* "Fauna of the Ross Sea". Part 5. General Account Station Lists and Benthic Ecology. *Bull. N.Z. Dep. scient. ind. Res.* No. 176, 76 pp.

Delépine, R. and Hureau, J-C. (1963). La vegetation marine dans l'archipel de Pointe Geologie (Terre Adelie). *Bull. Mus. natn. Hist. nat., Paris* **35**, No. 1, 108–15.

Dell, R. K. (1965). Marine biology. *In* "Antarctica" (T. Hatherton, ed.). Methuen, London; A. H. & A. W. Reed, Wellington; Frederick A. Praeger, New York.

Dunbar, M. (1968). "Ecological Development in Polar Regions". Prentice-Hall, New Jersey.

El Sayed, S. Z. (1966*a*). Biologie der Antarkischan Maere, *Umschau*, **66**, No. 8, 250–5.

El Sayed, S. Z. (1966*b*). Prospects of primary productivity studies in Antarctic waters. *In* "Symposium on Antarctic Oceanography", Scott Polar Research Institute, Cambridge, pp. 227–39.

El Sayed, S. Z. (1968). On the productivity of the Southwest Atlantic Ocean and waters west of Antarctic Peninsula. *In* "Biology of the Antarctic Seas III", Antarctic Research Series **2**, 15–48.

El Sayed, S. Z. and Mandelli, E. F. (1965). Primary production and standing crop of phytoplankton in the Weddell Sea and Drake Passage. *In* "Biology of the Antarctic Seas II", Antarctic Research Series **5**, 87–124.

El Sayed, S. Z., Mandelli, E. F. and Sugimura, Y. (1964). Primary organic production in the Drake Strait and Bransfield Strait. *In* "Biology of the Antarctic Seas I", Antarctic Research Series **1**, 1–12.

Filippov, B. A. (1965). The problem of hydrology of Antarctic coastal water (Text in Russian). *Trudy gos. okeanogr. Inst.* **87**, 64–76.

Foxton, P. (1956). The distribution of the standing crop of zooplankton in the Southern Ocean. *"Discovery" Rep.* **28**, 191–236.

Foxton, P. (1964). Seasonal variations in Antarctic waters. *In* "Biologie Antarctique" (R. Carrick, M. Holdgate and J. Prevost, eds). Hermann, Paris.

Hardy, A. C. (1967). "Great Waters". Collins, London.

Hardy, A. C. and Gunther, E. R. (1935). The plankton of South Georgia whaling grounds, 1926–27. *"Discovery" Rep.* **11**, 456 pp.

Hart, T. J. (1942). Phytoplankton periodicity in Antarctic surface waters. *"Discovery" Rep.* **21**, 261–356.

Herdman, H. F. P. (1966). The Southern Ocean. *In* "Encycloaedia of Oceanography" (R. W. Fairbridge, ed.), Reinhold, New York, pp. 837–46.

Holdgate, M. W. (1967). The Antarctic ecosystem. *Phil. Trans. R. Soc.* **252**, 363–89.

Hureau, J. C. (1964). Contribution à la conaissance de *Trematomus bernacchii* Boulenger. *In* "Biologie Antarctique" (R. Carrick, M. Holdgate and J. Prevost, eds). Hermann, Paris.

Ichimura, S. and Fukushima, H. (1963). On the chlorophyll content in the surface water of the Indian and Antarctic Oceans. *Bot. Mag., Tokyo* **76**, 395–9.

Ivanov, Yu. A. (1961). Frontal zones in Antarctic waters. *Okeanologicheskiye Issled.* **3**, 30–51.

Knox, G. A. (1968). Tides and intertidal zones. *In* "Symposium on Antarctic Oceanography", Scott Polar Research Institute, Cambridge, pp. 131–46.

Kopanev, I. D. (1962). Sunshine duration in Antarctica. *Soviet Antarct. Exped. Inform. Bull.* 31, 15–17.

Kort, V. G. (1962). The Antarctic Ocean. *Scient. Am.* **207**, 113–28.

Kort, V. G., Korotkevich, E. S. and Ledenev, V. G. (1965). Boundaries of the Southern Ocean. *Soviet Antarct. Exped. Inform. Bull.* **5**, 216–63.

Klumov, S. K. (1963). Nutrition and helminthological fauna of whalebone whales (Mysticceti) in the main fisheries areas of the world ocean. *Trudy in-ta okeanol, Akad. Nauk. SSSR.* 71.

Klyashtorin, L. B. (1964). Studies of primary productivity in Antarctica (Text in Russian) *Okeanlogiya* **4**, No. 3, 458–61.

Littlepage, J. L. (1965). Oceanographic investigations in McMurdo Sound, Antarctica. *In* "Biology of the Antarctic Seas II", Antarctic Research Series **5**, 1–38.

Littlepage, J. L. (1964). Seasonal variation in lipid content of two Antarctic marine crustacea. *In* "Biologie Antartique" (R. Carrick, M. Holdgate and J. Prevost, eds). Hermann, Paris.

Littlepage, J. L. and Pearse, J. S. (1962). Biological and oceanographical observations under an Antarctic ice shelf. *Science, N.Y.* **137**, 679–87.

MacGinitie, G. E. (1955). Distribution and ecology of the marine invertebrates off Point Barrow, Alaska. *Smithson, misc. Coll.* **128**, No. 9, 1–201.

Mackintosh, N. A. (1946). The Antarctic Convergence and the distribution and surface temperatures in Antarctic waters. *"Discovery" Rep.*, **23**, 179–212.

Mackintosh, N. A. (1960). The pattern of distribution of the Antarctic fauna. *Proc. R. Soc.* B **152**, 624–31.

Mackintosh, N. A. (1964). A survey of Antarctic biology up to 1945. *In* "Biologie Antarctique" (R. Carrick, M. Holdgate and J. Prevost, eds). Hermann, Paris.

Mackintosh, N. A. and Brown, S. G. (1953). Preliminary estimates of the southern populations of the larger baleen whales. *Norsk Hvalfangsttid.* **45**, 469–80.

Maksimov, I. V. and Vorobyev, V. N. (1965). Study of deep currents in the Antarctic Ocean. *Soviet Antarct. Exped. Inform. Bull.* **4**, No. 1, 17–19.

Mandelli, E. F. and Burckholder, P. R. (1966). Primary productivity in the Gerlache and Bransfield Straits of Antarctica. *Jl mar. Res.* **24**, 15–27.

Marr, J. S. W. (1962). The natural history and geography of the Antarctic krill (*Euphausia superba* Dana). *"Discovery" Rep.* **32**, 33–464.

Marshall, N. B. (1964). Some convergences between the benthic fishes of polar seas. *In* "Biologie Antarctique" (R. Carrick, M. Holdgate and J. Prevost, eds). Hermann, Paris.

Matthews, L. H. (1929). The natural biology of the elephant seal, with notes on other seals found at South Georgia. *"Discovery" Rep.* **1**, 235–56.

Meguro, H. (1962). Plankton ice in the Antarctic Ocean. *Antartic Rec.* **14**, 72–79.

Nemoto, T. (1968). Feeding of baleen whales and krill and the value of krill as a marine resource in Antarctica. *In* "Symposium on Antarctic Oceanography", Scott Polar Research Institute, Cambridge, 240–55.

Pasternak, F. A. and Gruzov, A. V. (1960). Benthonic research. *In Vtoraja Morshija Ekspeditsija na D/E "Ob" 1956–1957 gg. Trudy̅ Sov. antarkt. Eksped.* **7**, 126–42.

Pearse, J. S. (1963). Marine reproductive periodicities in polar seas: A study of two invertebrates at McMurdo Station, Antarctica. *Bull. ecol. Soc. Am.* **44**, No. 2, 43.

Pearse, J. S. (1965). Reproductive periodicities in several contrasting populations of *Odonaster validus* Koehler, a common Antarctic asteroid. *In* "Biology of the Antarctic Seas II", Antarctic Research Series **5**, 39–85.

Pearse, J. S. (1966). Antarctic asteroid *Odonaster validus* constancy of reproductive periodicities. *Science*, *N.Y.* **152**, No. 3730, 1763–4.

Phillpot, H. R. (1964). The climate of the Antarctic. *In* "Biolgie Antarctique" (R. Carrick, M. Holdgate and J. Prevost, eds). Hermann, Paris.

Propp, M. V., Gruzov, E. N. and Pushkin, A. (1966). Report on hydrobiological exploration with diving equipment at Mirny and Molodiozhanaya, Antarctica. (In the press.)

Ryther, J. H. (1963). Geographic variations in productivity. *In* "The Sea" (M. N. Hill, ed.). Vol. II. Interscience Publications, New York.

Saidova, K. L. M. (1961). Quantitative distribution of bottom foraminifera in Antarctica. *Dokl. Akad. Nauk. SSSR.* **139**, No. 4.

Saijo, Y. and Kawashima, T. (1964). Primary production in the Antarctic Ocean. *J. Oceanogr. Soc. Japan* **19**, 22–28.

Strickland, J. D. H. (1965). Phytoplankton and marine primary production. *A. Rev. Microbiol.* **19**, 127–62.

Sverdrup, H. U., Johnson, M. W. and Fleming, R. H. (1942). "Oceans: Their Physics, Chemistry and General Biology". Prentice-Hall, New York, 1087 pp.

Thomas, C. W. (1966). Vertical circulation off the Ross Ice Shelf. *Pacific Sci.* **20**, No. 2, 239–45.

Tickell, W. L. N. (1964). Feeding preferences of the albatrosses *Diomedea melanophris* and *D. chryostoma* at South Georgia. *In* "Biologie Antarctique" (R. Carrick, M. Holdgate and J. Prevost, eds). Hermann, Paris.

Tressler, W. L. (1964). Marine bottom productivity at McMurdo Sound. *In* "Biologie Antarctique" (R. Carrick, M. Holdgate and J. Prevost, eds). Hermann, Paris.

Tressler, W. L. and Ommundsen, A. M. (1962). Seasonal oceanographic studies in McMurdo Sound, Antarctica. *U.S. Navy Hydrographic Office Tech. Rep.* **125**, 141 pp.

Ushakov, P. V. (1962). Some characteristics of the distribution of the bottom fauna off the coast of Antarctica. *Soviet Antarct. Exped. Inform. Bull.* **4**, 287–92.

Ushakov, P. V. (1963). Quelques particularites de la bionomie benthique de l'Antarctique de l'Est. *Cah. Biol. mar.* **4**, No. 1, 81–89.

Volkovinsky, V. V. (1966). Studies on the primary production of the South Atlantic Ocean. *Second International Oceanographic Congress*, Moscow, 30 May–9 June 1966. Abstracts of Papers, Nauka Publishing House, Moscow, pp. 386–7.

Volkovinskiy, V. V. and Fedosov, M. V. (1965). Formation of primary productivity in Antarctic waters. (Text in Russian.) *Akad. nauk. SSSR Mezhduved geofiz. komt. proved MGG. Zrazdel progr. MGG: Okeanol. issled. Sb. statey* **13**, 115–22.

Voronina, V. M. (1966). Distribution of the zooplankton biomass of the Southern Ocean. *Oceanology* **6**, No. 6, 836–46.

Wyrtki, K. (1960). The Antarctic Circumpolar Current and the Antarctic Polar Front. *Dent. Hydrograph 2* **13**, 153–74.

Marine Biogeography of the Antarctic Regions

JOEL W. HEDGPETH*
Department of Oceanography, Corrallis, Oregon, U.S.A.

I. Introduction

The first attempt to summarize Antarctic distributions in a general way was that of Ekman (1935, 1953), which was based on the results of the first wave of intensive Antarctic research at the turn of the century. Ekman divided the benthic faunas of the shelf and near island regions into Antarctic and Antiboreal regions. His Antarctic region is that south of the Antarctic Convergence; his Antiboreal region is equivalent to the Subantarctic of most authors. Oceanographers in particular have not accepted Ekman's suggestion that the Subtropical Convergence be changed to Antiboreal Convergence. Some Soviet workers have used the term "notal" for the region between convergences, but not consistently. Vinogradova (1962), Andriashev (1962), and Lomakina (1964), for example, have used "notal", but Andriashev (1965) avoided the term. In view of the great ecological and systematic differences between the latitudinally comparable regions of northern and southern hemispheres, use of the well-known but always somewhat vaguely defined term "boreal" in the Southern Hemisphere would be misleading. Webster III has the term "notalian" defined as "the south temperate marine biogeographic realm that is bounded by the isocrymes of 68° and 44°F", but no authority is given for this term and fortunately it is not used by any of the authors consulted by me. Fleming (1963) dislikes the terms Neoaustral and Palaeoaustral and suggests Neonotian and Palaeonotian, but palaeontologists live in their own terminological haze anyhow. There seems no valid reason not to use Antarctic and Subantarctic, and many reasons to avoid a term like "notal" or its weaker modifications, which, if anything, refers to the top or back of something.

II. Distribution Patterns

According to Ekman's system the Antarctic was divided into a high Antarctic region, which in turn was subdivided into the West Antarctic,

* Present address: Marine Science Centre, Newport, Oregon, U.S.A.

including the Weddell Sea and the Antarctic Peninsula, and the East Antarctic, including the Ross Sea. The low Antarctic region included South Georgia. His Antiboreal region was divided into a South American region with a strong Antarctic component, a region of oceanic islands, and Kerguelen. Ekman was not consistent in his usage of "region" and "province" in this English version (1953) and used them indiscriminately and interchangeably.

This usage of region and province in Ekman's English edition may have been the result of the translator's impulse toward elegant variation, since *das Gebiet* of the German edition can mean either a region or a province, but preferably a region. In English province has more the connotation of an administrative or political unit and consequently carries with it the implication of conditions somewhat more precisely definable than justified by most biogeographic data. Quite possibly the late Professor Ekman, a Swede writing in German, was unaware that this loose translation would introduce uncertainties. In any event, it seems preferable not to use "province" for Antarctic distribution patterns.

Most of the contributors to the 11th Folio of the Antarctic Map Series (Bushnell and Hedgpeth, 1969) do not find clear evidence of distinct East and West subdivisions of the Antarctic. Kussakin (1967) considers as East Antarctic on the basis of isopods a region from the Weddell Sea around the continent to 90°W in the Bellingshausen Sea; this arc of 270° leaves only the Antarctic Peninsula as West Antarctic, with South Georgia considered as a separate province. Kussakin calls these subdivisions provinces (oblast); Andriashev (1965) recognizes a similar division into East and West Antarctic districts as part of a "Continental Province". Ekman did not consider South Georgia a separate part of his low Antarctic region, and the results of many recent systematic studies tend to confirm his opinion. There is, of course, indication that the fauna of the Antarctic Peninsula and island arc is somewhat different in composition from the "high Antarctic" region because of the interchange of elements between the Antarctic Peninsula and South America. Groups demonstrating such affinities are, among others, Bryozoa, Brachiopoda, Mollusca, and many echinoderms. On the other hand, where the information is based on groups represented for the most part by deep-water species, e.g. various types of corals, sipunculids, and echiurids, the distribution pattern is more clearly related to the position of the Convergences than to continental and island configurations.

According to Dell (1968) there are at least forty-eight species of Antarctic molluscs whose bathymetric ranges are greater than 500 m, and five have ranges exceeding 1000 m. Similar bathymetric ranges are noted for sponges (Koltun, 1964) and pycnogonids (Fry, 1964) and for representatives of other groups. I am not aware that there has been any demonstration of uniform population density for any of these markedly eurybathic species, and probably most of them are more characteristic of a narrower depth range. In any event such distributions tend to "soften" biogeographic boundaries based on limited presence or absence criteria.

There are various degrees of affinity, in so far as littoral species are concerned, between the outlying Subantarctic islands and New Zealand, South America, and South Africa (Holdgate, 1960). The source of the colonizing species tends to be the nearest larger neighbour to the west, especially in the case of Tristan da Cunha and South America. This distribution pattern is usually related to the West Wind Drift. According to Fell (1967) the New Zealand region is one of active speciation and has sent its colonists to the eastward via the West Wind Drift. Since New Zealand straddles cold temperate and subtropical environments, and Southern South America is predominantly cold temperate or Subantarctic with northward currents on both coasts, it should be expected that eurythermal New Zealand species might have a better chance of gaining foothold in southern South America. The Subantarctic islands are smaller, stenotpoic environments and therefore have proportionately fewer species to contribute to the eastward migration. From this it does not seem necessary to invoke rates of evolution or the Coriolis effect. Fell's suggestion that the evolutionary pattern could be traced westward in the tropics has been criticized with respect to insular speciation by Briggs (1967). Invoking the mysterious "Coriolis parameter" (whose value is zero at the Equator) is to say little more than the earth is a rotating spherical body.

In the general scheme for littoral regions proposed by Knox (1960) the Antarctic province includes Bouvet and Heard Islands as well as the South Sandwich Islands; South Georgia is considered a separate province although lying within the Antarctic region. The Antarctic Peninsula and Scotia Arc are considered to be the Scotian subprovince; a separate Rossian subprovince is recognized for the Ross Sea and adjacent regions. In the Subantarctic or cold temperate regions the scattered islands of Prince Edward and Marion, Crozet, Kerguelen, and Macquarie comprise the Kerguelenian Province, and the Subantarctic islands near New Zealand, but not the shore of South Island proper, are regarded as the Antipodean Province. The southernmost part of South America and the Falkland Islands make up the Magellanic Province. This scheme is based on consideration of information about plants as well as many groups of animals, but is concerned primarily with littoral or shallow water organisms. Therefore it does not take into consideration the benthos of depths below the limits of algal growth. Most of our information for the benthos concerns the animals of this lower region, and includes a number of groups showing strong affinities with the tip of South America. Furthermore, it does not seem possible to defend independent or subprovincial status for the Ross Sea; as work progresses on group after group, supposed Ross Sea endemics fall by the wayside.

There is still no clear agreement among biogeographers as to the limits or comparative ranking of regions, provinces or other biotic subdivisions. For the purposes of the Antarctic Folio Series the major divisions, i.e. Antarctic and Subantarctic, are regarded as "regions" rather than "provinces" (Fig. 1). The Antarctic region, including all of the Scotia Arc and the pelagic waters below the Antarctic Convergence, has two major subdivisions which may be

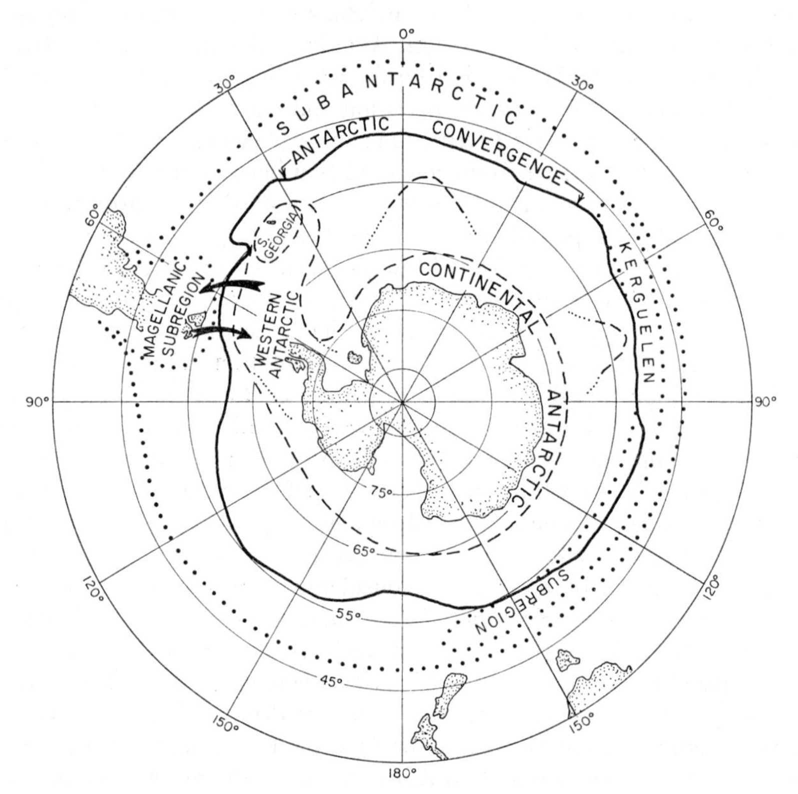

FIG. 1. Biogeographic regions of the Antarctic.

regarded as subregions or provinces, according to taste. These are the high Antarctic or continental Antarctic, south of the Antarctic Divergence, roughly equivalent to East Antarctic of some workers, and the "western" Antarctic including the Antarctic Peninsula and Scotia Arc. From this broad viewpoint it does not seem that South Georgia should be regarded as an independent biogeographic entity, but may rate status as a subprovince or "district".

The Subantarctic region includes the vast oceanic area south of the Subtropical Convergence (except that the limits of this region on the two sides of South America are not yet defined), and the shallow waters of the tip of

South America. Although the southern part of New Zealand lies within the Subtropical Convergence, the biota is not regarded as "Subantarctic" but "cold temperate". There is certainly less evidence of interchange between New Zealand and the Subantarctic regions proper than between South America and the Antarctic regions. An eastward distribution pattern has been recognized for the islands near the Antarctic Convergence from Kerguelen to Macquarie. These islands are usually regarded as comprising a Kerguelen subregion, province, or district. The status of such isolated islands as Bouvet and Heard is uncertain because of inadequate information, but they appear to be more Antarctic than Subantarctic.

III. Bipolarity

This perennial favourite of biogeographers dies hard. As late as 1967 Sir Alister Hardy, in his book "Great Waters", refers to *Priapulus caudatus* as "known only from the north and south, particularly in the polar regions, with no specimens in between" (Hardy, 1967, p. 406), although Lang (1951) convincingly demonstrated that the Arctic and Antarctic forms were actually separate species (see also Hedgpeth, 1957). As systematic refinement continues, fewer and fewer completely discontinuous species are recognized. Koltun (in Bushnell and Hedgpeth, 1969), recognizes only four authentically discontinous or "bipolar" species of sponges in the 300 Antarctic and 200 Arctic species known. In several groups, e.g. Stylasterine and Scleractinian corals, brachiopods, bryozoa and molluscs, no bipolar species are recognized. Much of the original emphasis on bipolarity was based on groups in which it is difficult to delineate species clearly, especially the so-called "Gephyrea", a zoologically indefensible grouping of sipunculids, echiurids, and priapulids. Some of these are still considered bipolar, but the material is not convincing. As already indicated, the bipolarist's favourite, *Priapulus caudatus*, has fallen by the wayside, and recent information suggests that priapulids may be much more widespread throughout the oceans of the world than previously suspected (see Murina and Starobogatov, 1961; Sanders and Hessler, 1962; van der Land, 1968).

There are no bipolar pycnogonids, and, as with many other groups, the total facies of the Antarctic fauna is different from the Arctic, even when we set aside the indigenous ten-and twelve-legged forms. There is a single bulky species of *Colossendeis* in the Arctic basin proper (*Colossendeis proboscidea*), whereas there are several of these conspicuous animals in shallow Antarctic waters, where they are numerous enough to be significant components of the bottom communities. The Arctic and Antarctic are similar in lacking brachyuran crabs, although large anomuran crabs occur in such cold northern regions as the Bering Sea. Recently several specimens of an anomuran crab identified as *Paralomis spectabilis*, a species previously known from waters off Iceland and southern Greenland were reported from 67°23′S, 179°53′E at a depth of 500–900 m. (Birstein and Vinogradov, 1967). If the determination is correct, we may have another "bipolar" species, at least until specimens are found in intermediate regions. In both Arctic and Antarctic the ecological role of brachyuran crabs is taken over in part by idotheid isopods. *Mesidothea* and *Glyptonotus* are superficially similar in appearance and belong to the same family.

Nevertheless, there is little in common between the highly diversified Antarctic fauna and its dense epifaunal assemblages and the more monotonous predominantly infaunal assemblages of the Arctic basin. On the basis of Soviet investigations of the benthos of various regions of both polar seas it appears that the Antarctic biomass is several times to an order of magnitude greater, and that the percentage composition of the major invertebrate groups is markedly different (see Ushakov, 1963; Zenkevitch, 1963; Bullivant, 1967). Except for cold water and long polar day and night, there is little in common between the two polar environments. The Antarctic is a ring of cold water around a continent with the bottom deepening towards the rest of the world, while the Arctic is an almost enclosed mediterranean sea. Probably the Antarctic seas have had a longer and less-interrupted connection with the seas of the world, but, more significantly, have had a much longer interrupted period of continuity as marine waters since Mesozoic times. The Arctic, on the other hand, may have been completely frozen over during some of the glacial periods, or may have been completely isolated as a basin of reduced salinity. Accordingly, when the world was cold and polar faunas should have been continuous, there may not have been two polar seas in which formerly continuous populations could have persisted until the present time. In any event, our present knowledge of invertebrate systematics offers no convincing evidence of past continuity.

But attractively simple ideas die hard, and even though Stiasny (1935) was convinced that he had slain the dragon by suggesting equatorial submergence ("Es gibt kein Bipolaritätsproblem mehr."), Murphy (1928) was correct in remarking that the old theory turns up in one way or another. Thus the idea that there are faunal and floral elements in Northern and Southern Hemispheres that are "relicts" of a former continuous distribution across the Equator is still very much alive. Hubbs (1952) suggested the term antitropical for latitudinal discontinuities, and Brinton (1962) discussed the "biantitropical" distributions of euphausiids, suggesting that during times of cooling of the oceans the presently separated populations would move toward the Equator and become continuous, while during warm periods (as at present) they are separated and comparatively "bipolar".

References

Andriashev, A. P. (1962). Bathypelagic fishes of the Antarctic. 1. Family Myctophidae. *Rez. biol. issl. Sov. Antarkt. Eksp.* **1**, 216–94.

Andriashev, A. P. (1965). A general view of the Antarctic Fish Fauna. *In* "Biogeography and Ecology in Antarctica" (P. Van Oye and J. Van Meighem, eds). Junk, The Hague, pp. 491–550.

Birstein, J. A. and Vinogradov, L. G. (1967). Occurrence of Paralomis spectabilis Hansen (Crustacea, Decapoda, Anomura) in the Antarctic. *Rez. biol. issl. Sov. Antarkt. Eksp.* **3**, 381–8.

Briggs, J. C. (1967). Dispersal of Tropical Marine Shore Animals: Coriolis Parameters or Competition? *Nature, Lond.* **216**, (5113), 350.

Brinton, E. (1962). The distribution of Pacific Euphausiids. *Bull. Scripps Instn. Oceanogr. non-tech. Ser.* **8**(2), 51–270.

Bullivant, J. S. (1967). The fauna of the Ross Sea. 5. Ecology of the Ross Sea benthos. *Mem. N.Z. Oceanogr. Inot.* **32**, 49–75.

Bushnell, V. C. and Hedgpeth, J. W. (eds) (1969). Distribution of selected groups of marine invertebrates in waters south of 35° S. latitude. "Antarctic Map Folio Series", Folio 11. American Geographical Society, New York.

Dell, R. K. (1968). Benthic faunas of the Antarctic. *In* "Symposium on Antarctic Oceanography", Santiago Chile, 13–16 September 1966. Scott Polar Research Institute, Cambridge, pp. 110–18.

Ekman, S. (1935). "Tiergeographie des Meeres." 542 pp., 244 figs. Akademische Verlagsgesellschaft, Leipzig.

Ekman, S. (1953). "Zoogeography of the Sea." xiv + 417 pp. Sidgwick & Jackson, London.

Fell, H. B. (1967). Resolution of Coriolis Parameters for Former Epochs. *Nature, Lond.* **214**, 1192–8.

Fleming, C. A. (1963). Paleontology and southern biogeography. *In* "Pacific Basin Biogeography" (J. Linsley Gressit, ed). Bishop Museum Press, Honolulu, pp. 369–83.

Fry, W. G. (1964). The pycnogonid fauna of the Antarctic continental shelf. *In* "Biologie Antarctique". Hermann, Paris, pp. 263–70.

Hardy, A. (1967). "Great Waters". A voyage of natural history to study whales, plankton and the waters of the Southern Ocean in the old Royal Research Ship *Discovery* and with the results brought up to date by the findings of the R.R.S. *Discovery II*. Collins, London, 542 pp.

Hedgpeth, J. W. (1957). Marine biogeography. *In* "Treatise on Marine Ecology and Paleoecology." *Mem. geol. Soc. Am.* **67**(1), 359–82, 16 figs, 1 pl.

Holdgate, M. W. (1960). The fauna of the mid-Atlantic islands. *Proc. R. Soc.* B, **152** (949), 550–67.

Hubbs, C. L. (1952). Antitropical distribution of fishes and other organisms. *Seventh Pac. Sci. Congr.* **3**, 374–30.

Knox, G. A. (1960). Littoral ecology and biogeography of the southern oceans. *Proc. R. Soc.* B **152**,(949), 577–624.

Koltun, V. M. (1964). Sponges of the Antarctic. Part 1. Tetraxonida and Cornascuspongida. *Rez. biol. issl. Sovet. Antarkt. Eksp.* (1955–58 gg) **2**, 6–131, 25 figs, 15 pl.

Kussakin, O. G. (1967). "Isopoda and Tanaidacea from the coastal zones of the Antarctic and Subantarctic." *Rez. biol. issl. Sov. Antarkt. Eksp.* **3**, 220–380.

Lang, K. (1951). Priapulus caudatus Lam. and Priapulus caudatus forma tuberculato-spinosus Baird represent two different species. *Ark. Zool.* **2**, 2(11), 565–8.

Lomakina, N. B. (1964). The euphausiid fauna of the Antarctic and Notal regions *Rez. biol. issl. Sov. Antarkt. Eksp.* **2**, 254–334.

Murina, V. V. and Starobogratov, Y. I. (1961). On the systematics and zoogeography of priapulids. *Trudy. Inst. Okeanol.* **46**, 179–200.

Murphy, R. C. (1928). Antarctic zoogeography and some of its problems. *In* "Problems of Polar Research". American Geographical Society, New York, pp. 355–79, 1 fig.

Sanders, H. L. and Hessler, R. R. (1962). *Priapulus atlantisi* and *Priapulus profundus*. Two new species from bathyal and abyssal depths of the North Atlantic. *Deep Sea Res.* **9**, 125–30, 5 figs.

Stiasny, S. (1935). Das Bipolaritätsproblem. *Archs. néerl. Zool.* **1**, 35–53.

Ushakov, P. V. (1963). Quelques particularités de la bionomie benthique de l'Antarctique de l'Est. *Cah. Biol. mar.* **4**, 81–89.

van der Land, J. (1968). A new aschelminth, probably related to the Priapulida. *Zoöl. Meded., Leiden* **42**, (22), 237–50, 18 figs.

Vinogradova, N. G. (1962). Ascidiae simplices of the Indian part of the Antarctic (in the collections of the Soviet Antarctic Expedition). *Rez. biol. issl. Sov. Antarkt. Eksp.* **1**, 196–215.

Webster III. (1965). "Webster's Third New International Dictionary of the English Language Unabridged", P. B. Grove (ed). G. & G. Merriam, Springfield, Mass.

Zenkevitch, L. (1963). "Biology of the Seas of the U.S.S.R." Translated by S. Botcharskaya. London, George Allen & Unwin, 955 pp., illus.

Ecosystem Adaptation in Marine Polar Environments

M. J. DUNBAR
McGill University, Montreal, Canada

The word "adaptation", when used in the evolutionary context, is usually taken to apply to the adaptation of individuals, and hence of species, to changing environments, or to the perfection of adjustment to a stable environment. The mechanism by which this adjustment is made, maintained, and spread through the specific population, has been the chief concern of students of evolution. In the study of polar floras and faunas, the emphasis has been overwhelmingly upon the problems imposed on individuals, and hence on species, by the generally low temperature régime, in both aquatic and terrestrial communities, so that we have a considerable literature on the means that have been adopted by plants and animals to avoid the limiting effects of low temperature, to maintain active metabolism and growth in spite of the low temperature, or to avoid low temperatures by migration or dormancy.

It is only quite recently that the evolution of the ecosystem as a whole has been given serious attention, although the first hint of the importance of this approach was made by Alfred Russel Wallace just ninety years ago. The theory that high-latitude ecosystems are younger and therefore less diverse than tropical systems was first put forward in nineteenth-century terms by Wallace (1878), and it has been revived much more recently by several authors (e.g. Fischer, 1960; Dunbar, 1960, 1968).

It has been widely held, and in fact it has often been considered to be axiomatic, that the decisive difference between polar and tropical environments, the factor responsible for the differences in their living communities, is the low temperature level characteristic of the high latitudes. This belief I have recently challenged (Dunbar, 1968), particularly where aquatic environments are concerned, but also for terrestrial regions. It has become increasingly clear, since the first suggestions of Krehl and Soetbeer (1899) and Krogh (1916), and more so since the experimental studies of Thorson (1936), Spärck (1936), Fox (1936, etc.), Fox and Wingfield (1937), Dehnel (1955), and others, that poikilothermic as well as homoiothermic living organisms, can and do adapt to low temperatures very readily, especially in terms of metabolism and locomotor activity, and also, if the situation demands it, in terms of growth rate. That is, when polar, temperate, and tropical populations of the same or closely related species are compared, the Q-10 law is flagrantly and happily disobeyed. Examples of this are now very numerous, and have been summarized in general reviews (Bullock, 1955; Fry, 1958; Dunbar, 1957).

If low temperature is not a serious problem in adapting to Pleistocene conditions in high latitudes (and I take it we are agreed that we live in the Pleistocene period), then the explanation for the very great differences between polar and tropical ecosystems, manifested in species diversity, growth rates, body sizes and so on, must be sought elsewhere. We cannot point to low temperature as being effective at the ultimate level and only to a limited degree at the proximate level. In considering these problems, involving as they do physiological responses to external factors and the evolution of ecosystems, it is extremely important to keep the proximate and ultimate levels of causation and of explanation strictly separate; to confuse them leads to logical anarchy.

Besides the generally lower temperature régimes of the high latitudes, the Pliocene-Pleistocene change brought other important consequences, such as: (1) the presence of sea ice; (2) an Arctic Ocean régime highly stable in the vertical column and therefore very unproductive; (3) a very unstable, and therefore productive, Antarctic Ocean; (4) a highly oscillating basic food supply (inorganic nutrients for plants and plant food for herbivores), the oscillation being annual in period. This is particularly marked in the Arctic, owing to the great extent of sea ice and the intense vertical density stratification, which keep the nutrient concentrations low in the euphotic zone and cause them to be rapidly used up in the spring.

For the purposes of this paper it is this last of the legacies of the Pleistocene event, the seasonally oscillating environment, that is most significant, especially when considered together with the generally low productivity in the Arctic. For the herbivorous animals depending on the phytoplankton for their livelihood, the short plant production season, which may be only three to five weeks long, and the very low food supply during the rest of the year, make demands which encourage the following developments or adjustments:

(1) Growth rates from egg to maturity which fit the periods of phytoplankton abundance. For most planktonic herbivores this means a considerable extension of the life cycle when compared with the same species in temperate waters, so that spawning is delayed until the time of the next phytoplankton bloom. It is probable, as pointed out by Conover (1964), that micro-zooplankton and organic matter in the water form an important secondary food source for these

herbivores at potentially all times of year; nevertheless they breed not more than once a year in the Arctic.

(2) Large body size, which is associated logarithmically with fecundity (high egg number) in the female. This assures an adequate breeding stock despite the mortality during the year. If the egg number is not large, then the eggs themselves must be large and yolky, so that survival rates are increased. In either case the energy reserves must be high.

(3) A small number of species; if the number of species is too large the survival of all species will be in hazard, assuming that the total food supply is severely limited, owing to the natural mortality during the long period during which spawning does not occur.

These adjustments are, in fact, found in the ecosystems of high northern latitudes; slow growth rates, large body size, and few species. And food chains tend, in consequence, to be short and simple: diatom, herbivorous zooplankter, fish or whale or seal. One of the standard specific examples is from the Antarctic: *Fragilariopsis antarctica*⟶*Euphausia superba*⟶*Balaenoptera musculus* (blue whale).

Such simple systems, however, tend to be unstable, especially where the biomass is low, as in the Arctic, and it is reasonable to wonder whether they are, in fact, anywhere near saturation. They are subject to serious population oscillations, again particularly if there is low total energy or biomass, since both lags and overproductions in specific populations occur readily, leading to local extinction and breakdown of the community. The standard examples of this are from terrestrial environments, which are easier to observe, such as that in which the lemming is involved; but there is evidence from our work in the far north (Nansen Sound complex) that the same thing is demonstrable in marine systems.

Greater ecological stability is achieved by increasing the number of species (species diversity), increasing the biomass, reducing specific fecundity, increasing growth rates, and spreading the feeding load over a much larger portion of the year; this implies that herbivores must develop a degree of omnivorous habit, using detritus, micro-zooplankton, and dissolved organic material. It is to be noted that these objectives are not the same as those already evolved in response to the oscillating environment; in fact, the two evolutionary processes, if they exist together, are to a great extent in competition with each other.

Evidence suggesting that selective evolution toward greater ecological stability in polar and cool temperate regions is in fact going on around us has been marshalled elsewhere (Dunbar, 1968). In the evolutionary context with which we are concerned here, the interest lies in the possibility that differentiation of morphological pattern and food habit, within species and probably sympatrically, is an active process in these regions.

The number of species in tropical environments, both terrestrial and marine, is at first bewildering in its lavishness, and many a stranger to tropical biology has been appalled by the tasks faced by his tropical colleagues. Closer examination of tropical faunas, however, reveals that the species themselves are well disciplined taxonomically, that is to say they do not present serious problems of decision to the systematic expert other than by their sheer number. In temperate faunas, and especially, it seems, in subpolar areas, intraspecific variation, mutants and "varieties", plague the systematist at almost every turn. That some such intraspecific variation exists also in warmer waters is admitted, as, for instance, the example of certain Mediterranean copepods described by Battaglia (1958), but these are much less impressive than the taxonomic jungle of the higher latitudes. I am excluding from consideration here, as irrelevant to the argument, local variant populations on a small geographic scale, such as changes in intertidal populations corresponding to degree of exposure to the air or to wave action, and also obvious allopatric geographic races such as distinguish Hudson Bay from the Beaufort Sea.

Examples which are relevant and which may be offered are the following:

1. The genus *Gammarus*. The former "*Gammarus locusta*" has been shown to consist of several species, forming a complex in which overlap of geographic range is often very large indeed. *G. locusta*, in the modern sense, is confined to the shores of north-west Europe, but including Iceland; *G. oceanicus* is temperate and Subarctic on both sides of the Atlantic; *G. setosus* extends further north into Arctic water, and *G. wilkitzki* is more strictly Arctic still. There are also other species.
2. The genus *Calanus*. The splitting up of the former *Calanus finmarchicus* into a number of species has much in common with the *Gammarus* case, but here we are dealing with planktonic populations, which perhaps increases the theoretical ecological interest. Both cases suggest very strongly a recent evolutionary divergence with the effect of increasing the ecological diversity. In the broad regions of overlap between *C. helgolandicus* and *C. finmarchicus* (s.s.), and between *C. finmarchicus* and *C. glacialis*, one wonders how the Gaussian principle of exclusion could apply, unless significantly different ecological, perhaps feeding, demands have also been evolved. In addition to these three, in the North Atlantic and the Arctic areas, there is *C. hyperboreus*, Subarctic and Arctic in distribution, and very similar morphologically to the others.
3. The genus *Parathemisto*. There are at least two separable forms, or "morphs", of *P. gaudichaudi*, formerly considered to be separate species, known as "*bispinosa*" and "*compressa*"; both are known from the northern

and southern hemispheres, and there is third form, *thomsoni*, known in the south only. They differ in the shape and setation of the third and fifth peraeopods and in the development of dorsal spines.

4. The genus *Thysanoessa*. *T. inermis*, *T. raschii*, and to a lesser extent *T. longicaudata*, form a close trio of euphausids occupying much the same regions and water masses. *T. longicaudata* has elongated second thoracic legs, and there is a variant of *inermis*, known as "*neclecta*", which has similar modified second legs.

5. The genus *Hyperia*. There is a variant, apparently a somewhat rare variant, of *Hyperia galba*, known as "*H. spinigera*", known from Svalbard, northern Norway, Labrador, Hudson Strait, the west coast of Ireland and the south coast of England, and from the Antarctic.

6. The genus *Aglantha*. The Trachymedusan *Aglantha digitale*, very abundant in northern waters, exists in several colour variants which have so far not been explained.

7. Chaetognatha. *Sagitta elegans* and *Eukrohnia hamata* in the Arctic Ocean possess well-developed "irridescent spots", so-called, on the fins. These are well supplied nervously, and may well be similar to the ciliary tufts described by Horridge and Boulton (1967) in *Spadella cephaloptera*. In the Arctic Ocean itself, a very high proportion (85–97%) of the individuals of *E. hamata* possess these organs, and in the northern Barents Sea some 20% of individuals of both *E. hamata* and *S. elegans* possess them; in the southern Barents Sea, however, they are absent from both species (Newbury, personal communication). These characters, associated as they probably are with the perception of vibrations in the water, may be associated with the lesser intensity of light which prevails in the Arctic Ocean, and with the low density of prey. They may also have other significances, and in particular be related to the types of prey organisms eaten.

8. The genus *Eucalanus*. Johnson (1939) drew attention to the systematic problems of the group "commonly lumped more or less indiscriminately by some authors under the name *Eucalanus elongatus* without reference to varieties established by Giesbrecht (1892)". Several forms, now raised to specific rank, are found in the North Pacific, recorded under the specific or subspecific names *bungii*, *elongatus*, *californicus* and *inermis*. This situation is not unlike that of the former *Calanus finmarchicus*.

To these examples should be added others of a somewhat different sort, namely examples of anomalies of geographic distribution which suggest the evolution of mutant stocks which differ physiologically but not morphologically from the main body of the specific population; "cryptomorphs" which might well differ also in food habits. Such examples are to be found in the euphausid *Meganyctiphanes norvegica*, an Atlantic species which is found unexpectedly in north-east Greenland waters; the north-east Greenland population of *Gammarus oceanicus* and of *Thysanoessa longicaudata;* and *Parathemisto gaudichaudi* in northern Foxe Basin.

In the face of these interesting variations and anomalies, the next step is to discover in what ways they differ from their cousins, or conspecific partners, in their ecological positions and necessities. This unfortunately has not yet been done, nor is it likely to be done for some time, for the material and the problems are both large; it is one of the facets of the IBP study we are beginning at McGill in the Gulf of St Lawrence, and there is a good deal of work being done along these lines in several countries. Despite the lack of detailed information, one may be excused for indulging in a little pleasurable anticipation, and discussing what few facts are at hand. Differentiation in ecological demands and necessities, probably including food requirements and food-getting abilities, is to be expected, involving sophistication of the food-chain pattern within the system as a whole.

An excellent recent summary of what is known or suspected about the food habits of marine organisms, especially the plankton, has been provided by Raymont (1963), from whose work it emerges that "our knowledge of specific dietary requirements is . . . fragmentary". The pattern that appears so far is that most planktonic animals display considerable lability in food habits. Even the most clearly herbivorous forms, such as species of *Calanus* and *Euphausia*, appear to ingest animal food occasionally, and others, such as individual species of *Thysanoessa*, may be herbivorous, carnivorous, or omnivorous (Raymont, 1963; Nemoto, 1967). The latter paper is an example of the precise study of food habits in relation to morphological characters in planktonic groups that is needed. The Hyperiid amphipods appear to be predominantly carnivorous (e.g. Dunbar, 1946, for *Parathemisto libellula*); nothing is known of any difference in food habits between the two (or three) morphs of *P. gaudichaudi*.

Omnivores are common in the zooplankton. Raymont (1963) writes that "the animals probably change their diet to a considerable extent depending upon the availability of food". In ecological theory, the omnivorous habit can mitigate the restricting effects of the simple ecosystem, because it allows change of diet to respond either to the scarcity or the superabundance of any given food organism, thus acting as a dampening influence on specific population oscillation. This is interesting in itself, for it suggests that too intense attention to "trophic levels" in marine ecology may not be the most productive approach to the economy of the sea. It does not, however, reduce the weight of the argument presented here, which is, in brief, that the evidence suggests strongly that there is a continuing present evolution toward greater diversification and subdivision of niches, including that part of the niche represented by food habit and position in the general food web, in polar seas.

References

Battaglia, B. (1958). Ecological differentiation and incipient intraspecific isolation in marine copepods. I.U.B.S. Ser. B (Colloques), No. 24, 259–68.

Bullock, T. H. (1955). Compensation for temperature in metabolism and activity of poikilotherms. *Biol. Rev.* **30**, 311–42.

Conover, R. J. (1964). Food relations and nutrition of zooplankton. *Proc. Symp. Exp. Mar. Ecol., Occasional Publ. No.* **2**, Grad. School Oceanogr., Univ. Rhode Island, 81–89.

Dehnel, P. A. (1955). Rates of Growth of gastropods as a function of latitude. *Physiol. Zoöl.* **28**, 115–44.

Dunbar, M. J. (1946). On *Themisto libellula* in Baffin Island coastal waters. *J. Fish. Res. Bd. Can.* **6**, 419–34.

Dunbar, M. J. (1957). The determinants of production in northern seas: A study of the biology of *Themisto libellula* Mandt. *Can. J. Zool.*, **35**, 797–819.

Dunbar, M. J. (1960). The evolution of stability in marine environments; natural selection at the level of the ecosystem. *Am. Nat.* **XCIV**, 129–36.

Dunbar, M. J. (1968). "Ecological Development in Polar Regions." Prentice-Hall, Englewood Cliffs, N.J. 119 pp.

Fischer, A. G. (1960). Latitudinal variations in organic diversity. *Evolution* **XIV**, 64–81.

Fox, H. Munro (1936). The activity and metabolism of poikilothermal animals in different latitudes. *Proc. zool. Soc. Lond.* **1936**, 945–55. Also ibid, **1938**, 501–5, and **1939**, 141–56.

Fox, H. Munro and Wingfield C. A. (1937). The activity and metabolism of poikilothermal animals in different latitudes, II. *Proc. zool. Soc. Lond.* **1937**, 275–82.

Fry, F. E. J. (1958). Temperature compensation. *A. Rev. Physiol.* **20**, 207–20.

Giesbrecht, W. (1892). Systematik und Faunistik der pelagischen Copepoden des Golfes von Neapel und der angrenzenden Meeresabschnitte. "Fauna und Flora des Golfes von Neapel," 19; 831 pp., Berlin.

Horridge, G. A. and Boulton, P. S. (1967). Prey detection by Chaetognatha via a vibration sense. *Proc. R. Soc.* B **168**, 413–19.

Johnson, M. W. (1939). The study of species formation in certain *Eucalanus* copepods in the North Pacific. *Proc. 6th Pacific Science Congress* **III** 565–8.

Krehl, L. and Soetbeer, F. (1899). Untersuchungen über die Temperaturabhängigkeit von Lebensprozessen bei verschiedenen Wirbellosen. *Pflüger. Arch. ges. Physiol.* **77**, 611.

Krogh, A. (1916). "Respiratory Exchange of Animals and Man." Longmans, Green, London.

Nemoto, T. (1967). Feeding pattern of euphausids and differentiations in their body characters. *Info. Bull. Planktology Japan:* Comm. No. Dr Y. Matsue's 60th birthday, 151–71.

Raymont, J. E. G. (1963). "Plankton and Productivity in the Oceans." Pergamon Press, New York. 660 pp.

Spärck, R. (1936). On the relation between metabolism and temperature in some marine lamellibranchs and its ecological and zoogeographical importance. *K. danske Vidensk. Selsk. Skr.* **13**, 1–27.

Thorson, G. (1936). The larval development, growth, and metabolism of Arctic marine bottom invertebrates compared with those of other seas. *Meddr Grønland* **100** (6), 1–55.

Wallace, A. R. (1878). "Tropical Nature and Other Essays." Macmillan, London and New York. 356 pp.

Discussion

Marine Ecosystems

ECOSYSTEM ADAPTATION

W. S. BENNINGHOFF

Among vascular plants there are parallels with Dr Dunbar's thesis. In high Arctic situations species have many ecotypes and micro-species and exhibit high incidence of polyploidy. Conversely, in low latitudes there are few ecotypes, good Linnean species, and low polyploidy. This situation may be a response to physical environmental stresses in high latitudes where there are steep gradients of physical conditions and to biotic environment stresses in low latitudes which evoke an all-or-none response. As a consequence of the Pleistocene glaciations high-latitude and low-latitude species were mixed. Some "high-latitude" multiversant types became weed species colonizing open disturbed ground in temperate latitudes. In South Polar regions, in contrast, this interplay did not happen, for biogeographical reasons associated with the configurations of land and sea.

M. J. DUNBAR

I am told that similar intraspecific variation occurs in high-latitude frogs, salamanders, and lepidoptera. The existence of the diversity is as important ecologically as its cause.

P. K. DAYTON

Dr Dunbar spoke of the evolution of ecosystems as units by a Darwinian mechanism. What units? And what mechanism?

M. J. DUNBAR

As units, take groups of species living together in a geographically defined area. With a few species only, population numbers show a high oscillation and there is a significant chance of local extinction of a species when its numbers are in a trough. This could throw the whole system out, as there may be no other species available to fill the same niche, and extinction of the whole system is theoretically possible. Replacement would be by immigration from adjacent areas. In Darwinian terms the immigrant population will differ from that eliminated, and species or ecotypes less liable to oscillation will be favoured. Thus selection tends to reduce the amplitude of population fluctuations. If two species come in where one was before, the niches being subdivided, there is a further tendency towards stability.

G. A. KNOX

The concept of increased stability through increased diversity may be related in the high productivity and biomass of Antarctic waters, especially in the Antarctic benthos. But we must remember that these systems are *not* diverse compared with temperate regions. The faunas are disharmonic like those of oceanic islands: for example, there are no crabs and Dell has shown that there are fewer molluscs, with the absence of families and with fewer species per genus than in New Zealand and other temperate regions. The Antarctic fauna is currently gaining members via the Scotia Ridge, but not in the New Zealand sector.

P. K. DAYTON

If the two mechanisms stated are assumed, then the number of species present will relate closely to time elapsed. But there are also considerations of area and of saturation, as considered by McArthur and Wilson. Even if much of the hypothesis of saturation can be challenged, this must be considered. It is by no means certain that productivity would have moved up and down with stability.

M. J. DUNBAR

Is there any evidence for the correlation suggested between stability and time? Islands are probably different. Antarctica isn't an oceanic island. I do not see any contradictions here with McArthur and Wilson's thesis.

R. W. MORRIS

But Antarctica has a high level of endemism and in this sense *is* an island.

M. J. DUNBAR

At the moment there is a balance between the high Arctic fauna and the environment, with well-known oscillations in response to food supply. We cannot be sure —only suspect—that we are moving toward a more stable situation. The question is not whether we will have tropical diversity in the polar regions but whether we will attain stability.

BIOGEOGRAPHY OF ANTARCTIC MARINE ANIMALS

K. G. MCKENZIE

Dr Hedgpeth spoke of a eurybathic fauna. Are the populations of such species uniform throughout the depth range?

J. HEDGPETH

Some species are very wide-ranging from surface waters down to as much as 2000 m, but they are not uniformly abundant at all these depths.

K. G. MCKENZIE

What proportion of benthic animals have planktonic larvae?

J. HEDGPETH

The proportion of animals with planktonic larvae is probably much less than has been thought. In many cases supposedly planktonic larvae have been shown to settle immediately after release, and much of the dispersal of benthic animals is probably by slow crawling.

G. A. KNOX

Dr Hedgpeth suggested that most Antarctic species were more widespread around the continent than had been supposed. I have just finished a monograph on the polychaete fauna of the Ross Sea, recording some 120 species, and many of these were formerly recorded only from East Antarctica. There are only two or three species peculiar to the Ross Sea.

Similarly, studies of the echinoid fauna by Dr Dawson of the New Zealand Oceanographic Institute reveal that only one species found on the New Zealand slope region even gets as far as Balleny Islands and that none reaches the Ross Sea. Thus the link between Australasia and Antarctica appears far less marked than that between South America and the Peninsula.

Part III

PLANKTON AND ITS PELAGIC CONSUMERS

Plankton and its Pelagic Consumers

In this section the initial review by S. Z. El Sayed summarizes recent discoveries which have qualified earlier emphasis on the extreme high productivity of the Antarctic Ocean, and demonstrated great regional variability in biomass, production and productivity. The subsequent short papers bring together data from the extensive Soviet oceanographic cruises, and that by E. Balech suggests that the importance of diatoms in the Antarctic phytoplankton has been overstressed. Taken together, these papers form a reasonably comprehensive review of their field and, in conjunction with G. A. Knox's paper in the preceding section, a satisfactory lead in to the literature (attention should, perhaps, be drawn to J. S. Bunt's papers, especially that in SCAR (1968), which are not cited in the present section).

The papers on zooplankton are, in contrast, far from comprehensive, and this is partly because of a lack of modern ecological studies of many groups. More general information can be obtained from papers referred to in G. A. Knox's review paper in the preceding section, or from the paper by David in the SCAR Symposium on Antarctic Oceanography (SCAR, 1968) which lists the *Discovery* Reports on this subject. However, the present section does give information concerning the Copepoda, which predominate in the general Antarctic zooplankton, and the "krill" (*Euphausia superba*), which forms striking aggregations and may account for half the total zooplankton biomass. The Soviet papers on krill in this section do not contain bibliographies: for this, reference may be made to the monograph by Marr (1962). The food chain leading from phytoplankton via krill to whalebone whales has long been celebrated: the paper in this section by Y. E. Permitin emphasizes that many fish species, even belonging to groups of generally benthic habit, may also consume krill, as do several species of seals and birds. Finally, the role of whale species as consumers of krill production is considered by B. A. Zenkovich, and while he does not give references to the considerable literature, these may be found in the review by N. A. Mackintosh in the following section.

References

Marr, J. W. S. (1962). The natural history and geography of the Antarctic krill (*Euphausia superba* Dana). *"Discovery" Rep.*, Vol. XXXII, pp. 35–463.

SCAR (1968). "Symposium on Antarctic Oceanography". Scott Polar Research Institute, Cambridge.

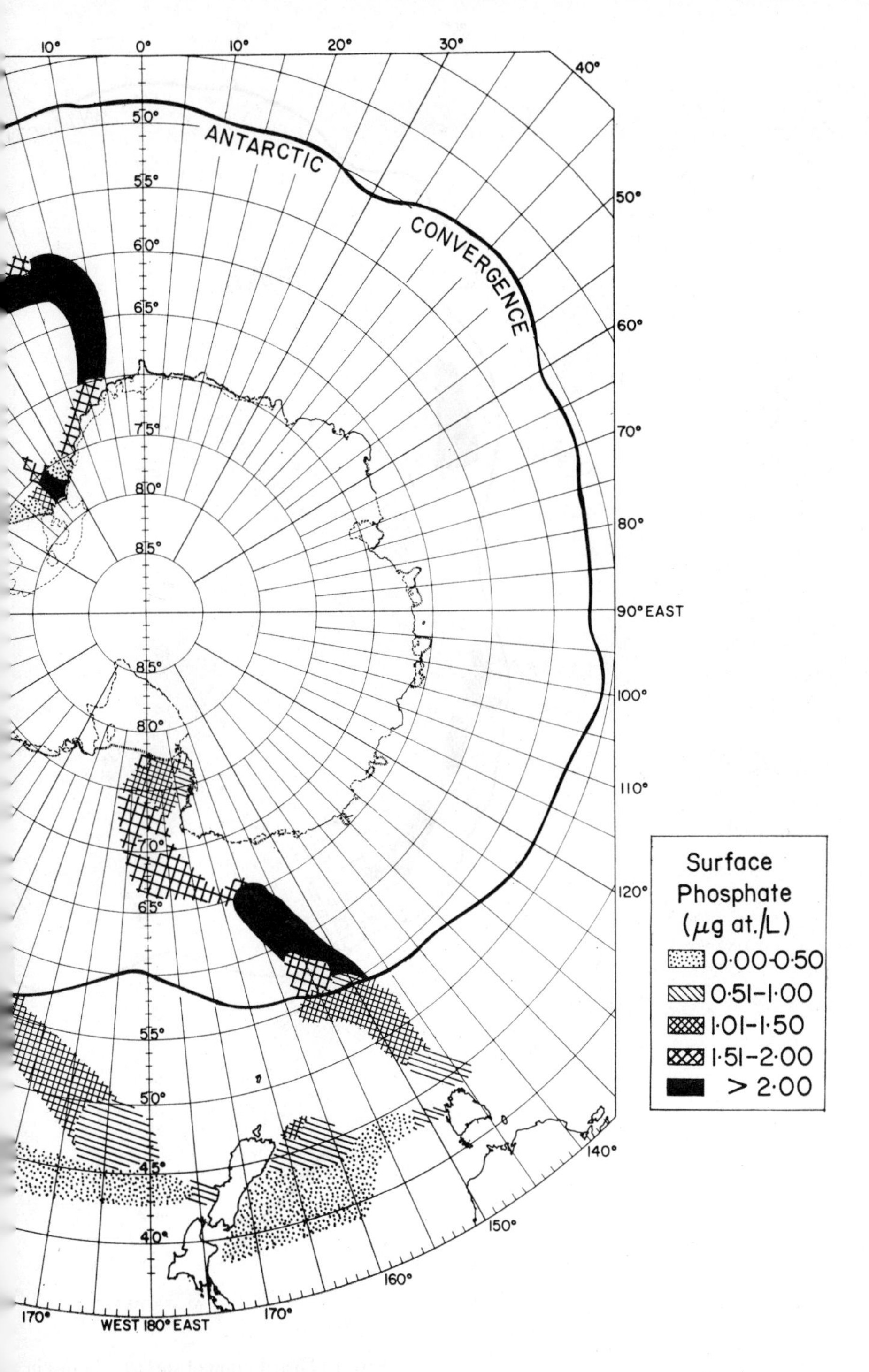

n of surface phosphates in the study areas.

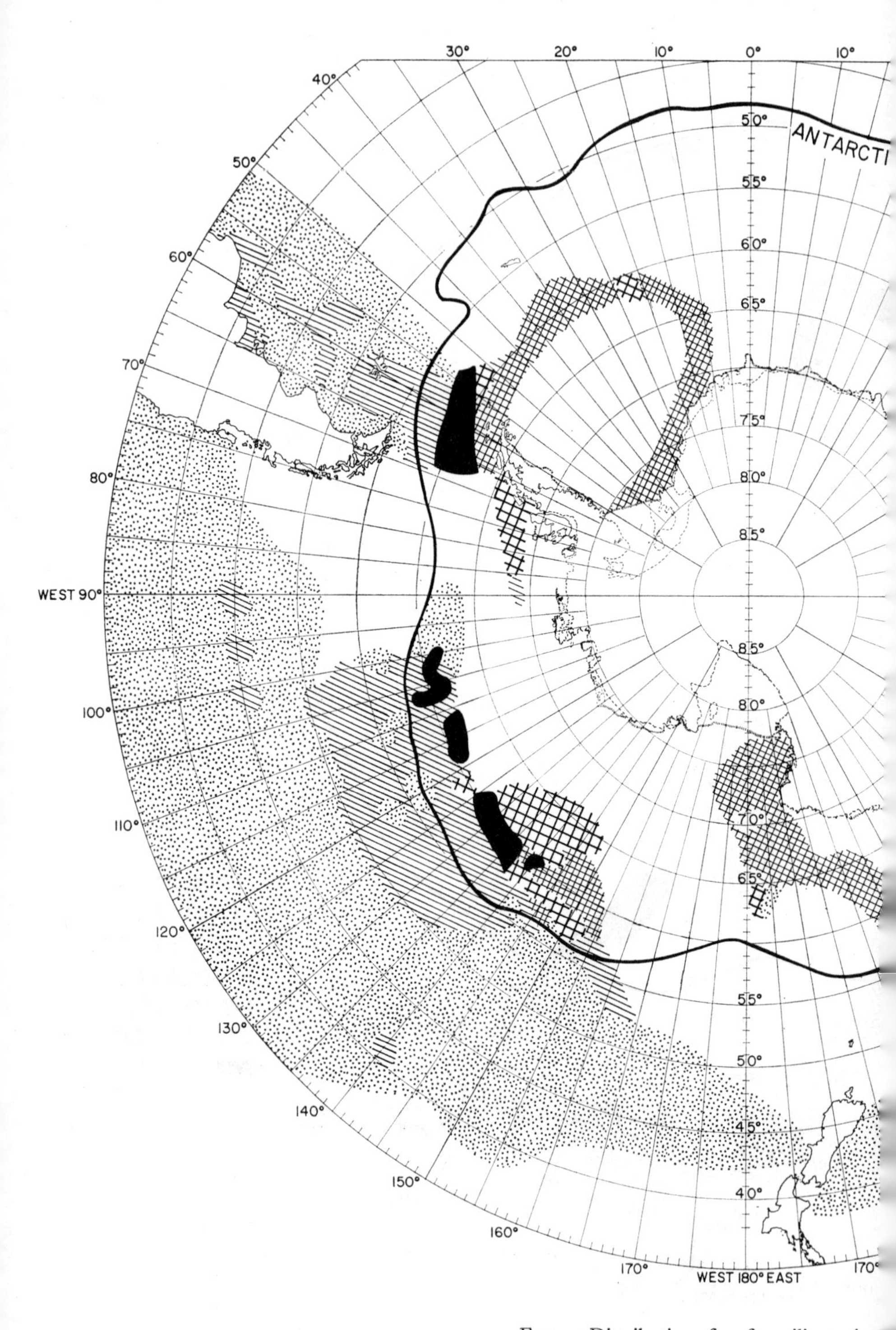

FIG. 10 Distribution of surface silicates in

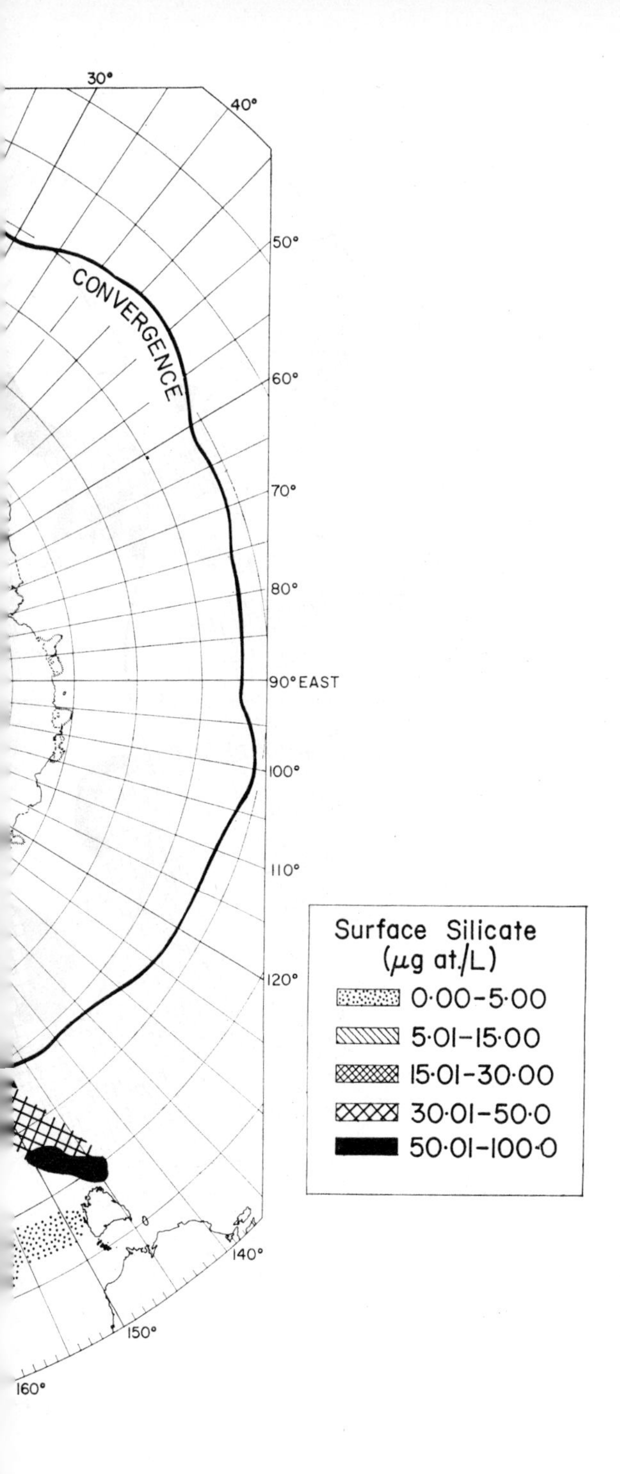
30°
40°
50°
60°
70°
80°
90° EAST
100°
110°
120°
140°
150°
160°
CONVERGENCE
Surface Silicate
(μg at./L)
0·00–5·00
5·01–15·00
15·01–30·00
30·01–50·0
50·01–100·0
70°
80°
WEST 90°
100°
110°

reas.

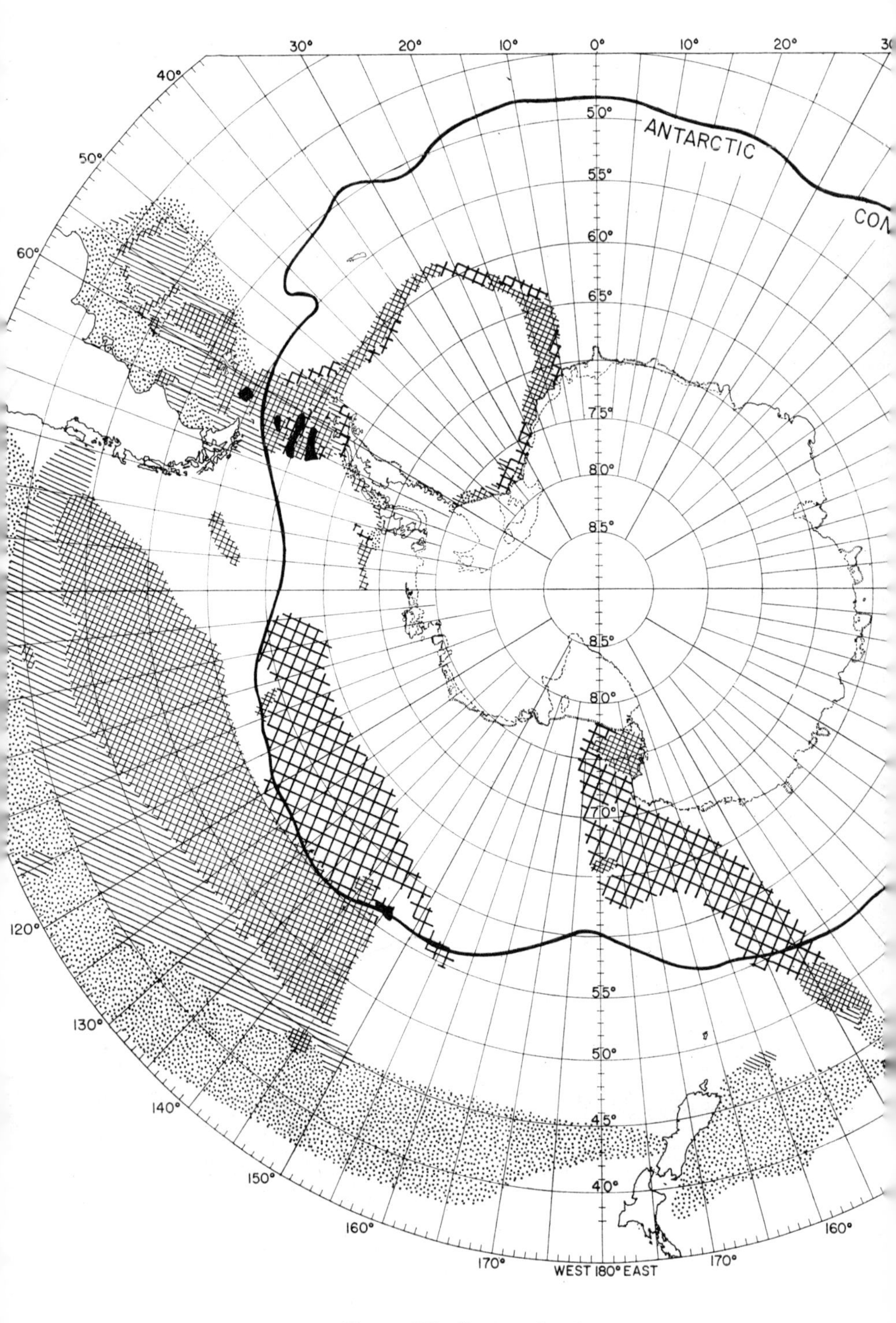

FIG. 11 Distribution of surface nitrates in the study areas.

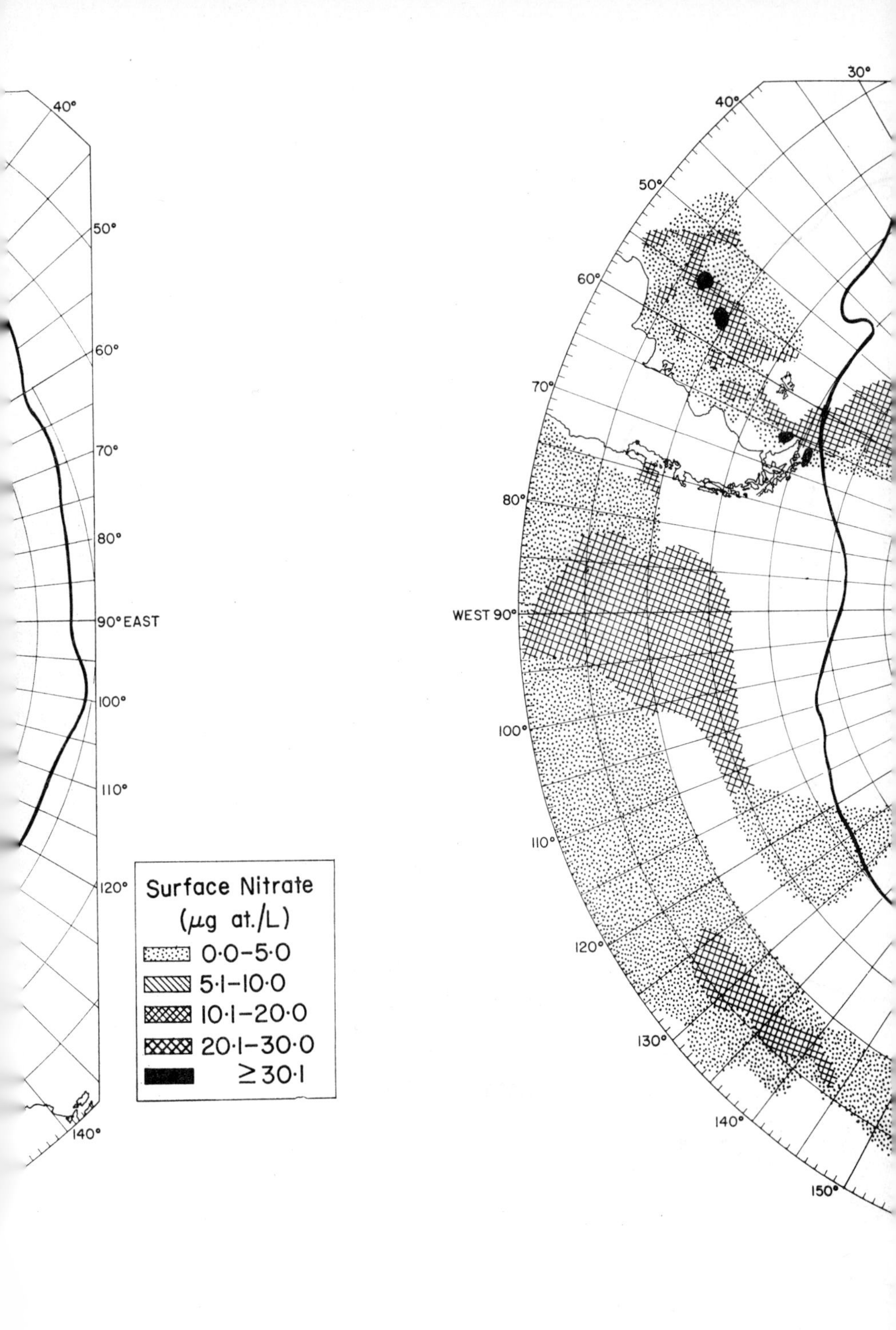

40°
50°
60°
70°
80°
90° EAST
100°
110°
120°
140°
30°
40°
50°
60°
70°
80°
WEST 90°
100°
110°
120°
130°
140°
150°
Surface Nitrate
(μg at./L)
0·0–5·0
5·1–10·0
10·1–20·0
20·1–30·0
≥30·1

FIG

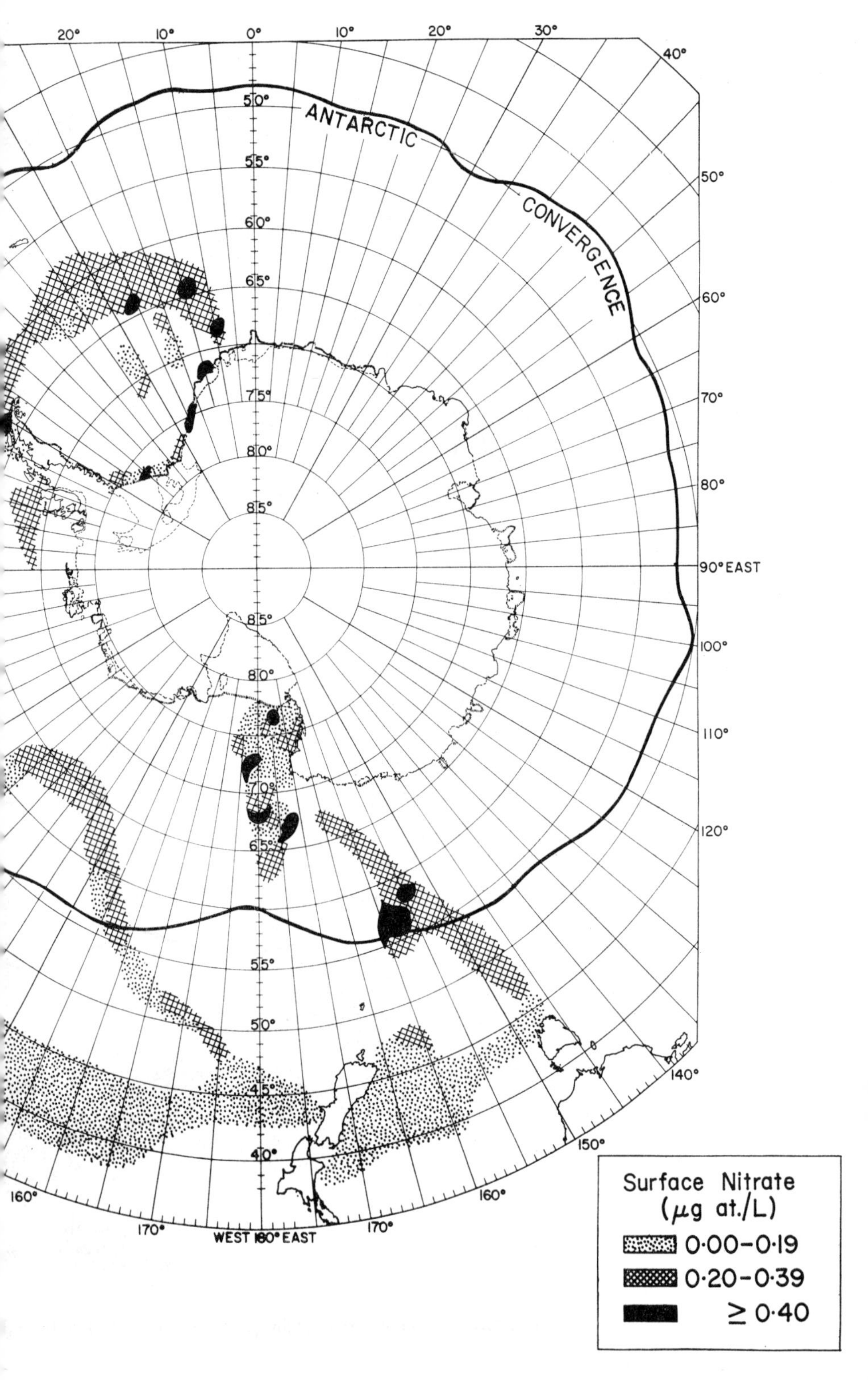

12 Distribution of surface nitrates in the study areas.

On the Productivity of the Southern Ocean
(Atlantic and Pacific Sectors)*

SAYED Z. EL-SAYED
Department of Oceanography, Texas A & M University, College Station, Texas, U.S.A.

I. Introduction

The legacy which J. D. Hooker has left us, concerning the extreme richness of the Antarctic waters in marine plant life, dates back to the time when the famed botanist-surgeon of the *Erebus* and *Terror* expedition (1839–43), under James Clark Ross, sent some of his plankton samples to the German diatomist, Ehrenberg, who published in 1844 the first paper on Antarctic diatoms. During the past one hundred years the numerous phytoplankton investigations carried out in the Antarctic have served to perpetuate the belief in the proverbial fertility of the Antarctic seas. However, it is only recently that the first measurements of primary organic production of the Antarctic waters, using the radioactive ^{14}C uptake method, were made. (See Klyashtorin, 1961; Ichimura and Fukushima, 1963; Saijo and Kawashima, 1964; El-Sayed *et al.*, 1964; El-Sayed and Mandelli, 1965; Mandelli and Burkholder, 1966; Volkovinsky, 1966; and El-Sayed, 1967, 1968*a*, *b*.)

In the present paper the standing crop and primary productivity of the phytoplankton in Antarctic and Subantarctic waters will be assessed, based on the author's investigations of these waters over the past six years. In these investigations studies were also made of the distribution of the nutrient salts and particulate and dissolved organic carbon, and of the species composition of phytoplankton. However, emphasis in this paper will centre mainly on the geographic and seasonal variations of the phytoplankton standing crop and primary production of the Antarctic and Subantarctic waters, in both the Atlantic and Pacific sectors. Due to their significance in explaining the distribution of the phytoplankton, a brief discussion of the distribution and abundance of the nutrient salts (phosphates, silicates, nitrates and nitrites) will be included in the present paper. For detailed information regarding

* This study was supported by grants from the Office of Antarctic Programs, National Science Foundation, G-207, G-915.

productivity parameters, distribution of nutrients salts, dissolved and particulate organic carbon, etc., reference should be made to El-Sayed (1968*a*, *b*).

The results of the investigations to be reported herein are based on the data collected during nine cruises made in the Atlantic sector of the Southern Ocean, between 1962 and 1965, aboard the Argentine research vessels *Capitan Canepa* and *Commandante Zapiola* and aboard the ice-breaker, *General San Martin*. Data obtained during nine cruises of the USNS *Eltanin* in the Pacific sector, between 1965 and 1967, are also included.

II. Methods

The photosynthetic activity of the phytoplankton was measured by the ^{14}C uptake method according to Steemann Nielsen (1952), with the modifications suggested by Strickland and Parsons (1960), and more recently by Steemann Nielsen (1964). Phytoplankton standing crop (in terms of chlorophyll *a*) was estimated by the method used by Richards and Thompson (1952), as modified by Creitz and Richards (1955). The concentration of chlorophyll *a* was estimated, using the revised equations given by Parsons and Strickland (1963).

Studies of nutrient salts included determination of the amounts of phosphates (following the method of Robinson and Thompson, 1948), nitrates (Mullin and Riley, 1955), nitrites (Bendschneider and Robinson, 1952), and silicates (Robinson and Thompson, 1948).

TABLE 1

The standing crop of phytoplankton, primary production, and nutrient salts in the Atlantic sector of the Antarctic and Subantarctic (from El-Sayed, 1968*b*)

	Min.	*Max.*	*Mean*	*Std. Dev.*	*No of Observ.*
Chl *a* (mg/m^3)	0·01	118·35	0·89	1·31	518
*Chl *a* (mg/m^2)	0·72	81·38	15·94	14·17	79
^{14}C (mgC/m^3 hr)	0·02	97·44	5·25	8·65	458
*^{14}C (mgC/m^2 hr)	3·43	337·49	50·70	17·49	87
PO_4 ($\mu g-at/L$)	0·01	2·90	1·21	0·53	442
†PO_4 (mg/m^2)	38·22	437·95	225·66	69·58	173
SiO_3 ($\mu g-at/L$)	0·1	100·0	29·1	21·5	385
†SiO_3 (g/m^2)	0·18	13·64	3·82	2·33	150
NO_3 ($\mu g-at/L$)	0·1	94·9	11·9	8·5	437
†NO_3 (g/m^2)	0·18	8·52	2·26	1·03	170
NO_2 ($\mu g-at/L$)	0·01	2·73	0·19	0·18	415
†NO_2 (mg/m^2)	1·50	71·75	22·80	10·35	170

* Integrated values in the euphotic zone.
† Integrated values based on the depth of approximately 150 m.

The pertinent data for chlorophyll *a*, ^{14}C uptake, and nutrient concentrations for the combined Atlantic and Pacific sectors are summarized in Tables 1 and 2.

TABLE 2

The standing crop of phytoplankton, primary production, nutrient salts, and particulate and dissolved organic carbon (POC and DOC) recorded during *Eltanin* Cruises 18–28 (less Cruise 22) in the Pacific Sector of the Antarctic and Subantarctic (from El-Sayed, 1968*b*)

	Min.	*Max.*	*Mean*	*Std. Dev.*	*No. of Observ.*
Chl *a* (mg/m^3)	0·01	5·80	0·26	0·34	723
*Chl *a* (mg/m^2)	0·23	41·32	12·62	6·32	217
^{14}C (mgC/m^3hr)	0·03	22·50	1·22	1·69	656
*^{14}C (mgC/m^2hr)	3·54	194·73	32·01	23·93	213
PO_3 ($\mu g-at/L$)	0·01	4·66	1·09	0·46	350
*PO_4 (mg/m^2)	0·84	457·00	42·98	37·01	146
Si ($\mu g-at/L$)	0·1	79·9	13·5	13·5	368
*Si (g/m^2)	0·01	5·41	0·57	0·59	154
NO_3 ($\mu g-at/L$)	0·1	30·2	12·9	5·5	313
*NO_3 (g/m^2)	0·01	2·93	0·63	0·41	161
NO_2 ($\mu g/-at/L$)	0·01	1·23	0·18	0·11	296
*NO_2 (mg/m^2)	0·6	33·8	10·7	6·7	146
POC (mgC/L)	0·003	0·520	0·058	0·051	149
*POC (gC/m^2)	2·46	18·84	5·52	2·27	153
DOC (mgC/L)	0·25	2·66	0·95	0·27	156
*DOC (gC/m^2)	14·1	243·1	58·3	23·4	157

* Integrated values in euphotic zone.

III. Results

A. DISTRIBUTION OF PHYTOPLANKTON STANDING CROP IN THE AREAS INVESTIGATED

The distribution of chlorophyll *a* in the surface-water samples (Fig. 1) shows discernible geographic variations in the areas investigated.

In the Atlantic sector chlorophyll *a* exhibits a high degree of variability related to the complexity of the different water masses in that region. In the northern and middle Drake Passage the pigment values were noticeably lower than those along much of the Argentine continental shelf. Low values of chlorophyll *a* in the Drake Passage coincided with the position of the Antarctic Convergence. High pigment concentrations were found in the southern Drake Passage, in the region north of South Shetland Islands, and between the South Orkney and South Sandwich Islands.

In the eastern and southern Weddell Sea the paucity of phytoplankton was notable, except in the region along the Edith Ronne and Filchner Ice Shelves, between 30° and 40°W. During the recent International Weddell Sea Oceanographic Expedition (January–March 1968) the author encountered, on February 10, 1968, off the Filchner Ice Shelf, a very extensive bloom of phytoplankton which covered an area of more than 6100 square miles (Fig. 2). Chlorophyll *a* concentrations during this bloom were extraordinarily high,

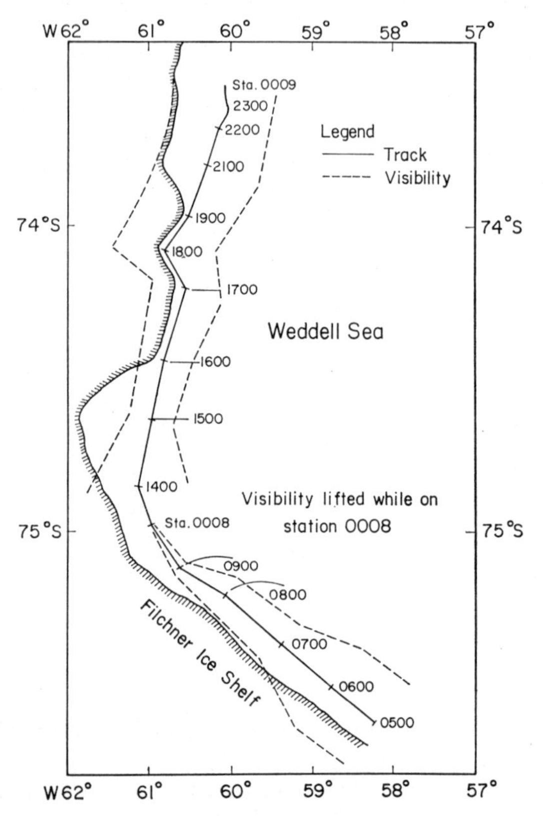

FIG. 2. Cruise track of the ice-breaker USCGC *Glacier* during the bloom of phytoplankton.

reaching 123 mg/m³ at station 0008. Although similarly high chlorophyll values have been encountered in polluted estuarine waters (Dr Charles Yentsch, personal communication), the existence of such high concentrations in marine habitats elsewhere has seldom been reported in the literature. Interestingly, the high productivity of the waters affected by the bloom was also reflected in high concentrations of nutrient salts (e.g. phosphates, 2·02 μg at./l, nitrates, 2·49 μg at./l, and silicates, 68 μg at./l), and in the teeming of the bloom region with Adelie penguins, crab-eater seals, and other marine vertebrate life. (See Siniff *et al.*, 1970: this symposium.)

The region to the west of the Antarctic Peninsula was also noted for its rich phytoplankton populations; surface chlorophyll *a* concentrations as high as 18 mg/m^3 were recorded by the author from the Gerlache Strait (El-Sayed, 1968*a*). High values (25 mg/m^3) were also reported by Burkholder and Mandelli (1965) from the same strait. In the Bellingshausen Sea, low values, similar to those of the northern Drake Passage, were found.

In the Pacific sector, except for isolated pockets ranging between 0·50 and 0·99 mg/m^3 chlorophyll *a*, surface phytoplankton standing crops were generally poor ($< 0{\cdot}50$ mg/m^3). On the other hand, the coastal regions off New Zealand, Tasmania, and the Ross Sea showed much higher chlorophyll *a* values than the oceanic areas. Off the coast of Chile, high phytoplankton concentrations were always found.

In terms of integrated pigment values for the euphotic zone (i.e. values integrated through a column of water extending from sea surface to the depth to which 1% of surface light intensity penetrates), substantially high values were found in the Scotia Sea, the south-western Weddell Sea, west of the Antarctic Peninsula, and off New Zealand, Tasmania, and the Ross Sea. Except for the area of low phytoplankton standing crop in the northern Drake Passage, the integrated chlorophyll *a* data in the areas investigated were moderately rich.

When all chlorophyll *a* observations in the Atlantic sector were compared with those made in the Pacific sector, it was found that average surface chlorophyll *a* in the former (1·20 mg/m^3) was about five times higher than in the latter (0·26 mg/m^3). However, in terms of integrated values, the Atlantic figures are not markedly higher than those for the Pacific (15·17 mg/m^2 and 12·62 mg/m^2, respectively). Caution should be exercised in interpreting these results, however. For instance, while a great many of the stations occupied in the Atlantic sector were located in the highly fertile coastal regions of the south-west Atlantic Ocean and west of the Antarctic Peninsula, most of the stations occupied in the Pacific sector were in oceanic regions which are noted for their low productivity.

B. Distribution of ^{14}C Uptake

The distribution of primary productivity in surface-water samples from both the Atlantic and Pacific sectors (Fig. 3) is more or less similar to that of phytoplankton standing crop. Generally high values were reported from the Argentine continental-shelf waters, as compared to the Drake Passage (El-Sayed, 1968*a*). Very high photosynthetic rates were recorded in the northern and south-western Weddell Sea. Exceptionally high primary productivity values were found in the Bransfield and Gerlache Straits (11·83 and 13·13 mgC/m³ hr, respectively). In the Bellingshausen Sea, however, primary production was low (1·46 mgC/m³ hr).

In the Pacific sector, essentially all the stations occupied gave low rates of photosynthesis (< 5·0 mgC/m³ hr); however, patches of relatively high photosynthetic rates were recorded between 170° and 180°W. Primary production in the euphotic zone in the study areas shows relatively low photosynthetic activity in the Drake Passage, in the eastern Weddell Sea, in the Bellingshausen Sea, and in the Pacific sector between 75° and 150°W—except for isolated pockets of moderately high photosynthetic activity. High carbon assimilation values were found south-east of Tierra del Fuego, in the vicinity of the South Orkney Islands and the south-western Weddell Sea, west of the Antarctic Peninsula, and off New Zealand, Tasmania, and the Ross Sea. As in the case of the phytoplankton standing crop, the primary productivity of surface-water samples in the Atlantic sector was about four times the Pacific value (4·87 mgC/m³ hr, compared to 1·22 mgC/m³ hr). In terms of integrated values, the Atlantic stations were not substantially more productive than the Pacific stations (42·82 and 32·01 mgC/m² hr, respectively).

C. Vertical Distribution of Standing Crop of Phytoplankton and ¹⁴C Uptake in the Atlantic and Pacific Sectors

The vertical distribution of chlorophyll *a* and ¹⁴C uptake in the euphotic

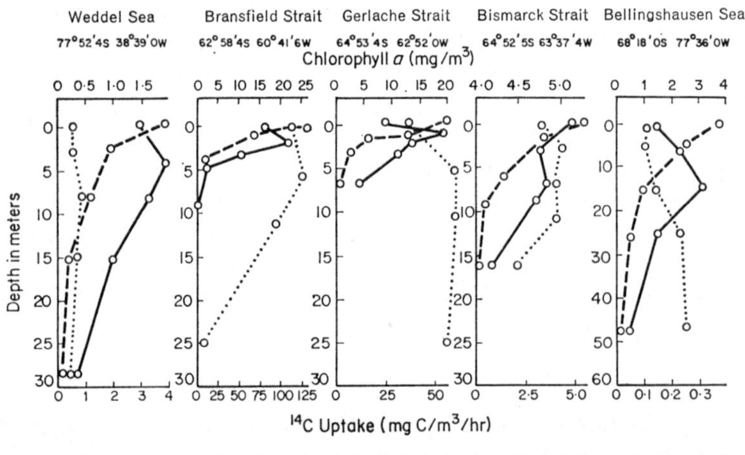

FIG. 4. Distribution of chlorophyll *a*, ¹⁴C uptake, and percent light penetration at different depths at selected stations in the Weddell Sea and the region west of the Antarctic Peninsula. o · · · · o Chl *a* (mg/m³); o——o ¹⁴C uptake (mgC/m³ hr); o— — —o % light.

zone at stations occupied in the south-west Atlantic Ocean and west of the Antarctic Peninsula were discussed by El-Sayed (1968*a*); a few stations representing the various areas studied are plotted in Fig. 4. This figure shows that chlorophyll *a* values, by and large, tended to be evenly distributed from the surface to the depth of the euphotic zone, with a tendency toward higher values at the subsurface levels than at the surface. Carbon assimilation, on the other hand, showed higher values at or near the surface; these decreased gradually to minimum values at depths ranging from 7 m in the Gerlache Strait to 48 m in the Bellingshausen Sea. The same figure shows that the more shallow the euphotic zone, the greater the productivity. Thus at the Bransfield and Gerlache Straits stations, which exhibited the highest primary production encountered (5·26 gC/m^2 day and 3·8 gC/m^2 day), the depths of the euphotic zone at these stations were 8 and 7 m, respectively. On the other hand, at the Bellingshausen Sea station, where the euphotic depth is 47 m, the amount of organic production was much lower (0·15 gC/m^2 day) than that found in the Bransfield and Gerlache Straits.

The vertical distribution of the phytoplankton standing crop and primary production in the euphotic zones of the Pacific sector for the combined stations of each cruise made by the USNS *Eltanin* are plotted in Fig. 5. This figure shows marked variations in the vertical distribution of chlorophyll *a*, ^{14}C uptake, and light penetration between the various cruises. Except for Cruises 27 and 28, where the chlorophyll values tended to increase with depth, the vertical distribution of the phytoplankton standing crop showed, in general, a more or less homogeneous distribution in the euphotic zone. The distribution of the pigment concentration below the euphotic zone was examined from the data collected during Cruise 27; these are plotted in Fig. 6. This figure shows that chlorophyll concentration at several stations is higher at depths below the euphotic zone than above it. This corroborates Hasle's findings (in press), in which substantial parts of the phytoplankton populations in the samples examined from the South Pacific were found below the euphotic zone.

Carbon assimilation at the stations occupied in the Pacific sector (Fig. 5) showed high values at the surface, which decreased gradually to minimal values at depths ranging from 42 m (Cruise 27) to 94 m (Cruise 23). During Cruise 26, however, the highest photosynthetic activity was recorded at a depth of 6 m rather than at the surface. This subsurface increase could perhaps be attributed, in part, to the photo-inhibition of surface phytoplankton caused by the early austral summer in the Tasman Sea, where this cruise was made.

The depths of the euphotic zone in the Pacific sector also showed considerable variations between cruises; the average depths ranged from 50 m for Cruise 27 (between Tasmania and the Ross Sea) to 105 m for Cruise 23 (west of the Drake Passage between 55° and 65°S). It is noteworthy that the average depth of the euphotic zones for all the combined cruises in the Pacific sector (based on 213 observations) was about 80 m. If the transparency

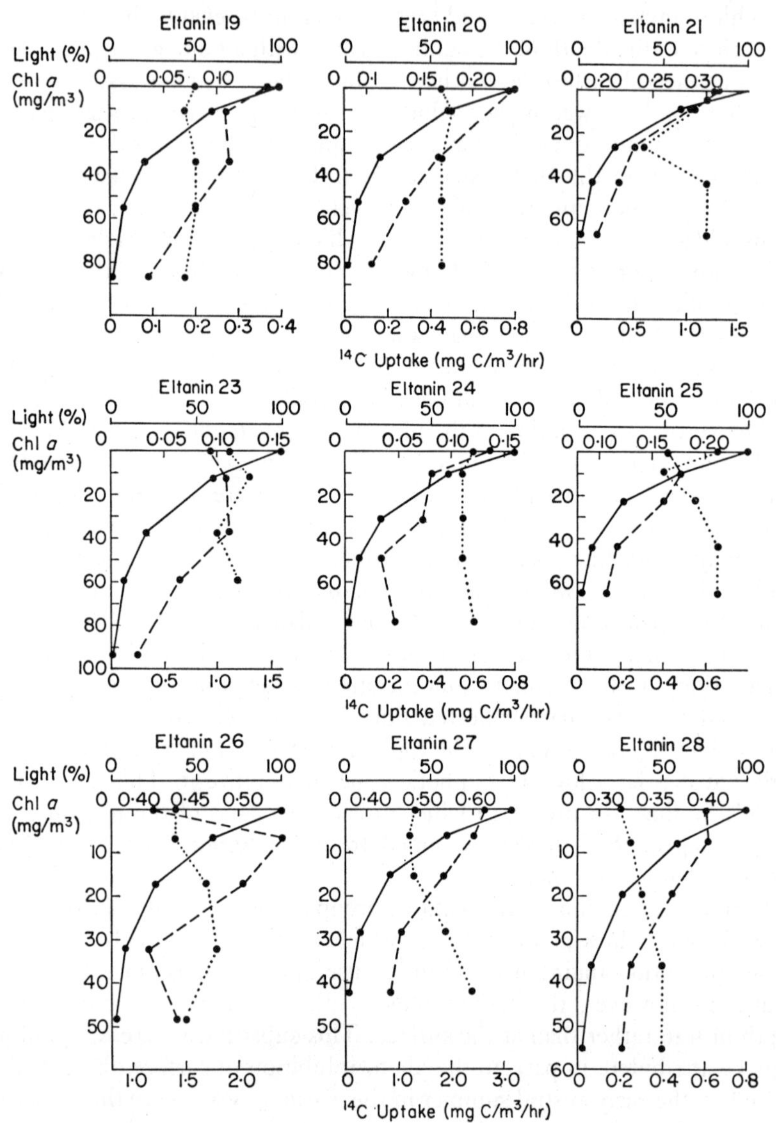

FIG. 5. Vertical distribution of average chlorophyll *a* and ^{14}C uptake and percent light penetration at different depths in the euphotic zones during *Eltanin* Cruises 19–28 (less Cruise 22) in the Pacific sector. •——• % Light; • - - - - • ^{14}C uptake (mg C/m³ hr); • · · · · · · · • Chl *a* (mg/m³).

of sea water can be used as an indication of the phytoplankton abundance in the water column, as demonstrated by Atkins *et al.* (1954), Hart (1962), and Hasle (in the press), there is little doubt that the clear waters of the Pacific sector of the Antarctic do indeed reflect the paucity of their phytoplankton populations.

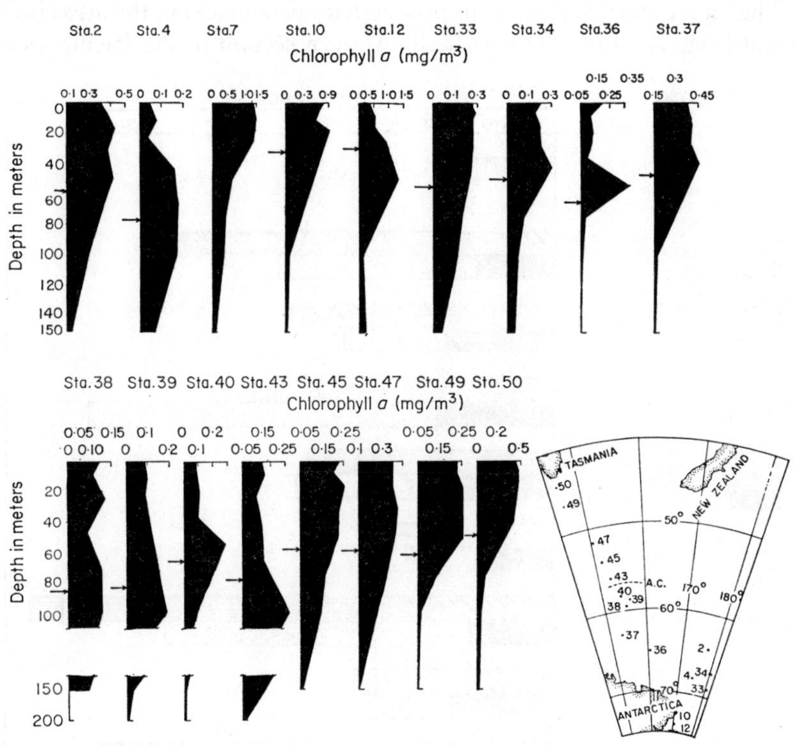

FIG. 6. Vertical distribution of chlorophyll *a* at several stations occupied during *Eltanin* Cruise 27. Position of arrows indicates depth of euphotic zone.

D. Latitudinal and Longitudinal Variations in Phytoplankton Standing Crop and Carbon Assimilation in the Areas Investigated

Since the areas covered by this investigation encompass large geographical regions which are bounded to the north by 40°S latitude, to the south by the coast of Antarctica, to the east by 20°W, and the west by 140°E, it is instructive to study the latitudinal and longitudinal variations in the productivity parameters in these vast regions. For this reason, the data collected in surface-water samples, as well as in the euphotic zones, in both the Atlantic and Pacific sectors, were averaged by 5° latitude and are plotted in Fig. 7. This figure shows the regions between 70° and 75°S latitude to be among the richest areas investigated. In terms of carbon fixation, the areas between 35° and 40°S, and between 60° and 65°S, displayed higher values than any other area studied, except for the phenomenal richness of the region between 70° and 75°S.

The longitudinal variations in productivity parameters in the areas investigated (Fig. 7) clearly show that the western section of the Pacific sector,

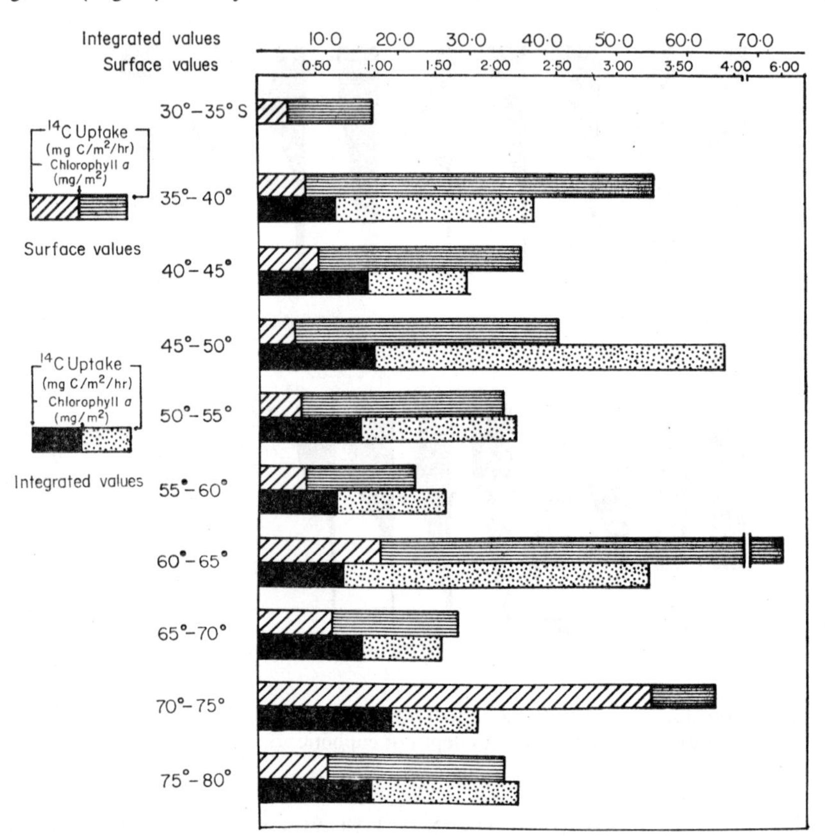

FIG. 7. Latitudinal variations of surface and integrated chlorophyll *a* and ^{14}C uptake values in the areas investigated in the Atlantic and Pacific sectors.

between 140°E and 170°W (less 150°–160°E), is conspicuously richer in chlorophyll *a* than is the central south Pacific. These high chlorophyll *a* concentrations are due primarily to the proximity of the water samples collected to the coastal regions of New Zealand, Australia, and Tasmania [demonstrating the "land-mass effect" described by Doty and Oguri (1956)]. The low chlorophyll values encountered between 150° and 160°E (i.e. in the

Tasman Sea) are of the same order of magnitude as those found in the oceanic regions of the Pacific sector. Highest chlorophyll *a* concentrations in the areas investigated were found between 60° and 70°W longitude. The proximity of the observations made in the Atlantic sector to land masses reflects the generally higher phytoplankton standing crops in that sector as compared to the Pacific regions studied.

In terms of ^{14}C uptake values, longitudinal variations of surface and integrated values show a more or less similar trend to that of the chlorophyll *a* distribution (Fig. 8).

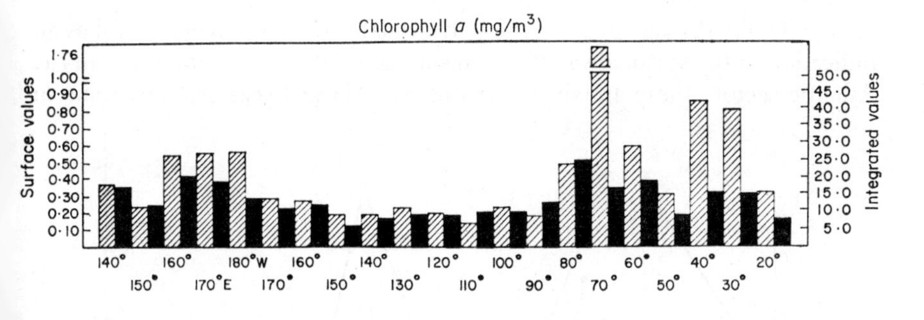

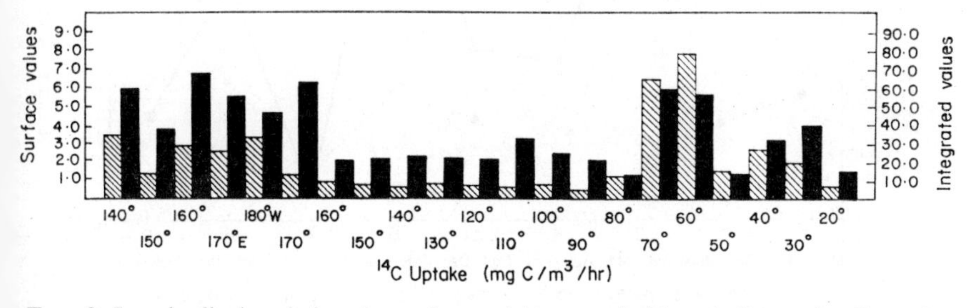

FIG. 8. Longitudinal variations in surface and integrated chlorophyll *a* and ^{14}C uptake values in the areas investigated in the Atlantic and Pacific sectors. ▧ Surface values; ■ integrated values.

E. DISTRIBUTION OF INORGANIC NUTRIENT SALTS

The distribution of phosphate, silicate, nitrate, and nitrite concentrations are shown in Figs. 9, 10, 11, and 12. Despite marked variations in the distribution of the inorganic salts, their pattern of distribution is more or less similar in both the Atlantic and Pacific sectors. By and large, low concentrations of these nutrients are found along the Argentine coast, in the northern Drake Passage, in the Bellingshausen Sea, in the Pacific waters north of the Antarctic Convergence, and in the Tasman Sea. Moderately high values are found in the southern Drake Passage, west of the Antarctic Peninsula, and south of Tasmania. Very high values of nutrient concentrations are located in the Bransfield Strait, the Weddell Sea, and to the north of the Ross Sea.

When comparing the nutrient concentrations in both sectors of the Antarctic, it was found that the distribution of surface phosphates, nitrate, and nitrite showed, in general, similar values. Silicate concentration, on the other hand, was more than doubled in the Atlantic stations as compared to the Pacific ones.

F. Seasonal Variations in the Distribution of Chlorophyll *a* and ^{14}C Uptake

The Drake Passage data are the only available data which are useful as an indication of the seasonal variations in surface productivity parameters in the Atlantic sector; these are shown in Fig. 13. Marked seasonal variations in

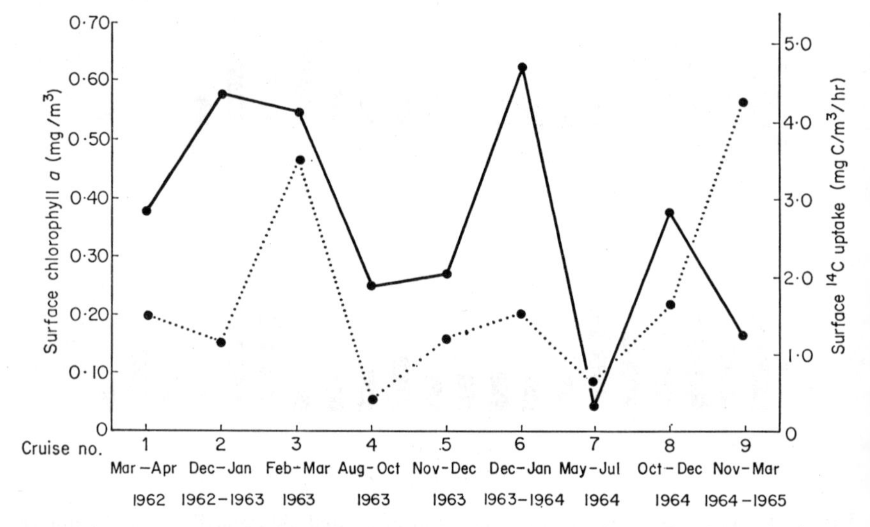

FIG. 13. Seasonal variations in the distribution of chlorophyll *a* and ^{14}C uptake in the Drake Passage. ●——● Surface chl *a* (mg/m³); ●·····● Surface ^{14}C uptake (mgC/m³ hr).

chlorophyll *a* levels are discernible in this figure; higher values were recorded during the summer cruises than during the late fall and early spring. Lowest chlorophyll *a* values (0·04 mg/m³) were obtained during midwinter (Cruise 7). Photosynthetic activity of phytoplankton was as expected, relatively high during the austral spring and summer cruises, as compared to the fall and early winter.

The seasonal variations of surface and integrated pigment and primary productivity data collected in the Pacific sector during the nine cruises of the *Eltanin* (Cruise 19 through Cruise 28, less Cruise 22) are plotted in Fig. 14.

Here again, as one would predict, substantial increases in the phytoplankton standing crop and photosynthetic activity of the primary producers were noted during the austral spring and summer cruises, while considerably lower productivity values were found during the fall and winter cruises.

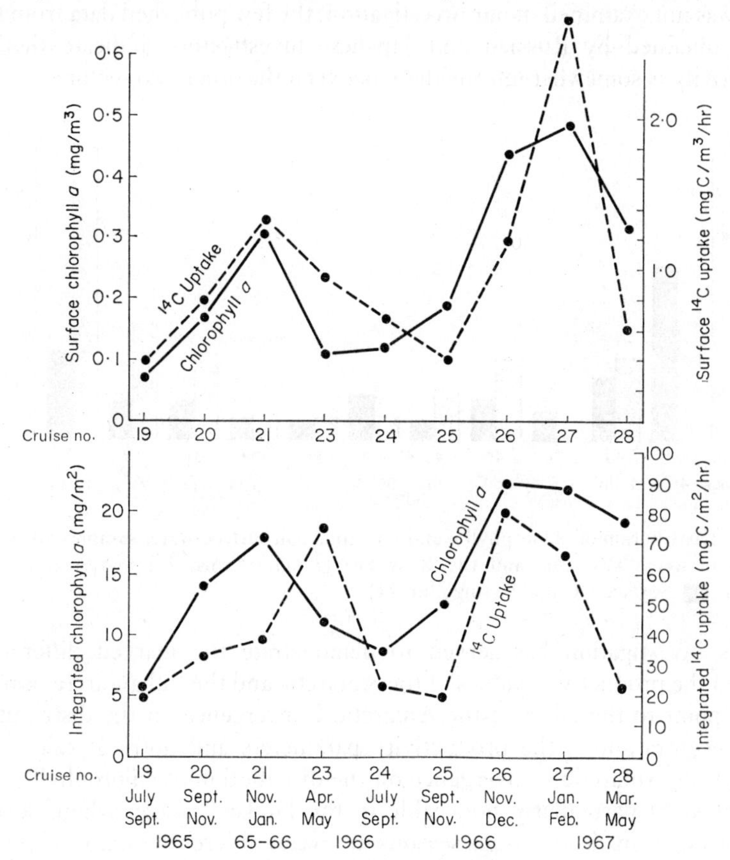

FIG. 14. Seasonal variations in the distribution of chlorophyll a and ^{14}C uptake in the Pacific sector.

Hart (1942) observed similar seasonal variations in phytoplankton population which he related to seasonal changes in the physical and chemical conditions in the Southern Ocean.

IV. Discussion

In the preceding pages an attempt has been made to summarize the existing data on the geographic distribution and seasonal variations of the phytoplankton standing crop and primary productivity in the Atlantic and the Pacific sectors, based on the author's investigations in these regions. Despite the vastness of the areas studied, it is safe to say that we now have a fair knowledge of the basic productivity of both sectors. Although the Indian sector was not examined in our investigation, the few published data from this sector, obtained by Russian and Japanese investigators, indicate that its productivity is somewhat intermediate between the other two sectors.

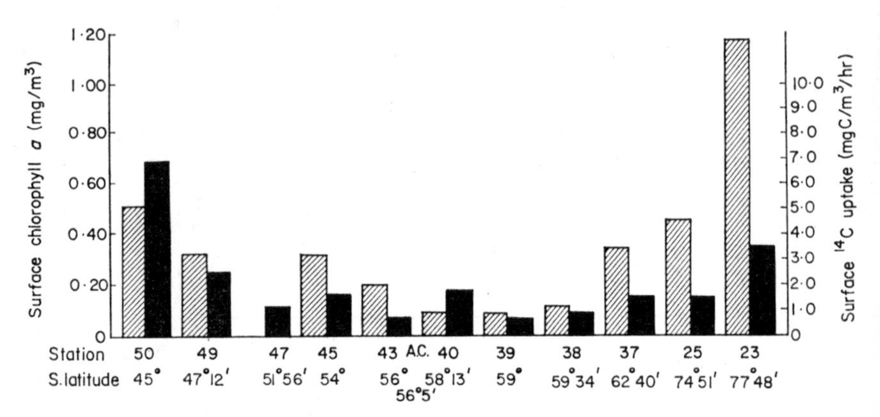

FIG. 15. Distribution of chlorophyll *a* and ^{14}C uptake in surface-water samples taken in a transect between Tasmania and the Ross Sea (*Eltanin* Cruise 27). ▨ Surface chl *a* (mg/m^3); ■ Surface ^{14}C uptake (mgC/m^3 hr).

This investigation has served to demonstrate the marked differences between the productivity values of the Antarctic and the Subantarctic waters, and to point to the effect of the Antarctic Convergence on the distribution and concentration of the productivity parameters and nutrient salts. The effect of the Antarctic Convergence on the distribution of chlorophyll *a* and ^{14}C uptake is particularly noticeable in the Drake Passage, where several crossings were made at various seasons in several different years. Low phytoplankton standing crop and photosynthetic activity at the Antarctic Convergence have been reported by El-Sayed *et al.* (1964), and El-Sayed and Mandelli (1965). Although the data collected during a recent cruise between Tasmania and the Ross Sea (*Eltanin* Cruise 27) did not demonstrate this as clearly as did data obtained in the Drake Passage, it is evident in Fig. 14 that the phytoplankton standing crop and primary productivity are much higher south of the Convergence than north of it.

Corroborative evidence of the effect of the Convergence on the distribution and abundance of the phytoplankton was also manifested in the quantitative analysis of the phytoplankton samples collected during *Eltanin* Cruise 27 (Marumo, 1968; unpublished). It is noteworthy that in his study of the species composition of the diatom samples collected on this cruise, Marumo was able to demonstrate the existence of a special flora which is typically associated with the Antarctic Convergence. This flora, besides its abundance in diatom species, includes species which are peculiar to this region such as *Corethron criophilum "inerme"*, *Coscinodiscus excentricus*, *Rhizosolenia rhombus*, and *R. simplex*. This seems to corroborate Hendey's (1937) suggestion that there might be an "Antarctic Convergence Flora" which is very abundant in species and genera. Cassie (1963), in her study of the phytoplankton between New Zealand and the Ross Sea, also mentioned such a flora, with its relatively large number of species. Beklemishev (1958) also pointed to the existence of a mixture of floras from Subantarctic and Antarctic waters at the Convergence in the Indian sector of the Antarctic.

The effect of the Antarctic Convergence on the distribution of the nutrient elements is also quite noticeable in the maps provided in Figs. 9, 10, 11, and 12. In general, the nutrient distribution shows higher concentrations south of the Convergence than north of it. However, it is interesting to note that although the concentration of the nutrient elements north of the Convergence is lower than in the Antarctic waters proper, even the lowest levels of concentrations are higher, in general, than are the winter maxima of temperate regions.

Our studies have also served to underscore the conspicuous regional differences in the productivity parameters of the Southern Ocean, and the striking differences between the productivity of the oceanic and neritic regions. For instance, an earlier publication (El-Sayed, 1968*a*), based on the data collected from the Atlantic sector, showed that in terms of chlorophyll *a* concentration and ^{14}C uptake, values obtained from Antarctic surface neritic waters are five times as high as those obtained in the oceanic waters. Similar regional differences were also noted for the Subantarctic waters. Subsequent findings, based on data from the Pacific sector, serve to uphold the validity of these conclusions and to substantiate our belief that the proverbial richness of the Antarctic waters is factual only with regard to coastal and inshore regions, and not with regard to the oceanic regions. These conclusions are in substantial agreement with those of Hart (1942) based on the extensive *Discovery* data on quantities of phytoplankton pigments in the Atlantic, Pacific, and Indian sectors of the Southern Ocean.

References

Atkins, W. R. G., Jenkins, P. G. and Warren, F. J. (1954). The suspended matter in sea water and its seasonal changes as affecting the visual range of the Secchi disc. *J. mar. biol. Ass. U.K.*, 33, 497–509.

Beklemishev, K. W. (1958). Svyza' raspredelenga fitoplanktona Indookeanskogo sektora Antartiki s gidrolo gicheskimi usloviyami. *Dokl. Akad. Nauk SSR*, **119**, 694–7.

Bendschneider, K. and Robinson, R. J. (1952). A new spectophotometric method for the determination of nitrite in sea water. *J. mar. Res.* **11**, 87–96.

Burkholder, P. R. and Mandelli, E. F. (1965). Carbon assimilation of marine phytoplankton in Antarctica. *Proc. natn. Acad. Sci. U.S.* **54**, 437–44.

Cassie, V. (1963). Distribution of surface phytoplankton between New Zealand and Antarctica, December 1957. *T.A.E. Sci. Rep.* **7**, 1–11.

Creitz, G. I. and Richards, F. A. (1955). The estimation and characterization of plankton populations by pigment analysis, III, A note on the use of Millipore membrane filters in the estimation of plankton pigments. *J. mar. Res.* **14**, 211–16.

Doty, M. S. and Oguri, M. (1956). The island mass effect. *J. Cons. Int. Explor. Mar.* **22**, 33–37.

El-Sayed, S. Z. (1967). Biological productivity investigations of the Pacific Sector of Antarctica. *Antarctic J. U.S.* **11**, 200–1.

El-Sayed, S. Z. (1968*a*). On the productivity of the Southwest Atlantic Ocean and the waters west of the Antarctic Peninsula. *Biology of the Antarctic Seas*, *III*, *Ant. Res. Ser.* **11**, 15–47.

El-Sayed, S. Z. (1968*b*). Primary productivity and benthic marine algae of the Antarctic and Subantarctic. Antarctic Map Folio Series, Folio 10. American Geographical Society.

El-Sayed, S. Z. and Mandelli, E. F. (1965). Primary production and standing crop of phytoplankton in the Weddell Sea and Drake Passage. *Biology of the Antarctic Seas*, *II*, *Ant. Res. Ser.* **5**, 87–106.

El-Sayed, S. Z., Mandelli, E. F. and Sugimura, Y. (1964). Primary organic production in the Drake Passage and Bransfield Strait. *Ant. Res. Ser.* **1**, 1–11.

Hart, T. J. (1942). Phytoplankton periodicity in Antarctic surface waters. *"Discovery" Rep.* **21**, 261–356.

Hart, T. J. (1962). Notes on the relation between transparency and plankton content of the surface waters of the Southern Ocean. *Deep Sea Res.* **9**, 109–14.

Hasle, G. R. (in the press). An analysis of the phytoplankton of the Pacific Southern Ocean: abundance, composition and distribution during the "Brategg" Expedition. Hvalrad. Skr.

Hendey, N. I (1937). The plankton diatoms of the Southern Seas. *"Discovery" Rep.* **16** 151–364.

Ichimura, S. and Fukushima, H. (1963). On the chlorophyll content in the surface water of the Indian and the Antarctic Oceans. *Bot. Mag.*, *Tokyo* **76**, 395–9.

Klyashtorin, L. B. (1961). Primary production in the Atlantic and Southern Oceans according to the data obtained during the fifth Antarctic voyage of the diesel-electric *Ob. Dokl. Akad. Nauk SSSR* **141**, 1204–7,

Mandelli, E. F. and Burkholder, P. R. (1966). Primary productivity in the Gerlache and Bransfield Straits of Antarctica. *J. mar. Res.* **24**, 15–27.

Marumo, R. (1968). The study of phytoplankton in the section along 43° between Australia and South America. *Texas A & M Research Foundation*, *Technical Report.* (Unpublished.)

Mullin, J. B. and Riley, J. P. (1955). The spectrophotometric determination of nitrite in natural waters. *Anal. Chem. Acta.* 12, 464–80.

Parsons, T. R. and Strickland, J. D. H. (1963). Discussion of spectrophotometric determination of marine-plant pigments, with revised equation for ascertaining chlorophylls and carotenoids. *J. mar. Res.* 21, 155–63.

Richards, F. A. and Thompson, T. G. (1952). The estimation and characterization of plankton populations by pigment analysis, II, A spectrophotometric method for the estimation of plankton pigments. *J. mar. Res.* 11, 156–72.

Robinson, R. J. and Thompson, T. G. (1948). The determination of phosphates in sea water. *J. mar. Res.* 7, 33–41. The determination of silicate in sea water. *J. mar Res.* 7, 49–55.

Saijo, Y. and Kawashima, T. (1964). Primary production in the Antarctic Ocean. *J. oceanogr. Socl Japan* 19, 190–6.

Siniff, D. B., Cline, D. R. and Erickson, A. W. (1970). Population densities of seals in the Weddell Sea, Antarctica in 1968. (This volume.)

Steemann Nielsen, E. (1952). The use of radioactive carbon (C^{14}) for measuring organic production in the sea. *J. Cons. Int. Explor. Mer.* 18, 117–40.

Steemann Nielsen, E. (1964). Recent advances in measuring and understanding marine primary production. *J. Ecol. Jubilee Suppl.* 52, 119–30.

Strickland, J. D. H. and Parsons, T. R. (1960). A manual of sea water analysis. *Bull. Fish. Res. Bd. Can.* 125.

Volkovinsky, V. V. (1966). Studies of primary production in the waters of the South Atlantic Ocean, Second International Oceanographic Congress, Moscow, 30 May–9 June 1966, *Abstracts of Papers*, Moscow: Nauka Publishing House, pp. 386–7.

Phytoplankton of the Southern Ocean

V. V. ZERNOVA
Institute of Oceanology, Academy of Sciences, Moscow, U.S.S.R.

I. Introduction

This report results from the examination of phytoplankton samples which were obtained during the first three cruises of RS *Ob* in the Indian and Pacific sectors of the Antarctic Ocean during the southern summer and autumn of 1956–58 (Fig. 1).

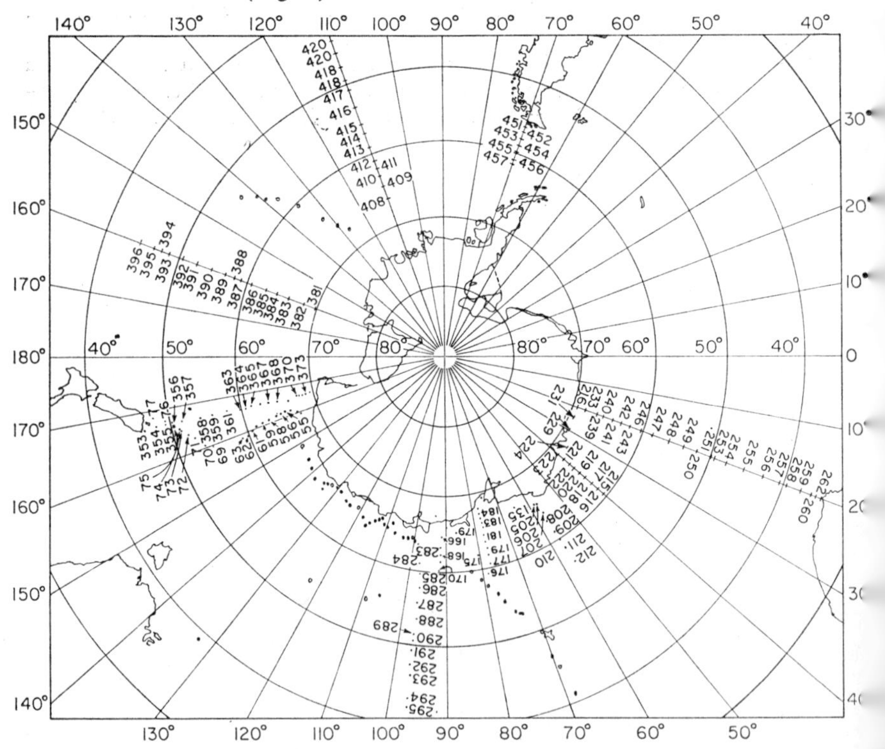

FIG. 1. Positions of the observations obtained in the I–III commissions of RS *Ob*. From the numbered positions sediment samples were studied; from the positions without numbers only net samples were studied.

The samples were collected using Nansen bottles from depths of 0, 10, 25, 50, 75, and 100 m, and also by closing Juday nets with a mouth aperture 38 cm in diameter, and the silk cone made of gauze with 38 meshes/cm from depths of 0–10, 10–25, 25–50, 50–100, and 100–200 m. Over 1000 bottle samples from 160 stations were studied.

Quantitative assessments of the phytoplankton are possible from the Nansen bottle samples, whereas the net hauls generally permit only qualitative descriptions of the flora, except along one section at 77°E on the second cruise of the *Ob*, where quantitative data were also collected.

The bottle samples included abundant small and medium-sized cells, which were not adequately collected by the Juday net. The net hauls, however, contained many robust species, such as *Coscinodiscus bouvet*, *Rhizosolenia curvata*, and *Ceratium pentagonum*. Taken together, net and bottle samples give a more or less complete picture of the Antarctic phytoplankton.

II. Abundance, Composition and Seasonal Variation

Diatoms constituted over 99% of the total number of cells in the samples. Among them 80 species of Bacillariphyta were identified. The genus *Chaetoceros* was represented by 17 species, and *Rhizosolenia* by 12 species. The Pyrrophyta were represented by 17 species, the Chrysophyta by 2 species, and the Xanthophyta by one only. These figures may be compared with those in earlier reports in which the quantity of diatom species varies from 80–90 (Hustedt, 1958; Kozlova, 1964) to 200 (Van Heurck, 1909; Karsten, 1905). Such variations in the data are due not only to differences in the time and place of the investigations but also to the use of different methods for collecting and studying the material.

It is known that the great abundance of phytoplankton in the South Ocean is connected with the exceptional richness of the diatom flora. Phytoplankton standing crops in the Antarctic vary from 10^4 cells/l in the 0–100 m layer generally to over 10^5 cells/l in areas of "blooming". The most numerous species in our samples (more than 10^5 cells/l) were *Chaetoceros neglectus*, *Ch. dichaeta*, *Ch. atlanticus*, *Corethron criophilum*, *Nitzshia sp.*, and *Fragilariopsis sp. Chaetoceros atlanticus*, *Corethron criophilum* and *Rhizosolenia alata* were generally less abundant, with populations of 10^5–10^4 cells/l.

In our material, which was obtained in January–April, "summer" and "autumn" species predominate, whereas "spring" species were numerous only in January. The seasonal characteristics of the species proposed by Hart (1942) have been adopted by us. The earliest samples which we received from the second commission of RS *Ob* were collected in Indian Ocean on 15–19 and 23–28 January 1957 from sections along 91°E and 77°E between 60°S and the coast of Antarctica. On the crossing along 91°E a maximum of more than

10^5 cells/l was found in the 0–25 m layer near to the zone of Antarctic Divergence (65°S, station 166, Fig. 2). Northwards, the total quantity of diatoms was less than 10^5 cells/l, varying between 10^4 and 10^5 cells/l in the 10–100m layer, while to the south a comparable number of cells was found in the 0–50 m layer. In the south *Amphiprora Kjellmanii*, *Chaetoceros neglectus*, *Biddulphia weissflogii*, and *Rhizosolenia hebetata f. semispina* were predominant. Some of these species are neritic and ice-edge forms, which are relatively important from the beginning to the peak of the main seasonal increase (Hart, 1942). They can therefore be considered as spring forms. Passing northward along this section, the spring forms found in the south were replaced by summer forms farther to the north.

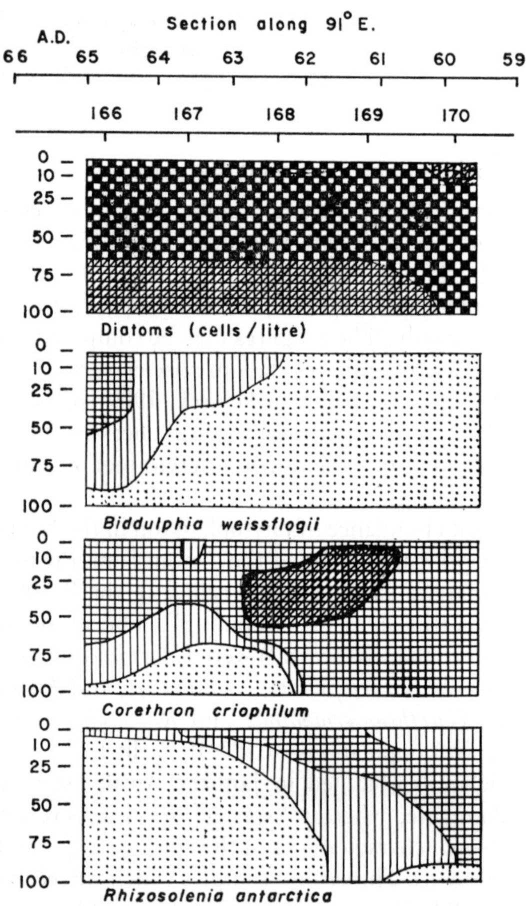

FIG. 2. Phytoplankton abundance (cells/l):

1; 1–100; 100–1000; 1000–10000; 10000–100000; <100000

The distribution of phytoplankton along the section 77°E resembles that along 91°E (Fig. 3). The main population peak was found near the Antarctic coast, to the south of the Antarctic Divergence. The species composition was already somewhat different. For instance, *Nitzschia closterium* was the most abundant species, in the neritic zone. The number of *Biddulphia weissflogii* was reduced and it was encountered only south of the Divergence, while *Chaetoceros atlanticus* was present only to the north. In the central area (stations 181–183) maxima of some spring and summer species, notably *Chaetoceros heglectus*, *Ch. dichaeta*, *Rhizosolenia hebetata* f. *semispina*, *Rh. antarctica*, and small forms of *Dactyliosolen antarctica*, were found.

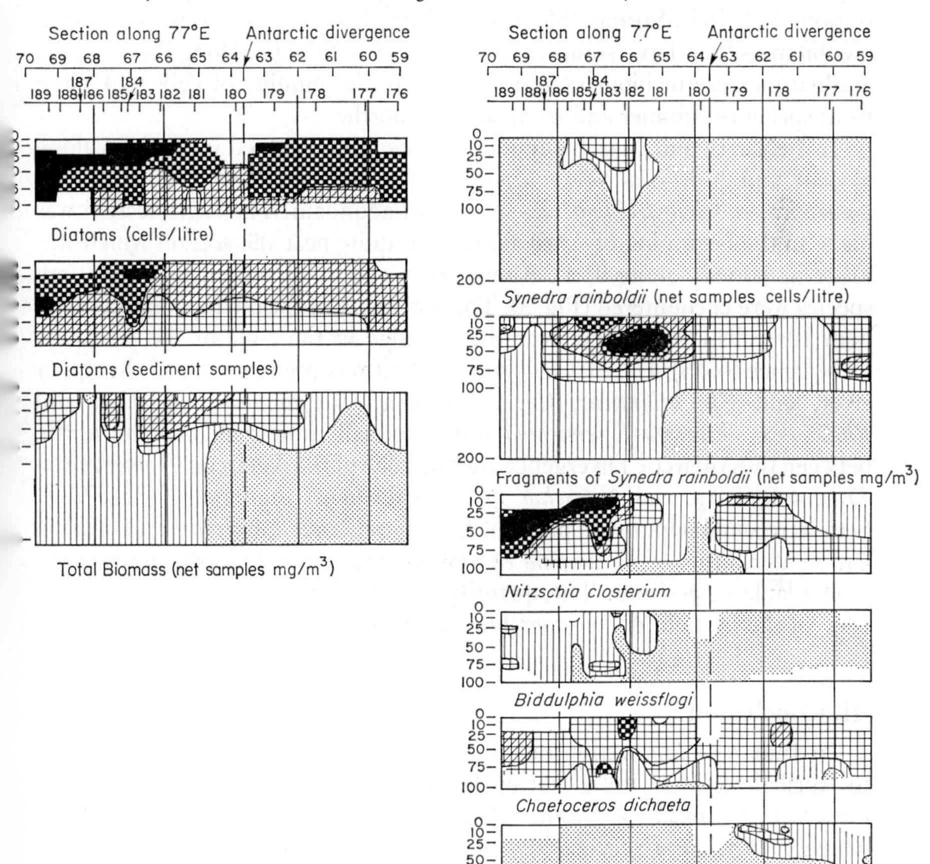

FIG. 3. Biomass mg/m³ or cells/litre: < 1; 1–10; 10–100; 100–500; 500–1000; > 1000. For Key to cells per litre, see Fig. 2.

Along this section, as mentioned previously, quantitative net collections of phytoplankton were also made. In the samples broken pieces of *Synedra reinboldii* were in great abundance. In bottle samples only rare fragments of this large form were obtained (Fig. 2). The maximum of *S. reinboldii* was found to the south of the Antarctic Divergence (65°–67°S), where in the 0–25 m layer it totalled more than 100 cells/l, while in the deeper layers and toward the boundary of this area only broken pieces were found. The biomass of the fragments (2884 mg/m^3 at 25 m depth at station 181) was twice as great as the biomass of the sediment phytoplankton even in the area of peak population along this section (1017–1380 mg/m^3 respectively, at 10 m and stations 182, 183). Spring "blooms" of *Nitzschia closterium* contribute much less biomass than large summer species like *S. reinboldii*. Along the section a gradual increase in biomass and decrease in the number of cells took place from spring to summer and from south to north.

In February and March summer species predominated in sections along 57°, 40° and 20°E. *Chaetoceros atlanticus*, *Corethron criophilum*, *Fragilariopsis antarctica*, and *Nitzschia* species were most abundant. The latest section was made in the beginning of April along 97°E quite near the section which was made in January along 91°E. Along this section only summer and autumn species were encountered (Fig. 3). The maximum of the phytoplankton (more than 10^5 cells/l was found near the ice edge in the zone of the Antarctic Divergence (63°S). Here *Chaetoceros dichaeta* was predominant in the upper layer, and *Ch. atlanticus*, *Ch. criophilum*, *Dactyliosolen antarctica*, and *Rhizosolenia hebetata f. semispina* were especially abundant. To the north, between the Antarctic Divergence and the zone of the Antarctic Convergence, *Fragilariopsis sp.* and *Nitzschia sp.* were the most numerous forms. Only here were small population peaks of *Rhizosolenia chunii*, *Corethron criophilum*, and winter forms of *Eucamphia balaustium* encountered. In the autumn the phytoplankton declines. The quantity rapidly decreases and only near the edge of the ice field do summer-blooming species remain abundant.

III. Conclusion

In Indian Ocean section of the Antarctic over the period from January to April there is an initial spring blooming of ice-edge forms (*Biddulphia weissflogii*, *Eucamphia balaustium*, *Chaetoceros neglectus*, *Nitzschia closterium*), which then decline very rapidly in summer, when the bulk of the phytoplankton is composed of big forms such as *Chaetoceros criophilum*, *Rhizosolenia alata*, *Rh. chunii*, *Rh. hebetata f. semispina*, *Dactyliosolen antarctica*, and *Corethron criophilum*. The quantity of these species, in fact, gradually decreases from December to March. In late summer species of the genus *Chaetoceros* (*Ch. atlanticus*, *Ch. dictaeta*, *Ch. castracane*) can be especially numerous. This periodicity in composition, quantity, and biomass of the phytoplankton is certainly governed by seasonal changes in the environment. A similar picture was found in the Pacific sector of the Antarctic Ocean, and the distribution of the phytoplankton in both sections of the Southern Ocean is summarized in Fig. 5.

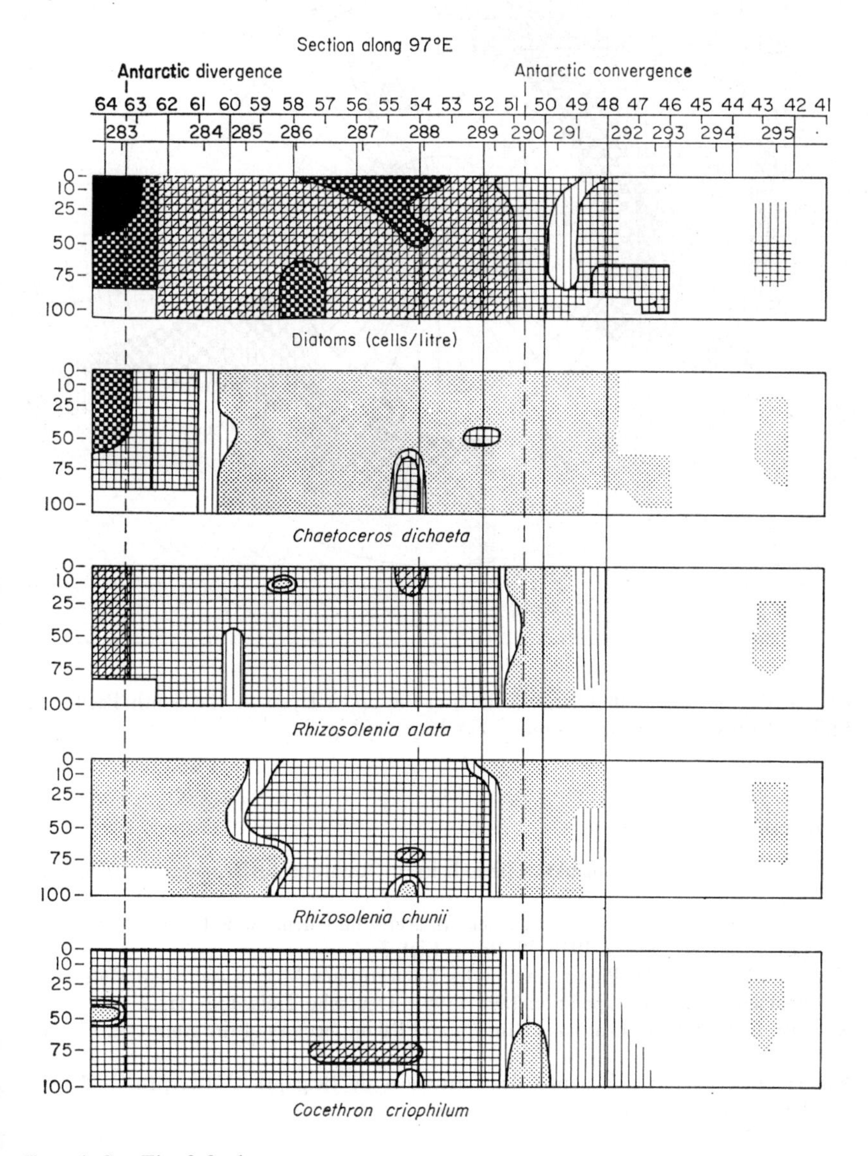

FIG. 4. See Fig. 2 for key.

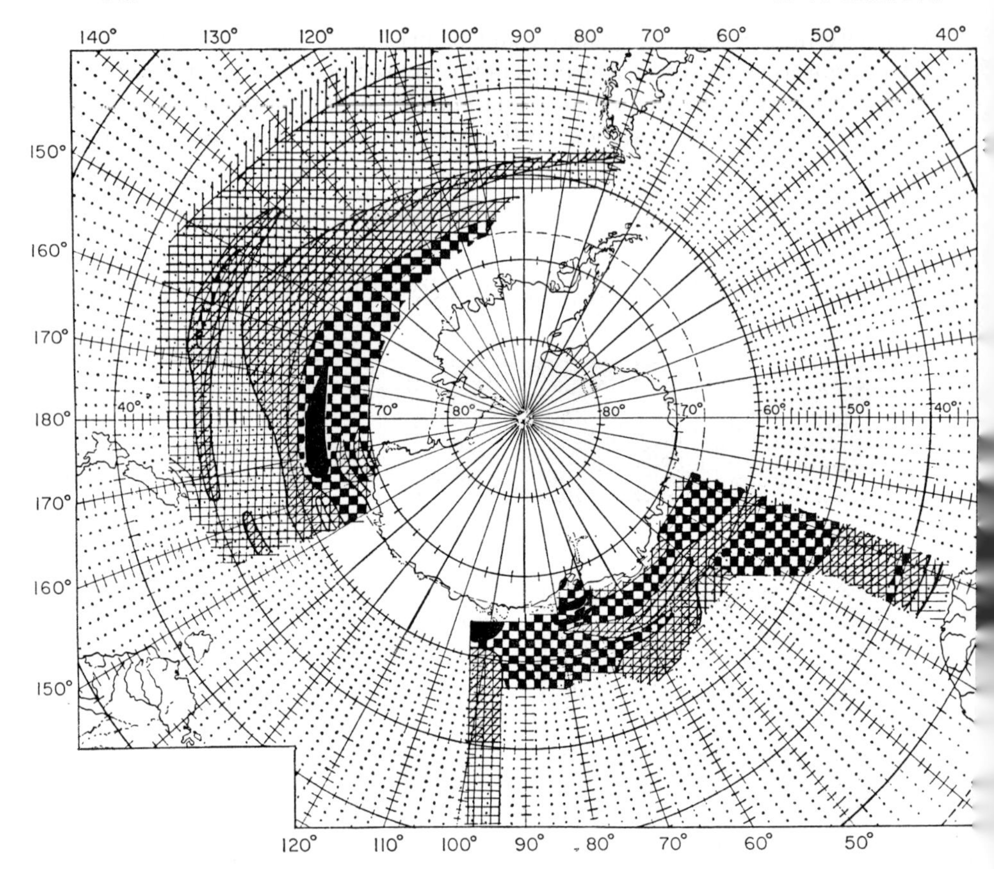

FIG. 5. Phytoplankton abundance (cells/l) in the upper layers of the South Pacific and Indian Oceans in the austral summer. For Key, see Fig. 2.

References

Hart, T. J. (1942). Phytoplankton periodicity in Antarctic surface waters. "*Discovery*" *Rep.* 21.

Hustedt, F. (1958). Diatomeen aus der Antarctis und dem Südatlantik. *Wiss. Ergebn. Dtsch. Antarkt. Ezped.* 1938–39. Bd. 2, Lief. 3.

Karsten, G. (1905). Das Phytoplankton des Antarktischen Meeres nach dem Material der deutschen Tiefsee-Expedition 1898–1899.—Deutsche Tiefs. Exp. II, 2.

Kozlova, O. G. (1964). Diatoms of Indian and Pacific Sectors of the Antarctic. Moscow, Nauka.

Van Heurck, J. (1909). Synopsis des Diatomées de Belgique. Antwerpen, 1880–1885. Diatomees. *Exp. Antarct. Belge.* Anvers.

The Distribution and Endemism of some Antarctic Microplankters

E. BALECH
Estación Hidrobiológica de Puerto Quequén, Argentina

I. Introduction

The study of the microplankton collected by twelve Antarctic expeditions, in addition to a great number of Subantarctic plankton samples gathered over many years, has permitted a reinterpretation of current opinions on the composition of Antarctic plankton (Balech, 1958*a*, *b*, 1959, 1962).

Hitherto most authors discussing Antarctic phytoplankton have considered diatoms only. All the other groups have been dismissed as negligible both from the point of view of primary productivity and floristic studies. Mention is usually made only of one species of silicoflagellates, one or two *Ceratium* species and about the same number of *Peridinium* spp. The present paper demonstrates the inadequacy of such generalizations.

II. Plankton Groups

A. Silicoflagellates

The investigations described here have shown that the silicoflagellate *Dictyocha speculum* is generally abundant in the Antarctic, and sometimes outnumbers any species of diatom. Though it is smaller than most diatoms, and its chloroplasts are pale, it should not be neglected as an important contributor to the planktonic biomass and even as a primary producer.

B. Ceratium spp

The genus *Ceratium* shows a general avoidance of Antarctic waters, except for two species: *C. pentagonum grandis* and *C. lineatum*. Even these two are usually confined to the stations closer to the Convergence. They are only found occasionally, and mostly in insignificant numbers, in more definite Antarctic situations. This result seems to conflict with the work of Hart (1934), but most of the stations where Hart collected Ceratia in abundance were rather close to the Convergence, or around South Georgia, where there are many conspicuous and well-known Subantarctic features (Hardy and Gunther, 1935). Conversely *Ceratium* is significantly absent from most samples taken well inside the Antarctic, including those collected over three years at Terre Adélie (Balech, 1958*b*) and from Gerlache Strait and the Weddell Sea (Balech and El Sayed, 1965).

Some other species of the same genus have been obtained from time to time, in general as single individuals and in rather deep hauls. These are regarded as occasional invaders of the Antarctic Ocean, where they cannot thrive.

C. Other Dinoflagellates

Mangin (1915), Peters (1928), and Wood (1954) have reported a total of thirty-two species of dinoflagellates in the Antarctic, more than two-thirds of them belonging to the genus *Peridinium*. The rest are *Dinophysis* and *Gonyaulax*. An additional thirty species of thecate dinoflagellates and half a dozen naked ones have been added in the present study. The latter group had not previously been reported from the Antarctic, where they are, in all probability, much more abundant than they seem to be, for they must be destroyed or become highly deformed and thus almost unrecognizable, during sampling and fixation. None the less they are unlikely to be important as primary producers, since most of them lack chloroplast, or have a few very pale plastids. Most of the species, even those with chlorophyll, are phagocytes, since they usually show very strong trichocysts and contain ingested small flagellates and diatoms. This is a fact to bear in mind when determining productivity by chlorophyll extraction.

Some corrections and eliminations from the lists were necessary before the total number of known Antarctic species could be assessed. After deletion of some evident misidentifications or very dubious determinations, and some Subantarctic species which transgressed only a little into the Antarctic (here termed occasional invaders), a list of fifty species of dinoflagellates normally obtained in surface Antarctic waters was obtained. This number is much lower than that usually found in warm waters, but it is much higher than was previously thought. Many species are small and easily deformable, and therefore generally overlooked by planktologists primarily interested in diatoms.

Of these fifty species, 80% are exclusively Antarctic. Only one, *Diplopeltopsis minor*, seems to be truly cosmopolitan. The designation of a species as exclusively Antarctic does not imply that it does not occasionally occur north of the Convergence. In fact, six of these dinoflagellates, and three of the Antarctic tintinnids, were found at some Subantarctic stations. Conversely, there are some Subantarctic plankters which have been occasionally found in Antarctic waters (six or seven species of dinoflagellates and four tintinnids). The degree of mixing seems to vary considerably from year to year, and probably also from season to season. During the winter of 1964 it was rather high.

Such mixed planktonic populations could be produced by two mechanisms. First, waters sinking at the Convergence could bring some species to a surface station in the Subantarctic zone by upwelling, and secondly some eddies could be isolated at the Convergence and carried by a Subantarctic current far beyond the Antarctic front. The second explanation seems to fit the known facts better in the cases of some Antarctic species found from time to time along or off the Argentine littoral where no indications of upwelling could be found.

Conversely, upwelling is suggested by the plankton composition at some stations in the Drake Passage (Balech, 1962). In one occupied on April 1, 1958, at 55°50′S, 65°W, a small isolated patch with a mixed Subantarctic-Subtropical population was found. In the winter of 1964 a few stations had a species, *Oxytoxum belgicae*, previously known only from Arctic waters. In this connection, however, two stations were particularly worthy of note, one at 57°49′S, 65°42′W, and the other at 58°19′S, 62°52′W. Both had two typical "shade" genera of the tropics: *Heterodinium* and *Heteroschisma*, and also the species *Oxytoxum diploconus*, known from warm waters. It should be stressed that the temperature of the first of those stations was 3·38°C, and of the second one was 2·44°C. Station 68, situated farther north at 57°38′S, 63°30′W was much colder with a temperature of 0·25°C. These observations seem to provide for the first time some evidence that in this place or near by the Convergence was replaced by a divergence. Peculiar planktonic populations also seem to give some hints of divergence near two stations in the Weddell Sea, one at 66°55′7S, 11°39′W, occupied on December 25, 1963, and the other at 64°40′S, 15°54′6W, January 10, 1964 (Balech and El Sayed, 1965).

II. Discussion

In terms of biomass and number of individuals, in most samples the diatoms overwhelmingly exceed the dinoflagellates. In several, however, the dinoflagellates contribute an important share of the planktonic bulk, and in a few stations they exceed the diatoms.

There are still insufficient samples to allow any subdivision of the Antarctic Ocean on the basis of plankton distribution. It seems, however, that from this viewpoint it is rather homogeneous. The differences found seem to be only quite local and/or temporary: some, found in earlier studies, disappear as sampling goes on.

Among other groups, it is noteworthy that the radiolaria are more abundant in the Antarctic plankton, especially in the north of the region, than in most of the other seas studied by the author. Some of them, because of their xanthella, are primary producers. One very small colonial organism, which could not be determined, was on occasion the most important photosynthetic organism in the samples.

Tintinnid ciliates, which were studied in some detail, are interesting for two reasons: first, they are very active consumers of phytoplankton, including rather large diatoms: and secondly, they seem to be the best indicators of Antarctic waters, since all their species but one are endemic. The only exception, *Cymatocyclis parva*, also occurs in the southern Subantarctic, where it seems to thrive better.

The endemism in the Antarctic proceeds in the following ascending order: silicoflagellates, diatoms, dinoflagellates, and tintinnids. The only silicoflagellate known in Antarctic waters can be found in both hemispheres in different water masses. The percentages of endemism for dinoflagellates and tintinnids are 80% and almost 100% respectively. The degree of endemism of the diatoms was not established but it is significantly lower and probably only about half that in the dinoflagellates.

True bipolarity was not found among the dinoflagellates or the tintinnids. However, bipolarity of forms, i.e. a close resemblance between some Antarctic and Arctic species was encountered. The formation of excrescences is a common feature in the Arctic as well as in Antarctic species. However, it attains a much higher degree of morphological distinctiveness in the Antarctic. The Antarctic *Peridinium applanatum* has its counterpart in the Arctic *P. bulbosum*. The anomalous *P. minusculum*, of the Northern Hemisphere is strikingly similar to the Antarctic *P. defectum*, but differs in plate pattern. Since previous authors did not analyse in detail the theca of the dinoflagellates they overlooked specific characters, thus failing to recognize the endemism of most of the Antarctic species. *Dinophysis ovum*, *Peridinium subinerme*, *P. depressum*, *P. pyriforme*, *P. cerasus*, *P. pellucidum*, *P. decipiens* *P. granii*, and *P. ovatum* are among species wrongly reported from the Antarctic in consequence.

References

Balech, E. (1958*a*). Plancton de la Campaña Antártica Argentina, 1954–1955. *Physis B. Aires* **21** (60), 75–108.

Balech, E. (1958*b*). Dinoflagellés et Tintinnides de la Terre Adélie (Secteur français antarctique). *Vie Millieu* **8** (4), 382–408.

Balech, E. (1959). Operación Oceanográfica Merluza. V° Crucero. Plancton. *Serv. Hidrograf. Naval* **618**, 1–43.

Balech, E. (1962). Plancton de las campañas oceanográficas Drake I y II. *Serv. Hidrograf. Naval* **627**, 1–57.

Balech, E. and El-Sayed, S. Z. (1965). Microplankton of the Weddell Sea. *Antarctic Res. Ser.* **5**, 107–24.

Hardy, A. C. and Gunther, E. R. (1935). The plankton of the South Georgia whaling grounds and adjacent waters. *"Discovery" Rep.* 11, 1–546.

Hart, T. J. (1934). On the phytoplankton of the South-west Atlantic and the Bellingshausen Sea. *"Discovery" Rep.* 8, 3–268.

Laccmann, H. (1909). Die Tintinnodeen der deutschen Südpolar Expedition 1901–1903. *Dt. Südpol.-Exped.* 11, 340–496.

Mangin, L. (1915). Phytoplankton antarctique. *Exped. Antarct. "Scotia"* (1902–1904), 1–134.

Peters, N. (1928). Die Peridineenbevölkerung der Weddellsee mit besonderer Berusksischtigung der Wachstums—und Variations-formen. *Int. Revue ges. Hydrobiol. Hydrogr.*

Wood, E. J. F. (1954). Dinoflagellates in the Australian region. *Aust. J. mar. Freshwat. Res.* 5 (2), 171–351.

Diatoms in Suspension and in Bottom Sediments in the Southern Indian and Pacific Oceans

O. G. KOZLOVA
Institute of Oceanology, U.S.S.R. Academy of Sciences, Moscow

I. Introduction

Research on diatoms in surface waters, the main water mass and bottom sediments was undertaken as part of a study of the sedimentation process in the Indian and Pacific ocean sections of the Antarctic. Samples of diatoms in suspension, collected by membrane filters and separators, and in the uppermost layers of bottom sediments were examined. Attention was paid particularly to the numbers and species of Antarctic diatoms in the suspension and to their role in the process of sedimentation.

A. The Number of Diatoms in the Surface Waters of the Indian and Pacific Sectors of the Antarctic Ocean

The following regularities were discovered in the quantitative distribution of diatoms in the surface waters of the southern part of the Indian Ocean:

1. The largest quantity of diatoms is characteristic of the waters to the east wind drift, south of the Antarctic Divergence zone. The number of diatoms varies from 250×10^6 to 1×10^9 cells per m^3 in the coastal waters of the Antarctic during the spring and summer seasons (Fig. 1). The high nutrient content of the water, which is not entirely exhausted even at the peak of diatom numbers in summer, is conducive to the wealth of diatoms in the coastal regions of the Antarctic.

In the zone of the Antarctic Divergence, in the centre of the area of upwelling water north of Enderby land, the number of diatoms decreases to on the average one-third to one-tenth that at other coastal stations outside the zone of divergence.

2. In the open zones of the oceans, between the Antarctic Divergence and Convergence, the number of diatoms in summer averages 14×10^6 to 15×10^7 cells per m^3, reading $3 \times 10^8/m^3$ in a few areas. Thus in the open deep-water areas of the Indian Ocean sector of the Antarctic there are, on average, only one-quarter the number present in the coastal areas.

3. In the Subantarctic waters north of the Antarctic Convergence zone the lowest numbers of diatoms were found, totals varying between 3×10^5 and 12×10^6 cells/m³ of water. The limited number of diatoms in the Subantarctic waters may be explained by their low nutrient content.

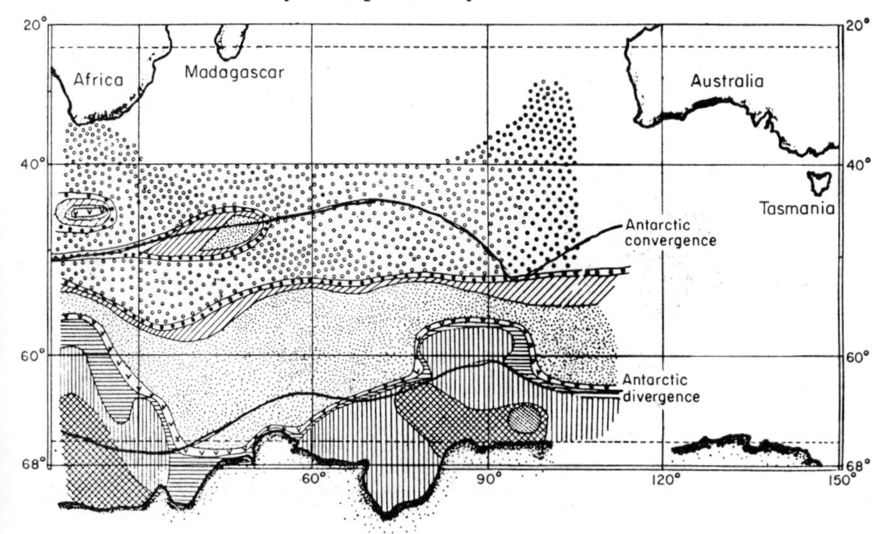

FIG. 1. Number of diatoms per cu. m from the 0–7 m layer in the Indian Ocean sector of the Antarctic (samples obtained on the second voyage of the *Ob*). Maximum (fine cross-hatching), 10^9 cells/m³; heavy cross-hatching, $600–800 \times 10^6$/m³; vertical shading $400–600 \times 10^6$ etc.

In the Pacific as well as in the Indian sector of the Antarctic the waters south of the zone of the Antarctic Divergence are characterized by a great number of diatoms. Up to 54×10^7 cells/m³ were found in samples collected in summer along King George V Coast (Fig. 2). The waters south of the zone of the Antarctic Divergence (along the Oates Coast, Victoria Land, and in the northern part of the Amundsen Sea) are characterized by diatom numbers between 2×10^8 and 4×10^8 cells/m³ in summer as well as autumn.

North of the zone of the Antarctic Divergence the number of diatoms in the Pacific sector of the Antarctic Ocean proved to be between 7×10^6 and 10^7 cells/m³: that is, only one-seventh on average of the numbers south of this zone. The smallest number of diatoms, between 9×10^4 and $5{\cdot}7 \times 10^6$ cells/m³, is characteristic of the waters north of the Antarctic Convergence zone.

In the Pacific sector of the Antarctic Ocean the distribution of the number of diatoms in suspension thus shows the same peculiarities as in the Indian sector, and in both regions the hydrological frontal zones proved to be essential borders in the quantitative distribution of diatoms.

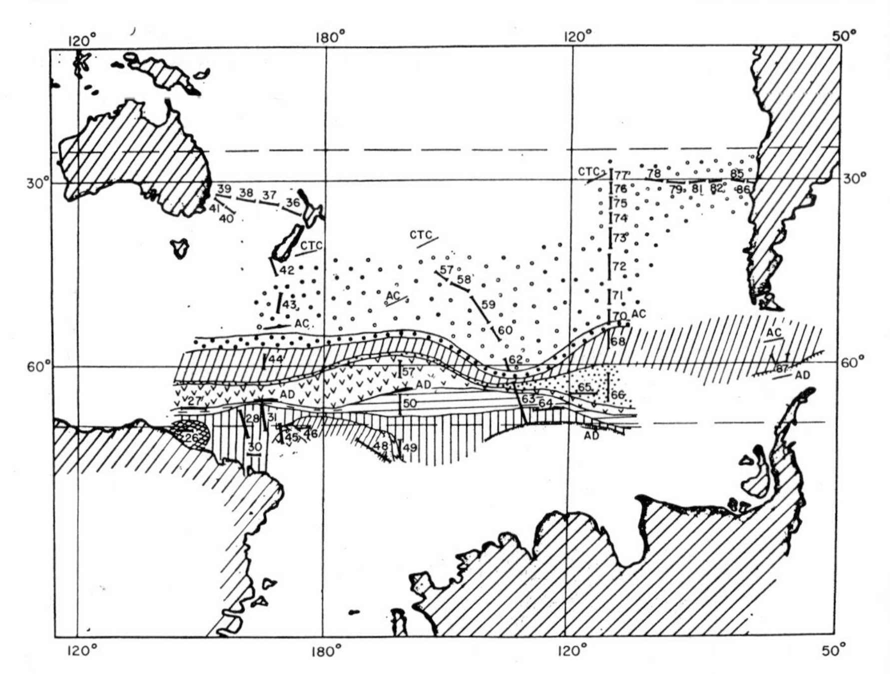

FIG. 2. Number of diatoms per cu. m from the 0–7 m layer in the Pacific Ocean sector of the Antarctic (samples obtained on the third voyage of the *Ob*). Collecting stations numbered. Cross-hatching, over 400 × 10^6 cells/m³ (maximum 540 × 10^6); vertical shading, 200–400 × 10^6 etc. AC Antarctic convergence; AD, Antarctic divergence; CTC, Sub-tropical convergence.

B. The Number of Diatoms in the Upper Layer of Bottom Sediments

The absolute number of diatoms per gm was determined for each type of sediment encountered, and was shown to depend primarily on the type of sediment, its granulometric composition and location.

In terrigenous (iceberg) sediments of the Antarctic continental shelf the content of diatoms in low-ranging from 55 × 10^3 to 5 × 10^6 cells/gm sediment. These figures are considerably less than diatom numbers in suspension in the waters of the same zone (from 2 × 10^8 to 5·9 × 10^8 cells/gm of suspension).

In terrigenous-organogenous sediments of the continental slope of the Antarctic the average number of diatoms is three times more than in the zone of typical iceberg sediments. Cell totals fluctuating between 7 × 10^4 and 1·5 × 10^7/gm sediment are characteristic of the continental slope, even relatively near the coast. The total is directly related to the content of the terrigenous material in the sediments. The content of diatoms in the terrigenous-organogenous sediments of the continental slope amounts to 9–25% of the number of diatom cells in the suspension above this zone.

In the zone of ocean diatom oozes the number of diatoms in suspension and in the sediments is almost the same, making up from 3×10^7 to 11×10^7 cells/gm of suspension and from $1{\cdot}5 \times 10^7$ to $10{\cdot}3 \times 10^7$ cells/gm of sediment. This arises mainly from the excellent preservation of the diatom species inhabiting the open ocean, and upon the insignificant contribution of terrigenous material to the bottom sediments.

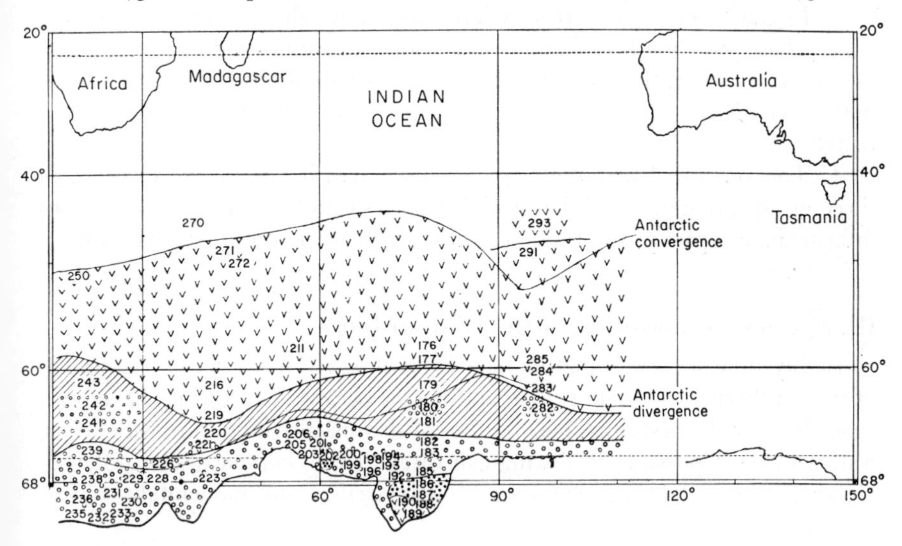

FIG. 3. Number of cells in 1 gm of deposit from the surface of the ocean bed. Figures indicate stations. 'V' hatching, $1–2 \times 10^6$ cells/gm. Oblique shading, $8 \times 10^5–10^6$; circles, below 8×10^5/gm.

II. The Vertical Distribution of Diatoms

In the different zones of the southern part of the Indian and Pacific Oceans the following regularities in diatom distribution in the water were observed.

1. In the coastal areas of the Antarctic, above the area of iceberg sediments, the surface layer down to 100 m is characterized by high numbers of diatoms in spring and summer. In the depths ranging from 100 to 1000 m the number of diatoms drops gradually and in the near-bottom layers it amounts to only between 0·8 and 9% of the number of diatoms in suspension in the surface layers.

2. A great number of diatoms also characterizes the layers from 0 to 100 and from 0 to 300 m in the open areas of the ocean above the area of diatom

oozes. But the number of diatoms falls sharply in the deeper layers. However, at some stations it increases in the abyssal and near-bottom layers of the ocean and may amount to from 10 to 130% of the number in suspension in the surface layers. Thus, more diatoms reach the bottom in the open areas than in the coastal areas of the ocean.

3. In waters of more northerly latitudes, above the area of foraminiferal oozes, there are abundant diatoms in summer and autumn down to 300–500 m. Below these depths the number of diatoms falls sharply and in the near-bottom layers constitutes from 2 to 6% of the number in the surface suspension.

4. The vertical distribution of diatoms makes it possible to distinguish three groups, one of which has a high power of preservation, the second an intermediate capacity, and the third with almost no power of preservation.

III. Species Composition of the Diatom Flora

Eighty-nine species of diatom have been observed in suspension in waters of the southern part of the Indian and Pacific oceans. Ten species have been described for the first time. Peculiarities of diatom distribution in the surface waters made it possible to distinguish three diatom complexes, of different biogeographical nature: Antarctic, Subantarctic, and moderately warm-water.

Antarctic diatoms are the most cold-water diatoms. To a great extent, they are ice species capable of photosynthesis and multiplication at temperatures below zero (−0·5° to −1·9°C) or low temperatures above zero (up to +1·5°C) and under considerable fluctuations of salinity. The Antarctic complex of diatoms develops mainly in the waters of the East Wing Drift.

The Subantarctic species of diatoms require warmer conditions than the Antarctic species. They display vegetative activity mostly in summer, in temperatures only slightly above zero (+1 to +5°C) and relatively stable salinities between 33·8 and 34·5°/00. Unlike the Antarctic complex, they do not develop near the edge of the ice. The main area of distribution of Subantarctic diatoms lies in the waters of the West Wind Drift, and the Antarctic Convergence zone forms the northern limit of their distribution.

Among Antarctic and Subantarctic diatoms may be distinguished a group of widespread species that are more or less evenly distributed in both zones, in the coastal and in the open areas of the ocean.

The moderately warm-water complex of diatoms inhabits the waters mostly north of the zone of the Antarctic Convergence.

Mixed complexes of species develop in the region of the junction and interpenetration of waters of western and eastern drifts as well as in the area of Subantarctic and moderately warm waters.

The diatom flora represented in the surface layer of the bottom sediments shows a latitudinally zoned distribution similar to that in the surface plankton. No signs were found of dead diatoms being transferred horizontally for great distances.

References

Hart, T. J. (1942). Phytoplankton Periodicity in Antarctic surface waters. *Discovery Rep.* 21.

Hustedt, F. (1958). Diatomeen aus der Antarctis und dem Südatlantik. *Wiss. Ergebn. dt. antarkt. Exped.* 1938–39. Bd. 2, Lief. 3.

Karsten, G. (1905). Das Phytoplankton des Antarktischen Meeres nach dem Material der Deutschen Tiefsee-Expedition, 1898–1899. *Deutsche Tiefs. Exp.* **II**, 2.

Kozlova, O. G. (1964). Diatomovyye vodorosli Indiyskogo i Tikhookeanskogo sektorov Antarktiki. (Diatom algae of the Indian and Pacific Ocean sectors of the Antarctic). Moscow, "Nauka" Publishing House, 1964.

Van Heurck, H. (1909). Synopsis des Diatomees de Belgique. Antwerpen, 1880–1885. Diatomées. *Exp. Antarct. Belge.* Anvers.

Regularities in the Distribution of Planktonic Foraminifera in the Water and Sediments of the Southern Ocean

N. V. BELYAEVA
Institute of Oceanology, U.S.S.R. Academy of Sciences, Moscow, U.S.S.R.

The foraminifera present in samples of plankton taken at forty-five stations and in forty-four samples of separation obtained during the cruises of RV *Ob* in the Southern Ocean have been studied (Belyaeva, 1964, 1968, 1969).

The planktonic foraminifera had a total frequency of occurrence* in water samples of 0·66. Only one species, *Globigerina bulloides*, was present at most stations (frequency of occurrence, 0·66). *Globigerina pachyderma* was very rare (frequency of occurrence 0·05), and comprised less than 10% of the total population of planktonic foraminifera in the water. Both species belong to the family Globigerinidae.

The distribution of planktonic foraminifera in the samples of sediments taken by Soviet Expeditions were also studied, and the number of specimens per gramme of dry sediment recorded. Data from McKnight (1962) and Pflum (1966) about the numbers and species of planktonic foraminifera per gramme of sediment were also used. A map showing the total amount of planktonic foraminifera in the sediments of the Southern Ocean south of 60°S has been compiled from all these data, a total of 177 stations being involved (Fig. 1).

Data on the distribution of planktonic foraminifera obtained by foreign expeditions at a total of 363 stations were also used in order to compare the frequency of occurrence (p) at different depths (Table 1) (Earland, 1934, 1936; Heron-Allen and Earland, 1922; Huberson, 1934; Blair, 1965; Kennett, 1966; Parr, 1950; Pirie, 1914; Uchio, 1960; Warthin, 1934; Wiesner, 1931).

Planktonic foraminifera were recorded at 111 stations out of 177 (Table 2, Fig. 2) in quantities of from 0·04 to 8451 specimens/gm. The distribution of planktonic foraminifera in recent sediments is related to their productivity in the 200 m water layer, the topography of the sea bottom, and depth. A low concentration (less than 100 specimens/gm) is predominant at all depths

* The frequence of occurrence is occurrence expressed in fractions of a unit.

($p = 0{\cdot}49$). The low concentration of planktonic foraminifera in the sediments of continental shelf and slope (Fig. 1) is due to their low concentration in the water over the shelf and slope and to dilution by terrigenous material. Planktonic foraminifera are absent from sediments at depths greater than 3200 m because of the dissolution of calcium carbonate in their shells (Fig. 2).

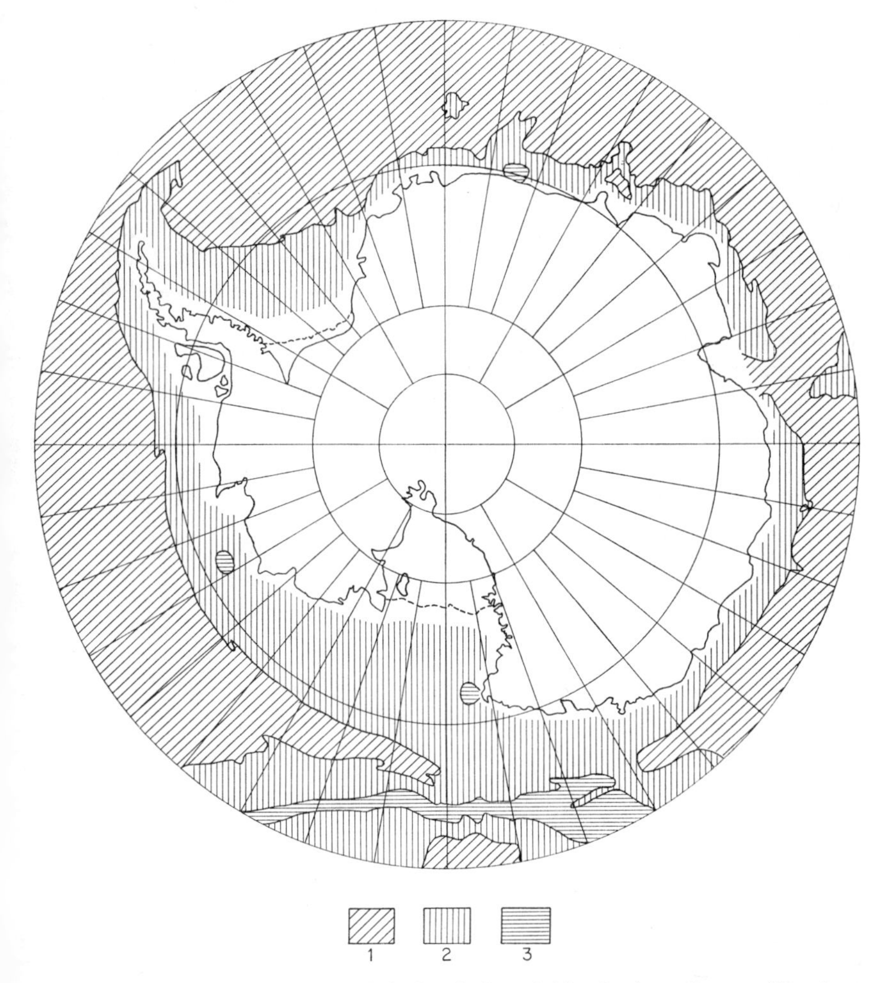

FIG. 1. Quantitative distribution of planktonic foraminifera in the sediment of Southern Ocean (in specimens/gm): 1 = no specimens, 2 = 1 — 1000, 3 = more than 1000.

The maximum concentration of planktonic foraminifera in the sediments was found on the submarine ridges and sea mounts with depths above this critical limit.

TABLE 1

The frequency of occurrence of planktonic foraminifera at different depths (from sources cited in text)

Depth *m*	*Number of stations*	*Number of stations at which planktonic foraminifera were noticed*	*Frequency of occurrence* (p)
0–200	17	11	0·65
200–500	45	26	0·58
500–1000	38	19	0·50
1000–2000	17	6	0·35
2000–2500	6	4	0·67
2500–3000	11	8	0·73
3000–3500	9	7	0·78
3500–4000	10	7	0·70
4000–4500	10	4	0·40
4500–5000	23	7	0·30
over 5000	3	2	
Total for all depths	186	99	0·53

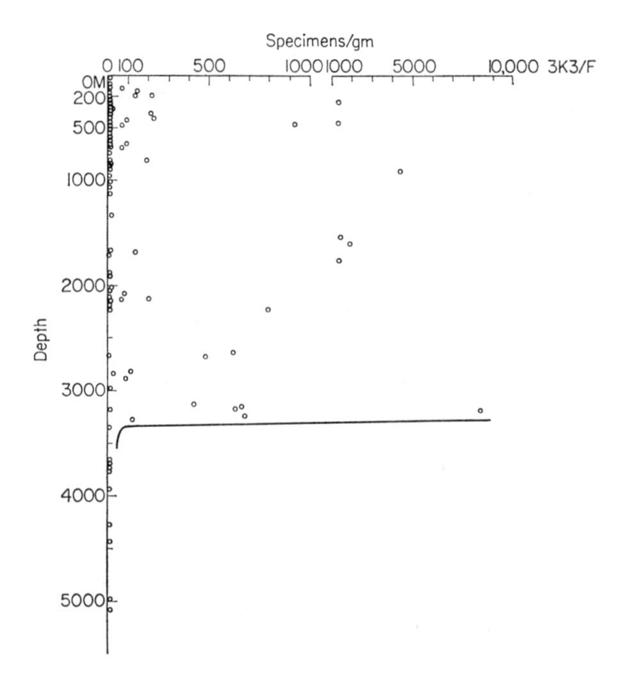

FIG. 2. The quantitative distribution of planktonic foraminifera in sediments at different depths.

TABLE 2

The distribution of planktonic foraminifera in the sediments of the Southern Ocean*

Depth (m)	*Number of stations*	*Number of stations at which foraminifera were recorded*	*Number of specimens*			*Total frequency of occurrence*	*Numbers of stations at which certain numbers of foraminifera were found (specimens/g) and frequency of occurrence of planktonic foraminifera at them*									
							<1/gm		*1–100/gm*		*100–500/gm*		*500–1000/gm*		*>1000/gm*	
			max.	*min.*	*mean*		*Number of stations*	*p*	*Number of stations*	*p*	*Number of stations*	*p*	*Number of stations*	*p*	*Number of stations*	*p*
0–200	10	10	217	0·04	55	1·0	2	0·20	5	0·50	3	0·30				
200–500	40	31	1462	0·04	101	0·78	12	0·30	14	0·35	2	0·05	1	0·02	2	0·05
500–1000	45	25	4382	0·04	105	0·55	20	0·44	3	0·07	1	0·02			1	0·02
1000–2000	18	12	1939	0·08	272	0·66	3	0·17	5	0·28	1	0·05			3	0·17
2000–2500	12	10	789	0·04	85	0·83	3	0·25	5	0·40	1	0·08	1	0·08		
2500–3000	12	7	623	0·05	106	0·58	2	0·17	2	0·17	2	0·17	1	0·08		
3000–3500	11	7	8451	0·04	939	0·63	1	0·09	1	0·09	2	0·18	2	0·18	1	0·09
3500–4000	11	5	3	0·04	0·4	0·45	4	0·36	1	0·09						
4000–4500	7	2	2	0·2	0·3	0·28	1	0·14	1	0·14						
4500–5000	6	1	0·68	0·68	0·1	0·16	1	1·0								
over 5000	5	1	0·12	0·12	0·02	0·20	1	1·0								
Total for all depths	177	111	8451	00·4		0·62	50	0·28	37	0·21	12	0·07	5	0·02	7	0·04

* From material collected by R V *Ob* and "Deep Freeze" (Belyaeva, Mc-Knight and Pflum).

TABLE 3

The distribution of *Globigerina pachyderma* in the sediments of the Southern Ocean

Depth (m)	*Number of stations*	*Number of stations at which* G. pachyderma *was recorded*	*Total frequency of occurrence*	*Numbers (of specimens)* specimens/gm *min.*	*max.*	*mean*	% *of all foraminifera min.*	*max.*	*mean*
0–200	10	9	0·90	0·04	184	43	31	100	76
200–500	40	30	0·75	0·04	1309	99	74	100	72
500–1000	45	23	0·51	0·04	4352	104	50	100	49
1000–2000	18	11	0·61	0·16	1937	265	81	100	59
2000–2500	12	10	0·83	0·04	789	95	94	100	82
2500–3000	12	7	0·58	0·05	623	102	75	100	55
3000–3500	11	7	0·63	0·04	8439	936	97	100	66
3500–4000	11	3	0·27	0·04	0·1	0·02	100	100	27
4000–4500	7	2	0·28	0·04	0·04	0·01	20	50	10
4500–5000	6	1	0·16	0·04	0·04	0·01		100	16
over 5000	5	0							
Total for all depths	177	103	0·58						

TABLE 4

The distribution of *Globigerina bulloides* in the sediments of the Southern Ocean

Depth (*m*)	*Number of stations*	*Number of stations at which* G. bulloides *was recorded*	*Total frequency of occurrence*	*Numbers (of specimens) (specimen/gm)* min.	max.	mean	*% of all foraminifera* min.	max.	mean
0–200	10	6	0·60	0·04	46	10	0·3	100	20
200–500	40	14	0·46	0·04	204	11	0·2	100	5
500–1000	45	6	0·13	0·03	28	0·6	0·6	100	7
1000–2000	18	5	0·28	0·04	37	2	0·1	18	1
2000–2500	12	2	0·16	0·1	0·5	0·05	2·6	5·6	0·7
2500–3000	12	1	0·08	0·08	0·08	0·006	0·25	0·25	0·02
3000–3500	11	3	0·27	0·2	12	1	0·05	0·7	0·1
3500–4000	11	2	0·18	0·6	3·5	0·3	100	100	19
4000–4500	7	2	0·28	0·04	0·16	0·10	80	50	65
4500–5000	6	0							
over 5000	5	0							
Total for all depths	177	41	0·23						

Two species were identified and counted and the results expressed as specimens/gm dry sediment and as a percentage of the total population of planktonic foraminifera. *Globigerina pachyderma* is predominant in the sediments at all depths, with a total frequency of occurrence 0·58. A maximum of 8439 specimens/gm was recorded (Table 3). The species accounted for the entire population of planktonic foraminifera at most stations. The vertical distribution and abundance of *G. pachyderma* is shown in Table 3. The frequency of occurrence of *Globigerina bulloides* in the sediments is 0·23, and a maximum of 200 specimens/gm of this species was recorded (Table 4). This distribution of both species is in accordance with the data obtained by Bé (1960) in the Arctic basin.

The total frequency of occurrence of planktonic foraminifera, their quantity, and the number of species are lower in the Antarctic than in other zones of the world ocean. The critical depth in this zone is at 3000–3200 m. But carbonate sediments are found south of 60°S, and for these to form, the presence of planktonic foraminifera in the water, the absence of terrigenous dilution, and the absence of dissolution of $CaCO_3$ are all necessary.

References

Belyaeva, N. V. (1964). Raspredelenie planktonnix foraminifer v vodax i ocadkax Indiickogo okeana. *Trudy Inst. Okeanol.* **68**.

Belyaeva, N. V. (1968). Planktonnie foraminiferi v ocadkax Tixogo okeana. *Okeanol.* **8**, Pt. I.

Belyaeva, N. V. (1969). Raspredelenie planktonnix foraminifer v ocadkax Mirovogo okeana. *Vop. Mikropaleont.* **12**.

Bé, A. W. H. (1960). Some observations on Arctic planktonic foraminifera. *Contrib. Cushm. Found. Foram. Res.* **II**, Pt. 2.

Blair, D. (1965). The distribution of planktonic foraminifera in Deep-Sea cores from the Southern Ocean, Antarctica. (Thesis). Contrib. Sedimentol. Res. Lab. Dept. Geol. Florida University.

Earland, A. (1934). The Falklands sector of the Antarctic (Excluding South Georgia). *"Discovery" Rep.* **10**.

Earland, A. (1936). Additional records from the Weddell Sea sector from material obtained by the SY *Scotia*. *"Discovery" Rep*, **13**.

Heron-Allen, E. and Earland, A. (1922). Protozoa. Pt. II—Foraminifera. *British Antarctic ("Terra Nova") Exp.* 1910. *Zool.* **6**, 2.

Huberson, E. (1934). *"Discovery" Rep.* **9**.

McKnight, W. M. (1962). The distribution of foraminifera off parts of the Antarctic coast. *Bull. Am. Paleont.* **44**, 201.

Kennett, J. (1966). Foraminiferal evidence of a shallow calcium carbonate solution boundary Ross Sea, Antarctica. *Science*, N.Y. **153**, 3732.

Parr, W. (1950). Foraminifera. *B.A.N.Z. Antarctic Res. Exp.* 1929–31. *Rep.* Ser. B. V, Pt. 6.

Pflum, C. (1966). The distribution of foraminifera in the eastern Ross sea, Amundsen sea and Bellingshausen sea, Antarctica. *Bull. Am. Paleont.* **50**, 226.

Pirie, H. (1914). Deep-sea deposits. Scottish Nat. Antarct. Exp. 1902–04. *Trans. R. Edin.* **XLIX**, Pt. III, No. 10.
Uchio, T. (1960). Planktonic foraminifera of the Antarctic Ocean. *Biol. Res. Japan. Antarct. Res. Exp.*, **12**.
Warthin, A. (1934). Foraminifera from the Ross sea. *Am. Mus. Novit.* N **721**.
Wiesner, H. (1931). Die Foraminiferen der Deutschen Südoplar-Exp. 1901–1903. *Dt. Südpol. Exped.* **XX**.

Seasonal Cycles of some Common Antarctic Copepod Species

N. M. VORONINA
Shirshov Institute of Oceanology, Academy of Sciences, Moscow, U.S.S.R.

I. Introduction

The knowledge of the seasonal cycles of common species is a prerequisite for understanding plankton distribution patterns.

The bulk of mesoplankton are copepods, which compose 73% of the total biomass. Among this group three species have the greatest importance: *Calanoides acutus*, *Calanus propinquus*, and *Rhincalanus gigas*. That is why they have been chosen for discussion in this paper.

The material was collected during three cruises of the RV *Ob* during the second part of the summer in 1956, 1957, and 1958 in the area between 20° and 165°E. The 38 cm diameter vertical closing Juday net (made of silk with 38 meshes per cm) was used. At each station six different depths were usually hauled within the upper 500 m. These were: 10–0, 25–10, 50–25, 100–50, 200–100 and 500–200 m. A total of 563 samples from 129 stations were analysed. The number, age composition, and biomass of the species mentioned above were determined for each sample. Kamishilov's formula (1951) expressing the relationship between weight and length in *Calanus* was used in order to determine the biomass.

A. The Life Cycle of Rhincalanus gigas

The life cycle of one of the species, *R. gigas*, which is more broadly distributed than the other two, has been examined in detail. Data on the age composition of its population along two meridional sections (Fig. 1) show that late in summer *R. gigas* was absent from the southernmost stations or was represented by overwintered copepods. Somewhat to the north the young of a new generation appeared and farther to the north the average age of the new brood gradually increased. In this sequence the more mature population is typical of the Divergence zone. In the northern waters no dominance of stages V and VI has been ever observed. It can be suggested this is due to

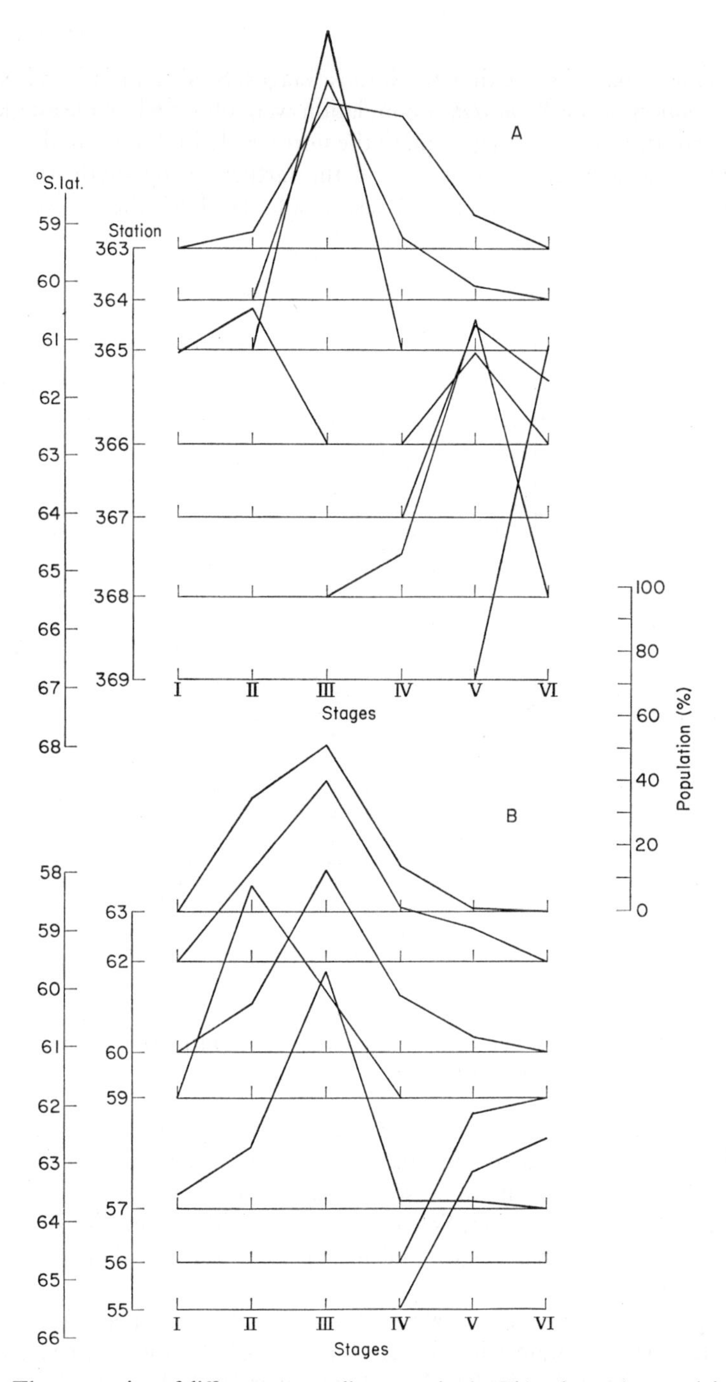

FIG. 1. The proportion of different copepodite stages in the *Rhincalanus gigas* stock in the 0–500 m layer. A, Section South from New Zealand, March–April 1958. B, Section South from New Zealand, March 1957.

copepods sinking before they reach those stages. Similar variations in the age composition of the *Rhincalanus* population were observed by Ottestad (1932) and Ommaney (1936). In general in the northern latitudes it was always more advanced at a particular season, and the farther to the south, the more it lagged behind in development. These results establish the different timing

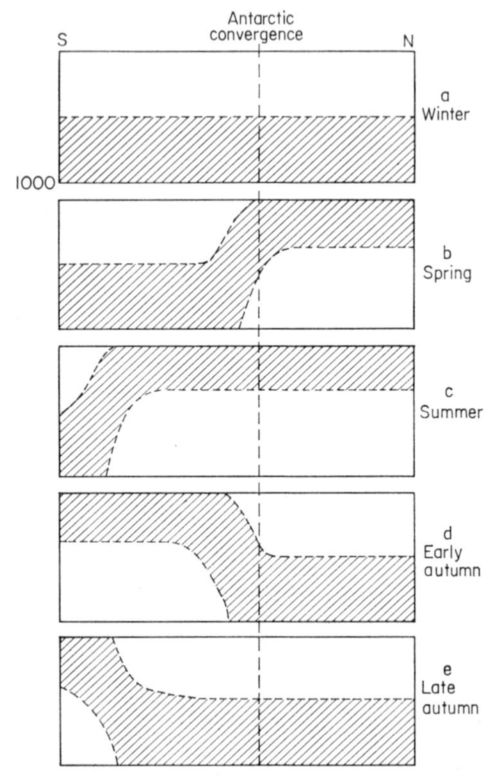

FIG. 2. Seasonal changes in the zone inhabited by the bulk of *Rhincalanus gigas* population (indicated by cross-hatching).

of the main phases of the annual cycle, notably the ascending migration in spring, breeding, and the autumnal descent into deep waters, in different latitudes. All this results in seasonal changes in distribution of the bulk of the *Rhincalanus* population. Schematically this is shown in Fig. 2. Confirmation of this theory has been found in papers on the distribution of *R. gigas* by several authors.

Figure 2a represents the almost complete absence of *R. gigas* from the Antarctic surface waters in winter. Ommaney (1936, Fig. 11) has published data establishing this for late June–September 1932. According to our data,

Rhincalanus descend below 500 m in autumn in the Subantarctic. According to Mackintosh (1937, Table IV), in September the lower boundary of distribution of *R. gigas* lies below 1500 m.

There are very few data for the spring period. But in the *Discovery* section in the east Pacific sector in October 1932 *R. gigas* was found at all stations to the north of the Antarctic Convergence throughout the 250 m layer in quantities which increased northwards. Conversely, to the south of the Convergence the species was practically absent from the surface waters (Ommaney, 1936, Table IIIc). This situation is represented in Fig. 2b. Breeding in the Subantarctic is likely to take place in November–December.

Summer is the period when the majority of the population of *R. gigas*

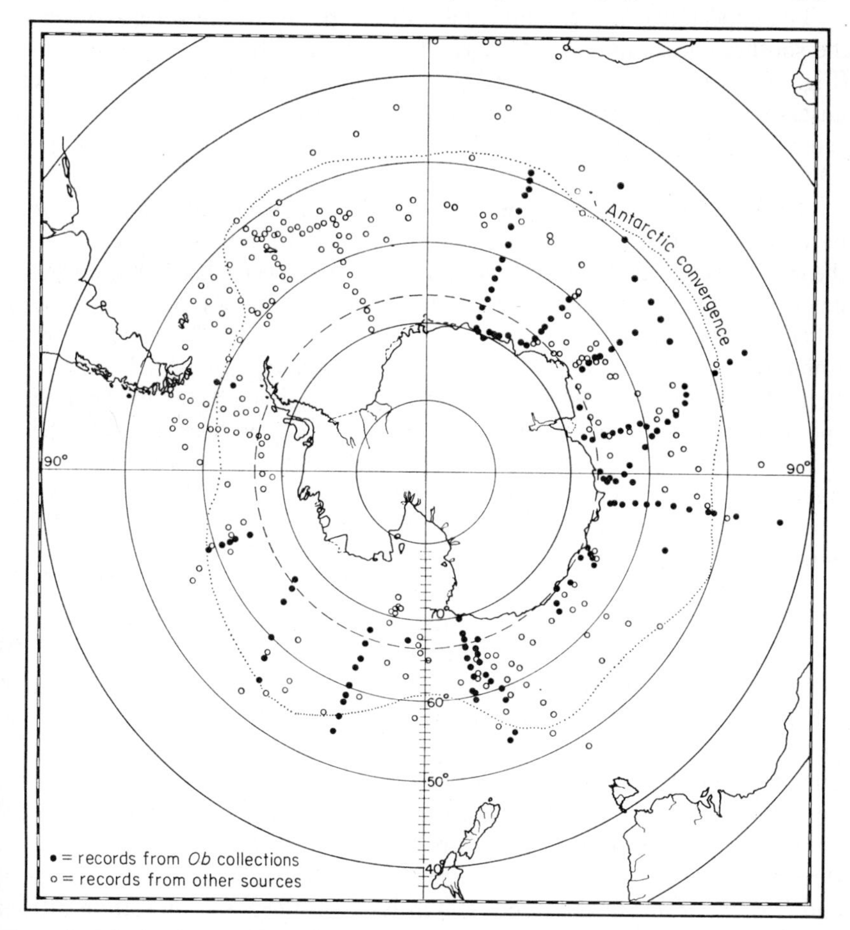

FIG. 3. Distribution of *Rhincalanus gigas*: ●, Data from *Ob* collections; ○, Data from other sources; . . . ., Antarctic convergence.

inhabit the surface waters of both Antarctic and Subantarctic. Only in the southernmost areas, with the lowest temperatures have they not ascended from the deep water (Fig. 2c). The autumnal migration of *R. gigas* downwards from the surface layers to deeper water obviously takes place earlier in the Subantarctic. Our data from the section along 98°E and the results of Naumov (1964) for the sections along 160° and 109°W make this plain (Fig. 2d). In April 1957 and 1958 the plankters were not discovered in the upper 500 m layer in the parts of these sections to the north of Antarctic Convergence. In conditions of circumpolar water transfer such absence cannot be the result of regional or annual features in plankton composition, but is undoubtedly connected with seasonal peculiarities in its vertical distribution.

The appearance and the breeding of this species in the surface water in the southern areas in April–May is evident from Ommaney's and our data (Fig. 2e). It is only in this period that breeding begins here. Ommaney was mistaken in interpreting this phenomenon as the appearance of a second generation. *R. gigas* remains in the Antarctic surface water until late June (Ommaney, 1936, Fig. 11).

All these facts show that the zone of surface water inhabited by *R. gigas* moves during the summer from the north to the south. Lack of appreciation of the seasonal differences in the distribution of this species has led to errors in determining its biogeographical characteristics. In this way Ottestad (1932) called it Subantarctic, Vervoort (1957) and Naumov (1964) considered it as Antarctic, Beklemishev (1958) as lower Antarctic, while Schmaus and Lenhofer (1927) believed that it inhabited the surface water in Antarctica and descended to deeper waters north of 50°S. It is now clear that the data of these authors reflected only the different seasonal distributional pattern in *Rhincalanus*. Its range, taking all the finds together, is shown in Fig. 3, from which it is apparent that *R. gigas* inhabits both Antarctic and Subantarctic zones.

During the summer period each of the species investigated has two maxima of biomass concentration in the surface layer. The first occurs in spring following the upward migration and growth of overwintered plankters. This maximum is caused only by the redistribution of plankters within the inhabited layer and is not followed by an increase in their total number. The greater biomass maximum is observed in each species when the IV copepodite stage dominates its population. In the preceding period the biomass is low due to the low weight of the early stages, while later on it decreases because of the autumnal migration and the dispersal of the population throughout the deep water. The dependence of the total biomass of *R. gigas* and *Calanus acutus* in the upper 500 m layer on the age composition of the population is shown in Fig. 4. It is clear that this factor is more important than local differences in numbers. Since the time of domination of each copepodite stage comes earlier in the north and is progressively later in the southern regions, the timing of the summer biomass maximum has the same changes in space.

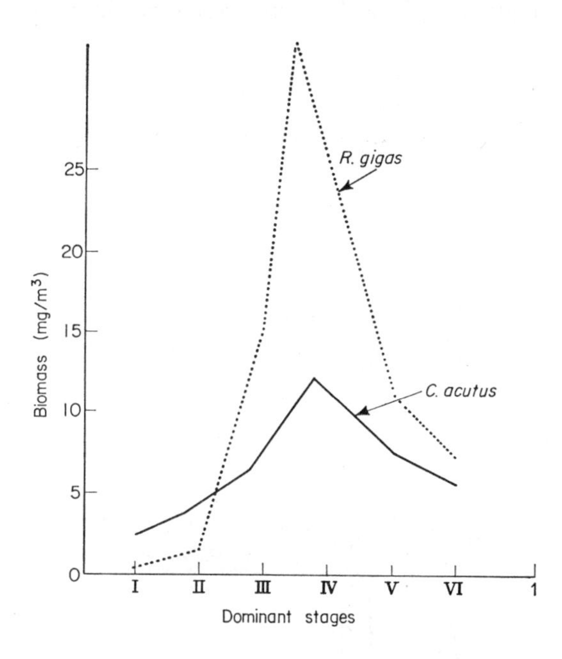

FIG. 4. Relationship between *R. gigas* and *C. acutus* biomass and the age composition of their stock. Data from about 100 stations are used in this figure.

Besides seasonal biomass maxima there exist peaks caused by the mechanical transport of plankton to the Convergence and Divergence zones by the meridional components of the current. There water moves in a vertical direction, but the pelagic animals which can actively maintain a constant vertical distribution can obviously stay and accumulate at a preferred depth. The redistribution of plankton biomass by currents was considered in a previous paper (Voronina, 1968). In summer, when the majority of the plankton inhabits the surface layers, such aggregations emerge as a rule in the zones of downward water movement. In winter, when plankton is concentrated in deep water, aggregations are found in the zones of upward water movement. This is why a maximum of overwintering copepods is found in spring in the Divergence zone. Owing to favourable food conditions, a numerous brood is produced in this area. This rich plankton is carried with the Antarctic surface water in a northward direction. Its displacement from the Divergence depends both on the time and on the velocity of the current. The position on different sections of *R. gigas* maximia which had arisen at the Divergence is shown in Fig. 5. A belt of increased numbers is also clearly seen on a *Rhincalanus* distribution map. A most pronounced biomass peak occurs when the plankters in such patches reach the older copepodite stages.

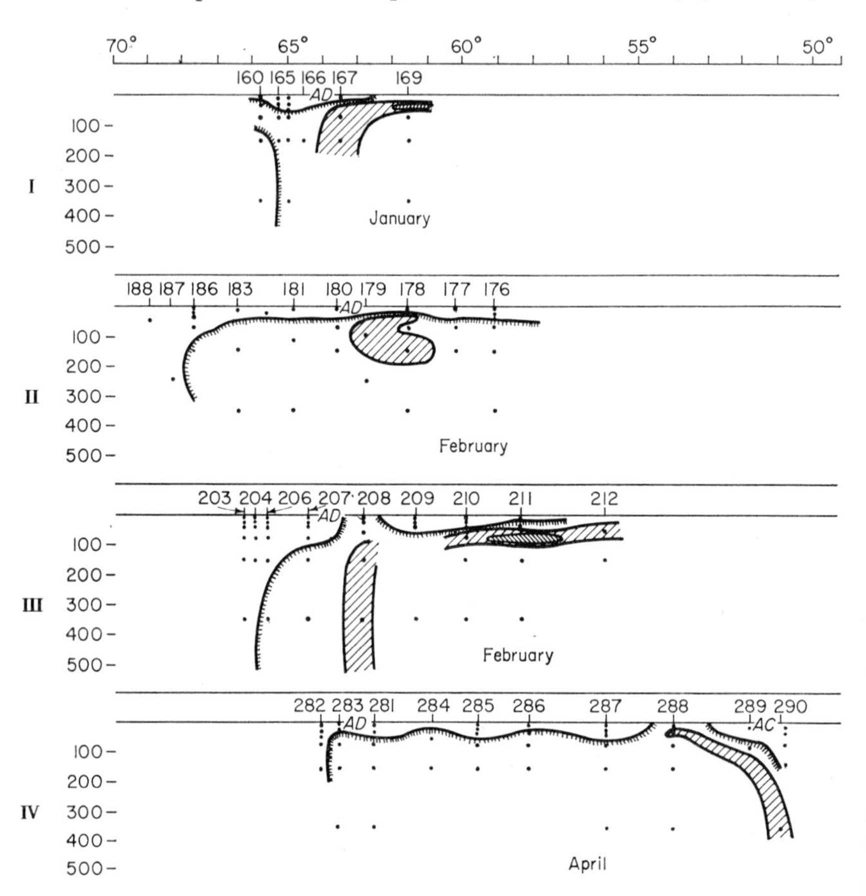

FIG. 5. Distribution of *R. gigas* along four sections. I. The section along 91°E, January 1957; II. The section along 77°E, February 1957; III. The section along 58°E, February 1957; IV. The section along 98°E, April 1957.
AC, Antarctic Convergence; AD, Antarctic Divergence; Heavy line, boundary of distribution; Unshaded within line, less than 100 specimens/m³; Light hatching, 100–999 specimens/m³; Close hatching, over 1000 specimens/m³.

B. The Life Cycle of Other Copepod Species

The ranges of distribution of *C. acutus* and *C. propinquus* are narrower than that of *R. gigas*. But the annual cycles of all these copepods are similar in the existence of meridional differences in the timing of breeding. The cycles of *R. gigas* and *C. acutus* are also similar in the existence of such differences in the timing of seasonal migrations. This is why the boundaries of distribution of *C. acutus* in the surface water also vary with the season. As is shown in Fig. 6, the distribution of all three copepods is widest at the beginning of summer and progressively narrows with the passage of time.

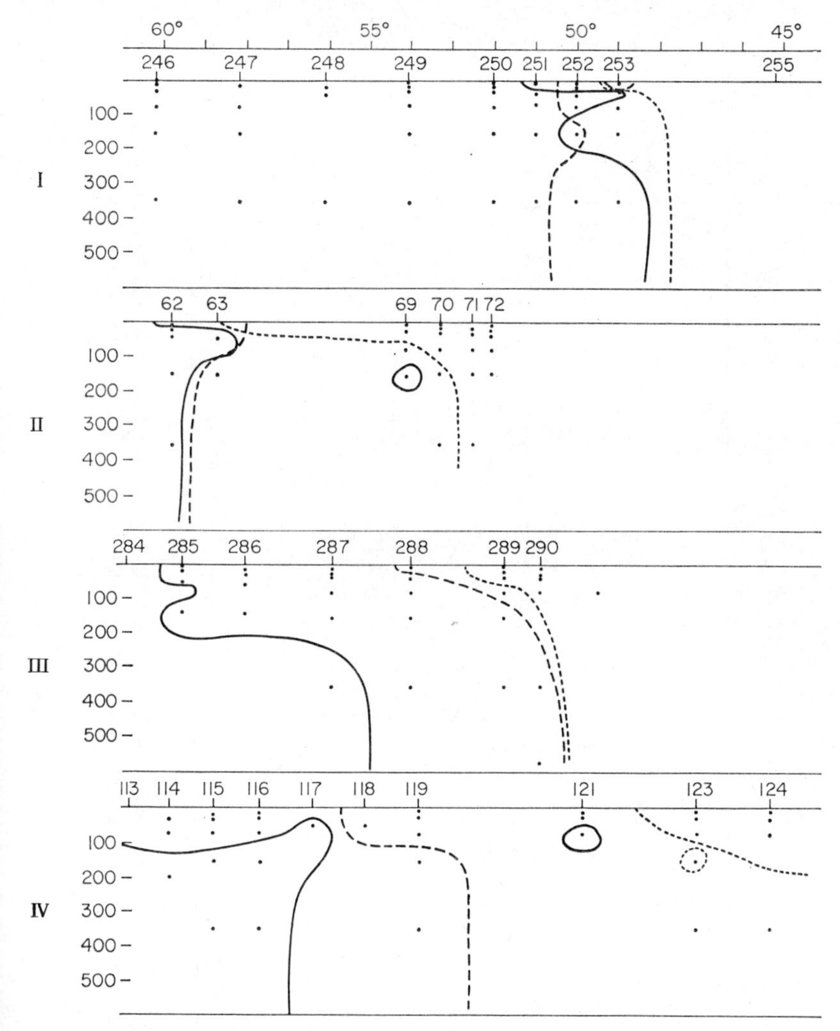

FIG. 6. The northern boundaries of three copepod species at different times. I. Section along 20°E, February–March 1957; II. Section south from New Zealand, March–April 1956; III. Section south from New Zealand, March 1958; IV. Section from Mirny to Aden, May 1956. ————, *C. acutus*; – – – – –, *C. propinquus*, ..., *R. gigas*.

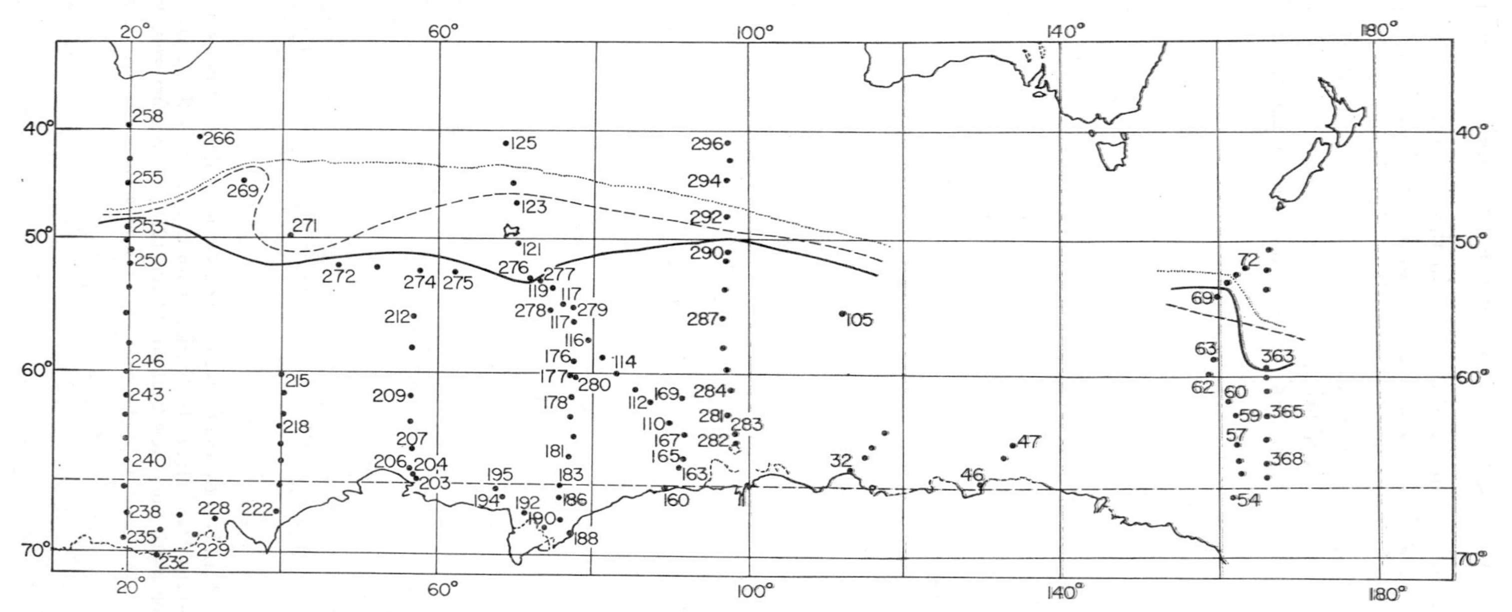

FIG. 7. The northern boundaries of distribution of three copepod species in the 500–0 m layer in the second part of the summer. ————, *C. acutus*; – – – –, *C. propinquus*; ...., *R. gigas*.

The biomass maxima of *C. acutus* and *C. propinquus* also depend on the age composition of their populations and on their redistribution by currents. But the cycles of these species differ in their timing. The breeding period, the time of domination of each copepodite stage, and the time the summer biomass maximum is attained in a particular region generally occurs in a distinct order, first in *C. acutus*, then in *C. propinquus*, and last in *R. gigas*. In late summer *C. acutus* leaves the surface water earlier than *R. gigas*. Such differences in the timing of seasonal downward migration results in the northern boundary of distribution of *C. acutus* being the southernmost and that of *R. gigas* the northernmost of all three species (Figs. 6 and 7).

Different timing in the summer biomass maximum in these copepods provides a mechanism leading to the spatial isolation of their maxima. As a rule the maximum biomass of *C. acutus* is developed in a more southern position

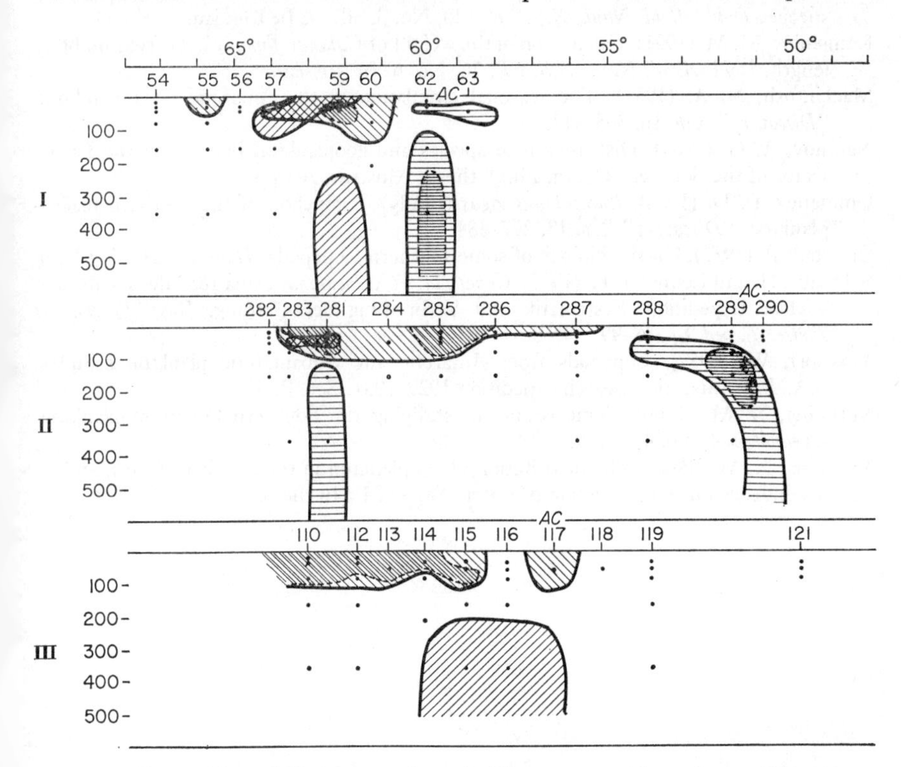

FIG. 8. The position of biomass maxima of different copepod species on *Ob* sections. I. Section south from New Zealand, March–April 1956; II. Section along 98°E, April 1957; III. Section from Mirny to Aden, May 1956. AC, Antarctic Convergence; [hatching], *C. acutus* > 25 mg/m³; [hatching], *C. acutus* > 50 mg/m³; [hatching], *C. propinquus*, > 25 mg/m³; [hatching], *C. propinquus* > 50 mg/m³; [hatching], *R. gigas* > 25 mg/m³; [hatching], *R. gigas* > 50 mg/m³.

from that of *C. propinquus* or in a deeper layer, while the maximum of *R. gigas* is the northernmost of them (Fig. 8). It seems that in the Antarctic Convergence zone, where there is a mechanical concentration of the plankton, the prevailing species succeed one another in the same order.

The biological importance of all these facts is obvious. The sequence in appearance in the plankton of the numerous herbivorous species increase the intensive grazing period and the degree of phytoplankton utilization. The spatial differences in the maxima of different species decrease the competition between them.

References

Beklemishev, C. W. (1958). The biogeographical nature of some Antarctic zooplankton species. *Dokl. Akad. Nauk. S.S.S.R.* **120**, No. 3, 507–9. In Russian.

Kamshilov, M. M. (1951). Calculation of the weight of *Calanus finmarchicus* from its body length. *Dokl. Akad. Nauk. S.S.S.R.* **76**, No. 6. In Russian.

Mackintosh, N. A. (1937). The seasonal circulation of the Antarctic macroplankton. *"Discovery" Rep.* **16**, 365–412.

Naumov, A. G. (1964). Distribution of species and zooplankton biomass in the Pacific sector of the Southern Ocean. Ph.D. thesis, Moscow, 208 pp.

Ommaney, F. D. (1936). *Rhincalanus gigas* (Brady), a copepod of the southern macroplankton. *"Discovery" Rep.* **13**, 277–384.

Ottestad, P. (1932). On the biology of some southern Copepoda. *Hvalråd. Skr.* **5**, 61 pp.

Schmaus, H. and Lenhofer, K. (1927). *Copepoda.* 4: *Rhincalanus* Dana 1852 der Deutschen Tiefsee Expedition. Systematik und Verbreitung der Gattung. *Wiss. Ergebn. dt Tiefsee-Exped.* **8**, 358–99.

Vervoort, W. (1957). Copepods from Antarctic and Subantarctic plankton samples. B.A.N.Z. Antarctic research expedition 1929–1931, Ser. B. **3**.

Voronina, N. M. (1966). Some results of studying the Southern Ocean zooplankton. *Okeanolgia* **4**, No. 4, 681–9.

Voronina, N. M. (1968). The distribution of zooplankton in the Southern Ocean and its dependence on the circulation of water. *Sarsia* **34**. (In the press.)

The Biology and the Distribution of the Antarctic Krill

R. R. MAKAROV, A. G. NAUMOV and V. V. SHEVTSOV
Department of Fisheries and Oceanography, Moscow, U.S.S.R.

I. Introduction

In recent years the Antarctic krill, *Euphausia superba* Dana, has been attracting special attention in connection with the study of possibilities for more complete use of world ocean biological resources. This crustacean occurs in fairly large quantities in the Southern Ocean and serves as food for whales and many other Antaractic animals. *Euphausia superba*, being permanently found in massive concentrations, is a highly attractive prospect for a fishery.

Soviet fishery research expeditions began to ascertain the possibilities of utilizing the Antarctic krill in the Atlantic sector of the Southern Ocean in 1962. Methods of search have now been worked out and experimental work has been done on the krill concentrations found.

II. Location of Krill Swarms

The search for krill concentrations has been based on regular relationships which have been demonstrated between the distribution of *E. superba* and a number of environmental features. Daily visual and hydroacoustic observations were of considerable importance in locating the krill concentrations. For the first time a trawl was used for the capture of krill, and this eliminated the problem of gear avoidance by large specimens, which had taken place while using plankton nets.

Echograms registering the presence of krill concentrations were checked by hauls with the midwater trawl. The systematic check of the tracings of the acoustic devices by means of trawling allowed the particular trace pattern produced by krill swarms to be identified, and this in turn greatly facilitated the search for krill concentrations suitable for trawling. Visual observations from the vessels served to detect patches of krill nearer the surface than the acoustic devices and consequently not registered by them.

III. Size, Age and Sex Composition of Krill Swarms

The study of the size distribution in mature and immature specimens of *E. superba* showed that crustaceans of these age classes differ fairly well in size and, as a rule, do not mix. Immature specimens usually average from 31 to 38 mm in length, while the average size of mature specimens within the area investigated ranged from 45 to 49 mm. It is interesting that a slight increase in the average size of the mature crustaceans was noted on sailing from west to east. The sex ratio in the concentrations of immature specimens was equal and more or less constant. In concentrations of mature specimens, however, the sex ratio ranged widely.

The comprehensive data obtained by several expeditions allows the difference in size composition of *E. superba* concentrations in different years to be followed. Both in 1965 and 1967 the investigations were conducted at the same time—in February and March. Specimens of *E. superba* caught in 1965 were larger than those caught in 1967. This difference is evident throughout the whole area investigated and is apparently correlated with differences in the hydrometeorological regime. In 1965 it was warmer than in 1967. Because of the earlier spring, mature and immature specimens began feeding earlier. Rapid growth resulted, and the mature crustaceans began to breed. It is quite natural that by February 1965 individuals had become larger in size than in February 1967, when the development at several stages in the life cycle was delayed because of severe hydrometeorological conditions.

During the 1967 investigations swarms of spawning crustaceans were sighted in the area north-east, north, and north-west of the South Orkney Islands. The quantitative study of the ratio of spawned-out specimens to specimens which had still to spawn showed that spawning of *E. superba* was more advanced in the area north-west of the Islands than in the area to the north-east.

IV. Feeding of Krill

The study of *E. superba* feeding habits showed that phytoplankton is the main item of food. In certain seasons a well-defined diurnal rhythm of feeding with two periods of maximum activity—one in the daytime and the other at night—can be observed in areas rich in phytoplankton. There are further differences in feeding activity in *E. superba* related to reproductive condition, mature males feeding more actively than spawning females, and females that had spawned feeding more actively than other females.

V. Distribution of Krill

Krill distribution is closely connected with a number of environmental parameters and with the distribution of its phytoplankton food. Dense concentrations of *E. superba* were observed in the area where the waters of the West Wind drift mixed with those of the Weddell Current. The area is characterized by a high silicon content, by the specific temperature stratification of the waters and so on. Biologically, the area is the most productive region in the area investigated. The relief of the bottom, which determines the direction of currents, also affects considerably the location where the waters mix. The position of the area of high productivity changes with the seasons and from year to year as a result of the interplay of all these factors.

The krill concentrations can also be found on the periphery of the area of upwelling in the Antarctic divergence zone. Such concentrations were found by the Soviet Antarctic expedition on board the d/e *Ob* in 1957 and 1958. At the same time a massive phytoplankton bloom was observed in the peripheral part of the zone of upwelling, where there were quasi-stationary cyclonic eddies. The rate of vertical movement of the upwelling water does not exceed 8·2 cm/hr, and the concentration of krill cannot reasonably be explained in terms of passive movement. The concentrations must rather be regarded as resulting from trophic factors.

Krill concentrations are very rarely seen in the central oceanic region of the South Atlantic. The main mass of krill is located in the southern part of the Scotia Sea, in the areas adjacent to the island arc. The exact location of the concentrations depends on the periodically changing conditions of the environment. The available data show that the immature specimens are met with to the south of the island arc, in the waters of the Weddell Sea.

It is known that a part of the population of *E. superba* is moved by the Weddell Current from the Weddell Sea to the South Shetland and South Orkney Islands, and further eastward to the South Sandwich Islands. It is quite possible that *E. superba* concentrations move northward from this area to arrive in the waters around South Georgia, where they can be observed in considerable quantities. The complicated relief of the Scotia Sea, with its groups of islands and submarine ridges, leads to the formation of numerous gyrals and local eddy currents which can persist for rather long periods of time and prevent the krill from leaving the area and dispersing. According to observations made in 1965 and 1967, some concentrations remained at the same places in such areas for not less than five weeks.

The analysis of observations of krill concentrations made using acoustic devices, with sampling by trawling, led to the conclusion that the krill concentrations are located within the photic layer of water depths of less than 40 m, and very seldom occur below 70–90 m. The concentrations of crustaceans are lens-shaped swarms of different size, mosaically located. The distribution and the extent of the crustacean concentrations change at different times of the day. The greatest density of concentrations in subsurface layers of the water was recorded during daylight.

The krill patches were observed visually in a number of areas. The rise of swarms to the surface to form visible patches does not obviously depend on weather conditions. In different areas surface patches were observed both in calm weather and with a force seven wind. The abundance of sea birds feeding on krill concentrations in the surface waters helps to indicate the presence of such patches. The sizes of patches and the density of crustaceans in them fluctuate, and patches from 0·5 × 1 m up to 150 × 400 m or more were sighted. They contain either mature or immature specimens. Experimental catches and underwater photographs showed that the density of the crustaceans in a patch increases from the periphery to the centre; furthermore the crustaceans are located parallel to each other with their heads in the same direction. Densities of 15 kg per cu. m or more have been encountered.

The Consumption of Krill by Antarctic Fishes

YU. E. PERMITIN
VNIRO (All-Union Research Institute of Marine Fisheries and Oceanography), Moscow, U.S.S.R.

The available information about the abundance of krill (*Euphausia superba*) in the Antarctic is somewhat contradictory. There is a belief that the production of krill is greater than the world catch of fish. The ability of krill to form vast concentrations in the pelagic waters of the Antarctic, the fact that krill is easily available to those organisms which feed on it, and the high calorie content of krill suggest that it is a principal link in the complex trophic interactions of the Antarctic.

It has been difficult so far to define the proportion of the total biomsas of krill taken by different consumers. Whales have probably always taken the largest share. The role of fishes as consumers of krill seems, however, to be much more important than was believed earlier. A number of investigators—among them Lönnberg, Gunther, Tattersall, and more recently Marr, Nybelin, Olsen, and Andriashev—have found krill in the stomachs of Antarctic fishes. Investigations carried out by Soviet scientists in 1965, 1967, and 1968 on board the VNIRO research vessel *Academic Knipovich*, as well as studies on the feeding habits of some fishes commonly encountered in the Scotia Sea, showed that during the warmer months of the year krill was an important, and in some cases the main, food of some bottom-living or near-bottom-living as well as pelagic, bathypelagic, and epipelagic fishes. Krill was found in the stomachs of thirty-one fish species belonging to the twelve families Rajidae, Paralepidae, Myctophidae, Scopelarchidae, Muraenolepidae, Gadidae, Moridae, Macruridae, Nototheniidae, Bathidraconidae, Chaenichthyidae, and Trichiuridae.

However, the significance of krill and the frequency of its occurrence in the diet of these fishes varies and depends on the degree of the morphological adaptation of different species to its consumption. O. Nybelin considered the temporary movement of some bottom-living Antarctic fishes into pelagic waters as an adaptation enabling them to utilize the rich food resources of the krill zone which surpasses by far the productivity of benthos. As Belyaev and Ushakov (1957) demonstrated, the total biomass of benthos off the coasts of East Antarctica is on the average quite high, amounting to 450–500 g/m²; however, it consists mainly of the non-food benthos groups, such as Porifera, Bryozoa, and Ascidiae, which make up 60–90% of the total mass of organisms.

In analysing the bottom fauna of the Antarctic it is usually emphasized that the shelf area is quite small. The shelf area of the Scotia Sea, which in some places is as deep as 500 m, amounts to only 5·8% of the entire sea area. The low biomass of benthic organisms available as food and the small shelf area as well as the high abundance of easily available food (krill) in pelagic waters may have caused adaptive variability and partial transition of some primarily bottom-living Antarctic fishes belonging to families Nototheniidae, Chaenichthyidae, and Bathidraconidae to life in pelagic waters, feeding on krill.

Antarctic *Notothenia* provide an example of changes which occur in the outward morphological structure of some species in relation to their transition from a bottom-living habit to temporary life in pelagic waters where they can feed on krill. The demersal species *Notothenia gibberifrons* and *N. nudifrons* with inferior mouth, eyes on the upper part of the head, body somewhat flattened dorsoventrally and protective coloration feed mainly on benthic organisms such as Polychaetae, Gammaridae, and molluscs. Twenty-two benthic species occurred among other food items in *N. gibberifrons*. For example, 58% of fish had Polychaeta in their stomachs. However, krill also makes an important contribution to the diet of these fish, occurring in the stomachs of 44% of the 600-odd specimens examined. These fish do not migrate vertically to feed on krill. Their habitat is limited to the insular shelves in the Scotia Sea and along the Antarctic Peninsula.

Of all the Antarctic *Notothenia* species *N. larseni* has the most pronounced pelagic structure, with an elongated body, terminal mouth, eyes located almost at the level of the longitudinal axis of the body, and so on. *N. larseni* was often collected near the surface in the places where krill was concentrated. The main food components are macroplanktonic (krill) and pelagic (Hypperiidae) organisms which occurred in 64% of the fish examined (240 specimens). It is believed that the more the species is adapted for pelagic life, the wider its area of distribution will be. *N. larseni* accords with this hypothesis occurring off both West and East (Balleny Island) Antarctica.

N. macrocephala, which is widely distributed in the temperate waters of the South Ocean and occurs off Archipel de Kerguelen and Macquarie Island was found in the Scotia Sea off the South Orkney Islands and South Georgia. This eurythermal species has typical pelagic colouration: the upper part of the body and the head is dark blue, while the belly and the lower part of the body are silvery with a metallic sheen. The fish caught in the pelagial in the areas where krill concentrations occurred had their stomachs full of this crustacean. Like *Micromesistius australis*, *N. macrocephala* seems to spawn in the Subantarctic waters of the southern Hemisphere and to feed in the productive Antarctic waters in the areas where krill is concentrated. A most interesting discovery was recently made by Hureau (1966), who found that *N. macrocephala* has pelagic eggs.

The life of *Notothenia rossi marmorata* is closely connected with the pelagic krill zone of the Antarctic. The morphology of these demersal-pelagic fish, which are bigger than other Antarctic *Notothenia*, with powerful locomotor musculature and a big terminal mouth, allows them to perform vertical and horizontal migrations to the pelagial in search of krill and to feed actively on this organism. In the summers of 1965 and 1967 these fish were observed near the surface in krill concentration areas and 93% of the 200 fish examined had their stomachs full of krill. Between 1000 to 1900 specimens of krill 33 to 36 mm long were found in each stomach, and this was equivalent to 5·2–11·3% of the weight of fish.

According to our data, the habitat of *Dissostichus eleginoides* extends as far as South Georgia. In the stomachs of these big predatory fish we observed *Champsocephalus gunnari* and *N. larseni*, which feed mainly on krill. The small specimens examined had krill, Mysidacea, and Decapoda in their stomachs.

A close connection with krill was also observed in some species belonging to the family Chaenichthyidae. In these fish the degree of adaptation to feeding on krill seems also to be reflected by their morphology, and notably by body shape, fat content, colouration, and fine structure.

Champsocephalus gunnari often occurred in the pelagial. Some 73% of the 346 fish examined contained krill and 2% had pelagic Myctophidae in their stomachs. This species must be much more widely distributed than was believed earlier. Specimens were obtained in the Scotia Sea near South Orkney and South Shetland Islands.

Krill seems to be a very important component in the diet of *Pseudochaenichthys georgianus*. Like *Notothenia rossi marmorata*, these fish perform feeding migrations to the open sea, where krill concentrates. Their food range seems to be very narrow: krill was discovered in the stomachs of 36% and fish in the stomachs of 35% of the 280 specimens examined. *P. georgianus* has a number of adaptive characters related to the extension of its ecological niche into the open sea. Besides the poor calcification of the skeleton, which is typical of most Chaenichthyidae, *P. georgianus* is characterized by a more powerful body and consequently a higher locomotor function and a greater accumulation of fat in the flesh, body cavity, and liver, thus decreasing the specific weight of the body and increasing its buoyancy. As may be inferred from the investigations conducted by Aliev (1963), the buoyancy of pelagic and demersal-pelagic fish, as a rule, is close to neutral. Accumulation of fat is one of the factors contributing to a decrease in the specific weight of the body of fish and other marine animals and, consequently, an increase of buoyancy. A chemical analysis carried out by my colleague Mrs T. Dubrovskaya showed that in summer the fat content of *P. georgianus* amounted to 7·7% in the flesh and 21% in the liver. The demersal *Chaenocephalus aceratus* had a fat content as low as 1% in the flesh and 14·1% in the liver.

Within the family Chaenichthyidae pelagic adaptations are particularly conspicuous in *Neopagetopsis ionah*. This species, earlier observed in the waters of eastern Antarctica, was recorded in the Scotia Sea off the South Orkney and South Sandwich Islands as well as in the pelagial over great depths in the northern Weddell Sea. The morphology of *N. ionah*, which has highly developed paired fins, a notched tail, very poor calcification of the skeleton, and typical pelagic colouration, seems to confirm its pelagic mode of life. These pelagic features are particularly obvious in young specimens with a standard length from 191 to 242 mm. Nybelin (1947) and Andriashev (1960) pointed out that *N. ionah* seemed to spend their feeding period somewhere in the pelagial far from the shore and to feed on krill. The stomachs of the fish caught were full of krill. Thus the stomach of a specimen with an overall length of 265 mm contained seventy-eight specimens of crustaceans 15 to 40 mm long. The correlation of all data on the occurrence of *N. ionah* available so far seems to suggest that this species has a circumpolar distribution in the Antarctic.

Krill is an important component of the food of the bathypelagic Myctophidae of the Scotia Sea. It is believed that the factor limiting the utilization of krill by the Antarctic Myctophidae is the size of these fish. Krill occurred in the stomachs of 24–27% of the total of 277 small bathypelagic *Protomyctophum tenisoni* and *Electrona antarctica* examined (standard length up to 90 mm). In the bigger *Gymnoscopelus nicholsi* krill is the main component of the food, occurring in the stomachs of 83% of the total of 161 specimens examined. These bathypelagic fish seem to make vertical migrations to the surface waters to feed on krill.

Our data appear to suggest that only the adult population of *Micromesistius australis* occurs in the Scotia Sea, and that it migrates here from the Patagonian and Falkland areas. The stomachs of about 1000 fish analysed were full of krill. Merrett (1963) was the first to draw our attention to the fact that *M. australis* fed on krill. According to Harts (1946) this species breeds in the Patagonian and Falkland regions.

Krill is also a component of the food of *Raja georgiana*. The range of this species which is generally considered to be an endemic of the South Georgian region, extends to 60°S and probably even as far south as the Antarctic Peninsula. Large mature skates feed mainly on fish, but the stomachs of small immature skates contained benthic organisms such as Polychaeta, Mysidacea, and Decapoda, and krill (23% of the total of forty-three stomachs analysed).

The occurrence of *Paralepis atlantica prionosa*, *Anatopterus pharae*, *Pseudoicichthys australis*, *Notothenia macrocephala*, and *Paradiplospinus gracilis* in the epipelagial of the Scotia Sea seems to suggest that the epipelagic water of the Antarctic which is described by many authors as a highly productive krill zone is the feeding-place of not only whales, seals, birds, and Antarctic fishes, but also of fishes typical of the Subantarctic and Subtropical epipelagial of the Southern Hemisphere. This group of fishes is characterized by the wide separation of feeding and reproductive areas. Their breeding areas lie in the Subantarctic and Subtropical zones of the Southern Hemisphere. Long seasonal feeding migrations to the Antarctic such as their adult populations perform to feed on krill are only possible because of the existence of the warm intermediate deep water current which flows southwards in the Southern Ocean. The water masses that make up this current are of subtropical origin and in the South Atlantic they form a layer at depths between 200 and 1000 m (Deacon, 1933; Ivanov, 1961). It is this layer that is used by fish such as the Myctophidae *P. atlantica prionosa*, *A. pharae*, and others, and from this layer they ascend to the surface to feed on krill. In contrast to the morphological adaptations of the bottom-living fishes of Antarctic origin, belonging to the families Nototheniidae, Chaenichthyidae, and Bathidraconidae which ascend and move in the epipelagial to feed on krill, the latitudinal and vertical migrations of Subantarctic warm-water epipelagic fish to the Antarctic seem to be possible because these fish possess a high degree of temperature adaptation and are consequently able to tolerate wide movement between the different water masses in the Southern Ocean.

Conclusion

Krill (*Euphausia superba*) plays an important role in the trophic interactions of the fish fauna of the Southern Hemisphere. It is a major food source for a number of species and an additional one for an even greater number of Antarctic, Subantarctic, and even Subtropical fish.

References

Aliev, Yu. G. (1963). "Functional basis of the exterior structure in fish", 3–246.

Andriashev, A. P. (1960). Families of fishes new to the Antarctic. Paradiplospinus antarcticus, gen. et sp. n. (Pisces, Trichiuridae), *Zool. Zhurn.* XXXIX 2, 4, 7, 244–9.

Andriashev, A. P. (1965). A general review of the Antarctic Fish Fauna. *In* "Biogeography and Ecology in Antarctica", Tunk, Den Haag, pp. 491–550.

Belyaev, G. M. and Ushakov, P. V. (1957). Certain regularities in the quantitative distribution of bottom fauna in Antarctic waters, *Doklady Akad. Nauk, SSSR*, 112(I), 137.

Bigelow, H. B. and Schroeder, W. C. (1965). Notes on a small Collection of Rajids from the Sub-Antarctic Region, *Limnology and Oceanography* V, 10 R 38–R–49.

Bussing, W. A. (1965). Studies of the midwater of the Peru-Chile Trench. *In* "Biology of the Antarctic Seas", II-Antarct. Res. Ser., 5.

Deacon, G. E. R. (1933). A general account of the hydrology of the South Atlantic Ocean, *"Discovery" Rep.* 7, 171–238.

Haedrich, R. L. (1967). The Stromateoid fishes: Systematics and a Classification, *Bull. Museum Compar. Zool. Hon.* **135**, N 2.

Hureau, J. C. (1966). Biologie Comparée de quelques poissons antarctiques (Nototheniidae). Thése.

Hart, T. J. (1946). Report on trawling surveys on the Patagonian Continental Shelf, *"Discovery" Rep.* 23, 223–408.

Merrett, H. R. (1963). Pelagic gadoides in the Antarctic, *Norsk Hvalfangst-tid.*, **52**, No. 9.

Ivanov, Ju. A. (1961). On the factors forming the therming stratification in the Antarctic waters.

Moss, S. A. (1962). Melamphaidae II, a new Melamphaid genus *Sio* with a redescription of *Sio nordenskjoldi* (Lonnberg), *Dana Rep.* **56**.

Norman, J. R. (1937). Coast fishes. Part II: The Patagonia Region, *"Discovery" Rep.* **16**, 1–150.

Norman, J. R. (1938). Coast fishes. Part III: The Antarctic Zone, *"Discovery" Rep.* **18**, 1–105.

Nybelin, O. (1947). Antarctic fishes, *Sci. Res. Norw. Antarct. Exp.* 1927–1928. **26**, 1–76.

Parin, N. V. (1968). "Epipelagical oceanic Ichtiofauna", Moscow.

Permitin, Yu. E. (1966). Some new data on specific composition and distribution of fish in the Sea Scottia, *Probl. Ichthyol.* **6**, 3, 424–31.

Rofen, R. R. (1966). Family Paralepididae. *In* "Fishes of the Western North Atlantic", Part 5—Mem. Sears Found Mar. Res.

Rofen, R. R. (1966). Family Anotopteridae. *In* "Fishes of the Western North Atlantic", Part 5—Mem. Sears Found. Mar. Res.

Whales and Plankton in Antarctic Waters

B. A. ZENKOVICH
All-Union Research Institute of Marine Fisheries and Oceanography (VNIRO), Moscow, U.S.S.R.

I. The Food and Feeding Behaviour of Whales

For many years scientists have sought to determine the quantity of zooplankton eaten by whales, and I have collected data on whales feeding in various areas of the world ocean and in Antarctic waters for a considerable period. Records of the abundance of some species of whale have also been compiled. The number of whales caught from the beginning of whaling in the Antarctic, in 1904, until the end of 1965 has been calculated. Direct measurements have been made of the amount of food found in the stomachs of freshly killed whales which had been killed instantaneously by a single harpoon (important because wounded whales usually vomit their food). Either the volume (in litres) or weight of the food present was determined. This amount of food was regarded as that eaten by the whales at one time, provided that the stomach was full. But numerous observations over many years showed that in cold areas rich in food whales feed not less than four times per day, and sometimes even more often. Food is digested very quickly by whales, and if a whale which has just fed is killed by one harpoon, but is not examined until 3–4 hr after killing its stomach usually contains the remains of digested Crustacea only as a thin gruel. There are several considerations which should be taken into account when studying the feeding of whales. Whales inhabiting cold waters, in the vicinity of ice, probably consume much more food, and perhaps feed more often than whales living in moderate or warm waters, but digestion is the same under all these conditions. It could be that stomachs of whales in warm waters were only occasionally completely filled with food and that at other times they remained half empty. However, some whales killed in warm waters proved on examination to have full stomachs. Stomachs of whales taken near ice are as a rule always filled or almost filled. Except when such whales are lying without movement near the surface (perhaps asleep?), they feed very intensively, dive regularly and "spout" with corresponding frequency when appearing near the surface. Age and condition provide further variables. Large old whales are believed to feed more intensively than young whales and pregnant females also apparently feed more intensively than other whales.

It was noted long ago that very large whales usually fatten near ice, and this suggested that they fed on the crustaceans which are so densely concentrated in this area at the junction between the waters of ice zone and warmer waters. Whales, however, consume a great amount of phytoplankton and this is of great importance in their feeding, although it is not generally sufficiently considered in the literature. Phytoplankton is especially important in the cold zones of the world ocean. The role of phytoplankton as a health factor is considered in other papers.

Bearing in mind these general principles, the following conclusions about the food consumption of the different whale species can be drawn.

II. Abundance and Food Consumption of Whale Species

A. Blue Whales

In total 331,142 blue whales were caught in the Antarctic waters during whaling operations from 1904/5 to 1965/6. The stock at the beginning of whaling can be estimated as about 100,000 individuals. Food consumption at any one time—the content of full stomach—is one ton of planktonic organisms. Consumption per day is therefore about four tons of planktonic crustaceans, mainly Euphausiidae. Blue whales stay in the Antarctic on average for 120 days in each year. Thus, at the beginning of the whaling period the unexploited stocks of blue whales must have eaten about 50 million tons of planktonic organisms, mainly crustaceans, in Antarctic waters. At present blue whales have been virtually exterminated.

B. Fin Whales

During the same sixty-one-year period not less than 671,092 fin whales were caught. The stock at the beginning of whaling is estimated as 200,000. A fin whale eats 700 kg of planktonic crustaceans at one feed; individuals feed intensively, taking not less than four meals per day, and they stay in Antarctic waters not less than 120 days in the year. Thus, every fin whale ate about 2800–3000 kg of crustaceans per day or about 360 tons per season. In total fin whales ate about 72 million tons of planktonic crustaceans, mainly Euphausiidae, per annum in the Antarctic.

C. Humpback Whales

During the same period not less than 145,424 humpback whales were taken in the Antarctic and adjacent waters. The take of humpback whales in the whole Southern Hemisphere is included here because this is the only species caught with equal intensity outside the Antarctic and in the cold zone.

The catch of other whales in warm waters made up only an inconsiderable percentage of the total.

The humpback whale stock at the beginning of whaling is estimated as 50,000. Food consumption at one feed is 500 kg of planktonic crustaceans. Humpback whales feed, apparently, not less than four times per day. They also stay in the cold zone about 120 days. Thus, the daily consumption of a humpback whale is up to 2 tons of plankton or about 240 tons for a season, and the total initial stock ate 12 million tons of krill in the Antarctic per annum. At present the species is almost exterminated.

D. Sei Whales

In the period under consideration not less than 87,284 sei whales were caught in the Antarctic, about half of that quantity being taken in two recent seasons because pelagic fleets fished first for blue and humpback whales, then when these became rare, for fin whales and subsequently turned to sei whales after the recent great decline in fin-whale abundance.

The present stock of sei whales is estimated at 75,000. Their food consumption in the cold zone is about 300 kg at any one time. The species stays in the Antarctic waters for up to 100 days. Sei whales move much more rapidly than other whales, and according to our observations, feed more intensively than other baleen whales. It is assumed that they feed not less than five times per day. The daily consumption of every sei whale in the cold zone is thus about 1·5 tons of krill. Consequently, during a season every sei whale eats about 150 tons of planktonic crustaceans, and the total population of sei whales eats about 12 million tons (11,250,000 tons) of krill.

III. Discussion

Taken together, the unexploited stocks of large baleen whales therefore consumed about 150 million tons of planktonic crustaceans, mainly Euphausiidae per season in Antarctic waters. Taking the average weight of a blue whale as 100 tons, that of fin whale as 50 tons, a humpback whale as 40 tons, and that of sei whale as about 17 tons, the total weight of these whales at the beginning of whaling when whale stocks were not exploited was 23,250,000 tons. This figure applies not only to the Antarctic but to the whole Southern Hemisphere. All the whale species feed in intermediate and warm-water zones, where they find a sufficient amount of food, but their diet there slightly changes, and a great amount of cephalopods and small, mainly pelagic, fish are eaten in addition to planktonic crustaceans.

As was mentioned above, blue and humpback whales are now virtually exterminated, the number of fin whales greatly reduced, and only sei whales are comparatively numerous. Thus a great amount of food in the form of krill is not being used by whales.

Discussion

PRIMARY PRODUCTION

A. J. HORNE

Caution is needed in the interpretation of the high rates of primary productivity which have been reported by Dr El-Sayed. Prof. Fogg and myself have recently studied the primary productivity in the sea near Signy Island in a study to be published shortly. We have found that there is a short-lived peak of primary production, chlorophyll A and biomass which follows the ice break-up. Sampling whilst on a sea cruise could easily be at such a peak or in the low either side and an extrapolation from one point in time to a whole season could be misleading. Some of the spatial variability in productivity might disappear if all the values were related to comparable stages in the annual cycle.

G. E. FOGG

In the open waters, although nutrient concentration may be high, the rate of diffusion to the cells may still be limiting for plankton growth. With ice-attached organisms there will be better stirring, because of the relative movement of water and ice so that these organisms are less limited by nutrient supply.

M. PROPP

Many diatoms occur on floating ice and fast ice. Do we know about the productivity of such ice-supported organisms in the open sea?

S. Z. EL-SAYED

Dr J. S. Bunt is studying this at Miami. Enormous levels of phytoplankton bloom have been shown to occur beneath thin and pancake ice. Ice seems to attract diatoms mechanistically, or to indicate the natural preference of this epontic flora for this type of ice formation.

In the midst of the phytoplankton bloom I examined it was evident that the diatom cells were concentrated below the thin ice and less dense in open pools, some of which were very clear. The chlorophyll and ^{14}C uptake measurements have been correlated with the species of diatoms and dinoflagellates present.

COMPOSITION OF THE PHYTOPLANKTON AND EPONTIC FLORA

R. DELÉPINE

Between Kerguelen and Iles Crozet patches of Antarctic water with salinity and temperatures like that of water south of the polar front have been studied. The microflora closely corresponds with that described by Dr Balech in his paper.

J. KALFF

Are we sure that the importance of diatoms in the Antarctic phytoplankton is not being overemphasized?

G. HASLE

At maximum I have recorded a diatom standing crop of 2 to 3 $\times$ 10^6 cells/l near the pack ice, at the end of January and in February. Along the Peninsula in mid-to-late February 10^6 flagellate cells/l were recorded, but identification is not feasible due to poor preservation. In the Subantarctic the coccolithophorids are important, with up to 300,000 cells/l of *Coccolithus huxleyi* (also a Northern Hemisphere species). Dinoflagellates reached a maximum of 60,000 cells/l, and were mainly *Exuviaella baltica*, a small species, and unarmoured species. The mixture is a complex one, but I agree that diatoms do predominate in the Southern Ocean as a whole.

J. KALFF

Preservation is important. We just cannot go on using only formalin, which destroys whole groups of flagellates. Other preservatives must be experimented with.

M. J. DUNBAR

Do we know if the epontic algae are the same as those found in the phytoplankton after ice break-up? If the zooplankton standing crop is so high as compared with the phytoplankton, does it not imply that the phytoplankton turnover is rapid?

G. A. KNOX

J. S. Bunt is working on the relationship between ice-attached and plankton algae, but the results are not yet available. So far as rates of turnover are concerned, Dr El-Sayed has shown that blooming in the phytoplankton can be rapid.

G. HASLE

Samples from the South Pacific reveal that epontic diatoms constitute a major component of the phytoplankton, especially near the coast. *Fragilariopsis* species are among these forms, but this genus also includes forms growing on the ice that are not prominent in the plankton.

G. A. KNOX

Those that are released into the water column are presumably available to the detritus feeders.

H. JANETSCHEK

Does the percentage of nannoplankton increase as one approaches the continent? I ask because in high Alpine lakes nannoplankton forms predominate and there are few big plankton organisms.

G. A. KNOX

There is little information on the contribution made by nannoplankton.

C. R. GOLDMAN

About 50% of the plankton in Antarctic lakes are ultraplankton under 5–10 m long. Nannoplankton makes up over 80% of the total plankton.

G. HASLE

Small diatom species are most abundant, especially near the coast, and small *Fragilariopsis* may total millions of cells per litre.

T. J. HART

Ice-attached diatoms are also indirectly important because they absorb solar radiation and encourage ice break-up, facilitating the beginning of the main increase.

ZOOPLANKTON AND ITS CONSUMERS

K. G. MCKENZIE

Did Dr Voronina collect ostracoda as well as copepoda? Ostracods can be valuable as indicators of water masses, as we know from tropical Indian Ocean data.

V. VORONINA

Ostracoda were found, and their total numbers counted, but species were not identified and counted individually.

J. KALFF

Ultimately we must be concerned with production at the various trophic levels. Early nauplii and small adult copepods cannot consume these big diatoms we have heard about. Small flagellates must be very important and we ought to have figures for the small nannoplankton per unit volume.

G. A. KNOX

While small organisms are very important for nauplii of small copepods, adult krill feed mainly on large diatoms. Large blooms may be very important indirectly through the release of material on cell breakdown.

E. BALECH

In some Subantarctic waters *Biddulphia sinensis* may bloom, yet because small zooplankters cannot eat so large a diatom, phytoplankton abundance may be accompanied by a die-back of the zooplankton. Productivity of the higher trophic levels may therefore not be governed by photosynthesis but by the ability of the zooplankton to take diatoms.

N. A. MACKINTOSH

Professor Knox referred to the great difficulties of measurement of rates and quantities. This is evident in the comparison he made between Antarctic and Subantarctic standing crops of plankton based on Foxton's figures. The standing crops appeared the same, but krill was excluded from the Antarctic figures and were they included the Antarctic would appear much richer.

What is the ratio between the biomass of krill and other zooplankton? Marr gave a figure for krill of, I believe, 2·5 to 25 mg/m^2, but this was based in effect on a single sample from surface swarms in one area. He suggested that this could be representative of the Weddell and East Wind drifts, but it might not be. It would be dangerous to assume it was without further evidence. The apparent poverty of the Pacific sector is seen in the *Discovery* data, but whales and krill make their appearance there later than elsewhere. The retreat of the ice eventually exposes a zone comparable in productivity to other sectors, though relatively narrow and far to the south.

S. Z. EL-SAYED

The *Eltanin* worked mostly north of the Convergence, and our investigations in this region showed that chlorophyll levels were low. Dr Hays yesterday said that even at its poorest the Antarctic Ocean was never as poor as the Sargasso Sea. In fact, the Pacific sector of the Antarctic Ocean north of the Convergence is almost as poor as the Gulf of Mexico.

D. ASHTON

What is the migration pattern in krill?

N. A. MACKINTOSH

Essentially vertical rather than horizontal. Krill, like other Antarctic pelagic Crustacea, stay in a band of latitude, and this is done because the eggs sink into the southward-moving warm deep current while the young come into the surface waters which have a northward set. Adult krill could hardly swim one mile per day at maximum.

J. KALFF

In Arctic lakes algal stocks start to increase as soon as melting of the snow cover allows increased light penetration into the water. Maximum populations usually occur at approximately the time of ice break-up. I suspect that in the Antarctic seas, too, the greatest phytoplankton populations may occur at the retreating ice edge. The observed following of the retreating ice by the whales might be associated by their feeding on the krill concentrated in this zone of high phytoplankton biomass.

N. A. MACKINTOSH

My diagram was based on observations outside the ice edge. But I know of little information on how much open water there might be within the ice belt.

S. Z. EL-SAYED

Where do the biomass figures for Antarctic krill come from? Were there extrapolations from the rich areas of the Scotia Sea, for example?

P. A. MOISEEV

In my paper I spoke of the macroplankton of the whole ocean, not just of the Antarctic. There are no good data on the biomass of krill in the Antarctic. However, by analysis of whale stomach contents it is possible to estimate the krill consumption per whale year. This is a take-off value, and the total estimate of 100×10^6 metric tons/annum in the region as a whole results; of course, this figure is provisional only.

H. H. DE WITT

We have taken *Micromesistius* from the New Zealand shelf off South Island.

N. A. MACKINTOSH

The blue whiting (*Micromesistius*) occurs in the North Atlantic, where it is taken commercially. I understand it is concentrated on shelves and slopes, but larvae are found over the whole north-east Atlantic, suggesting open ocean breeding is possible, although I believe the eggs have so far been found only on shelves and banks.

T. ØRITSLAND

Predators like *Micromesistius australis* and other pelagic fishes eat krill all through the twenty-four hours in large numbers. The Leopard seal in the pack ice also relies on krill as a staple diet. In twenty-seven stomachs I found 51 krill on average in each, with 121 as the maximum. Only eight stomachs contained penguin remains.

N. A. MACKINTOSH

All this adds up; but one interesting question is how far these animals can range, for example, from their breeding sites. The great bird colonies in the region of the Antarctic Peninsula can hardly crop the ocean resources far away, but crabeater seals breeding on the pack ice are not similarly restricted by limited sites on land.

P. K. DAYTON

Bird colonies may be limited by the time and energy required and risk involved in foraging over substantial distances and periods of time. Krill may be too far off in terms of time, energy, or risk to be available. In contrast fish can reproduce anywhere in the ocean.

G. A. KNOX

Penguins are ashore only for a short period. Outside the breeding season they range very widely pelagically. We know that crabeater seals are widespread all through the pack-ice zone, and this places them in an ideal position as krill predators.

N. A. MACKINTOSH

What is the foraging range of penguins?

J. L. SLADEN

About 200 miles in the Adélie.

Part IV

THE PELAGIC RESOURCES OF THE SOUTHERN OCEAN

The Pelagic Resources of the Southern Ocean

For many decades Antarctic exploration has been falsely represented as an expensive luxury yielding no return except heroism, obscure scientific data, and endearing pictures of penguins. Yet the first explorations of many Subantarctic islands and the first detailed examination of the Antarctic mainland itself were made for economic reasons, as a part of the short-lived but lucrative sealing industry between 1790 and 1830. In the first half of the present century the Antarctic Ocean supported a valuable whaling industry that was the direct cause of major oceanographic researches, and the recent collapse of whaling occurred only because those responsible for its management were unwilling or unable to heed the warnings which that research produced. Today the vast biomass of krill in these same southern waters is attracting as much attention, and may prove as valuable a resource as seals and whales once did. The papers by Mackintosh, Moiseev, and Gulland in this section review this important field, the second of them calculating that the yield of world fisheries might be doubled by the exploitation of the available surplus of krill. The Soviet work on this subject, described by Moiseev, is one of the two currently active programmes: the other is Japanese and has been described by Nemoto (1968). This research is likely to be one of the most active growing points of Antarctic biology over the coming decade.

Reference

Nemoto, T. (1968). *In* "Symposium on Antarctic Oceanography". Scott Polar Research Institute, Cambridge.

Whales and Krill in the Twentieth Century

N. A. MACKINTOSH
Natural Environment Research Council, London, England *

I. Introduction

The whaling industry has provided both the stimulus and the facilities for collecting data on whales in the Antarctic, and for this reason we have better estimates of the quantities of the commercially important whales than of other major populations in that region. The reduction of the stocks of whales to about a tenth of their former size is probably the only effect of human activities in the Antarctic likely to be large enough to have a measurable effect on the ecosystem as a whole; and so we have the advantage of a measured factor the effects of which can be examined in comparative isolation from those of other factors. This paper, however, will, I hope, show the need for better quantitative data on other components of the fauna. It includes first a review of the past and present magnitudes of the stocks of whales and their future prospects, and then a discussion of the possible effects of their diminution on the quantities of krill and its other consumers.

II. Species and Migrations of Whales

Blue, fin, sei, minke, humpback, southern right, and sperm whales are the species which are or have been taken in the Antarctic since modern whaling began there in 1904. Sperm whales will not be considered here, because they are not consumers of krill and no estimates of their numbers have been made. Only males enter the Antarctic, and they must always have been much fewer than the original numbers of baleen whales; but their consumption of squid might have to be reckoned with in relation to total Antarctic production and consumption. Southern right whales, too, can be left out, for they belong rather to Subantarctic waters and have long been protected. The small minke or lesser rorqual is negligible in the catches, but will be referred to later as a consumer of krill.

Of the blue, fin, sei, and humpback the first two are far the most important

* Whale Research Unit, British Museum (Natural History), England.

to the industry on account of their greater size and original numbers (see Fig. 2). All four species migrate to the colder waters in summer and warmer in winter. Evidence supplied in a number of publications shows that the krill (*Euphausia superba*) must constitute the greater part of the food of blue, fin, and humpback whales (see Mackintosh, 1965, for a discussion of this point and references). I know of no firm estimate of the ratio of krill to total food, but it is probably at least 80% in blue and fin and even more in humpbacks, and they have only some four to five months to consume it in the Antarctic. Sei whales appear to be less dependent on the Antarctic krill. From the distribution of the catches in recent years, the comparatively late arrival of those that enter Antarctic waters, and the fact that their baleen is adapted for feeding on smaller organisms, it seems that sei whales feed more in lower latitudes outside the zone of abundant krill. Probably krill forms less than half the nourishment of the main stock, though penetration into the Antarctic may have increased with the reduction of the larger whales (Nemoto, 1962).

It should be remembered that the baleen whales' migrations are not mass movements at one time, but more in the form of a protracted procession, so that the stock in the Antarctic builds up gradually to a maximum about February and falls to a minimum about July or August, as indicated in Fig. 1.

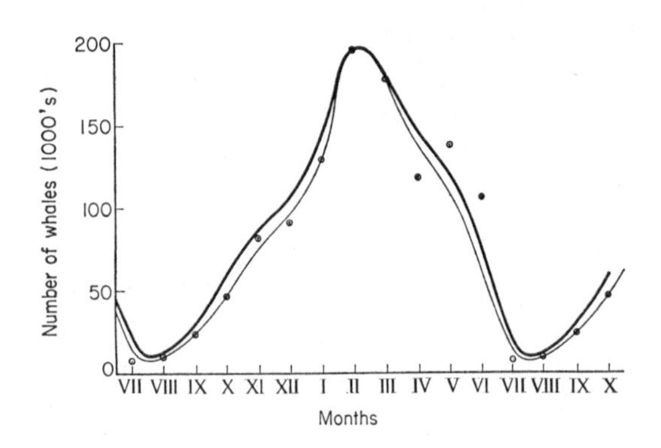

FIG. 1. Estimated seasonal variation in the combined numbers of blue, fin, and humpback whales in ice-free waters in the Antarctic. From Mackintosh and Brown (1956). The heavier line is the "best estimate".

In this figure the vertical scale is of absolute numbers in Antarctic waters of blue, fin, and humpback whales combined, as estimated from sightings in voyages of the RRS *Discovery II* in the period 1933–39. It is to be taken as less than the total stock at the time, and still less than the initial, or original, stocks, since depletion was already in progress in those years.

III. Biomass of the Catches

The history of the catches in the whole Antarctic is shown in Fig. 2, in which the numbers of each species taken (published in the International Whaling Statistics) are converted into weight to give a more correct impression of what has been taken out of the standing stock year by year. Weights

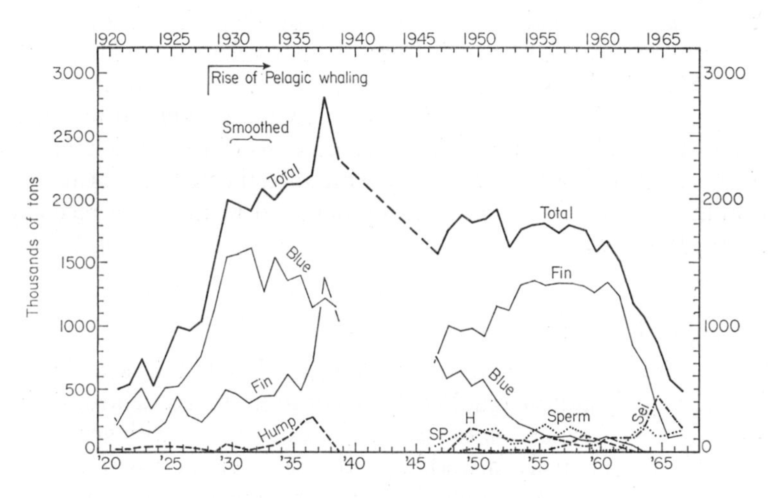

FIG. 2. Tonnage of Antarctic catches.

are less exact than numbers, but can be taken as fair approximations. Values in the diagram for the seasons of 1932–33 to 1958–59 are from a paper by Crisp (1962). For blue, fin, sei, and humpbacks he used formulae relating length to weight from Ash (1952, 1956, and personal communication), and for sperm a formula from Omura (1950). Many of the original records of the body weights of blue and fin whales are in a paper by Nishiwaki (1950). Lengths are available in the Statistics. On the same basis I have extended the calculations for the years since 1959 and before 1932, but have not gone back before 1920, since laborious tabulations are involved and the earliest catches are of minor significance.

Up to the 1920s the catches had no serious effect on the stocks as a whole, though about 1910–15 there was severe "overfishing" of humpbacks, mainly in the Atlantic sector. The total mass of the catches, however, would scarcely have reached 500 thousand tons in any of those earlier years.

It was the development of pelagic whaling from the late 1920s onwards that caused the real trouble, with catches of more than 2 million tons in the 1930s and not much less in the 1950s after the pause during the war. It can be assumed that the catches before 1928 reduced the numbers of whales, but that, with the exception of the Atlantic humpback stocks, they were still above the level at which the maximum yield can be taken (see below, p. 200). The excessive catches since 1929–30 were first concentrated on blue whales, and when that species became scarce it was the fin whales' turn. Recently attention has turned to sei whales, but four sei are the equivalent of only one blue or two fin,* and the steep fall in the tonnage of the catches in the 1960s reflects the severe reduction of the total mass of whales in the sea.

The reasons for this state of affairs are not relevant to this paper (see Ruud, 1956; Mackintosh, 1965, pp. 156 ff.), but it can be said that although the International Whaling Commission has not been able to maintain the stocks at a reasonable level it instituted restrictions without which the decline would have taken place more rapidly with an estimated loss of more than £50 million worth of products actually obtained in the more recent years (Gulland, 1966).

IV. Changes in Stock Sizes

Figure 2 is based on factual records of the catches, but the actual numbers in the sea, roughly indicated in Fig. 3, are not so easily ascertained. Estimates of stock sizes are included in the calculations of a group with special knowledge of population analysis working with the Scientific Committee of the IWC; and their findings are published in the Annual Reports of the Commission, Nos. 14 to 18, 1964 to 1968†. This group has been concerned primarily with current sustainable yields and the status of each species in the last six years, but the pooled data from national research units, together with the records of catches, have allowed calculations back to previous years, and forward to the condition of the stocks under various possible levels of future catching. The essential data for such calculations include catch per unit of effort from industrial sources, mortality rates from age determination and marked whales, rates of recruitment from observations on maturity and pregnancy, and information on the distribution and movements of distinct populations. Stock estimates from sightings have also been used. For the full treatment of the material reference can be made to the Commission's Reports; for short explanations of the essential principles see the 14th Report (1964,

* In "blue whale units" six sei count as equivalent to one blue, but Crisp shows that in body weight the ratio is nearer four to one.

† The constitution of the group has changed from time to time and its reports are not published under the authors' names. It started in 1961 as a committee of three scientists drawn from countries not engaged in Antarctic whaling: D. G. Chapman, K. R. Allen and S. J. Holt, who introduced the methods. They were joined by J. A. Gulland, and much of the recent work has been continued and further developed by him and L. K. Boerema as members of the Fish Stock Evaluation Branch in F.A.O.

p. 42) and Mackintosh (1965, pp. 184–98); see also Holt and Gulland (1964) and Gulland (1966).

Stock sizes in Fig. 3 refer to the numbers of whales entering the Antarctic feeding grounds. The total populations are almost certainly rather more, for some of the smaller, mainly immature, whales seem not to be fully represented

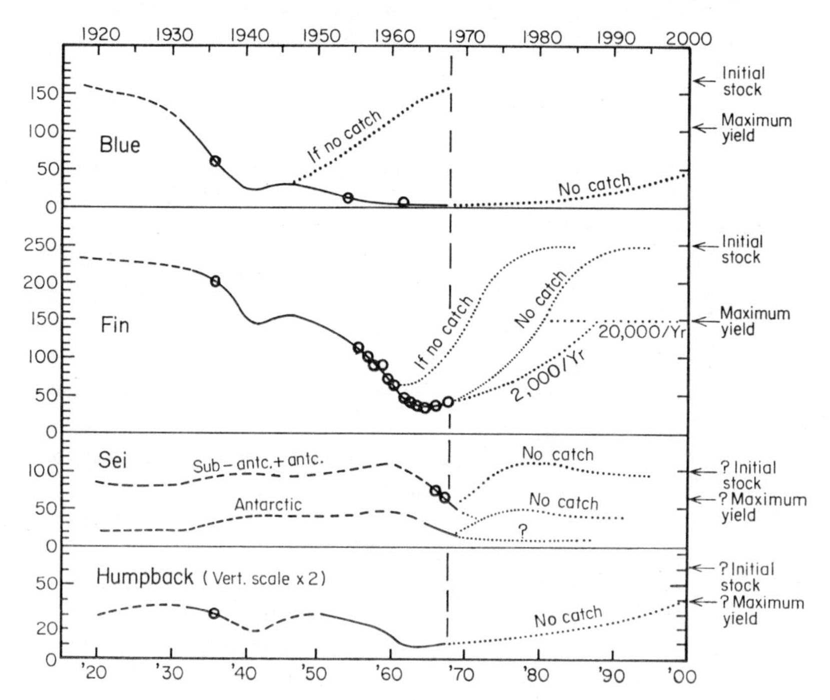

FIG. 3. Estimates of stock sizes in numbers of whales (thousands).

in the Antarctic. The curves are based largely on the group's findings, but I have taken account also of Mackintosh and Brown's estimates (1956) from sightings in the 1930s (middle date, 1936), and filled the gaps with interpolations or extrapolations, guided in part by variations in the catches.

These estimated quantities are at best approximately correct. For different species and different years they vary in accuracy or reliability, and they are subject to revision with more exact biological information, especially on age determination. The diagram, however, should give a broadly correct view of the course of events. Estimates of stock sizes in the 1960s are almost certainly the best approximations. Ringed points on the curves indicate those based on realistic data, and unbroken lines give a fairly reliable view of the trend of numbers. Pecked lines are without such good quantitative data, but should not be far wrong in so far as other calculations are well founded.

Initial stock sizes and the level of maximum yield, marked on the right side, are subject to an even wider margin of error, perhaps about ± 35%. The "initial" stock is the natural, more or less stable population before exploitation, at which recruitment balances mortality. When the stock (P) is reduced the rate of recruitment tends to exceed that of mortality, and the surplus or sustainable yield, P(r–M), is at a maximum at a certain ("optimum") stock size thought to be rather more than half the initial stock. The sustainable yield is the catch which can be taken without reducing the stock or allowing it to increase. At the maximum it appears to be about 4–10% of the stock according to the species. r–M is the net potential rate of increase and the basis for calculating future or hypothetical past stock sizes, either with no catches or with assumed catches in each future year. These are shown by dotted lines.

Taking the species in turn, the stock of blue whales must have been falling sharply in the 1930s. A small increase in the war years can be assumed, and if it had been allowed to continue unchecked the maximum yield might have been available from about 1960, but continued catching brought the stock down by 1963 to about 1000 or even less (excluding the pigmy blue whales which belong more to Subantarctic waters). Blue whales are now wholly protected, but it may be forty to fifty years before they can recover from such a low level to that of the maximum yield.

Later reduction of a probably larger stock has left the fin whales in a better condition. Fin and sei together are subject to an overall catch limit which is now below the estimated current sustainable yield for the two combined, but there is no knowing how the catch will be distributed between them, what future limitation there may be, or indeed whether Antarctic whaling will continue. If catching ceased now, the optimum stock might be reached by 1980. More likely is a catch of, say, 2000 fin a year, allowing for the maximum yield by about 1990, but even this may be too optimistic.

Less is known of the sei whale stocks at all stages, though better estimates are likely to come later. Catches were quite small for many past years, and an initial stock of the order of 100,000 may even have increased a little with the reduction of other baleen whales. (See Bannister and Gambell, 1965, for evidence of an increase at least in South African waters). Heavy taxation since 1960, however, in both Subantarctic and Antarctic, has brought the numbers down. The Antarctic component of the stock, probably rather less than half the total, is shown by a separate line in Fig. 3. Future prospects are unpredictable, but for the estimates which follow, of the biomass supported by krill, the uncertainties of the quantities of sei whales will make no large difference.

Southern humpbacks are segregated into six separate stocks (Mackintosh, 1965). Those in the Atlantic and south-west Indian Ocean must have been severely reduced in the early years, but should have partially recovered by now. Those of the south-east Indian and south-west Pacific are known to have been reduced to a remnant comparable to that of blue whales (Reports of the Commission, and Chittleborough, 1965). A probably small stock in the south-east Pacific should be stable. Humpbacks also are now protected, but the indicated future increase is a little misleading, because the reduced stocks will fare no better than the blue whales, whereas others may be beyond the optimum level by the end of the century. The dotted line, however, assists estimates of the total mass of all whales.

V. Biomass Supported by Krill

The curve in Fig. 4 is obtained from the estimated numbers of each species in Fig. 3, converted into weights from mean lengths and added up after

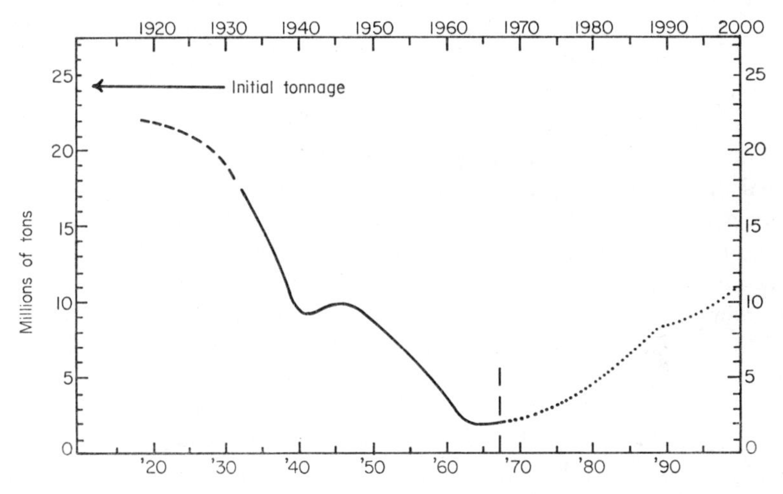

FIG. 4. Estimated biomass of baleen whales (excluding minke) supported by the krill.

deduction to allow for a minor part of total nourishment from food other than krill. Only the Antarctic part of the sei whale stock is included, and a small adjustment is made on the assumption that weight at length is a little less when stock size is at or near its ceiling.

There can be cumulative errors in the estimates of stock sizes and their conversion to weight, but it does seem that the biomass of whales supported by krill has fallen from over 20×10^6 tons to about a tenth of that amount. The curve, if correct, shows a deficit of 22×10^6 tons, and this suggests a corresponding potential surplus of krill. It has been pointed out that the reduction or removal of a consumer does not inevitably result in a surplus of its food. Nor can the possibility be excluded that there has always been a surplus of krill that dies uneaten; if so the amount normally consumed by whales could be a small fraction of the total production. The whales, however, must be one of the larger consumers of the krill in its later growth stages, and the question of what happens to the likely surplus calls for consideration, even if no clear answer can yet be found.

The amount of the potential surplus depends on the whales' rate of consumption, and here we come into difficulties through lack of adequate data. Several authors have made tentative estimates of feeding rates (e.g. Clarke, 1954; Nemoto, 1959; Ivashin, 1961; Marr, 1962; Klumov, 1963). It appears that a whale's stomach can accommodate up to some such quantity as a ton of krill per 40 tons of body weight, and there is evidence of feeding at certain times of day. The majority opinion seems in favour of about a ton a day as the mean feeding rate in a whale of this weight, though Ivashin indicates a much higher rate in humpbacks. But the average period spent by whales in the Antarctic is uncertain, and they are not likely to be feeding all the time. Indeed, the wide variations in the amount of food in stomachs examined and the percentage of empty stomachs (Mackintosh, 1942; Nemoto, 1959) suggest considerable irregularity in the rate of feeding.

With such uncertainties it seems that a near estimate of the true overall annual rate of consumption is scarcely within reach at present. In Fig. 5, however, the "deficit" of whales is converted into a range of possible values for the potential surplus of krill according to various possible rates of consumption. I suppose the rate could not be less than 1·5 times the body weight. For example one ton a day for sixty days' feeding, or less for more days, would be a very modest allowance for a 40-ton whale, as would 2 tons for an 80-ton whale. At the other extreme it seems not quite impossible that a 40-ton whale eats 5 tons a day for 120 days, or fifteen times the body weight. Within these limits a krill surplus could now be anywhere between about 33 million and 330 million tons. Indeed, the range is even greater than this, because estimates of the initial stocks of whales are by no means exact. It can only be said that, say, 100–150 million is a reasonably probable amount.

If such a surplus dies uneaten it will not be annihilated but might be lost to the consumers of krill. The krill, however, is the preferred food of a variety of animals other than whales, and since the food supply is generally a major factor in the limitation of populations it seems inherently probable that one or more of these consumers will take advantage of the greater supply to increase their own numbers. The questions are which of them are likely to do so and whether there are any signs of increased populations. It is the krill-eating vertebrates—seals, birds, and fish, and among other Cetacea the minke whale—that can be considered as the large whales' competitors, and it is the adolescent and adult krill, of about 20–60 mm, mostly in or approaching the second year of growth, that they eat.

The presumed surplus has not become suddenly available; whatever the amount, it can be presumed to have gradually increased, mainly over a period of forty years, so that competitors with a high reproductive potential have no obvious advantage over the slower breeders. Distribution and access to the krill are likely to be the more important factors.

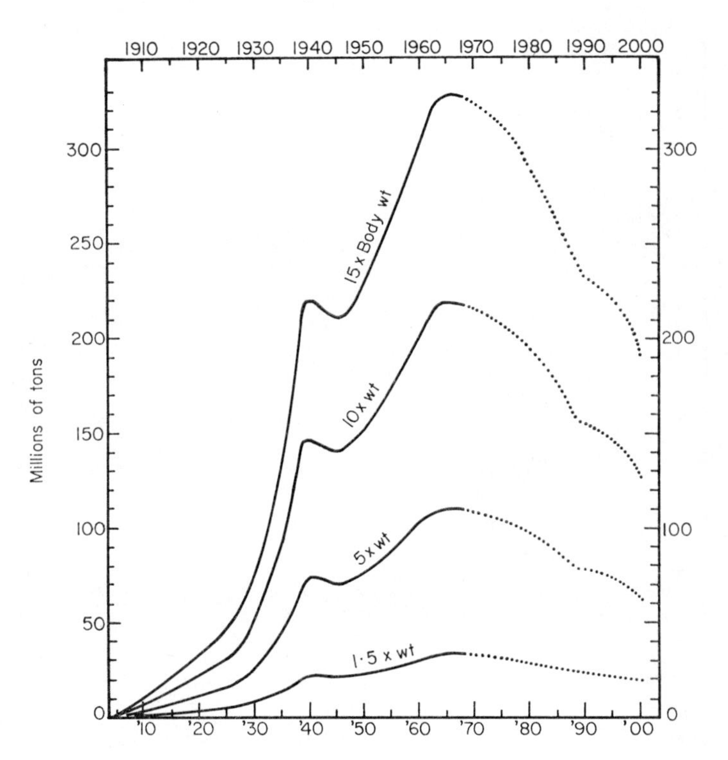

FIG. 5. Potential surplus of krill. Estimates according to various assumed annual rates of consumption by whales, in terms of multiples of a whale's body weight.

VI. Distribution of Krill and Grazing by Whales

Figure 6 is a map of the Antarctic whaling grounds up to about 1960. The shaded area is approximately the whole region covered by the pelagic factories over the years and through the summer months, and it should reflect roughly the distribution of the whales feeding on krill. The recent years are excluded because catching has spread largely into Subantaractic waters in the search for sei whales feeding on other plankton organisms, and the area covered would not then be related to the krill. As it is, the area is a very large one, completely circumpolar; and much of it is very remote from colonies of seals and birds at their breeding sites on the continental coasts and islands. Neither the whales nor the whalers, however, are spread all over this area at any one time. Split up by months, the whaling grounds are seen to constitute a narrower zone, lying in spring at the outer fringe of the total area and shifting south as the pack ice retreats.

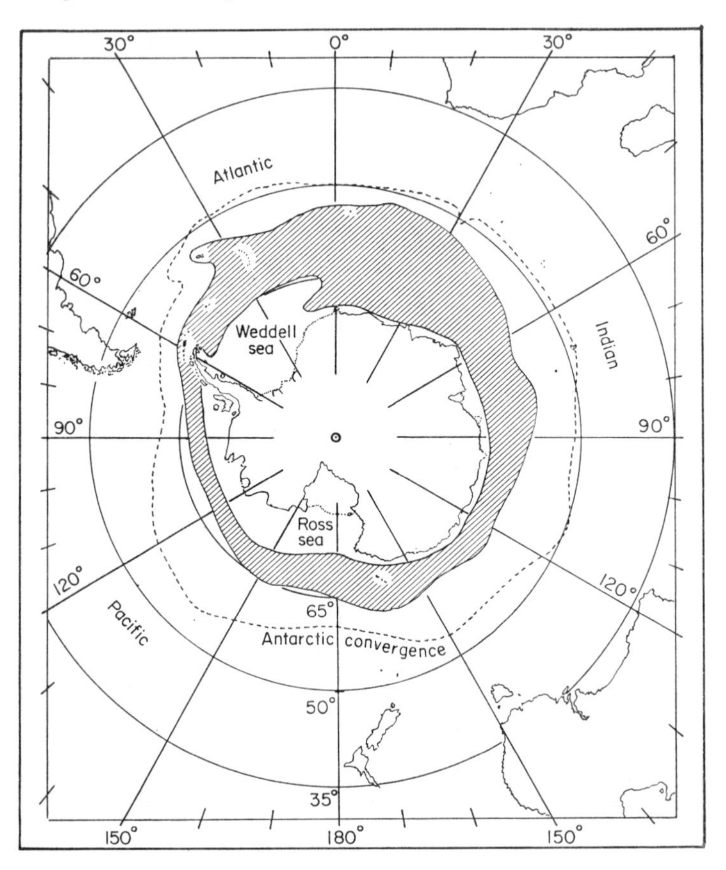

FIG. 6. Approximate area of the Antarctic whaling grounds prior to extension into lower latitudes in the 1960s.

The pack ice is a major factor in the distribution of whales and access to the krill. Its mean northern limit is reached in September and October (Mackintosh and Herdman, 1940), when it covers just over half the total ocean area south of the Antarctic Convergence, apart from any stretches of open water there may be within the ice belt. Figure 7 shows how its outer edge, usually a sharp transition from open water to packed sea ice, gradually retreats through the summer months. At its lowest ebb, about March, there is little left, and the continental coast is often clear of ice except in the Pacific sector and perhaps the Weddell Sea. Through the winter there is a similarly gradual advance from March to the maximum in September.

At the time of this early spring maximum the ice almost entirely covers the zone occupied by krill, apart from the stragglers between ice and Convergence which typically form the thinned-out extension of many plankton

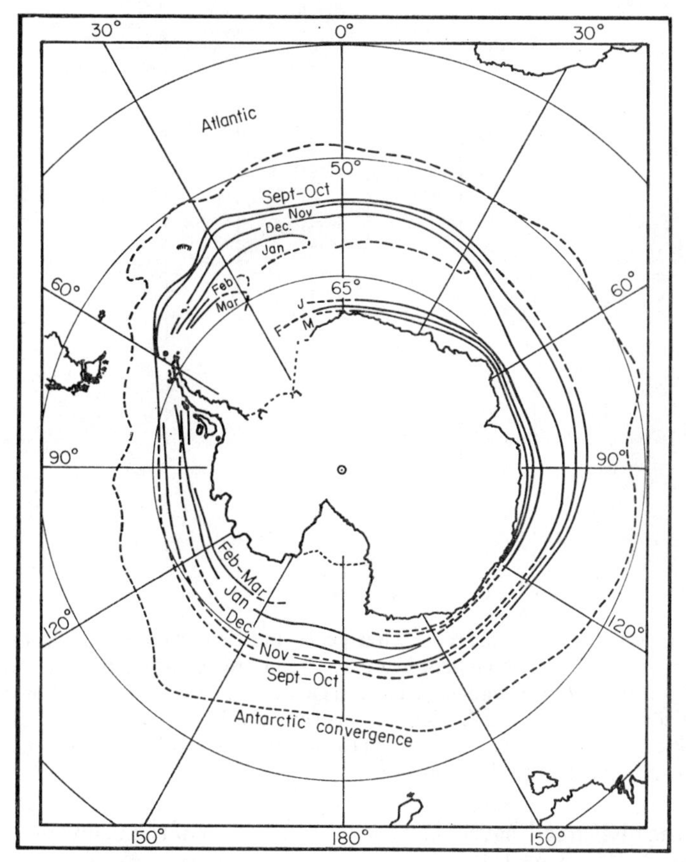

FIG. 7. Mean position of the pack-ice edge in the spring and summer months. From Mackintosh and Herdman (1940).

populations. After the retreat of the ice plenty of krill is found hundreds of miles south of the spring position of the ice edge, and it cannot have travelled there with the open water, for there is no general southward drift of the surface layer, and the krill's power of locomotion would scarcely allow for one mile a day even if it moved continuously in one direction. It must live under the ice, waiting, as it were, to be uncovered.

Figure 8 is the result of preliminary measurements of the zones of ice, feeding whales, and total area south of the Antarctic Convergence. It is from work in progress and should be taken as provisional, since some of the data have yet to be checked, but it is not likely to be altered appreciably except in so far as the pecked lines and hence the areas within the part marked "feeding zone" may need adjustment.

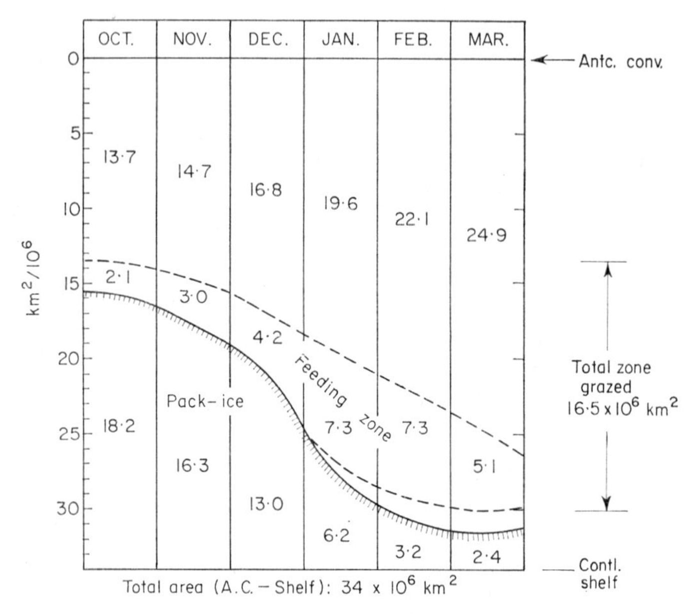

FIG. 8. Areas between the Antarctic Convergence and continental shelf, based mainly on data from 1931 to 1939. Numbers in each column are estimated areas, in millions of square kilometres, at the middle date of each month. Pecked lines and areas of the "feeding zone" are provisional. The gap between the lower pecked line and ice edge allows for certain waters, uncovered late in the season, where krill and whales appear to be scarce, notably in part of the Weddell Sea.

For the total area I have taken the mean position of the Convergence from Mackintosh (1946), and the edge of the continental shelf (from recent charts) in preference to the coast, because on the shelf *E. superba* appears to be replaced by *E. crystallorophias*. It is seen that in a total area of 34×10^6 km² the ice belt occupies from about 18·2 in October to 2·4 in March. These figures cannot be exact, because Convergence and ice positions are variable and the means are based on better data from some more than other months and regions. They should not be very far wrong, however, in view of recent checks on the positions of Convergence and ice edge by Gordon (1967) and Heap (1964) respectively.

The "feeding zone" is more difficult. It is that in which most of the whales assemble and the krill is relatively abundant, and from its nature it is a zone which can hardly be defined and measured accurately. It is derived from three sources of data and although details cannot be given here the steps can be summarized as follows. In a series of papers by Hjort *et al.* (1932–38) and another by Bergersen *et al.* (1939) the distribution of the whaling fleet was plotted on a series of charts for each month in the seasons 1930 to 1938. In any one month it would be differently distributed in different years, but a combination of the plottings in all years for each month separately shows a clear enough pattern in the form of a southward-shifting zone. This gave a first approximation to the feeding zone measured in Fig. 8, after the addition of a less-well-mapped strip in the Pacific sector which was not entered by the pelagic fleet until the mid-1950s. This, however, is a more restricted zone of whaling (see below). Inspection of the charts on which sightings of whales by the *Discovery II* from 1933 to 1939 had been plotted (those used by Mackintosh and Brown, 1956) showed that the observed concentrations of whales corresponded well enough with the "whaling zone" except that the latter could sometimes be enlarged or extended a little. This enlargement accords with expectation, since in the 1930s the whaling mostly kept near the ice edge in pursuit of blue whales, which tend to lie a little south of the fin, though their ranges overlap. The third step was to plot the quantities of krill in tow-net samples from the *Discovery* material, by orders of magnitude, in a manner similar to that adopted by Marr (1962), but broken down to single months rather than the three-month groupings he used. Here the picture is not quite so clear, since the interpretation of net samples of such a patchily distributed organism is always difficult. For each of the summer months the number of sample counts available varies from about 100 to 250, and they are fairly well scattered between Convergence and ice edge, with partial or complete circumpolar coverage. It can at least be said that nearly all the large samples do fall within the zone of whaling and whales, but there are not quite enough samples outside this zone to put beyond doubt the relative scarcity of krill above the longer pecked line in Fig. 8.

There is little doubt, however, that the grazing baleen whales sweep the southern half of the ocean south of the Convergence in some such way as is indicated in Fig. 8—gradually as the ice retreats—or at least that they did so before their numbers were so heavily reduced; that is, in the 1930s when nearly all the data discussed above were collected and when the stocks were still at a high level. From Fig. 8 it appears that the total area grazed is about 16·5 million square kilometres. It can be supposed that a large population of krill at first covers all this area, that it is then mostly under the ice, and that high concentrations accessible in open water tend to be confined at any one time to the relatively narrow and shifting feeding zone.

Changes in the shape of this zone are worth noting. For much of the summer it is a more or less continuous circumpolar band, except for the Pacific sector, but there are indications that it breaks up into a few regions of concentration about February and March. In much of the Pacific sector there is no feeding zone until December; here the continental coast lies far to the south, sea surface conditions tend to a southerly displacement, the krill lies in a narrow southerly belt covered by ice until near the turn of the year, and the whales do not make their appearance there much before that time. In the Atlantic sector, on the other hand, the drift from the Weddell Sea brings krill much farther north, creating a kind of loop in the feeding zone, with an outer belt of krill and whales which persists through most of the summer while the zone lies farther south in other sectors.

The feeding zone, as provisionally drawn in Fig. 8, is not sharply separated from the rest of the ice-free water. For example, not all the whales are packed into it. Especially in January and February it can be supposed that some will be left outside it, mopping up the outlying krill, and there will be late migrants on their way to the feeding zone or early ones departing from it. It is narrow in early spring (October) and becomes larger up to February, so that the population density of whales does not increase in proportion to the increasing number of whales in Antarctic waters shown in Fig. 1. In fact, density per unit area seems rather less at the peak numbers, but it is hard to be sure of this with the data available.

VII. Other Vertebrate Consumers of Krill

If a potential krill surplus is evenly spread over a grazing area of $16{\cdot}5 \times 10^6$ km^2, then at, say, 100×10^6 tons it would amount to only about 6 tons per km^2 (= 20·6/sq. nautical mile). Many of the missing 90% or so of whales, however, would not have arrived in the early part of the summer, so it can be supposed that the krill surplus is rather more concentrated in the southern part of the krill zone, where the ice has receded in January and February. However this may be, the potential surplus is essentially circumpolar, and the consumers most likely to take advantage of it are presumably those which can spread their feeding in a circumpolar direction and far from land. Even if the krill does tend to accumulate in the higher latitudes there will be much of it, for example in the Pacific sectors or eastern part of the Weddell drift, that is so distant from the more numerous breeding sites of penguins, other birds, and most seals, as to be beyond their likely foraging range.

The crabeater seal is an obvious candidate, since it is so widely distributed over the pack ice and not tied to breeding sites on land; but the population seems to have shown little if any increase. A rough estimate by Eklund (1964) puts the total in comparatively recent years at 5–8 million. The adult body weight is around 500 lb (Bertram, 1940; King, 1964) and the mean weight must be substantially less. Even if there were now as many as 10 million their biomass would scarcely amount to $1\frac{1}{2}$ million tons, and any part of this which might represent an increase over the original crabeater stock would be a trivial amount to set against a missing 22 million tons of whales. Other krill-eating seals may take part of the krill surplus more locally, but they are almost certainly much fewer than the crabeaters.

There are good local estimates here and there of populations of birds, but there appears to be no basis for realistic estimates of the total mass of the krill-eating species. Some oceanic birds can wander over the whole Antarctic ocean, and the possibility of a large increase cannot be excluded, but considering the number of even the larger birds equivalent to the weight of one whale it is hard to believe that they can have increased enough to equal, say, half the deficit of whales without drawing attention to themselves either at sea or at their breeding sites.

Another likely beneficiary is the small minke whale, but this, too, seems not to have filled the hiatus. Arseniev (1961) gives 7·675 metric tons as the mean of nine weighings at a mean length of 27 ft (8·3 m). This is rather high according to the formulae for other species, and it might be a little above that of the population as a whole. Even so an extra million minkes would equal only a third of the missing large whales, and would not be likely to have escaped notice. Mr S. G. Brown and I recently made a preliminary analysis of organized sightings over three years by several ships in the Scotia and Weddell Sea regions,* and the number (per unit distance steamed in good visibility) of small whales seen, which were or might have been minkes, seems far too small to suggest any such general increase.

There remain the oceanic fish and possibly the squid, if indeed any population has increased on the surplus krill. A fish now known to form dense shoals feeding on krill is the southern species of the blue whiting, *Micromesistius australis* (see Merrett, 1963; Marti, 1967; Mikheyev, 1967). Merrett's paper, reporting such shoals in the southern part of the Scotia Sea, appears to be the first record of this species in Antarctic waters, though it was previously known from the Patagonian Shelf (Norman, 1937; Hart, 1946). Spawning is said to take place on the continental shelf, but I understand that such a fish, by analogy with its northern counterpart, is not likely to be always dependent on shallow water for spawning. Merrett found high concentrations some 600 miles from the Patagonian Shelf, and if it can spawn in oceanic waters might it not spread farther afield than the Scotia Sea? Or perhaps there may be other fish feeding on the krill which have not yet been

* Brown and Mackintosh, 1968; unpublished report to the International Whaling Commission. The programme of sightings was adopted by S C A R at the invitation of the I W C and is continuing.

found or reported. One night in the RRS *William Scoresby*, in 1931, the late Mr E. R. Gunther and I saw a bathypelagic fish, with bright luminous organs, feeding on a swarm of krill a few feet from the surface in calm weather. Perhaps there may be other surprises in store. At least it is worth searching for fish in other regions when swarms are located.

As to the squid there is, I believe, no information whatever on their quantities or population density in the Antarctic. Nor do I know of any data on their diet. It can only be said that they may have taken to eating krill, like so many other animals. No doubt they should be borne in mind as a possible but unknown factor in the consumption of krill.

So in the field covered in this paper there is little we can be certain of beyond the magnitude of the reduction of the stocks of whales. There is evidence, though it is not decisive, that the crabeater seals and minke whales have not increased so as to take the place of the larger baleen whales; and other seals and birds are less likely to have done so. If any consumers of the adolescent and adult krill have taken advantage of the surplus, it would seem on balance of probability to be the fish.

One important point is that available information, so far as it goes, suggests that the mass of whales, in their original numbers, was far greater than that of other known consumers. If that is so, perhaps their total consumption was not very far short of the overall annual production of post-larval krill, unless there has always been a surplus that dies off uneaten.

I see no way of settling these problems without the collection of better quantitative data in the Antarctic. With modern techniques it should not be too difficult now to obtain more realistic estimates, for example of krill density, and to ascertain more of the quantities and distribution of fish. It is clearly important also to keep a watch on the stocks of whales in future, whether the industry continues or not. The SCAR programme of sightings mentioned above was organized for this purpose, and it may be hoped that comparable sightings can be extended in regions additional to the south-west Atlantic.

VIII. Summary

The stocks of baleen whales feeding in the Antarctic have been reduced, mainly in the past forty years, by about 85–90%. It is hoped that the decline has now been halted, but the prospects of recovery depend on the future of whaling; and the time required for the maximum or any other level to be restored differs considerably in blue, fin, sei, and humpback whales. A rough estimate suggests that of these whales the biomass supported by the Antarctic krill has been reduced by round about 20 million tons, not much more than half of which is likely to be regained by the end of the century. To calculate the potential surplus of krill, which is presumed to result, we need better data on the rate of consumption, but the surplus seems unlikely to be less than about 30 million tons, and might be far more. This could allow a huge increase in other consumers of krill, but the surplus would be spread over a vast circumpolar zone, grazed by the whales as the ice retreats. Populations that seem most likely to benefit are those capable of widespread feeding and not tied to limited breeding grounds, such as the small minke whales, crabeater seals, and oceanic fish, but the first two seem not to have greatly increased, and the advantage, if any, could be with the fish or squid.

References

Arseniev, V. A. (1961). Lesser rorquals of the Antarctic, *Balaenoptera acutorostrata* Lac. *Rep. Conf. Sea Mammals, 1959. Ichthyol. Commiss. USSR. Acad. Sci.* **12**, 125–32.

Ash, C. E. (1952). The Body Weights of Whales. *Norsk Hvalfangsttid.* **41**. No. 7, 364–74.

Ash, C. E. (1956). Variation in Blubber Thickness with length in Fin Wales. *Norsk Hvalfangsttid.* **45**. No. 10, 550–4.

Bannister, J. L. and Gambell, R. (1965). The Succession and Abundance of Fin, Sei, and other Whales off Durban. *Norsk Hvalfangsttid.* **54**. No. 3, 45–60.

Bergersen, B., Lie, J. and Ruud, J. T. (1939). Pelagic Whaling in the Antarctic. VIII. The Season 1937–1938. *Hvalråd Skr.* **20**, 1–42.

Bertram, G. C. L. (1940). The Biology of the Weddell and Crabeater Seals: with a study of the Comparative Behaviour of the Pinnipedia. *Sci. Rep. Brt. Grahamld Exped.* **1**, No. 1, 1–139.

Chittleborough, R. G. (1965). Dynamics of two populations of the humpback whale, *Megaptera novaeangliae* (Borowski). *Aust. J. mar. Freshwat. Res.* **16**, No. 1, 33–128.

Clarke, R. (1954). Whales and seals as Resources of the Sea. *Norsk Hvalfangsttid.* **43**. No. 9. 489–510.

Crisp, D. T. (1962), The Tonnages of Whales taken by Antarctic Pelagic Operations during Twenty Seasons and an Examination of the Blue Whale Unit. *Norsk Hvalfangsttid.* **51**. No. 10, 389–93.

Eklund, C. R. (1964). Population studies of Antarctic seals and birds. *In* "Antarctic Biology". (R. Carrick, M. Holdgate and J. Prévost eds). pp. 415–19.

Gordon, A. L. (1967). Structure of Antarctic Waters Between 20°W and 170°W. Antarctic Map Folio Series, *Am. Geogr. Soc.*, Folio 6, pp. 1–10.

Gulland, J. A. (1966). The Effect of Regulation on Antarctic Whale Catches. *Cons. perm. int. Explor. Mer.* **30**, No, 3, 308–15.

Hart, T. J. (1946). Report on trawling surveys on the Patagonian continental shelf. *"Discovery" Rep.* **23**, 223–408.

Heap, J. A. (1964). Pack Ice. *In* "Antarctic Research" (R. Priestly, R. J. Adie and G. de Q. Robin eds). London.

Hjort, J., Lie, J. and Ruud, J. T. (1932–38). Pelagic Whaling in the Antarctic. *Hvalråd. Skr.*, Nos. 3–18.

Holt, S. J. and Gulland, J. A. (1964). Measures of Abundance of Antarctic Whale Stocks. *Rapp. Cons. Explor. Mer.* **155**, 147–51.

International Whaling Commission (1964–68). *Reports* 14–18. Office of the Commission, London.

International Whaling Statistics (1930–68). Nos. 1–60. Oslo.

Ivashin, M. V. (1961). On the periodicity of feeding the hunched whale in the southern part of the Atlantic Ocean. *Byull. mosk. Obshch. Ispyt. Prir.* **66**, No. 6, 110–15.
King, J. E. (1964). "Seals of the world." British Museum (Natural History).
Klumov, S. K. (1963). Food and helminth fauna of whalebone whales (Mystacocoeti) in the main whaling regions of the world ocean. *Trudy Inst. Okeanol.* **71**, 94–194.
Mackintosh, N. A. (1942). The southern stocks of whalebone whales. *"Discovery" Rep.* **22**, 197–300.
Mackintosh, N. A. (1946). The Antarctic Convergence and the distribution of surface temperatures in Antarctic waters. *"Discovery" Rep.* **23**, 177–212.
Mackintosh, N. A. (1965). "The Stocks of Whales." Fishing News (Books) Ltd, London.
Mackintosh, N. A. and Brown, S. G. (1956). Preliminary Estimates of the Southern Populations of the Larger Baleen Whales. *Norsk Hvalfangsttid.* **45**, No. 9, 469–80.
Mackintosh, N. A. and Herdman, H. F. P. (1940). Distribution of the pack-ice in the southern ocean. *"Discovery" Rep.* **19**, 285–96.
Marr, J. (1962). The natural history and geography of the Antarctic krill (*Euphausia superba* Dana). *"Discovery" Rep.* **32**, 33–464.
Marti, Y. Y. (1967). The first cruise of the research vessel Akademic Knipovich in Antarctic waters. *Okeanologiya*, **7**, No. 3, 421–6.
Merrett, N. R. (1963), Pelagic Gadoid Fish in the Antarctic. *Norsk Hvalfangsttid.* **52**, No. 9, 245–7.
Mikheyev, B. I. (1967). On the Biology and Fisheries of Certain Fishes from the Patagonian Shelf (Falkland Region). *In* "Antarkticheskiy Kril" (R. N. Burnkovskiy, ed.). Atlant. Sci. Res. Inst. Fish & Oceanogr., Kaliningrad.
Nemoto, T. (1959). Food of baleen whales with reference to whale movements. *Sci. Rep. Whales Res. Inst.*, Tokyo **14**, 149–290.
Nemoto, T. (1962). Food of baleen whales collected in recent Japanese antarctic whaling expeditions. *Sci. Rep. Whales Res. Inst.*, Tokyo **16**, 89–103.
Nishiwaki, M. (1950). On the Body Weights of Whales. *Sci Rep. Whales Res. Inst.*, Tokyo **4**, 184–209.
Norman, J. R. (1937). Coast Fishes. Pt. II. The Patagonian Region. *"Discovery" Rep.* **16**, 1–150.
Omura, H. (1950). On the Body Weight of Sperm and Sei Whales located in the Adjacent Waters of Japan. *Sci. Rep. Whales Res. Inst.*, Tokyo **4**, 1–13.
Ruud, J. T. (1956). International Regulation of Whaling. A Critical Survey. *Norsk Hvalfangsttid.* **45**, No. 7, 374–87.

Some Aspects of the Commercial use of the Krill Resources of the Antarctic Seas

P. A. MOISEEV
Institute of Fisheries and Oceanography, Moscow, U.S.S.R.

I. Introduction

In recent years the problem of supplying ever-increasing human populations with food, and particularly with animal protein, has received close attention from the governments of almost all countries as well as from UNO and its specialized organizations. Even at present, with a world population of about 3·5 billion, some 60% of mankind are starving or have an unsatisfactory diet, and some thirty to thirty-five years hence, when the number will have nearly doubled to reach about 6·5 billion, it will be necessary to increase the production of foodstuffs and particularly of food containing animal proteins to three times the present level if the whole population is to have an adequate diet.

Severe problems involved in the development of animal husbandry on a commercial scale or fish culture in fresh waters force many countries to look upon the development of the biological resources of the world ocean as the most promising way of meeting the need for animal protein. Approximate estimates show that in order to continue to meet about 15% of these requirements from the ocean it is necessary to raise the total catch of fish and other marine organisms to 130–150 million tons by the year 2000. At present the total catch of aquatic organisms from the ocean is about 60 million tons (including statistically unrecorded landings). Our estimations, based on the analysis of the biological productivity of the world ocean and the results of investigations carried out by Soviet scientists, suggest that the total catch of fish, big invertebrates and marine mammals could be increased by 20 to 30 million tons, taking the total yield from the ocean up to 80 or 90, but not more than 100 million tons. These calculations assume that commercial fisheries would be properly managed, new fishing grounds developed, and species such as skipper, small tuna fish, anchovy, squid, etc., caught more intensively.

II. Potential New Fishery Resources

Quantitative estimates of the primary production of the world ocean and of secondary production by animals of different trophic levels suggest that mankind is far from using fully the biological resources of the ocean, for it is only big animals which occupy the third, fourth, or sometimes even the fifth or sixth trophic levels that have been fished so far.

Data presented by various Soviet investigators and particularly those by Bogorov (1965), Zenkevich (1963), Koblents-Mishke (1965), Syomina (1967), and some others, adjusted in the light of later information, suggest that the contribution of the main biological groups to the oceanic resources which are of commercial interest to man may be estimated as follows (figures are for raw weight in billion tons):

Producers		*Consumers*	
Phytoplankton	330	Zooplankton	15·0
Phytobenthos	0·2	Zoobenthos	1·0
Total	330·2	Nekton	0·3
		Total	16·3

Thus the yield of fish, large invertebrates and marine mammals is only one-fiftieth of the zooplankton production consumed by them. If we compare their yield with the total zooplankton production of the world ocean (50 million tons), the disparity would be even greater.

Therefore, one of the most promising but technologically difficult ways of increasing the biological yield of the ocean is the commercial use of animals occupying lower trophic levels, and particularly zooplankton. However typical mesoplanktonic organisms, although very abundant, are generally widely dispersed, and their concentration rarely exceeds a few grammes per cubic metre. It is quite obvious therefore that until methods of forming dense concentrations of mesoplankton are developed it will be impossible to begin a fishery on this component of the zooplankton.

At the same time relatively big zooplanktonic organisms composing the macroplanktonic group and belonging mainly to Euphausiacea, constitute a relatively abundant biological resource with a production of not less than 10 billion tons over the world ocean. There is an urgent need for study and development of means of utilizing this resource.

III. Investigation of Krill Resources

Investigations recently conducted by Soviet scientists show that the Antarctic krill (*Euphausia superba* Dana) is the most promising object of potential fishery, because of the nature and size of its concentrations, its behaviour, and technical and chemical properties.

When baleen whales were relatively abundant they consumed annually up to 150 million tons of krill within a period of three to four months, which confirms the rather high production of this macroplanktonic organism in Antarctic waters (Table 1). Investigations of distribution, biology and condi-

TABLE 1

Abundance of Antarctic Populations of Baleen Whales and the food consumed by them (according to B. Zenkovich)

Species	*Number (thousands of whales)*	*Caught from 1904 to 1966 (thousands)*	*Mean mass (tons)*	*Food consumed daily (tons)*	*Time spent in Antarctic (days)*	*Annual food consumption tons* × 10^6
Blue whale	100	131·1	100	4	120	50
Fin whale	200	671·1	50	2·8–3·0	120	72
Humpback whale	50	145·4	40	2	120	12
Sei whale	75	87·3	17	1·5	100	12
	425	1034·9				146

tions for catching Antarctic krill in bulk initiated by Soviet scientists in 1962 established that in a number of areas south of 60°S krill forms shoals with dense concentrations during the period from December to March, the density amounting to 10 or even 16 kg/m³. These concentrations, extending for several hundred metres, are somewhat irregular. They usually occur in the upper layer (down to 5 m) and very rarely move to depths over 40 m. The densest concentrations were observed in the daytime and sometimes they could be detected visually. Observations conducted in the Scotia Sea over several years show that krill concentrations occur every year, their location, composition of populations and behaviour pattern changing in relation to hydrometeorological conditions.

Experimental catches of krill were taken from the concentrations located. The catches were taken with an otter-trawl into which a fine-meshed bag had been inserted, and were rather stable, amounting to 5–6 tons per haul. Undoubtedly, other more effective methods can also be developed. Individual *Euphausia superba* in the Scotia Sea can be as long as 60–70 mm and weigh up to 1 g. The animal contains (wet wt) up to 7% of fat and 16% of protein, which makes it a valuable potential source of fodder and food products.

However, the investigations and experimental fishing show that the biological studies are very time-consuming and the development of commercial operations involves many difficulties. It should be noted that the life cycle of krill seems to span at least four or four and a half years: its concentrations are differentiated by age groups and it performs rather extensive vertical migrations. Due to the fact that krill concentrations mainly occur in the water layer above the ship's keel, detection of concentrations by means of hydroacoustic devices presents difficulties and it is consequently not always possible to shoot the trawl directly to the place of concentration. Further technical and economic problems arise in the processing of krill into various products, and in marketing.

But taking into account the high production of krill in Antarctic waters, the fact that the standing crop appears largely unconsumed by other animals in these seas, the positive results of Soviet investigations into the biology of krill and its fishery as well as the urgent necessity of finding additional protein resources, it seems well worth while for all countries to intensify their efforts to study the possibilities of establishing a commercial krill fishery in Antarctic waters. Success in investigations of this kind would probably allow us to double the present catch of aquatic organisms from the world ocean.

References

Bogorov, V. G. (1965). Qualitative estimation of animal and plant populations of the ocean. *DAN*, USSR, **162**, No. 5.

Koblents-Mishke, O. I. (1965). Estimate of Primary production of two Pacific Ocean. *Okeanologia*, **5**, No. 2.

Syomina, G. I. (1967). Phytoplankton, Pacific Ocean. "Biology of the Pacific Ocean", book **1**. Moscow, Nauka.

Zenkevich, L. A. (1963). "Biology of the U.S.S.R. seas," Moscow, U.S.S.R. Academy of Sciences.

Zenkovich, B. A. (1969). Whales and plankton in the Antarctic. Collected papers, marine mammals. Moscow, Nauka.

The Development of the Resources of the Antarctic Seas*

J. A. GULLAND
Fisheries Department, FAO, Rome, Italy

I. Introduction

It is generally accepted that with many people in the world hungry now, and with the total population steadily increasing, the world is facing the danger of an increasing food shortage, especially a shortage of animal protein. It is also widely believed that much of the latter could or should come from the world's oceans, which make up 70% of the Earth's surface. The success of fisheries over the past ten to fifteen years in increasing the total marine harvest (fish, whales, crustaceans and molluscs) at a fairly steady rate of around 7% per year, to a total of some 50 million tons in 1967 would seem to confirm these hopes.

However, this total has been confined almost entirely to a limited number of groups of animals: the medium-sized and valuable animals, mostly living on the bottom, vulnerable to such gear as trawls and bottom lines (e.g. cod, sea bream, flatfish, etc.); the smaller shoaling fish, such as herring and anchovy, which can be caught very effectively by purse-seines; and (though less important) the very large animals such as whales which can be economically harvested even in the open oceans. Various estimates have been made of the total potential of these resources, with general agreement that they probably do not exceed 100–200 million tons, i.e. about twice to four times the present catch. If the present rate of increase in total catch were maintained, these levels would be reached in about ten to fifteen years.

Two important conclusions can be drawn; first that there should be a very great improvement in the arrangements for the conservation and management of the types of fish presently exploited, and secondly, that if the oceans are to fulfil the more optimistic expectations some other types of fish or other animals must be utilized. It is with this latter thought in mind that renewed attention is being paid to the exploitation of the Antarctic seas.

* Most of the data on the resources are summarized from a report on the Antarctic prepared for FAO under its Indicative World Plan, by Prof. G. Hempel of Keil. The views expressed are those of the author and not necessarily those of FAO.

II. Traditional Antarctic Resources

The exploitation of these rich resources is, of course, no new thing. The exploitation and near extermination of some of the Subantarctic marine animals (fur seals, right whales) goes back a century, and the very important pelagic whaling operations for blue, fin and (later) sei whales are nearly fifty years old. Indeed, in the peak years of the 1930s Antarctic whaling accounted for 10% of the total marine harvest (up to 2 million tons out of 20 million), which was probably more than that taken from the whole of the rest of the world except the coastal areas of the North Atlantic and the North and Western Pacific.

The failure to achieve rational management of the whales, and the successive decline in blue and fin whale stocks to levels where the present harvest is very much less than the optimum is well known (Chapman, 1964). Even with optimum management the maximum possible harvest is not great in relation to world protein demand—probably around 6000 blue whales, 20,000 fin whales and 5000 sei whales, giving a total of 1 to 1½ million tons. Thus, while it is clearly most desirable to achieve proper management of the whale stocks, and procure from them their potential yield, the major future interest in the Antarctic must be in other animals.

The whaling data do show one aspect of the Antarctic resources which may be important in future exploitation, and that is the great lack of uniformity of distribution round the Antarctic. The statistics of Antarctic whaling distinguish six areas according to longitude (chosen in accordance with what was known about the separation of blue whale stocks). These statistics show that since the 1931–2 season—when good collection of statistics was started—nearly two-thirds of the total catch were taken in Areas II and III, which make up roughly one-third of the total Antarctic Ocean, from Drake Passage eastwards to Kerguelen.

These figures may be biased, reflecting catches rather than stocks or potential, because of the concentration of catching operation in these areas—though this bias may not be great, since the catches, particularly of blue whales, have nearly completely removed the stocks from all areas. Information that is more nearly free from such bias is provided by the estimates of the initial stocks of sei whales in each area before intense exploitation began. These estimates, adapted from FAO (1968), and the total catches of each species from the 1931–2 season to the 1966–7 season, in terms of total numbers, and percentage in each area are given in Table 1.

The relatively high production of whales in the Atlantic sector agrees with other observations, e.g. of primary production, and krill; also within each area there are smaller regions of high abundance, such as those of whales and krill off South Georgia. In fact, patches of local abundance of decreasing

TABLE 1

Percentage Distribution of Whales in the Different Whaling Areas, as Shown by the Total Catches 1931/2–1966/7, and the Estimated Abundance of the Unexploited Sei Whale Stock

Area	II 0–60°W	III 0–70°E	IV 70–130°E	V 130°E–170°W	VI 170–120°W	I 120–60°W	*Total* (*No.*)
Catches							
Blue	20·3	40·7	29·9	6·2	2·4	0·5	189,157
Fin	31·1	37·7	15·0	7·0	5·9	3·3	513,344
Humpback	5·4	27·5	43·5	14·2	4·3	5·1	28,629
Sei	49·5	17·9	9·2	12·0	6·9	4·5	81,668
Sperm	21·6	32·8	21·0	19·2	3·0	2·4	99,207
Initial sei whale stock*	35	17	10	17	13	8	125,000

extent can be described down to the local intense swarms of krill, or smaller. These irregularities are helpful to exploitation by man (and possibly by other predators), since by concentrating in the high-density regions much higher catch rates can be achieved than when operating on a uniform density. However, this patchiness can make analysis of data difficult, especially where there may have been a tendency for most data to be collected in the richer regions.

III. Total Production

The primary production in the Antarctic expressed as carbon fixation per unit area is fairly high compared with most parts of the open ocean, though less than in some of the most productive areas (e.g. some subtropical upwelling areas). Figures quoted for the average production per year have ranged from 40 to 100 gC/m^2 (Currie, 1964; El Sayed and Mandelli 1965; Ryther 1963). Multiplying these by the area south of the Antarctic Convergence—10 to 20 $\times$ 10^6 km^2 according to the season—gives a total carbon fixation of 0·4 to 2 $\times$ 10^9 tons. Taking (mainly for ease of computation) a 1 : 10 conversion ratio from carbon to live weight, a total production of 4 to 20 $\times$ 10^9 tons live weight is suggested.

Ecological efficiency, defined here as the ratio of the production by successive levels in the food chain, appears to be highly variable in the sea, tending to be higher in areas of high primary production, and in latitudes where production is seasonal. There are also big differences according to the general

* Abundancy of animals of the exploited size only.

biological characteristics of the organism. A figure of 10% efficiency has been quite widely used, and lacking better information, is probably not unreasonable to use for the Antarctic. This would give the following estimates of production (using a central value for primary production).

Phytoplankton	10,000 million tons
Herbivores	1000 million tons
First stage carnivores	100 million tons

There is little direct evidence on the production of zooplankton. More data is available on standing crop, expressed sometimes as density per m^2 and sometimes per m^3. A central value is about 10 g/m^2, or a total for the whole Antarctic of 150 million tons. Of this total perhaps half is krill (Vinogradov and Naumov, 1958). The ratio of production to standing crop is unknown, but if the mean life span of the zooplankton animals is taken as one year, then the two are equal, and the production is 150 million tons. These estimates are subject to considerable errors due, for example, to the patchiness of both animals and sampling. Also many of the nets used, especially in early work, were not efficient catchers of the larger animals, such as krill; this would make the figures underestimates of the real standing crop.

A lower bound to the production of krill is given by the consumption of whales. When the whale stocks were at their maximum they probably ate at least 50 million tons per year. There is no evidence to suggest what proportion this was of the total annual krill production.

These calculations thus provide three independent (though extremely rough) estimates of the annual production of krill, the dominant zooplankton species, as follows:

From primary production:	500 million tons (assuming krill is half the total herbivore production)
From zooplankton standing crop:	over 75 million tons
From whale consumption:	at least 50 million tons

Probably the true production is nearer the larger figure, since there are good reasons why the other two could be quite serious underestimates. However, for the present it does not seem worth while to attempt to make a closer estimate, even if the data were good enough, since the same important conclusion can be made from all the estimates—krill has a potential at least as great, in terms of weight, as all the presently exploited fish stocks combined (Burukovskii, 1965).

For practical purposes, if harvesting of krill is being considered, the important figure is not so much the annual production as the sustained yield that can be taken; this will be lower than the total production, due to losses to other predators, disease, etc. This potential yield almost certainly cannot be estimated with any great accuracy until harvesting occurs at a level sufficiently high to have some detectable effect on the stocks. If harvesting by man can be considered as initially a substitution for harvesting by whales, then a lower limit to the potential harvest is above 50 million tons, less the consumption by the presently greatly reduced whale stocks, which is no more than a fifth of the original consumption.

It has been suggested that the decrease of whale stocks, and their reduced krill consumption, has been followed by an increase of krill, and of other animals eating krill. There seems to be no evidence that this has happened, nor indeed are there good theoretical reasons why it should necessarily happen, at least to any great extent. Virtually nothing is known of the factors controlling the abundance of krill, or of the animals eating krill, of which grazing and food supply are, for the two populations respectively, only two of a large possible range. These uncertainties do not, however, seriously affect the conclusion that a very large harvest of krill is biologically possible.

Krill is not the only potential resource. The theoretical food-chain calculations suggest a production of 100 million tons of carnivores, of which baleen whales are only a part. Other parts are the penguins, seals and other birds and mammals. Rough estimates of these are known, and their total potential, probably because of the limitation set by breeding requirements, is not high: rather less than that of the large baleen whales.

Little is known quantitatively about the fish in the Antarctic. Many of the most productive areas are over deep water so that the rich bottom communities supporting the major trawl fisheries of the world cannot develop. In some areas, for example off the South Orkney, and South Shetland Islands, large catches of fish have been taken by bottom or mid-water trawls; the species involved include Nototheniids, *Micromesistius australis*, and myctophids. Little is known about the extent of suitable fishing grounds, but if these are not too limited, the total potential could be considerable.

These fish feed mainly on krill, but there are other predatory fish, and also other organisms, such as squid which may feed on krill, and which add to the total potential.

IV. Development and Management of the Resources

These conclusions—that there is certainly a very large potential of krill, and probably a substantial potential of fish and possibly squid, are about as far as the biologist can take matters at present for the immediate purposes of exploitation. The next logical step, if harvesting is to take place, lies with the technologists. The problems include finding the most effective catching method, including the best times and places to fish, where there is some need for biological and oceanographic advice on the likely distribution patterns; processing either into a form suitable for direct human consumption, or for animal food; and distribution and marketing. If these problems can be solved and a useful product can be produced at an economical price, then experience of other fisheries shows how rapid development could be. The Peruvian anchoveta catch increased from a few thousand tons to nearly 10 million tons in less than ten years. Distance need not be a great difficulty; the long-range operations of Japan and U.S.S.R. are well known, but even such a relatively poor country as Korea has a substantial fishery in the Atlantic.

The history of all too many fisheries have unfortunately shown how rapidly a newly developed fishery can reach the stage of overexploitation, making conservation and management necessary, and this stage is again one where the biologist has a vital role to play. Experience also shows how desirable it is to make the arrangements for collection and analysis of data, and for the introduction of management measures, as early as possible.

The near extinction of the Antarctic whaling industry illustrates the disasters that can follow poor management—though there are biological reasons (essentially the low fecundity of whales) why the disaster for whales was more complete than is likely for an industry based on fish or invertebrates. Many factors have been involved in this failure, but two points may be considered here in relation to the future management of other resources—the quality and timing of the scientific advice, and the authority of the International Whaling Commission.

In the 1950s the whale stocks were not too greatly depleted, so that not too severe a reduction in the total quota, plus a more selective protection for the blue whale, could have maintained the stocks. Unfortunately the scientists could not at that time, through disagreement, give clear advice on the state of the stocks, and on the consequences of the possible actions by the Commission. This is no criticism of the scientists involved, who were not experts in the quantitative aspects of population dynamics, but does underline the need for such experts to be brought in as early as possible. Unfortunately by the time this was done by the IWC, and the Committee of Three Scientists presented their report, the decline in the stocks had become extremely serious. Their restoration to the optimum level could no longer have been done almost painlessly, but would have required, if achieved rapidly, large, if short-run, sacrifices by those carrying out whaling.

These sacrifices were not accepted by the countries involved, nor could they be enforced by the Commission, on which the immediate whaling interests have the dominant voice. Thus the stocks continued to decline, and the loss of catch (compared with the potential) has become much greater than if the short-term sacrifices had been accepted.

The Whaling Commission is only one of several such commissions, and has not been clearly the least successful. This lack of success arises because it, and other commissions, have little power. The whale stocks belong to no one, certainly not to the Commission, so that it is no one's direct interest to manage the stocks correctly. The individual interest is to maximize the share from the stocks in the present and immediate future. The final solution to this problem seems to require a fundamentally new approach to management, possibly including new concepts of the ownership of the oceanic resources (Gulland, 1968). More immediately any nation contemplating the exploitation of the resources of the Antarctic seas must also consider how the resources should be managed, and the scientists involved should consider how proper advice on such management should be provided.

References

Burukovskii, R. N. (ed.), (1965). "Antarkticheskii Krill. Biologiiai Promysel". Kaliningrad, (Antarjucheskii Naukno-issledovatel'skii Institut Rybnogo Khoziaistua i Okeanografii).

Chapman, D. G. (1964). Final report of the special committee of Three Scientists. *Rep. int. Commn. Whal*, 14, 39–92.

Currie, R. I. (1964). Environmental factors in the ecology of Antarctic seas. *In* "Biologie Antarctique" (R. Carrick, M. Holdgate and J. Prévost, eds). Hermann, Paris. 87–94.

El-Sayed, S. Z. and Mandelli, E. F. (1965). Primary production and standing crop of phytoplankton in the Weddell Sea and Drake Passage. *Antarct. Res. Ser.* 5, 87–124.

FAO (1968). Report on the effects on the baleen whale stocks of pelagic operations in the Antarctic during the 1967/68 season, and on the present status of those stocks. Document presented to the 1968 session of the International Whaling Commission (mimeo).

Gulland, J. A. (1968). The management of Antarctic whaling resources. *J. Cons. perm. int. Explor. Mer.* **31** (3), 88.

Ryther, J. H. (1963). Geographic variations in productivity. In "The Sea—Ideas and Observations on Progress in the Study of the Seas" (M. N. Hill, ed.). J. Wiley & Sons, New York. Vol. **20**, 347–80.

Vinogradov, M. R. and Naumov, A. G. (1958). Quantitative distribution of plankton in Antarctic waters of the Indian and Pacific Ocean (in Russian). *Inf. Byull. sov. antarkt. Eksped.*, 1955–8 (3), 31–34.

Discussion

BIOLOGY OF WHALES

A. W. Erickson

Do the mortality figures take into account the whales killed but lost? Has this been *measured* (rather than guessed)?

J. A. Gulland

There are really two categories. First, whales harpooned, killed, but lost prior to working up. These are recorded, and the loss is known to be very small—below 1% of the kill. But we have no data for whales shot but lost because the harpoon comes out while the whale is alive: some of these may die later. It is unlikely that this is a large figure.

R. W. Morris

Is there any information about metabolic efficiency in whales? Theoretically they should be very efficient.

N. A. Mackintosh

I doubt if there are data. The situation is complicated. The whales are in continuous movement which uses energy even though it is slow. On the other hand, the surface: volume ratio is low and insulation is high.

J. A. Gulland

There are really two efficiencies. The whale is highly efficient in itself, but whale populations are clearly not efficient. One can crop only 10% of the population per annum at maximum as compared with 60% per annum in fish.

R. W. Morris

But blue whales grow very fast.

A. Gulland

After completion of growth they have to keep going for a very long period.

N. A. Mackintosh

In fact, the growth rate is less rapid than it was at first thought to be.

E. Balech

The 10% figure for efficiency of conversions of material worries me: I believe much higher efficiencies are normal. Averages are hard to use, since there must be wide variations with species and temperature.

J. A. Gulland

This is important. First, this conversion rate isn't the right figure. The conversion of food eaten to weight put on is in the 30–40% range. Ecological efficiency includes other factors such as the proportions of food consumed devoted to growth and to maintenance, and the effectiveness of a predator in grazing its prey. Calculations for whales at maximum sustainable yield indicate a potential harvest to man of 2×10^6 tons/annum. Total deaths, equal in the steady state to the production, may total 4×10^6 metric tons. The standing crop was about 100×10^6 metric tons. The ecological efficiency was low (4%): much energy may have been devoted to maintenance. In the North Sea the fish harvest is 1% of the input through the two or more trophic levels involved. An ecological efficiency better than 10% is required for the North Sea fish populations.

CHANGES CONSEQUENT UPON THE REDUCTION OF WHALE STOCKS

G. A. Knox

It is clear that *Euphausia superba* is even more important than we had imagined. Many estimates of standing crop have been made, but it looks as if about 150×10^6 metric tons per annum were consumed by whales when the latter were at peak. If other consumers took 100×10^6 metric tons, we have a total consumption of 250–300 $\times 10^6$ metric tons per annum. What proportion of the total adult *Euphausia* production does this represent?

S. Z. El-Sayed

Will the gaps in the ecosystem left by the removal of the blue and humpback whales be filled by the multiplication of some related species? It seems theoretically possible for another whale to take over that enormous "lebensraum". On the Californian coast, when the sardine stock were reduced by the fishery, anchovy increased and is now the basis of another thriving fishery.

N. A. Mackintosh

An increase of whales might also be checked as a whole if other organisms have expanded to take more of the krill production. But against this idea there is the undoubted recovery of fur seals and of grey whales in the past half-century.

J. A. Gulland

The oscillations between anchovies and sardines are interesting. Mortality early in life is a very important influence in this case.

H. H. De Witt

Fossil scales in sea-bottom cores suggest that the anchovy was usually the commoner off California, and that the recent predominance of sardines was atypical and resulted from the oscillations both species show.

J. A. Gulland

This kind of thing emphasizes how little we know about the subtler aspects of population regulation.

S. Z. El-Sayed

But surely there is no denial that overfishing may have contributed to the most recent reversal in their proportions?

E. Balech

The sardine problem is a different one. The species has had cycles of abundance through the centuries in the absence of fishing. The whale populations, on the other hand, have been reduced directly by the fishery.

B. Stonehouse

It is unwise to assume that the removal of whales has necessarily left a gap in the ecosystem that man can fill. Krill is important to fish, and also to birds, and for every whale removed there could well be a compensating increase by fish or birds. The role of birds may be considerable. There are populations of up to 5 million penguins in some small areas in Antarctic and Subantarctic. Each takes about 500g/day of food, largely krill, and when feeding chicks the food collected may rise fourfold. There is little positive evidence of expansion of birds during the period over which whales have declined, but we have very few data for colonies over more than twenty years. *Pygoscelis antarctica* has increased in South Georgia, and perhaps elsewhere.

I. Everson

Is it not considered that bird populations may be restricted by the lack of availability of breeding space?

M. W. Holdgate

Even though vast bird colonies exist in some areas, such as the Peninsula, Scotia Arc, and Subantarctic islands, there are great lengths of Antarctic coastline on which no colonies could be established. If you take the breeding biomass of birds at an area like Pointe Géologie, where there is a high concentration, and distribute this over the sea area north of it, the amount of birds per unit area is almost trivially small. This might suggest that even if birds did increase they would not make a great inroad on any hypothetical "surplus" of krill.

If penguin colonies have expanded there may be evidence in the soils. In the South Sandwich Islands Dr Longton found some evidence of marginal change around a colony from examination of the vegetation and soil profile.

T. J. Hart

In the days of shore-based whaling stations there were large petrel populations around the stations, supported on whale offal. When the stations closed there was a noticeable die-back. This does seem to demonstrate that bird populations can adjust themselves to take an available surplus.

B. Stonehouse

One hundred tons of whale would not be replaced by 100 tons of birds. The same food might support only 1 ton of birds, with their higher energy production and heat losses.

I know of no evidence of Antarctic bird population limitation by crowding and competition at the breeding grounds. Penguin colonies seem, subjectively, to have plenty of spare space. Possibly this results from a reduction in the stocks over recent centuries. We must in any event look for evidence of recent population expansion or increased breeding efficiency. Antarctic krill is, of course, eaten not only by Antarctic residents but also by Arctic and temperate zone migrants. There are thus many breeding stocks involved.

J. A. Gulland

Dr Holdgate's reference to biomass in birds is not really the appropriate parameter. Food-consumption figures are what we need. Even if the biomass is low, consumption could be high in an organism like a bird.

UTILIZATION OF KRILL AND OTHER RESOURCES OF THE SOUTHERN OCEAN BY MAN

J. T. RUUD

Dr Gulland's paper was a most valuable one, and I entirely support his thesis that some measure of international control over the utilization of the resources of the high seas is essential. I would emphasize that the scientists, such as Dr Mackintosh and myself, were aware of the need for proper whale-stock evaluation. But at the time—in the 1930s—there were only about twenty people in the whole world working on whales. We had to develop methods from scratch, and it was indeed through the efforts of British and Norwegian scientists that the valuable statistic of catch per unit effort (catch per catcher's day's work) was introduced.

From the beginning Dr Mackintosh and I tried to get distinct quotas set for different species, so that we could adjust cropping to the changes of their individual stocks, but we could never get this accepted by the industry, which has consequently been able to overexploit each species in turn, starting with the blue as the largest and most rewarding harvest, and passing to fin and sei.

J. A. GULLAND

The last thing I was trying to do was to criticize the scientists whose advice was not followed. I was criticizing those who thought that so important an industry could get along with so few research scientists. It was obvious that research on so many elements in the system was needed—krill, whales, population dynamics and habitat conditions. In fact, the work in the 1930s did provide the basis for the present understanding of whale population dynamics and did delay the collapse of the industry. More scientists and more resources might have led to even better understanding and prevented that collapse altogether.

R. E. LONGTON

The uncontrolled exploitation of krill on a large scale is an alarming prospect because of the central position of these animals in so many food chains. Overcropping could have drastic effects on populations of fish, birds, whales and seals, and indeed on the whole Antarctic marine ecosystem. Dr Gulland has stressed how rapidly a fishing industry can develop and lead to overexploitation. We must decide now whether we should aim to take the maximum possible quantity of krill or curb our demands and protect the secondary consumers. The latter course seems more desirable, as there are other areas where world food production can be increased to meet foreseeable demands. It is thus clear that both fundamental research on the population dynamics of krill and international discussion on rational exploitation should begin now. The experience of whaling has shown that once an industry, with its huge capital investment, has developed it is too late to exercise effective control.

J. A. GULLAND

I did once suggest—perhaps naïvely—that the whaling fleets should come under international ownership, but this was not taken up. I agree that if one is to control an industry it is important to get in with your regulations *before* exploitation starts, just as we are attempting to do with Antarctic sealing.

N. A. Mackintosh

It would be very refreshing to work that way! In krill fishery the total we should be thinking about is not the total available but the total in fishable swarms for economic cropping. The uneven distribution of krill might amount to built-in protection. We certainly need more data on distribution of density. I guess the krill never form uniform high concentrations over a wide range of latitude: it is more likely that the higher concentrations are in a narrow band that moves southward with the receding ice. We want to know how wide the band is, and how much of it is harvestable.

G. G. L. Bertram

I want to make four points:

1. We started by talking about human needs. Our problem, in meeting this need sensibly, does not arise from scientific limitations but from the inadequacy of any legal framework governing the *ownership* of high sea resources such as fisheries. It is interesting to note the speed at which the floor of the North Sea was divided among the riparian nations as soon as the sea-floor gas and possible oil reserves were recognized. Yet worldwide legal arrangements over high-seas fisheries remain totally inadequate. The competitive greed to exploit any unowned resources, which is everywhere resulting in overfishing to our detriment, must be replaced by a rationality which can only come via recognition of legal ownership, whether vested in a nation or an international agency.
2. We must avoid a "year 2000" fixation! That year is no more important than any other in planning what we hope will be the future of mankind.
3. In the long term the cheapest way of harvesting krill may be to allow whales to reover and crop them.
4. Rather than ships designed as whales, if we do collect krill mechanically it may be done better by anchored platforms with automatic, wind-driven filter pumps.

B. Stonehouse

If krill were exploited, which parts of the population would be taken? Could yet get a better production from young or old? Can you select in the field?

P. A. Moiseev

We cannot answer this question yet. We guess the life span of krill to be four or five years, and that the animal reaches maturity and can first spawn at two to two and a half years old. It may be that 25–30% of the krill standing crop is catchable, but it is still too early to say.

T. J. Hart

When we consider using excess krill, one thing to remember is that there are carnivorous zooplankton species that take krill in its first year. *Euphausia superba* is unusual among planktonic crustacea in taking more than one year to complete its cycle. Planktonic predators like *Parathemisto* and *Sagitta* certainly take some young stages.

It is important to remember that the mortality of first-year krill may be very high. Their predators may go through a more rapid life cycle than they (krill) do.

K. G. McKenzie

How does the protein in krill compare with that in other edible Crustacea?

P. A. MOISEEV

I have no data here, but my memory is that some other Crustacea are richer in protein.

J. A. GULLAND

What is the composition of the protein? In particular the lysine and methionine levels may be important.

P. A. MOISEEV

As approximate percentages of the whole protein:

lysine	12	alanine	6
arginine	8	tryptophane	2
thianine	7	glutamine	12
valine	8	triasine	7
leucine	15	servine	2
phenyl alanine	6	cystine	8
		asparagine	11

L. IRVING

The nutritional value of krill must be compared with that of vertebrate food. When considering the possible use of plankton as emergency rations for survivors from ships or aircraft at sea it was thought that the chitinous exoskeletons would present problems, since they would be abrasive and indigestible. However, many vertebrates eat Crustacea without difficulty. Salinity levels were also thought likely to be high and to present a problem, but in practice they are only equivalent to or slightly less concentrated than sea water. Processing for human consumption is therefore likely to be practicable. I have myself lived on plankton for several days and it is quite satisfactory, although rather dull.

P. A. MOISEEV

Our scientists are working on the processing of krill for human consumption; preliminary results are good. It can be the base for many pleasant products; the aroma is good and palatability high. While krill may not be imminent as a human food, there seem to be no problems and we are confident it will be used in some years' time.

G. A. KNOX

We have had a lot of talk about "excess" or "surplus" krill, and this is dangerous. We are dealing with a highly dynamic, little-known system and whatever krill is not taken by a consumer will in any event revert to the system via the decomposers. What we want to know is how much krill there is, what its productivity is, and what would be the maximum sustainable yield.

W. J. L. SLADEN

All this emphasizes how important it is that all SCAR nations devote more efforts to the study of the pack-ice ecosystem.

G. A. KNOX

Among the other consumers of krill one must not forget the epipelagic fishes. What about using these fishes as krill consumers, and exploiting them?

P. A. MOISEEV

It is possible. There are Antarctic fish, such as *Notothenia* species, which may be commercially exploitable, but there are probably not very many. Some fish migrate from the north into Antarctic waters to feed and might also be catchable.

M. J. DUNBAR

Some time ago I read of a scheme to introduce Northern Hemisphere food fishes, including cod and herring, into the southern ocean, and I understood that Soviet scientists were behind the plan. Is this still seriously considered as a possibility.

P. A. MOISEEV

I don't know about it. There is one southern fish that resembles a herring somewhat. The plan you refer to is not talked about at present.

J. T. RUUD

I made a note of the fact that Dr Moiseev said that there were still technical and economic problems to be solved. It seems that there is therefore no immediate danger of the invasion of the Antarctic by fishermen. An experimental fishery research programme is obviously what we need at present. I agree with Dr Bertram that even a modern vessel may find it hard to compete for efficiency with a whale. By 1990 we have seen that the fin whale may be back to a croppable level and the blue might also recover if all whaling ceased now. In the long term it might be in everybody's interests to stop whaling now and let the stocks recover, so that we have a really viable whaling industry as our main means of cropping krill in the not too distant future.

Part V

MARINE BENTHOS

Marine Benthos

In most parts of the world the analysis of floral and faunal zonation in the intertidal zones has been a major preoccupation among marine biologists. G. A. Knox (1960) attempted a comparative summary of such zonation patterns for the Antarctic and Subantarctic and extended this in his paper in the SCAR Symposium on Antarctic Oceanography (Knox, 1968). The latter paper remains the most recent and comprehensive review in this field, and the brief contributions by Propp, Gruzov and Pushkin and Gallardo and Castillo in the present section should be examined in relation to it, and to the supporting papers by Price and Redfearn, and Etcheverry in the same volume. All these authors have emphasized the relatively barren nature of the ice-scoured Antarctic littoral and upper sublittoral, where rich growths of algae and concentrations of animals are restricted to pools and crevices. As Dayton, Robilliard and Paine and the Soviet contributors in the present section point out, faunal and floral diversity and biomass increase with depth, and strikingly large biomasses are encountered at around the 50–300 m levels (see, for example, the data obtained by Ushakov set out in Fig. 5 in the review paper by Knox in Part II of this volume). As might be expected, however, the increasing number of papers is beginning to reveal the diversity of Antarctic sublittoral zonation patterns which appear to be related not only to substratum and shelter from ice scour, but to the duration and opacity of the sea-ice cover, which will clearly have a major influence on plant growing seasons. With information now available for Mac Murdo (Dayton, Robilliard and Paine, this section) Terre Adelie (Delepine and Hureau, 1963), Haswell Islands (Propp, this section), Molodezhnaya (Gruzov and Pushkin, this section), the South Orkney Islands (Price and Redfearn, 1968), the South Shetland Islands (Gruzov and Pushkin, this section; Gallardo and Castillo, this section) and several points on the coast of the Antarctic Peninsula (Ageitos de Castellavos and Perez, 1963; Etcheverry, 1968; Delepine, Lamb and Zimmermann, in preparation), qualitative and quantitative differences between the littoral and sublittoral biotas of the Antarctic coastlands are beginning to emerge just as they are doing in the field of planktonic primary productivity. The next few years should see advance toward a meaningful comparative evaluation.

Recent advances have also been made in the analysis of the trophic interrelations of the benthic fauna, and these, *inter alia*, have demonstrated the fallacy of the belief, widely held until recently, that the large slow-growing sponges and colonial polyzoa of the Antarctic sublittoral were unavailable in food chains except through the decomposers. In the present section, P. M. Arnaud demonstrates the wide adoption of scavenging by the Antarctic benthic fauna and attributes this to the seasonal periodicity of plankton production, as a result of the ice regime. His paper and those by M. H. Thurston and M. White will indicate the results to be looked for from more detailed autecological studies of Antarctic benthic species.

References

Ageitos de Castellavos, Z. J. and Perez, J. C. L. (1963). Algunos aspectos bioecológicos de la zona intecotidal de cabo Primavera (costa de Danco, Peninsula Antártica.). *Inst. Antártico Chileno*, Contr. No. 72.

Delepine, R. and Hureau, J.-C. (1963). La vegatation marine dans l'archipel de Pointe Geologie (Terre Adélie). Apercu preliminaire. *Bull. Mus. Hist. Natlle, Paris.* 35, No. 1, 108–15.

Etcheverry, H. (1968). Distribution of benthic algae on the continental platform of the Antarctic Peninsula. *In* "Symposium on Antarctic Oceanography". Scott Polar Research Institute, Cambridge.

Knox, G. A. (1960). Littoral ecology and biogeography of the southern oceans. *Proc. R. Soc.* 152, No. 949, 577–624.

Knox, G. A. (1968). Tides and intertidal zones. *In* "Symposium on Antarctic Oceanography." Scott Polar Research Institute, Cambridge.

Price, J. H. and Redfearn, P. (1968). The marine ecology of Signy Island, South Orkney Islands. *In* "Symposium on Antarctic Oceanography." Scott Polar Research Institute, Cambridge.

Bottom Communities of the Upper Sublittoral of Enderby Land and the South Shetland Islands

E. N. GRUZOV AND A. F. PUSHKIN
Zoological Institute, Academy of Sciences, Leningrad and *Murmansk Marine Biological Institute, Academy of Sciences, Murmansk, U.S.S.R.*

I. Introduction

The scuba diving technique has opened the way for new studies of life in the coastal shallow seas. Standard hydrobiological methods, generally insufficient for the solution of many problems of marine ecology, are employed in the Antarctic with great difficulty. This appears to account for the almost complete lack of information on communities of the upper sublittoral in Antarctic seas.

Propp (1970) has outlined our joint work in the Davis Sea in 1965–66. This work laid a foundation for ecological research in the shallow Antarctic seas and yielded the first information about biocoenoses of Haswell Islands. This region was chosen for study purely for technical reasons, since there was almost no information on bottom communities for any part of the coast. Naturally enough, after this work was finished the question of the representativeness of the region selected immediately arose.

The absence of macrophytes previously reported from various areas of the Antarctic, from this region, suggests that it is aberrant rather than typical. Furthermore, the uniformity of the whole coast and similarity between all transects did not allow us to detect the influence of local hydrological, hydrochemical and other conditions upon the composition and nature of the biological communities.

The only way to answer all these questions is by carrying out analogous investigations in other parts of the Antarctic coast. That is why the authors of the present paper, supported by S. N. Rybakov as underwater photographer, and V. I. Luleev as mechanic, took part in the 13th Soviet Antarctic Expedition.

Work was carried out at Molodezhnaya (Enderby Land) in December 1967 (from the ice) and in mid-March 1968 (in open water). In February 1968 dives were made in Ardley Bay, near Bellingshausen Station (King George Island, South Shetland Islands). Some dives were also undertaken at Mirny

Station and off the coast of the Antarctic Peninsula. Research at Enderby Land was expected to establish the extent to which the data obtained in the Davis Sea could be extended to other parts of east Antarctica, and the studies in the South Shetland Islands to yield material for comparison of the east and west Antarctic. All collections, including quantitative samples of animals and plants, were made directly under water at depths down to 55 m. Areas of the most typical biocoenoses were photographed, though, due to the greater turbidity of the water, the pictures were not so good as those taken in the Davis Sea. During the expedition 169 dives were made, ninety-seven hours were spent under water and ninety-five samples of benthos were taken. The main collections are still being processed.

II. Benthic Communities at Molodezhnaya and Mirny Stations

Underwater landscapes at Molodezhnaya Station differ from those at Mirny. There are extensive muddy and sandy areas which are practically absent from Haswell Islands. The benthic populations of rocky ground, especially in shallow waters, also show marked differences which primarily depend on the illumination of the sea bottom.

We distinguish two types of rocky upper sublittoral. The first is characteristic of steep coasts with ice shelves. Under such shelves there are always huge snowdrifts which absorb most of the solar radiation. If, in such areas, the bottom is steep enough and the edge of the snowdrift lies over a depth of 20 m or more, the illumination of the bottom is insufficient for the development of macrophytes. Such areas are very similar to those at Mirny.

The upper zone (up to 7–8 m) is practically lifeless. At depths from 8 to 15 m there are starfishes (*Odontaster validus*), sea urchins (*Sterechinus neumayeri*), very occasional sponges, restricted to trenches, and some other forms. There are also small colonies of the alcyonarian *Eunephthya* which are not rare, but have a very small biomass. This zone can be compared with the *Eunephthya* zone at Mirny.

Near low coasts snowdrifts are absent and the ice is fairly transparent. The snow cover in the region of Molodezhnaya Station is in general not so thick as at Mirny. Below the lifeless zone, at depths from 2 to 5 m, the rocks are covered by diatoms. This zone is inhabited by amphipods and gasteropods. At 5–7 m a zone of macrophytes which are absent from Haswell Islands begins. Two to three species of red algae occur to a depth of 10 m and brown algae (*Desmarestia* sp.) to 20–25 m. Among animals in this zone *Odontaster validus* and *Sterechinus neumayeri* have the greatest biomass. There are also some species of sponges, nemertines (*Lineus*), sedentary polychaetes, and other forms.

At depths from 30 to 50 m no algae at all were recorded. *Sterechinus neumayeri* is the most abundant species, though sponges and ascidians have the greatest biomass. Many alcyonarians, Echinodermata, Pantopoda and Crustacea, are present here. Differences between transects at this depth are almost negligible and the whole zone resembles that of sponges at Mirny. On steep slopes the fauna and flora is richer. In the middle of March the bottom is densely covered with diatoms.

On the whole, the biomass of animals in Molodezhnaya is much lower than that at Mirny. The fauna in this region is much poorer in species primarily because of the absence of passive filter-feeding animals. This can apparently be correlated with weak currents in the region of station.

The fauna of mud and sand was studied only down to 15 m. The biocoenoses of mud include bivalves, *Laternula elliptica*, irregular sea urchins (*Abatus sp.*) and burrowing polychaetes. On the surface one can observe starfishes (*Odontaster validus*) and gasteropods. The fauna of sand is very poor.

Short observations at Mirny station added almost nothing to our knowledge of this region. Mention should be made, however, of the presence of a thick layer of bottom ice near the coast. This layer extended to a depth of 15 m, i.e. just to the upper limit of the zone of *Eunepthya*. The bottom ice appears to inhibit the development of life in the uppermost horizons of the sublittoral.

The preliminary data collected by the 11th Soviet Antarctic Expedition suggested that the areas around Molodezhnaya and Mirny differed considerably from one another. Observations made in 1967–68, however, have shown that the zonation pattern of the biocoenoses at these stations is the same in identical biotopes. It is significant that most of the same species occur both at Mirny and Molodezhnaya. The same picture may therefore be expected throughout the whole area from Enderby Land to the Davis Sea. At the same time the number of different biotopes at Molodezhnaya is greater and it is apparently more typical of the upper sublittoral of east Antarctica.

III. Benthic Communities in the South Shetland Islands

The littoral zone is either lifeless or very poor. In addition to scarce diatoms there are also some species of chiton and gasteropods (*Patinigera*).

At depths of 2–3 m and below there is a zone of abundant, mainly green and red, algae belonging to five to seven species. The number of species of animals is increased, primarily by starfishes, sea urchins, sponges and ascidians. *Patinigera*, however, still remains among the dominants and there are several other species of gasteropod. None the less, the fauna as a whole is very poor. At a depth of 8–10 m red algae are replaced by brown ones and starfishes (*Labidiaster* sp.) appear. The biomass of animals increases with increasing depth.

At a depth of 30 m a zone of mud inhabited by ascidians, sea urchins (*Abatus* sp.), starfishes and brittle stars begins. Vast colonies of synascidians reaching from 7 to 10 m in length are characteristic of this zone. Serolidae, *Laternula*, etc., are found in mud below shallower water (at around 10 m). Biomass is greater and the fauna richer on steep rocks than on gentle slopes. The area appears to resemble the South Orkney Islands most closely in its ecology*.

Some dives were made in Fildes Strait, which is characterized by strong tidal currents following at up to 4–5 knots. The bottom is rocky in its character.

At low tide, small rock pools are isolated in the littoral zone, and these contain red and green algae. Under stones amphipods (two to three species) are very abundant, and there are some species of planarian.

In the upper sublittoral red algae form dense thickets inhabited by starfishes, gasteropods (*Patinigera*) and amphipods. Brown algae appear below, at depths down to 15–20 m. Their thalli lack epiphytes and attached animals. Under the crown of algae currents are weak and the entire surface of the rocks is covered with animals. The fauna is very rich and the number of species greatly exceeds that in Ardley Bay. Sponges and ascidians have the greatest biomass. There are many hydroids and alcyonarians, and bryozoans, all groups of Echinodermata, polychaetes and crustaceans are very abundant. Unfortunately there was insufficient time to study this region in detail.

Thus, the observations carried out in 1968 reconfirmed the faunistic differences between the east and west Antarctic. These differences are ecological as well as biogeographical. Before a more detailed account of zonation in east Antarctica can be given, further investigations are necessary, mainly to the east of Mirny.

References

Price, J. H. and Redfearn, P. (1968) (eds). The marine ecology of Signy Island, South Orkney Islands. *In* "Symposium on Antarctic Oceanography", Polar Research Institute, Cambridge.

Propp, M. V. (1970). The study of bottom fauna at Haswell Islands by scuba diving. (This volume).

* See J. H. Price and P. Redfearn (1968).

The Study of Bottom Fauna at Haswell Islands by Scuba Diving

M. V. PROPP
Murmansk Marine Biological Institute, Academy of Sciences, Murmansk, U.S.S.R.

I. Introduction

The use of scuba diving is convenient for exploring marine-bottom communities near shore. It can be applied even when a thick layer of ice covers the sea surface. More than 140 scientific dives were made during the summer season of 1965–66 near Haswell Islands in the east Antarctic, and sixty more dives were carried out in the 1967–68 season. One hundred and twenty quantitative samples were collected. Underwater photography and a study of statistical regularities in the distribution of the large bottom invertebrates were also employed.

This work made it possible to describe the bottom communities of this region and to compare them with those of the North Atlantic, where the authors had previously carried out similar investigations.

II. Benthic Communities

In the vicinity of Haswell Islands there are to be found mostly hard bottoms. The littoral zone is lifeless, while the sublittoral communities include numerous species with high biomass. The following bottom communities prove to be the most common ones:

1. The bottom community of diatoms, the asteroid *Odontaster validus* and the hydroid *Tubularia ralphy* is to be found on rocky ground at depths of 2–10 m. The most common diatoms belong to the genera *Pleurosigma*, *Fragilariopsis*, *Amphiprora*, *Achnantes* and *Nitschia*. These diatoms develop abundantly in spring and summer, forming a layer on the bottom which may be several centimetres thick. For the rest of the year the bottom in shallow water is covered by a thick cover of ice crystals, formed when the sea freezes and destroyed in the end of December or in the beginning of January. The total animal biomass reaches 20–25 g/m^2, but the number of species is generally comparatively small (twenty to forty).

2. The bottom community of the red alga *Phyllophora antarctica*, calcarous algae and the sea urchin *Sterechinus neumayeri*, is to be found at the depth of 6–25 m. Bottom ice also forms in the zone occupied by this community, but in smaller quantities than in the preceding case. The total animal biomass in this community is 450 g/m^2 and the number of animal species is also greater, reaching forty to sixty.

It should be mentioned that both these shallow-bottom communities are most characteristic of regions where the fast ice is transparent. If a thick layer of snow covers the ice (this depends on the orientation of the shore with regard to the direction of the winds) the characteristic features of the bottom communities are not so definitely expressed.

3. The bottom community of Alcyonaria (*Eunephthya* sp.) is found at 25–30 m. This community is characterized by its varied fauna, including more than seventy to eighty species, and its total biomass averages about 1000 g/m^2.

4. The bottom community of the sponges *Rosella racovitzae* and *Scolymastra joubini*, the hydroid *Oswaldella antarctica* and some Ascidiacea occupies depths more than 30 m. This community includes several hundreds of different species, the total biomass of which goes up to 3 kg/m^2. This is the richest of all the communities discovered, both in total biomass and the number of its species.

As far as can be judged, similar bottom communities are widely spread in many parts of the east Antarctic. The region of Haswell Islands differs, however, in that macroscopic algae are nearly absent, *Phyllophora antarctica* being the only representative. The area suitable as a habitat for large bottom algae seems to be too small to be sufficient for the maintenance of populations of algae with planktonic spores (*Phyllophora* can reproduce vegetatively).

III. Discussion

The Antarctic sublittoral bottom communities have some features in common with the corresponding communities of the North Atlantic, though the number of bipolar species is very small.

Algae predominate near the upper edge of the sublittoral in both Arctic and Antarctic. In the Haswell Islands they are chiefly microscopic diatoms, while in the North Atlantic they are mainly large *Laminaria* spp. However, in many other regions of the Antarctic large brown algae, such as *Phyllogigas* and *Desmarestia*, are important. These algae are ecologically similar to the Arctic *Laminaria*. At the same time an abundant development of bottom diatoms can be expected in the High Arctic. It would be interesting to find out if bottom ice exists in the Arctic and if so, how it influences animals and plants.

Bottom communities of herbivorous sea urchins and calcarous algae are to be found at greater depths than the communities mentioned above. The sea urchin *Sterechinus neumayeri* is particularly widespread in the Antarctic, while *Strongylocentrotus droebachiensis* is most common in the North Atlantic. The ecological similarity of these communities is obvious at first sight.

With the increasing depth, attached seston-eaters predominate in the communities. These animals can actively seize the heavier particles from the bottom water. Such are Alcyonaria in the Antarctic and Cirripedia in the North Atlantic. At greater depths in the sublittoral larger organisms with powerful filtering apparatus predominate. In the east Antarctic different sponges and ascidians belong to this group, and in the Arctic chiefly Spongia and Bivalvia.

It must be mentioned that side by side with these elements of similarity there are considerable differences. Thus, the bottom communities of the Antarctic are two or three times richer in species than those of the Arctic. It would be interesting to establish the degree to which the metabolic rates of common species of algae and invertebrates are similar in the Arctic and Antarctic.

Quantitative Observations on the Benthic Macrofauna of Port Foster (Deception Island) and Chile Bay (Greenwich Island)

V. A. GALLARDO AND J. CASTILLO
Departmento de Zoology, Universidad de Concepción, Chile

I. Port Foster

On 21 and 31 December 1967 a limited survey of the bottom was carried out by the authors to observe the effects of the volcanic eruption of 4 December on the infauna of Port Foster. Fifteen 0·1 m^2 and one 0·2 m^2 Petersen grab samples and five dredge hauls gave evidence that most of the bottom had been covered by a layer of ash of a minimum thickness of 30 cm. Bottom samplers caught little or no infauna in the greater part of Port Foster and dredges from the same area showed no residues of the previously existing infauna. Comparisons with yields from samples taken in a previous year at Port Foster and outside the bay give an idea of the extent of the mortality. Near the entrance of Port Foster, where the bottom did not show considerable ash covering, animals were more numerous. A dredge haul here caught many specimens of living *Ophionotus victoriae* Bell, 1902, together with many dead ones. All Echinoids were dead and in an advanced state of decomposition. Mortality in this case was presumably due to chemical and/or physico-chemical factors.

Other causes of mortality in the bottom fauna of Port Foster were the uplift of the bottom and a formation of a new islet at Telefon Bay, the high concentration of toxic compounds and the high temperature reached by the water nearby. Further alterations of the ecosystem were indicated by the absence of fish and other sea life at the time of the observations. Turbidity of the water and the presence of sulphur compounds may have also altered the productivity of the surface layers.

Port Foster is now an excellent spot to study the re-establishment of the ecosystem as the habitat slowly returns to normality.

II. Chile Bay

Preliminary analysis of quantitative samples taken in Chile Bay at depths varying from 15 to 350 m disclosed interesting features for Antarctic sub-littoral infaunas. Down to about 100 m the macroinfauna is highly diversified, the number of species per sample being high and the number of individuals per species comparatively low, although not quite as low as in tropical in-faunas. In other words, no dominant species is found in these bottom deposits in this investigation. The biomass of the fauna appears comparatively low.

Below about 100 m samples differ sharply in having a clearly dominant species (*Maldane sarsi antarctica* Arwidsson, 1911) which makes up about 50% of the total number of individuals per $0{\cdot}1m^2$ Petersen grab sample. In this zone the biomass surpasses that in the shallower waters.

The features briefly described above have interesting evolutionary and ecological implications. North temperate and cold water sublittoral infaunas in general have shown to be little diversified and generally have strongly dominant species; on the other hand, tropical sublittoral infaunas are re-markably diverse and normally without dominant species. It would appear that the extreme environmental conditions and geological instability accounts for the low diversity and immaturity of most northern ecosystems, while in the Antarctic sublittoral, although the environment is also harsh (mainly because of the extreme low temperatures) the benthic ecosystems have attained maturity because of the long geological stability or permanence of this environment.

Benthic Faunal Zonation as a Result of Anchor Ice at McMurdo Sound, Antarctica

PAUL K. DAYTON, GORDON A. ROBILLIARD AND
R. T. PAINE
Department of Zoology, University of Washington, Seattle, Washington, U.S.A.

I. Introduction

Gradients in faunal diversity with latitude, and the vertical zonation of marine communities have received much attention from marine ecologists. Thorson (1946) and Ekman (1953) summarize literature which emphasizes a great tropical diversity which is dramatically reduced at high latitudes. Pianka (1966, 1967) has emphasized that any or all of a complex of factors, including the evolutionary age of the fauna, environmental heterogeneity and stability, competition, predation, and primary productivity may be the fundamental causative factor of this phenomenon. Improved sampling techniques have recently added another dimension to the problem, for Hessler and Sanders (1967) have found that the extremely homogeneous and stable deep-sea environment harbours a surprisingly diverse fauna.

The zonation especially characteristic of most marine rocky littoral areas is a related phenomenon, both because comparable abundance-diversity trends characterize transects from high to low levels and because many of the same processes are causally involved, although only on a local scale. An extensive literature has been summarized by Lewis (1964), who particularly emphasized the role of physical factors. More experimental studies (Connell, 1961; Paine, 1966) have indicated the importance of interspecific interactions, suggesting that any future synthesis of causal processes will be complex.

The rich Antarctic fauna (Dearborn, 1965), the high latitude, the extreme physical stability (Tressler and Ommundsen, 1962; Littlepage, 1965) and the seasonal but predictable primary productivity emphasize the potentially important contribution investigations of Antarctic marine communities may make to many ecological generalizations. The excellent logistic and laboratory support offered by the U.S. Navy and the National Science Foundation at McMurdo Sound plus the opportunity to work from stable annual sea ice has permitted an extensive diving programme designed to obtain basic information about the patterns of distribution and abundance of the dominant epibenthic animals and the biological interactions which characterize the shallow-water benthic communities.

Given the stable Antarctic environment and a relatively homogeneous substratum, biological interactions would *a priori* be expected to be most important in the evolution and maintenance of the benthic community. This may be so in deep (>33 m) water associations. Ice phenomena (Dayton *et al.*, 1969), however, are the dominating influences on the shallow (0–33 m) environment. Sea ice forms annually in the intertidal zones, to depths as great as 4 m. The scouring effect as this ice mass floats with the tides effectively eliminates sessile macroscopic organisms from intertidal or immediate subtidal levels. In the McMurdo region ice floes from the near-by shelf occasionally scrape the bottom to depths of at least 15 m. Further, in the spring (October–December) of 1967, ice crystals in the form of large platelets 10–15 cm in diameter and 0·2 to 0·5 cm thick froze and formed a mat on the bottom in depths down to approximately 15 m. Aggregates of this anchor ice were seen in depths down to 33 m, and it has been demonstrated to be capable of lifting weights of at least 25 kg (Dayton *et al.*, 1969). It was clear that the relevance of these ice phenomena to both animal distribution and biological interactions required study.

Dearborn (1965), working with a variety of oceanographic sampling devices, surveyed and described the various bottom types in McMurdo Sound and presented a very complete compilation of the fauna obtained in various grabs and dredges. Dearborn and Bullivant and Dearborn (1967) attempted to catalogue all the McMurdo bottom types and Ross Sea faunal assemblages. The shallow-water benthic communities investigated by us generally fell within Dearborn's much more general Bottom Types 1, 2 and 3. Our paper, emphasizing the results of physical and biological interactions, does not attempt to list all species (especially the smaller ones comprising the infauna of the sponge mat) occurring in this habitat.

II. Methods

Two of us (P.K.D. and G.A.R.) made a total of 178 dives between 14 October and 11 December 1967. Dives were made at Cape Armitage, Hut Point, Arrival Heights, the Cinder Cones, Turtle Rock, Cape Evans, Cape Royds, Horseshoe Bay, and the Dailey Islands. Except at Cape Armitage and Hut Point, dives were generally made in the open through holes blasted in the annual sea ice. In a few instances natural tide cracks and seal holes were utilized. Dives at Hut Point and Cape Armitage were made through blasted holes over which were placed heated huts. Standard wet suits and scuba equipment were used; no significant modifications were found necessary. The average duration of the dives was 40 min; the longest dive was 1 hr 35 min. The average working depths were 20–45 m, although a number of dives were made to 60 m.

The results presented in this paper are ancillary but essential to our experimental study of Antarctic trophic dynamics which involved the establishment of cages designed to exclude specific types of predator. In addition to establishing these cages and their controls, observations were made on the relative abundance, size relationships, and feeding interactions of the larger animals. A Nikonos underwater camera with flash attachment was used for the photographic aspects of the study.

Our observations refer only to depths of 60 m or less at Cape Armitage and the north side of Hut Point. Other localities were characterized by different faunas and floras, probably due to differences in substrate, currents, sedimentation, etc. For descriptions of different bottom types, reference should be made to Bullivant and Dearborn (1967).

III. Results

Ice scouring by drifting floes occurs only rarely and was not observed in the spring of 1967. Anchor ice, however, does have a pronounced effect on the benthic animals (Dayton *et al.*, 1969). The mats of ice crystals grow to be as much as 0·5 m thick and entangle benthic animals present on the substratum. Motile animals crawl on to the surface of the ice, where they also often become entrapped. Portions of this anchor-ice mat become detached from the substratum and float to the undersurface of the annual sea ice, where the animals are effectively trapped. We frequently observed individuals of the fish genus, *Trematomus*, the echnoid *Sterechinus neumayeri*, the asteroid *Odontaster validus*, the nemertean *Lineus corrugatus*, the isopod *Glyptonotus antarcticus*, and various pycnogonids frozen into the undersurface of the sea ice. In one instance twelve *S. neumayeri* and forty *O. validus* were frozen into the undersurface of 1 sq m of the sea ice. It is interesting to note that entrapped animals are not necessarily killed by these large ice crystals, and we observed many, particularly *O. validus* and *Lineus*, which escaped and fell unharmed to the bottom. Those that do not escape are carried out to sea each summer when the ice breaks up. These ice phenomena, in addition to the effect of the annual sea-ice scouring, produce the marked faunistic zonation of the bottom discussed below.

A. Zone I

At both Cape Armitage and Hut Point this shallow zone extends from 0 to approximately 15 m and is characterized by a general organic barrenness. At Cape Armitage the substratum is a pebble slope, and at Hut Point it consists of pebbles and volcanic debris.

It appears that the ice scouring and heavy anchor-ice formation effectively clear most of the motile and sessile animals that are able to establish themselves each year during ice-free periods. The detritus-feeding echinoderms, *S. neumayeri* and *O. validus*, as well as *Lineus*, *Glyptonotus*, and a few pycnogonids and fish forage into Zone I. *Lineus* and *Glyptonotus* appear to be scavengers; the pycnogonids eat coelenterates, which are rare in Zone I; and the fish are active predators. Indeed, the predation of the bathydraconid fish, *Gymnodraco acuticeps*, on *Trematomus bernacchii* and *T. nicolai* was the only active interaction observed in Zone I.

B. Zone II

Except for a shoal area at Cape Armitage where a strong current reduces anchor ice formation and a few sponge species occur in as little as 23 m, the upper limit of Zone II is reasonably well defined at 15 m, while the lower limit is sharply defined at 33 m. The substratum is of cobble and lava, and there are numerous sessile animals. The alcyonarian, *Alcyonium paessleri*, and the actinarians, *Artemidactis victrix*, *Isotealia antarctica*, *Urticinopsis antarctica*, and *Hormathia lacunifera*, are the largest and most conspicuous sessile components of Zone II. The stoloniferan, *Clavularia frankliniana*, and the hydrozoans, *Tubularia hodgsoni* and *Lampra parvula*, are numerically dominant. *Clavularia* grows from stolons and is heavily clumped in some areas. *Lampra parvula* also has a patchy distribution. There are a few scattered individuals of the hydroid, *Halecium arboreum*, and a few clumps of sponges in the lower part of Zone II. In most areas the large ascidians, *Cnemidocarpa verrucosa*, are also present.

The most conspicuous motile animals of Zone II are again *Odontaster*, *Sterechinus*, *Lineus*, and the fishes, *Trematomus bernacchii* and *T. centronotus*. The pycnogonids, *Thavmastopygnon striata*, *Colossendeis robusta* and *C. megalonyx*, are also common.

All the alcyonarians and hydroids feed on suspended particles; the observed diets of some of the macroscopic invertebrate carnivores are given in Table 1. The actinarians, *Isotealia* and *Urticinopsis*, frequently feed on the large medusae which in shallow areas often get close enough to the bottom to be captured. *Urticinopsis*, however, feeds predominantly on echinoderms, which comprise 77% of its diet. Its most frequent prey, the echinoid *Sterechinus*, protects itself against this predation by camouflaging itself with bivalve shells and other debris (*cf.* Arnaud, 1964, who described this as protection against sunlight). The camouflage often includes a thick mat of hydroids. Twenty *in situ* experiments demonstrate that when a camouflaged urchin makes contact with an anemone, the anemone places its tentacles over the potential prey, touches the hydroids, and then often retracts its tentacles, thereby releasing the urchin. Sometimes, when the urchin was apparently

TABLE 1

Dominant Predators and Their Prey in Zone II

Predator	*Observations*	*Prey*	*% of diet*
Urticinopsis antarcticus	75	*Sterechinus neumayeri*	65·3
		Scyphozoans	21·3
		Diplasterias brucei	5·3
		Odontaster validus	4·0
		Perknaster fuscus antarcticus	1·3
		Acodontaster hodgsoni	1·3
		Urticinopsis antarcticus	1·3
Thavmastopycnon striata	32	*Artemidactis victrix*	81·3
		Clavularia frankliniana	9·4
		Unidentified sponge	3·1
		Unidentified hydroid	3·1
		Unidentified anemone	3·1
Colossendeis robusta	25	Tiny unidentified hydroid on sponge	48·0
		Clavularia frankliniana	40·0
		Tubularia hodgsoni	12·1
Colossendeis megalonyx	5	Tiny unidentified hydroid on sponge	100·0

aware of the anemone tentacles, it released its camouflage and made its escape, leaving the anemone with the shell debris. In 80% of the experiments with camouflaged prey the urchin escaped. The camouflage was then removed and the urchin induced to crawl against the same anemone. This was always fatal to the urchin. Since *Urticinopsis* employs a "sit and wait" feeding strategy, it would be advantageous to them not to have any close neighbours. Our frequent observations of two anemones with their tentacles entwined may represent a kind of territorial behaviour. Although in one case this relationship resulted in cannibalism, in most cases the two simply moved apart. The entire sequence is shown in Figs. 1, 2, 3 and 4.

The other predation observations in Zone II were on pycnogonids. *Thavmastopygnon striata* definitely eats both the anemone, *Artemidactis victrix*, and the stoloniferan, *Clavularia*. *Colossendeis megalonyx* is mostly seen eating a small unidentified hydroid which grows on the clumps of sponge, and *Colossendeis robusta* eats the same hydroid as well as *Tubularia hodgsoni*. Among the fish, *Gymnodraco* is reasonably common and still eats small *Trematomus*. The stomach contents of *Trematomus* were almost 100% scaleworm with an occasional crustacean (see also Dearborn, 1965).

FIG. 1. Three of the camouflaged echinoids, *Sterechinus neumayeri.*

FIG. 2. One of the same echinoids, having been induced to crawl against an actinarian *Urticinopsis antarctica*, escapes, leaving parts of its camouflage.

FIG. 3. The same *Sterechinus* with its camouflage removed is captured and eventually eaten by the same *Urticinopsis*.

FIG. 4. Possibly a form of territorial behaviour by *Urticinopsis*.

C. Zone III

Zone III begins abruptly at 33 m and continues down to an undetermined depth. Because of a sharp cliff at the 30 m level at Cape Armitage, the transition from Zone II to Zone III is best observed at Hut Point. Here, within a vertical distance of 3 m, the substratum changes from a cobble rocky bottom to one of a thick mat of sponge spicules and bivalve shells. Thirty-three

TABLE 2

Dominant Predators and Their Prey in Zone III

Predator	*Observations*	*Prey*	*% of diet*
Diplasterias brucei	71	*Limatula hodgsoni*	97·2
		Trophon longstaffi	2·8
Odontaster meridionalis	17	*Polymastia invaginata*	29·4
		Homaxonella sp.	23·5
		Rossella racovitzae	17·6
		Mycale acerata	17·6
		Calyx arcuarius	5·9
		Adocia tenella	5·9
Acodontaster conspicuus	88	"*volcano sponge*"*	53·4
		Tetilla leptoderma	31·8
		Rossella racovitzae	7·9
		Haliclona dancoi	3·4
		Polymastia invaginata	1·1
		Sphaerotylus antarcicus	1·1
		Homaxonella sp.	1·1
Perknaster fuscus antarcticus	38	*Mycale acerata*	39·5
		Polymastia invaginata	23·7
		Tetilla leptoderma	15·8
		Icodictya setifer	7·9
		Haliclona dancoi	5·3
		Rossella racovitzae	2·6
		Kirkpatrickia variolosa	2·6
		Homaxonella sp.	2·6
Austrodoris mcmurdoensis	147	"*volcano sponge*"*	50·3
		Rossella racovitzae	25·2
		Polymastia invaginata	8·2
		Haliclona dancoi	6·8
		Calyx arcuarius	4·8
		Sphaerotylus antarcticus	2·0
		Tetilla leptoderma	0·7
		Microxina benedeni	0·7
		Homaxonella sp.	0·7

* Volcano sponge was the field identification of *Scolymastra joubini* and *Rossella nuda*, which were not differentiated.

metres appears to be the lower limit of ice formation in the water column in this area (Dayton *et al.*, 1969), possibly because of a halocline effect of the sort proposed by Hela (1958). This halocline effect would lead to the establishment of an abrupt, predictable, boundary between Zones II and III, for even if anchor-ice formation as deep as 33 m were unusual, the very slowly growing sponges would not be expected to survive long above this level, nor would the spicule matrix be able to accumulate.

The sponge spicule mat is almost always more than a metre deep and the surface is totally covered with many as yet unidentified species of sponges. These in turn furnish a substratum for numerous other epibenthic sessile organisms. The most conspicuous of these are the actinarians *Stomphia selaginella*, *Artemidactis victrix*, and a few individuals of *Urticinopsis antarcticus*, the hydroids *Lampra parvula*, *L. microrhiza*, *Halecium arboreum* and many other unidentified hydroids, a few sabellid polychaetes, some bryozoans and a great many molluscs. The most conspicuous mollusc was the bivalve *Limatula hodgsoni*. The rich infauna of the sponge spicule matrix was demonstrated by Dearborn (1965), who recorded more than 12,500 individual animals representing an unspecified number of species per cubic decimetre of the sponge mat.

Asteroids are the most conspicuous motile animals in Zone III. Four of the asteroids (*Acodontaster hodgsoni*, *A. conspicuus*, *Perknaster fuscus antarcticus*, and *Odontaster meridionalis*) are definitely sponge predators (Table 2). *Odontaster validus*, always extremely common, was seen on a few occasions to eat sponges and hydroids, but it generally seems to be a detritus feeder (Pearse, 1965). *Diplasterias brucei* specializes on molluscs, usually *Limatula hodgsoni*. Three *Macroptychaster accrescens* were found at Cape Armitage. In other areas this species swallows *Odontaster validus* and *Sterechinus* whole, but since these *Macroptychaster* were rare in our study area, we did not cut them up to check for recent feedings.

A large dorid opisthobranch, *Austrodoris mcmurdoensis*, was very commonly seen eating large white sponges (Table 2). Another common gastropod, *Trophon langstaffi*, drilled bivalves, particularly *Limatula hodgsoni*. The same fish and pycnogonids of Zone II were common in Zone III.

IV. Discussion

Sufficient data have been presented to evaluate the relative roles of physical and biological stresses in structuring the shallow-water benthic community at McMurdo Sound, Antarctica. It now appears that physical stresses result in a vertical zonation of the dominant sessile organisms (Fig. 5). Within these zones biological interactions are of varying degrees of significance. It is probably noteworthy that the fauna of Zone I, physically the most disturbed

FIG. 5. Vertical zonation of fauna. A few motile animals forage into Zone I, which is otherwise barren of sessile animals. The sessile animals of Zone II are almost exclusively coelenterates, while those of Zone III are predominantly sponges.

zone, is characterized by motile detritus feeders and an absence of competitive interaction and significant predation. Presumably the basic reason for this is that the lack of a consistent and predictable physical environment has prevented both the evolution of permanent residents and the establishment of high densities of the transitory species, either or both of which would enhance the probability of meaningful biological interactions taking place.

The upper limit of Zone II is again not determined by biological factors. The most cogent hypothesis is that this limit represents the lower level of predictable annual removal of sessile fauna by ice scouring and heavy anchor ice. Slow growth and recruitment rates might increase the temporal interval between which scouring and anchor-ice uplift must act to maintain the observed transition. Within Zone II there is a vertical gradient of an increasing luxuriant growth with increasing depth, reflecting a decreasing probability of physical disturbance.

The upper limit of Zone III has a sharp boundary where the slow-growing long lived sponges become effective. This is probably the result of two processes:

(1) the sponges exclude completely the epifauna of Zone II;
(2) the relative physical stability, permitting organic debris to accumulate, allows the substratum to change from a hard rocky bottom to a thick mat of sponge spicules.

Apparent competition in which sponges and hydroids grow over each other has been seen in the transition area. The substratum change allows the development of an infauna and reduces or eliminates the solid substratum necessary for most of the sessile organisms of Zone II. The importance of this is emphasized by the fact that those *Urticinopsis* which do occur in Zone III have settled on relatively tiny clam shells. Without a solid attachment, they can be easily lifted off the bottom by the medusae they catch. The boundary between Zone II and Zone III, then, results from both biological and physical processes.

Zone III is noteworthy because of its extreme physical stability and its relatively greatly increased biological tempo. The differences are emphasized by the greater faunistic densities, higher standing crop, and greater trophic complexity. Extensive diving produced the still preliminary observations on the numerous higher-order predators in Zone III (Table 2) and no evidence of conspicuous overexploitation of the prey. The one known echinoderm predator, *Macroptychaster accrescens*, is not big enough to eat most of the sponge-eating asteroids and is far too rare to effect any differences anyway. The only hypothesis we can propose is that the abundant filter and detritus feeders, particularly the omnivorous and extremely common *Odontaster validus* (characteristic densities up to $15/m^2$), are eating the settling young of most of the other asteroids. This hypothesis could be supported by the observation that the size distribution of most of the other species seems to be skewed far to the right, as only full-grown adults were seen. Even the exceptions to this generalization might support the theory, as *Odontaster validus* itself has a normal size distribution with all size classes represented, as does *Diplasterias brucei*, which broods its young to a well-developed stage. Young *Perknaster antarcticus fuscus* were also found, but we know nothing of its reproductive biology.

The trends revealed by the comparison of our three zones may be relevant to current hypotheses on the causes of trends in organic diversity with latitude. We find with increasing physical stability, where the important parameter is reduction in ice effects, that the macroscopic epifauna, and presumably the microscopic infauna as well, become more abundant and diverse, and that biological interactions are more obvious. Presumably the availability of primary producers to all three shallow zones is equivalent. One of the current hypotheses on species diversity (Paine, 1966) indicates that an increased tempo of predation can lead to increased diversity. Pianka (1966, 1967) has pointed out that another current hypothesis, that of competitive interactions, makes predictions opposite those generated by the predation hypothesis. Our data presently show only that increased diversity is accompanied by increased biological interaction. The basic question of whether the observed coexistence is furthered by competition or predation will only be answered by additional observation and the completion of the cage studies. Finally, we should point out that our understanding of the maintenance of high diversity in a physically stable, low-temperature marine environment will be immediately applicable to deep-sea communities, with many similar biological and physical characteristics.

Acknowledgements

The outstanding co-operation and help by the personnel in the U.S. Navy photographic laboratory at McMurdo Sound is gratefully acknowledged. The following specialists have promptly helped us identify specimens: C. Hand, coelenterates; J. Dearborn, echinoderms; J. Hedgpeth, pycnogonids; J. Bullivant, bryozoans; R. Dell, molluscs; A. Brinckmann-Voss, hydroids; and V. M. Kolton, porifera. S. P. Heller made Figure 2. L. Wilmot assisted in the preparation of the manuscript. This research was supported by the National Science Foundation Grant GA 1187.

References

Arnaud, P. (1964). "Echinodermes littoraux de Terre Adélie (Holothuries exceptées) et Pélécypodes commensaux d'Echinides antarctiques." Expeditions Polaires francaises, publ. No. 258, Paris. 72 pp.

Bullivant, J. S. and Dearborn, J. H. (1967). General accounts, station lists, and benthic ecology. The Fauna of the Ross Sea, Part 5, New Zealand Oceanographic Institute Memoir No. 32. *Bull. N.Z. Dept. scient. ind. Res.* **176**.

Connell, J. H. (1961). The effects of competition, predation by *Thais lapillus*, and other factors on natural populations of the barnacle *Balanus balanoides*. *Ecol. Monogr.* **31**, 61–104.

Dayton, P. K., Robilliard, G. A. and De Vries, A. L. (1969). Anchor ice formation in McMurdo Sound, Antarctica, and its biological effects. *Science, N.Y.* **163**, 273–5.

Dearborn, J. H. (1965). "Ecological and faunistic investigations of the marine benthos at McMurdo Sound, Antarctica." Doctoral dissertation, Stanford University, California.

Ekman, S. (1953). "Zoogeography of the Sea." Sidgwick and Jackson, London. XIV, 417 pp.

Hela I. (1958). The Baltic as an object of ice studies. *In* "Arctic Sea Ice". Washington, D.C. (U.S. National Academy of Sciences—National Research Council Publication 598).

Hessler, R. R. and Sanders, H. L. (1967). Faunal diversity in the deep sea. *Deep Sea Res.* **14**, 65–78.

Lewis, J. R. (1964). "The Ecology of Rocky Shores." English Universities Press, London. 323 pp.

Littlepage, J. L. (1965). Oceanographic investigations in McMurdo Sound, Antarctica. *Antarctic Res. Ser.* **5**, 1–37.

Paine, R. T. (1966). Food web complexity and species diversity. *Am. Nat.* **100**, 65–75.

Pearse, J. S. (1965). Reproductive periodicities in several contrasting populations of *Odontaster validus* Koehler, a common Antarctic asteroid. *Antarctic Res. Ser.* **5**, 39–85.

Pianka, E. R. (1966). Latitudinal gradients in species diversity: a review of concepts. *Am. Nat.* **100**, 33–46.

Pianka, E. R. (1967). On lizard species diversity: North American flatland deserts. *Ecology* **48**, 333–51.

Thorson, G. (1946). Reproduction and larval development of Danish marine bottom invertebrates. *Meddr. Kommn. Danm. Fisk.-og. Havunders., Ser. Plankton*, **4**, 1–523.

Tressler, W. L. and Ommundsen, A. M. (1962). Seasonal oceanographic studies in McMurdo Sound, Antarctica. *U.S. Navy Hydrographic Office Technical Report* TR-125, 141 pp.

Frequency and Ecological Significance of Necrophagy among the Benthic Species of Antarctic Coastal Waters

PATRICK M. ARNAUD
Station Marine d'Endoume, Marseille, France

I. Introduction

The Antarctic benthic fauna displays a remarkable frequency of normal or facultative necrophagy. Attention has already been drawn to this in a study of the echinoderms of Terre Adélie (Arnaud, 1964), and several necrophagous species belonging to other animal groups were mentioned briefly by Arnaud and Hureau (1966).

More complete information is now available, and this allows certain qualitative and quantitative aspects of the necrophagous habit in the waters of Terre Adélie to be described precisely, and an explanation of the significance of this phenomenon to be attempted.

II. Methods

This study was undertaken in the Archipel de Pointe Géologie, adjacent to Dumont d'Urville Station (66°40′S: 140°01′E), using two systems which attract animals using baits: traps and lines.

A. Traps

These were generally cylindrical, 100 cm long and 45 cm in diameter, covered with a hexagonal wire mesh and having two terminal entrances. Spindle-shaped traps with a single entrance were also used. These traps were weighted, baited with penguin flesh or more rarely with beef, and left on the sea bed for at least 24 hrs. The results thus obtained come from 111 traps, of which seven were used by J-C. Hureau in 1961.

The species taken in the traps have been considered to be necrophages except for a few which were caught very rarely and were capable of entering the traps accidentally without being attracted by the baits. These species are described here as "probable accidentals".

B. LONG LINES

Such lines, bearing one or more hooks, have been used in open water or under sea ice. The results from twenty-two lines (of which five were used by J-C. Hureau) are analysed below.

III. Results

The results obtained in Terre Adélie are set out in Tables 1 and 2, under four headings: method of capture, time of the year, depth of collection and species captured. Periods of the year are defined as follows:

"Winter period" (from about the end of February until mid-December): sea ice present, insolation reduced, phytoplankton very scanty.

"Summer period" (from about mid-December until the end of February): sea generally free of ice, intense insolation, abundant phytoplankton. The groups of animals present in the collections will now be considered in turn.

A. NEMERTEA

One species, *Lineus corrugatus*, was taken in the traps throughout the year (130 individuals) and even by line (two individuals). One single trap, left for 48 hrs at a depth of 30 m and taken up on 19 January contained not less than thirty-nine individuals; 24 hrs later it contained twenty-seven new individuals. This frequency is the more remarkable in a species which can be up to 120 cm in length and 2 cm in diameter.

That this species is necrophagous has been known for many years. Joubin (1905), when redescribing it under the name *Cerebratulus charcoti*, mentioned and figured a large hook baited with a lump of seal meat, found in the interior of an individual of this species brought back by the French Antarctic Expedition of 1903–5. This author drew attention to the abnormality of the necrophagous habit for a nemertine.

Two examples will illustrate the voracity of this species: one individual, taken on 23 July in Terre Adélie, had the body split in three places through having engulfed in the trap a piece of meat weighing 56 gm: another, collected on 26 October, was distended by a lump of meat weighing 61 gm and measuring $9 \times 3 \times 1{\cdot}5$ cm.

B. GASTEROPODA

One species only has been taken often enough in the traps for it to be clear that it was attracted by the bait: *Neobuccinum eatoni*, which is also the largest gasteropod in Terre Adélie. This species seems, from the point of view of its feeding habits, to occupy a position, in the Antarctic, analogous to that of *Buccinum undatum* on the Atlantic coasts of Europe.

C. Pycnogonida (identified by F. Arnaud)

Several *Nymphon australe* have been taken in traps in depths of between 24 and 35 m, during summer only. This pycnogonid is the most common on the sea bed off Terre Adélie and we have obtained many hundreds by dredging.

Three other species were collected in traps between 85 and 320 m: these large pycnogonids were inside the traps and not grasping the exterior, thus demonstrating that they were not picked up accidentally.

D. Amphipoda (identified by D. Bellan-Santini)

The counts of amphipods, often taken in abundance by the traps, have only limited significance, because they detach themselves from the bait and leave the traps in hundreds while the trap is being hauled to the surface.

Down to 120 m, *Orchomenella nodimanus* is the species most commonly captured, the maximum catch being 2600 individuals, at a depth of 30 m on 19 April 1962. It is generally accompanied by much smaller numbers of *Waldeckia obesa*. The maximum count for this species was 2207 individuals, also from a depth of 30 m, on 17 May 1962.

As the single trap placed 320 m deep showed, these two species are replaced at greater depths by two other species, *Orchomenella plebs* and *O. rossi*, which are often also caught in traps in the Ross Sea (Bullivant and Dearborn, 1967).

E. Isopoda

Only three individuals of *Antarcturus* sp. have been taken in the traps. *Glyptonotus antarcticus*, frequent in traps in the Ross Sea (Pearse and Giese, 1966*a*), was never obtained.

F. Echinodermata

The catches of echinoderms in the traps during winter have already been analysed in detail (Arnaud, 1964): here we need only note that five species of asteroids, two of ophiuroids, one echinoid and one holothurian have been taken (cf. Table 1).

The summer catches during my second period of field-work have yielded the same species, except for three: *Odontaster validus* and *Cuenotaster involutus*, not taken in summer, and *Astrotoma agassizii*, not observed in winter, but caught in the summer at a depth of 120 m.

G. Pisces

Three species, *Notothenia neglecta*, *Trematomus bernacchii*, and *T. hansoni*, were caught in large numbers, by traps or lines, in both summer and winter.

Two other species, *Gymnodraco acuticeps* and *G. victori*, were only taken by line, and in smaller numbers.

IV. Discussion

The preceding results demonstrate that, in the Antarctic, necrophagy occurs in diverse animal groups. Numerous instances of a similar habit in fishes, amphipods, gasteropods and starfishes are well known from other regions of the globe. But it is not the same for nemertines, ophiuroids, echinoids, holothurians or pycnogonids, among which necrophagy has rarely, or even never, been reported.

In a previous study (Arnaud, 1964) it was supposed that the necrophagous habit was linked to the discontinuity in the plankton cycle, which could operate in two ways:

(*a*) it placed the plankton-feeding and seston-eating species (suspension-feeders) and those consuming the detritus layer on the sea bed (deposit-feeders) at a disadvantage compared with the necrophagous species for which food was available throughout the year;
(*b*) it obliged species which consumed plankton or detritus during summer to substitute a necrophagous habit in winter.

It was not possible to reach any conclusions about necrophagy in summer for lack of data.

If the "probably accidental" species and those which have only been caught during summer in depths of 85 m or greater (and which are consequently not comparable with the winter catches, restricted to depths of less than 50 m) are not considered, it may be said that all the remainder have been taken throughout the year except for seven species, only obtained in winter. These seven consist of three asteroids (*Odontaster validus*, *Cuenotaster involutus* and *Saliasterias brachiata*), one pycnogonid (*Colossendeis frigida*), one isopod (*Antarcturus* sp.) and two fishes (*Gymnodraco acuticeps* and *G. victori*). Between these species, *Odontaster validus* shows the most obvious seasonal occurrence in catches (721 individuals in winter, no individual in summer).

It is therefore surprising to recall that Pearse (1965) records the capture of large numbers of *O. validus* in traps *during summer* in the Ross Sea. Moreover, that author indicates that traps set at Cape Royds between 16 and 22 November in the zone formerly covered by sea ice, after the latter had broken out, caught no *Odontaster* at all even though the species was very abundant there: conversely, many individuals were taken a kilometre away but in advance of the ice edge on 7 December.

If Pearse's comments are compared with our observations at Terre Adélie, it can be deduced that *Odontaster validus* is only necrophagous when there is an insufficient supply of vegetal food. Such food is generally reduced in winter, under the sea ice.

Conversely, when the break-up of the ice creates favourable conditions for a vegetal increase, *O. validus* reverts to a plankton and benthic diatom-consuming habit. Such an explanation accounts for the absence of summer catches at Terre Adélie and near the ice edge at Cape Royds—in both cases, in open water—in contrast to numerous catches under the sea ice where this remains in place. In other words, *O. validus* is a seasonal necrophage in those sectors where the sea ice is only present in winter, and necrophagous throughout the year where the ice does not break out.

Two observations by Pearse confirm this hypothesis; on one hand he reports numerous *Odontaster* feeding on seal faeces on the sea bed under the ice, and on the other he notes the rarity of diatoms in the stomachs of *O. validus* taken in traps and their abundance in those taken using a net in open water. Finally, we can note that this species adopts a very characteristic attitude on the sea bed (as shown, for example, in photographs published by Bullivant, 1959), with the arms recurved upwards towards their distal ends: this clearly indicates that it collects suspended particles.

The necrophagous habit has probably arisen for similar reasons in *Cuenotaster involutus* and *Saliasterias brachiata.*

Turning to the echinoid *Sterechinus neumayeri*, represented only by a single individual in the summer catches, because this species at this season in open water feeds predominantly on benthic diatoms and multicellular algae (Pearse and Giese, 1966*b*). In winter, or beneath the sea ice, these sources of nourishment are insufficient and the animals become necrophagous or consume detritus. Among the other species of facultative necrophage which probably belong to the same category, *Ophiosparte gigas* may be mentioned, and perhaps *Waldeckia obesa* and *Nymphon australe*, species which are far more rarely taken in the traps in summer than in winter.

V. Conclusions

The two hypotheses suggested above have been confirmed: necrophagy is, in the Antarctic, normal in many species, while in others, of which *Odontaster validus* is typical, it is facultative or supplementary. In these species the habit can be considered an adaptation to the cycle of planktonic and benthic diatoms which is temporarily unfavourable to suspension-feeders or to consumers of the superficial layer of the sea floor (deposit-feeders).

It seems that this tendency to necrophagy will be similarly well developed at great depths, since it has been demonstrated, in particular in the expeditions of Prince Albert of Monaco, that normal or facultative necrophagous species are there undoubtedly, and for reasons similar to those we have already considered, at an advantage by comparison with the others.

TABLE 1

Results using Traps in Terre Adélie

	Winter period									Summer period									
Depth (m)	10–15	16	21	22	24	30	35	40	50	10	15	20	30	40	85	90	105	120	320
Number of collections	2	19	23	8	3	18	1	2	6	1	3	4	3	5	7	2	2	1	1
Species obtained																			
Nemertea *Lineus corrugatus*		6	29	3					1	3	11	12	65						
Gasteropoda *Neobuccinum eatoni*			1						1			3	5						
Pycnogonida *Nymphon australe*					5	15	1												
Pentanymphon antarcticum																			1
Colossendeis glacialis															1				
Ammothea glacialis																			1
Amphipoda *Waldeckia obesa*		25	200		100	2300		2	20					2				11	
Orchomenella nodimanus		61			150	4000			25		69			23		1792			
O. plebs																			139
O. rossi																			30
Isopoda *Antarcturus* sp.							1	2											
Asteroidea *Diplasterias brucei*	1	22	23	9	1	1					11	1	12						
Lysasterias perrieri			1								1		1						
Saliasterias brachiata	5																	2	
Odontaster validus			721																
Cuenotaster involutus					1	4		2											
Ophiuroidea *Ophiosparte gigas*		6			1	17		2						2					
Ophionotus victoriae			23											7					
Astrotoma agassizii																		3	
Echinoidea *Sterechinus neumayeri*	1	1	4					1	2				1						
Holothuroidea Sp. indet.							2	1	2				1						
Pisces *Notothenia neglecta*	3	2	45	3							7	16				1			
Trematomus bernacchii		2	15	2		8	5	9	27	1	11	10	3	17	13		2		
T. hansoni		9	34	2	2	23		11	29					10	71		15		1
Probable Accidentals																			
Polychaeta		1																	
Gasteropoda *Toledonia hedleyi*			1																
Marseniopsis mollis									1										

Table 2

Results using Lines in Terre Adélie

	Winter period						*Summer period*	
Depth (m)	3–6	7–8	8–16	20–23	31–35	50	5–10	40
Number of collections	2	2	6	5	2	2	2	1
Species obtained								
Nemertea *Lineus corrugatus*	1							1
Pycnogonida *Nymphon australe*								1
Colossendeis frigida					1			
Amphipoda *Waldeckia obesa*	Numerous							
Asteroidea *Diplasterias brucei*								5
Psilaster charcoti								2
Ophiuroidea *Ophiosparte gigas*			3			1		10
Holothuroidea Sp. indet								14
Pisces *Notothenia neglecta*	1	2	1	13	6		1	
Trematomus bernacchii	2	3	24	34	16	1	3	
T. hansoni	1		53	17	3	4		
Gymnodraco acuticeps				5				
G. victori				1	1			

Acknowledgement

I am most grateful to J-C. Hureau for making available to me the results of his own catches, and to D. Bellan-Santini for identifying amphipods.

References

Arnaud, P. (1964). Echinodermes littoraux de Terre Adélie (Holothuries exceptées) et Pélécypodes commensaux d'Echinides antarctiques. *Publ. Expéd. polair. Fr.* **258**, 1–72, Figs. 1–4, Pl. 1–2.

Arnaud, P. and Hureau, J. C. (1966). Régime alimentaire de trois Téléostéens Nototheniidae antarctiques (Terre Adélie). *Bull. Inst. océanogr. Monaco* **66** (1368), 1–24, Figs. 1–5.

Bullivant, J. S. (1959). Photographs of the bottom fauna in the Ross sea. *N.Z. Jl. Sci.* **2** (4), 485–97, Figs.1 –10 (3 col.).

Bullivant, J. S. and Dearborn, J. H. (1967). The fauna of the Ross sea. 5. General account, station lists and benthic ecology. *Bull. N.Z. Dep. scient. ind. Res.* **176**, 1–77, Figs. 1–6, Pl. 1–23.

Joubin, L. (1905). Note sur un némertien recueilli par l'Expédition antarctique du Dr Charcot. *Bull. Mus., Hist. nat., Paris,* **11** (5), 315–318, Fig. 1.

Pearse, J. S. (1965). Reproductive periodicities in several contrasting populations of *Odontaster validus* Koehler, a common antarctic Asteroid. *In* "Biology of the Antarctic Seas", 2, G. A. Llano (ed.), *Antarctic Res. Ser.* **5**, 39–85, Figs. 1–28.

Pearse, J. S. and Giese, C. (1966a). The organic constitution of several benthonic invertebrates from McMurdo Sound, Antarctica. *Comp. Biochem. Physiol.* **18**, 47–57, Fig. 1.

Pearse, J. S. and Giese, C. (1966b). Food, reproduction and organic constitution of the common antarctic Echinoid *Sterechinus neumayeri* (Meissner). *Biol. Bull. mar. biol. Lab., Woods Hole* **130** (3), 387–401, Figs. 1–5.

Résumé

Des récoltes de poissons et invertébrés benthiques ont été faites en Terre Adélie (Antarctique de l'Est) entre 5 et 320m de profondeur, pendant toute l'année. L'étude qualitative et quantitative de ces captures sert de base à des remarques sur la fréquence et la signification de la nécrophagie parmi la faune du précontinent antarctique. Au total, 28 espèces sont concernées, appartenant aux groupes suivants; Némertes (1), Gastéropodes (1), Pycnogonides (5), Amphipodes (4), Isopodes (1), Ophiurides (3), Astérides (6), Echinides (1), Holothurides (1) et Poissons (5).

Quelques unes de ces espèces ont été prises au cours de la période estivale (quand la mer était libre de glace) aussi bien que pendant la période hivernale (quand la mer était couverte de glace) et sont donc considérées comme nécrophages permanentes (normales ou facultatives).

D'autres, au contraire, sont seulement des nécrophages hivernales: ainsi l'Astéride *Odontaster validus*, planctonophage et mangeuse de Diatomées et algues pluricellulaires benthiques en été, et l'Echinide *Sterechinus neumayeri*, mangeur du film superficiel des sédiments et algivore en été, deviennent nécrophages ou détritophages en hiver. Pour ces espèces, la nécrophagie paraît être un régime de remplacement ou d'appoint lorsque leur nourriture normale est insuffisante ou absente.

Ce phénomène semble être en rapport avec la variation annuelle du cycle phytoplanctonique et du cycle phytobenthique des eaux antarctiques. Cette hypothèse est confirmée par le fait que, dans les zones non libérées par les glaces en été (c'est à dire celles où la nourriture végétale disponible reste tout l'année insuffisante), ces mêmes espèces sont nécrophages toute l'année.

Vertical Zonation of Marine Vegetation in the Antarctic (abstract)

R. DELEPINE, I. MACKENZIE LAMB and M. H. ZIMMERMANN
Laboratoire de Biologie Végétale Marine, Paris, France, Farlow Herbarium, Harvard University, Cambridge, Massachusetts, U.S.A. and Harvard Forest Station, Petersham, Massachusetts, U.S.A.

The authors have studied the vertical zonation of marine and paramaritime vegetation at a number of localities in the Antarctic and have extended their knowledge by a review of the literature.

The vegetation of the supra-littoral, littoral and infra-littoral (s.l.) zones has been described for each of the areas studied, and inter-comparison facilitated by the preparation of summary tables.

It has proved possible to analyse the general features of these zonation patterns and to consider them in relation to biogeographical data. Some comparisons with the situation in the Arctic have also been made.

Note. The text of this paper was not received in time for publication in full, and the data will appear elsewhere.

Growth in *Bovallia gigantea* Pfeffer *(Crustacea: Amphipoda)*

MICHAEL H. THURSTON
National Institute of Oceanography, Wormley, Surrey, England

I. Introduction

About 230 species of gammaridean amphipods have been described from the Antarctic Peninsula, the Weddell Sea, and islands of the Scotia Ridge. The Gammaridea form an important part of the shallow-water benthic fauna in all Antarctic seas. The large size and great abundance of many species make them ideal subjects for growth and life-history studies.

The reports of those expeditions which have collected amphipods in the Atlantic sector of Antarctica show that two families, the Lysianassidae and the Pontogeneiidae, form an important part of the fauna of the region. The lysianassids, which may be taken in large numbers in baited traps, are frequently associated with deposit bottoms, while the pontogeneiids are characteristically found among *Phyllogigas*, *Desmarestia* and other large algae in the shallow sublittoral of Antarctica.

The pontogeneiid *Bovallia gigantea* was described from South Georgia by Pfeffer (1888) and has since been recorded from many localities in Graham Land and throughout the Scotia Ridge. It is associated with large and small algae from the littoral to depths of 40 m. The species is a large and easily identified one, being strongly dentate dorsally, red or brown in colour, and reaching a maximum length of 52–53 mm.

Collections of the marine flora and fauna were made in 1964–65 at the British Antarctic Survey Station on Signy Island, South Orkney Islands, using aqua-lung techniques and conventional collecting methods. This included 33,000 amphipods belonging to over sixty species. The present paper results from the examination of over 500 specimens of *Bovallia gigantea* which were obtained.

II. Fecundity, Development, Moulting and Growth in Amphipoda

A. Fecundity

The fecundity of *Gammarus chevreuxi* Sexton has been discussed by Sexton (1924), *Rivulogammarus pulex* (L.) and *Crangonyx pseudogracilis*

Bousfield (as *C. gracilis*) by Hynes (1955), *Rivulogammarus duebeni* (Lilljeborg), *Marinogammarus marinus* (Leach) and *Marinogammarus obtusatus* (Dahl) by Cheng (1942) and *Pontoporeia affinis* Lindstrom by Mathisen (1953). In each of these species the number of eggs produced is proportional to the volume of the female concerned. Jensen (1958) has concluded that this

FIG. 1. Female *B. gigantea*, length 49 mm.

situation is generally true among the Malacostraca. Kinne (1961) has confirmed this for *Gammarus salinus* Spooner and also shown that fecundity is significantly higher at lower temperatures.

B. Rate of Development

Hynes (1954) has shown that in *R. duebeni* incubation occupies 14 days at 18°C and 55 days at 5°C. In a later paper the same author (Hynes, 1955) has provided data for *C. pseudogracilis*. In this species hatching occurs 14–17 days after laying at 15°C and after 48 days at 3·5°C. Clemens (1950) has also demonstrated the effect of temperature on the rate of development of eggs in *Gammarus fasciatus* Say. At 24°C 7 days are required for development, at 20°C the period is 9 days, at 15°C 22 days, while at10°C hatching occurs only after 41–45 days. A study of the winter-breeding glacial relict *P. affinis* by

Mathisen (1953) in lakes in southern Norway has shown that development takes more than 3 months at 3–4°C.

C. Frequency of Moulting

Moult-frequency data are provided for a number of species by Sexton (1924), Clemens (1950) and Kinne (1960, 1961). In all of the species of *Gammarus* studied by these authors the pattern of moult frequency is similar. Juvenile animals moult at more frequent intervals than do adults and the frequency continues to drop throughout life. Moult frequency is increased at higher temperatures. The moult at which sexual maturity is attained is constant within a species, but may vary considerably among closely-related species. Sexton (1924) gives seven, ten and twelve moults for *G. chevreuxi*, *R. pulex*, and *Gammarus locusta* (L.) respectively.

D. Growth Rates

Growth rates for *G. salinus* are given by Kinne (1960) and for *Gammarus zaddachi* Sexton by Kinne (1961). In the two species of *Gammarus* growth is rapid and at 19–20°C females may become sexually mature in under 30 days and males in 35 days. Sexton (1924) provides data which show that maturity in *G. chevreuxi* is attained in 70 days in summer and 180 days in winter. *R. pulex* requires 3–4 months in summer and 7 months in winter to attain maturity (Hynes, 1955). Ecological observations by Hynes (1955) show that *R. pulex*, *Rivulogammarus lacustris* (Sars), and *Gammarus tigrinus* Sexton live for 14–15 months, females producing four to six broods of young. In contrast to these data *P. affinis* has been shown to grow much more slowly, requiring nearly two years to reach a length of 8 mm, and breeding only once before dying at an age of 26–27 months (Mathisen, 1953).

Kurata (1962) has recently discussed growth in Crustacea and shown that graphical methods using size increase per moult and moult interval can give useful information about growth rates.

III. Growth in *Bovallia gigantea*

A. Material and Methods

Specimens of *Bovallia* were present at thirty-six stations worked at Signy Island in 1964–65. Most of these stations were at depths of 20 m or less and in areas with partial or complete algal cover on rock, boulder or boulder and sand bottoms. Specimens were obtained during all months of the year except November, a month in which no stations on suitable substrates were worked. It is very probable that the population is a static one, showing no migration of the kind described for some Antarctic lysianassids by Hodgson (in Walker, 1907).

A total of 588 specimens were obtained. Twenty-four of these were damaged and were discarded. The following observations, therefore, are based on 564 specimens, consisting of 211 males, 29 ovigerous females, 258 non-ovigerous adult and sub-adult females and 66 juveniles. The sex ratio of male to female is 1 : 1·36.

Each specimen was sexed and the length measured from the tip of the rostrum to the apex of the telson. The state of development of ova of ovigerous females was also noted.

B. Results

Ovigerous females were obtained in February, March, April, June, July and September. It proved possible to assign each of these females to one of five arbitrary but reasonably distinct categories depending on the developmental conditon of the eggs.

These categories were:

(i) ovum with close-packed yolk cells, but no trace, in the preserved material, of any embryonic tissue;
(ii) early embryo with yolk cells surrounded by embryonic tissue and with traces of metameric segmentation;
(iii) embryo with somites and limb-buds present;
(iv) late embryo with articles of all appendages complete and traces of pigment in eyes;
(v) hatchling stage with some at least of the embryos hatched and free in the brood pouch.

Developmental stages of eggs of twenty-nine ovigerous females are shown in Table 1.

Table 1

Distribution in Time of the Stage of Development reached by the Eggs of Twenty-nine Ovigerous Females

Date	*Station No.*	*Development Stage* i	ii	iii	iv	v	*Total*
26 February 1965	22	1	—	—	—	—	1
1 March 1965	16	2	—	—	—	—	2
4 March 1965	12, 13	9	—	—	—	—	9
15 April 1964	46, 47, 48	5	—	—	—	—	5
19 April 1964	54	2	—	—	—	—	2
29 June 1964	49	—	1	1	—	—	2
1 July 1964	59	1	2	1	—	—	4
14 September 1964	52	—	—	—	1	—	1
20 September 1964	53	—	—	1	1	1	3
						Total	29

Although the sample is not large, it is apparent that eggs were laid in late February and March, that early development was very slow and that hatching occurred in late September and in October. The 7-month interval between laying of eggs, and hatching and release of juveniles is considerably in excess of that reported for any other amphipod species. An incubation period of 3–3½m onths has been reported for *Pontoporeia affinis* and 2–2½ months for *Pallasea quadrispinosa* Sars (Mathisen, 1953). Both of these species breed in waters of 3°C to 5°C as opposed to *Bovallia*, which is exposed to temperatures of +1°C to −2°C.

The number of eggs produced by *Bovallia* (Table 2) was found to be proportional to (length)^3 of the female. This species is therefore similar to those described by Sexton (1924), Cheng (1942), Hynes (1955) and Kinne (1961) and conforms to the pattern demonstrated by Jensen (1958).

TABLE 2

Relation between Number of Eggs and Length of Incubating Female

Station No.	*No. of eggs*	*Length of ♀ (mm)*
12	80	41
13	91	44
13	96	45
13	116	46
13	126	46
53	139	49

Relative to the size of the female, eggs are rather small. Twenty first-stage eggs had an average length of 1·531 mm (range 1·33–1·73 mm), a width of 1·153 mm (range 1·04–1·23 mm) and a volume of 1·0679 mm^3 (range 0·9079–1·2879 mm^3). The corresponding measurements of twenty fourth-stage eggs were: length 2·060 mm (range 1·97–2·17 mm), width 1·491 mm (range 1·36–1·60 mm), depth 1·846 mm (range 1·75–1·97 mm) and volume 2·9824 mm^3 (range 2·6573–3·2922 mm^3). The increase in volume during development is therefore nearly threefold, a figure comparable to those given by Spooner (1947) for *Gammarus locusta* (L.) and *Gammarus zaddachi* Sexton. Using data given by Spooner (1947), it can be shown that the eggs of *Bovallia*, although absolutely much larger, are relatively smaller than those of *G. locusta* and *G. zaddachi*. The relatively small eggs of *Bovallia* might be expected to result in a short period of development and less well-developed hatchlings. It has, however, already been shown that the period of development is very long. It is probable, therefore, that low temperature is mainly responsible for the length of this period.

The restricted breeding and hatching periods shown by an examination of the eggs of ovigerous females give rise to well-marked year groups within the population. Length/frequency histograms for juveniles, males and females show clearly the growth increments of these year groups.

Hatchlings are released from the female brood pouch in late September and in October, when they are 3·5–4 mm long. By December a length of

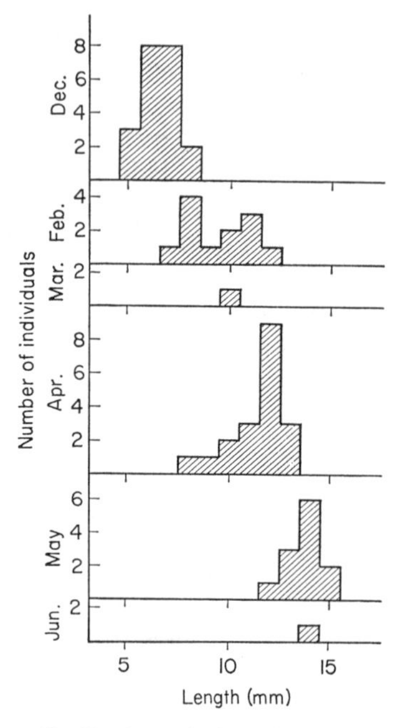

FIG. 2. Length-frequency distribution of sixty-six juvenile *B. gigantea* grouped by months.

6–7 mm has been reached and the juveniles, although lacking the carinate pleon so characteristic of the adults, are readily recognizable by the stout antennae and broad carpal articles of the gnathopods. Growth continues at a rate of nearly 2 mm per month until at an age of 8 months and a length of 13–14 mm males become recognizable by the development of rudimentary genital papillae. Females become recognizable when vestigial oostegites are developed at an age of about 12 months and a length of 17–18 mm. Up to this age, the growth rate of the two sexes is similar, but thereafter females grow rather faster than males. At the end of the second year males have reached a length of 28 mm, and are sexually mature during the breeding season, which occurs 28–29 months after they have hatched. This is confirmed by specimens 30 mm and 31 mm in length which were taken in February and March and which had sperm strands issuing from the genital papillae. Although the variation in number of specimens taken in each month is due in part to the sampling programme, there appears to be a genuine reduction in numbers of males subsequent to breeding. Growth of those animals which survive for a third year is much reduced, averaging about 4 mm. The presence of specimens of 39–40 mm length is unexplained. No evidence is available to show

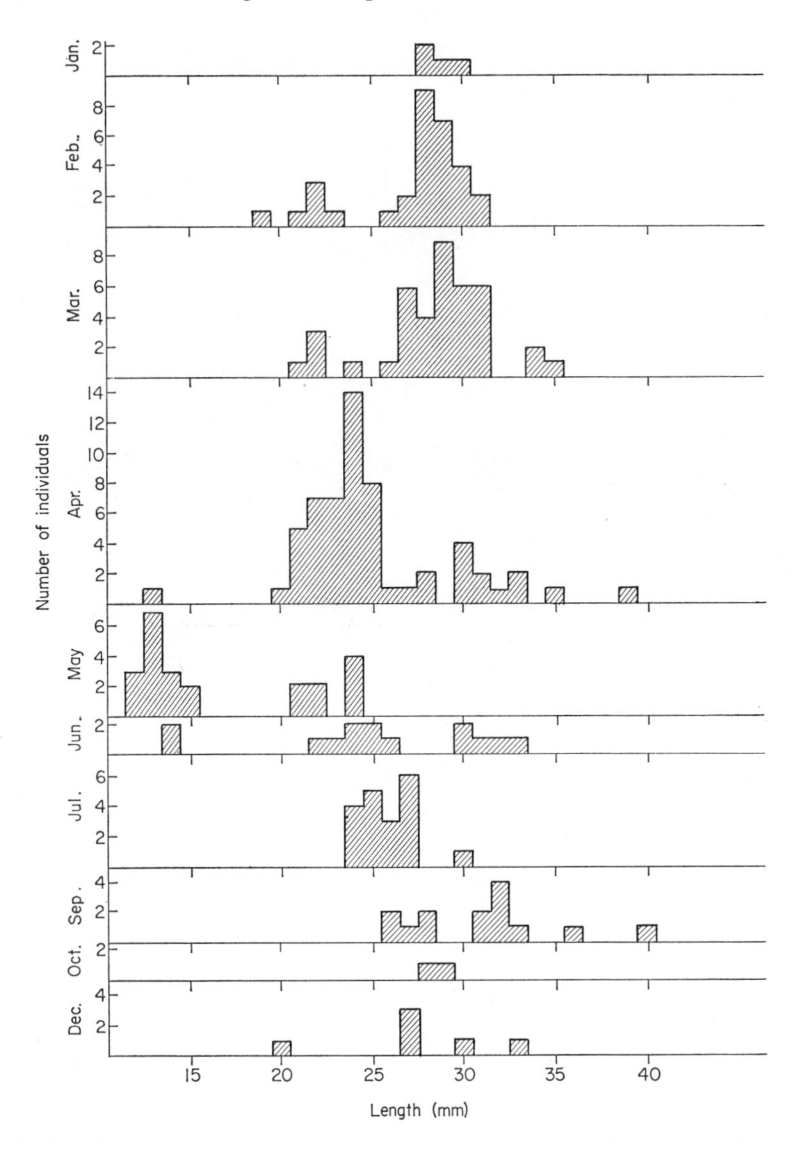

FIG. 3. Length-frequency distribution of 211 male *B. gigantea* grouped by months.

whether or not these older animals are capable of breeding for a second time. Baker (1959) found a similar situation in *Euphausia triacantha* Holt and Tattersall, but was unable to show whether these animals had grown more rapidly or, as appears more likely, were a year older than the rest of the breeding population.

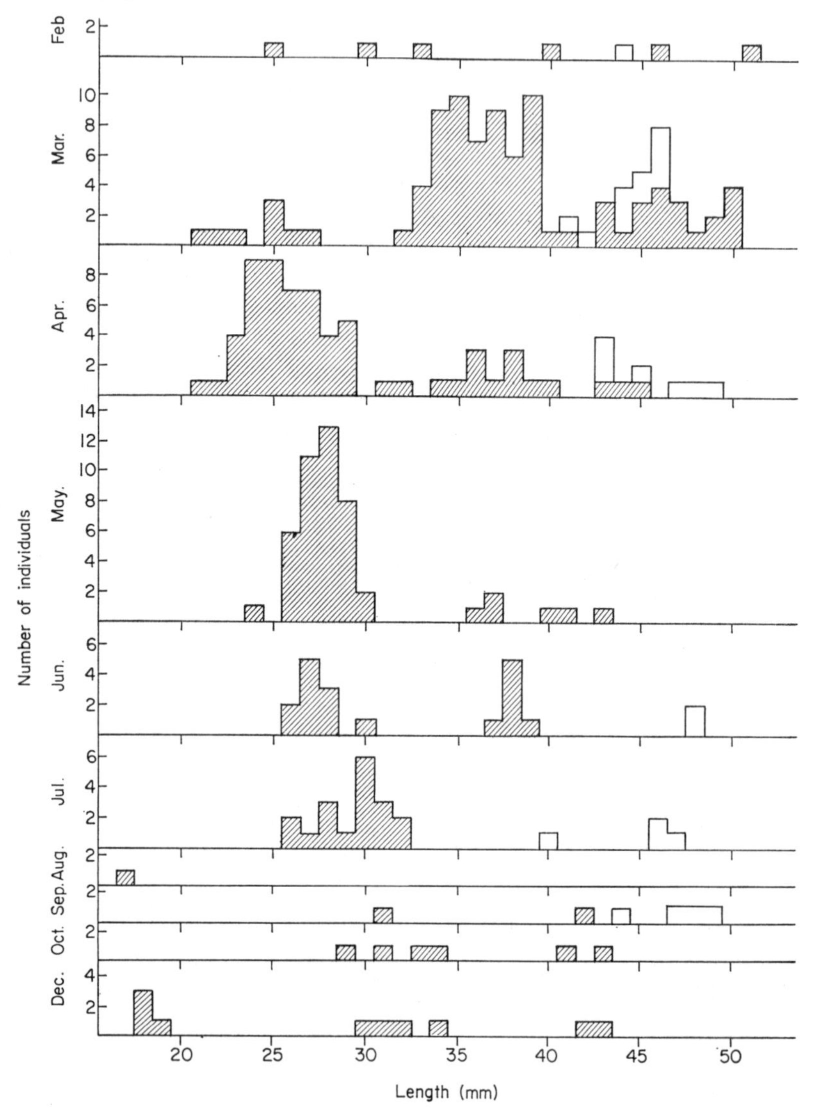

FIG. 4. Length-frequency distribution of 287 female *B. gigantea* grouped by months. Unshaded areas represent ovigerous females, shaded areas non-ovigerous females.

Females at an age of 2 years attain a length of about 32 mm, 4 mm more than males of the same age. A further growth increment of 10 mm occurs during the third year. Breeding takes place in February and March at an age of 41–42 months. Eggs are carried through the winter and hatchlings released in the following spring. The spent females generally die after the young have been liberated, although some appear to survive until the following breeding season. It is unlikely that these females breed again, as most exhibit degeneration of branchiae and oostegites, symptoms which precede death in *Pontoporeia affinis* (Mathisen, 1953).

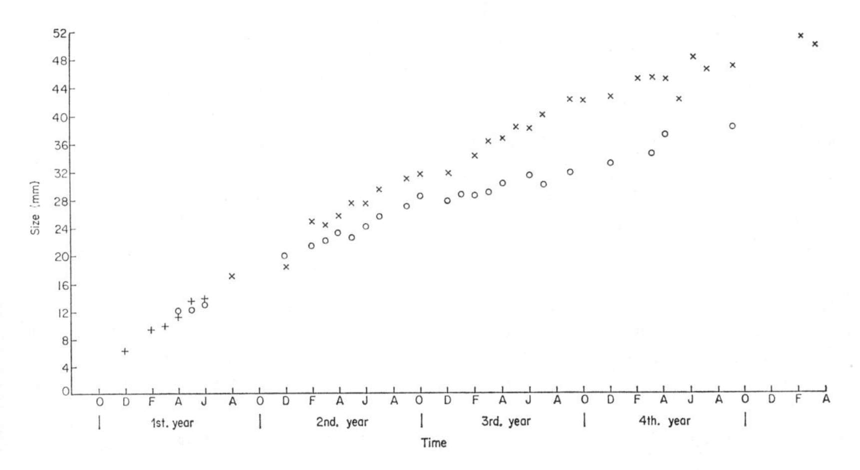

FIG. 5. Growth curve for *B. gigantea*. 0 = male, x = female, + = juvenile.

The growth curve shows the disparity between males and females. If the difference in length of life is taken into account, and only those animals less than 30 months old are considered, the sex ratio is reduced from 1 : 1·36 males to females to 1 : 1·13. Little information is available concerning size increments at moulting in the Amphipoda, but the excellent drawings of moults given by Sexton (1924) for *G. chevreuxi* enable growth factors to be calculated. The linear increase over the first eight moults is by a factor of 1·25 per moult. This figure is close to 1·26 (2^{-3}) a factor considered significant by Przibram (1929), as it represents a doubling of the body volume.

If the growth factor of *Bovallia* is the same as that of *G. chevreuxi*, then male *Bovallia* will undergo nine moults to reach maturity and females eleven moults. Work in progress at Signy Island suggests, however, that a growth factor of 1·25 is too high, so that the number of moults required to reach maturity would be correspondingly greater.

The populations of pontogeneiid amphipods at the islands of the Scotia Ridge are probably strongly isolated due to their shallow-water habitat. The different ages at which males and females become mature in *Bovallia* may aid the exchange of genetic material within each population.

In a rather more general context, it is of interest to note that the pattern of autumn mating and spring hatching and release of young appears to be common in Antarctic amphipods.

References

Baker, A. de C. (1959). Distribution and life history of *Euphausia triacantha* Holt and Tattersall. *"Discovery" Rep.* 29, 309–40.

Cheng, C. (1942). On the fecundity of some Gammarids. *J. mar. biol. Ass. U.K.* 25, 467–75.

Clemens, H. P. (1950). Life cycle and ecology of *Gammarus fasciatus* Say. *Contr. Stone Lab. Ohio Univ.* 12, 1–63.

Hynes, H. B. N. (1954). The ecology of *Gammarus duebeni* Lilljeborg and its occurrence in fresh water in Western Britain. *J. Anim. Ecol.* 23, 38–84.

Hynes, H. B. N. (1955). The reproductive cycle of some British freshwater Gammaridae. *J. Anim. Ecol.* 24, 352–87.

Jensen, J. P. (1958). The relation between body size and egg number in marine malacostrakes. *Meddt. Danm. Fisk.-og Havunders*, N.S. 2, No. 19, 25 pp.

Kinne, O. (1960). *Gammarus salinus*—einige Daten uber den Umwelteinfluss auf Wachstum, Häutungsfolge, Herzfrequenz und Eientwicklungsdauer. *Crustaceana* 1, 208–17.

Kinne, O. (1961). Growth, moulting frequency, heart beat, number of eggs, and incubation time in *Gammarus zaddachi* exposed to different environments. *Crustaceana* 2, 26–36.

Kurata, H. (1962). Studies on the age and growth of Crustacea. *Bull. Hokkaido reg. Fish. Res. Lab.* 24, 1–115.

Mathisen, A. O. (1953). Some investigations of the relict crustaceans in Norway with special reference to *Pontoporeia affinis* Lindström and *Pallasea quadrispinosa* G. O. Sars. *Nytt Mag. Zool.* 1, 49–86.

Pfeffer, G. (1888). Die Krebse von Süd-Georgien. *J. hamb. wiss. Anst.*, 5, 77–142.

Przibram, H. (1929). Quanta in biology. *Proc. R. Soc. Edinb.* 49, No. 18, 224–31.

Sexton, E. W. (1924). The moulting and growth stages of *Gammarus*, with descriptions of normals and intersexes of *G. chevreuxi*. *J. mar. biol. Ass. U.K.* 13, 340–401.

Spooner, G. M. (1947). The distribution of *Gammarus* species in estuaries. Part 1. *J. mar. biol. Ass. U.K.* 27, 1–52.

Walker, A. O. (1907). Amphipoda. *Nat. Antarctic Exped.* 1901–1904, *Zool.* 3, 1–39.

Aspects of the Breeding Biology of *Glyptonotus antarcticus* (Eights) (Crustacea, Isopoda) at Signy Island, South Orkney Islands

MARTIN G. WHITE
British Antarctic Survey Biological Unit, Monks Wood Experimental Station, Abbots Ripton, Huntingdon, England

I. Introduction

Glyptonotus antarcticus, a large marine idotheid isopod, was originally described by James Eights (1852) from a specimen that he collected on a shore in the South Shetland Islands. The genus has, since then, been the subject of a number of systematic and morphological papers prompted by its capture from other regions about the Antarctic Continent and from islands south of the Antarctic Convergence (Miers, 1881; Pfeffer, 1887; Tait, 1917; Collinge, 1918; Tattersall, 1921; Calabrese, 1931; Monod, 1926; Nordenstam, 1933; Sheppard, 1957). Sheppard (1957) reviewed the status of the genus and after re-examination of preserved material concluded that it was monotypic. *Glyptonotus acutus* Richardson (1906) and *Glyptonotus antarcticus* var. *acutus* Tattersall (1921) appear to be at one extreme of a continuous polymorphic series linking specimens collected from the deeper bathymetric range and those from near the shoreline.

The biology of this species was investigated from the British Antarctic Survey Biological Station at Signy Island (60°43′S, 45°38′W), South Orkney Islands, between February 1966 and February 1968. Specimens were collected by five main methods, a 1 m Agassiz dredge, a 2 m beam trawl, baited traps and hand sampling from the intertidal belt or deeper than this by scuba diving. Similar trapping methods have been used by Finnish scientists in the Baltic to sample the closely related isopod *Mesidotea entomon* (Linn.) (Haahtela, 1962), and scuba diving is recognized as an efficient sampling method where species are secretive or their habitats are inaccessible to remote collecting methods. The Antarctic epibenthos is such a habitat, since ice scour restricts the biota to sheltered sites.

Diving was conducted throughout the year from small craft whilst the coasts were ice free, or through holes cut in the fast ice. Specimens were retained for observation and experiment either in laboratory tanks through which sea water was constantly circulated to simulate environmental conditions or in metal cages which were returned to the sea.

II. Observations

Of 1593 specimens examined at Signy Island 515 were females. Ovigerous females were found during each month of the year. The contents of the marsupia were shown to be at different stages of development in different individuals at any one time, indicating that the species is able to breed successfully throughout the year.

Male *Glyptonotus* attain maturity upon development of a pair of accessory copulatory styles on the second pair of pleopods, the appendix masculina. These males carry the pre-adult female by grasping the forward edge of the thorax with three pairs of gnathopods. This association has been observed to continue for as long as 190 days. Fidelity is high during the thirty or so days preceding the ecdysis of the female to maturity, but males carry females promiscuously before then. The stimuli associated with this behaviour were not determined, but the mechanism ensures that a mature male is present for the fertilization of ripe ova, and since this is coincident with moulting it also serves the function of protecting the vulnerable female.

Copulation has rarely been observed among Isopoda, although the phenomenon of pre-copulative pairing is common. It is usually inferred that where species have intromissive structures, these are used to transfer semen or spermatophores to the female. In some genera hypodermic insemination is suggested. *Glyptonotus* was observed in coitus on nine occasions. The male manipulates the female so that their ventral sides are in apposition and then the second pair of pleopods are flexed forward so as to locate the proximal ends of the appendix masculina with the penal appendages which are on the articular membrane behind the coxal plates of the last thoracic somite. A groove facilitates the transfer of bundles of spermatozoa to the short oviducts of the female. Over the next 48 hours the fertilized eggs are deposited in the ventral marsupium. The total number of eggs produced by individual females is variable, but there is a positive correlation between the size of the female and the number of eggs deposited in the marsupium. The mean number of eggs per female at Signy Island was 512 and that at McMurdo Sound was 746 (Dearborn, 1967), coincident with the greater size of mature females from the Ross Sea.

The metamorphosis and growth in the marsupium was observed in six females retained in cages at 7 m below mean tide level. The completion of the cycle, from eggs being deposited to release from the marsupium, varied between 577 days and 626 days.

The dry weight fell during development from a mean for the egg at laying of 3·5 mg to 2·4 mg for the instar prior to release when the exoskeleton was strengthened with inorganic salts. The initial loss of weight indicates that although the development is protracted, there is little or no transfer of nutrients from the female to the developing larvae through the thin ventral

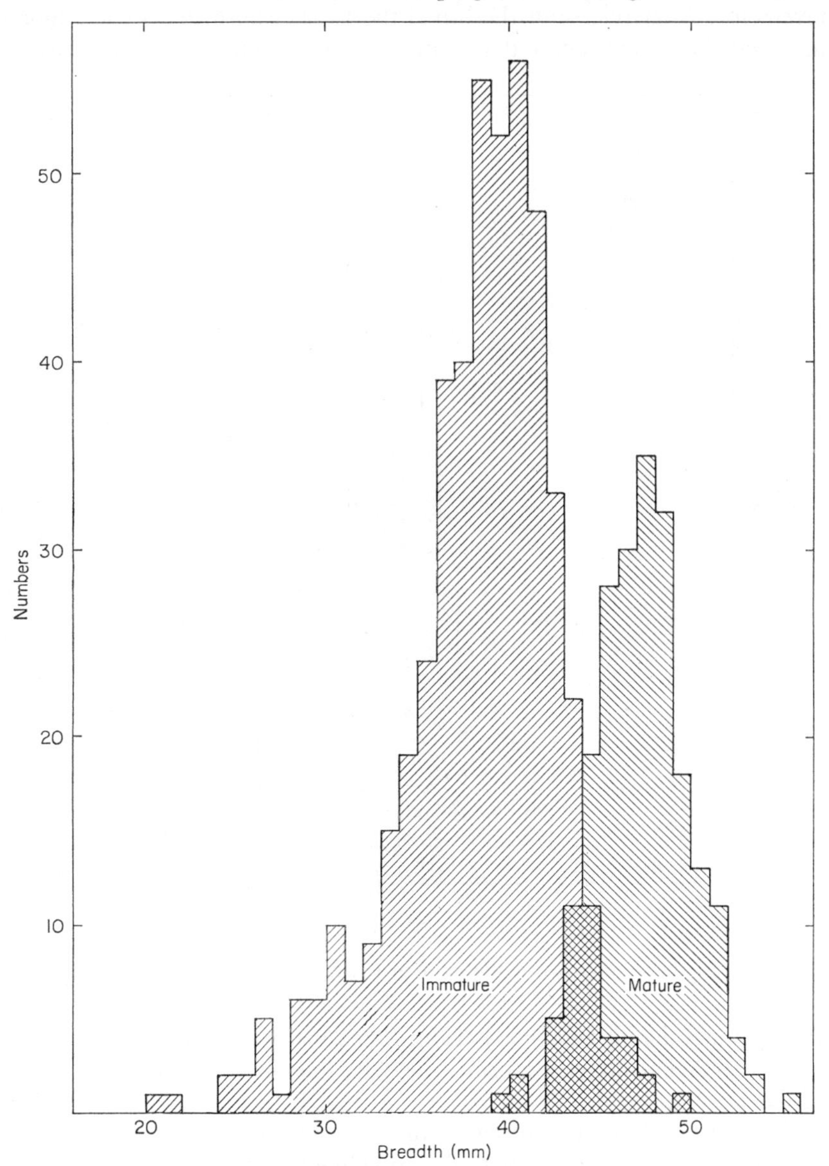

FIG. 1. Size distribution in male *Glyptonotus antarcticus*.

body wall, this flexible integument apparently being an adaptation to accommodate the developing larvae. The eggs develop synchronously and the larvae are released as miniature adults by the parent female swinging the oostegites laterally more vigorously than during the normal ventilatory movements. After release of the brood the females normally become moribund and die within a few days without feeding, but a small proportion

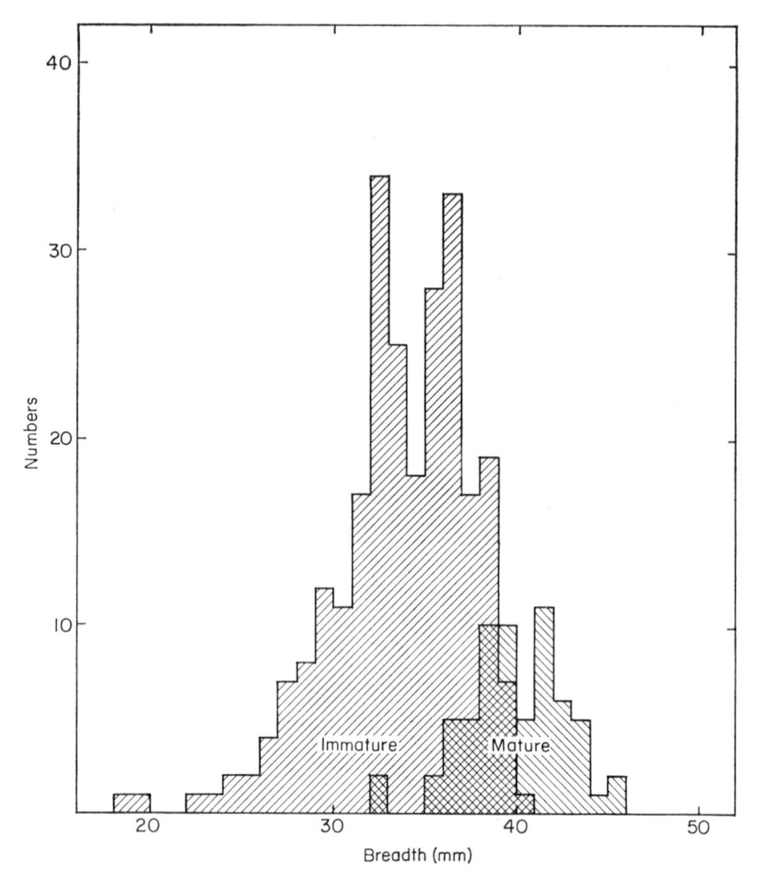

FIG. 2. Size distribution in female *Glyptonotus antarcticus*.

(*c*. 2–3%) may moult and breed again. Some males survive copulation and remate if they encounter a receptive female, but the majority stop feeding and die.

Thirty-two ecdyses were observed in detail. The normal sequence was for the exoskeleton to be shed in two halves dividing between the fourth and fifth free thoracic somites, the posterior half preceding the anterior by a period of

22–100 hrs. The new exoskeleton is insufficiently robust to allow normal locomotion or feeding for about 36 hrs. after moulting.

The distribution of different size classes within the population are difficult to determine by biometric examination of a large sample, because the classes overlap and blur the formation of peaks of a size/frequency histogram (Figs 1 and 2). By direct observation and measurement the ecdysis frequency was found to be not less than 100 days and sometimes longer than 730 days. Smaller individuals ecdyse more frequently than larger ones, but there is no indication of a seasonal cycle. A minimum of eleven moults are required to attain maturity, with size increases expressed as mm linear breadth of 0·9, 1·3, 1·5, 2·0, 2·5, 3·1, 4·0, 4·9, 6·4, 8·5, and 8·7 for males and 0·9, 1·3, 1·5, 2·0, 2·5, 3·1, 4·0, 5·0, 6·0, 7·3, and 4·1 for females, after release from the marsupium at a mean breadth of 3·7 mm.

The sex of individuals can be determined from the external morphology by the fifth or sixth instar. The sex ratio within the population at Signy Island differs from that observed by Dearborn (1967) at McMurdo Sound. Specimens collected by baited traps indicated that the sex ratio was 7 males : 3 females and samples taken by hand, where any bias owing to differing feeding habits between the sexes is negated, gave a ratio of 5 : 3. At McMurdo Sound the ratio is reversed and females exceed males by 6·6 : 1. The significance of the disparity is not obvious, and no observations were made to determine the sex ratio at release from the marsupium for either population.

III. Discussion

Linear breadth of the fourth free thoracic somite was the measurement used to determine size. This parameter is more stable than length, as it does not vary with the amount of fluid in the perivisceral cavity or the muscular tonus of the thoracic musculature. Observation and measurements were made of moulting individuals and the increase in size at each used to infer the maximum increment from one size class to the next. This information was collated to construct a table for the minimum number of ecydses from a mean size at release from the marsupium of 3·7 mm to mature male (40–56 mm) and mature female (32–44 mm). This was found to be 11 with an average growth factor of 1·26 for males and 1·25 for females. These factors conform closely with that of 1·26 determined by Przibram (1929), which implies that the body volume doubles at each increment. It assumes maximal increase in size at each moult throughout development; however, the factor will be reduced and the number of moults to maturity increased where individuals ecdyse with small or negative increases in size, as has been observed for *Euphausia superba* (Mackintosh, 1967) and *Bovallia gigantea* (D. Bone, personal communication.

The breeding biology of benthic invertebrates from Antarctic seas is largely unknown, but where autecological investigations have been made the reproductive cycles have often been shown to be seasonal. Pearse (1963, 1964) reports that the common omnivorous asteroid *Odontaster validus* and the amphipod *Orchomenella proxima* are winter breeders which release young feeding stages in late winter or early summer. The amphipod *Bovallia gigantea* (Thurston, 1968) is also recorded as a winter breeder at the South Orkney Islands, releasing young stages in late winter. Similar seasonal reproductive cycles are described by Thorson (1936, 1950) for Arctic invertebrates, and it is suggested that these cycles directly or indirectly are adaptations for the release of young feeding stages when food is most plentiful during the short summer phytoplankton bloom. Green (1957) notes that the isopods *Sphaeroma hookeri* as reported by Kinne (1954) and *Idotea emarginata* as reported by Naylor (1955) breed throughout the year and suggests that it is advantageous for species where the fecundity is low and the juvenile mortality high. Similarly *Glyptonotus antarcticus* breeds throughout the year at the South Orkney Islands and at McMurdo Sound (Dearborn, 1967). The lack of any apparent breeding cycle may be of advantage where maturation and exposure to predation are prolonged. It is improbable that there is any advantage to be gained by linking the reproductive cycle with seasonal fluctuations in the environment where the species is a highly mobile predator/scavenger with a catholic diet.

References

Calabrese, G. de (1931). Observaciones sobre des especies antarticas del género *Glyptonotus* Eights. *Physis, Buenos Aires*, **10**, 323–6.

Collinge, W. F. (1918). Some observations upon two rare marine isopods. *J. zool. Res.* **1**, No. 2, 63–78.

Dearborn, J. H. (1967). Food and reproduction of *Glyptonotus antarcticus* (Crustacea, Isopoda) at McMurdo Sound, Antarctica. *Trans. R. Soc. N.Z.* **18**, No. 15, 163–8.

Eights, J. (1852). Description of a new animal belonging to the Crustacea, discovered in the Antarctic Seas by the author. *Trans. Albany Inst.* **2**, 331–4.

Green, J. (1957). The feeding mechanism of *Mesidotea entomon* (Linn.) (Crustacea: Isopoda). *Proc. zool. Soc. Lond.* **129**, 245–54.

Haahtela, I. (1962). Spånakäringen-Biologi och Fångst. *Sartr. Fiskeritidskrift för Finland* **1**, 1–10.

Kinne, O. (1954). Eidonomie, Anatomie und Lebenszyklus von *Sphaeroma hookeri* Leach (Isopoda). *Kieler Meersforsch.* **10**, 100–20.

Mackintosh, N. A. (1967). Maintenance of living *Euphausia superba* and Frequency of Moults. *Norsk Hvalfangsttid.* **5**, 97–102.

Miers, E. J. (1881). Revision of the Idoteidae. *J. Linn. Soc.* (*Zool.*) **16**, 1–88.

Monod, Th. M. (1926). Tanaidacés Isopodes et Amphipodes. *Resultats due Voyage de la "Belgica" 1897–99, Rapports Scientifiques, Zoologie*, 1–67.

Naylor, E. (1955). The life cycle of the Isopod *Idotea emarginata*. *J. Anim. Ecol.* **24**, No. 2, 270–81.

Nordenstam, A. (1933). Marine Isopoda of the families Serolidae, Idotheidae, Pseudidotheidea, Arcturidea, Parasellidea and Stenetriidae, mainly from the South Atlantic. *Further Zool. Res. Swedish Antarctic Expedition 1901–1903*, Vol. 3, Part 1, 1–284.

Pearse, J. S. (1963). Marine reproductive periodicity in Polar Seas: A Study on two invertebrates at McMurdo Sound. *Bull. ecol. Soc. Am.* **44**, Part 2, 43.

Pearse, J. S. (1964). Reproductive Periodicities in Several Contrasting Populations of *Odontaster validus* Koehler, a Common Antarctic Asteroid. Ph.D. dissertation, Stamford University.

Pfeffer, G. (1887). Die Krebse von Süd-Georgien nach der Ausbente der Deutschen Station 1882–83. *Jb. hamb. wiss. Anst.* **4**, 41–150.

Przibram, H. (1929). Quanta in Biology. *Proc. R. Soc. Edinb.* **49**, part 3, No. 18, 224–31.

Richardson, H. (1906). Crustacés Isopodes (Premier memoire). *Expédition Antarctique Francaise (1903–1905) Sci. Nat. Doc. Sci.* 1–21 p.

Sheppard, E. M. (1957). Isopod Crustacea Part I: The sub-order Valvifera. Families: Idotheidae, Pseudidotheidae and Xenarcturidae Fam. n. With a supplement to Isopod Crustacea, Part I. The Family Serolidae. *"Discovery" Rep.* **29**, 141–98.

Tait, J. (1917). Experiment and observations on Crustacea. Part 4. Some structural features pertaining to *Glyptonotus*. *Proc. R. Soc. Edinb.* **37**, 246–303.

Tattersall, W. M. (1921). Crustacea. Part 6. Tanaidacea and Isopoda. *British Antarctic (Terra Nova) Expedition 1910. Nat. Hist. Report* 3 (Zool.), Part 8, 191–258.

Thorson, G. (1936). The larval development, growth and metabolism of Arctic marine bottom invertebrates. *Meddr. Grønland* **100**, No. 6, 1–155.

Thorson, G. (1950). Reproductive and larval ecology of marine bottom invertebrates. *Biol. Rev.* **25**, No. 1, 1–45.

Thurston, M. H. (1968). Notes on the life history of *Bovallia gigantea* (Pfeffer) (Crustacea, Amphipoda). *Br. Antarctic. Surv. Bull.* **16**, 57–64.

Discussion

Benthos

ZONATION AND PRODUCTIVITY

G. A. KNOX

The zonations in Dr Delepine's pictures seemed to have a barren zone between the *Durvillea* zone and that of *Ulothrix* and green algae. Do lichens of the genus *Verrucaria* occur in that zone?

R. DELEPINE

All the black colouration on the slides at this level was due to *Verrucaria*, which is characteristic of the upper supralittoral to mid-littoral, below the zone of *Ulothrix* and *Urospora*. Several species are involved, *V. striata* being prominent.

S. Z. EL-SAYED

Is there any information about the productivities of benthic algae in inshore Antarctic and Subantarctic waters?

R. DELEPINE

There was almost no data. In the Subantarctic at Kerguelen, the standing crop of *Macrocystis* in the upper 50 cm of water amounts to 10 kg (wet wt)/m^2. This material, cut and removed in February/March this year, has now been replenished, giving a productivity rate of 20 kg/m^2 year.

G. A. KNOX

The barren nature of ice-abraded Antarctic shores has been stressed. But the crevices of rocky shores hold fine sediments and these can support a rich interstitial fauna of copepods, bivalves, gasteropods, nudibranchs and mites.

J. HEDGPETH

Dr Delepine's photographs reminded me of the inhospitable shores of the Galapagos Islands, which, of course, are barren for other reasons. These superficial resemblances between shores inhabited by very different organisms under very different climates are quite interesting.

M. PROPP

We have not described the same zonation pattern in our area as Dr Dayton has outlined, but it may be that the discrepancy is in part due to differences in the way in which we have defined communities and zones. The similarity may be greater than is apparent, because of differences in terminology. In Mirny, the sea is only free of ice for about one month each summer, whereas the stronger winds at McMurdo take the ice out to sea early, and the water can remain ice free into March or April. This makes a large difference in the season when the benthic algae and diatoms can grow.

R. DELEPINE

Dr Zinova (1966: Novitates Systematicae plantarum non. vascularum) referred to eight species of algae only, which surprised me, as there are at least twenty species in Terre Adélie. Has any work been done on the sublittoral algae around Mirny or elsewhere?

M. PROPP

I regret that I showed few pictures with algae in them, as the underwater camera was unserviceable when we were working at Molodeznhaya Station, where there is a substantial sublittoral algal zonation. Here from 2–5 m there are no plants, but there are numerous large diatoms under the transparent ice, between 5 and 9 m. *Leptosomia* then becomes prominent with *Desmarestia* abundant down to 20 m. This pattern is seen only on rocky shores. In other places there are no such algae near the shore. In late spring and early summer a growth of *Monostroma* develops on many rocks.

R. DELEPINE

Do you find small red algae under the *Desmarestia* or *Phyllogigas*?

M. PROPP

Material was collected, but I cannot tell you what it consisted of, as it is all with Dr Zinova for determination.

H. JANETSCHECK

How abundant are ophiuroids in the Antarctic inshore waters? Are they ever found upside down?

M. PROPP

Ophiuroids are very common, especially below 20 m. The biomass may be up to 10–20 g/m^2 and up to ten species may be involved. I have never seen them other than in a normal position.

I. M. LAMB

At what depth did Dr Propp photograph the crinoids he showed us? At Melchior crinoids like these were found mainly below 50 m.

M. PROPP

Crinoids are very abundant at Mirny below 20 m, but rare in shallower waters. There are three or four species and my photograph is of the commonest, which is easily recognized because it has twenty arms.

INTERRELATIONSHIPS OF BENTHIC ORGANISMS

V. A. GALLARDO

Would Professor Knox comment on the relative prominence of infauna and epifauna in the Antarctic?

G. A. KNOX

There is a reasonably developed infauna in the softer shelf deposits and this becomes more conspicuous in deeper water. Rocky shelf areas and areas littered with erratics mainly support an epifauna.

C. R. GOLDMAN

How important do you feel bacteria are to the filter-feeders?

G. A. KNOX

This is unknown: indeed, the energetics of seston-feeders has not been studied. They may mainly depend on detritus, but undoubtedly bacteria contribute towards their food. There is evidence from Russian work that Antarctic bacteria are very efficient at breaking down detritus, and bacteria associated with the epontic micro-algae must contribute to the food cycle.

V. A. GALLARDO

Professor Knox showed some figures in which the benthos was listed partly as available food for other organisms, and partly not thus available. Would he please explain this.

G. A. KNOX

It has been suggested in the literature that some elements in the benthos, such as large sponges, are not available to higher trophic levels, and it was estimated that as much as 40–60% of the biomass might be in this category. In my review I suggested that this view would prove to be mistaken. It is now quite clear that the idea is erroneous: we have just seen pictures of nudibranchs and other animals grazing these sponges.

H. H. DEWITT

Do sponge-eating benthic organisms breed freely in McMurdo Sound?

P. K. DAYTON

J. Dearborn, who has completed a detailed thesis on the benthic communitites of the Sound, has more data and he has certainly recorded young animals. I have seen some reproduction in nudibranchs and asteroids and J. L. Littlepage also has some evidence.

A. L. DEVRIES

With such efficient predation by starfish and amphipods, what room is there for bacterial decomposition?

P. K. DAYTON

There is some evidence that bacterial activity is reduced in the cold water of the Sound. Seal meat protected from amphipods can persist almost unchanged for six weeks.

H. H. DEWITT

Fish skeletons also get cleaned rapidly, but do not decompose further.

M. H. THURSTON

Which species of Amphipoda were present on the seal carcass in Mr Dayton's slide. What is their normal density?

P. K. DAYTON

The species shown was an *Orchomenella*, perhaps *O. plebs*. Some members of this genus have been seen swimming around and feeding on diatoms. At least three species have been found on carcasses. Dr J. Pearce has more extensive data on the ecology of these amphipods.

M. H. THURSTON

At least two *Orchomenella* species, *O. plebs* and *O. rossi*, are likely to be involved, and there is a third, smaller species I have seen behaving in the same way on the Peninsula. The mouth parts of all these suggest a carnivorous habit, but they could equally well be omnivorous.

P. K. DAYTON

The range of these amphipods probably lies rather deeper at McMurdo than our relatively shallow scuba observations. Seal remains in 300–400 m of water are always cleaned by amphipods, whereas in shallower water *Odontaster* and similar benthic animals may feed on them.

G. A. KNOX

Do you agree that these detritus-feeders get the bulk of their energy from seal faeces at seal colonies?

P. K. DAYTON

We made preliminary counts of the relative abundance of seal faeces and the detritus-feeding animals and concluded that seal faeces, in relation to diatom detritus, comprise a relatively insignificant portion of the total intake.

K. G. MCKENZIE

Reviewing today's papers, it is evident that attention has been concentrated on macro-assemblages. I hope the smaller groups will not be neglected. Ostracoda Radiolaria and Foraminifera are abundant as fossils in sediments and would therefore be helpful in Antarctic palaeobiogeography, if their present distribution in the region were known.

COLONIZATION OF NEW ISLET AT DECEPTION ISLAND

R. DELEPINE

When Dr Gallardo visited Deception, was there any colonization of the new volcanic island by algae?

V. A. GALLARDO

I was at Deception Island on 27th and 31st December and at that time nothing was living on the island, which was very hot.

R. DELEPINE

Benthic diatoms were the first colonists of Surtsey very soon after the eruption.

V. A. GALLARDO

We did not look for diatoms at Deception Island.

RAFTING OF ANIMALS TO THE SURFACE BY ICE

P. K. DAYTON

Anchor-ice uplift provides a good explanation for the presence of some animal remains on the surface of the ice shelves. Swithinbank and others (*Science*, *N.Y.*, 1961) invoked an unlikely theory of Debenham's to explain the presence of fish and delicate invertebrate remains around the Dailey Islands in the McMurdo Sound Region. It is now almost certain that seals captured these fish and lost them in the platelet ice in the tide cracks at the Dailey Islands. We have observed this to happen at the Dailey Islands. The invertebrate remains, however, were probably uplifted by anchor ice from the bottom. It has been calculated that surface ablation of the ice in this area is approximately 0·5 m/yr: an equal amount is assumed to be accumulating from below. Thus the delicate invertebrate remains would accumulate undamaged on the surface. We have seen algae, rocks, and invertebrates frozen all through annual sea ice (in one case within 3 in of the surface).

The sponge spicules described as composing a supralittoral amongst lichens behind Scott Base and on Observation Hill most likely were blown there after working their way to the surface of the ice shelf.

NECROPHAGY

M. J. DUNBAR

We must remember that hungry omnivores can eat very strange things. In West Greenland I once found two pieces of turkey, one corn cob, and an empty Lucky Strike packet in a cod stomach.

R. DELEPINE

What are the proportions of animals caught by net, line or trap in temperate areas?

P. ARNAUD

So far as fishes are concerned, we should ask an ichthyologist. Many invertebrate species such as asteroids, amphipods, crabs (e.g. *Carcinus maenas*) and Palinuridae are caught by traps in temperate seas. Some other groups could perhaps be caught, but unfortunately such apparatus has almost never been used extensively by scientists.

M. H. THURSTON

In the amphipods, one family the Lysianassidae has a mandible so shaped as to suggest a necrophagous habit; and this would mean one-eighth of the known Gamaridea are necrophagous—400 species out of about 3200.

R. DELEPINE

What is the proportion of necrophagy in other groups?

P. ARNAUD

In Terre Adélie, more than half the species of asteroids and ophiuroids are necrophagous, as well as five out of fifteen species of fishes. Data are not yet available for other groups.

P. K. DAYTON

Although asteroids I have studied are effective predators, any of them would stop and eat a dead fish placed in their path. Almost any hungry invertebrate would probably eat anything that is dead.

R. DELEPINE

Can Dr Hureau give comparable figures for the Subantarctic?

J. C. HUREAU

At Kerguelen fishes are readily netted, but cannot be caught in traps. I believe all the species take living prey and are not necrophagous except *Notothenia cyanobrancha*.

P. Arnaud

These differences may reflect differences in metabolism. Benthic fishes in Terre Adélie, especially *Trematonus bernacchii* and *T. hansoni* are known from Wohlschlag's work to have a low metabolism, and to be slow moving, and this may account for their preference for dead food. In Kerguelen, moreover, the plankton cycle does not have such marked seasonal periodicity.

BIOLOGY OF AMPHIPODA AND ISOPODA

K. G. McKenzie

The Ostracoda species Dr Elofson studied off the Skagerak produced occasional large individuals quite outside the normal range. The size at maturity ranges up to a normal maximum of 1 mm, but there are rare, peculiar, large individuals of 1·1 to 1·2 mm mean length. This may be a general problem in many Crustacean groups.

M. Propp

Several *Glyptonotus* were observed at Mirny, but only in deeper water, below 30 m. I have never seen phototropism in this species; it was found only below transparent ice. I will send examples to Mr White.

G. A. Knox

There seems to be a contrast in the breeding habits of *Glyptonotus* and *Bovallia*. The year round availability of food to the former does not necessitate the timing of reproduction to coincide with a marked seasonal periodicity in food. Does *Bovallia* have any seasonal restriction of food supplies available to newly hatched individuals which may account for its limited breeding season?

M. H. Thurston

Pontogeneiids are usually omnivorous, taking algae and debris. I have found no animal remains in the gut, and there would appear to be plenty of available food at all seasons.

M. White

I have watched *Bovallia* at Signy Island. They sit in the water whirling their antennae and drawing in a current, and their mouth parts are working, perhaps seizing particles. Antarcturids observed in the same habitats exhibit similar behaviour and these are certainly phytoplankton filter-feeders.

K. G. McKenzie

The adult male *Glyptonotus* pictured was covered with *Spirorbis*. Were these only found on the adults?

M. White

They were especially numerous on the exoskeleton of adults, but some were also present on younger animals. I tried using them as an indicator of age, but without success since the life history of these polychaetes is imperfectly known.

Part VI

FISHES

Fishes

In most of the world's seas the fish fauna has been an especial object of study because of its economic importance. This has not been so in the Antarctic. Here, while the fish species present have become fairly well known and been the subject of substantial reviews (e.g. Andriashev, 1965), there is, as G. A. Knox pointed out in his review paper in Part 2, still no reliable estimate of their biomass or productivity and relatively little information on the autecology of most species. The first two papers in the present section do not fill this gap, although they do provide important information about, on the one hand, the curious group of fishes closely associated with floating ice and the diatom and crustacean system it supports, and on the other about the fish fauna of the semi-isolated Ross Sea basin. A. P. Andriashev's paper can usefully be examined in conjunction with his important contribution to the SCAR Symposium on Antarctic Oceanography (1968) and with the paper by N. B. Marshall (1964) in the proceedings of the first SCAR Symposium on Antarctic biology in which convergent features of the benthic fishes of polar seas were discussed.

Conversely the physiology of Antarctic fishes, which maintain activity in water consistently below 0°C and sometimes below the natural freezing points of their body fluids, has attracted much attention. The United States biological laboratory at McMurdo has been the base for important investigations of their metabolism, led by Wohlschlag (1964). Interest has likewise focused on the respiratory physiology of the Chaenichthyid fishes lacking blood-carrier pigments. In the present section this subject is reviewed, and new evidence presented by I. Everson and R. Ralph. Most of the section is, however, devoted to the physiology of freezing resistance. A. L. de Vries produces evidence for an "antifreeze" substance (a protein containing carbohydrate) in the blood of inshore fishes at McMurdo: conversely R. N. Smith concludes that the freezing-point depression of the blood of related species in the slightly warmer waters of the South Orkney Islands is largely due to sodium chloride. Clearly this apparent discrepancy is of the highest interest and merits further comparative investigation. Another important line of study is presented in the paper by R. W. Morris and R. E. Feeney in this section, for both are concerned in different ways with the efficiency of physiological systems at low temperatures. Dr Morris provides evidence that heat generated by muscular activity during cold stress may have survival value in polar fishes, and that at such times the circulation may be concentrated in the core of the body, thus retaining centrally such heat as is available. R. E. Feeney illustrates how enzyme-substrate reactions in Antarctic polar fishes may be adapted for high efficiency at very low temperatures. Since the study of adaption to extreme polar conditions is one of the most evidently justifiable fields of investigation in Antarctica, we may expect this whole field to be an important growing point in the future.

References

Andriashev, A. P. (1965). A general review of the Antarctic fish fauna. *In* "Biogeography and Ecology of Antarctica". Den Haag, Junk.

Andriashev, A. P. (1968). The problems of the life community associated with lower layers of the Antarctic fast ice. *In* "Symposium on Antarctic Oceanography", Scott Polar Research Institute, Cambridge.

Marshall, N. B. (1964). Some convergences between the benthic fishes of polar seas. *In* "Biologie Antarctique". Paris, Hermann.

Wohlschlag, D. E. (1964). Respiratory metabolism and ecological characteristics of some fishes in McMurdo Sound, Antarctica. *Antarctic Res. Ser.*, 1, 33–62.

Cryopelagic Fishes of the Arctic and Antarctic and their Significance in Polar Ecosystems

A. P. ANDRIASHEV
Zoological Institute, U.S.S.R. Academy of Sciences, Leningrad, U.S.S.R.

I. Introduction

Despite the seeming homogeneity of the life conditions in the pelagic zone of the ocean, we cannot neglect the ecological heterogeneity of its fish fauna. This depends primarily on such biological parameters as constant or temporary occupation of the pelagic zone (including natural connections with the coast at various stages of the life cycle); peculiarities of the vertical pattern of the distribution of fishes in midwater in the ocean (including the occupation of constant vertical zones, and vertical migration daily, with age, or in response to other factors); ability for distant migrations and overcoming marine currents; the nature of adaptations to the life in midwater; relations with the floating substratum, etc. It is particularly important to consider the evolutionary age of "pelagicity", that is whether a species belongs to true necton families adapted to the pelagic mode of life long ago, e.g. many sharks, pomfrets, marlins and other true pelagic forms or originates from coastal or bottom-dwelling families and has only recently adapted to temporary or constant life in the pelagic zone, e.g. some white-blooded fishes of the family Chaenichthyidae (*Champsocephalus gunnari*, *Neopagetopsis ionah*, etc.) and Antarctic herring (*Pleuragramma antarcticum*) of the family Nototheniidae and other "secondarily pelagic" forms.

Recently Nicholas Parin in his monograph "Epipelagic fish fauna of the ocean" (1968) has attempted a classification of various ecological groups of epipelagic fishes. Of all the groups of his system the so-called cryopelagic fishes peculiar only to polar seas, are of the greatest interest in present circumstances.

The author suggested the use of the term "cryopelagic" for fishes which actively swim in midwater (in coastal zones or in the open sea), but during their life cycle are associated in some way or other with drifting or fast ice (Andriashev, 1968). Both young and adult fishes can be associated with ice or water immediately below the ice. These relationships are usually trophic in their nature, but in some cases ice provides fishes with a shelter from predators or even a substratum for sucking. The association of fishes with ice can be observed easily and often. The more intimate aspects of their behaviour are, however, still little known and the explanations cited for this association are often little more than imperfectly substantiated assumptions. The aim of the present short paper is to draw the attention of polar biologists to the problem of the relationship between fish and sea ice, within the overall context of cryobiology.

II. Cryopelagic Fishes of the Arctic

I am not quite sure who made the first observations and first reports on the connection of fishes with sea ice. I believe, however, that they concerned the polar cod (*Boreogadus saida*) described by Ivan Lepechin as early as the eighteenth century.

Everybody who has sailed in the Arctic seas, especially aboard ice-breakers, will probably recall the following trivial picture. Astern of the ice-breaker are dozens of kittiwakes (*Rissa tridactyla*). From time to time they throw themselves down, picking small dark-silvery fishes from the surface of ice. This is the polar cod (*Boreogadus saida*), or "saika" in Russian. These observations, though naïve enough, are quite reliable. The very fact of the polar cod's presence on the surface of overturned pieces of ice shows that before the passage of the ship it was under or in the lower surface of the ice.

According to many eyewitness observations (see A. Jensen, 1948), polar cod often occur in ice holes, cracks, hollows and cavities in the lower surface of the ice. They are most common among broken ice or near the ice edge. Here, as the ice thaws and breaks up phyto- and zooplankton develop and provide food for polar cod. It is possible that the fish also feed on organisms of the amphipod-diatom ice community inhabiting the lower "fluffy" ice layer. This peculiar ice biocoenosis is known now both from the Arctic and Antarctic (S. Jensen, 1948; Bunt, 1963; Meguro *et al.*, 1967; Andriashev, 1968; etc.). At the same time polar cod apparently use sea ice as shelter from the numerous enemies attacking them from both water and air.

Polar cod are abundant animals and make distant migrations, and their enormous autumn-winter pre-spawning swarms are well known. The species is also very widely distributed, not only along the shelf areas in the Arctic Basin but also in higher latitudes. Many years ago Nansen observed polar cod at 84°N; in the collections of the Zoological Institute there are specimens caught recently near the North Pole.

Due to the above peculiarities polar cod plays a very important part in the Arctic polar ecosystems. On the one hand, it is one of the main consumers of Arctic plankton; on the other, it is a common food of Greenland seal (*Pago-*

phoca groenlandica), ringed seal (*Phoca hispida*), bearded seal (*Erignathus barbatus*), white whale (*Delphinapterus leucas*), narwhal (*Monodon monoceros*) and other marine mammals, many marine birds (including gulls, guillemots, etc.) and fishes (Klumov, 1937; Andriashev, 1954).

Another species of cod can now be added to the Arctic cryopelagic fishes. In 1948 the well-known Danish ichthyologist A. Jensen described a new genus and species, *Phocaegadus megalops*, and reported that seals caught it by chasing it until it jumped from the water and became stranded on the ice. As was established later (Andriashev, 1954, 1957; Nielsen and Jensen, 1967), this fish had been found first and described almost a century ago by Peters and is now known under the name "glacial cod"* (*Arctogadus glacialis*). It is little studied, but like polar cod is widely distributed not only off Greenland but also in the high latitudes of the Polar Basin over abyssal depths.

It has been caught repeatedly in "shot-holes" on drifting stations ("North Pole.—6", "NP—10", "NP—16", and American station "Charlie"); it was on "Charlie" that about a thousand fishes were caught in one day in winter through "shot-holes" and "hydro-holes" (Walters, 1961). Glacial cod, like polar cod, are plankton-eating fish and serve as food for seals. This means that they play a similar part in the ecosystem of the Polar Basin to cryopelagic polar cod. In this context a unique observation made by an American submarine off Greenland (Anonymous, 1965) should be mentioned. Sailors saw fishes which stood vertically, their heads turned upwards, eating plankton from the lower ice surface. I believe these fish were glacial cod feeding on the amphipod-diatomous ice community rather than salmon, as the eye-witnesses thought.

III. Cryopelagic Fishes of the Antarctic

Though underwater investigations using SCUBA diving are now developing rapidly, this method, unfortunately, is little used in the Arctic. That is why we are almost without direct observations on northern cryopelagic fishes. In the Antarctic the situation is somewhat better.

Long ago, during the wintering of the German expedition aboard the *Gauss*, the presence of some fishes, including *Trematomus borchgrevinki*, in the sub-ice water of the Davis Sea was established. These half-forgotten observations have now been confirmed and supplemented. Large winter sub-ice swarmings have been found recently in two species, *T. borchgrevinki* and *T. newnesi* (Andriashev, 1967). Both species were caught through holes at the lower surface of the fast ice, where they feed on krill and other

* Some American authors use other common names: Arctic cod (*Boreogadus saida*) and Polar cod (*Arctogadus glacialis* (*Arctogadius glacialis*); see "A list of common and scientific names of fishes . . ." Ann Arbor. Mich., 1960).

crustaceans. Fishes occurred under the ice near the coast (Mirny) and far out in the open sea (Novolazorevskaya).

Observations made by SCUBA divers on young *T. borchgrevinki* are especially interesting. Young fishes hide themselves in hollows and cavities of the lower surface of fast ice "in much the same way that fish can be spotted in small rock caves in temperate areas" (Peckham, 1964). Our SCUBA divers observed large shoals of young *T. borchgrevinki*, which at the slightest danger instantly hid themselves in loose diatom-rock ice. Apparently, this productive amphipod-diatom layer of ice serves for fishes as a feeding ground and refuge.

IV. Attachment to Ice in Antarctic Fishes

Wonderful observations on Antarctic fishes and sea ice were made this year at Enderby Land (69°S, 13°E) by Eugene Gruzov and Alexander Pushkin (Gruzov *et al.*, 1967). Working at depths down to 30 m on the vertical wall of a tabular iceberg, they observed fishes attached to the smooth surface of the iceberg, with their heads turned up and down. After these fishes were caught and placed in an aquarium, they swam a little and settled on its glass wall. Identification has shown that these were young (fingerlings) of the common Antarctic coast fish *Trematomus nicolai*, which like other percoid fishes has no special sucking disc. They attach to ice using wide ventral fins which have, however, a normal structure (I 5). In doing so the fish stretches its ventral fins maximally and clings to the surface of the iceberg. Thus, a peculiar crimped plane is formed consisting of six rays and the fin membrane which produces a sucking effect.

I believe the adaptive significance of this unique phenomenon may be explained as follows. The vertical wall of the iceberg is a rich feeding ground where young fishes can obtain attached diatoms and small crustaceans. All species of notothenoid fishes, however, including *Trematomus*, have no swim-bladder. Therefore, keeping close to an iceberg while feeding would require the expenditure of much energy on maintaining the animals in midwater. Their peculiar ice-sucking capacity enables them to keep on the vertical ice surface with minimum expenditure of effort. Dr E. Gruzov observed and caught near the wall of the iceberg specimens of other species of *Trematomus*, which are not yet identified.

All this indicates that not only young of *T. borchgrevinki* but also of *T. newnesi* and some other species have a cryophilic stage in their life cycle.

Unfortunately, we know almost nothing about the biology of other pelagic species of this family, such as *Pagothenia antarctica*, *Aetothotaxis mitopteryx*, *Pleuragramma antarcticum*, etc. It is very likely that in future new discoveries concerning their cryophily will be made.

V. Cold Adaptation and Stenothermy of Cryopelagic Fishes

Fishes of polar seas and especially cryopelagic species differ in cold adaptation and stenothermy. According to my superficial observations made in the northern part of the Chukchi Sea (about 73°N) polar cod remained healthy and actively swam to and fro in an aquarium at a temperature a little below zero. With a slight increase in the temperature of water (to 2–4°C) the fishes became less mobile and swam slowly at the surface. After several pieces of sea ice were placed in the aquarium, the fishes became animated again and their activity was restored.

Experiments carried out by Dr P. F. Scholander and his colleagues between 1953 and 1962 have shown that polar cod and some other Arctic fishes have a blood freezing-point about 1°C below zero (to −1·5°C in winter) and are supercooled by about 0·2–0·7°C (Scholander *et al.* 1957; Marshall, 1965).

Interesting information on temperature tolerance has been obtained recently for Antarctic fishes*. It is known that in temperate fishes the greatest swimming activity is observed at temperatures slightly lower than seasonal maxima (Fry, 1957). In cryopelagic *T. borchgrevinki* the greatest swimming activity was established at freezing temperatures (from −1·9° to −1·7°C); it declined at −0·8° and ceased about 2°C (Wohlschlag, 1962). The same species, in experiments by Somero and DeVries (1967), was active enough at −2·5°C, but died when the temperature was increased to 5–6°C. Experiments on metabolic level carried out by Wohlschlag (1962, 1964) in the laboratory at McMurdo are especially significant, for they showed convincingly the maximum of stenothermy and cold adaptation in *T. borchgrevinki* and some other species of the genus.

It should be noted that direct contact with sea ice is a normal mode of life for some Antarctic fishes which hide in the lower layer of fast ice and in cavities of icebergs, or suck on ice surfaces, and does not cause freezing of their body fluids.

VI. Taxonomic Rank and Morphological Parallelism in Cryopelagic Fishes

The taxonomic rank of cryopelagic fishes among other forms of the family is indicative, to a certain extent, of the degree of adaptation of these fishes to their peculiar mode of life.

Polar and glacial cod are assigned by all ichthyologists to two distinct genera, *Boreogadus* and *Acrtogadus*. Each of these genera has characters not occurring in any other Gadoid fishes, e.g. the presence of palatine teeth in *Arctogadus*, and a special structure of the scale covering and zigzag lateral line in *Boreogadus*.

* See also papers by A. L. DeVries, R. N. Smith, R. W. Morris and R. E. Feeney in this volume.

The most characteristic Antarctic cryopelagic species, *T. borchgrevinki*, is still referred to a large endemic Antarctic genus *Trematomus*, which includes thirteen species (Andriashev, 1964). Recently, however, it has been suggested that *T. borchgrevinki* (together with the allied species *T. brachysoma*) should be separated into a distinct genus due to the peculiar structure of their lateral line organs (DeWitt, 1964; Andriashev, 1964). Thus, without going into details, we may say that the taxonomic rank of cryopelagic species attains, in general, the generic level. This speaks indirectly in favour of the long adaptation of these forms to a peculiar mode of life, associated more or less with sea ice.

Cryopelagic fishes of the Arctic and Antarctic are distant from one another in the systematic position. They belong to different orders of Teleostei —Gadiformes and Perciformes. Nevertheless, they have similar morphological features which would be regarded only as morphological parallelisms. These involve mainly the system of lateral line organs, associated with the perception of movement and various water fluctuations.

In most of the species of the families Gadidae and Nototheniidae the seismosensorial system has a normal structure, consisting of canals in the skull bones and a body canal formed by tubular scales. In these canals, which open to the exterior by pores, there are neuromasts responding to water fluctuations. Cryopelagic fishes both in the Arctic and Antarctic tend to replace the system of neuromast-containing canals by a system of free neuromasts on the body and head. It is inappropriate to discuss the complex reasons for these changes in detail here. It should be noted, however, that the changes in the lateral line organs (interruption of canals on the head, reduction of pores, development of free neuromasts, etc.) indicate the degree to which these Notothenoid fishes have evolved adaptations for pelagic life.

VII. Conclusions

Cryopelagic fishes are normally confined to polar seas, where they are widely distributed within the zone of ice cover. They lead a pelagic mode of life under ice and are especially associated with a peculiar amphipod-diatom ice bicoenosis. The ice biotope is used by cryophilic fishes as a feeding ground and a refuge from numerous enemies.

Cryopelagic fishes of the Arctic (*Boreogadus*, *Arctogadus*) and Antarctic (*Trematomus borchgrevinki*, etc.) evolved independently in different orders of Teleostei. Under the influence of a similar mode of life they acquired some analogous characters, which may be regarded as morpho-physiological parallelisms.

Cryopelagic fishes are a good example of bipolarity of life forms. They are well adapted to cold, stenothermic and abundant. They play a similar and very important part in the northern and southern polar ecosystems, being the main consumers of plankton and representing at the same time the main food for numerous marine mammals, birds and fishes.

In conclusion I would like to make a more general comment. Recent investigations in the Arctic and especially the Antarctic have yielded many new interesting facts about the relationship between organisms and sea ice. We may state that as a result of efforts of scientists from various countries the features of a new branch of hydrobiology, which may be provisionally called "marine cryobiology", are now being defined.

The main aim of work in this field is to study, in nature and by experiment, complex and still imperfectly described causal connections between organisms and communities and various types of sea ice. Research is required on physical and chemical characteristics of ice biotopes, morpho-physiological adaptations of cryophilic species, biological structure and productivity of ice biocoenoses, and their role in polar ecosystems.

References

Andriashev, A. P. (1954). Fishes of the Northern Seas of the U.S.S.R. Zool. Inst. Ac. Sci., Leningrad (in Russian). English translation by Israel Progr. Sci. Transl., No. 836, 1964, 1–617.

Andriashev, A. P. (1957). A codfish species [*Arctogadus glacialis* (Peters)] new to the fauna of the U.S.S.R. caught at the drifting station "North Pole—6". *Zool. Zh.* XXXYI, No. 11, 1747–9 (in Russian). English translation by Israel Progr. Sci. Transl., No. 765, 1963, 55–58.

Andriashev, A. P. (1964). A general review of the Antarctic fish fauna. *In* "Explor. Fauna Seas" II (X), 335–86 (in Russian). English ed.: *Monogr. biol.* XY, 1965, 491–550.

Andriashev, A. P. (1967). Microflora and fauna associated with the Antarctic fast ice. *Zool. Zh.*, XLYI, No. 10, 1585–93 (in Russian).

Andriashev, A. P. (1968). The problems of life community associated with lower layers of the Antarctic fast ice. *In* "Symposium on Antarctic Oceanography," Scott Polar Research Institute, Cambridge.

Anon (1965). Greenland fishing of Atlantic Salmon. *Atlant. Salmon J.* Fall, 28–32.

Bunt, J. S. (1963). Diatoms of antarctic sea-ice as agents of primary production. *Nature, Lond.* 199, 1255–7.

DeWitt, H. H. (1964). A redescription of Pagothenia antarctica, with remarks on the genus *Trematomus* (Pisces, Nototheniidae). *Copeia* 4, 683–6.

Fry, F. E. (1957). The aquatic respiration of fish. *In* "The Physiology of Fishes" (M. E. Brown, ed.), Vol. I, 1–63.

Gruzov, E. N., Propp, M. V. and Pushkin, A. Th. (1967). Biological communities of the inshore areas of the Davies Sea (from data of diving observation). *Inf. Byull sov. antarkt. Eksped.* 65, 124–41 (in Russian).

Jensen, A. S. (1948). Contribution to the ichthyofauna of Greenland 8–24, *Spolia Zool. Mus. haun*, 9, 1–182.

Jensen, S. (1948). *In* A. S. Jensen, 1948, 1. c., 132.

Klumov, S. K. (1937). Saika, Boreogadus Saida (Lepech.) and its significance in Arctic life. *Izv. Acad. Sci. U.S.S.R.* (biol.), **1**, 175–88 (in Russian).

Marshall, N. B. (1965). "The Life of Fishes". Weidenfeld and Nicolson, London, pp. 1–402.

Meguro, H., Ito, K. and Fukushima, K. (1967). Ice flora (bottom type): a mechanism of primary production in polar seas and the growth of diatoms in sea ice. *J. Arctic* **20**, No. 2, 114–33.

Nielsen, J. G. and Jensen, J. M. (1967). Revision of the arctic cod genus Arctogadus (Pisces, Gadidae). *Meddr. Grønland* **184**, No. 2: 1–28.

Parin, N. V. (1968). Epipelagic fish fauna of the ocean. *Trudy Inst. Okeanol.* (in Russian).

Peckham, V. (1964). Year-round SCUBA diving in the Antarctic. *Polar Rec.* **12**, No. 77, 143–6.

Scholander, P. F., Van Dam, L., Kanwischer, J. W., Hammel, A. T. and Gordon, M. S. (1957). Supercooling and osmoregulation in arctic fish. *J. cell. comp. Physiol.* **49**, 5–24.

Somero, G. N. and DeVries, A. L. (1967). Temperature tolerance of some Antarctic fishes. *Science*, N.Y. **156**, No. 3772: 257–8.

Walters, V. I. (1961). Winter abundance of Arctogadus glacialis in the Polar basin, *Copeia* **2**, 236–7.

Wohlschlag, D. E. (1962). Metabolic requirements for the swimming activity of three Antarctic fishes. *Science*, N.Y. **137**, No. 3535, 1050–1.

Wohlschlag, D. E. (1964). Respiratory metabolism and ecological characteristics of some fishes in McMurdo Sound, Antarctica. *Antarctic Res. Ser.* **1**, 33–62.

The Character of the Midwater Fish Fauna of the Ross Sea, Antarctica*

HUGH H. DEWITT
Department of Marine Science, University of South Florida, St Petersburg, Florida, U.S.A.

I. Introduction

During cruise 27 of the USNS *Eltanin*, in January and February of 1967, thirty-five tows were made with a 10 ft Isaacs-Kidd midwater trawl south of 65°S latitude in and to the north of the Ross Sea. Twenty-one of these tows were taken over the continental shelf of the Ross Sea, from the northern edge to the south-west corner near Ross Island (Fig. 1). They represent the first collections made with a midwater trawl in this large, relatively shallow sea, and permit us to characterize the midwater fishes found there.

Since no metering or closing mechanisms were used with the trawl, making the hauls of limited value for quantitative purposes, the data presented below are averages or percentages based upon the total number of hauls in the Ross Sea. Immediately after retrieving a sample all fishes were sorted out and preserved separately. Species of the suborder Notothenioidei were shipped first to the University of Southern California and then to the University of South Florida, where the work resulting in this paper was completed. The Notothenioidei from stations 1872 through 1934 (Fig. 1) were counted and then weighed to the nearest one-tenth gramme after excess moisture had been blotted from them with a cloth. Some material from two hauls (stations 1891 and 1915) were lost during shipment to the United States when a 30 gallon drum was lost overboard during a storm. The surviving material from these stations has been used for distributional purposes only.

II. The Fish Fauna of the Ross Sea

As the *Eltanin* moved south from the Southern Ocean over the continental shelf of the Ross Sea, a very sudden change was observed in the species of midwater fishes collected. All of the species normally abundant in the

* Contribution No. 8 from the Marine Science Institute of the University of South Florida.

Southern Ocean disappeared and were replaced by species of the suborder Notothenioidei, a group whose members are primarily benthic as adults. Therefore nearly all of the species captured occurred only as juveniles or larvae. This abrupt faunal change is illustrated in Figs 2 and 3, where the patterns of occurrence are presented for eight families of fishes. Note that

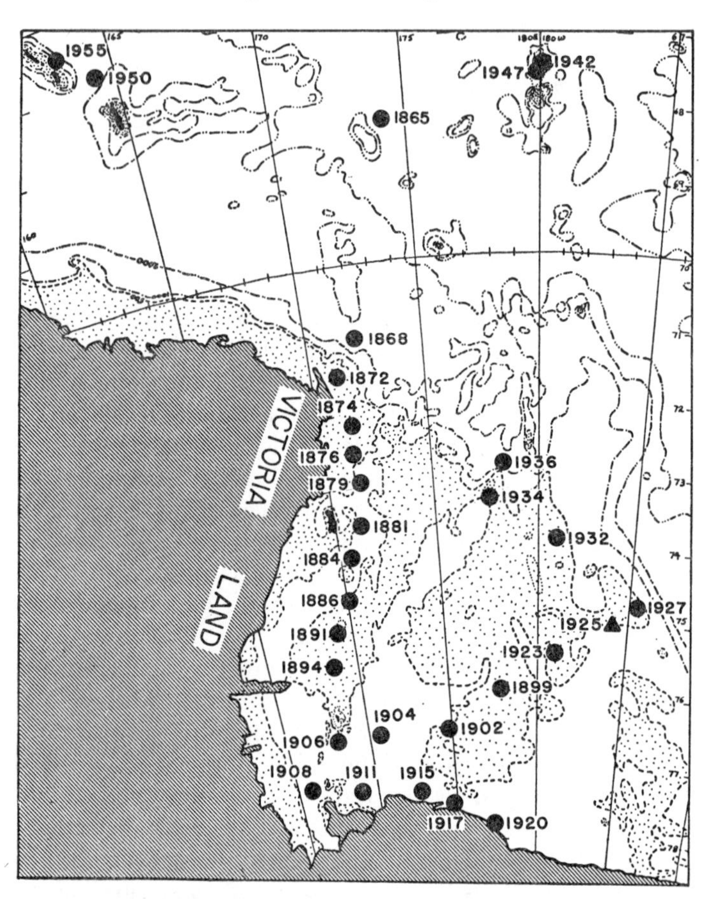

FIG. 1. USC *Eltanin* stations in and to the north of the Ross Sea where midwater fishes were collected; circles represent catches with a 10 ft Isaacs-Kidd trawl; the triangle represents a Blake trawl haul; stippled areas are less than 500 m in depth.

the Myctophidae, Gonostomatidae, Bathylagidae and Paralepididae are nearly entirely excluded from the Ross Sea and, except for the last, extend south only on to the edge of the continental shelf (Fig. 2). The Paralepididae are represented in the Ross Sea by one specimen at station 1884 and possibly one more at station 1920 (a badly damaged head). On the other hand, the families

Nototheniidae, Harpagiferidae, Bathydraconidae and Channichthyidae (all belonging to the suborder Notothenioidei) are of wide occurrence in the Ross Sea and, except for the family Nototheniidae, are nearly entirely restricted to the waters over the continental shelf (Fig. 3). In addition to the families mentioned above, the families Macruridae and Liparidae were represented in the

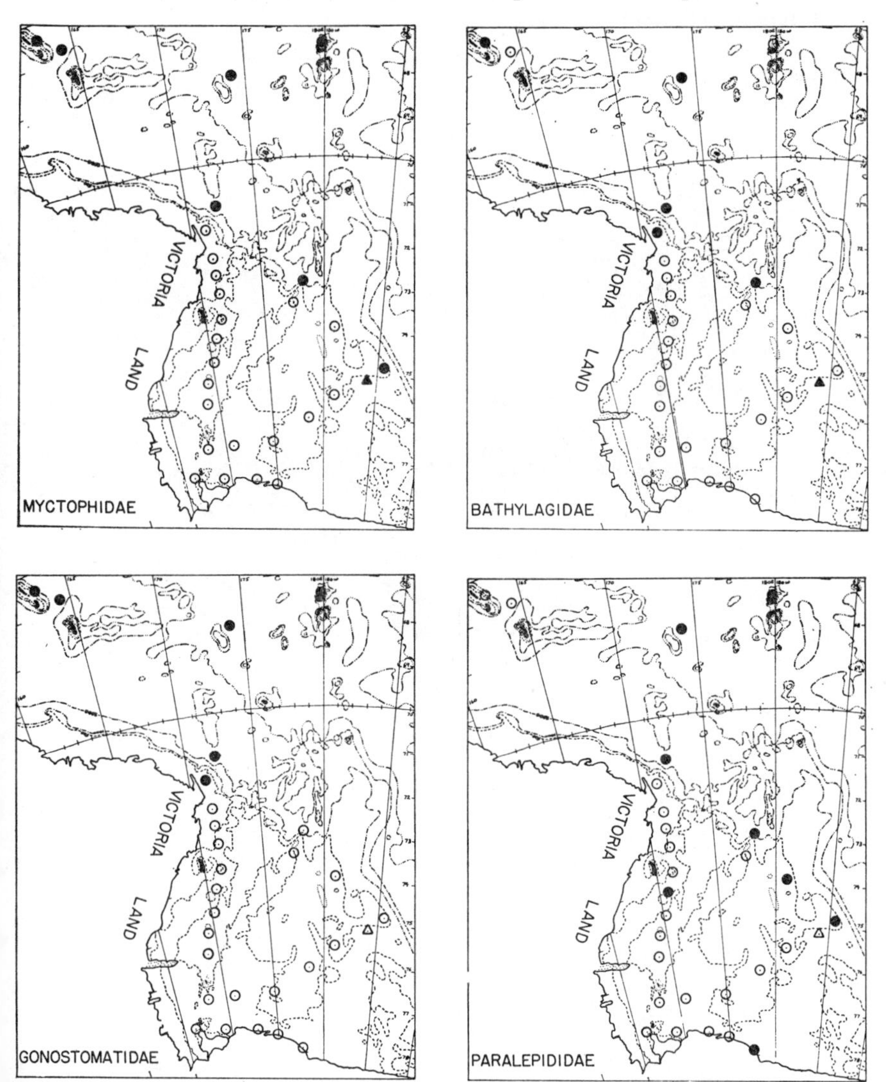

FIG. 2. Patterns of occurrence in Ross Sea midwaters for four families of fishes. Solid circles represent stations with positive records.

Ross Sea midwaters by one and seven juvenile specimens, respectively. The total number of non-nototheniiform fishes obtained over the continental shelf was twenty-five, constituting only 0·7% of the fishes captured there. The only adults obtained in the Ross Sea midwaters were one specimen of *Neopagetopsis ionah* and about a hundred specimens of *Pleuragramma antarcticum* with lengths greater than 100 mm.

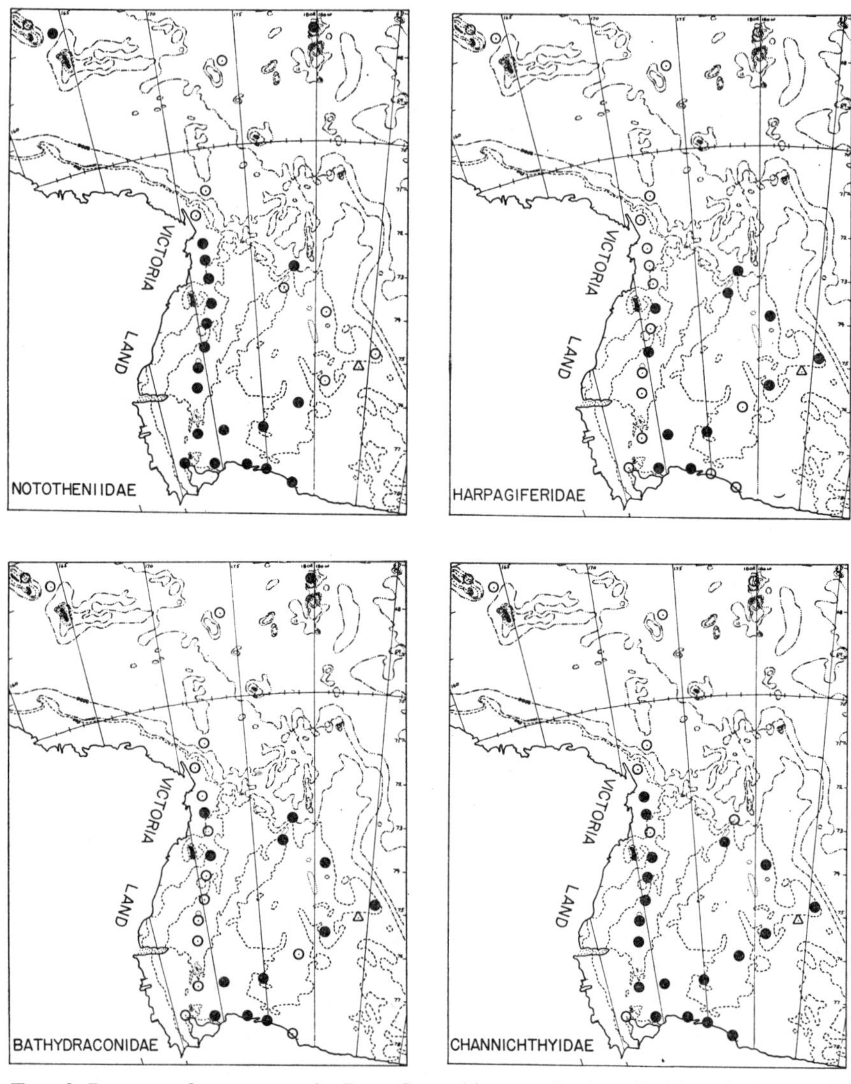

FIG. 3. Patterns of occurrence in Ross Sea midwaters for four families of fishes. Solid circles represent stations with positive records.

Pleuragramma antarcticum was found to be the overwhelmingly dominant species of midwater fish. Fig. 4 presents the relative proportions, by number and weight, of the four notothenoid families, with the data for *P. antarcticum* shown separately from those for the rest of the family Nototheniidae. The extreme preponderance of the single species is clearly evident. Note also that the average size, as indicated by the differences in percentages expressed by numbers and weights, is larger for *P. antarcticum* than for the other families (if the single large specimen of *Neopagetopsis ionah* is removed from the Channichthyidae). This results from the absence of adults of all species except *P. antarcticum* (and *N. ionah*). The actual size ranges of the four families and *P. antarcticum* are given in Table 1.

TABLE 1

Ranges of Total Length of Notothenioid Families in Ross Sea Midwaters. The figure in parenthesis refers to the single large specimen of *Neopagetopsis ionah*

Nototheniidae (excluding *Pleuragramma antarcticum*)	25–32 mm
Pleuragramma antarcticum	8–232 mm
Harpagiferidae	12–28 mm
Bathydraconidae	14–67 mm
Channichthyidae	13–69 (381) mm

A further fact clearly shown by Fig. 4 is the insignificant number of specimens of the family Nototheniidae, other than *P. antarcticum*, which are present in the Ross Sea midwaters. This indicates that juveniles of the genus *Trematomus*, the dominant benthic group of the family in the Ross Sea, do not normally stray far from the bottom. In the peninsular region, and at Scott and Balleny Islands, where the closely related genus *Notothenia* is the dominant benthic group, fair numbers of pelagic juveniles have been obtained (Fig. 3, and unpublished *Eltanin* data).

There are indications that the presence of *P. antarcticum* influences the distribution and abundance of the families Harpagiferidae, Bathydraconidae and Channichthyidae. Each of the latter shows a lower average number of

TABLE 2

Average Number of Specimens per Haul for Three Families of Fishes when captured with and without *Pleuragramma antarcticum*. Figures in parentheses are numbers of hauls

	With P. antarcticum	*Without* P. antarcticum
Harpagiferidae	2·2 (5)	17·5 (4)
Bathydraconidae	2·8 (6)	10·2 (4)
Channichthyidae	4·6 (12)	14·2 (5)

specimens per haul when taken with *P. antarcticum* than when taken without this species (Table 2). It also appears, from the patterns of occurrence (Fig. 3), that the Harpagiferidae and Bathydraconidae are more severely limited than are the Channichthyidae. Of the fourteen hauls in which *P. antarcticum* was captured, only five also contained Harpagiferids and only six also contained Bathydraconids. I plan to investigate the food of *P. antarcticum* to determine whether the above interpretations are correct.

III. The Relation between Midwater Fish Faunas and Water Masses

The Ross Sea is relatively broad and shallow, shallowest to the north and east, where the average depth is between 300 and 400 m at the shelf edge, and

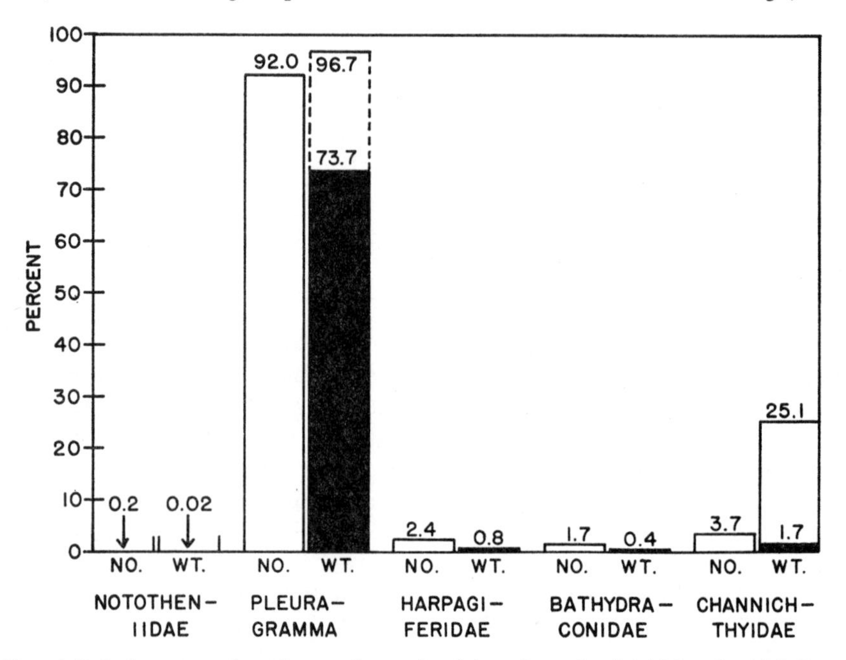

FIG. 4. Relative proportions, by number and weight, of notothenioid fishes found in Ross Sea midwaters. Open bar and solid bar for *Pleuragramma* represent, respectively, relative proportions when large channichthyid is disregarded (solid bar of Channichthyidae) or included (open bar of Channichthyidae).

deepest to the south-west, where soundings of about 1000 m have been recorded (Fig. 1). Three broad troughs lead from the edge of the continental shelf into the south-west basin, with minimum sill depths of from 550 m to a little less than 500 m. A body of water with these dimensions would ordinarily be a suitable habitat for many pelagic fishes found in the adjacent ocean. An area useful for comparison is the San Pedro Basin off the coast of southern California. Paxton (1967) and Lavenberg and Ebeling (1967) have recently studied the midwater fishes of this basin, which, although much smaller, has depths somewhat similar to those of the Ross Sea. It lies between the mainland to the east and Santa Catalina Island to the west, and is connected to other deeper basins to the north-west and south-east. The basin has a maximum depth of 912 m and a sill depth of about 750 m. Fifty-two species of pelagic fishes have now been recorded for the San Pedro Basin (Lavenberg and Ebeling, 1967).

The area off southern California is known as a region of transition into which three water masses enter and mix (Emery, 1954). Pacific Equatorial water is found in the basin in modified form below 350 m; Pacific Subarctic and Eastern North Pacific Central waters are brought in by the California Current in the upper 200 m. Fifteen species of Myctophidae, associated with all three of these water masses, are found in the basin (Paxton, 1967). Twelve of the fifteen species are vertical migrators and traverse all three water masses in their daily movements. However, only two of the migrators have horizontal distributions throughout the three water masses. In general, the horizontal distributions of the majority of pelagic fishes seem to coincide with the limits of surface water masses. This phenomenon appears to hold also in the Southern Ocean, where Andriashev (1962) has shown that the Antarctic Convergence has an important influence upon the distribution of

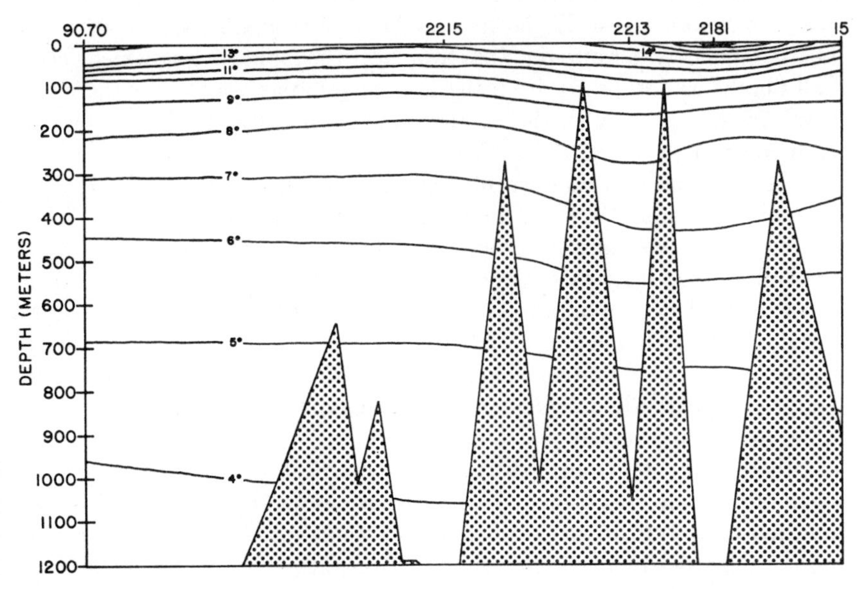

FIG. 5. Temperature cross-section from the open Pacific Ocean into the San Pedro Basin (data from Emery, 1954).

the Myctophidae, although he mentions that some species may avoid it in deeper waters.

In Paxton's study of the San Pedro Myctophidae, temperature was considered to be the most important factor influencing distribution, as it was the only parameter investigated which showed any correlation with distribution patterns (excluding light as a factor in daily vertical migrations). A temperature cross-section from the open Pacific into the San Pedro Basin (Fig. 5) shows that, although there is a definite thermocline, temperatures are rather uniform at any particular depth across the whole region. It would seem that the three water masses entering the basin remain discrete enough to allow their associated faunas to enter also.

The Ross Sea presents a very different picture. Two major water masses are present (Countryman and Gsell, 1966): the Upper Water, characterized by low salinity (34·00–34·75° per thou.) and, during the summer, relatively high temperatures at the surface (−1–1·5°C); and the Shelf Water, characterized by very low temperatures (less than −1·80°C) and high salinity (34·75–35·00° per thou.). Antarctic Circumpolar Water, an extension of the warm deep water of northern origin which rises to, or nearly to, the surface near the Antarctic Continent, penetrates to a varying extent between the Upper and Shelf Water masses. Rapidly cooled and modified as it moves south, the Antarctic Circumpolar Water is finally blocked by the Shelf Water. The isolated cells of warmer water shown in Fig. 6, based upon temperature data from *Eltanin* cruise 27 (Jacobs and Amos, 1967), illustrate the intrusion of Circumpolar Water into the Ross Sea. Note the rapid cooling which occurs at all depths as one passes from the Southern Ocean south over the continental shelf, especially in the deeper waters where the isotherms become nearly vertical.

Experiments by a number of workers (Doudoroff, 1938, 1942, 1957 [review]; Alabaster, 1964) on the effects of temperature changes on fishes, both at lethal levels and in temperature gradients, have shown that lower temperatures are at least as important as, and perhaps more important than, higher temperatures in limiting the distributions of fishes. Reports of natural mortality due to temperature changes have nearly always been related to cooling rather than heating (Doudoroff, 1942). Acclimation to cold temperature is apparently independent of acclimation to warm temperature, and occurs much more slowly.

Although the horizontal distributions of most pelagic fishes (at least myctophids) may be correlated with surface water masses, Paxton's data indicate that in transitional regions deeper water may be more important in limiting the range of a species than is surface water. Of the fifteen species of myctophids found in the San Pedro Basin, two were non-migrators and were associated with the Pacific Equatorial water mass; one species migrated, but remained below 150 m; and eight species remained below 50 m, that is, below the thermocline. The absence of non-migrators of northern distribution was related to the presence of Pacific Equatorial Water below 350 m.

The striking decrease in temperature in deeper water as one enters the Ross Sea seems the most logical explanation for the absence there of the

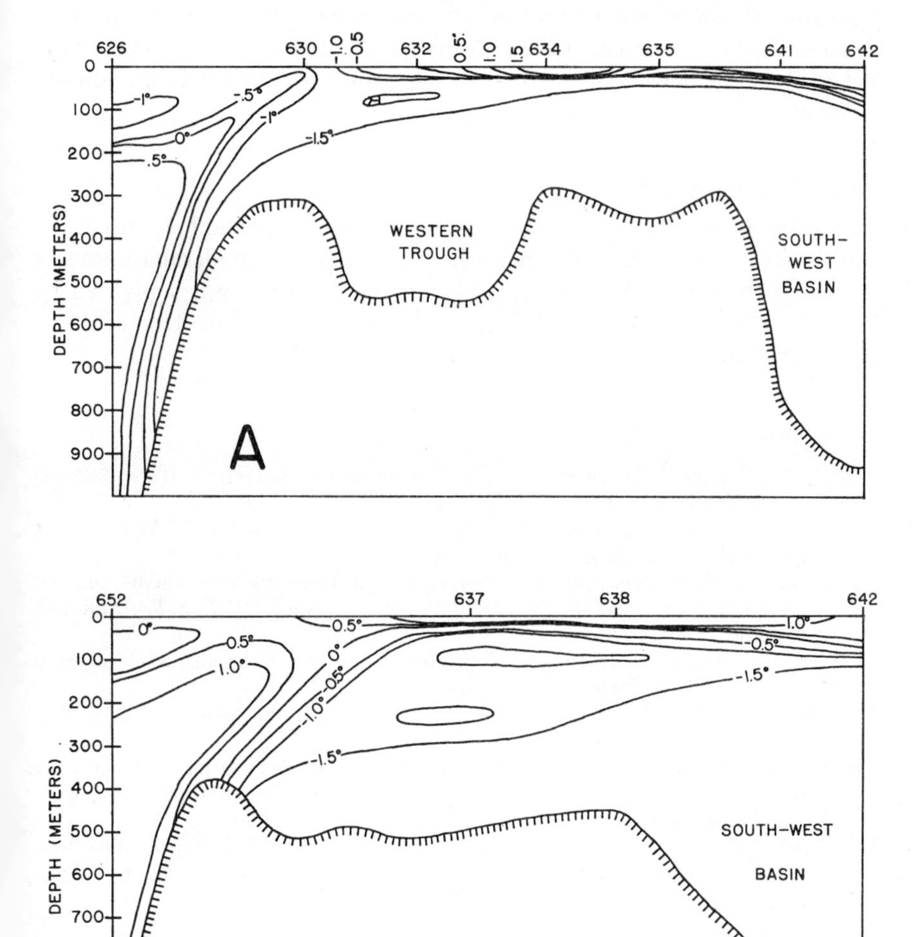

FIG. 6. Temperature profiles across the Ross Sea, from *Eltanin* cruise 27 data (Jacobs and Amos, 1967) which closely follow midwater trawl sample locations (cf. Fig. 1). A, north-south section along western edge of Ross Sea. B, north-east/south-west section from north-east edge of Ross Sea to near Ross Island.

pelagic fishes of the Southern Ocean. The closing of this extensive region to more northern fishes has left the Ross Sea essentially without a midwater fish fauna, there being only one species, *Pleuragramma antarcticum*, which exists there in any great numbers. This situation, in which a large pelagic habitat is occupied essentially by only one species, would seem to be unstable. Probably *P. antarcticum* has evolved into a midwater form from some *Notothenia*- or *Trematomus*-like ancestor (DeWitt, 1964), and some of the pelagic juvenile notothenioids represent species moving towards a midwater existence.

Acknowledgements

I acknowledge the help of the personnel of the Antarctic Program at the University of Southern California, who provided me with identification and counts of the non-nototheniiform fishes. The field-work was supported by grant G-448 from the National Science Foundation to the University of Southern California.

References

Alabaster, J. S. (1964). The effect of heated effluents on fish. *Advances in Water Pollution Research*, Vol. 1, pp. 261–92.

Andriashev, A. P. (1962). Bathypelagic fishes of the Antarctic. I. Family Myctophidae. *Issled. fauni morei*, **I**, (IX), 216–94 (in Russian).

Countryman, K. A. and Gsell, W. L. (1966). Operations Deep Freeze 63 and 64, summer oceanographic features of the Ross Sea. *U.S. Naval Oceanog. Off. Tech. Rept.* TR-190, v + 193 pp.

DeWitt, H. H. (1964). A redescription of *Pagothenia antarctica*, with remarks on the genus *Trematomus* (Pisces, Nototheniidae). *Copeia* **1964**, 683–6.

Doudoroff, P. (1938). Reactions of marine fishes to temperature gradients. *Biol. Bull. Mar. biol. Lab., Woods Hole.* **75**, 494–509.

Doudoroff, P. (1942). The resistance and acclimatization of marine fishes to temperature changes. 1. Experiments with *Girella nigricans* (Ayers). *Biol. Bull. mar. biol. Lab., Woods Hole* **83**, 219–44.

Doudoroff, P. (1957). Water quality requirements of fishes and effects of toxic substances. *In* "The Physiology of Fishes", M. E. Brown (ed.), Vol. 2. Chap. IX, pp. 403–30. Academic Press, New York.

Emery, K. O. (1954). Source of water in basins off Southern California. *J. mar. Res.* **13**, No. 1, 1–21.

Jacobs, S. S. and Amos, A. F. (1967). Physical and chemical oceanographic observations in the southern oceans. USS *Eltanin* cruises 22–27, 1966–1967. *Lamont Geological Observatory, Columbia Univ., Tech. Rept.* No. 1-CU-1-67, 287 pp., 2 charts.

Lavenberg, R. J. and Ebeling, A. W. (1967). Distribution of midwater fishes among deep-water basins of the Southern California Shelf (pp. 185–201). *In:* "Proc. Symp. Biol. California Islands", R. N. Philbrick (ed.), Santa Barbara Botanic Garden, Inc.

Paxton, J. R. (1967). A distributional analysis for the lanternfishes (family Myctophidae) of the San Pedro Basin, California. *Copeia* **1967**, 422–40.

Respiratory Metabolism of *Chaenocephalus aceratus*

INIGO EVERSON AND R. RALPH
British Antarctic Survey Biological Unit, Monks Wood Experimental Station, Huntingdon, England, and Department of Zoology, University of Aberdeen, Scotland

I. Introduction

The absence of any respiratory pigment in the family Chaenichthyidae is a phenomenon of immense physiological interest. It is a fact with which Antarctic whalers may have been familiar for a long time, but was not recorded until quite recently (Matthews, 1931; Ruud, 1954). The blood, although devoid of a pigment, has been shown to contain a few erythrocytes (Martsinkevich, 1958; Hureau, 1966), which are, however, insignificant as blood-oxygen transporters.

The physiological problems attendant upon an absence of respiratory pigment centre around the two questions:

(*a*) Is the oxygen consumption rate comparable with that in red-blooded fish?
(*b*) How does the fish transport oxygen around its body?

Hureau (1966) measured the respiratory rate of *Chaenichthys rhinoceratus* from Archipel de Kerguelen (lat. 49°21′S, long. 70°12′E) and found it was much lower than in nototheniids which had haemoglobin. However, his experiments were carried out at 11°C, several degrees above the maximum sea temperature at Kergulen (Mackintosh, 1946). The solubility of gases in fluids is governed by temperature, so that at a higher temperature oxygen will have a lower solubility both in sea water and also in a haemoglobinless fish's blood. The difference in metabolic rate recorded by Hureau may therefore have been due to the higher temperature as well as the difference in respiratory pigment, and not solely to the latter factor.

Ruud (1954) demonstrated the low oxygen-carrying capacity of *Chaenocephalus* blood. In a later paper (1965) he mentioned that the heart size appeared larger and suggested that the blood volume was much greater than in a normal teleost, and that this large blood volume was the fish's major physiological asset.

These observations are discussed further in the present paper, in conjunction with measurement of oxygen consumption rate of *Chaenocephalus aceratus* at Signy Island. The work described forms part of a more extensive programme which has been reported in greater detail elsewhere (Ralph and Everson, 1968).

II. Methods and Results

The fish used in this study were kept in as near natural conditions as possible by continuously pumping water direct from the sea through the holding tanks. The tank water was therefore well aerated and at the same temperature as the natural environment.

Respiration rates were determined by calculation of the rate at which a fish of known size removed oxygen from a known volume of sea water.

The general equation relating oxygen consumption rate (Y mg 0_2/hr) to weight (X gm) may be expressed by the special case of the modified exponential equation:

$$Y = aX^b$$

which, if the logarithmic transformation is applied, may be solved by the method of least squares in the form:

$$\log Y = \log a + b \log X.$$

For *C. aceratus* the equation is:

$$\log Y = +\ 0{\cdot}842 + 0{\cdot}271 \log X.$$

The b value (+ 0·271) is much lower than the normally expected value of around + 0·8. However, it must be borne in mind that the experiments were carried out only on mature females, all of very similar size. Olsen (1955) has found that *C. aceratus* caught at South Georgia showed very little growth after attaining sexual maturity although growth up to maturity was fairly rapid. Zeuthen (1953) quotes several cases where workers had studied the metabolism of poikilotherms over a weight range near the maximum size of the species concerned. In all cases very low *b* values were found. The low *b* value is thus only representative of the respiratory rate near the maximum size, the same relationship not holding for the total size range of the fish.

The results of oxygen consumption rate plotted against weights for *C. aceratus* and also two species of *Notothenia* are shown in Fig. 1 and it will be seen that the results for the chaenichthyid fall within the range of those for the red-blooded fish.

To make realistic comparisons between the oxygen consumption rates of various species, values for fish of the same size must be calculated. For this purpose 1 kg has been taken as the standard size, since it falls within, or very close to, the size range of all the species considered. Table 1 gives the calculated results using data from Ralph and Everson (1968) and also from Wohlschlag (1964).

The results indicate that in spite of a total absence of any respiratory pigment the chaenichthyid respired at more or less the same rate as red-blooded fish of similar size. Fox (1954) has suggested that other fish may be able to

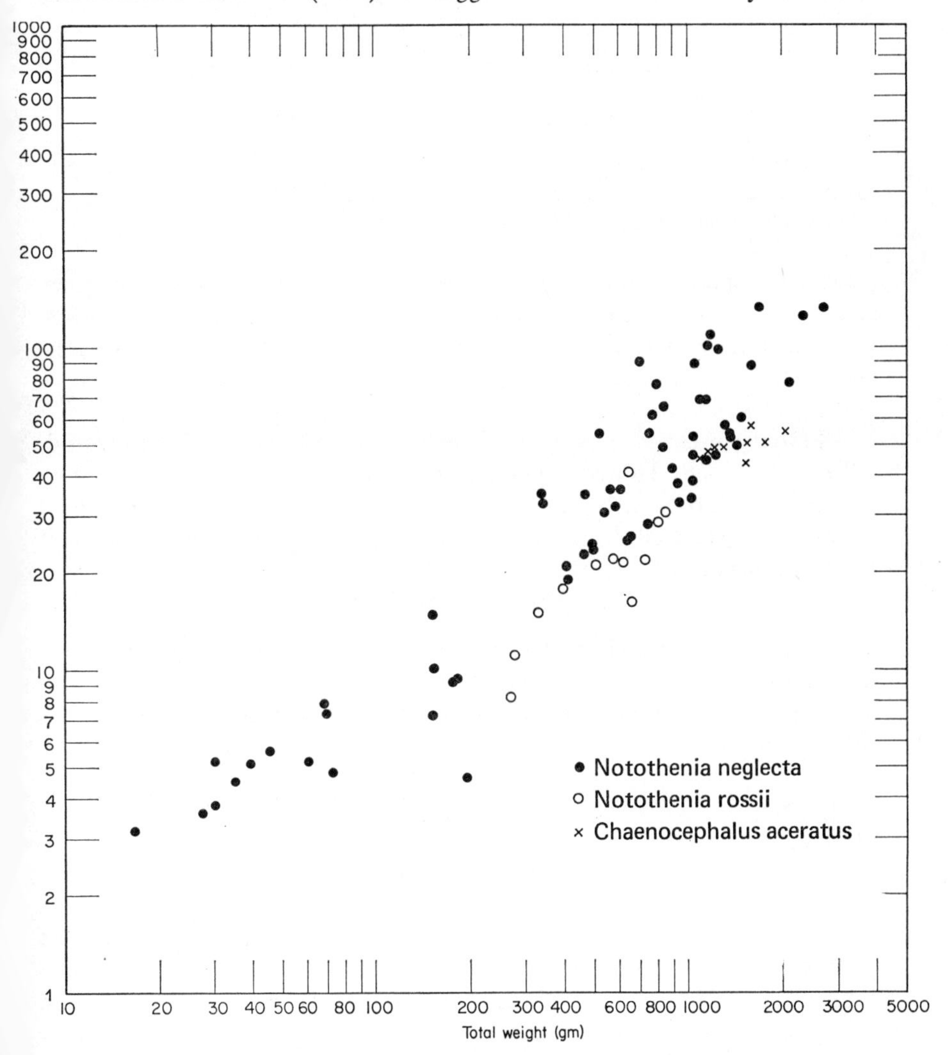

FIG. 1. Relationship between weight and oxygen consumption in *Chaenocephalus aceratus* and two *Notothenia* species. (Data for the latter from Ralph and Everson, 1968.) ●, *Notothenia neglecta*; O, *Notothenia rossii*, X, *Chaenocephalus aceratus*.

exist without haemoglobin and Anthony (1961) found that gold fish could survive with 99% of their haemoglobin inactivated by carbon monoxide.

TABLE I

Respiratory rates in Antarctic Fishes weighing 1 kg. (rom Ralph and Everson, 1968.)

	Respiratory rate *mg O_2/hr.*	*Temperature* *°C.*
Notothenia neglecta	55·2	−0·5 to +1·7
N. rossii	38·2	0·0 to +1·7
Chaenocephalus aceratus	45·2	+0·4 to +1·5
**Trematomus bernacchii*	42·3	−1·8 to −0·8
**T. borchgrevinki*	56·4	−1·74

* From Wohlschlag, 1964.

The transport of oxygen to the respiring tissues by the blood vascular system may be examined by means of a theoretical model. The oxygen, when available to the fish, is dissolved in sea water and when transported throughout the fish's body is dissolved in blood. The oxygen-carrying capacities of both solvents are known.

The oxygen-carrying capacity of chaenichthyid blood is 6·7 ml/l (Ruud, 1954) or 9·57 mg/l. However, not all the oxygen carried in the blood will be released in the tissues, but an equilibrium will be reached when the blood is, say, 25% saturated. In this case, the effective oxygen-carrying capacity of the blood would be:

$$9{\cdot}57 \times 0{\cdot}75 = \text{about } 7{\cdot}5 \text{ mg/l.}$$

During one hour a chaenichthyid weighing one kg consumes 45·2 mg of oxygen (Table 1) and this must be dissolved in the blood in order that it may be transported around the body. In one hour the heart must therefore pump through the gills:

$$\frac{45{\cdot}2}{7{\cdot}5} = \text{about 6 litres}$$

of blood.

This is about ten times the resting heart pumping rate of the cod, *Gadus morrhua* (Johansen, 1962), and for the chaenichthyid system to be as effective as the cod system at rest the heart must therefore be capable of pumping a much larger volume of blood. Ruud (1965) reported a disproportionately large heart in chaenichthyids and more recently we have found (with E. Twelves) that the heart weight (for comparative purposes heart weight is the weight of the bulbus arteriosus and the ventricle together) of preserved *C. aceratus* is over three times that of red-blooded fish of the same size. This would provide quite an effective compensatory mechanism.

The theoretical model envisaged above has only taken account of the uptake of oxygen by the fish's gills. Walvig (1951) has shown histologically the suitability of the skin of *C. aceratus* for gaseous interchange. It is not known, however, exactly how effective this mechanism is nor the proportion of oxygen that is absorbed in this manner by the chaenichthyid, but it is known that in the eel *Anguilla* the skin performs a very important respiratory function and at low temperatures *all* the oxygen needed can be obtained in this manner (Jones, 1964). The same system may be equally important for the chaenichthyid.

References

Anthony, E. H. (1961). Survival of Goldfish in the presence of Carbon Monoxide. *J. exp. Biol.* 38, 109–25.

Fox, H. Munro (1954). A comment on the article by Professor Ruud. *Nature, Lond.* 173, 850.

Hureau, J-C. (1966). Biologie de *Chaenichthys rhinoceratus* Richardson et problèmes du sang incolore des Chaenichthyidae, Poissons des Mers Australes. *Bull. Soc. zool. Fr.* 91, 735–51.

Johansen, J. (1962). Cardiac Output. *Comp. Biochem. Physiol.* 7, 169–74.

Jones, J. R. E. (1964). "Fish and River Pollution". p. 6. 1st Ed. Butterworth, London.

Mackintosh, N. A. (1946). The Antarctic Convergence and the distribution of surface temperatures in Antarctic waters. *"Discovery" Rep.* 23, 177–212.

Martsinkevich, L. D. (1958). Cellular composition of blood in white-blooded fishes (Chaenichthyidae) of the Antarctic. (In Russian.) *Inf. Byull. sov. antarkt. Eksped.* 3, 67–68.

Matthews, L. H. (1931). "South Georgia: The British Empire's Sub-Antarctic Outpost". p. 36. Wright and Marshall, London.

Olsen, S. (1955). A contribution to the systematics and biology of chaenichthyid fishes from South Georgia. *Nytt Mag. Zool.* 3, 79–93.

Ralph, R. and Everson, I. (1968). The respiratory metabolism of some antarctic fish. *Comp. Biochem. Physiol.* 27, 299–307.

Ruud, J. T. (1954). Vertebrates without erythrocytes and blood pigment. *Nature, Lond.* 173, 848–50.

Ruud, J. T. (1965). The Icefish. *Scient. Am.* 213, 108–14.

Walvig, F. (1951). The integument of the icefish *Chaenocephalus aceratus. Nytt Mag. Zool.* 6, 31–36.

Wohlschlag, D. E. (1964) Respiratory metabolism and ecological characteristics of some fishes in McMurdo Sound, Antarctica. *In* "Biology of the Antarctic Seas", Washington. American Geophysical Union, Antarctic Research Series, Vol. 1, pp. 33–62. (National Academy of Science—National Research Council Publication No. 1190.)

Zeuthen, E. (1953). Oxygen uptake as related to body size in organisms. *Q. Rev. Biol.* 28, 1–12.

Freezing Resistance in Antarctic Fishes

ARTHUR L. DEVRIES
Department of Food Science and Technology, University of California, Davis, California, U.S.A.

I. Introduction

The Antarctic Ocean in the vicinity of McMurdo Sound is extremely cold. During 1961 Littlepage (1965) found that sea-water temperatures near McMurdo Station averaged −1·87°C and varied by only 0·2°C both with depth and season. In McMurdo Sound the months of December through April are designated as the hydrographic summer season. Water temperatures during this period cluster around a mean of −1·80°C. During the winter hydrographic season, May through November, water temperatures cluster very closely around a mean of −1·90°C. This distinction is small but nevertheless important, because −1·90°C is the freezing-point of the McMurdo Sound water. McMurdo Sound usually freezes over during April and the sea ice increases in thickness until December, at which time a slight rise in water temperature results in melting. From July throughout the remainder of the winter minute ice crystals and large ice platelets (0·5 mm thick by 8–10 cm in diameter) are regularly observed in the upper 30 m of the water column. The ice platelets have been observed as masses of anchor ice frozen to the ocean floor and as a matrix of platelets frozen together in an irregular fashion beneath the annual solid sea ice. Several fishes of the genus *Trematomus*, belonging to the family Nototheniidae, are closely associated with these types of ice. The platelet layer beneath the solid ice is used by *Trematomus borchgrevinki* as a part of its habitat. This fish is often observed resting on ice platelets in this layer (Fig. 1). *Trematomus borchgrevinki* has also been observed swimming into holes and tunnels in this layer when pursued by Weddell seals. The benthic fishes, *T. bernacchii* and *T. hansoni*, have both been observed sitting on masses of anchor ice (Fig. 2). These same two fishes are also found in the deep water of the Sound. Another species, *T. loennbergi*, together with a zoarcid and liparid, inhabits only the deep water of the Sound.

In my study serum freezing-points were determined and used as a measure of freezing resistance in these fishes. Some supercooling studies were also carried out.

II. Material and Methods

All of the fishes studied were caught with baited traps except *T. borchgrevinki*, which was caught by hook and line.

FIG. 1. *Trematomus borchgrevinki* resting on an ice platelet in the sub-ice platelet layer. (Photograph by P. K. Dayton.)

Blood was collected hypodermically from the heart and allowed to clot for 6 hrs at 0°C and the serum drawn off. The serum freezing-points were measured with a Fiske Osmometer. Chlorides were determined according to the method of Keys (1937). Non-protein nitrogen was measured by the micro-Kjeldahl method, urea by the ammonia-diffusion method and the free amino acids by the ninhydrin method (Natelson, 1965). Protein was determined according to the method of Lowry (Lowry *et al.*, 1951).

FIG. 2. *Trematomus bernacchii* resting on a patch of anchor ice in 20 m of water. (Photograph by P. K. Dayton.)

III. Results and Discussion

The deep water of the Sound has been designated Zone I (Fig. 3). This zone is inhabited by the zoarcid *Rhigophila dearborni* and the liparid *Liparis sp.* Freezing-points (Table 1) indicate the zoarcid and liparid are supercooled by 0·4°C and 1·0°C, respectively. These fishes survive in a supercooled state and are in little danger of freezing because in the deep water there is no ice present to seed them. That ice is necessary to seed such supercooled fishes is shown by the observation that when caught in traps during the winter the zoarcids are seeded and freeze when raised through the ice-laden surface waters. During most of the winter minute ice crystals are suspended in the upper 30 m of the water column. In the summer, when the ice crystals are absent, the zoarcids can be raised through the surface water without freezing. However, if the zoarcids are put into a container of sea water at −1·8°C and a small quantity of crushed ice is added, they are at once seeded and freeze.

Trematomus loennbergi, in contrast to the zoarcids and liparids, has a freezing-point which is close to the freezing-point of sea water. This fish was only occasionally observed to freeze when exposed to the ice-laden water during the winter, indicating that it was considerably more resistant to freezing than the zoarcids.

Trematomus bernacchii and *T. hansoni* captured in Zone I at a depth of

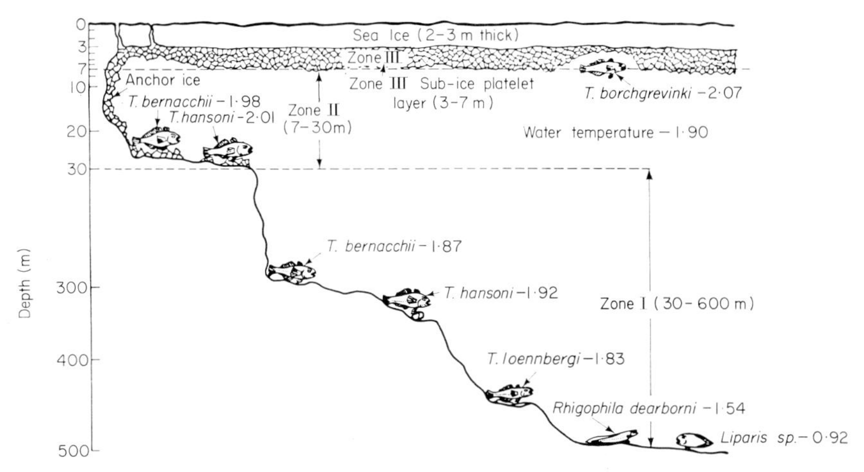

FIG. 3. Sketch of McMurdo Sound showing the habitats of the fishes and blood-serum freezing-points.

300 m had freezing-points of −1·92° and −1·87°C, respectively. Individuals of these same two species caught in the shallow water (Zone II) where anchor ice is present to depths of 30 m had lower freezing-points than those from the deep-water populations. Statistical comparisons showed that the shallow and deep-water populations of *T. hansoni* were different ($p < 0{\cdot}01$). The shallow- and deep-water populations of *T. bernacchii* were also different. Water temperatures at the shallow and deep sites are the same. The only differences between the two sites are ones of ice and pressure. At 300 m no ice is present and the fishes experience 30 atmospheres of pressure. It is interesting to note that if the freezing-points of the deep-water populations were measured at that depth, their freezing-points would be identical to those of the shallow-water populations.

Trematomus borchgrevinki living in the sub-ice platelet layer (Zone III) had a mean serum freezing-point of −2·07°C. It is not surprising that this fish has the lowest freezing-point, since the coldest water and most ice occurs at the ice-water interface.

In my study of freezing resistance I also investigated two *Notothenia* species inhabiting the waters near the Balleny Islands. The Balleny Islands are located on both sides of the Antarctic Circle, 1200 km north of McMurdo

TABLE 1

Summary of Data on Blood Sera of Antarctic Fishes. Data are expressed as mean ± standard error. Numbers of samples are indicated in parentheses

Location	Species	*Serum freezing-point* °C	*Serum chloride* nM/1	% *ΔFP due to* NaCl†	*Serum concentration (mg/100ml)**				
					Non-protein nitrogen	*Urea nitrogen*‡	*α-Amino nitrogen*	*Carbohydrate as glucose*	*Lowry protein*
McMurdo Sound (water temp. −1·9°C)									
Zone I	*Liparis sp.*	−0·88 & −0.97	234 & 241	93	54(1)				
	R. dearborni	−1·52±0·105 (23)	233±12·0 (5)	52	60±3·5 (3)			88±9·4 (3)	125 (1)
	T. loennbergi	−1·83±0·010 (21)	233±5·3 (3)	43	274±22·2 (3)				
	T. bernacchii	−1·87±0·008 (14)	254±4·4 (14)	46	343±24·7 (14)			587±24·5 (6)	1120±91·5 (9)
	T. hansoni	−1·92±0·015 (13)	258±3·3 (13)	46	375±17·9 (13)			594±43·1 (5)	1620±65·8 (7)
Zone II	*T. bernacchii*	−1·98±0·007 (25)	254±1·9 (25)	44	481±10·3 (25)	52±2·0 (22)		880±30·6 (8)	1900±83·4 (8)
	T. hansoni	−2·01±0·019 (24)	259±4·3 (24)	44	480±12·0 (14)		12±1·2 (3)	838±41·5 (7)	1830±93·0 (7)
Zone III	*T. borchgrevinki*	−2·07±0·014 (28)	235±1·6 (26)	39	504±8·5 (26)	61±1·3 (6)	20±4·0 (5)	831±35·0 (10)	1890±67·8 (10)
Balleny Islands (water temp. +1·0°C)									
	N. kempi	−0·84±0·005 (20)	191±1·9 (20)	77	120±2·0 (20)			121±6·4 (16)	420±24·2 (12)
	N. larseni	−1·52±0·014 (20)	202±3·0 (20)	46	136±4·2 (19)			279±5·8 (12)	710± 6·6 (9)

* Determinations made on 10% TCA filtrates. † Sodium chloride estimated on basis of chloride measurements. ‡ Determinations made on whole serum.

Sound. During February 1965 the water temperature at 150–450 m where these fishes were collected was +1°C. The surface-water temperature was −1·5°C. The serum freezing-points for *Notothenia kempi* and *Notothenia larseni* indicate that these fishes are less resistant to freezing than the *Trematomus* species. The absence of the genus *Notothenia* from McMurdo Sound can probably be attributed to the fact that it is not very resistant to freezing.

In most temperate marine fishes sodium chloride is responsible for about 85% of the serum freezing-point depression (Gordon, 1964). The total sodium chloride concentration in the sera of the Antarctic fishes was estimated by assuming that sodium was present at the same concentration as chloride. The fraction of the serum freezing-point depression due to sodium chloride was calculated (Table 1). In the *Trematomus* species sodium chloride accounts for less than half of the serum freezing-point depression. What is the remainder due to?

In a few temperate marine fishes, such as the sharks and *Latimeria*, non-protein nitrogen compounds are responsible for 30–40% of the serum osmotic pressure. As an example, the serum freezing-point depression of *Squalis acanthias*, a shark, is 1·9°C, of which 34% is attributable to the non-protein nitrogen compound urea. Therefore, concentrations of non-protein nitrogen (NPN) were measured in 10% tri-chloroacetic acid (TCA) filtrates of serum from Antarctic fishes. In general, the concentrations of non-protein nitrogen in the *Trematomus* and *Notothenia* species increase as serum freezing-points decrease (Table 1). The zoarcid, *Rhigophila dearborni* is an exception. NPN concentrations in *T. borchgrevinki* are five times higher than those found in temperate marine fishes. Urea and free amino-acid analyses showed that these compounds were not responsible for the high NPN concentrations. Total carbohydrate and protein soluble in TCA were also measured and found to increase with decreasing serum freezing-points. These high levels are attributable to the presence of a carbohydrate-containing protein which will be discussed later.

Since sodium chloride accounted for such a small fraction of the serum freezing-point depression in the *Trematomus* fishes, the question of the substances responsible for the remaining fraction of the serum freezing-point depression arose. One would not expect high concentrations of ions such as K, Mg, and Ca to be responsible because of the importance of their ratios in the function of nerve conduction. Since time and quantity of blood sera were limiting, a new approach was tried. This approach involved removal of the small serum components such as ions and low molecular weight organic compounds by dialysis. Dialysed serum of *T. borchgrevinki* had a freezing-point of −0·6°C, which is 30% of the freezing-point of the whole serum. Most of the material responsible for depressing the freezing-point of the dialysed serum was a protein containing carbohydrate. This compound was termed an antifreeze. The antifreeze from this fraction was purified by Sephadex gel filtration. Ultracentrifugation and Sephadex gel filtration studies indicated the antifreeze was homogenous. Electrophoretic studies indicated that the antifreeze was not homogeneous but migrated towards the anode as three closely grouped bands which were readily stained with a carbohydrate stain, but not with protein stains.

Several chemical and physical properties of the antifreeze purified by Sephadex gel filtration were studied. The freezing-points of aqueous solutions of the antifreeze were measured and were plotted against concentration (Fig. 4). At low concentrations the antifreeze is as effective as sodium chloride in depressing the freezing-point of water. However, at high concentrations it is less effective. Calculation of the molecular weight from the freezing-point data (Fig. 4) gave a value of 30 g. However, it was found that in dialysis experiments the antifreeze would not pass through a dialysis membrane. This indicates it is probably somewhat larger than 20,000 g. From osmotic pressure measurements obtained with a membrane osmometer a molecular weight of 12,000 g was calculated. Data from analytical ultracentrifugation

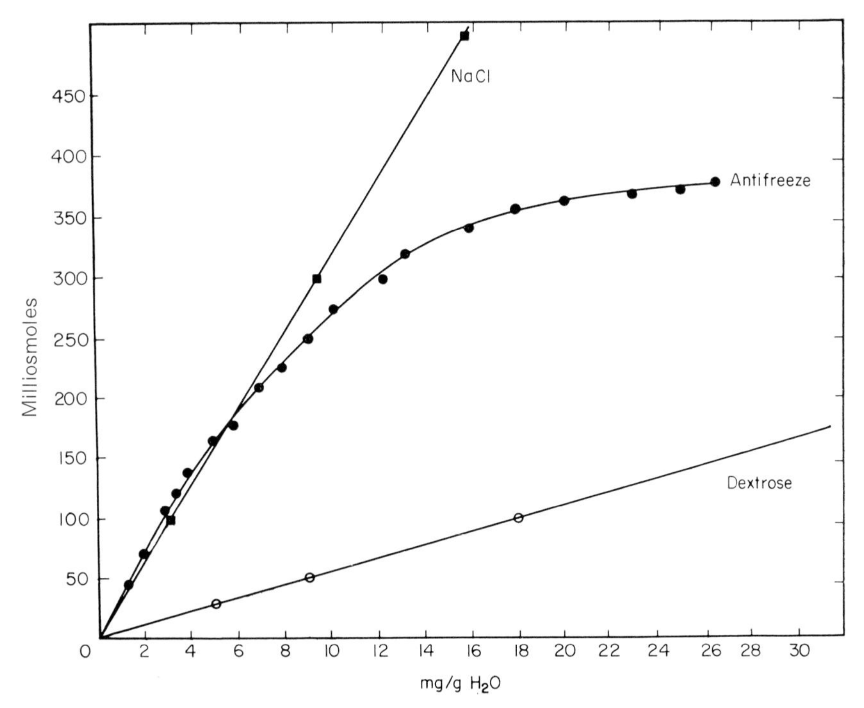

FIG. 4. Freezing-points as a function of concentration for aqueous solutions of antifreeze, sodium chloride and dextrose. A 100 milliosmolar solution has a freezing point of $-0{\cdot}186°C$.

and Sephadex gel filtration also indicated that the molecular weight of the antifreeze was approximately 20,000 g. Studies with calibrated ultrafiltration membrances indicated a molecular weight larger than 10,000 g and smaller than 50,000 g.

Freezing-points of aqueous solutions of antifreeze, sodium chloride and dextrose were measured as a function of molal concentration (Fig. 5). A molecular weight of 25,000 g was assumed for calculation of the molal concentration of the antifreeze. A 1 molal solution of glucose has a freezing-point of −1·86°C, while a 1 molal solution of sodium chloride has a freezing-point of about −3·6°C. Since the depression of freezing-point is dependent on the number of particles in solution, one would expect the antifreeze to depress the freezing-point of water to the same extent as glucose at a concentration of 0·001 molal. However, this does not happen; instead, the antifreeze appears to be a thousand times more effective than glucose in depressing the freezing-point of water.

Chemical analysis indicated that the antifreeze was 50% protein and 25% carbohydrate by weight. Bovine serum albumin and glucose were used as standards. The antifreeze is completely soluble in 10% trichloroacetic acid.

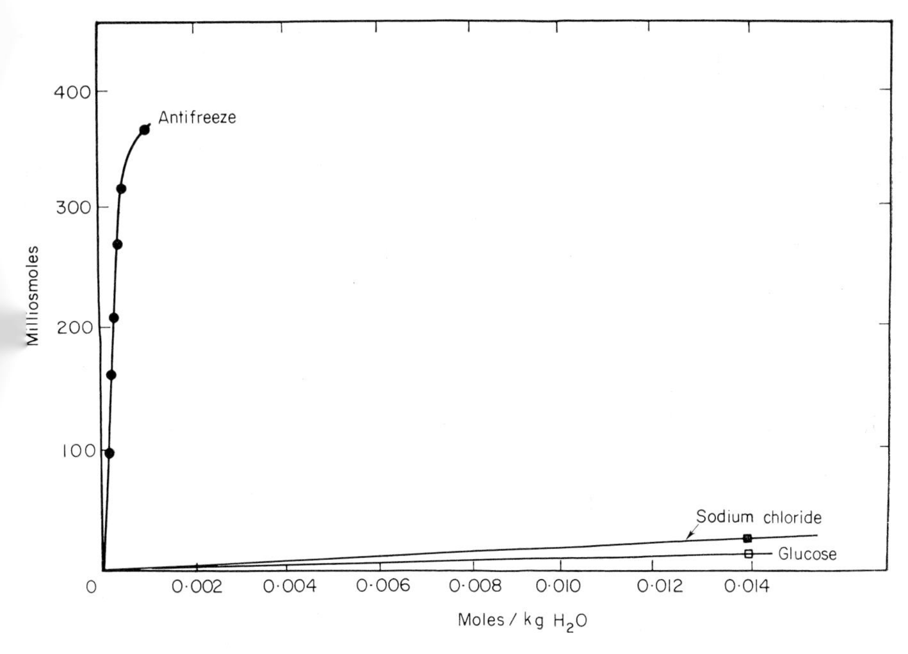

FIG. 5. Freezing-points as a function of molal concentration for aqueous solutions of antifreeze, sodium chloride and dextrose. A 100 milliosmole solution has a freezing point of 0·186°C.

This property explains the high concentrations of NPN, carbohydrate and protein which were observed in the serum of the *Trematomus* fishes.

The mechanism of the antifreeze activity is at present unknown. Binding of water, making it less available to ice formation, is probably involved. I am presently investigating this problem at the University of California, Davis, and in addition I am also carrying out a more complete chemical and physical characterization.

References

Gordon, M. S. (1964). Adaptation to the Environment. *In* "Handbook of Physiology", Sec. 4, (D. B. Dill, ed.) American Physiological Society, Washington, D.C., pp. 697–713.

Keys, A. (1937). The microdetermination of chlorides in biological materials. *J. biol. Chem.* **119**, 389–403.

Littlepage, J. L. (1965). Oceanographic investigations in McMurdo Sound, Antarctica. *In* "Biology of the Antarctic Seas", Vol. II, (M. O. Lee, ed.), pp. 1–37. Amer. Geophys. Union, Washington, D.C.

Lowry, O., Rosebrough, N. J., Farr, A. L. and Randall, R. J. (1951). Protein measurement with the Folin phenol reagent. *J. biol. Chem.* **193**, 265–75.

Natelson, S. (1965). "Microtechniques of Clinical Chemistry", Charles C. Thomas, Chicago, Illinois, pp .1–578.

Note Added in Proof

Studies subsequent to those presented in this paper have shown that the antifreeze is composed only of alanine, threonine, N-acetylgalactosamine and galactose. These residues appear to exist in the antifreeze molecules as repeating units of alanine, alanine and threonine to which a disaccharide is attached. The disaccharide is composed of galactose and N-acetylgalactosamine and is linked O-glycosidically through the latter to the threonine residue. Chemical modification of the antifreeze indicates that the *cis*-hydroxyls of carbons 3 and 4 of the galactose residues are the sites responsible for the freezing-point depressant activity. Preliminary studies suggest that water molecules are structured about these *cis*-hydroxyls by means of hydrogen bonding.

The Biochemistry of Freezing Resistance of Some Antarctic Fish

R. N. SMITH
British Antarctic Survey Biological Unit, Monks Wood Experimental Station, Huntingdon, England

I. Introduction

The freezing resistance of Arctic fish has been studied by Scholander and his colleagues (Scholander *et al.*, 1953; Scholander *et al.*, 1957; Gordon *et al.*, 1962), but by 1966 there had been no comparable study of Antarctic fish, though some initial experiments had been carried out by Everson and Ralph at Signy Island. They investigated *Notothenia neglecta* and *Notothenia rossii* and found that the blood of both species was supercooled for some six months of the year when the sea temperature fell below approximately −1°C. In addition, supercooled *Notothenia neglecta* were found to survive contact with ice for up to several hours before death occurred; whereas *Notothenia rossii* under the same conditions died within a relatively short time. These facts appeared worthy of further investigation, and in 1966 a research programme was initiated to study the freezing resistance of Antarctic fish. The work was carried out at Signy Island in the South Orkneys and this paper is a preliminary account of some of the results obtained.

II. Analytical Study of Blood Sera

A. Material and Methods

The two main species studied were *Notothenia neglecta* and *Notothenia rossii*, and the initial approach was a comparative analytical study of their blood sera. Fish were caught on lines or in baited traps and blood was obtained by heart puncture. Serum specimens were analysed for:

total nitrogen by the Kjeldahl method;
protein by the biuret method, with a bovine plasma albumin standard;
total carbohydrate by the phenol/sulphuric method (Dubois *et al.*, 1956) using a glucose standard;
reducing sugar by the method of Hagedorn and Jensen (1923*a*, *b*) using a glucose standard;

urea by an adaptation of the spectrophotometric method of With *et al.*, (1961);
sodium and potassium by flame photometry on diluted samples;
and chloride by the potentiometric titration method of Ramsay *et al.*, (1955).

Serum freezing-points were measured using an apparatus based on that described by Ramsay and Brown (1955).

B. RESULTS

The results of the analyses are shown in Table 1. Standard deviations are included, though in some cases the sample numbers are too small for these to have much significance. In both species the osmoconcentration of the serum is largely due to sodium chloride.

It will be noticed that *N. neglecta* serum is a more concentrated solution than *N. rossii* serum both in summer and winter, particularly with regard to protein and total carbohydrate concentrations. In addition, in both species the concentrations of the serum components increase in winter, with the exception of potassium in *N. neglecta* serum and urea in *N. rossii* serum. In the latter case the apparent decrease may be due merely to the small sample numbers. The differences between summer and winter fish are more marked in the case of *Notothenia rossii*, particularly with regard to total nitrogen, protein and total carbohydrate concentrations. Of the serum components that increase in winter in both species, only the reducing sugar concentration in *N. neglecta* serum increases to an extent comparable with the increase in *N. rossii* serum.

The freezing-point determinations confirm the fact that the blood of both species is supercooled in winter by an amount not exceeding 0·8°C approximately, and the continued survival of the two species emphasizes the stability of the supercooled state under natural conditions. Since supercooled *Notothenia rossii* are more susceptible to death resulting from contact with ice than *Notothenia neglecta*, it is tempting to infer from the results of the serum analysis that those components whose concentrations markedly increase in *N. rossii* serum in winter are the ones most likely to confer upon the supercooled state some measure of stability. Additionally, it may be postulated that reducing sugar is of major importance in this respect, since it increases markedly and to approximately the same extent in both species in winter. However, in the absence of confirmatory evidence such conclusions must inevitably be regarded as being extremely tentative. The cryoprotective action of various solutes on erythrocytes has been reviewed (Meryman, 1966). In particular, it has been demonstrated (Tamman and Buchner, 1935; Lusena, 1955) that relatively small amounts of certain alcohols, glycols, sugars and proteins effectively retard crystallization velocities during freezing.

TABLE 1

Results of Serum Analysis

	N. neglecta (summer)			*N. neglecta* (winter)		
	$\bar{x}$	s	n	$\bar{x}$	s	n
Total nitrogen, mg/ml	9·1	1·3	30	11·8	1·3	12
Protein, mg/ml	63.4	10.9	33	71·9	6·2	30
Total carbohydrate, mg/ml	13·6	1·4	33	16·3	2·0	30
Reducing sugar, mg/ml	4·7	1·0	22	9·7	0·9	30
Urea, mg/ml	4·4	3·5	10	9·5	2·2	30
Sodium, mM	248	12	17	259	12	44
Potassium, mM	3·6	1·1	16	2·9	1·6	36
Chloride, mM	212	11	21	242	13	48
Freezing point, °C	−0·92	0·02	7	−1·08	0·04	15

	N. rossii (summer)			*N. rossii* (winter) Averages of two results
	$\bar{x}$	s	n	
Total nitrogen, mg/ml	5·4	0·9	15	8·8
Protein, mg/ml	36·5	9·6	15	50·0
Total carbohydrate, mg/ml	8·7	2·7	15	15·2
Reducing sugar, mg/ml	2·8	0·7	9	6·0
Urea, mg/ml	6·7	2·3	9	5·0
Sodium, mM	217	16	9	237
Potassium, mM	2·4	0·7	9	6·2
Chloride, mM	196	7	9	238
Freezing point, °C		n.d.		−1·06, −1·07

$\bar{x}$ = sample mean; s = standard deviation; n = sample number.

Viscosity alone is unlikely to explain this effect and alternative hypotheses to be considered include the masking of nuclei and the poisoning of crystal growth surfaccs by thc inclusion of these solutes. It is possible that some such mechanism may actively assist in the stabilization of supercooled *N. neglecta* blood, though the eventual death of fish exposed to freezing conditions demonstrates the incomplete effectiveness of such a process, if indeed it does occur.

III. Experimental Study of Freezing

A second approach to the problem of how Antarctic fish resist freezing involved the exposure of fish to freezing conditions and the investigation of some of the experimental variables. These experiments were all carried out on *Notothenia neglecta*. Eleven fish were put, one or two at a time, in a refrigerated aquarium at a temperature of —1·8 to —2·0°C. Ice crystals were present in abundance in the aquarium and continual stirring ensured contact of the fish with ice for the duration of the experiments. Cloacal temperatures of the fish were measured at intervals with a thermometer and survival times were recorded. Death was generally preceded by vigorous convulsions and was assumed to have occurred when the fish lay motionless on their backs with the gill covers wide open. No fish subsequently recovered after reaching this stage. Blood samples were taken soon after death and the serum was analysed for protein, total carbohydrate and reducing sugar. In addition the serum freezing-points were determined. Survival times for the eleven fish were plotted against the following parameters:

> Weight; length; skin thickness; initial temperature of the fish; serum protein content; serum total carbohydrate content; serum reducing sugar content; and serum freezing-point.

In no case was there any apparent correlation. The results of the serum analysis lay, with one exception, within the extremes found for summer and winter fish. The exception was due almost certainly to seawater contamination during sampling. These results were not unexpected, since the experiments were carried out in November when the sea temperature was rising after winter. No fish died before its body temperature fell below its serum freezing-point, and in most cases the body temperature fell to within 0·1°C of the aquarium temperature. Ice formation in the eyes of the fish generally occurred during the experiments, but bore no apparent relation to survival times. A single determination indicated that the freezing-point of the mucilaginous eyeball contents lay within the range of serum freezing-points. Of those factors investigated, only one bore any relation to the survival times, and this was the behaviour of the fish. Although the relationship cannot be expressed on a quantitative basis, it became apparent during the experiments that active fish died relatively quickly under freezing conditions, while fish that lay quietly in the aquarium survived for much longer periods, the maximum observed being 8¼ hrs. Active fish opened their mouths wider than quiescent fish and occasionally "coughed" as though to expel ice crystals from their mouths. Quiescent fish opened their mouths only very slightly and were not observed to "cough".

These facts suggested that the gills of *Notothenia neglecta* were the sites at which the initiation or nucleation of freezing by contact with ice occurred, and that nucleation through the remainder of the body surface either did not occur or was not lethal. This hypothesis was tested by cooling the fish to about −1·8°C in an ice-free aquarium and then freezing part of the gills or the body by contact with ice crystals at about −20°C. Survival times for gill-frozen fish ranged from 5 to 150 min, and for body-frozen fish from 120 to 255 min. In each case one fish survived, but the surviving gill-frozen fish developed partial paralysis of the body, and the surviving body-frozen fish subsequently succumbed after a portion of its gills was frozen. To date these experiments have been carried out on a small number of fish only, but the data obtained show that either body-freezing or gill-freezing can be lethal. In addition it appears that on average gill-frozen fish die sooner than body-frozen fish, but further experiments are required to verify this point.

In the initial freezing experiments in which the fish were in continual contact with ice, the survival times were mostly of the order of 100 min or less, which suggests that nucleation occurred at the gills. If nucleation could occur through the remainder of the body surface, then the unusually high survival times observed, e.g. 8 and 8¼ hrs, would be unlikely to occur. Further data are required to elucidate this point and additional experiments have been planned for the Antarctic summer of 1968–69.

Freezing experiments comparable to those just described have not yet been carried out on *Notothenia rossii*, but a comparative study of the gills and skin of *N. rossii* and *N. neglecta* is in progress. Microscopic examination of gill sections shows that the diffusion distance in *N. rossii* gill is less than that in *N. neglecta* gill. This factor may contribute to the greater susceptibility to nucleation of *N. rossii* compared with *N. neglecta.*

Under laboratory conditions (and therefore presumably in nature), the initial reaction of *N. neglecta* or *N. rossii* is to swim away when ice is encountered. Cloacal temperature measurements using a thermistor show that, for both species, the body temperatures of inactive fish are within 0·2 or more frequently 0·1°C of the water temperature. In addition, the vigorous movements and convulsions of *N. neglecta* dying under freezing conditions do not produce a rise in body temperature prior to death. This suggests that the contribution of heat production to freezing resistance is minimal.

Plots of body temperature versus time were made for several *N. neglecta* that died under freezing conditions. In general the initial cooling curve was fairly smooth and levelled out close to the aquarium temperature if death did not occur first. Shortly after death a temperature rise of approximately 0·2–0·3°C occurred, probably due to release of latent heat as a result of ice formation in the body. The temperature then fell and levelled out at approximately −1·4°C in the case of summer fish, and a single determination at the end of winter gave a corresponding value of −1·85°C. These figures may represent "whole-body freezing-points", and the value of −1·85°C may result from adaptation to winter conditions. Further experiments are required to resolve this point. If, indeed, a winter "whole-body freezing-point" of −1·85°C is characteristic of *N. neglecta*, then the hypothesis that nucleation does not occur through the skin under natural conditions would appear to be correct.

The actual mechanism by which freezing death occurs is so far unresolved. Ice formation, although it occurs to a limited extent only, is no doubt a contributory factor. Ice formation invariably occurs in the eyes, but does not appear to be lethal, and apart from this there is no evidence as to where else in the body ice formation actually occurs in *N. neglecta*. Very approximate calculations based on the slight post-mortem temperature rise show that, if freezing is assumed to be confined to the blood, then it occurs to an extent of only 0·3% by volume. In addition to this the results of the serum analysis on fish killed by freezing confirm that freezing of the blood and resultant concentration of blood solutes is minimal.

In winter, supercooled fish would appear to be in no danger of death by freezing unless nucleation by contact with ice occurs. *N. neglecta* was found at all depths in which fishing was carried out, namely from about 1–10 fathoms. At these depths contact of the fish with ice is possible if unlikely. Aqualung divers at Signy Island have reported ice scour on the sea bed and in winter copious amounts of anchor ice have occasionally been observed. In this connection it may perhaps be argued that if *N. neglecta* never came into contact with ice and did not therefore require such a marked freezing resistance, then it would not be so well adapted to its present environment. *N. rossii* was far more scarce in winter than in summer, and the only two specimens obtained in winter were caught at a depth of 10 fathoms. Perhaps the main defence of *N. rossii* against freezing in winter is the avoidance of ice by migration and/or living at depths at which ice is unlikely to be encountered.

IV. Studies on *Trematomus newnesi*

Some specimens of *Trematomus newnesi* were caught during and towards the end of winter. The fish were small, only 3–4 cm in length, so comprehensive serum analysis could not be carried out. However, the serum freezing-points of fourteen fish were determined. They covered a close range and averaged −1·01°C. Sodium and chloride determinations on three of the larger serum samples showed that the freezing-point depression was primarily due to sodium chloride. Protein, total carbohydrate and reducing sugar determinations on a combined serum sample gave values within the ranges covered by summer and winter *N. neglecta* serum. The freezing resistance of a number of *Trematomus newnesi* was demonstrated by their ability to survive contact with ice at −1·8°C for 60 min, after which time the experiment was discontinued. Contact of ice with the gills was unlikely to occur, since the ice crystals were too large to enter the fishes' mouths. It would seem that *T. newnesi* resembles *N. neglecta* in that nucleation apparently does not occur through the skin. These observations provide an interesting contrast with the *Trematomus* fishes of McMurdo Sound studied by DeVries (1970). The "antifreeze" compound present in McMurdo fishes was either not present in the Signy Island fish or else it was present only in such a small concentration as to be negligible.

V. Summary

In winter both *Notothenia neglecta* and *Notothenia rossii* were found to be supercooled by about 0·7°C. Analysis showed that in each species the osmo-concentration of the blood serum increased slightly in winter. This was largely due to an increase in sodium-chloride concentration.

Previous workers have shown that supercooled *N. neglecta* in contact with ice can resist death by freezing for periods of several hours. This phenomenon was investigated and experimental freezing of fish indicated that "seeding" of the fish by contact with ice does not occur through the skin, but is liable to occur at the gills.

Similar, but less comprehensive experiments were carried out on specimens of *T. newnesi*. These fish were found to resemble *N. neglecta* in their resistance to freezing.

In all three species the freezing-point depression of the blood serum was found to be largely due to sodium chloride. The "antifreeze" found in the blood of some polar fishes was either absent or else present in such small concentration as to be negligible.

Acknowledgement

I wish to express my gratitude to my colleagues on Signy Island for their valuable assistance.

References

DeVries, A. L. (1970). "Freezing Resistance in some Antarctic Fishes". Paper presented at the SCAR Symposium on Antarctic Ecology. Cambridge. (This volume.)

Dubois, M., Gilles, K. A., Hamilton, J. K., Rebers, P. A. and Smith, F. (1956). Colorimetric method for determination of sugars and related substances. *Analyt. Chem.* 28, No. 3, 350–6.

Everson, I. and Ralph, R. *Personal communication.*

Gordon, M. S., Amdur, B. H. and Scholander, P. F. (1962). Freezing resistance in some northern fishes. *Biol. Bull. mar. biol. Lab., Woods Hole* 122, 52–62.

Hagedorn, H. C. and Jensen, B. N. (1923*a*). Zur Mikrobestimmung des Blutzuckers mittels Ferricyanid. *Biochem. Z.* 135, 46–58.

Hagedorn, H. C. and Jensen, B. N. (1923*b*). Die Ferricyanidmethode zur Blutzuckerbestimmung. II. *Biochem. Z.* 137, 92–95.

Lusena, C. V. (1955). Ice propagation in systems of biological interest. III. Effect of solutes on nucleation and growth of ice crystals. *Archs Biochem. Biophys.* 57, No. 2, 277–84.

Meryman, H. T. (Ed.). (1966). "Cryobiology". Academic Press, London.

Ramsay, J. A. and Brown, R. H. J. (1955). Simplified apparatus and procedure for freezing point determinations upon small volumes of fluid. *J. scient. Instrum.* 32, 372–5.

Ramsay, J. A., Brown, R. H. J. and Croghan, P. C. (1955). Electrometric titration of chloride in small volumes. *J. exp. Biol.* 32, 822–9.

Scholander, P. F., Flagg, W., Hock, R. J. and Irving, L. (1953). Studies on the physiology of frozen plants and animals in the arctic. *J. cell. comp. Physiol.* 42, Suppl. 1, 1–56.

Scholander, P. F., Van Dam, L., Kanwischer, J. W., Hammel, H. T. and Gordon, M. S. (1957). Supercooling and osmoregulation in arctic fish. *J. cell. comp. Physiol.* 49, 5–24.

Tamman, G. and Buchner, A. (1935). Die Unterkülungsfähigkeit des Wassers und die lineare Kristallisationsgeschwindigkeit des Eises in wäßrigen Lösungen. *Z. anorg. allg. Chem.* 222, 4, 371–81.

With, T. K., Petersen, T. D. and Petersen, B. (1961). A simple spectrophotometric method for the determination of urea in blood and urine. *J. clin. Path.* 14, 202–4.

Thermogenesis and its Possible Survival Value in Fishes

ROBERT W. MORRIS
University of Oregon, Eugene, Oregon, U.S.A.

I. Introduction

Studies of the respiratory quotient of bony fishes have demonstrated values significantly greater than 1·0 in a number of species (Morris, 1967). Two years ago similar studies were conducted on the Antarctic nototheniid, *Trematomus bernacchii*, and high RQ values were also found in this species. However, such studies are complicated by the fact that carbon dioxide is apparently released as bicarbonate in the urine and there appears to be a long micturation interval in this species (Potts and Morris, in the press).

A high respiratory quotient (greater than 1·0) is usually interpreted as indicating something in the nature of synthesis, such as conversion of carbohydrate to fat. However, such an RQ could easily indicate oxidation of an accumulation of some intermediate. A third possibility would be that it resulted from some sort of anaerobiosis. Evidence of anaerobic activity in a cypriniform species under cold stress was reported as long ago as 1958 by Blazka, but it appears that the true extent and possible survival value of such mechanisms have not been investigated further.

II. Methods

A few years ago the author began to study direct calorimetric methods which might permit simultaneous measurement of oxygen consumption and heat production. Despite many technical difficulties in 1967 a system which would give reproducible results was perfected. The apparatus is illustrated in Fig. 1. Except for the thermometer, the entire apparatus is kept in a walk-in refrigerator, the temperature of which is controlled within approximately ±1·0°C. Leads to the two thermometer probes are 12 ft long and are taken into the apparatus through a small hole in the side of the refrigerator. The two metering pumps which pull water through control and experimental flasks are calibrated to move water at the same rate and can easily be set so that their rates agree to within 0·1%. The lines leading from each flask to its respective pump are fitted with $\frac{3}{8}$ in side arms plugged with serum caps which permit periodic sampling with a hypodermic. These samples are analysed for oxygen and carbon dioxide on a Fisher Model 25V gas chromatograph.

The characteristics of the system were determined using a controlled heat source in the experimental flask. Since the inlet tube extends to the bottom

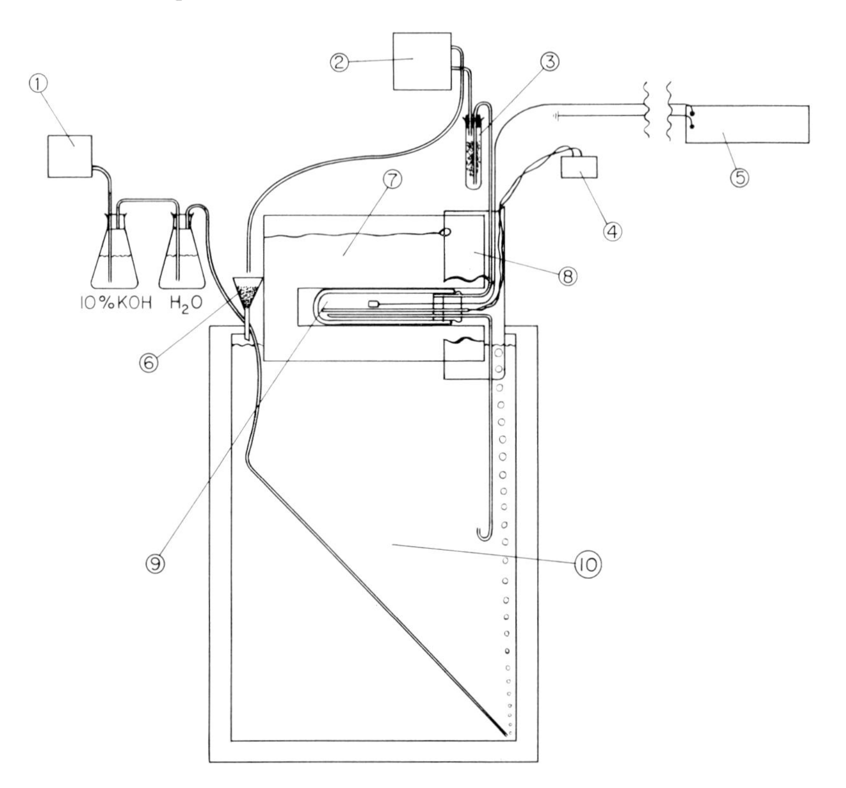

FIG. 1. Apparatus used in measuring heat production of small ectotherms: (1) air pump; (2) Beckman solution metering pump (paired); (3) glass wool filter; (4) constant voltage source adjustable up to 1·0 volt; (5) Hewlett-Packard, two channel quartz crystal thermometer; (6) funnel with glass wool filter; (7) Styrifoam block 10 in × 12 in × 18 in; (8) $\frac{5}{16}$ in Neoprene shield wrapped around end of Styrifoam block; (9) one-litre Dewar flask (paired), each provided with water inlet and outlet, and a thermometer probe; the experimental flask is provided with an 83 ohm heater fed by the voltage source; (10) 55 gal insulated drum of water.

of the flask, permitting the inflowing water to heat before it starts to mix with the water already in the flask, the system functions as a heat-conserving countercurrent. Twenty-five tests demonstrated a range of apparent heat production from 121 to 140% of that expected. Hence, to be on the conservative side, all of the experimental results were multiplied by 0·70 in order to calculate the actual yield.

In a regular run a fish was placed in the experimental flask. The flasks were filled with water from the drum, stoppered and put in place in the Styrifoam block. The pumps were started and air bubbles were bled from the system.

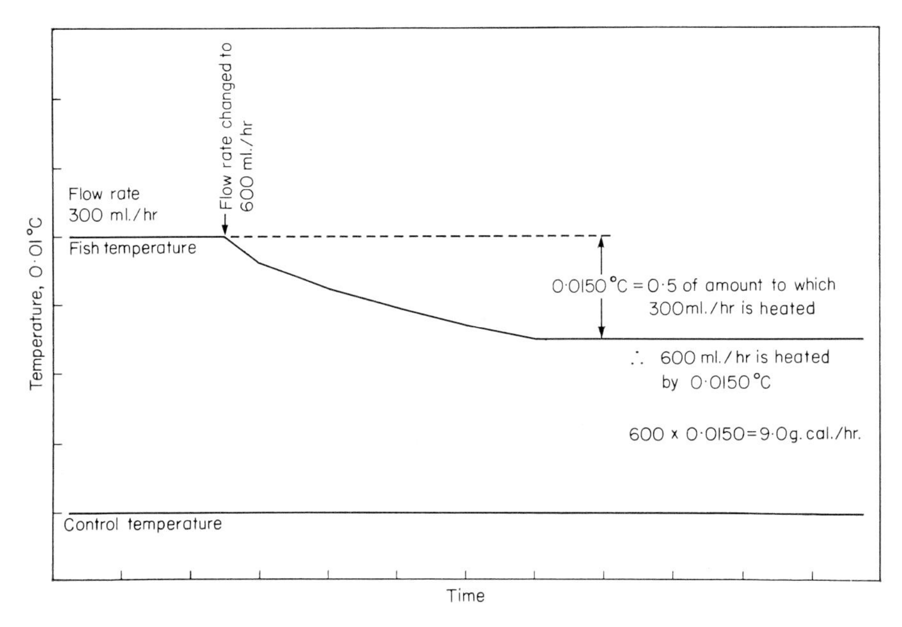

FIG. 2. Theoretical configuration of temperature record of a calorimetric run. 9·0/g cal must be corrected by ×0·7 to take account of the characteristics of the system: the true heat production was therefore 6·3 g cal/hr.

The block was then put in place, floating on the surface of the water in the drum and the pumps were set to deliver 300 ml/hr. The system was allowed to stand undisturbed overnight and the following morning the temperature record was begun, the probes being read alternately, about every half-hour. After two to four hours of thermometer readings, when it was seen that the system was stable and that the two temperature records were running in parallel, the flow rate of the pumps was changed to 600 ml./hr. The thermometer readings were continued for a period of from 6 to 10 hrs, until the system had again stabilized. Two or three water samples were taken from each water train during the morning before the flow rate was changed and again some hours later when the system had recovered stability. A hypothetical record showing something like what was expected appears in Fig. 2.

The pattern of an actual run usually appeared as the lower pair of lines in Fig. 3. The fall and subsequent rise after flow rate change occurred because the drum was cooler than the room, while the pumps were a heat source.

III. Results

During the summer of 1967 twelve runs were made using as experimental fish, the tropical cichlid, *Aequidens portalegrensis*. The fish ranged from 1·4 gm (average weight of four specimens used in one run) up to 21·0 gm in wet weight. Average hourly oxygen consumption ranged from 0·50 ml up to 1·07 ml and the observed heat production ranged from 3·57 to 11·34 gm

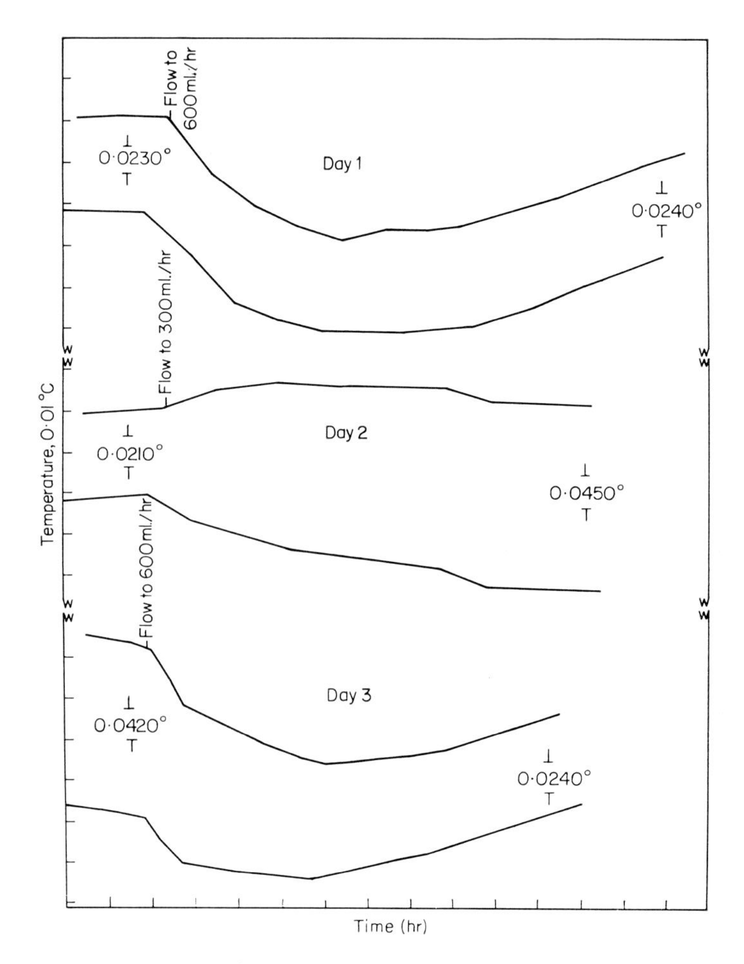

FIG. 3. Actual appearance of temperature record of a three-day calorimetric run. The lower line is the control in each case.

cal/hr. The observed heat production exceeded that which would be expected (on the basis of 5 gm cal/ml of 0_2) by margins ranging from 33% up to 200%.

On one occasion during July 1967 a run was made in which the experimental and control temperature records remained practically parallel throughout the duration of a 12 hr run. Interpretation of such a result could mean either that the fish was producing no heat at all or that after changing the water-flow rate from 300 to 600 ml/hr heat production was approximately doubled. Neither of these alternatives was at all appealing. However, the author was unable to find anything technically wrong with the run. Again on August 18, 1967, a similar result was obtained. The temperature record of this run appears as the uppermost pair of lines in Fig. 3. On this occasion the fish was allowed to remain in the apparatus through the second night, and the temperature readings were resumed on the second day. On this day the flow rate was returned to 300 ml/hr and the resulting record is shown in the second pair of lines in Fig. 3. This run was continued through day 3, and the result is shown in the bottom pair of lines in Fig. 3. Here, the result was in the pattern originally expected. The fish in this run weighed 14·4 gm and twelve sets of oxygen consumption measurements ranged from 0·64 to 0·78 ml/hr. The author could find nothing technically wrong with this run and was forced to conclude that the rate of heat production had indeed changed almost simultanteously with change in water-flow rate and without any apparent relationship to oxygen consumption.

Collateral studies of an exploratory nature have shown that these animals are excreting quite a large amount of organic intermediates and that their anaerobic metabolism apparently amounts to a considerably greater fraction of the total than has heretofore been suspected.

Turning now to the problems of the Antarctic fishes: *Trematomus bernacchii* is a member of the family Nototheniidae, endemic to the Antarctic seas and circumpolar in its distribution. During much of the year the population in McMurdo Sound is subjected to temperatures at which the sea water is freezing. Specimens are found even in fairly shallow water where anchor ice is growing.

Under laboratory conditions, several species of *Trematomus* demonstrate a peculiar cold-stress behaviour when the temperature is lowered beyond about −1·85°C. The fishes lie on the bottom of the tank and, with mouth agape, the pectoral fins beat out of phase with each other at a steady rate of about 20–30 strokes per minute. The gills become progressively more pale as circulation is reduced and blood is withdrawn from the periphery of the body. Figure 4 shows two fish that had been removed from holding tanks and immediately cut open. The upper fish in the figure had been held at −1·95°C and the lower fish at −1·0°C, for a period of 24 hrs prior to dissection.

In studies two years ago the author and his collaborators found the freezing-point of the urine of these fish to be approximately 0·8°C higher than ambient temperature during cold stress. Urine may amount to as much as 4·0% of the total body weight. Urine from several dozen specimens was sampled, but ice crystals were never found in the urinary bladder. The blood of these fish was

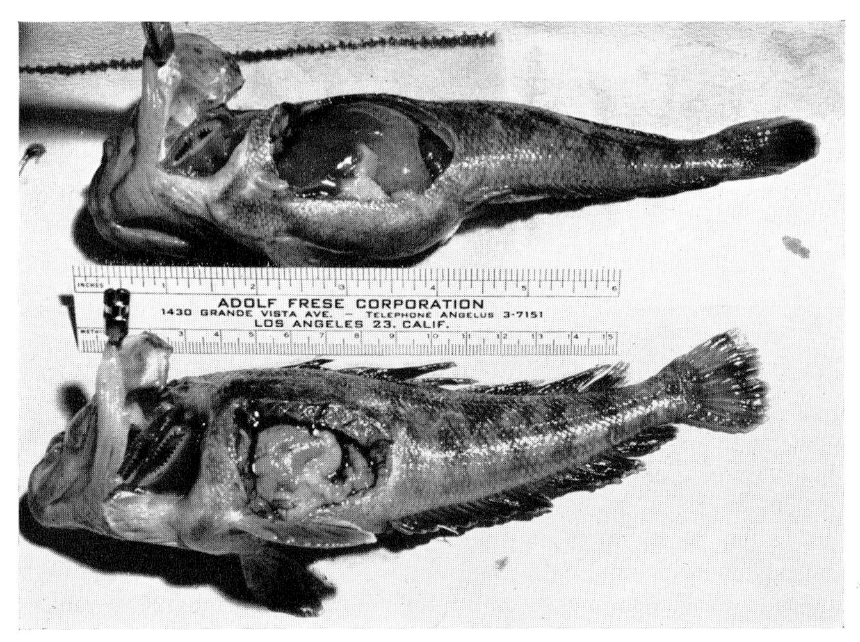

FIG. 4. Two fish cut open to show the relationship between blood distribution and cold stress. (Photo by G. C. Grigg.)

shown by A. L. DeVries (*personal communication*) to be well fortified with anti-freeze substances, so that its freezing point was maintained at a level below ambient temperature even during cold stress. Therefore, it would appear that restriction of circulation during cold stress would be unnecessary to prevent the blood from freezing. Hence, the most reasonable hypothesis would seem to be that the restriction of circulation during cold stress is a mechanism for preventing heat loss from the visceral core. Activity of the pectoral fins, as well as respirometric measurement, indicate that the animal is not in a state of suspended animation during cold stress and that there must be production of considerable amounts of metabolic heat. It appears not inconceivable that this heat is managed to an extent sufficient to impart substantial survival value.

References

Blazka, P. (1958). The anaerobic metabolism of fish. *Physiol. Zoöl.* **31**, 117–28.

Morris, R. W. (1967). High respiratory quotients of two species of bony fishes. *Physiol. Zoöl.* **40**, 409–23.

Potts, D. C. and Morris, R. W. (1969). Some body fluid characteristics of the Antarctic fish, *Trematomus bernacchii*. "Marine Biology". (In the press.)

Biochemistry of Proteins and Enzymes of Antarctic Fish

ROBERT E. FEENEY
College of Agricultural and Environmental Sciences,
University of California, Davis, U.S.A.

I. Introduction

Our laboratory is engaged in studying homologous proteins from different species. The studies are designed to provide:

(*a*) descriptive information which might be useful for taxonomy and
(*b*) information on the molecular properties of the protein which might be useful in relating the function of proteins to their structures (in a manner similar to the application of comparative anatomy to understand limb and organ function).

Studies of protein structure and function and of the probable course of molecular evolution are being undertaken both on cold adapted species (marine organisms) and independently developing homeotherms (penguins).

Penguin egg-white proteins have proved to differ extensively from homologous proteins from the whites of other avian species (Feeney *et al.*, 1966; Feeney *et al.*, 1968). For example, Adélie penguin ovomucoid differs extensively from all other avian ovomucoids. Many other avian ovomucoids have the biochemical property of inhibiting either the bovine proteolytic enzyme α-chymotrypsin or the bacterial proteolytic enzyme subtilisin, but only penguin ovomucoid is a very strong inhibitor of the bacterial enzyme and a weak inhibitor of the animal enzyme (Bigler and Feeney, 1969). We are currently using these differences in function in an effort to understand how the ovomucoids cause the inhibition of the enzymes. These differences are probably a result of the extensive genetic variability commonly encountered in egg-white proteins (Feeney and Allison, 1969). Blood-serum proteins of three different penguin species have been compared with the serum proteins of other avian species and man and with egg-white proteins of the Adélie penguin (Feeney *et al.*, 1968; Allison and Feeney, 1968). These comparisons have helped to show relationships between the blood protein, serum transferrin, and the egg-white protein, ovotransferrin. There are no particular temperature adaptations necessary in the blood, muscles or eggs of penguins, because physiological temperatures of these are nearly the same as those of the chicken.

In the case of the poikiliothermic Antarctic fish, however, the proteins are synthesized and function at very low temperatures. Temperature adaptations resulting in structural differences at the molecular level might therefore be anticipated. As part of our programme of protein chemistry, we have been studying blood-serum proteins and muscle enzymes from the three cold-adapted Antarctic fish—*Trematomus borchgrevinki*, *Trematomus bernacchii*, and *Dissostichus mawsoni*. We have completed some comparative descriptive observations and are now studying some of the structure-function relationships (Feeney *et al.*, 1967; Greene and Feeney, 1968; Osuga and Feeney, 1969).

II. Experimental Studies

A. Procurement of Fish

The fish were obtained at McMurdo Sound, Ross Island. The species of *Trematomus*, which have been shown to be obligatorily adapted to low temperature (Somero and DeVries, 1967), were obtained in November 1965, in November through January 1966, and in November and December 1967. They were collected using traps and hand lines. The *D. mawsoni* were obtained in November and December 1966, and were captured from a seal. A total of thirteen specimens of *D. mawsoni* were obtained, nine of which were alive and in excellent condition with an average weight of approximately 25 kg.

B. Muscle Enzymes

Muscle specimens were taken immediately after the fish were killed. The specimens were not allowed to warm more than a few degrees centigrade before they were refrigerated for immediate investigation or before they were frozen and transported in dry ice for later investigation. The enzymes which have been studied in these three species are as follows:

1. *Aldolase*
   Fructose-1,6-diphosphate ⇆ Dihydroxyacetone phosphate + Glyceraldehyde-3-phosphate.
2. *Glyceraldehyde-3-phosphate dehydrogenase* (*GAPD*)
   Glyceraldehyde-3-phosphate + $PO_4^{=}$ + DPN ⇆ 1,3-diphosphoglyceric acid + DPNH.
3. *Lactic acid dehydrogenase* (*LDH*)
   Pyruvate + DPNH ⇆ Lactate + DPN.

These three enzymes are all important in the metabolism of carbohydrate. They all exist as polymers (tetramers) of subunits and are under allosteric control.

Certain determinations have been made directly on extracts of the muscle. These have included total enzymatic activities and enzymatic activities in gel-electrophoretic patterns. The principal work has been on the isolation and characterization of the purified enzymes. Both the LDH and the GAPD have handled quite well under these procedures and are presently being prepared in a high state of purity. Crystallization of aldolase and GAPD has been achieved. The LDH, however, has not yet been crystallized, but a study of the effects of temperature on its activities has not revealed anything unsual about its properties. In fact, *D. mawsoni* LDH and rabbit LDH had very similar catalytic activites of 0°C and 37°C and also had approximately the same heat lability at higher temperatures. In contrast, the aldolase, although it was crystallized, has been difficult to handle. At a certain stage of purity, including crystallization, the enzymatic activity of preparations of aldolase has been unstable to further methods of fractionation. Amino-acid analyses and physical analyses by ultracentrifugation have been done on several of the preparations of these enzymes.

A more detailed study of the *D. mawsoni* GAPD has recently been completed (Greene and Feeney, 1968). The enzyme has been purified by ammonium-sulphate fractionation and DEAE chromatography. Its molecular and kinetic properties have been compared to those of rabbit-muscle GAPD. Their sizes are comparable ($S_{20,w}$rabbit GAPD = 7·71, $S_{20,w}$fish GAPD = 7·65). Studies of the effects of temperature indicated first that their heat stabilities were similar, and secondly that the fish enzyme had a lower apparent activation energy above 5°C than the rabbit enzyme, while they appeared similar at lower temperatures. The Arrehenius plot for the rabbit-muscle GAPD was therefore linear, but the Arrehenius plot for that from *D. mawsoni* showed a transition point at 5–7°C. Thirdly, the *D. mawsoni* GAPD was more active than the rabbit GAPD at −2°C. In general, however, the *D. mawsoni* GPDH did not appear to possess any unique "cold-adapted" molecular properties which might allow exceptionally high activity at low temperatures.

C. Blood Proteins

Both fresh and frozen blood plasma were studied. Protein patterns were obtained for the different species by disc and starch-gel electrophoresis. From these patterns it was possible to differentiate male from female *T. borchgrevinki*. Thirty fish were sexed in this way. From eighteen plasma samples it was also evident that the three different-coloured fishes in the group classified *T. bernacchii* could be subdivided into at least two groups.

There were large differences in the plasma of six *D. mawsoni*, indicating many divergences. Photographs of the acrylamide-gel electropherograms of these six fish are seen in Fig. 1. Partial purification of several of the serum proteins has been achieved. The effect of temperature on the stability of the serum transferrin and the rate of blood clotting has been studied. Preliminary

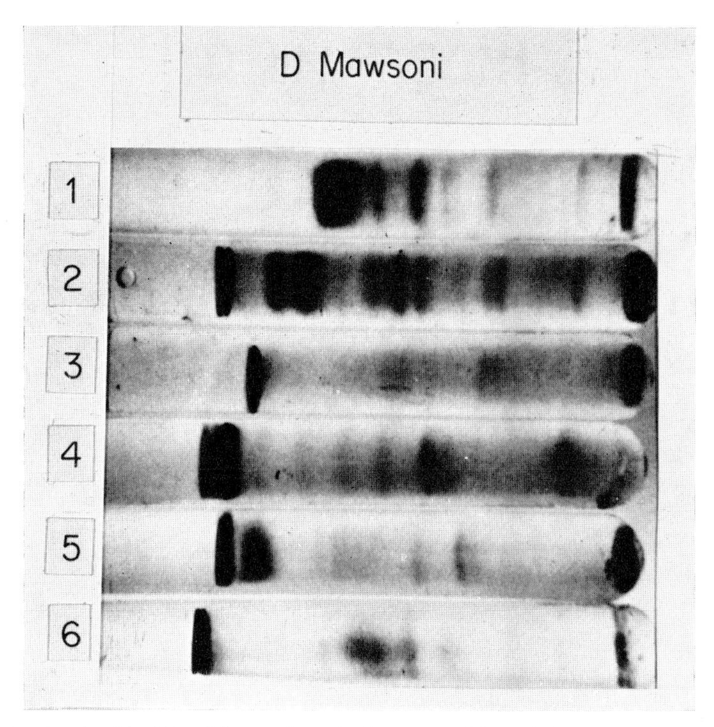

FIG. 1. Acrylamide Disc Electrophoretic Patterns of Blood Serum of Six Different *Dissostichus mawsoni* using the standard 7% gel according to Davis (1964).

results show that *Trematomus* serum transferrin does not have an unusual heat lability, but that a heat-labile factor in the blood is required for clotting.

III. Discussion

The effect of temperature on biological systems is one of the more important and more interesting subjects in biology. As compared to chemical reactions in non-biological systems, temperature relationships in biological systems are restricted to a comparatively narrow range of temperature. This temperature range is, indeed, usually only over half the temperature range between the freezing-point of water at 0°C and its boiling-point at 100°C, namely 0–50°C. A few organisms will grow at warmer temperatures and some of the more commonly considered constituents, such as enzymes, may retain their structural integrity and activity at temperatures considerably higher than 50°C, but most of them are quite labile at temperatures slightly above this 50°C. When viewed on the absolute temperature scale, this range of functional activity in biological systems is really a relatively small one.

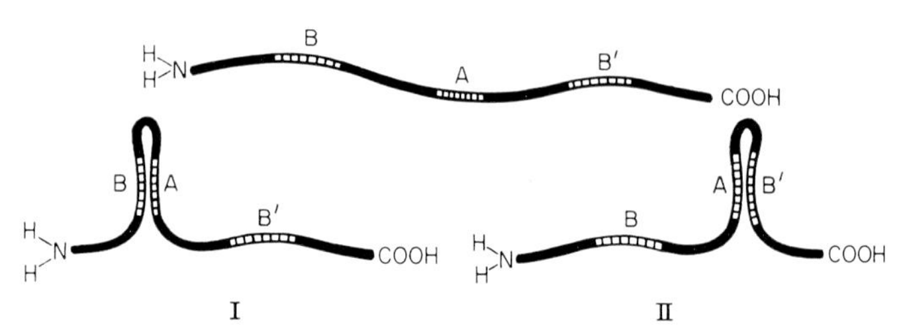

FIG. 2. Segment of protein, shown extended and bound to itself in two alternative metastable configurations. (From Dayhoff and Eck, 1968, p. 60.)

In considering the effect of temperature on biological reactions, one of the first necessities is to get rid of the emotional attachment to the requirement for good biochemical activity only at temperature ranges between 20°C and 40°C, namely slightly below or near the normal temperature of mammals and birds, including man. When viewed on the absolute-temperature scale, and when the myriad of possible catalytic activities are considered, there is no reason why intensely active biochemical systems cannot exist at 0°C. It is thus a falsity to consider that organisms living at this temperature must necessarily be sluggish. In fact, it is perhaps more appropriate to wonder why all poikiliothermic animals, plants and micro-organisms cannot function well at low temperature (Ingraham and Maaloe, 1967). It is, however, a fact that most organisms do not function well at these temperatures. In addition, many of the truly cold-adapted species do not function well at higher temperatures. The fact is that we are dealing with complex systems which are not affected by temperature in the same way as simple chemical reactions. It is these differences that set off the simple chemical systems from the more complex ones in living organisms and fascinate the biochemist. We want to know what the molecular differences or molecular relationships that account for these resistances or susceptibilities to different temperatures are. Biochemists now believe that proteins exist in many different conformational structures. These are in equilibrium with one another and the particular predominating form is a function of the environmental conditions. The different forms may have different degrees of biochemical activity and different degrees of lability to side effects (e.g. chemical attack, such as oxidation or hydrolysis and unidentified effects causing "irreversible denaturation".) One of the main environmental factors commonly affecting proteins is temperature. Figure 2 shows the way that proteins may be affected by temperature (Dayhoff and Eck, 1968). One way of looking at Fig. 2 is that it represents the main forms that a protein may assume at different energy levels. At some particular level it may be so affected that the form assumed for practical purposes cannot revert to the other forms and such a state might be "irreversible denaturation". On the other hand, one of the forms might occur at a rather sharp temperature transition and might still retain its biochemical activity but behave in a different way (e.g. show higher or lower activity). This would be called a "transition" point as is discussed below for *D. mawsoni* GAPD.

In considering cold adaptation at the molecular level, the following are several possibilities:

1. The enzymes may function well at low temperatures, but may have lost the capability of retaining their native structure at the temperatures commonly encountered by species living in the warmer environments of 15–40°C. These enzymes would thus be denatured at these warmer temperatures and termed "heat labile".

2. There are novel enzyme systems for activities existing in the cold temperatures.

3. There is much more enzymatic activity in the tissues of the low-temperature adapted species than is found in the tissues of non-cold-adapted species. Thus, such higher enzymatic activity would allow the species to exist in the cold temperatures, whereas the enzyme systems of the warmer species would be lowered so greatly by a reduction in temperature that function would be impossible. These greatly increased activities in the cold-adapted species could be accomplished in several ways:

(*a*) There could be much higher levels of enzymes in the tissues. These enzymes would thus be similar to the enzymes from the non-cold-adapted species, but their concentrations would be manyfold higher—say twenty- to fiftyfold higher. This does not seem probable, because there is not room in tissues for all the enzymes to be increased by this amount.

(*b*) The enzymes are similar to the ones found in non-cold-adapted species, but they are made "hyper-active" by special activators (allosteric type effects).

(*c*) The enzymes are "hyper-active" enzymes as compared to the ones from non-cold-adapted species. Thus, the "catalytic power" or "turn-over number" of the enzymes from the cold-adapted species would be much higher than that of enzymes from the non-cold-adapted species.

There are other features that might be anticipated in enzymes from cold-adapted species, but the above list is representative of the main possibilities. The loss of heat stability (1 above) is not really germane to the problem under discussion. Loss of resistance to higher temperature might be expected in some instances because the enzyme does not have to function at these higher temperatures and the resistance at these temperatures is therefore an unnecessary characteristic. It is a "negative" matter in regards to the low-temperature adaptation because it might or might not be related to higher enzymatic activity at low temperatures.

The possibilities listed under 2 and 3 above, however, are germane to the problem, because they concern how the species can function at low temperatures rather than why it cannot function at high temperatures. Any of these alternatives might be expected, depending upon the particular tissues and the particular substance. It is obvious that situation 3(*a*) could not occur generally because, as stated above, there would not be room in the cells for all the necessary enzymes. The biochemist interested in molecular function would usually be most interested in molecular adaptations causing changes in function at low temperatures. These may or may not be found. In the present work we apparently have found evidence, at least in a limited way for several of the situations listed under 3, and for one example of situation 1. The latter might be the loss of heat stability of one of the factors necessary for blood clotting. The several examples of type 3 include the perhaps higher lability of aldolase, and the transition point for the GAPD at 5–7°C.

Other studies of the proteins and enzymes described in this article as well as of other systems are presently under way in our laboratory. One particular example is a programme on haemoglobins. Another is a study of the "antifreeze" substance in the blood serum of *T. borchgrevinki* (DeVries and Wohlschlag, 1968). This "antifreeze" is described elsewhere in this symposium. There are a variety of other problems that should be studied. Some of these are obvious from the above discussion. Others, however, are interrelated in a complex way with the general structures and physiological functionings of the organisms.

References

Allison, R. G. and Feeney, R. E. (1968). Penguin Blood Serum Proteins. *Archs. Biochem. Biophys.* **124**, 548–55.

Bigler, J. C. and Feeney, R. E. (1969). Inhibition of Subtilisin by Avian Ovomucoids. *Archs. Biochem. Biophys.* (In the press.)

Davis, B. J. (1964). Disc Electrophoresis—II. Method and Application to Human Serum Proteins. *Ann. N.Y. Acad. Sc.* **121**, Art. 2, 404–27.

Dayhoff, M. O. and Eck, R. V. (1968). "Atlas of Protein Sequence and Structure 1967–68". Silver Spring, Maryland: National Biomedical Research Foundation.

DeVries, A. L. and Wohlschlag, D. E. (1968). Freezing resistance in some antarctic fishes. *Science, N.Y.*

Feeney, R. E., Osuga, D. T., Lind, S. B. and Miller, H. T. (1966). The egg-white proteins of the Adélie penguin. *Comp. Biochem. Physiol.* **18**, 121–30.

Feeney, R. E., Miller, H. T. and Komatsu, S. K. (1967). "Properties of Proteins from Cold-Adapted Antarctic Fish". Abstract J-185, from the Seventh International Congress of Biochemistry, Tokyo, Japan, August 1967.

Feeney, R. E., Allison, R. G., Osuga, D. T., Bigler, J. C. and Miller, H. T. (1968). Biochemistry of the Adélie Penguin: Studies on egg and blood serum proteins. *In* "Antarctic Bird Studies". Vol. 12, Antarctic Research Series, American Geophysical Union.

Feeney, R. E. and Allison R. E. (1969). "Biochemical Evolution of Proteins. Proteins of Blood Plasma, Milk and Egg White". Interscience-Wiley, New York.

Greene, F. C. and Feeney, R. E. (1968). "Properties of Glyceraldehyde-3-Phosphate Dehydrogenase from an Antarctic Cold-Adapted Fish". Abstract from the 156th National Meeting of the American Chemical Society, Atlantic City, N.J. (September 1968).

Ingraham, J. L. and Maaloe, O. (1967). Cold Sensitive Mutants and the Minimum Temperature of Growth of Bacteria. *In* "Molecular Mechanisms of Temperature Adaptations" pp. 297–309. American Association for the Advancement of Science.

Osuga, D. T. and Feeney, R. E. (1969). "Properties of Muscle Lactic Dehydrogenase from Antarctic Cold-Adapted Fish". (In preparation.)

Somero, G. N. and DeVries, A. L. (1967). Temperature tolerance of some antarctic fishes. *Science, N.Y.* **156**, No. 3772, 257–8.

Discussion

Fishes

THE ECOSYSTEM ASSOCIATED WITH ICE

M. J. DUNBAR

I was interested in Professor Andriashev's "marine cryobiology". We have listened to his account of "ice-grazing" fish: we have heard about the fauna and flora of anchor ice and platelet ice. This reminds one of a thirty-year-old suggestion that water polymers (trihydrol, etc.) would stimulate algal cells. Experimental results by Barnes, Harvey and others confirmed this effect, but the work was abandoned, as the physicists showed that polymers quickly reverted to the monomer state as ice melted. However, organisms actually in contact with the ice may be able to use these polymers.

T. J. HART

You can get very odd chemical results from ice. *Nitschia frigida* was studied in Copenhagen harbour by Grontred in the first postwar years, and results showed very high supersaturation with oxygen near the diatom layer. These results were probably valid despite a controversy over the chemical techniques used.

RELATIONSHIPS OF NOTOTHENIIDAE

K. G. MCKENZIE

Dr DeWitt considered Nototheniidae primitive. Why?

H. H. DEWITT

Only because they are a most highly endemic family with uncertain relationships to other fish families.

K. G. MCKENZIE

Are there any fossils?

H. H. DEWITT

Two only, and neither of them useful for our purposes. One otolith has been found in the Miocene of New Zealand and one vertebra in the Snow Hill Tertiary rocks.

RESPIRATORY MECHANISMS

R. FEENEY

Surely the question arising from Dr Ralph's paper is why other fish need haemoglobin? Rather the same point applies to cold adaptation in micro-organisms: the problem is not how some grow at 0°–3°C but why they all cannot: their chemical processes should simply slow down. Abnormal control systems come in and stop growth.

R. W. MORRIS

Dr Ralph asked why haemoglobin was necessary. Surely it provides an emergency service, increasing the capacity of musculature. It is possible to knock out the haemoglobin in the blood of many fishes with carbon monoxide and yet allow normal functioning of the muscles—except in an emergency. Dr Ruud referred to the large amount of blood in Chaenicthyiid fishes. In my studies I have found that blood can make up to 10% of the body volume, thus confirming his observations.

I. EVERSON

How did Dr Morris draw samples of the colourless blood of Chaenicthyiids?

R. W. MORRIS

From the ductus Cuvier or common cardinal behind the last gill slits, using a heparinized syringe to stop clotting.

FREEZING RESISTANCE IN ANTARCTIC FISHES

R. N. SMITH

Dr De Vries assessed the contribution of NaCl to freezing-point depression on a basis of chloride determinations, and assumed the concentrations of chloride and sodium were the same. Is this valid? What factors were used in calculating freezing-point depressions from NaCl determinations?

A. L. DEVRIES

A literature survey of the composition of blood sera of both fresh and marine teleosts shows that the concentrations of serum chloride for *most* fishes are between 83% and 95% of the concentrations of the serum sodium. Therefore my estimates of the percentage of the serum freezing-point depression due to sodium chloride are somewhat low, but not far out of line. In addition I measured the serum-sodium concentration in *Trematomus borchgrevinki* and it was only 40 millimoles higher than the serum chloride concentration.

R. W. MORRIS

Chloride and sodium pass in and out of the urine independently. Can you assume uniform concentration and behaviour in body fluids? What about ionic interference?

R. N. SMITH

Direct measurement of freezing-point depressions is preferable to calculation of depressions from the concentrations of sodium, potassium, chloride, etc., in the blood serum. In such calculations it is usually assumed that a molal solution of any one ion depresses the freezing-point of water by 1·86°C. This leads to errors, since the cryoscopic effect varies with concentration and also with different solutes, the variation being most marked with strongly hydrated salts. However, the direct measurements of serum freezing-points carried out by Dr DeVries and myself show that McMurdo and Signy Island fish populations have distinct differences in their blood properties, and this is confirmed by chemical analysis.

A. L. DeVries

In my study I have not attached a great deal of importance to obtaining an accurate estimate of the total contribution of the inorganic ions to the freezing-point depression of the serum, because I have isolated a large molecular weight organic antifreeze which accounts for at least 30% of the freezing-point depression of the serum in most of the *Trematomus* fishes.

N. A. Øritsland

Red cells react to changing osmolarity of the plasma. Changing concentrations of free amino acids in plasma may be due to their outflow from the cells, as found by K. Függlli at our laboratory.

R. N. Smith

I have not measured free amino-acid concentrations in *Notothenia neglecta* serum, but there is probably only a very small change, if any, in response to the differing osmolarities of summer and winter fish serum. There is evidence of this lack of change in the fact that the difference between summer and winter serum freezing-points is accounted for by increases in salts, reducing sugar and urea, i.e. the expected cryoscopic effect of an increase in amino-acid concentration is not observed. Additionally, the serum freezing-points of fish killed by freezing conditions are similar to those of normal fish: it appears that nothing is released from the red cells in response to cold stress.

N. A. Øritsland

The relationship is not in cold stress but in changing osmolarity, as in a transition from marine to freshwater environments.

S. Z. El-Sayed

Did Dr Smith check the age of his experimental animals? Was this correlated with weight?

R. N. Smith

No. My data were not correlated for the size of the fish (the largest fish weighed about 600 gm) and I did not attempt a subdivision based on age.

I. Everson

Notothenia neglecta grows slowly at Signy Island, and the maximum standard lengths of females was about 52 cm and of males 42 cm. Dr Smith's largest fish were probably five or six years old. *N. rossi* may grow more quickly judging from Olsen's work at South Georgia.

J. T. Rudd

South Georgia waters are warmer and growth rates may differ.

BIOCHEMISTRY

H. H. DeWitt

Dr Feeney referred to the possible use of serum analysis in discriminating the races of *T. bernacchii*. This is a very variable species, judged by scales, lateral line characters, etc. I doubt if sera will be any more use in classification than these morphological characters.

R. E. Feeney

I agree with Dr DeWitt's comments on serum analysis in some respects, but disagree strongly with the general idea that biochemical taxonomy will not be a primary tool in many instances. I have confidence that some day we may be able to show small differences in taxonomic relationships by comparisons of integrated enzyme systems, say, for example, in the livers.

THERMOGENESIS

P. K. Dayton

Emphasis has been placed on the freezing-point of urine in Antarctic fishes. But is there any evidence that normal urine is produced under laboratory conditions? Removed from their normal benthic environment these fish may be under stress and show "laboratory diuresis".

R. W. Morris

Micturition, judged by the frequency of bladder expulsion, appeared to be at the normal rate for fishes.

R. N. Smith

I measured the cloacal temperatures of *Notothenia neglecta* and *N. rossi*, although my methods were less sophisticated than those of Dr Morris. Cloacal temperatures were all within 0·2°C, and generally within 0·1°C of water temperature, which is a little over 0°C in summer at Signy Island. If these temperature differences are maintained during winter and assuming that cloacal temperatures are characteristic of those in the rest of the body, then it would appear that thermogenesis contributes little towards the survial in winter of the fish I studied.

A. L. DeVries

In 1965 I measured body temperatures in *Trematomus bernacchii* in an aquarium where the water temperature was regulated at −1·86°C. A thermocouple was implanted 3 cm into the dorsal muscle mass, parallel to the vertebral column. Muscle temperatures were only 0·02–0·04°C above the temperature of the surrounding water. This technique has been criticized because of the possibility of conductance of heat through the wire to the surrounding water; however, the thermocouple wire was small and well insulated.

Part VII

THE BIOLOGY OF SEALS

The Biology of Seals

In recent years there has been much discussion of the possibility of cropping the seal stocks of the southern circumpolar zone, and especially the populations of crabeater seals (*Lobodon carcinophagus*), which may total 5–8 million individuals, making this the most abundant pinnipede in the world. T. Øritsland, in this section, reports on an exploratory voyage to test the feasibility of such Antarctic sealing. The Working Group on Biology of SCAR was asked in 1966 to provide information about seal numbers, distributions, available harvests and the optimal arrangements for regulating such an industry, should one develop. This information was required to guide SCAR's advice to the Antarctic Treaty Consultative Meetings, at which the need for an internationally agreed framework for the management of these resources was recognized. In 1968, concurrently with the Symposium, a sub-committee of specialists on seals met to formulate recommendations, and their findings are published in *SCAR Bulletin*, No. 32 (*Polar Record*, Vol. 14, No. 92, pp. 741–765, 1969).

In 1962 the first SCAR Symposium on Antarctic Biology received estimates of Antarctic seal stocks by R. M. Laws (1964), which, like the earlier generalizations of Scheffer (1958), could only be reached by a great deal of extrapolation. C. R. Eklund (1964), at the same meeting, reported on the first major direct census of seals from an ice-breaker in the pack. Since then programmes of this kind have become frequent among SCAR nations and examples are reported by Siniff, Cline and Erickson and Aguayo, and summarized by Øritsland in this section. These papers not only provide a more rigorous basis for calculation of the parameters which must be known if Antarctic sealing is to be properly managed, but indicate (as developed further in discussion) that the behaviour of the animals must be considered in evaluating the censuses. Carleton Ray's paper is of especial relevance here.

In the Arctic, biologists have for many years provided advice on the optimal sustained yield of seal stocks. A. W. Mansfield's paper foreshadows what will be required in the south should a sealing industry develop.

References

Eklund, C. R. (1964). Population studies of Antarctic seals and birds. *In* "Biologie Antarctique—Antarctic Biology". Hermann, Paris.

Laws, R. M. (1964). Comparative biology of Antarctic seals. *In* "Biologie Antarctique—Antarctic Biology". Hermann, Paris.

Scheffer, V. B. (1958). "Seals, Sealions and Walruses". Stanford University Press.

Biology and Population Dynamics of Antarctic Seals

TORGER ØRITSLAND
Institute of Marine Research, Directorate of Fisheries, Bergen, Norway

Four species (and genera) of phocids qualify as truly Antarctic and are grouped in the tribe Lobodontini: the Weddell seal (*Leptonychotes weddelli*), the crabeater seal (*Lobodon carcinophagus*), the leopard seal (*Hydrurga leptonyx*) and the Ross seal (*Ommatophoca rossi*).

The biology of these seals was reviewed (Carrick, 1964; Laws, 1964) at the first SCAR Symposium on Antarctic Biology in Paris, 1962. A serious attempt to estimate the stocks was reported to the Paris symposium by the late Dr C. R. Eklund (Eklund, 1964).

Since 1962 at least three additional reviews have appeared (Bonner and Laws, 1964; King, 1964; Stonehouse, 1965). Several attempts have been made to survey the seals of the Antarctic pack ice (see Table 1). The Weddell seal has been the object of intensive studies of physiology, behaviour and population dynamics in the Ross Sea region and elsewhere, and results of these studies are being published (Müller-Schwarze, 1965; Smith, 1966*b*; Stirling, 1967; Kooyman, 1967). Provisional results from studies made on an exploratory sealing expedition are available (Øritsland, 1970) and a broadly based investigation of seals in the pack ice has been launched by the United States (Siniff *et al.*, 1970). Finally, accumulated observations by various expeditions from several nations are being published or becoming available through translations (Zenkovich, 1962; Korotkevich, 1964; Solyanik, 1965; Mackintosh, 1967; Aguayo and Torres, 1967).

Assessments of coastal Weddell seal populations have been made for several areas, but coverage is still far from being complete. New data on the relative abundance of seals in the pack ice are available, and are summarized together with earlier data in Table 1. Previous stock assessments might be revised by these data, but density figures cover only limited areas, and also are confusingly inconsistent. In view of current research activities a reassessment therefore seems premature.

Aspects of the natural history of the Antarctic seals are summarized in Table 2. The table is not representative of our present knowledge about these

TABLE 1

Relative Abundance of Seals in the Antarctic Pack ice

Area	*Dates*	*Total no. of seals counted*	*Crabeaters*		*Leopards*		*Ross seals*		*Other sp.*		*References*
			No.	*%*	*No.*	*%*	*No.*	*%*	*No.*	*%*	
Weddell Sea 20°W–10°E (?)	Summers of 1950–52 (?)	113	92	81·4	8	7·1	13	11·5			Bonner and Laws, 1964
Ross Sea 166°–177°E Indian Ocean 105°–112°E	17 Dec. 1956– 10 Jan. 1957 25 Jan.– 28 Jan. 1957	846	785	(97·0) 92·8*	50	(2·2) 5·9*	11	(0·8) 1·3*			Eklund and Atwood, 1962 Eklund, 1964
Indian Ocean 65°E–165°E	7 Dec. 1957– 13 Feb. 1958	1,181	1,000	84·7*	59	5·0*	5	0·4*	117	9·9*	Zenkovich, 1962
W. of Terre Adélie ab. 130°E (?)	Jan. 1961	328	295*	90	7*	2			26*	8	Prévost, 1964
Weddell Sea– Scotia Sea 37°–55°W	25 Aug.– 31 Oct. 1964	861	729	84·7	110	12·8	15	1·7	7	0·8	Øritsland, 1970
W. Ross Sea 165°E–175°E (?)	Dec. 1965– Jan. 1966	572	275	48·1	30	5·2	17	3·0	250	43·7	Ray, 1966 and *personal communication*
S. Shetlands Palmer Peninsula 55°–65°W (?)	Dec. 1965– Mar. 1966	829– 845	737– 752	87·7– 88·1	83	10·0– 9·7	0	0·0	19	2·3– 2·2	Aguayo and Torres, 1967
Total		4,743	3,916	82·6	347	7·3	61	1·3	419	8·8	

seals, but an attempt has been made to review data which may be used as population parameters, or be relevant in planning and evaluating surveys and stock assessments.

TABLE 2

Summary of Biological Data on Antarctic Seals

	Weddell seal	*Crabeater*	*Leopard*	*Ross seal*
Distribution	Discontinuous circumpolar, coastal: 2, 4, 9, 10, 20, etc.	Circumpolar in pack ice: 2, etc.	Circumpolar in pack ice and southern temp. regions: 2, etc.	Circumpolar in pack ice: 1, 5, 25, etc.
Migration	Local movements: 4, 21, 22, 24, 26, 28, 29, 30, 33	Move towards coast in summer: 7, 9, 10, 19, 25, etc.	Regular visitor subantarctic islands in winter: 4, 7, 9, 10, 14, 16	—
General beh.	Semigregarious, intraspecific aggressiveness: 25, 27, 29	Semigregarious: 2, 9, 14, 17, 20, 25, etc	Solitary: 2, 4, etc.	Solitary: 1, etc.
Rhythm	Nocturnal: 22, 24, 28	Nocturnal: 33	Diurnal: 12, 15	
Food	Fish cephalopods, etc.: 1, 2, 3, 4, 6, 10, 11, 20, 23, etc.	Euphausids, fish, etc.: 2, 4, etc.	Fish, euphausids, penguins, cephalopods etc.: 2, 4, 5, 8, 12, 31, 32, etc.	Cephalopods, fish, etc.: 1, 2, 4, 25
Breeding	Sept.–Nov. acc. to locality, groups: 2, 3, 4, 6, 9, 11, 18, 20, 26, 28, 30, etc.	October, scattered pairs(?): 16, 31	November: 4, 8, 15	November: 31
Moult	Dec.–March: 2, 3, 4, 6, 11, 20, 26	Jan.–Feb., partly fasting: 1, 2, 9, 14	Jan.–Feb., no change in habits: 12, 15	January, fasting: 1
Longevity	15–16 years: 9, 30	29 + years: 31	26 + years: 31	12 years: 31
Mortality	High among pups: 6, 18	25–5%: 17, 31	8–5%: 31	—
Sex ratio	46–55% ♂: 9, 18, 26, 28	50% ♂: 9, 31	53–60% ♂, 50% ♂: 12, 15, 31	50% ♂: 31
Sex. mat. ♂	3–4 years: 2, 28	3–6 years: 31	3–7 years: 31	3–4 years: 31
Sex. mat. ♀	2–4 years: 6, 9, 18, 28	3–6 years, mean 3·5 years: 31	2–6 years, mean 5·1 years: 31	2–7 years: 31
Fertility	0·81–0·97: 9, 28, 30	0·80: 5. 0·76, increasing through young, decreasing through old age-groups: 31	0·61, increasing with age: 31	High (?): 31

References are given as numbers after the colon for each entry.

1 Hanson, 1902	12 Gwynn, 1953	23 Dearborn, 1965
2 Wilson, 1907	13 Paulian, 1953	24 Smith, 1965
3 Wilton *et al.*, 1908	14 Arseniev, 1957	25 Solyanik, 1965
4 R. N. R. Brown, 1915	15 K. G. Brown, 1957	26 Lugg, 1966
5 Matthews, 1929	16 King, 1957	27 Smith, 1966*a*
6 Lindsay, 1937	17 Laws, 1958	28 Smith, 1966*b*
7 Lindsay, 1938	18 Mansfield, 1958	29 Kooyman, 1967
8 Hamilton, 1939	19 Ingham, 1960	30 Stirling, 1967
9 Bertram, 1940	20 Korotkevich, 1964	31 Øritsland, 1970
10 Perkins, 1945	21 Prévost, 1964	32 Øritsland, unpubl.
11 Sapin-Jaloustre, 1952	22 Müller-Schwarze, 1965	33 Siniff *et al.*, 1970

References

Aguayo, L. A. and Torres, N. D. (1967). Observaciones sobre mamiferos marinos durante la Vigesima Comision Antartica Chilena. Primer censo de pinipedios en las Islas Shetland del Sur. *Revta Biol. mar.* **13** (1), 1–57.

Arseniev, V. A. (1957). Nablyudeniya za tyulenyami Antarktiki [Observations on the seals of the Antarctic]. *Byull. mosk. Obshch. Ispyt. Prir.* **62** (5), 39–44. [Engl. summary].

Bertram, G. C. L. (1940). The biology of the Weddell and crabeater seals. With a study of the comparative behaviour of the Pinnipedia. *Scient. Rep. Br. Graham Ld Exped* **1** (1), 1–139, Pl. 1–10.

Bonner, W. N. and Laws, R. M. (1964). Seals and Sealing. *In* "Antarctic Research", (Sir R. Priestly, R. J. Adie and G. de Q. Robin eds). Butterworths London. 163–90.

Brown, K. G. (1957). The leopard seal at Heard Island, 1951–54. *Interim Rep. Aust. natn. Antarct. Res. Exped.* **16** I–II, 1–34.

Brown, R. N. R. (1915). The seals of the Weddell Sea: Notes on their habits and distribution. *Rep. scient. Results Scott. natn. antarct. Exped.* **4** (13), 185–98, 9 pl.

Carrick, R. (1964). Southern seals as subject for ecological research. *In* "Biologie Antarctique: Antarctic Biology". (R. Carrick, M. Holdgate and J. Prévost eds). Hermann, Paris. 421–32.

Dearborn, J. H. (1965). Food of Weddell seals at McMurdo Sound, Antarctica. *J. Mammal.* **46** (1), 37–43.

Eklund, C. R. (1964). Population studies of antarctic seals and birds. *In* "Biologie Antarctique: Antarctic Biology". (R. Carrick, M. Holdgate and J. Prevost eds). Hermann, Paris. 415–19.

Eklund, C. R. and Atwood, E. L. (1962). A population study of antarctic seals. *J. Mammal.* **43** (2), 229–38.

Gwynn, A. M. (1953). The status of the leopard seal at Heard Island and Macquarie Island, 1948–1950. *Interim Rep. Aust. natn. Antarct. Res. Exped.* **3**, 1–33.

Hamilton, J. E. (1939). The leopard seal *Hydrurga leptonyx* (de Blainville). *"Discovery" Rep.* **18**, 239–64.

Hanson, N. (1902). Extracts from the private diary of the late Nicolai Hanson. *In* "Report on the Collections of Natural History made in the Antarctic Regions during the Voyage of the Southern Cross". (B. Shell and J. Bell, eds). Br. Mus. (Nat. Hist.), London 79–105.

Ingham, S. E. (1960). The status of seals (Pinnipedia) at Australian antarctic stations. *Mammalia* **24**, 422–30.

King, J. E. (1957). On a pup of the crabeater seal *Lobodon carcinophagus*. *Ann. Mag. nat. Hist. Ser.* 12, **10** (116), 619–24, Pl. 20.

King, J. E. (1964). "Seals of the World". Bri. Mus. (Nat. Hist.), London.

Kooyman, G. L. (1967). An analysis of some behavioral and physiological characteristics related to diving in the Weddell seal. *Antarct. Res. Ser. Am. geophys. Un.* **11**, 227–61.

Korotkevich, E. S. (1964) [1958]. Observations on seals during the first wintering of the soviet Antarctic Expedition in 1956–1957. *Transld. Inf. Bull. Sov. Antarct. Exped.* **1**, 146–7.

Laws, R. M. (1958). Growth rates and ages of crabeater seals, *Lobodon carcinophagus* Jacquinot & Pucheran. *Proc. zool. Soc. Lond.* 130 (2), 275–88.

Laws, R. M. (1964). Comparative biology of Antarctic seals. *In* "Biologie Antarctique: Antarctic Biology". (R. Carrick, M. Holdgate and J. Prévost eds). Hermann, Paris. 445–54.

Lindsay, A. A. (1937). The Weddell seal in the Bay of Whales. *J. Mammal.* 18 (2), 127–44.

Lindsay, A. A. (1938). Notes on the crabeater seal. *J. Mammal.* 19 (4), 456–61.

Lugg, D. J. (1966). Annual cycle of the Weddell seal in the Vestfold Hills, Antarctica. *J. Mammal.* 47 (2), 317–22.

Mackintosh, N. A. (1967). Estimates of local seal populations in the Antarctic, 1930/37. *Norsk Hvalfangsttid.* **56**, 57–64.

Mansfield, A. W. (1958). The breeding behaviour and reproductive cycle of the Weddell seal (*Leptonychotes weddelli* Lesson). *Scient. Rep. Falkld Isl. Depend. Surv.* **18**, 1–41, Pl. 1–6.

Matthews, L. H. (1929). The natural history of the elephant seal with notes on other seals found at South Georgia. *"Discovery" Rep.* **1**, 233–56, Pl. 19–24.

Müller-Schwarze, D. (1965). Zur Tagesperiodik der allgemeinen Aktivität der Weddell-Robbe (*Leptonychotes weddelli*) in Hallett, Antarktika. *Z. Morph. Okol. Tiere* **55**, 796–803.

Øritsland, T. (1970). Sealing and seal research in the south-west Atlantic pack ice, September–October 1964. (This volume).

Paulian, P. (1953). Pinnipèdes, cétacés, oiseaux des Iles Kerguelen et Amsterdam. Mission Kerguelen 1951. *Mem. Inst. scient. Madagascar*, Ser. A 8, 111–234, Pl. 1–30.

Perkins, J. E. (1945). Biology at Little America III, the West Base of the United States Antarctic Service Expedition 1939–1941. *Proc. Am. phil. Soc.* 89 (1), 270–84.

Prévost, J. (1964). Observations complementaires sur les pinnipedes de l'Archipel de Pointe Geologie. *Mammalia* 28, 351–8.

Ray, C. (1966). The ecology of antarctic seals. *Antarct. J.U.S.* **1** (4), 143–4.

Sapin-Jaloustre, J. (1952). Les Phoques de Terre Adélie. *Mammalia* **16** (4), 179–212, Pl. 3–7.

Siniff, D. B., Cline, D. and Erickson, A. W. (1970). Population densities of seals in the Weddell Sea, Antarctic–1968. (This volume).

Smith, M. S. R. (1965). Seasonal movements of the Weddell seal in McMurdo Sound, Antarctica. *J. Wildl. Mgmt.* 29 (3), 464–70.

Smith, M. S. R. (1966*a*). Injuries as an indication of social behaviour in the Weddell seal (*Leptonychotes weddelli*). *Mammalia* 30 (2), 241–6.

Smith, M. S. R. (1966*b*). Studies on the Weddell seal (*Leptonychotes weddelli* Lesson) in McMurdo Sound Antarctica. Ph.D. Thesis, Univ. Canterbury, Christchurch.

Solyanik, G. A. (1965) [1964]. Some information on antarctic seals. *Transld Inf. Bull. Sov. Antarct. Exped.* 5, 179–82.

Stirling, I. (1967). Population studies on the Weddell seal. *Tuatara* **15** (3), 133–41.

Stonehouse, B. (1965). Birds and Mammals. *In* "Antarctica". (T. Hatherton, ed.). Methuen, London. 153–86.

Wilson, E. A. (1907). Mammalia. *Natn. antarct. Exped. 1901–1904, nat. Hist.* **2** (1), 1–69.

Wilton, D. W., Pirie, J. H. H. and Brown, R. N. R. (1908). Zoological log. *Rep. scient. Results Scott. natn. antarct. Exped.* **4** (1).

Zenkovich, B. A. (1962). Sea mammals as observed by the round-the-world expedition of the Academy of Sciences of the USSR in 1957/58. *Norsk Hvalfangsttid.* **51**, 198–210.

Sealing and Seal Research in the South-west Atlantic Pack Ice, Sept.–Oct. 1964

T. ØRITSLAND
Institute of Marine Research, Directorate of Fisheries, Bergen, Norway

I. Introduction

A private exploratory sealing expedition in the MV *Polarhav* worked the pack ice of the western Atlantic sector of the Southern Ocean from 25 August to 31 October 1964. During the expedition material and data were collected for a study of Antarctic seals. This paper presents information on the abundance of seals in the pack ice, and provisional results which may be relevant to the population dynamics of crabeater, leopard and Ross seals (*Lobodon carcinophagus*, *Hydrurga leptonyx* and *Ommatophoca rossi*).

II. The Expedition, Observations and Catches of Seals

From 25 August to 22 September *Polarhav* operated east and north-east of the South Shetland Islands, penetrating as far as 190 nautical miles (347 km) from the ice edge, although most of the time was spent cruising and hunting further out in the pack (Fig. 1). Close pack ice with large newly broken floes predominated, but numerous leads facilitated navigation.

From mid-September north-westerly winds rapidly forced the ice edge southwards, and gradually compacted the pack. After a reconnaissance trip towards the Drake Passage, *Polarhav* worked an area north-west of the South Orkney Islands from 23 September to 9 October. The ship was beset just inside the ice edge south-west of the South Orkney Islands on 11 October, and drifted eastwards south of the islands until she was free to move again on 22 October. The rest of the time until the end of October was spent cruising along the compacted ice edge east of the South Orkney Islands.

As long as ice concentration increased with increasing distance from the edge (25 August to 9 October), conspicuously few seals were found in very open ice and in areas with ice cover of 8/10 or more. Seals were also scarce near the Drake Passage, but they appeared to be evenly distributed in pack ice of medium concentration throughout the rest of the area. Most seals were found singly on the floes, but young or subadult seals were also caught two to five together on individual floes. Hummocked floes seemed to be preferred, and the seals were often found close to or among mounds on the ice. During this period seals were counted from a helicopter on seven flights over the pack ice. Only seals within about half a nautical mile (0·9 km) from the aircraft

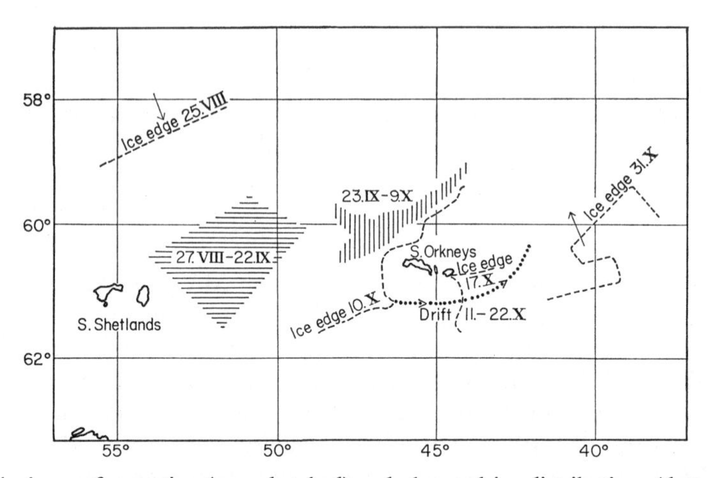

FIG. 1. Areas of operation (cross-hatched) and observed ice distributions (dotted lines) during the *Polarhav* sealing expedition in the south-west Atlantic in 1964.

could be definitely identified, and counts therefore were recorded without regard to species. Assuming that all seals within 1·5 miles from the aircraft were observed, densities have been calculated from counts and distances flown. The densities for these seven flights range from 0·10 to 0·31 (mean 0·23) seals per square n. mile (0·03–0·10; mean 0·07/km²).

After 10 October when the pack ice was very close and the edge compacted, the seals were concentrated with 5 n. miles (9 km) from open water. Very few seals were seen from the helicopter further in from the edge. During this period seals were counted on four flights over the pack near the ice edge. The calculated densities range from 0·29 to 0·85 (mean 0·56) seals per square n. mile (0·97 – 0·28; mean 0·18/km²). On a fifth flight seals were counted in an area with very open ice around the inner end of a bight in the edge, and the density here was calculated to 0·08 seals per square n. mile (0·027/km²).

On all the twelve flights a total of 964 seals were recorded and a distance of 900 n. miles (1650 km) flown. From these figures the mean density of seals on the ice in areas where seals occurred may be calculated to 0·36 seals per square n. mile (0·12/km²).

Except for three animals, all seals which could be reached from the ship were caught, but six seals slipped into the sea and were lost after being shot.

The total catch was 1127 seals, including 272 near-term foetuses and three newly born pups. It is believed that this catch is a representative sample of the seals in the area. The catch of subadult and adult seals, with correction for lost or by-passed animals which have all been identified with absolute certainty, can therefore be used to estimate the relative abundance of the species. The species composition was found to be 84·7% crabeater seals, 12.8% leopard seals, 1·7% Ross seals and 0·8% of other species.

III. Material and Methods

A procedure for rapid collection of selected material on board commercial sealing vessels has been outlined elsewhere (Øritsland, 1967). Material and data were collected for studies of age, maturity and annual cycle from the following subadault and adult seals:

Crabeater males	86
Crabeater females	132
Leopard males	33
Leopard females	51
Ross males	7
Ross females	8
Elephant males	4
Fur seal male	1
Total	322 animals

Feeding, growth, and parasitology were also studied, but these items are not included in this report.

In addition, sex and maturity in crabeater seals were recorded independently for a study of sex ratio and fertility in this species. Data on sex and length were also collected from near-term foetuses and newly born pups.

Provisional age determinations of subadults and adults were made by transmitted and reflected light on about 0·3 mm thick transverse sections cut from the lower canine teeth at the level of the jaw bone. Dentine layers were interpreted in accordance with the growth patterns established by Laws (1962) and, for the innermost very narrow layers in teeth from old animals, by analogy with Arctic seals.

Testes material has not yet been processed for histological examination, but measurements were taken, and the presence or absence of flowing sperm was ascertained in the field by cutting through the distal end of one epididymis. Bacculae were cleaned before measurements were taken, and linseed was used for volume determination. Ovaries were measured and cut by hand into

1–2 mm thick slices for macroscopic analysis. *Corpora lutea*, even of late preganacy, frequently contained a central fluid- or jelly-filled cavity, and luteal tissue was often found in recent *Corpora albicantia*. However, the classification of these bodies could be made without difficulty according to our practice with Arctic seals (Øritsland, 1964).

IV. Crabeater seals

A. Annual Cycle and Breeding Behaviour

The blubber layer of crabeater seals is thick: 228 measurements taken in the region of the sternum average 57 mm, and the greatest thickness was 92 mm, found in a 17-year-old female on 14 September. The measurements indicate that adult females (5 years or older) lose some blubber during October: the mean thickness for twenty-eight females measured from 1 to 8 October was 67 mm, and the corresponding mean for twenty-four females between 19 and 31 October was 53 mm. Measurements also suggest a slight decrease in adult males during the same month, but no trend has been discovered for subadult animals.

Pregnant females were caught regularly until the ship was beset on 11 October, but not later. Foetus lengths increased from a mean of 115 cm (twenty-five measurements, range 102–36 cm) for the period from 29 August to 10 September to 130 cm for 6 to 10 October (mean of thirty-five measurements, range 115–45 cm). A 15-year-old female with a 121 cm foetus was caught with blood flowing from the vagina on 2 September. The first newly born pup, however, which was found on 2 October measured 132 cm; and two pups found on 29 October were 147 cm and 161 cm long. The first pup may have been premature. The second could have been a few days or possibly one week old, and had started to moult. In the third pup moult was well advanced, and this animal was estimated to be about two weeks old. None of the three pups had erupted teeth.

It is regrettable that weather and ice prevented hunting during the critical period from 11 to 22 October, but the observations above suggest that crabeater seals in the western Atlantic sector of the Southern Ocean give birth in mid-October, and that pups may be 135–40 cm long at birth.

Sexually mature non-pregnant females were caught together with adult males from 10 September on. Such pairs became increasingly frequent towards the end of October: three pairs were found in September, six pairs from 1 to 21 October, and ten pairs from 22 to 31 October, the last two on the last day of the month. None of the nineteen females in these pairs had ovulated, but two of them, which were caught on 28 and 29 October, had mature follicles (diameter 28 mm) in one of the ovaries. The first female with a mature follicle was caught alone on 24 October, and three females which had ovulated very recently were caught alone on 28, 29 and 31 October.

Mature male crabeaters with free epididymal sperm were caught from 6 October onwards, and mature males without free sperm were found up to 10 October. Two 4-year-old males caught on 19 and 28 October, without epididymal sperm, were considered still immature or maturing.

Pregnant females were evenly distributed among other seals on the ice up to 11 October. The pairing of mature seals mentioned above, and the fact that each of the three females which had given birth were found in company with mature males, suggest that this species, like the hooded seal (*Cystophora cristata*) of the North Atlantic, associates in pairs during the breeding period.

The conspicuous absence of pregnant or lactating females in catches after 22 October (1·3% of crabeaters caught, compared with 42·9% before 11 October) suggests that breeding seals haul out further away from the ice edge than the non-breeders do. It may be remembered that at this time the seals were concentrated within 5 miles of the compacted edge of the ice, along which the ship hunted. There were no observations suggesting that crabeaters congregate in large breeding groups on the ice.

B. Age and Mortality

Sampling for studies of maturity and sexual cycle had priority, and because mature and maturing animals were selected for dissection whenever a choice had to be made, and females were preferred to males, the age material is not representative of the crabeater catch.

Age determinations were unambiguous up to 20 years for males and 16 years for females, but minimum ages had to be assigned to several animals in older age groups. The oldest male was found to be 25 years old, and two females were at least 29 years old (29+).

Except for a curious absence of 8–10-year-old males, most age groups were reasonably represented in the material. A curve which has been roughly fitted by eye to the age distribution of the males, and which allows for 50% mortality from birth to age 2 years and maximum life span of 30 years, suggests that annual mortality in males may be 8–9% through ages 2–10 years, and 5–6% in older age groups. The age distribution of older females suggests that mortality after age 11 years is similar to that in older males.

C. Sex Ratio

Independent counts were made of 176 near-term foetuses, 147 immatures, and 504 mature crabeater seals. Foetus counts show a prenatal sex ratio very close to 50:50 (49·4% males), and counts of immatures (53·7% males) are close enough to suggest that the ratio does not change appreciably during the first couple of years after birth. The count for mature animals is distorted, however (41·1% males), and suggests a difference between sexes in mortality or behaviour. One explanation might be that females in late pregnancy haul out more frequently or stay on the ice longer than males.

D. Sexual Maturity in Males

Measurements of reproductive organs from eighty-eight one-year-old or older males show a rapid growth in testes length from about 45 mm at 2 years to about 100 mm at 6 years, and a corresponding increase of baculum length and volume from about 80 mm and 2 cm^3 at 2 years to about 175 mm and 17 cm^3 at 6 years. Baculum volume increases very slowly in later years, but there is no appreciable change in length after 6–7 years. Free epididymal sperm was demonstrated in a few 3-year-old and older animals.

The evidence is far from being conclusive, but it may be tentatively concluded that male crabeater seals become sexually mature (attain puberty) at ages from 3 to 6 or 7 years. Further data will become available from a histological examination of testes and epididymis samples.

E. Sexual Maturity in Females

The youngest non-pregnant mature females (nullipara) were 4 years old when caught, and could have ovulated for the first time at an age of 3 years. Frequencies of females which had ovulated in each age group suggest 67% maturity at 3 years and 100% at age 4.

However, the size distribution of follicles and *Corpora* in each of the two ovaries from mature seals indicate that female crabeaters, like several other pinnipeds, have a regular one-year sexual cycle with a single ovulation each year. The number of *Corpora lutea* and *albicantia* was found to increase by 0·75/year from 2 to 10 years. Thereafter the formation of new *Corpora lutea* appeared to be balanced by a resorption of old *Corpora albicantia*. This suggests that *Corpora albicantia* are retained as macroscopically recognizable structures for five to six years after ovulation. All females which are not more than five years older than the youngest maturing age group therefore may be assigned to age at first ovulation by counting the *Corpora* in their ovaries. In this manner the age of puberty could be determined for twenty-four females, nine of which matured at an age of 3 years, thirteen at 4 years, one at 5 years, and one at 6 years. A cumulative graph of maturity based on this age distribution is shown in Fig. 2 (graph A). The graph suggests that the median age of maturity is close to 3·5 years in female crabeater seals.

F. Fertility

One 20-year-old female was caught on 2 September with two female foetuses, 122 and 119 cm long (double ovulation in same ovary), but all other pregnant seals had one foetus each. Reproductive success of mature females and fertility in the stock of females therefore may be measured in terms of annual rate of pregnancies.

Classified counts recorded throughout the season showed 226 pregnancies among 297 mature females, or a pregnancy rate of 0·76. It is probable, however, that breeding females were under-represented in catches after mid-October, and the counts up to 10 October showed that 224 of 258 mature

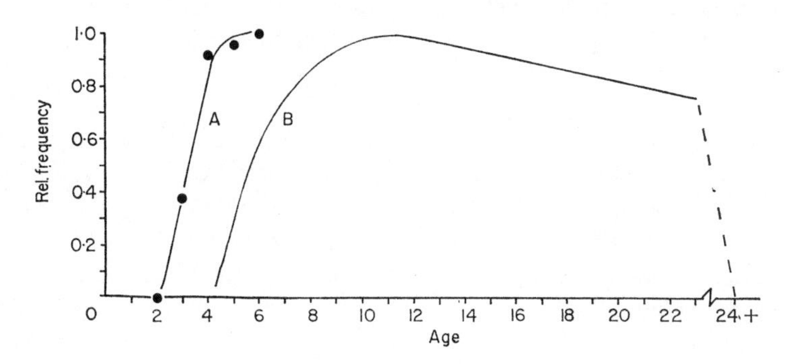

FIG 2. Sexual maturity (A) and fertility (B) of female crabeater seals.

females were pregnant. If near-term females did haul out and were caught more frequently than non-breeders, the pregnancy rate of 0·87 from the latter counts is a maximum figure for reproductive success of mature female crabeater seals.

Data from dissected seals indicate that reproductive success increases with age in the maturing and newly matured age groups. When all animals were assigned to age at last ovulation or breeding season, the ratios of pregnant to mature seals were found to be: 0:2 in age group 3; 3:5 in age group 4; 3:7 in age group 5; 3:4 in age group 6; 3:4 in age group 7; 1:2 in age group 8; 5:5 in age group 9, and 3:3 in age group 10.

The corresponding ratio for all 10 to 23-year-old females was 54:77 (average pregnancy rate 0·70). Smoothed rates for each of these age groups suggest that reproductive success decreases by about 0·02 per year from an apparent maximum at 10 years. None of the six females which were more than 24 years old was pregnant, a fact which suggests that reproduction ends rather abruptly at about this age.

The fertility of all females in the stock may be assessed by combining smoothed data on sexual maturity and reproductive success. The fertility graph (B) in Fig. 2 is a tentative interpretation of the data from this study, and shows how the rate of near-term pregnancies may change with age among female crabeaters. Hopefully it will be possible to correct this graph as new data become available from future studies.

V. Leopard Seals

A. Annual Cycle

The mean blubber thickness of eighty-four leopard seals was found to be 46 mm, with very little difference between sexes. The greatest thickness of 84 mm was found in a 13-year-old female caught on 19 September and this was also the longest animal measured (337 cm). Adult males appeared to lose some blubber through October, the mean of ten measurements from 28 September to 3 October being 53 mm, compared to 45 mm for ten measurements from 23 to 31 October. No trend was found for subadults or adult females.

Pregnant females were found from 2 September to 10 October, and again on 25 October. Measurements of ten foetuses indicate a growth from about 110 cm in early September to 140 cm in late October. If births take place in early November, a birth length of 150–60 cm is suggested.

Maturing or mature follicles were not found in ovaries from mature seals. However, free epididymal sperm was discovered in three males captured on 28, 29 and 31 October. The latest mature male without sperm was caught on 29 October.

B. Age and Mortality

Minimum ages were assigned to two males older than 18 years, and two females older than 13 years. For all other animals absolute ages could be determined. The oldest male was 23+ years and the oldest female 26+ years old, and most age groups were fairly well represented in the sample.

Allowing for 25% mortality during the first year, a curve fitted by eye to the age distribution of both sexes together suggests a mortality of about 8% per year from age 1 to 10 years, and about 5% per year in older age groups.

C. Sex Ratio

Sex was determined for eighteen foetuses, of which eight (44%) were males. The sample contains material from ten males and ten females in age groups 1–5, which is consistent with a hypothetical 50:50 ratio among immatures and maturing animals. Of the sixty-four older seals in the sample, twenty-three (36%) were males, and as in crabeater seals, the sex ratio may indicate a difference in behaviour between sexes. The sample comprises 76% of all sighted or captured leopard seals, and therefore may be representative of the animals which haul out on the ice during daylight hours at this time of the year.

D. Sexual Maturity in Males

In leopard seals rapid testicle growth occurs at ages from 2 to 5 years, and the accelerated growth of bacula is found in age groups from 2 to 7 years.

Production of sperm was demonstrated in two 5-year-old seals. From this evidence it is assumed that sexual maturity is attained by male leopard seals at ages from 3 to 6 years.

E. Sexual Maturity in Females

The youngest mature female was nearly 3 years old at capture, and she had probably ovulated when 2 years old. The youngest pregnant seal was nearly 6 years old, and had conceived at an age of 5 years. Direct estimates from the frequencies of mature animals in each age group suggest that the first animals mature at 2 years, and that 80% have reached maturity at 5 and 100% at 6 years. The numbers of *Corpora lutea* and *albicantia* increase by about 0·67 per year from 2 to 17 years. The increase is slower and the *Corpora albicantia* appear to persist longer than in crabeaters. The distribution of age at first ovulation of animals in the maturing or recently matured age groups suggests that female leopard seals ovulate for the first time at ages from 2 to 7 years, as indicated by the cumulative graph of maturity (Fig. 3). The median age of sexual maturity may be 5·1 years in this species.

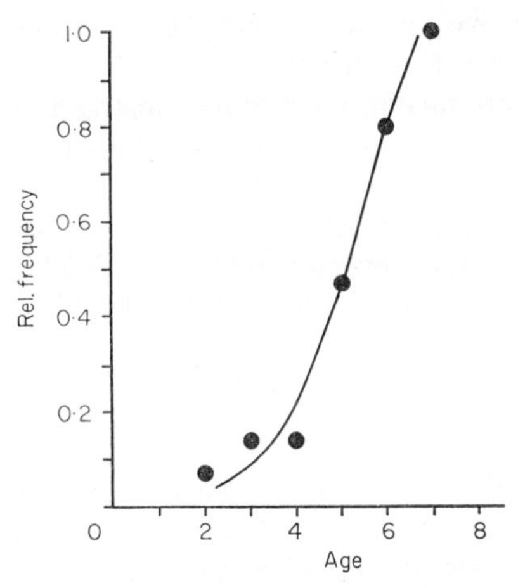

Fig. 3. Sexual maturity of female leopard seals.

F. Fertility

Twinning was not observed, and it seems safe to use the rate of pregnancies as a measure of fertility for the leopard seal. Among the dissected seals thirty-one were mature females, nineteen of which were pregnant. This suggests a pregnancy rate of 0·61. The data indicate an increasing fertility with age in the maturing age groups. Evidence was found in the reproductive organs of five mature seals which were from 3 to 6 years old at capture, that they had not conceived at their last ovulation. Failure of conception was also indicated in one 15-year-old seal, and six seals which were from 8 to 15 years old when caught had obviously aborted.

VI. Ross Seals

Scattered Ross seals were captured from 22 September to 31 October. The blubber thickness averaged 56 mm and showed no discernible increase or decrease during this period. The thickest layer (66 mm) was found in an 8-year-old male caught on 25 October. One foetus found on 23 September was 101 cm long, but six measurements which were recorded from 3 to 29 October suggest a growth from about 90 cm to about 100 cm during October. Mature follicles were not found, and none of the mature males captured up to 31 October was producing sperm. Few as they are, these observations suggest that breeding takes place in November, and that pups may be 105 cm long or even longer at birth.

Age determinations for twelve seals range from 2 to 12 years. Body lengths of the other three seals indicate that two males had ages within this range, whereas one female was probably older.

Of seven foetuses five were males, and the sex ratio of subadult and adult seals was seven males to eight females.

Although sperm production was not demonstrated, measurements of the reproductive organs suggest that male Ross seals become sexually mature when 3–4 years old.

All females had attained maturity, and the youngest which was caught at an age of nearly 3 years was pregnant and had ovulated for the first time when 2 years old. Ages at first ovulation could be assigned to seven seals, and the distribution is:

Age in years at first ovulation	2	3	4	5	6	7
Number of seals	3	1	1	1	0	1

It must be stressed, however, that it has been assumed from very limited evidence that *Corpora albicantia* are retained for a sufficient number of years.

One 6-year-old female had probably failed to conceive at the last breeding season, but all the other seven females were pregnant. A pregnancy rate of 0·88 can therefore be tentatively suggested.

References

Laws, R. M. (1962). Age determination of pinnipeds with special reference to growth layers in the teeth. *Z. Saugetierk.* 27, No. 3, 129–46.

Øritsland, T. (1964). Klappmysshunnens forplantningsbiologi [The breeding biology of female hooded seals]. *Fiskets Gang*, Vol. 50, No. 1, pp. 5–19. *Fisken Hav.*, 1964, No. 1, pp. 1–15. [English summary.]

Øritsland, T. (1967). Norwegian seal research. *Coun. Meet. int. Coun. Explor. Sea*, 1967, No. N:6, pp. 1–15. [Mimeo.]

Population Densities of Seals in the Weddell Sea, Antarctica, in 1968

D. B. SINIFF, D. R. CLINE AND A. W. ERICKSON
Department of Ecology and Behavioral Biology, University of Minnesota, Minneapolis, Minnesota, U.S.A.

I. Introduction

The Weddell Sea has not been penetrated to any great degree because of the heavy ice which persists there throughout the year. The International Weddell Sea Oceanographic Expedition (IWSOE) was initiated as a co-operative programme among several nations and scientific disciplines to explore this poorly known area. The 1968 cruise of the United States Coast Guard Cutter *Glacier* constituted part of this effort, and this paper reports on a seal census which was carried out during the cruise.

Reported observations on seal populations of the Weddell Sea are few. In his account of the 1903 cruise of the *Scotia*, Rudmose Brown (1913) discussed the species of seals encountered in the Weddell Sea, and their relative abundance. He also summarized the records of earlier cruises by the vessels *Discovery*, *Balaena* and *Challenger* in the Weddell Sea and adjoining waters. During the voyages of the *Scotia* the Weddell seal (*Leptonychotes weddelli*) was the commonest species encountered near the South Orkney Islands and off Coats Land. The crabeater seal (*Lobodon carcinophagus*) was described as "not uncommon" and the leopard seal (*Hydrurga leptonyx*) "without being common, was frequently seen". The Ross seal (*Omnatophoca rossi*) was described as "rarely seen". Most earlier papers refer to the population levels of Antarctic seals in the same subjective manner.

The Ross seal has been observed so infrequently that in 1940 Bertram was able to summarize all the records and report that less than fifty had been seen prior to that year. So far as we know, however, no comparable summary had been made for the subsequent period.

Gross estimates of seal numbers for Antarctica in general have been made by Scheffer (1958) and Laws (1964), while Laws (1953) gave similar estimates for the Falkland Islands and Dependencies, but these were for the most part subjective and were not based on any concerted census effort. The first attempt at a truly quantitative census of Antarctic seals was undertaken by Eklund and Atwood (1962) from ice-breakers moving through pack ice. A number of previous counts of seals in pack ice had been performed, but this was the first time that sampling was done in a manner permitting calculations to estimate density. The census methods used in the present study were similar to those described by Eklund and Atwood (1962) and Eklund (1964).

II. Shipboard Census

Counts were conducted from the ship's "flying bridge" 53 ft (16 m) above the waterline. Except in a few instances when seals were scarce,, two project biologists participated in the census. All seals seen within $\frac{1}{8}$ statute mile (200 m) on either side of the ship's track were counted, as were penguins, flying birds and whales, although only seals are considered in this paper. The $\frac{1}{4}$ mile wide census strip was chosen because of the difficulty of identifying species and the higher probability of not seeing animals at greater distances. Although we were equipped with 7×50 binoculars, positive species identification of an animal sleeping with its back toward the observer was usually impossible. Generally, however, noise from the passing ship was sufficient to elicit some reaction from seals within the census strip, and if they moved identification was usually possible because of readily definable behavioural characteristics. Seals within the census strip which could not be identified were tallied as unknowns and their numbers apportioned later according to the ratio of known animals.

In an effort to measure possible diurnal variations in the activity of seals in pack ice, counts were made during four different two-hour periods: 2400–0200, 0600–0800, 1200–1400 and 1800–2000. Effort was made to obtain an adequate number of counts during each sampling period. We were unable to count consistently within these time periods, however, because of the ship's schedule and incompatibility with other field projects (see Cline *et al.*, 1969). Moreover, changes in the 24-hour light regime with the approach of winter made 2400–0200 censuses impossible by the end of February, and the ship was usually stopped at midday for oceanographic work which interfered with the 1200–1400 count. Consequently, census counts during these two periods are poorly represented in the data.

Since no range-finder was available, a sighting board was constructed to delimit the transect width (Fig. 1). By aiming the top edge of the board at the horizon and then sighting along the angle line, the outer boundaries of the transects could be determined. Difficulties arose when animals were located near the outer limits of the transects, and in such instances several sightings were taken before deciding whether or not to include the animals in the census.

The ship's position was determined hourly by a navigational system which utilized a polar-orbiting satellite. The distance travelled during a sampling period was computed using these satellite-determined fixes. At times when hourly position data from the satellite were not available, estimates of distance travelled were obtained using the ship's average speed and time under way.

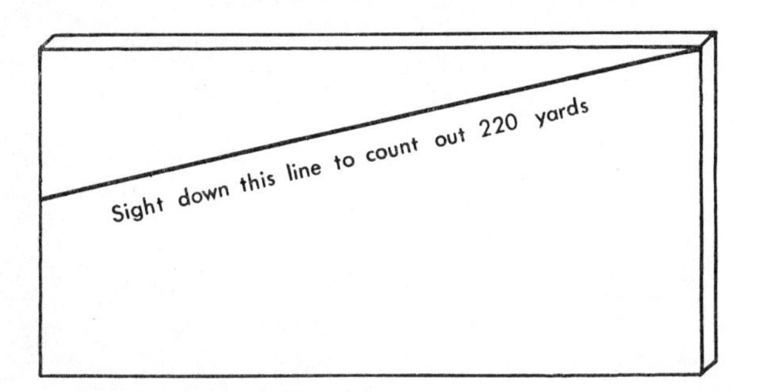

FIG. 1. Range-finding board used to determine transect width for shipboard censuses during the 1968 IWSOE

Because of the erratic path of the vessel through pack ice, however, the distance travelled during a census period was probably underestimated.

Basic environmental data such as air temperature, wind velocity and cloud cover were also recorded hourly by the *Glacier*'s meteorological section, in support of all the scientific programmes. Other data concerned with primary productivity and physical oceanography were collected at the oceanographic stations. When times of censuses coincided with these other measures of the marine environment, attempts were made to determine whether any of them was correlated with seal abundance. However, not all census data were included in these analyses, since the census counts and the oceanographic stations were not always coincident.

III. Aerial Census

Originally it had been planned to depend primarily on the ship's helicopters to accomplish the seal censuses. However, limited visibility and low cloud ceilings prevailed during the entire trip and drastically curtailed flying. Also, limitations of the navigational gear on board the helicopters and the ship precluded flights beyond view of the vessel (usually about 10 miles (16 km)). Hence, only seven useful census flights were accomplished during the cruise.

Census flights were made at an altitude of 300 ft (90 m) and because of the increased visibility at the higher altitude the transect width was increased to $\frac{1}{4}$ statute mile (400 m) on each side of the flight line. A sighting board similar

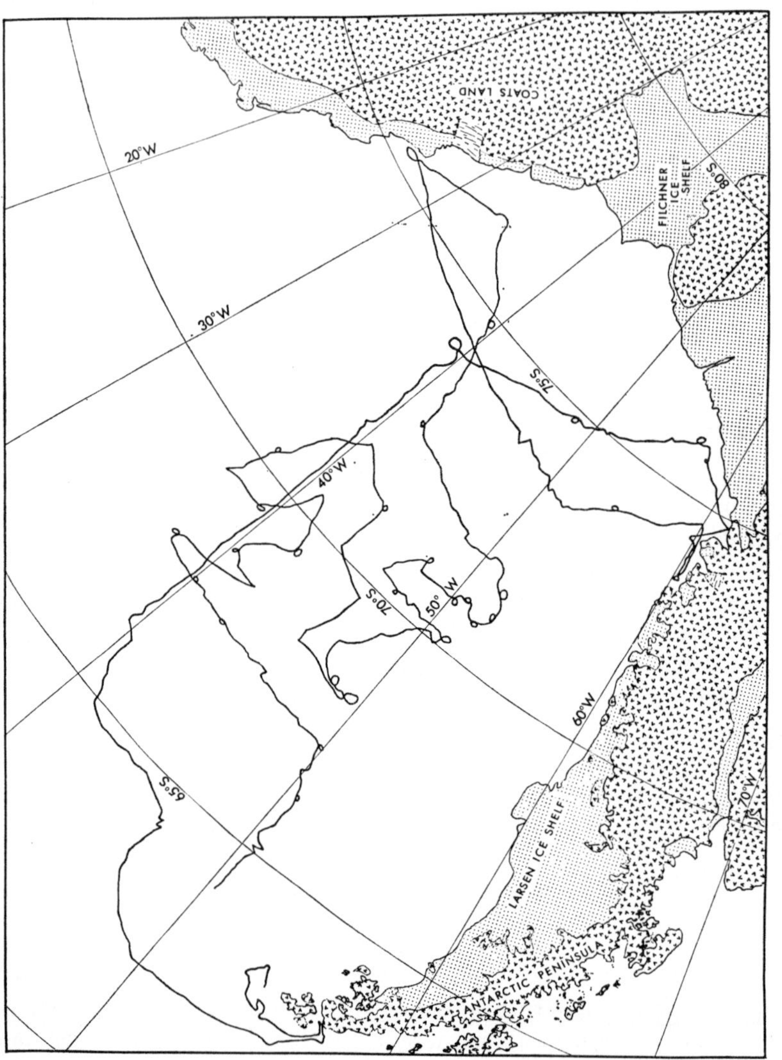

FIG. 2. Track of the USCGC *Glacier* during the 1968 IWSOE.

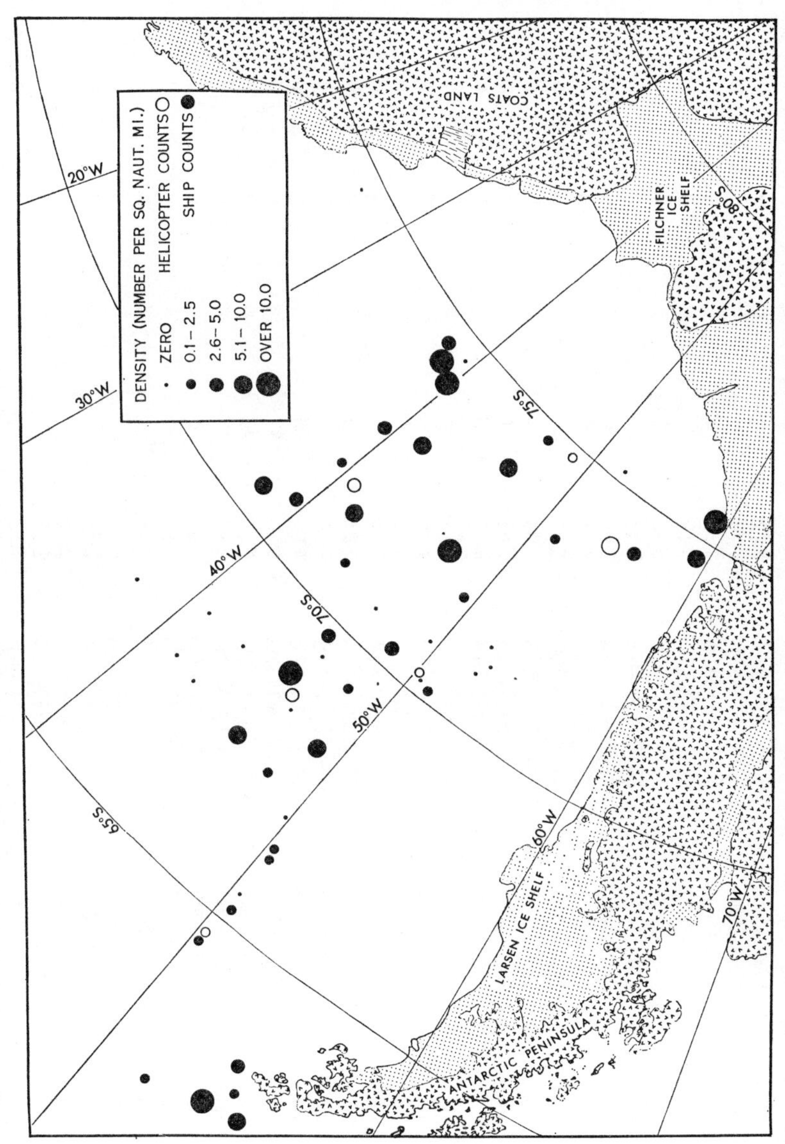

FIG. 3. Observed crabeater seal densities obtained from shipboard and helicopter census counts during the 1968 IWSOE.

TABLE 1

Basic Seal Census Data Obtained during the 1968 IWSOE Cruise of the USCGC Glacier

Shipboard Counts

Date	Time	Position	*Sq. NM censused*	*Number of seals counted* Crabeater	Weddell	Leopard	Ross	*Total*
30 Jan. '68	1300–1500	62–57S/54–07W	3·58	18	0	0	0	18
30 Jan. '68	1800–2000	62–54S/54–53W	3·84	4	6	1	0	11
1 Feb. '68	0600–0800	62–39S/55–41W	3·58	19	1	3	0	23
1 Feb. '68	1200–1400	62–22S/54–03W	3·19	58	0	5	1	64
1 Feb. '68	1800–2000	62–09S/52–19W	5·32	13	0	1	0	14
4 Feb. '68	1200–1400	70–53S/39–46W	4·99	16	0	0	0	16
4 Feb '68	1800–2000	71–50S/39–40W	2·93	6	0	0	0	6
5 Feb. '68	0000–0200	72–42S/39–44W	4·34	22	0	0	0	22
5 Feb. '68	1200–1400	74–10S/39–38W	1·11	106	0	0	0	106
6 Feb. '68	1200–1400	74–08S/39–23W	·43	7	0	0	0	7
7 Feb. '68	1800–2000	74–51S/48–16W	2·63	1	2	0	0	3
8 Feb. '68	1800–2000	75–12S/52–30W	4·15	0	4	0	0	4
10 Feb. '68	0600–0800	75–21S/59–25W	4·71	103	0	0	0	103
11 Feb. '68	1800–2000	74–43S/59–45W	3·86	38	0	0	0	38
12 Feb. '68	0000–0200	74–09S/56–00W	3·52	12	4	0	0	16
13 Feb. '68	0000–0200	73–33S/50–55W	5·41	4	0	0	0	4
13 Feb. '68	1200–1400	73–52S/46–12W	5·21	20	2	0	0	22
14 Feb. '68	0000–0200	74–37S/37–45W	4·84	13	2	2	0	17
17 Feb. '68	1800–2000	74–37S/39–37W	4·73	0	2	0	0	2
18 Feb. '68	0600–0800	73–07S/42–37W	5·10	39	0	0	0	39
19 Feb. '68	0600–0800	72–06S/47–11W	5·64	80	0	0	0	80
19 Feb. '68	1800–2000	71–47S/49–25W	5·88	1	0	0	0	1
20 Feb. '68	1800–2000	71–28S/52–46W	·24	0	0	0	0	0
21 Feb. '68	0600–0700	71–09S/52–54W	·56	0	0	0	0	0
21 Feb. '68	1800–2000	70–57S/52–37W	·15	0	0	0	0	0
23 Feb. '68	0600–0800	70–57S/49–36W	4·34	0	0	0	0	0
24 Feb. '68	1800–2000	70–29S/46–15W	2·54	0	0	0	0	0
25 Feb. '68	0600–0845	70–19S/48–37W	2·71	8	0	0	0	8
25 Feb. '68	1800–1930	70–15S/50–10W	1·95	0	0	0	0	0
26 Feb. '68	0600–0800	70–10S/51–06W	·85	1	0	0	0	1
[illegible]	[illegible]	69–07S/48–05W	3·93	3	1	0	0	4

[illegible]	[illegible]	68–51S/45–38W	1·74	87	0	0	0	87
1 Mar. '68	1745–1930	69–18S/46–16W	4·45	0	0	0	0	0
2 Mar. '68	0600–0800	69–46S/45–50W	4·41	17	1	0	0	18
2 Mar. '68	1800–2000	70–40S/43–42W	6·49	11	0	0	0	11
3 Mar. '68	0600–0800	71–28S/42–08W	4·99	28	0	0	0	28
4 Mar. '68	0600–0800	70–35S/38–07W	4·97	36	0	1	0	37
7 Mar. '68	0600–0700	68–41S/41–02W	2·65	0	0	0	0	0
7 Mar. '68	1200–1400	68–24S/43–03W	4·78	0	0	0	0	0
8 Mar. '68	0600–0700	67–58S/38–22W	2·91	0	0	0	0	0
8 Mar. '68	1400–1500	67–34S/41–30W	2·50	0	0	0	0	0
8 Mar. '68	1800–1900	67–32S/43–36W	1·09	0	0	0	0	0
9 Mar. '68	0600–0800	67–26S/46–28W	2·61	18	0	0	0	18
10 Mar. '68	0600–0800	67–21S/48–02W	4·06	6	0	0	0	6
11 Mar. '68	0600–0800	66–50S/50–00W	2·89	0	0	0	0	0
11 Mar. '68	1700–1900	66–24S/50–32W	2·95	2	0	0	0	2
12 Mar. '68	0600–0800	66–12S/50–53W	·87	2	0	0	0	2
12 Mar. '68	1700–1900	65–26S/50–19W	5·54	0	0	0	0	0
13 Mar. '68	0600–0800	65–14S/50–47W	3·26	3	0	0	0	3
13 Mar. '68	1700–1900	64–30S/50–29W	3·04	1	0	0	0	1
15 Mar. '68	0800–1000	64–06S/50–20W	4·34	67	0	2	0	69
		Totals	181·06	879	25	15	1	920
Average seals per sq. nm				4·85	·14			

Helicopter Counts

7 Feb. '68	2141–2155	74–56S/48–41W	11·90	10	40	0	0	50
12 Feb. '68	0920–0954	74–03S/54–38W	9·16	58	4	0	0	62
25 Feb. '68	1258–1316	70–14S/50–09W	5·69	11	3	0	0	14
27 Feb. '68	1542–1613	68–38S/47–20W	15·02	57	3	0	0	60
3 Mar. '68	1130–1148	71–48S/40–41W	10·16	39	0	0	0	39
13 Mar. '68	1321–1400	64–46S/50–33W	13·16	18	1	0	0	19
14 Mar. '68	0850–1000	64–06S/50–20W	29·52	67	6	0	0	73
		Totals	94·61	260	57	0	0	317
Average seals per sq. nm				2·75	·60			

to the one shown in Fig. 1 was used to define the transect zone. During each census flight the aircraft was followed by the ship's radar and a ground track relative to the ship was obtained. These ground tracks were measured to give the total linear distance of each census flight. The total area examined was then computed by simply multiplying the length of a census transect by its width.

IV. Results

Many factors contributed to the erratic track of *Glacier* in the Weddell Sea (Fig. 2). The small loops along the track represent locations where the ship manoeuvred for oceanographic or benthic sampling, and many of the abrupt turn-abouts indicate occasions when impenetrable pack ice was encountered. The census data obtained along this track (Table 1) indicated that the crabeater seal (*Lobodon carcinophagus*) predominated in the Weddell Sea seal population. Figure 3 shows the observed densities of crabeaters at the various census locations. It is evident that the greatest concentrations were observed at the periphery of the heavy pack ice and around the tip of the Antarctic Peninsula. The species had an aggregated distribution. Non-randomness in the dispersal of crabeaters was indicated by comparing the distribution data to the Poisson series and the negative binomial (Table 2) as suggested by Andrewartha (1961). This analysis indicates that the negative binomial distribution predicts the observed pattern.

TABLE 2

The Distribution of Densities compared to Poisson Series and Negative Binomial

Density (crabeaters/NM²)	*Number of census periods*	*Poisson*	*Expected number negative binomial*
0–2	31	10·7	31·0
2–4	10	18·6	9·9
4–6	7	15·9	5·6
6–8	4	9·1	3·7
8–10	1	3·9	2·5
10–12	0		
12–14	0		
14–16	2		
16–18	1	1·8 (10–12 to Over 22)	7·3 (10–12 to Over 22)
18–20	1		
20–22	1		
Over 22	1		
Totals	60	60·0	60·0

During this study only crabeater seals occurred in sufficient abundance to yield reliable information on group size. The number of crabeater seals per group was determined for all animals sighted within the $\frac{1}{4}$ mile (400 m) wide census strip. We roughly defined a group as consisting of all animals within close proximity to each other. When the ice floes were small (20–40 yds :18–37 m square) there was little problem, and all individuals on given floes were considered to be of the same group. However, when floes were larger, judgement was required and only seals within approximately 20 yds (18 m) of each other were considered to belong to the same group. This seldom presented a problem, however, as the animals were usually within 6–8 ft (1·8–2·5 m) of each other.

The frequency with which different-sized groups of crabeater seals were observed is presented in Table 3, which also shows that a mean of 2·2 seals

TABLE 3

Observed Crabeater Group Sizes Obtained during the 1968 IWSOE

Number of crabeater/group	*Observed frequency*	*% of total*
1	191	49·0
2	90	23·1
3	55	14·1
4	24	6·2
5	12	3·1
6	6	1·5
7	3	0·8
8	4	1·0
9	0	0·0
10	0	0·0
11	0	0·0
12	3	0·8
13	0	0·0
14	1	0·2
15	0	0·0
16	1	0·2
Totals	390	100·0
Average Average group size = 2·2		

occurred in each group. Kenyon (1967) gave data on group size from counts obtained during a cruise around the Antarctic Continent in January, February and March 1967. From this we computed an average of 1·3 seals per group for the crabeater, indicating less of a clumping tendency than in our data. We did not, however, observe densities even approaching those recorded by

Solyanik (1964), who stated, ". . . during the fall great permanent aggregations of crabeaters (up to 3000 specimens in the field of vision) assembled on the northern edge of the pack ice". The largest aggregation that we observed was a group of twenty-nine individuals on a floe outside the census strip.

Weddell seals (*Leptonychotes weddelli*) were sighted occasionally, but were only once the predominant species during a particular period. Weddells were typically found in the pack ice nearer the continent (Fig. 4) than were crabeaters. This distributional pattern has been observed many times before and is known to be typical of the species (Scheffer, 1958). Nevertheless, a few Weddells were found toward the centre of the Weddell Sea. We gained the general impression whenever *Glacier* attempted to penetrate the heavy pack ice off the Larsen ice shelf that this area was fairly devoid of all seal species including Weddells. However, complete penetration into this region is necessary to substantiate this.

Leopard and Ross seals were only infrequently encountered (Fig. 5). Density estimates for leopard seals show that this species was encountered in greatest numbers north and east of the Antarctic Peninsula. Only one Ross seal was sighted during the entire cruise.

Tests of several of the factors believed to have influenced the observed distribution of seals were made. In particular, the relationship between seal abundance, depth of the euphotic zone and chlorophyll concentration was considered. The density measurements for all seals were pooled and representative seal densities for a 60-mile radius of the euphotic zone and chlorophyll samples were obtained. Log transformations were made on these data before regression analysis was carried out. When the contribution of each independent variable was considered, chlorophyll abundance was determined as the most important (Table 4). Figure 6 shows a graphic display of this relationship and the least square regression line between chlorophyll abundance and seal density.

The crabeater was the only species present during enough of the census periods to provide sufficient data for examining diurnal variation. A one-way classification analysis of variance was carried out, testing between the four observation periods. A significant difference was indicated between the time period means (Table 5). Duncan's multiple range test (Kramer, 1956) was used to determine where the difference between means existed. The mean for the time period 1800–2000 was different from the means of time periods of 2400–0200 and 0600–0800 (Fig. 7). There was no significant difference (0·05 probability level) between the means of the time periods of 2400–0200, 0600–0800 and 1200–1400. These data indicated that the peak numbers of crabeaters were present at midday and that the lowest densities were noted during late afternoon and evening. These observations support to some degree

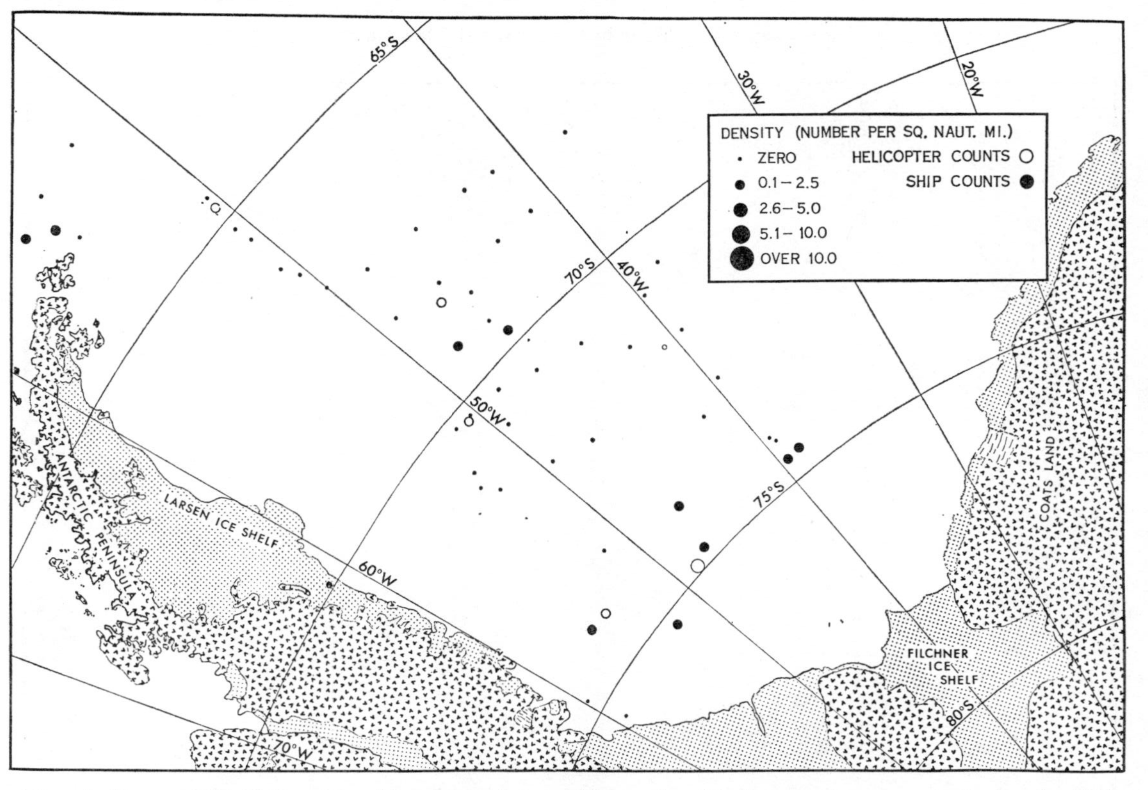

FIG. 4. Observed Weddell seal densities obtained from shipboard and helicopter census counts during the 1968 IWSOE.

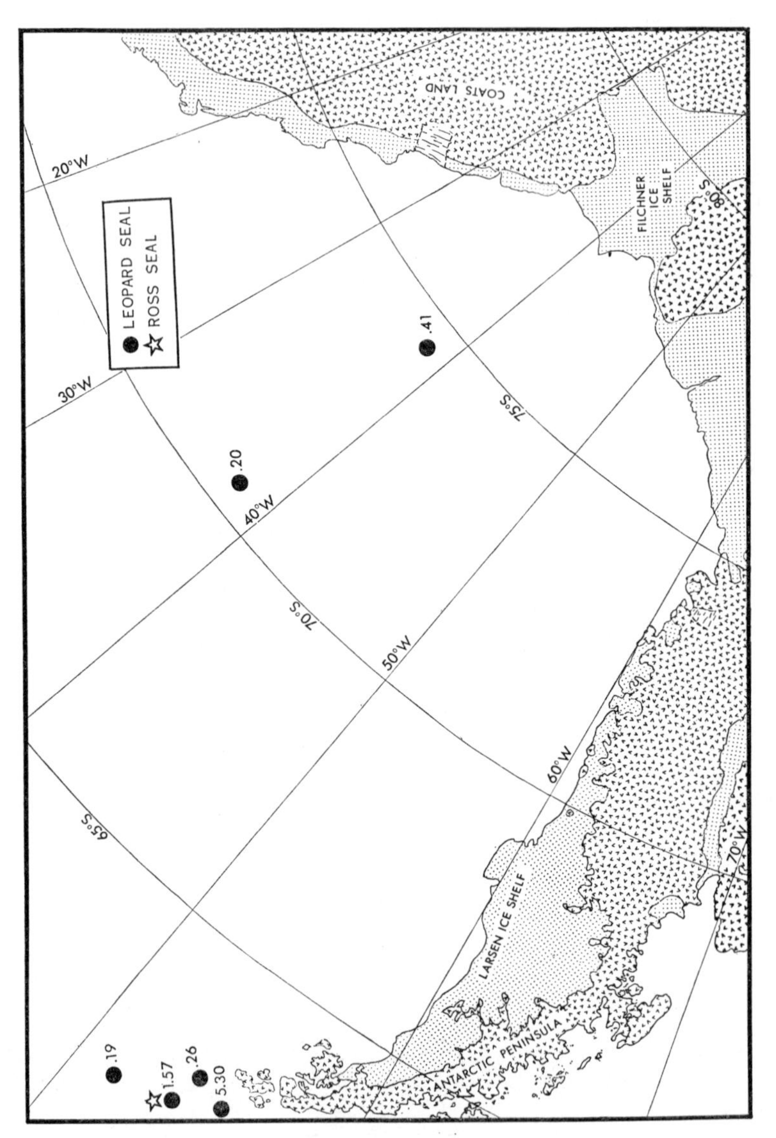

FIG. 5. Observed leopard seal densities and the Ross seal sighting as obtained during the 1968 IWSOE.

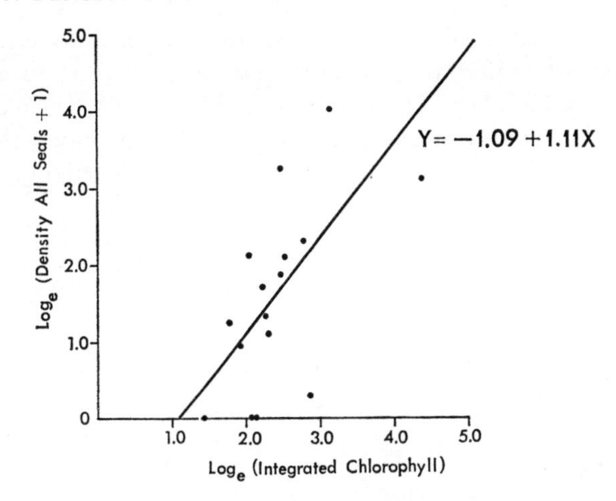

FIG. 6. Regression analysis showing relationship between seal density and chlorophyll *a* (mg/m^3).

TABLE 4

Regression Analysis of the Log (Density Total Seals) verses Log (Depth of Euphotic Zone) and Log (Integrated Chlorophyll)

Source	*d.f.*	*Sum of squares*	*Mean square*	*F*
Total	15	21·3960		
Regression	2	8·4935	4·2468	3·971*
Deviations from reg.	13	12·9025	1·0694	

Examining the Contribution of each Independent Variable with others held Constant

	Depth euphotic zone	*Integrated chlorophyll*
Regression coefficient	b_1 = 0·0356	b_2 = 1·1194
Variance of b_1	s_{b_1} = 0·2430	a_{b_2} = 0·3993
Student's computed "t" value	t_{b_1} = 0·1463	t_{b_2} = 2·8037*

* Significant 5% level.

the findings of Smith (1965), who reported peak abundances of Weddell seals on the ice between the hours of 1300 and 1800. However, he observed the lowest densities between midnight and 5 a.m. which differs from our observations. Our data, however, are at best indicative of possible diurnal patterns, since the data were derived from scattered seal populations and the observations were taken under many varying environmental situations.

Since the abundance of seals varied with time periods, it was necessary to consider these differences when relating population density to measures of the physical environment. The time perods of 2400–0200, 0600–0800 and 1200–1400 were not statistically different (Fig. 7). Therefore, these census periods were pooled and regression analysis was carried out to test for

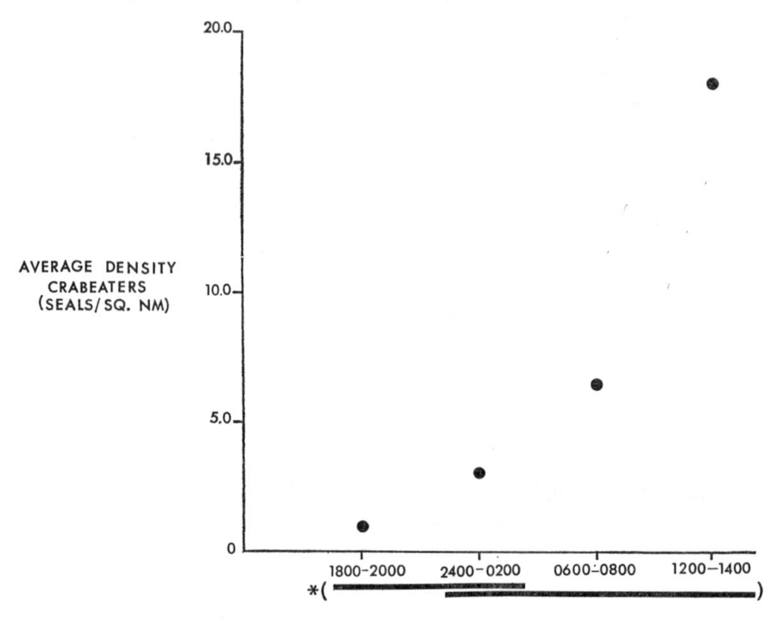

FIG. 7. Average crabeater seal density in relation to time of day.

TABLE 5

Analysis of Variance Testing for Differences in Density of Crabeater Seals obtained at Different Times of the Day (2400–0200, 0600–0800, 1200–1400 and 1800–2000)

Source	*d.f.*	*s.s.*	*m.s.*	*F*
Among	3	16·465	5·488	5·297*
Within	48	49·742	1·036	
Total	51	66·207		

* Significant 5% level.

possible relationships between the physical measurements of ice density, air temperature, cloud cover, wind velocity and abundance of crabeaters. This analysis indicated that ice density was the only parameter to show a relationship with seal density (Table 6). This relationship was inverse in nature,

TABLE 6

Regression Analysis of the Log (Density of Crabeater Seals 1·0) versus Ice Conditions, Cloud Cover, Air Temperature and Wind Velocity

Source	*d.f.*	*Sum of squares*	*Mean square*	*F*
Total	28	34·3497		
Regression	4	13·0506	3·2627	3·76*
Deviations from reg.	24	21·2991	0·8875	

Examining the Contribution of each Independent Variable with others held Constant

	Ice concentration	*Cloud cover*	*Air temperature*	*Wind velocity*
Regression coefficient	$b_1 = -0{\cdot}2615$	$b_2 = 0{\cdot}0851$	$b_3 = -0{\cdot}0350$	$b_4 = -0{\cdot}0328$
Variance of b_1	$s_{b_1} = 0{\cdot}0722$	$s_{b_2} = 0{\cdot}0923$	$s_{b_3} = 0{\cdot}0400$	$s_{b_4} = 0{\cdot}0330$
Student's computed "t" value	$t_{b_1} = -3{\cdot}621$*	$t_{b_2} = 0{\cdot}922$	$t_{b_3} = -0{\cdot}875$	$t_{b_4} = -0{\cdot}994$

* Significant 5% level.

so that increasing ice densities corresponded with decreases in crabeater abundance. These results are similar to those obtained by Eklund and Atwood (1962). A plot of the relationship between ice concentration and crabeater abundance is shown in Fig. 8.

V. Discussion

The range of average seal densities encountered during this cruise was somewhat lower than those reported by Eklund and Atwood (1962), but higher than recorded by Øritsland (1967: unpublished). In some areas crab-eater densities were very high (95·7/nm²:31·9/km²), but the average of 4·85 crabeaters/nm² (1·62/km²) is much less because many areas we entered were essentially devoid of seals. The average density figure is somewhat mis-leading because of the aggregated pattern of seals in the Weddell Sea. The influence of the diurnal activity cycle must also be considered. The suggested activity pattern implies that had all the counts been made around midday considerably higher densities would have been recorded.

The results of this census indicate that pack ice and seal distribution are related to the primary productivity of an area which in turn is undoubtedly related to physical, chemical and biological factors. The relationship between seal abundance and ice concentration may not be one of direct cause and effect, since primary productivity and the physical and chemical properties of the sea may also be relevant. The abundance of whales, penguins and flying birds is likewise undoubtedly influenced by many interacting factors and not merely dependent on a single environmental influence. For this reason, population studies of Antarctic species must form part only of an integrated multi-disciplinary research effort directed towards a complete understanding of the entire ecosystem.

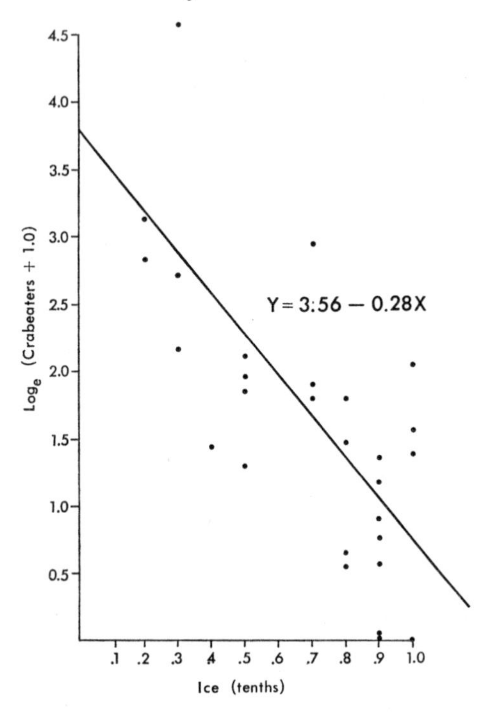

FIG. 8. Regression analysis showing relationship between seal density and ice concentration.

It has been suggested that Ross seals are most abundant in areas of concentrated pack ice (Laws, 1953; Eklund and Atwood, 1962). Our observations in the Weddell Sea do not support this hypothesis. During the last three weeks of the cruise *Glacier* repeatedly penetrated heavy pack ice, returning to more open water when cruise speeds fell below one knot. During these penetrations it was obvious that seal densities decreased with increasing ice concentration, and no Ross seals were sighted. These observations suggest that the Weddell Sea is not a stronghold for *Ommatophoca*: on the contrary it appears to be extremely rare there. Only one Ross seal was positively identified during the entire cruise and this was near the tip of the Antarctic Peninsula (Fig. 4). Some Ross seals may have been included in the "unknown" category, but if so the number must have been very small, since none of this species was positively identified once we left the vicinity of the Antarctic Peninsula.

Another possible variant which could have affected the census results was the sighting board used to judge distance. Environmental and observer difference may have caused variations in the width of our census strip. However, this is unlikely to have introduced a significant error since most seals were either clearly within or outside the census strip and we have no reason to believe that there was consistent over- or underestimation.

The relationship between the number of seals visible and the actual number present was unknown. Data from censuses at different times of the day indicate that the number of crabeaters hauled out is greatest around mid-day, but what proportion of the total population this may be requires further study. Basic behavioural observations such as this are essential if more precise census data are to be obtained.

Enough flights were made to show that counting seals is entirely feasible from the air and to indicate that this method is to be preferred to shipboard counts in future surveys, since aerial counts appear to be less biased. The area covered can be delimited more accurately, the animals can be readily observed, and a markedly greater area counted per unit of effort. Further studies comparing the accuracy of the two methods are planned.

These are some of the problems we encountered during the study. Certainly, in order to understand more fully the complete Antarctic ecosystem, studies on behavioural patterns, food selection, movement and migration, intra- and interspecific competition and other basic biological subjects are needed, and these would make census data more meaningful. When more of the data from the 1968 IWSOE have been tabulated we anticipate that it may be possible to establish further correlations between census counts of flying birds, penguins and seals and the other biologial and physical measurements which were made. It is hoped that such analyses may indicate additional factors influencing both the distribution and abundance of these animal populations.

Acknowledgements

Many people contributed to the success of this venture. Dr Sayed Z. El-Sayed of Texas A and M University provided the data on primary productivity. Captain Dawson and the crew of USCGC *Glacier* provided the logistic support and the physical measurements of the environment.

Special thanks are extended to members of *Glacier*'s Navy flight crew attachment and to Mr Robert Dale, NSF, 1968 IWSOE Scientific Co-ordinator. Support for this endeavour was provided by the National Science Foundation Grant GA-1325 from the Office of Antarctic Biology.

References

Andrewartha, H. G. (1961). "Introduction to the Study of Animal Populations", Univ. Chicago Press, Chicago. 281 pp.

Bertram, G. C. L. (1940). The biology of the Weddell and Crabeater seals. *Scient. Rep. Br. Graham Ld. Exped.* 1 (1), 84–120.

Cline, D. R., Siniff, D. B. and Erickson, A. W. (1969). Immobilizing and collecting blood from the Antarctic seals. *J. Wildl. Mgt.* 33 (1), 138–44.

Eklund, C. R. (1964). Population studies of Antarctic seals and birds. *In* "Biologie Antarctique" (R. Carrick, M. Holdgate and J. Prévost, eds) Hermann, Paris.

Eklund, C. R. and Atwood, E. L. (1962). A population study of Antarctic seals. *J. Mammal.* 43 (2), 229–38.

Kenyon, K. W. (1967). Antarctic seal observations, February 1967. Unpublished reports, U.S. Fish and Wildlife Service, Sandpoint Naval Station, Seattle, Washington. 17 pp.

Kramer, C. Y. (1956). Extension of multiple range tests to group means with unequal numbers of replication. *Biometrics* 12, 307–10.

Laws, R. M. (1953). The seals of the Falkland Islands and Dependencies. *Oryx* 2 (2), 87–97.

Laws, R. M. (1964). Comparative biology of Antarctic seals. *In* "Biologie Antarctique" (R. Carrick, M. Holdgate and J. Pérvost, eds). Hermann, Paris.

Øritsland, T. (1967). Unpublished summary of a report on Norwegian experimental sealing in Antarctic waters in 1964.

Rudmose Brown, R. N. (1913). The seals of the Weddell Sea: notes on their habits and distribution. Scottish Natl. Antarctic Exped., Sci. Res. Voyage "Scotia", Edinburgh, 1902–4 4 (Zool), 181–98.

Scheffer, Victor B. (1958). "Seals, Sea Lions and Walruses", Stanford Univ. Press and Oxford Univ. Press. 179 pp.

Smith, M. S. R. (1965). Seasonal movements of the Weddell seal in McMurdo Sound, Antarctica. *J. Wildl. Mgt.* 29 (3), 464–70.

Solyanik, G. A. (1964). Some information about the seals of the Antarctic. *Inf. Byull. sov. antarkt. Eksped.* 47, 54–59.

Census of Pinnipedia in the South Shetland Islands

ANELIO AGUAYO L.
Marine Biological Station, University of Chile, Chile

I. Introduction

A paper on our first pinnipede census in the South Shetland Islands was presented to the SCAR Symposium on Antarctic Oceanography held in Santiago de Chile in September 1966 (Aguayo and Torres, 1967, 1968). At that time it was hoped to repeat this census in 1966–67 and 1967–68, but unfortunately only isolated and partial counts proved possible in these seasons. The present paper, while presenting the results obtained, is mainly concerned with the methods developed for such a census, in the hope that a common technique can be established and that future pinnipede censuses in the Antarctic islands can be carried out through the collaboration of several SCAR nations.

II. Method

The observations were made by the naked eye from a helicopter flying at an altitude of 30–40 m and a speed of 60 mph. When the weather conditions were favourable, all counts were repeated, the aircraft flying in circles around the animals. When the number of animals was too large for direct counting (200 specimens was the normal limit), a careful estimate of the size of each group was made. The date and time of the observations was recorded in every case. Only occasionally could males, females and/or pups be counted separately, so the observations refer essentially to the total number of animals of each species seen. However, males, females and pups could be distingushed in two of the species recorded, *Mirounga leonina* and *Arctocephalus tropicalis gazella*.

III. Discussion

The totals given in Table 1 are minima, that is to say there can be more animals than are recorded, but under no circumstances less. The estimated error is approximately 15–20%.

TABLE 1

Marine Mammals counted during the Census of the South Shetland Islands in the Twentieth Chilean Antarctic Expedition

Place	*Mirounga leonina*	*Lobodon carcinophagus*	*Leptonychotes weddelli*	*Hydrurga leptonyx*	*Unidentified*	*Arctocephalus tropicalis gazella*	*Whale*	*Total*
Smith Island			11–11	3–3				14–14
Low Island	133–133	17–17	121–131	4–4	8–8			283–293
Snow Island	3300–3600	40–40	90–100	6–6				3436–3746
Deception Island		5–5	19–19					24–24
Livingston Island	10239–11003	278–391	211–223	23–23	15–18	200–210	14–14	10980–11882
Greenwich Island	163–183	130–138	31–31	4–4	12–16		1–1	341–373
Robert Island 1st census	273–338	42–42	165–170	1–1	39–39			
2nd census	230–240	9–9	228–248	2–2				
Mean number	257–289	26–26	196–209	1–2	19–20			*499–546
Nelson Island	574–599	33–33	985–1085	6–6				1598–1723
King George Island	6940–7515	761–811	249–254	26–26	55–60			8031–8666
Bridgeman, O'Brien, Eadie, Aspland and Gibbs Islands and Narrow Islet			25–25		30–45			55–70
Elephant, Cornwallis and Clarence Islands	2156–2426	51–51	39–39			257–297	1–1	2504–2814
Total number of animals	23762–25748	1341–1512	1977–2127	73–74	139–167	457–507	16–16	27765–30151

* The mean value for Robert Island has been used in arriving at the total number.

Our direct-count method could be improved considerably if aerial photographs could be taken from the helicopter. Carrara (1954) and Rand (1959) used this last method, but from an aeroplane. Rand's census had an error of approximately 6% (8129 ± 500), and he was able to differentiate males from pups. Photography, especially in continuous strips, from an aeroplane is, however, much more expensive than a direct count and it is not always easy to identify different pinnipede species, unless the pictures are taken from an inconveniently low altitude. Aerial photography from a helicopter may prove the most convenient method, since it could readily be combined with a direct count, allows photographs to be taken only in the areas where they are required, and from a carefully selected altitude, and is also intermediate in cost. This method is therefore proposed for future pinnipede censuses in the Antarctic Islands.

References

Aguayo, A. and Torres, D. (1967). Observaciones sobre mamíferos marinos durante la Vigésima Comisión Antártica Chilena. Primer censo de pinipedios en las Islas Shetland del Sur. *Rev. Biol. Mar. Valparaiso* **XIII**, pp. 1–57.

Aguayo, A. and Torres, D. (1968). A first census of Pinnipedia in the South Shetland Islands, and other observations on marine mammals. *In* "Symposium on Antarctic Oceanography, Santiago, Chile, 13–16 September 1966. Scott Polar Research Institute, Cambridge, pp. 166–8.

Carrara, I. S. (1954). "Observaciones Sobre el Estado Actual de las Poblaciones de Pinnipedios de la Argentina." Ministerio de Educación. Universidad Nacional de Eva Perón. Facultad de Ciencias Veterinarias (Publicacion especial). 17 pp.

Rand, R. (1959). The Cape Fur Seal: Distribution, Abundance and Feeding Habits off the South Western Coast of the Cape Province. *Investl. Rep. Div. Fish. Un. S. Afr.* 34, 1–65. Cape Town.

Population Ecology of Antarctic Seals

CARLETON RAY
Department of Pathobiology, School of Hygiene and Public Health, The Johns Hopkins University, Baltimore, Maryland, U.S.A.

I. Introduction

Knowledge of numbers and population structure is basic to the understanding of any animal. For pagophilic seals, this has not been achieved, mostly because of insufficient census coverage and inadequate logistic capability within their pack-ice and marine habitats.

Seal censuses in the pack have been reviewed by Øritsland (1970). Counts nearer shore are reviewed by Laws (1953) and Mackintosh (1967). Attempts have occasionally been made to extrapolate total population numbers, but it is clear that counts to date are merely indications of relative abundance. None has been able to take into account the aquatic phase of these species' amphibious lives, and none has a baseline of physiological-ecological-behavioural data upon which to determine relative abundance of seals on the ice (where they may be counted) to those in the water (where they cannot).

For the Weddell seal baseline data are being made available through a wide variety of studies. Work in progress on population dynamics and dispersal will probably prove most useful of all (Stirling, 1967). It is now possible to predict proportionate numbers of Weddell seals on ice, through knowledge of thermoregulation (Ray and Smith, 1968) and behavioural rhythms (Smith, 1965), and to detect animals underwater during the pupping-courtship season by listening for their sounds. By a combination of such knowledge it is apparent that virtually all Weddell seals will be on ice at midday when the sun is strong and wind low, subsequent to all reproductive behaviour or during the moulting season.

This paper is not an attempt to calculate population. It presents data on an improved helicopter census method with clues to aerial and underwater identification of Antarctic lobodontines at a distance.

II. Methods

The work was done aboard the *Wind*-class ice-breaker *Burton Island* during late December 1965 and early January 1966. Aboard were two helicopters of which the Bell G2, with its excellent visibility, was almost exclusively used. The ship's route is shown in Fig. 1, with each of eighteen flights indicated. Sampling covered the western Ross Sea, mostly at locations where mixed shore and pack ice were encountered.

Locations for flights were chosen more or less at random when good ice

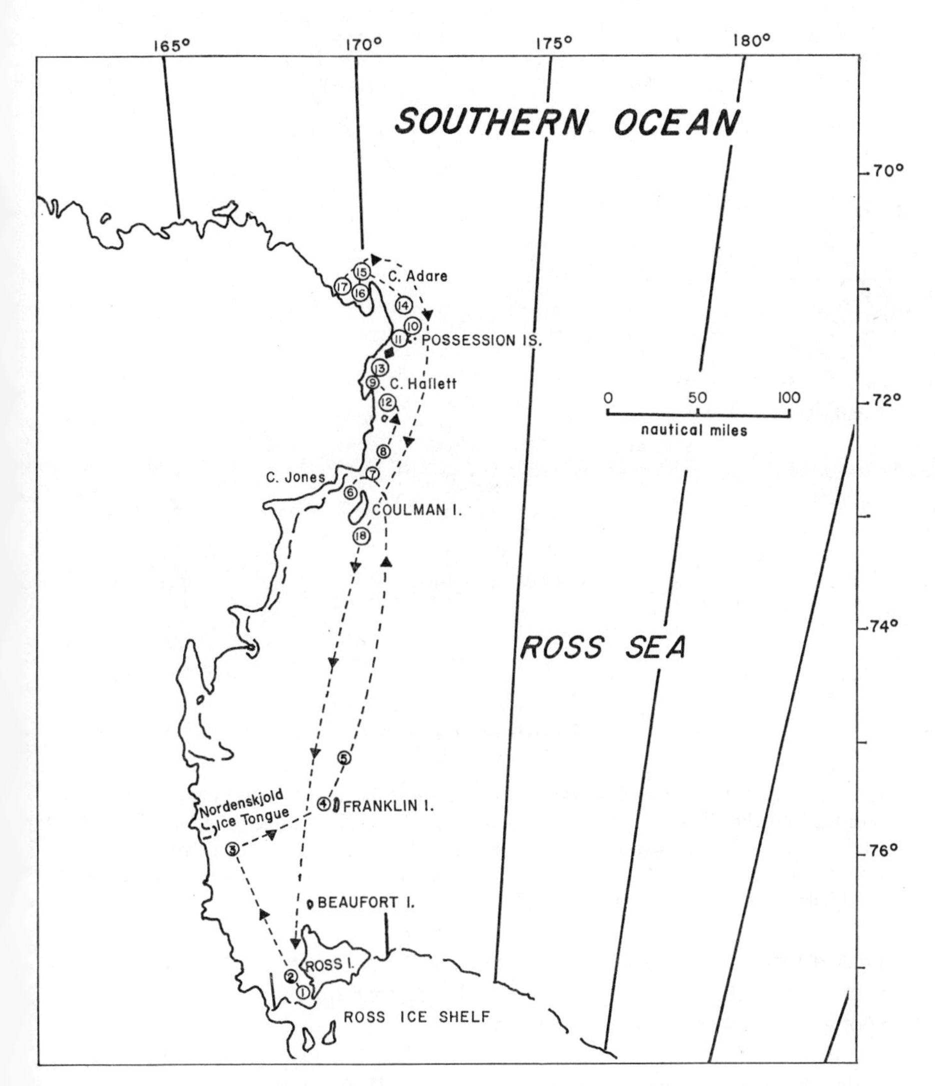

FIG. 1. Voyage of the ice-breaker *Burton Island* from 29 December 1965 through 13 January 1966. Helicopter census flights are indicated in circles and their exact locations are set out in Table I.

was encountered. The ship was stopped and motors and fathometer shut down so as to reduce underwater ambient sound. Times were synchronized between helicopter and ship and the flight was plotted on the ship's manoeuvring board. Figure 2 shows a typical flight. Coverage proved possible in a track 1000 m wide with the helicopter flying at 160 m altitude at 60 knots.

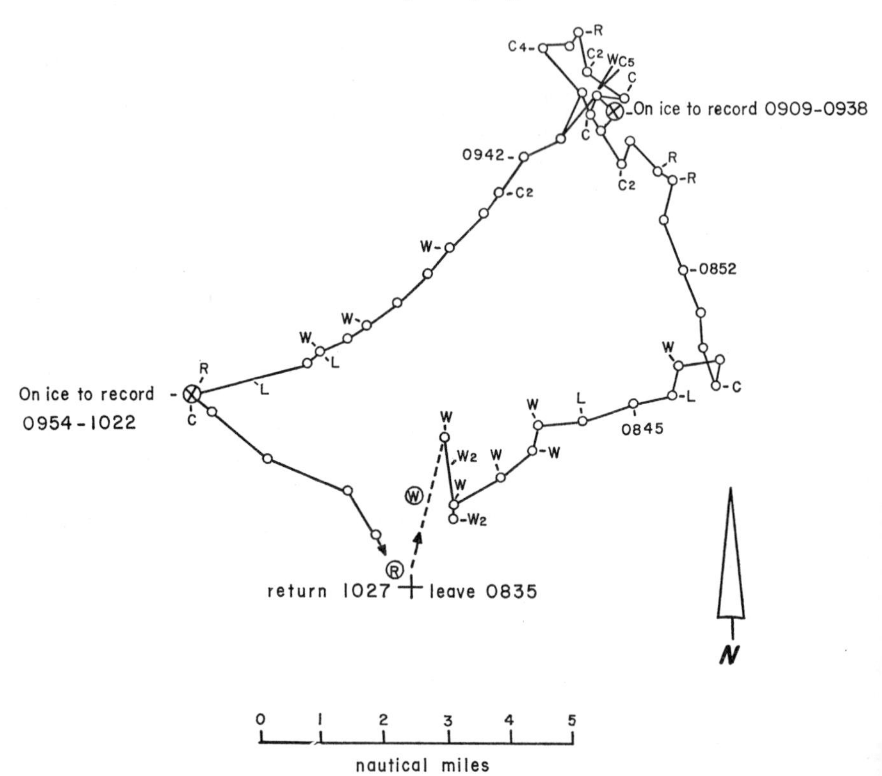

FIG. 2. Flight 15: a manoeuvring-board tracing. The large cross indicates the ship's position and the direction of flight is indicated. Minute intervals are indicated by small circles (some left out for clarity of the diagram). Positions of two tape recordings, made from floes, are indicated by the encircled crosses. Locations of seals are also indicated: W, Weddell; C, crabeater; L, leopard; R, Ross.

Descent from this height was made occasionally for positive identification of some seals. It was possible to plot, by noting times when each seal was spotted, the locations of all animals seen.

On almost all flights underwater recordings were made, usually among seals: there were twenty-three recordings in all. Recording equipment was a Nagra III B tape recorder with LC-50 (Atlantic Research) hydrophone and Woods Hole (Watkins) amplifier-preamplifier. Analysis playback was by means of a Crown (B 800 series) recorder and spectrograms were made with a Kay Electric Vibralyzer. The entire system was essentially flat from 50 to 10,000 cps.

Seal numbers per square nautical mile were calculated both from records of times of sightings and aircraft speed and from the manoeuvring board. A few manoeuvring-board plots were incomplete due to the difficulty of radar-tracking near headlands. We estimate missing not more than 10% of seals, as most of the ice covered was not heavily hummocked. A few trial shipboard counts proved much less reliable. The aloft conning tower is only 20 m from the water and even in lightly hummocked ice seals were obscured.

III. Results

A. Distance Identification of Adult Seals

Fortunately, Antarctic phocids are not difficult to distinguish from one another (cf. Scheffer, 1958; King, 1964). There is no sexual dimorphism in pattern or colouration and there is no markedly different juvenile coat. All pups probably bear lanugo fur during the first month or more of life. The pups of all but the Weddell have been little (crabeater) or not at all (leopard, Ross) observed alive and must be watched for.

The most useful means of distance identification are silhouette, behaviour and colouration. The degree of wetness of the fur alters colouration, generally darkening the animal. Moult occurs in January for all species and generally makes whatever colours or patterns are present stronger and "cleaner". Each species will be considered, the most salient features italicized.

1. Crabeater seal (*Lobodon carcinophagus*). Figures 3a and b. Moderately sized, and streamlined (to 2·5 m and 225 kg). Snout elongate. *Colour entirely silvery to creamy* with some flecking on the shoulders, sides and flanks. Coat often scarred.

Usually on large open floes of open to close pack. Singly or in small groups, occasionally in large aggregations. Nervous and attentive, *when disturbed raising head slightly as if in a "point", but remaining belly down.* If pressed, speedily travels over ice, aided by a "swimming" motion of the rear flippers and alternate "clawing" of the foreflippers; will occasionally roll. Speediest and most active of Antarctic seals, both in and out of water.

2. Weddell seal (*Leptonychotes weddelli*). Figures 4a and b. Large and heavy bodied (to almost 3 m and 500 kg). Head proportionately small with moderate snout. *Colour dark, only slightly lighter ventrally, and flecked liberally with dark and light spots.*

In large aggregations on shore ice, particularly during austral spring. Also found singly in the pack, preferring hummocked ice. *Behaviour upon disturbance is usually to roll on the side with one flipper raised in "salute"*. Travels slowly on ice.

FIG. 3a. (Above) Crabeater seal, *Lobodon carcinophagus*, from ice. Note streamlined shape, long snout, light colour and lack of strong pattern. The apparently strong line of dorso-ventral demarcation is due to the wetness of the belly and is not a real colour pattern. b. (Below) Crabeater seal, from air. Two seals are on a large, open floe, the favourite habitat. Note the "pointing", alert posture of the individual on the left.

FIG. 4a. (Above) Weddell seal, *Leptonychotes weddelli*, from ice. Note overall dark colouration with abundant spotting. Typical posture is shown: on side, with exposed flipper raised in "salute". b. (Below) Weddell seal, from air. Note location of seal in hummocked ice where it might be obscured from shipboard observer.

FIG. 5a. (Above) Leopard seal, *Hydrurga leptonyx*, from ice. Note dark dorsum and silvery venter, both liberally spotted. Typical posture shown: head raised in a direct, deliberate gaze, flippers to sides. b. (Below) Leopard seal, from air. Note huge head, pointed snout, neck constriction, slender shape. The species is easily frightened by helicopters, and this one is heading to the water.

FIG. 6a. (Above) Ross seal, *Ommatophoca rossi*, from ice. Note dark dorsum, light venter, streaking on side of head and throat and some spotting at the dorsoventral demarcation. Note also blunt snout and posture with head held high, throat inflated and mouth open. Animal is in moult and pattern is relatively weak.
b. (Below) Ross seal, from air. Note similar posture to that seen above. The species is easily approached, even by helicopter.

TABLE 1

Flight*	Date	NM^2	Flying time	Location and ice condition	Weddell Pelagic	Weddell Fast	Crabeater Pelagic	Crabeater Fast	Leopard Pelagic	Leopard Fast	Ross Pelagic	Ross Fast	Total seals	Summation
1	29 Dec.	90	2:30	Erebus Bay, fast ice	—	2455	—	—	—	—	—	—	2455	
					100%									
2	30 Dec.	12	:37	McMurdo Sound, close pack	3	—	4	—	—	—	—	—	7	Density per NM^2
					43%		57%							
3	30 Dec.	10	:23	10 miles SE Nordenskjold Ice Tongue, very open pack	1	—	—	—	—	—	—	—	1	WS 0·1 —55 (shore ice)
					100%									CS 0·2 —5·8
														LS 0·06—0·5
4	31 Dec.	22	:52	5 miles NW Franklin I., very open to very close pack	10	—	6	—	5	—	—	—	21	RS 0·04—0·4
					48%		28%		24%					
5	31 Dec.	22	:61	33 miles NNE Franklin I., very open to very close pack	34	—	9	—	—	—	—	—	43	Per cent pelagic—each species
					79%		21%							
6	1 Jan.	14	:34	4·5 miles ESE Cape Jones, fast ice	—	141	—	—	—	—	—	4	145	WS 8 % (inc. McM)
					97%						3%			WS 33% (not inc. McM)
														CS 99%
7	2 Jan.	28	:54	16 miles NE Cape Jones, close pack to fast ice	14	115	7	—	—	—	7	—	143	LS 97%
					90%		5%				5%			RS 77%
8	2 Jan.	28	:61	32 miles NE Cape Jones, very open to very close pack	38	—	11	—	3	—	—	—	52	Shore-ice composition (not inc. McM)
					73%		21%		6%					
9	3 Jan.	19	:44	Southern Moubray Bay, close pack to fast ice	27	17	4	—	1	—	2	—	51	WS 98·3%
					79%		12%		3%		6%			CS 0·6%
10	4 Jan.	26	:60	Cape McCormick, very open to very close pack	23	—	52	—	3	1	1	—	80	LS 0·2%
					29%		65%		5%		1%			RS 0·9%

11	4 Jan.	No count made			—	—	—	—	—	—	—	—	—	Pack-ice composition (not inc. McM)
12	5 Jan.	16	:36	5 miles S Cape Hallett, close to very close pack	28 82%	—	4 12%	—	—	—	2 6%	—	34	WS 43·8% CS 48·1%
13	6 Jan.	10	:32	Cape Roget, open pack to fast ice	13 92%	245	15 6%	3	2 1%	—	1 1%	1	280	LS 5·2% RS 2·9%
14	7 Jan.	13	:28	Cape Downshire, very open to very close pack	10 36%	—	12 43%	—	6 21%	—	—	—	28	Pack-ice composition (not inc. WS)
15	7 Jan.	15	:42	1 mile W Cape Adare, very open to very close pack	8 11%	—	62 83%	—	5 6%	—	—	—	75	CS 85·4% LS 9·3% RS 5·3%
16	9 Jan.	12	:32	SE Robertson Bay, very open to very close pack	12 15%	—	70 84%	—	1 1%	—	—	—	83	
17	12 Jan.	25	:40	SW Robertson Bay, very open to very close pack	18 40%	—	19 42%	—	4 9%	—	4 9%	—	45	
18	12 Jan.	25	:62	5 miles S Coulman I., very open to very close pack	11 100%	—	—	—	—	—	—	—	11	
Totals		387	14:09		250	2973	275	3	30	1	17	5	3554 (572 pelagic)	

* Flight numbers are referrable to locations indicated on Fig. 1. NM^2 = square nautical miles. Counts for each species are given separately for fast and pack ice; the percentage figure under these lumps total numbers and is a percent of all seals seen on that flight. Density/NM^2 is a range of values calculated from total nautical miles covered. Per cent pelagic refers to the percentage of each species seen on pack ice versus that of the same species seen on fast ice. Shore ice composition refers to the percentage of each species seen there and pack ice composition similarly refers to percentage of each species seen on pack ice. Lastly, the Weddell seal was excluded from a calculation of pack ice composition in order to make these data comparable with other censuses where few if any of that species were encountered.

3. Leopard seal (*Hydrurga leptonyx*). Figures 5a and b. *Very long and slender* (to almost 4 m and 450 kg). *Large headed with a marked constriction at the neck*. Snout long. Dark dorsally, silvery ventrally and liberally spotted with both lighter and darker spots.

Usually solitary. Widely ranging from open pack to close pack over many latitudes. The wariest of Antarctic seals. *Upon moderate disturbance, usually faces intruder with head raised in a direct look*. Usually deliberate in actions. Travels with agility in a manner similar to the crabeater seal, but not so speedily and with little use of the foreflippers.

4. Ross seal (*Ommatophoca rossi*). Figures 6a and b. Moderately sized with medium build (to 2·25 m and 225 kg). *Snout very blunt. Dorsum dark with little spotting, sharply turning silvery on venter; streaked on side of head and throat and spotted or streaked on sides and flanks*. Superficially like the Weddell seal in appearance and probably occasionally confused with it.

Usually on heavy pack, occasionally on shore ice. Apparently localized in occurrence. Very easily approached by helicopter or on foot. *When disturbed, raises the head, inflates the trachea and soft palate with air, and with open mouth makes trilling and "chugging" sounds*. Travels slowly on ice.

B. Census Results

Results are presented in Table 1. Seals were most numerous from Coulman Island northward. South of that point only Weddell seals were abundant, and few others were seen. The impracticability of correlation of seal species with ice coverage was apparent throughout. Commonly, coverage has been measured in tenths, and even at best this is misleading in its implication of accuracy. It is probably best to use the terminology of Armstrong *et al.* (1966), in which very open pack = 0·1–0·3, open pack = 0·4–0·6, close pack = 0·7–0·9, and very close pack = almost 1·0. Fast ice is defined as sea ice attached to shore. On this voyage ice was extremely mixed and impossible to characterize over large areas.

It is best to make note of temperature, wind, sky cover and other environmental vectors during all counts. These interrelate as an "effective temperature" which delimits "tolerance limits" for in-air exposure (Ray and Smith, 1968). The estimated effective temperatures were uniformly a little above freezing, but the number of flights too small for correlations of seal abundance with weather.

In-air flying time was 14 hrs 9 min and about 387 nm^2 were covered. Coverage of this area might comprise ten days of continuous ship time, in which many seals might be missed among even lightly hummocked ice. A total of 3554 seals was seen, 572 of them pelagic, i.e. not on fast ice. Erebus Bay Weddells comprised 2455 of this total, and are eliminated from some calculations so as not to bias the data.

The Weddell seal was the commonest species observed, overwhelmingly so on shore ice (98·3%), and second most numerous on pack ice as well (43·8%). It has generally been overlooked that the Weddell seal is commonly pelagic near shore. Even excluding Erebus Bay, 33% of all Weddells seen were on pack ice, all singly. These individuals were adult and juvenile, but probably non-breeders. The latter probably remain near colonies well into the austral summer and are easily counted there. Flight 1, made on a calm, sunny day, is illustrative of statements made above, namely that virtually all Weddell seals in areas of fast ice may be counted during favourable weather, subsequent to the reproductive season. The figure of 2455 seals is in close agreement with the population estimates of Smith (1965) and Stirling (*personal communication*) for Erebus Bay, McMurdo Sound.

As expected, the crabeater seal was the commonest species of the pack ice even near shore. It appeared to become commoner northward and comprised 48·1% of all seals seen there or 85·4% excluding the Weddell seal: 99% of the crabeaters were seen on pack ice. Leopards were about equally common everywhere, totalling 5·2% of individuals seen on pack ice, or 9·3% excluding the Weddell seal. Ross seals appear to concentrate in pockets of local abundance and were about half as abundant as leopards. Ninety-seven per cent of the leopard seals were also seen on pack ice, but only 77% of the Ross seals. The Ross seal no doubt owes some of its "rarity" to a fondness for heavy ice, where it is difficult to observe.

Density of seals per nautical mile varied greatly, but seals appear not to be as abundant in the Western Ross Sea as in the Weddell Sea. The highest pack-ice density was 5·8/nm^2 for the crabeater compared with up to 95·7/nm^2 seen by Siniff, *et al.* (1970) in the Weddell Sea.

C. Underwater Sound

It is not the intent here to describe seal sounds in detail. The identification of sounds among the great variety heard can be extremely difficult. However, underwater sound can be of aid in detection of seals and perhaps give an indication of relative abundance as well.

It is highly significant that no Weddell seal sounds were heard at any location during this voyage. These sounds are probably of social significance and are heard abundantly in the austral spring (Ray, 1967). Sonograms of some of the calls have been published by Schevill and Watkins (1965) and Kooyman (1968).

Sonograms attributable to leopard and Ross seals are presented in Figs 7 and 8. For both species, in-air and underwater sounds have been compared for purposes of identification; the identity of the leopard seal sound appears positive, but that for the Ross seal is somewhat tentative. Crabeater sounds have not been identified.

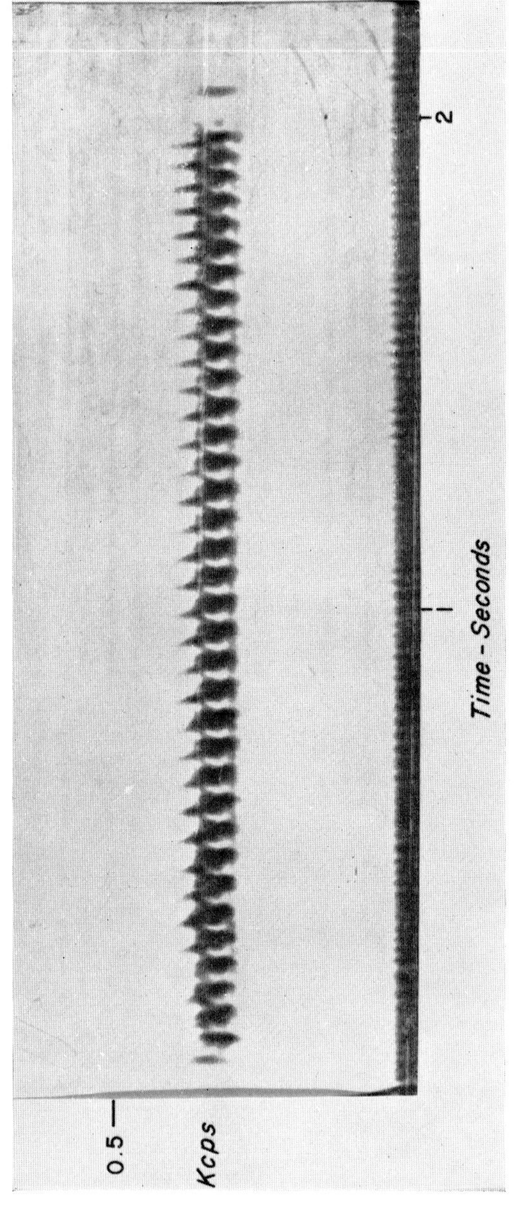

FIG. 7 (Above) Call of the leopard seal, *Hydrurga leptonyx*, underwater. A 100 cps band width filter was used in analysis.

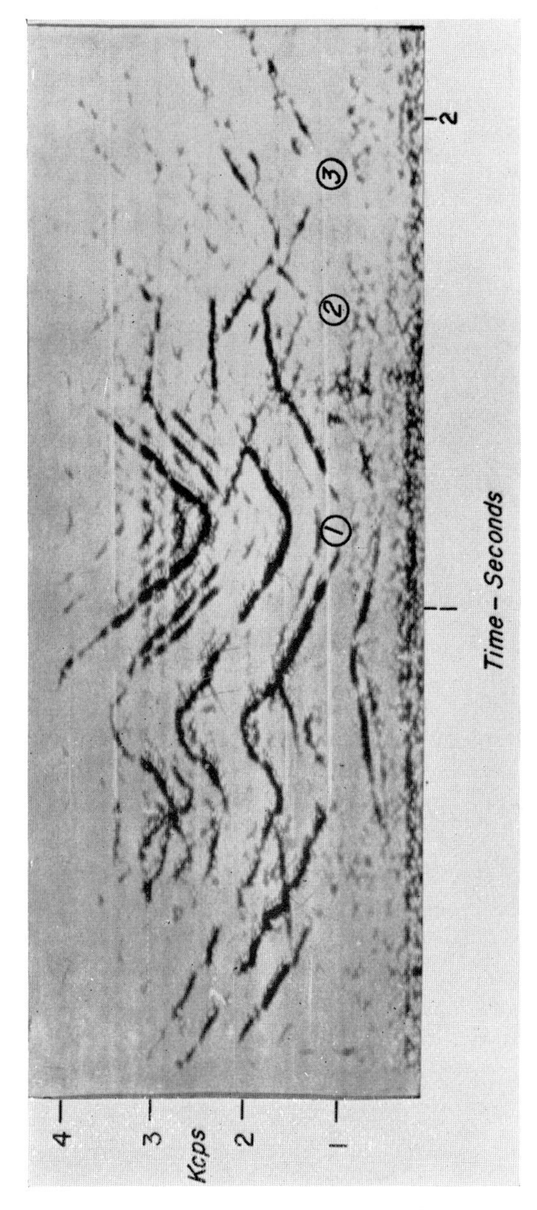

FIG. 8. (Below) Probable calls of chorusing Ross seals, *Ommatophoca rossi*, underwater. Three different individual calls are indicated by numbers placed at the 1000 cps point of each. A 500 cps band-width filter was used in analysis.

The leopard-seal call is a pulsed, narrow-band, and about 300 cps. Its haunting quality is unmistakable, once heard. The Ross seal can produce pulsed sounds as well, but the characteristic underwater sound is an unpulsed moan of varying frequency or a similarly structured buzzing.

During flights 8–17, sightings of Ross and leopard seals and underwater recordings were made almost simultaneously. For both species it appeared that the numbers of seals calling underwater always exceeded the numbers seen locally on ice. Leopard seals called singly, the relative intensities of calls revealing sounds made by different individuals. Figure 8 in particular is interesting in that it indicates chorusing of at least three Ross seals and choruses of differing intensity were heard. Obviously many seals of both species were missed in aerial census.

IV. Conclusion

Attempts to census pagophilic seals by on-ice counting are of little value prior to understanding of their behaviour, physiology and ecology. To date, there are no reliable data on more than relative abundance for any species but the Weddell (and then only locally). Even these data are of dubious value, as methods have not been standardized. Ratios of abundance between species are probably totally valueless due to lack of comparative behavioural data.

Major clues to in-air to aquatic proportionality are:

(1) the determination of the thermal "tolerance zone" as an indication of the quality of weather which influences hauling out on ice;
(2) the identification and behavioural significance of underwater sound as an indication of seal presence, or perhaps even of abundance;
(3) the evaluation of daily and seasonal rhythms of activity on ice or in water.

These must be studied separately for each species. An excellent start has been made for the Weddell seal. For crabeater, leopard, and Ross seals data are almost totally lacking. It seems to me that these three species are considerably more aquatic—they are certainly less accessible—than the Weddell. Therefore, it will be difficult to obtain significant data for them.

Other questions also remain:

(1) What is the relationship between the pack ice and food, hydrology and the benthos?
(2) What are the limiting factors which determine carrying capacity for each species?
(3) Are "pagophilic" seals obligate or facultative in their relationship with the ice?
(4) To what extent is the pack ice an "ecosystem"?

The western Ross Sea represents an ideal location for detailed ecological work which will lead to answers to these questions. Logistics are available and weather is generally good during the austral spring and summer. All species of lobodontines are readily available. I urge strongly that seal observations and oceanographic studies be expanded simultaneously and that increased cognisance be taken of physiological and acoustic clues to seal behaviour. Counting methods should be standardized, perhaps in the fashion indicated here or by Siniff *et al.* (1970). Time of study must be concentrated in the austral spring, the time of maximal social and reproductive behaviour of these species. Until such modifications in methods are made and until our efforts become essentially ecological, seal censuses will remain of interest, but totally inadequate.

Acknowledgements

Work was supported by grants from the National Science Foundation, Office of Antarctic Programs, to the New York Zoological Society and the Johns Hopkins University. Special thanks are extended to Commander C. L. Gott, USN, and to the officers and men of the ice-breaker *Burton Island* for their interest and cooperation.

Messrs W. E. Schevill and W. A. Watkins advised on acoustics and made the included sonograms (Figs 7 and 8). Aid in the identification of *Hydrurga* sounds was provided by the following who have heard these sounds at Cape Crozier: D. G. Ainley, G. Harrow, R. L. Penney, R. J. Peterson, W. J. L. Sladen and R. C. Wood.

References

Armstrong, T. E., Roberts, B. B, and Swithinbank, C. W. M. (1966). "Illustrated Glossary of Snow and Ice." Scott Polar Research Institute, Cambridge.

King, J. E. (1964). "Seals of the World". Brit. Mus. (Nat. Hist.), London.

Kooyman, G. L. (1968). An analysis of some behavioral and physiological characteristics related to diving in the Weddell seal. "Antarctic Research Series." Vol. II, *Biology of the Antarctic Seas III*. Amer. Geophys. Union, Washington, D.C.

Laws, R. M. (1953). The seals of the Falkland Islands and Dependencies. *Oryx* 2, 87–97.

Mackintosh, N. A. (1967). Estimates of local seal populations in the Antarctic, 1930/37. *Norsk Hvalfangsttid.* **67** (3), 57–64.

Øritsland, T. (1970). Biology and population dynamics of Antarctic seals. 361–6. (This volume).

Ray, C. (1967). Social behavior and acoustics of the Weddell seal. *Ant. Jour.* U.S. **2** (4), 105–6.

Ray, C. and Smith, M. S. R. (1968). Thermoregulation of the pup and adult Weddell seal, *Leptonychotes weddelli* (Lesson), in Antarctica. *Zoologica* **53** (1), 33–46, Pl. 1–2.

Scheffer, V. B. (1958). "Seals, Sea Lions and Walruses". Stanford University Press, Stanford, Calif. and Oxford University Press, London.

Schevill, W. E. and Watkins, W. A. (1965). Underwater calls of Leptonychotes (Weddell seal). *Zoologica* **50** (1), 45–46.

Siniff, D. B., Cline, D. R. and Erickson, A. W. (1969). Population densities of seals in the Weddell Sea. 377–94. (This volume.)

Smith, M. S. R. (1965). Seasonal movements of the Weddell seal in McMurdo Sound, Antarctica. *Jour. Wildl. Man.* **29** (3), 464–70.

Stirling, I. (1967). Population studies on the Weddell seal. *Tuatara* **15** (3), 133–41.

Weddell Seals of Signy Island

E. A. SMITH AND R. W. BURTON*
British Antarctic Survey Biological Unit, Monks Wood Experimental Station, Abbots Ripton, Huntingdon, England

I. Introduction

This paper describes some observations of Weddell seals by members of the British Antarctic Survey on Signy Island, where a research station has operated since 1947.

In 1948–49, R. M. Laws (unpublished) made fairly detailed observations and counted cows and pups. In 1952–53, A. W. Mansfield (1958) made a much more detailed study of breeding biology and reproduction. Subsequently, sporadic counts were made by staff at Signy Island and work was put on a more regular footing in 1960. Since then, annual seal reports have been written, some by biologists and others by non-scientists.

Although reporting has inevitably varied in thoroughness and frequency over these twenty years, data on pup numbers, and on distribution during the breeding season have been collected with reasonable continuity. Every accessible pup has been tagged, together with samples of adult females. More detailed observations of behaviour during breeding seasons are now being obtained in order to test some provisional conclusions derived from previous accounts and to assist interpretation of certain aspects of Weddell seal social behaviour in the light of increasing knowledge of other species.

It has been possible to extract from the reports reliable information on the numbers and distribution of pups. Table 1 shows that the counts of pups have remained fairly constant for twenty years. This is reassuring in view of the proximity of the human settlement, the handling of pups for tagging, and of the nearness of Coronation Island, to which, presumably, the animals could readily withdraw. It is interesting to compare this reaction with that in the more elaborately social terrestrial breeding colonies of the grey seal (*Halichoerus grypus*). In this species, escape reactions of even breeding animals are intense, except for a few lactating cows, and the tenacity with which a breeding site is maintained in succeeding years is easily diminished by human activities.

* Present address: Weston House, Albury, Surrey, England.

TABLE 1

Pupping of Weddell Seals on Signy Island

Year	*No. Pups Born*	*Reported by**	*Date of 1st pup*
1947	250	?	24 August
1948	250–300	Mansfield	24 August
1955	250–300	Cordall and Tickell	?
1960	*c.* 350	Pinder	14 August
1961	*c.* 300	Pinder and Jones	22 August
1962	300	Topliffe	13 August
1963	250	Topliffe	19 August
1964	315	Burton	23 August
1965	over 200	No count possible	20 August
1966	250	Bacon	20 August
1967	350	Mole and Spencer	10 August

First pup born during third week of August (mean date 16th). Peak date of pupping first week of September (mean date 7th).

* References in this column are to unpublished reports held by British Antarctic Survey.

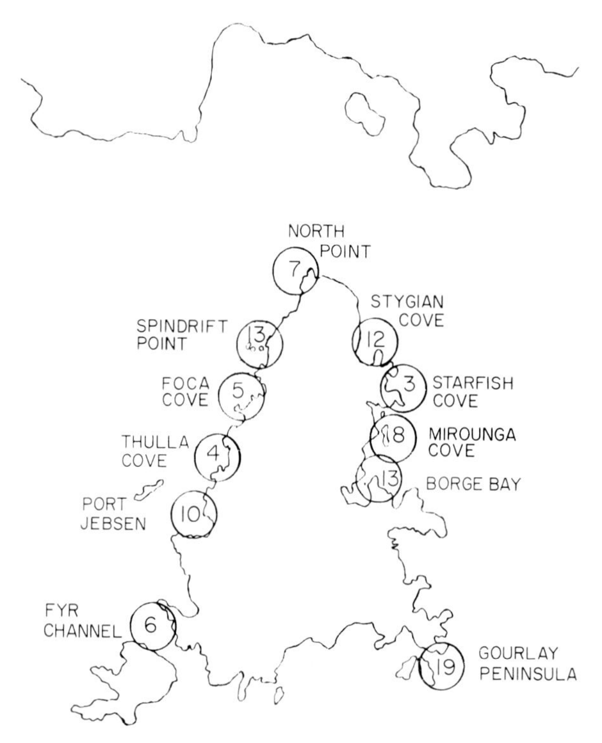

FIG. 1. Map showing pupping sites of Weddell Seals on Signy Island. Figures indicate pup numbers as percentage of average output over six years, 1960–65 inclusive.

Figure 1 shows that pupping over several seasons has been widely and fairly evenly spread around the island. Table 2 gives details of the pup tagging achieved in the same period.

TABLE 2

Weddell Seals on Signy Island—Pup Tagging

WEST COAST	1960	1961	1962	1963	1964	1965	1966	1967
North Point	19	4	3	45	28	7		
Spindrift Rocks	41	17	14	23	52	42		
Foca Cove	50	—	11	4	5	9		
Thulla Cove	2	2	—	23	12	17		
Jebsen Point	11	54	2	11	70	8		
Fyr Channel	—	16	—	36	41	—		
Total	123	93	30	142	208	83		
Island percentage	(36)	(50)	(11)	(65)	(68)	(45)		
EAST COAST								
Stygian Cove	40	—	80	23	18	23		
Starfish Cove	1	—	31	4	3	5		
Mirounga Cove	46	—	60	—	—	10		
Borge Bay	112	5	45	5	14	9		
Gourlay Pen.	20	91	15	46	64	55		
Total	219	96	231	78	99	102		
Island percentage	(64)	(51)	(89)	(35)	(32)	(55)		
Island total	342	189	261	220	307	185	229	335
Other areas	60	17	21	12	49	8	93	—
Total tagged	402	206	282	232	356	193	322	335

II. Distribution of Breeding Females

The results obtained between 1960 and 1967 confirm Mansfield's main conclusions. It has been established that the breeding season extends from the third week of August until the population disperses after the second week in November. No more than fifty animals have been counted in summer around the island.

Clearly the seals haul out on snow and ice in preference to shingle, which is itself preferred to boulders. It may be this fact which accounts for low summer numbers, but we think it more likely that factors associated with social behaviour are basic.

In summer, when wind drives accumulations of floes into the bays, it is common to see numbers of Weddell seals on them, rather than on the adjacent coast. Lack of suitable hauling-out places cannot alone account for the sparseness of seals in summer, for counts remain low in autumn and winter. In most years virtually none has been seen in July and August just before the rapid build-up that precedes breeding. It is likely therefore that the animals range more widely at this time, feeding at sea and building up reserves as most species of seal do before breeding. Normally the Weddell seal is to be regarded as a coastal species and few have been recorded more than a few miles from the coast during census counts in pack ice (Eklund and Atwood, 1962).

Breeding females become distributed in relation to sea-ice conditions and are concentrated especially in areas of broken and pressured ice with easy access to and from the sea. When sea ice surrounds the island, that on the west side is invariably broken because of the packing of the ice by prevailing winds and the greater abundance of islets and grounded bergs, while that on the east side tends to be smooth with few openings. However, Weddell seals are well known to be able to travel for considerable distances beneath shelf and fast sea ice and have the means of locating cracks and holes efficiently, so that even in years with extensive ice they are able to occupy east coast sites. The apparently haphazard concentration of cows over the broad area is probably influenced by incipient early arrivals at certain holes and cracks.

Cows appear to haul out and pup first of all on the west coast, spreading later to the east in years when ice is especially broken. However, in 1961, when there was fast ice along the east coast while ice was particularly broken along the west coast and at Gourlay Peninsula, only 5% of pups were born on the east coast.

In seasons with little or no sea ice, cows haul out and pup at the ice edge or on suitable beaches and may even go inland where the terrain is suitably flat. For instance, in 1962, after sea ice broke out, several cows pupped on the frozen freshwater lakes near the east coast.

Fortunately, as in the grey seal, Weddell individuals can be identified by coat-pattern markings without being handled. Prolonged watching of known individuals is likely to throw light on the sizes of "whelping grounds" and behaviour concerned with the establishment, maintenance and duration of them. Cow-pup fidelity is *apparently* great, but current observations are intended to show whether it is the pupping area or *the* pup or *any* pup which becomes the object of defensive behaviour. Experiments replacing and displacing pups are planned, and suckling frequency and whether feeding is generally elicited by maternal or pup behaviour are under scrutiny.

III. Pup Mortality

The causes of pup death in the Weddell seal are likely to include stillbirth, inanition (through maternal indifference), loss to predators (leopard seal and killer whale), damage by adults (e.g. maternal aggression) and accidental loss by trapping in ice clefts, freezing in ice holes and drowning during sudden and large-scale ice break-up. Clearly the last effect can be the greatest and most variable, for it can disrupt colonies (*a*) by directly causing the death of a proportion of pups, (*b*) by separating others from their cows and causing starvation and (*c*) by causing the movement of survivors still attended by cows to remaining areas of fast ice.

In conditions where ice is stable, cows and pups generally remain together and in one area (in relation to a particular ice crack or breathing hole) until weaning. Lindsey (1937) gives a figure of 18% for pup mortality in one colony in the Bay of Whales, where the ice remained fast throughout the season. Mansfield (1958) observed that on Signy Island, where conditions are less severe than in the Bay of Whales, the loss of precocious pups by freezing into seal holes would be less, and mortality during a season when ice remains fast would probably be less than 18%. But in stable ice dead pups are usually hidden by snowdrifts, so that estimates of mortality are difficult to obtain.

In 1964, however, when 315 pups were born, the snow cover melted from the surface of the sea ice, exposing all or very nearly all dead pups. Seventeen cadavers were seen, suggesting a pre-weaning mortality of the order of 5%. Some were stillborn, and others undersized, but most had become accidentally trapped in ice clefts and crushed or drowned, while some had apparently died after attack by adults. Such mortality as occurs is thus unlikely to be due to infections such as those seen in the temperate breeding colonies of the grey seal (Appleby, 1964). Grey seals breeding in the freezing conditions of the Baltic or north-east Canada are likewise not subject to infection. Coulson and Hickling (1966) have suggested a basic mortality of about 8·5% for this species, when not subject to crowding.

Mansfield (1958) suggested that when the ice broke up during the breeding period pup mortality might reach 30–50%. No counts of dead pups and survivors under these conditions have been possible in recent years.

IV. Moult of Pups and Lactation

Spot checks of the progress of moult in seventy-five pups were made in 1962 and indicated that it usually commences when the pup is three to four weeks old and is completed at five to seven weeks. More careful observations made in 1963 by F. Topliffe indicated that moulting begins along the edges of the fore and hind flippers, the loss of hair becoming noticeable at about three weeks after birth. By the time moulting is completed on the flippers hair has begun to be shed from the face, especially about the eyes, and from the central area of the abdomen. The first areas to moult appear to be those parts of flippers and abdomen that get rubbed against the ground and of the face that are rubbed against the mother when suckling. Next a strip of hair is shed along the mid-dorsal line, and this band widens outwards, as does that along the mid-abdominal line, until only a narrow band of woolly fur is left along each flank. This disappears at six to seven weeks after birth. These observations are in broad agreement with those cited by Mansfield (1958) and Lindsey (1937). Pups have frequently been seen to take to the water in their natal coat, and although swimming ability is present in the first week of life, they usually enter the water for the first time when two or three weeks old.

After swimming has begun there is little movement in years when ice remains unbroken; almost every pup is weaned within 50 m of its birth site. When ice breaks up pups and cows may, however, move considerable distances, in several instances more than 8 km.

A number of pups at least six weeks old have been observed suckling and it is suggested that weaning normally occurs at six to seven weeks. A few pups four to five weeks old with their moult only half completed have been found in good health and may already have been abandoned by their mothers. In other cases fully moulted pups have been observed still suckling in mid-November, more than seven weeks after birth.

V. Adult Movement

In addition to observations of the local movements of cows and pups induced by changes in ice configuration during a breeding season, a current experiment is aimed at showing the degree to which cows return to the same place to breed in succeeding years. Results summarized in Table 3 show that, despite the fairly regular size of the breeding group on Signy Island, there is considerable movement of individual animals to and from Borge Bay in succeeding seasons. That this is a function of ice conditions is indicated by a comparison of the last two columns in the table.

This reinforces the point that redistribution in succeeding years, while having an element of traditional site selection, is clearly attributable to the greater influence exerted by transient ice configuration. The records suggest that it is valid to refer to the South Orkney Islands Weddell seal population, less so to refer to a distinct Signy Island population, and invalid to assume any precise linkage of animals to breeding grounds on particular stretches of coastline. When ice conditions do not favour breeding on Signy Island the population disperses towards the other South Orkney Islands.

In 1964 some recoveries were made during summer visits to Coronation and other islands up to 25 km from Signy Island. The animals encountered which had been marked as pups on Signy Island were: a 3-year-old male and three out of five yearlings and twelve pups at Saunders Island, a 3-year-old

TABLE 3

Recoveries of Breeding Cows Tagged in Borge Bay

Year	No. tagged	Percentage recovered							
		After 1 yr	*After 2 yrs*	*After 3 yrs*	*After 4 yrs*	*After 5 yrs*	*After 6 yrs*	*Average age-class recovery rate*	*Approx. duration (days) of ice cover after 1 August*
1962	51	4	16	6	10	6	8	8·3	50
63	18	17	22	17	22	17		19	120
64	19	21	16	10	5			13	70
65	30	27	14	7				15	76
66	55	5	0					2·5	40
67	32	0						—	—
Average annual recovery rate:		12	13	10	12	12	8		

male and a pup on Michelsen Island and a 3-year-old male and a 2-year-old female and a female pup on Powell Island. A cow tagged as a breeding female in Borge Bay in 1962 was also encountered on Powell Island in 1964.

VI. Breeding Biology

Recent observations and tagging experiments on Signy Island have tended in the main to confirm the findings of other workers. Additional information has included an instance of a birth to a 3-year-old cow. Mansfield (1958) postulated maturation at three years and an average longevity of nine years.

A female tagged as a pup by Laws in 1948 has been recovered five times. On three occasions between 1960 and 1965 she produced a pup, but although she appeared among the breeding animals in 1967 and again in 1968 (her nineteenth and twentieth years) she did not pup.

Several instances have been recorded in which two pups have been seen attending a single cow. Adoption has been assumed or described on several occasions and recent reports include two authentic cases of twin births.

VII. Male Activities

It was noted that the first members of the local population seen basking in sunny, calm weather in early spring (August) were males. They always lay within easy reach of tide cracks, stress cracks or holes, giving access to the water.

As much as two weeks sometimes elapsed before the first females were observed, but at this period there is a direct correlation between fine weather and seals hauling out, whereas by September the females gather near the shore in more permanent small groups, often in coves where they can haul out through tide cracks on to the fast ice. When basking in calm weather males are often associated with these pods of cows, and frequently fight among themselves, as is evident from newly inflicted bite marks about their hind-quarters and genitalia. A dominant bull usually emerges, and where several bulls have been observed near a newly established pod of females, by the time the cows are ready to accept copulation only a single bull is left. For example at Polynesia Point during August 1967 three males were observed basking along the tide crack, yet by the second week in September when two cows had pupped on the Paal Harbour side of the Point only one male was seen in the area. A week later a bull was heard making prolonged whistling sounds beneath the ice near the cows, followed by coughing noises at the surface in a near-by ice hole. This behaviour was repeated several times, and after a period of about a quarter of an hour one of the cows followed the bull into the water (M. G. White, *personal communication*).

Observations of the behaviour of adult male Weddell seals towards the end of the period of pupping are rare. Mansfield (1958) reported fights between bulls from August onwards which he attributed to renewal of testicular activity. He quotes G. de Q. Robin, who described a fight which lasted for 20 min, mainly in the water, with the contestants biting each other around the head and hind flippers.

Recent examinations of wounded bulls show that most wounds are inflicted around the genitalia and hind flippers; the skin around the penis opening is often badly lacerated. Damage to rear flippers is even more common and they may be severely mutilated with parts of digits missing. A film by A. J. M. Walker of Weddell seal bulls fighting has been scrutinized. All attacks were concentrated towards the posterior end of each animal.

One of us (R.W.B.) observed a fight between two bulls on an offshore ice floe. The animals ignored the observer in a dinghy moored alongside the floe as they lay head to tail biting at each others hind flippers. During this encounter the genitalia were not attacked. The fight consisted of bouts of violent activity between periods during which the animals lay head to tail without reacting to each other. All the bouts of biting were initiated by the same bull. After 15 min of intermittent fighting, the dominant bull entered the water, swam about, and then suddenly hauled out again on to the floe and attacked the other seal aggressively. Both animals took to the water, where the aggressor was seen to charge broadside into the other and this attack took the animals beneath the ice, where they disappeared.

The male Weddell seal's habit of attacking its opponent's hindquarters is in marked contrast with the sparring behaviour of several non-Lobodontine species such as the elephant seal and grey seal. In the latter, damaged hind flippers and genitalia are extremely rare; frontal attacks are the rule and the snout, head and neck are damaged by bites and lunging foreflippers.

VIII. Discussion

Continuing studies of Weddell seals on Signy Island, including long-term recoveries of marked individuals and prolonged observations of behaviour are important, because successful conservation will depend on knowledge of population dynamics and because several aspects of Pinniped phylogeny are usefully approached on a comparative basis.

The Weddell seal may be regarded as semi-colonial (i.e. some degree of territoriality is manifested) and the species is dependent on land, or ice associated with land, for breeding. In this respect it differs from other Lobodontine species, for no others are colonial and all can breed on pack ice.

There are, however, several features of similarity between the Weddell seal and the grey seal *Halichoerus grypus*, which has been studied in detail by one of us (E.A.S.). These may be summarized as follows:

1. A return to the same breeding grounds in succeeding years to form aggregations which may vary in size, location and composition according to ambient conditions.
2. Marked defensive behaviour by cows, whether of the whelping area or of a pup.
3. Marked aggressive behaviour in bulls, in relation to a particular site.
4. Presence in both species of groups breeding on ice connected with land and groups breeding on ice-free beaches. The breeding season of ice breeders coincides with the spring break-up of ice.
5. Apparent neglect of immediately new-born young and absence of attempts by cows to assist pups in swimming. But if disturbed by human activity or ice break-out before weaning, cows and pups may move together several miles.
6. Presence of degrees of maternal solicitude which have been described in very similar terms. There have been instances of intense apparent tenacity and defence of a pup—even a dead one—in both species, but there are also instances of apparent carelessness and haphazard neglect or even killing of pups. Furthermore, nursing of pups not related to the cow in question has been seen in both species.

Davies (1957) has postulated the history of grey seal populations during the later stages of northern glaciation. Since glacial recession the species has been restricted to three groups. These populations, reviewed by Smith (1966), are in the Baltic (9·5% of the world population, invariably breeding on ice in late winter or early spring), north-west Atlantic (9·5% of the population, breeding on ice when ice forms and on skerries and islets in ice-free years in late winter and early spring) and north-east Atlantic (81% of the population, never encountering ice and breeding in the autumn).

Thus the grey seal is basically ice breeding, like all Phocinae, but it is of particular interest that numbers are now highest and rates of increase most marked where grey seals breed in conditions no longer dominated by ice formation (Smith, 1966).

For all seals it is clearly an advantage to conduct processes of parturition, lactation, pup moult and even mating in a stable, undisturbed habitat and this is provided by fast ice.

A study of pagophilous seal species suggest that (except for the N.E. Atlantic group of grey seals) there has been advantage in breeding at the *end* of the annual period of ice cover. Most probably the advantage is to permit rapid dispersal of young away from land predators in places where food would be immediately available. In fact, one of the most arresting features of Weddell seal biology is the variation in the timing of the breeding season with latitude to give an apparent correlation between breeding and the period of ice break-up (Table 4). Figure 2 shows this effect in detail for Signy Island. The average breeding season (the dates of first pup, peak daily birth-rate and

TABLE 4

Weddell Seals on Signy Island

Comparison of breeding seasons			
54°17′S	South Georgia	Mid-September	Vaughan 1968
60°43′S	Signy Island	Late August	Brown 1913 Pinder 1960
68°S	Graham Land	Early September	Bertram 1940
71°30′S	Cape Adare	Early September	Barrett-Hamilton 1902
77°50′S	E. Ross Sea	Mid-October	Wilson 1907
78°34′S	Bay of Whales	Early October	Lindsay 1937

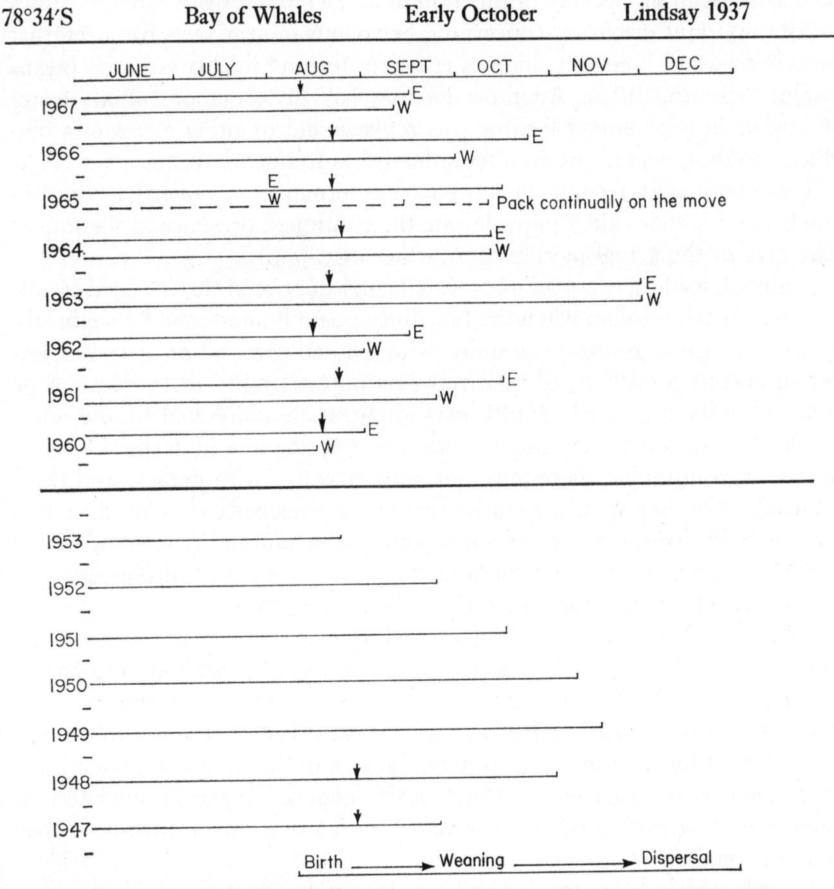

FIG. 2. Pupping of Weddell Seals on Signy Island. Arrows indicate dates of first pup. Horizontal lines indicate duration of ice cover, records for east and west coasts being shown separately after 1960.

last pup, derived from reports) between 1947 and 1967 evidently straddle the period during which ice break-up has occurred. Furthermore, it appears that the date of the birth of the first pup does not vary with ice break-up.

If there is gradual climatic amelioration, the preferred breeding conditions become gradually shorter in duration over a long period. In these circumstances there is clearly an advantage for pups and cows to complete processes of breeding and weaning more speedily or to change their breeding season. In general the former course appears to have been followed and, as earlier ice break-up places breeding animals at risk, it is probable that food requirements and/or social factors have brought about the retention of basic spatial and temporal breeding patterns. But this has meant that successful dispersal of pups after weaning becomes a function of accelerated growth rate.

An important discovery concerning behaviour in grey seals has been that in their crowded breeding colonies cow-pup feeding fidelity is by no means absolute (Smith, 1966). Adoptive feeding has been demonstrated; foster feeding or supplementary feeding (the replacement of either a cow or a pup which has disappeared, by another animal) has frequently been observed, as well as contingent feeding (a temporary alternative to normal feeding in which a cow suckles alien pups despite the continued presence in the immediate area of the actual mothers and/or her own pup).

Adoptive feeding is not an unexpected consequence of the crowded conditions which can develop when the breeding season is shortened by ice break-up. In a dense aggregation of animals individual recognition becomes less certain and in conditions of relatively low pup mortality there may not be sufficient milk produced rapidly enough by each individual of the adult female stock to bring every pup to optimum weaning weight in the shortened period. In conditions where pup mortality increases with density and there is a need for rapid growth and early weaning, a propensity for shared feeding can allow for competition for milk among the pups surviving neo-natal causes of mortality. In these conditions the rate of increase of population is at its height (11% per year on the Farne Islands recently).

The "sociality index" of McLaren (1967) arranges seal species in an order from "solitary and promiscuous" (value 2) to "gregarious and harem forming" (value 6). Those species with low values are characteristically ice breeders and those with high values are beach breeders, though this is not just a straightforward manifestation of the wealth of space available on fast ice in comparison with shores. (Grey seals "choose" apparently deleterious conditions of crowding when surrounded with space which previously they have occupied).

In seals which do not have a high sociality index there is invariably complete mutual feeding fidelity; in such species as *Phoca vitulina* or *Hydrurga leptonyx* loss of cow-pup contact would mean starvation. In a densely aggregated socially breeding species such contact could readily be lost if there was failure in signal recognition or, more particularly, if aggregations became redistributed by changing ice configuration, a position exemplified by the Weddell seal. Indeed, changing ice conditions provide important clues to the development of social behaviour in seals. For it may be said that Weddell seals and grey seals represent two stages in Lobodontine and Phocine evolution; the stages are different in sociality and correlate with the differences in the influence of ice on the two species.

McLaren has pointed out that there is no need to postulate group selection in the evolution of seals and the trends suggested in this paper would support his contention that sociality can readily be explained in ordinary evolutionary terms. Certainly there is no evidence that grey seal aggregations have developed in order to regulate numbers in accordance with food availability for adult stock. Both species are widely ranging catholic and opportunist feeders in productive seas. Smith (1968) has suggested that the apparent preference for dense aggregations in grey seals was first brought about when the choice of breeding site became limited after ice recession. This gave rise to the conditions in which young could disperse successfully and quickly because close contact allowed for food sharing among suckling pups.

McLaren also suggests that deferred maturity and pup mortality which increases with density can be explained as the excesses of sexual selection. The stage reached by grey seals compared with Weddell seals examplifies this. Grey seal females mature at 6–7 years (Hewer, 1964) and Weddell seals at 3–4 years; the oldest grey seal cow known to have reproduced was 36 and so far no Weddell seal older than 20 years has been encountered. A form of density-dependent pup mortality attaining 20–25% in some instances has been described by Coulson and Hickling (1966).

Holdgate (1967) refers to evidence that ice recession in the Antarctic is in progress today. With this in mind it is tempting to regard the Weddell population as one which could be undergoing the environmental vicissitudes which affected grey seals during the later stages of the northern glaciations. The comparative study of behaviour in the two species is thus of interest. Phenomena such as territoriality and adoptive feeding are particular examples of adaptions, inchoate features of which may be discernible in Weddell seals.

Detailed observations and quantitative studies have therefore formed part of the research programme on Signy Island. Now that human disturbance as a masking feature is no longer present on South Georgia the status and organization of the small "colony" at Larsen Harbour (Vaughan, 1968) will repay study.

References

Appleby, E. C. (1964). Observations on Wild Grey Seals in Britain. *Tijdschr. Diergeneesk.* 89, Suppl. 1.

Barrett-Hamilton, G. E. H. (1902). Southern Cross Collections. *Mammalia*, **1**, 1–66.

Bertram, G. C. L. (1940). The Biology of the Weddell and Crabeater Seals. *Sci. Rep. British Grahamland Exped.* 1934–37, 15, 1–139.

Brown, R. N. R. (1913). The Seals of the Weddell Sea. Notes on their Habits and Distribution. *Rep. Scot. Nat. Antarct. Exped.*, 1902–4, **4**, 185–98.

Coulson, J. C. and Hickling, G. (1966). The Breeding Biology of the Grey Seal *Halichoerus grypus* (Fab.) on the Farne Islands, Northumberland. *J. Anim. Ecol.* **33**, 3, 485–512.

Davies, J. L. (1957). The Geography of the Grey Seal. *J. Mammal.* 38, 297–320.

Eklund, C. R. and Atwood, E. L. (1962). A Population Study of Antarctic Seals. *J. Mammal.* **43**, 2, 229–38.

Hewer, H. R. (1964). The Determination of Age, Sexual Maturity, Longevity and a Life-table in the Grey Seal (*Halichoerus grypus*). *Proc. Zool. Soc. Lond.* **142**, 593–624.

Holdgate, M. W. (1967). Signy Island. (*In* a Discussion on the Terrestrial Antarctic Ecosystem organized by J. E. Smith) *Phil. Trans. R. Soc. Lond.* Ser. B, No. 777, **252**, pp. 167–392.

Lindsay, A. A. (1937). The Weddell Seal in the Bay of Whales. *J. Mammal.* 18, 127–44.

Mansfield, A. W. (1958). The Breeding Behaviour and Reproductive Cycle of the Weddell Seal (*Leptonychotes weddelli* Lesson). *Falkland Islands Dependencies Survey Sci. Rep.* **18**, 41 pp.

McLaren, I, (1967). Seals and Group Selection. *Ecology* **41**, 1, 104–10.

Pinder, R. (unpublished). Base H. Biological Reports 1960. Seals. British Antarctic Survey.

Smith, E. A. (1966). A Review of the World's Grey Seal Population. *J. Zool., Lond.* **150**, 463–89.

Smith, E. A. (1968). Adoptive Suckling in the Grey Seal. *Nature, Lond.* **217**, 5130, 762–3.

Vaughan, R. W. (1968). The Status of the Weddell Seal (*Leptonychotes weddelli*) at South Georgia. *Br. Antarct. Surv. Bull.* **15**, p. 71–74.

Wilson, E. A. (1907). Mammalia (Whales and Seals). *Brit. Nat. Antarct. Exped.* 1901–04, *Nat. Hist. N.Y.* 2, 1–66.

Population Dynamics and Exploitation of Some Arctic Seals

A. W. MANSFIELD
Fisheries Research Board of Canada, Arctic Biological Station, St Anne de Bellvue, Quebec, Canada

I. Introduction

Five species of seals are found in the Canadian Arctic. The commonest and most widely distributed is the small ringed seal, *Pusa hispida*, which forms the backbone of the Eskimo economy in most areas. Widespread, but far less common than the ringed seal, is the bearded seal or squareflipper *Erignathus barbatus*. This is a considerably larger species, much prized for its hide, which is used for making boot-soles and skin line. The harp seal *Pagophilus groenlandicus* is a locally abundant summer migrant which is taken in small numbers by the Eskimos of southern Baffin Island and northern Labrador. When congregated during the breeding season in more southern waters, it forms the basis of a large commercial fishery. The hooded seal *Cystophora cristata* frequents the same breeding areas as the harp seal, but is found only as a rare migrant to the north-eastern Canadian Arctic. The harbour or common seal *Phoca vitulina* is abundant in eastern and western Canada, and is found as a rare and local resident throughout the eastern Arctic.

All of these species are the subject of continuing research by the Fisheries Research Board of Canada, with the greatest effort concentrated on the harp seal and ringed seal. It is to these two species that the remainder of this paper will be devoted. Since some background is necessary for an understanding of the methods of population assessment to be described, a brief account of the life histories of these two species will be given.

II. Life History of the Harp Seal

The harp seal is a highly migratory species which follows the seasonally changing pack ice of the North Atlantic (Fig. 1). In early May the moulting adults, followed soon by the moulted pups or beaters, begin to move northwards along the Labrador coast. The migration is subsequently deflected by ice towards the open-water coast of West Greenland. In July, as break-up of the ice continues, the seals enter Parry Channel and Jones Sound to the north of Baffin Island. Small numbers move into Frobisher Bay and Cumberland Sound in south-eastern Baffin Island and fewer still move westwards into Hudson Bay, reaching Southampton Island and as far south as the Belcher Islands. The movement out of the Canadian archipelago begins in September, and by early November large numbers pass the northern tip of Labrador on their way south. Some immature seals remain behind in West Greenland throughout the winter.

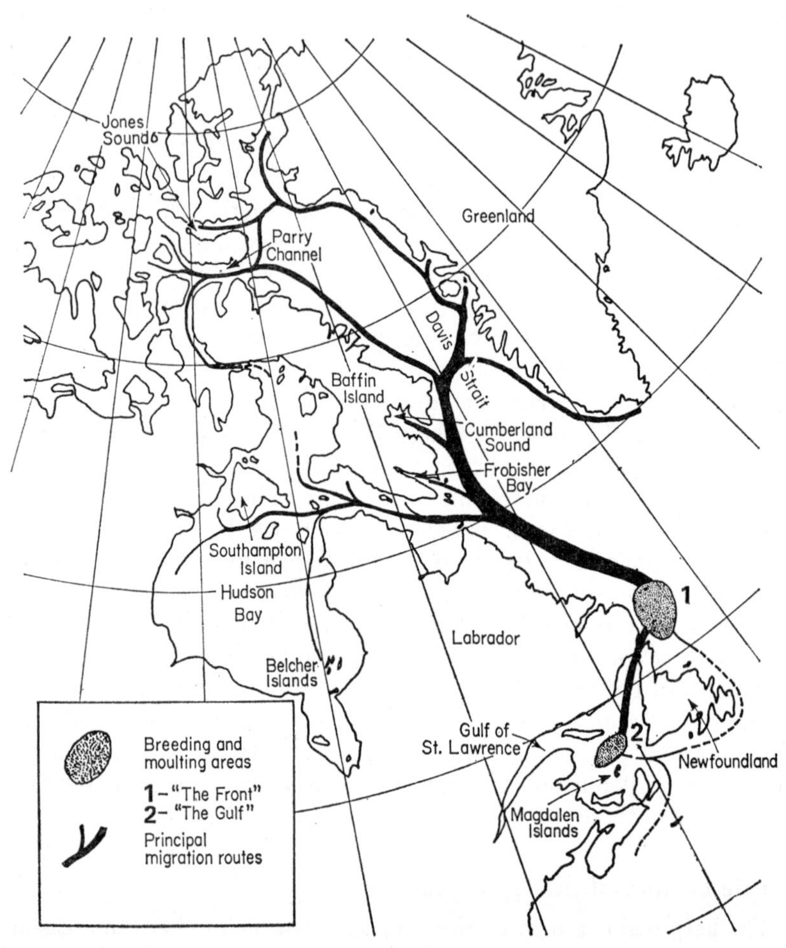

FIG. 1. Breeding and moulting areas, and principal migration routes of the harp seal.

In January part of the population goes through the Strait of Belle Isle into the Gulf of St Lawrence, while the remainder moves down the east coast of Newfoundland. In late February harp seals are found on the young ice usually to the north or west of the Magdalen Islands in the Gulf of St Lawrence and off the southern coast of Labrador. These breeding areas are known as the "Gulf" and "Front" respectively (Fig. 1). Both the timing of the whelping season and the general location of the whelping herds are fairly constant, though births may be delayed for a week by late formation of pack ice. When pack ice is absent seals resort to brash and pancake ice which becomes frozen in to a narrow strip along windward coasts. Such an event took place in the spring of 1953 when the seals in the Gulf whelped along the north shore of the Magdalen Islands (Sergeant, 1965*b*).

The size of the whelping groups is variable, but generally only two or three large patches are formed. These may vary in area from 5 to 100 square miles with a seal density of from 1000 to 5000 per square mile.

The pup is suckled by its mother for a period of 2 – 2½ weeks. In this short time the average body weight increases from about 18 lb (8·2 kg) at birth to 70 lb (32·8 kg) at weaning, most of this growth resulting from the accumulation of a thick layer of blubber underneath the skin. After weaning the pup basks on the ice and completes the moult of its foetal coat or *lanugo*, attaining a coat of short hair like the adult, but bearing only a lightly spotted pattern. Independent feeding of the pups on euphausids and some capelin (*Mallotus villosus*) begins in early April, these food organisms gradually replacing the accumulated fat store as a source of energy. In early May the pups begin their long northward migration to the Arctic, travelling perhaps up to 30 miles per day with rests at intervals on ice floes.

About the time of weaning, the adult male seals, which have been waiting in groups within and around the whelping areas, mate with the females. This occurs in the water if the ice is loose or on the ice if the water leads have closed up. In April and early May the immature and adult seals only feed intermittently and begin to moult. During this time they bask a great deal in the sunshine on the ice fields. When moulting is over they begin their migration, moving northwards in small groups of ten to twenty animals; thus the annual cycle is completed.

The Canadian population of harp seals is only one of three which inhabit the North Atlantic. Two others occur: one which congregates in the breeding season on the West Ice, that is the pack ice to the north and west of Jan Mayen Island; and the other on the pack ice in the White Sea. Both migrate northwards in summer to the waters about Spitzbergen and Franz Josef Land.

III. Population Assessment of the Harp Seal

A. Aerial Photographic Survey

The whelping and moulting habits of the harp seal make the species particularly amenable to study by aerial photography. The Russians pioneered the work on the White Sea herds in 1926 (Dorofeev and Freimann, 1928; Nazarenko and Yablokov, 1962) and the same method has been used in Canada with some success by members of the Fisheries Research Board (Fisher, 1955; Sergeant, 1963, 1964).

The technique is relatively simple. The patches are located and their general form determined. Strips of photographs are then run across each patch along known bearings and at a known altitude. From the photographs, the scale of which is known, the density of seals may be estimated and then applied to the total area of the patch. This in turn may be estimated by making a mosaic of the photographs and extrapolating for the parts not covered. The adult seals are readily visible in photographs taken at 2000 ft, but low altitude runs between 500 and 1000 ft, or telephoto shots from higher altitudes, are necessary to discern the pups adequately.

While the technique of aerial photography is simple in theory, the method calls for a high degree of skill in navigating. The relative bearings of flight lines across seal patches must be known with fair accuracy, and errors in altitude must be minimal, since they affect the scale of the photographs. Should the patch of seals contain unusually large ice floes, the interior parts of which are usually lightly colonized, the extrapolation of seal density from the flight lines to the remainder of the patch may introduce large errors. Such large floes commonly occur in the Gulf, but on the Front the swells from the Atlantic Ocean break up the ice, giving rise to smaller floes and denser patches of seals.

Once the patches have been located and adequately photographed, and this is no mean task on the Front in view of the distances to be flown and the variability of the weather, there are still many factors which can influence the population estimates. White-coated pups are difficult to detect owing to their cryptic colouration and their habit of lying under overhanging ice blocks. Moreover, it has always been necessary to photograph them before the opening of the sealing season at a time when an unknown proportion of adult females has given birth. When counting adults, similar difficulties are imposed, since the proportion of males to females is not known. At the beginning of our studies it was assumed that all of the adults in the breeding patches were breeding females, but we have since found that adult males, easily recognizable by their rutting odour, are present in the patches in an unknown proportion. Finally the diurnal habits of the adult females have never been known with any certainty, though a few counts of undisturbed pups and adults have been made recently from low-flying helicopters (Sergeant, 1967). In clear weather the proportion of females seen in a patch of well-grown pups may rise to nearly 80% soon after noon, but on overcast days, especially in mid-morning, the proportion may drop as low as 25%. The highest recorded attendance was in a patch of new-born young where

89% were accompanied by females. Clearly much more needs to be known about the behaviour of adults in the whelping patches in the Gulf and on the Front, but this has rarely been possible in the past owing to the early start to the sealing season and the great disturbance resulting from the mass killing of pups.

Recently, Russian biologists under the leadership of L. A. Popov (Popov, 1966), began a detailed study of undisturbed seals in the White Sea. This followed the Soviet Union's ban on commercial sealing in the White Sea for a period of five years beginning in 1965. During the breeding season, a field party was landed on the ice by helicopters and remained for twenty-five days drifting with a large group of seals.

The results of their behavioural studies are of great interest, since they show a greater diurnal variation in numbers of seals on the ice than Sergeant was able to find. On fine sunny days, when aerial photographs would normally be taken, the adult females are practically absent in the morning hours. In the middle of the day about 45–55% are present, and 70–80% are found on the ice in the evening. However, these figures do not represent the percentages of adult females in the total population, since an increasing proportion of adult males enters the whelping patches as the females near the end of lactation and enter oestrus. For this reason Popov suggests that aerial censuses, in conjunction with counts on the ice, could best be made earlier in the season when few males are present.

Estimation of the numbers of seals in moulting patches is also beset with similar difficulties. In April the more open nature of the ice on the Front and its speed of movement to the south cause the moulting herds to shift their position relative to the ice every few days. This necessitates surveying all the patches of seals within a short period, preferably in one day, and rechecking several times if possible. The best period of survey is at the end of April, when all the adult females have hauled out to moult, and only the young of the year and some immature seals are not represented. In the Gulf of St Lawrence this method is of no use, since break-up of the ice occurs early and few seals are able to moult on the floes.

Despite the many uncertainties involved in counting seals directly, the results are useful in showing the trend in numbers of breeding seals over a long period of time. However, since some estimate of the maximum sustainable yield of seals is required in order to set realistic quotas, other, more indirect methods of assessment must be used.

B. Marking Experiments

A useful, but expensive, method of estimating the production of young is by marking a large number of white coats before hunting begins. Such a method calls for an easily applied mark, usually metal or plastic discs pinned to upper and lower surfaces of the tail or a sheep ear tag clipped to the membrane between tail and hind flipper, and a large enough party of men with adequate helicopter support. The services of a powerful ice-breaker are also necessary when pack ice is heavy, as on the Front, and where distances from shore bases prohibit the use of land-based helicopters. Rewards are paid for the return of tags from ships, aircraft and land-based operators, and these must be substantial enough to ensure that tags are not retained by the hunters as souvenirs.

The total of young seals born at the time of tagging may be calculated by simple proportion from the return of tags and the number of seals killed; hence it is important to know the completeness of the returns. In the Gulf returns from individual ships have varied greatly, depending on their success in entering the main areas of tagging. On the other hand, returns from aircraft operators and landsmen have been much better dispersed and are considered to represent a more random sampling of the tagged population. They give rise to a better estimate of numbers of young produced. For example, in 1964 returns of tagged seals from ships gave an estimated pup production of approximately 154,000, while returns from aircraft operators and landsmen gave an estimated production of 120,000. The latter figure may be compared with 93,000 adult seals estimated in the same group of seals by aerial photographic survey (Sergeant, 1965*a*).

On the Front, where aircraft do not operate and few seals are caught by landsmen, returns from Canadian vessels resulted in an estimate of production of 193,000 pups. Perhaps 10% of the young were born after this date to give a total of 213,000. This was increased to a final estimate of 225,000 when allowance was made for pups killed in an untagged patch. The total catch of 168,000 pups on the Front, when considered together with the low escapement of tagged pups to the Arctic, suggest that this estimate of production is realistic (Sergeant, 1967).

IV. Sustainable Yield of Harp Seals

A. Life Tables

While marking experiments can provide a satisfactory estimate of pup production, the maximum sustainable yield of young seals can only be deduced by constructing life tables for hypothetical balanced populations. The basis of such life tables is an accurate method of determining the age of individual seals by means of dentinal annuli in the teeth (Laws, 1953; Sergeant, 1963). Samples of jaws of harp seals have now been obtained, over a number of years in some cases, from West Greenland, south-east Baffin Island, northern Labrador, the north shore of the Gulf of St Lawrence and the moulting patches in the Gulf and on the Front. These age samples have allowed reasonably accurate estimates to be made, not only of mortality rates at different ages, but also of variation in survival rates following kills of known magnitude. Collections of reproductive material have also allowed determination of age-specific birth rates. From the life tables constructed with these data it has been estimated that the sustainable yield of young seals on both the Front and in the Gulf is about 36% of production, provided that kill levels of older seals are low (Sergeant, 1967).

B. Age-class Survival

It is possible to check the accuracy of these estimates of production and sustainable yield by analysing the survival of particular age groups. In such a long-lived species as the harp seal recruitment is probably fairly steady from year to year, since natural mortality of young animals does not appear to show sharp fluctuations. However, hunting mortality varies markedly from year to year, depending on ice conditions, years of heavy hunting being followed by reduced survival and years of light hunting by increased survival.

In the Gulf of St Lawrence age samples of migrant seals have been collected from the net fisheries at La Tabatière on the north shore since 1953. In these samples many younger immature seals are absent because of later migration, but it is believed that the four-year-olds are nearly fully represented. From life tables it is estimated that survival at this age in an exploited population, reproducing at full efficiency, will be about 8% of the total population, or about 10% of the La Tabatière sample where some immatures are absent. When the annual take of pups in the Gulf is compared with their survival as 4-year-olds (Table 1), it appears that the sustained yield lies in the region of 90,000 young seals (Sergeant, 1966*a*). At 36% of production,

Table 1

Catch and Survival of Young Harp Seals from the Gulf of St Lawrence

Year class	*Catch*	*Subsequent survival*	
		Moulting sample	*Netted samples*
1967	91,000	No data	No data
1966	84,000	No data	No data
1965	90,000	No data	No data
1964	81,000	Good	Good 0·12*
1963	95,000	Poor	Poor 0·07
1962	91,000	Poor	Good 0·13
1961	43,000	Good	Good 0·16
1960	84,000	Good	Good 0·17
1959	72,000	Good	Good 0·13

* Four-year-olds expressed as proportion of total netted sample.

this would give a total of 250,000 pups born, about twice as many as have been estimated by aerial photography.

Confirmation of this sustainable yield has been obtained from a sample collected in April 1966 among moulting harp seals in the northern Gulf of St Lawrence (Fig. 2). The sample provides qualitative information on the survival after one year, which is in good agreement with the quantitative results

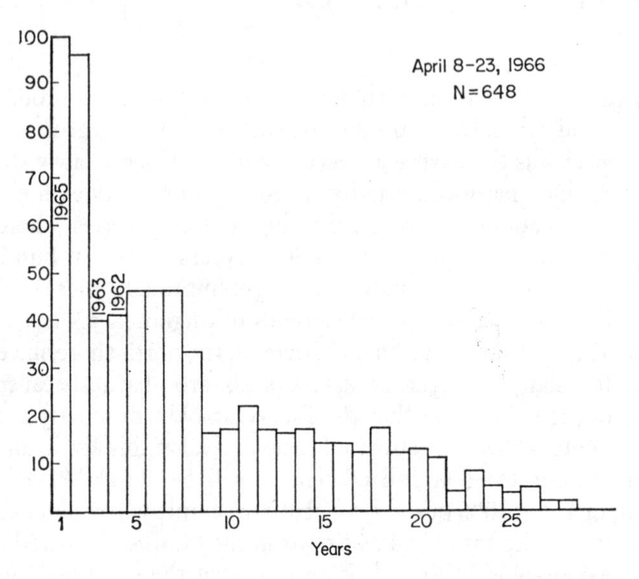

FIG. 2. Age sample of moulting harp seals from the Gulf of St Lawrence.

obtained from the netted samples (Table 1). In the past five years the quota of 50,000 young seals which may be taken by ships and aircraft operating in the southern Gulf of St Lawrence has operated to keep the total catch down to an average of 81,000, the balance of 31,000 seals being made up by landsmen's catches, and catches of moulted pups by ships in the northern area of the Gulf.

On the Front, age samples of moulting seals have also been used to show relative survival (Fig. 3). The results are in extremely good agreement for the two years 1967 and 1968. Very poor survival of the year classes 1963 and 1964 may be correlated with catches of the order of 160,000 and 170,000, and good survival of year class 1960 after a catch of 81,000. However, for more recent year classes the correlation breaks down, particularly for 1966, when a catch of 167,000 was followed by good survival (Table 2).

In seeking to explain this lack of correlation between catch and subsequent survival of the 1966 year class, we must consider whether the Gulf and Front populations of the harp seal are entirely separate entities. Meristic studies (Khuzin, 1967; Yablokov and Sergeant, 1963), biochemical studies (Naevdal, 1965), and tagging studies (Rasmussen and Øritsland, 1964; Sergeant, 1965*b*) have shown that interchange between the Canadian and East Greenland populations is nil or very small, but some exchange does occur between the

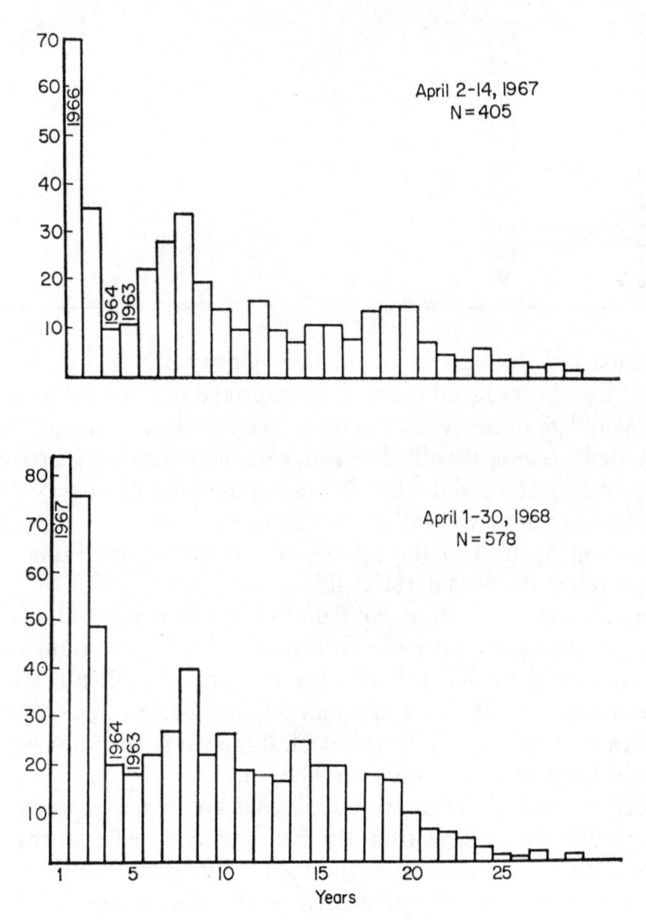

FIG. 3. Age samples of moulting harp seals from the Front.

East Greenland and White Sea populations. In Canada, recent tagging of several thousand pups in the Gulf of St Lawrence has shown a movement to the Front at one year of age (Sergeant, 1968). Tentatively it appears that about one-sixth of the young born in the Gulf in 1966 moved to the Front in 1967, and that these stayed on as 2-year-olds in their adopted herd. It cannot be decided as yet whether this movement is a new phenomenon, resulting

TABLE 2

Catch and Survival of Young Harp Seals from the Front

Year	*Catch* (X 10^3)	*Survival* *Poor*	*Fair*	*Good*
1959	173	X		
1960	81			X
1961	107		X	
1962	114		X	
1963	159	X		
1964	168	X		
1965	90		X	
1966	167			X
1967	185		X	
1968	98		No date	

from the marked decrease in population density of seals on the Front, or whether it has always taken place. It is suspected that these 1-year-old seals, which remain late in the Arctic, move directly to the Front herd because the Strait of Belle Isle is usually blocked with ice when they arrive there in February and March, and also because unusually good feeding may be obtained in eastern Newfoundland at this time. However, in April, when the ice is more open, most of the 1-year-olds appear to leave the Front, presumably to rejoin the herd in the Gulf.

It is an important practical problem to know how much diffusion occurs between the two herds, since the Gulf herd is believed to number about $1\frac{1}{2}$ million, slightly below its optimal level of about $1\frac{3}{4}$ million seals, while the Front herd is greatly depleted, from an original level of $3\frac{1}{4}$ million seals to a present low of 1 million. However, such diffusion is hard to measure, since the tags used appear to drop off with time.

Further evidence that the two populations are largely separate may lie in the finding that female seals from the Gulf attain sexual maturity about one year later than female seals from the Front: five years compared with four years if we consider the 50% pregnancy level (Sergeant, 1966*b*). This reduction in age appears to be a function of population density, since the mean age at sexual maturity has dropped by nearly one year in both populations over a period of 10 to 15 years, in which time both have been reduced by hunting, though admittedly this has been much greater on the Front than in the Gulf (Fig. 4).

There is now some uncertainty about the value of this method since the most recent samples of age and reproductive material from the Gulf, collected in March 1968, show a decrease in the mean age at sexual maturity to 4·3 years, from the previous four years average of five years. However, a possible explanation for this change lies in the heavy kills of young in 1962 and 1963, which lowered the number of animals now aged 6 and 5 years. This may have reduced competition and so permitted earlier maturation of survivors (Sergeant, 1968).

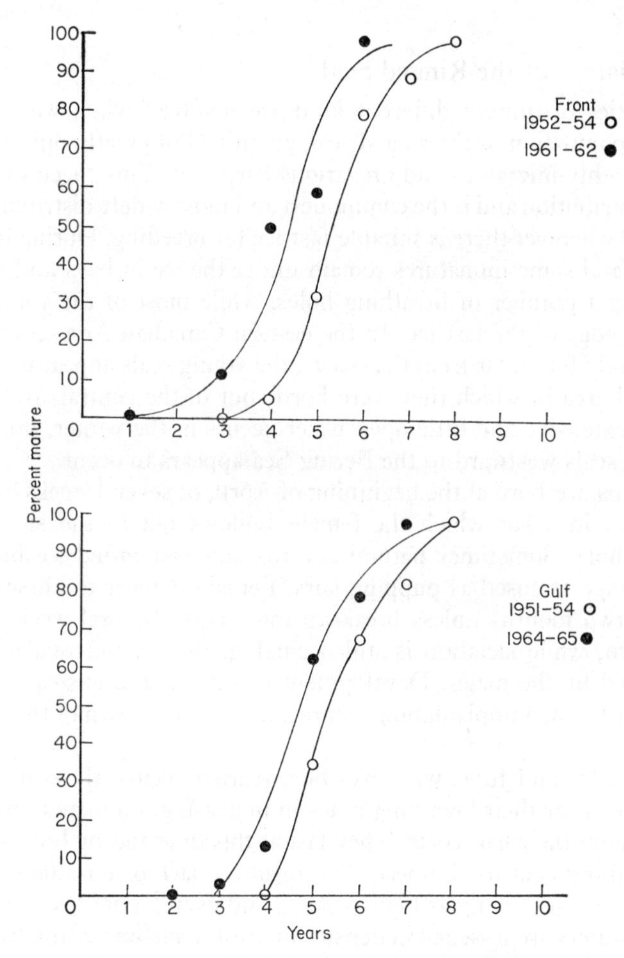

FIG. 4. Ages at sexual maturity of female harp seals from the Gulf and Front.

On the Front, the mean age at sexual maturity cannot be determined with any accuracy from the small number of females collected in 1968, but it appears to lie close to 5 years, rather than 4 years as previously estimated. The reasons for this change are not clear at the present time, since there is no evidence of mixing of year classes which would have reduced the age in the

Gulf or raised it on the Front. It may be tentatively concluded from all these observations that the Gulf and Front populations are largely separate, but that crossing-over of immature seals from the Gulf to the Front occurs intermittently. In future years this conclusion will be tested by repeated tagging of young in the Gulf.

V. Life History of the Ringed Seal

Difficulties of quite a different kind are involved when we attempt to assess the population of the ringed seal, an animal of greatly differing habits from the highly migratory and gregarious harp seal. This species is circumpolar in distribution and is the commonest and most widely distributed Arctic seal, found wherever there is suitable fast ice for breeding. During the winter the adults and some immatures remain under the ice in bays and fjords by maintaining a number of breathing holes, while most of the younger seals stay at the edge of the fast ice. In the eastern Canadian Arctic, where open water is rarely found far from the coasts, the young seals appear to remain in the general area in which they were born; but in the central Arctic, where fast ice is extensive and little open water occurs in the winter, migration of the young seals westward to the Bering Sea appears to occur.

The pups are born at the beginning of April, or several weeks later in the high Arctic, in a lair which the female hollows out in the snow over a breathing hole. Sometimes natural caverns amongst rafted ice blocks in a pressure ridge are used as pupping lairs. Females appear to nurse the pups for up to two months unless break-up intervenes. Several weeks after the pup is born, while lactation is still occurring, the females ovulate and are impregnated by the males. Development of the embryo is suspended until early August, when implantation occurs and normal growth of the embryo is resumed.

During May and June, whenever fine weather occurs, the seals come out on to the ice near their breathing holes in increasing numbers to bask in the sun and moult their hair coats. They fast at this time and by break-up of the ice the blubber is at its thinnest. The resulting lack of buoyancy results in hunting losses by sinking as high as 50%, and even higher losses may occur if surface waters are lessened in density by fresh melt-water from the sea ice. Once the ice is broken up, ringed seals usually remain in the water, very few being seen hauled out on the pack.

The diet of the ringed seal varies considerably. When inshore, epibenthic *Mysis*, prawns and the polar cod *Boreogadus saida* are commonly taken, but offshore the ringed seal feeds exclusively on macroplankton such as the pelagic crustacean *Parathemisto*. Since food may be chosen from many points on the food web, it does not appear to limit the distribution of this species;

nor does it seem to limit the abundance, since the ringed seal may be scarce where food is plentiful and common in regions of low productivity (McLaren, 1962).

VI. Population Assessment of the Ringed Seal

Estimation of the numbers of ringed seals by direct counting is a difficult task owing to the scattered distribution of this species. During the open-water season, when seals appear to disperse up to about 10 miles from shore, counts may be made from shipboard on calm days. The ship is held on a straight course at a known speed and the observer scans the water ahead over an arc of 180°, counting the seals which appear within his field of view. The limit of visibility may be determined by throwing over the side an object, similar in size to a seal's head, and timing its disappearance from view. This distance is rarely more than one-third of a mile.

If the average times which a seal spends on the surface and under water are known, an estimate of the density of seals per unit area of water surveyed is possible, using a formula developed by McLaren (1961). Even though these times vary widely (from 12 to 130 sec on the surface, and 18–720 sec under water, using figures from recent observations on seal behaviour), the bias introduced by using average values is probably not serious, and could not be eliminated without the use of an unnecessarily complicated formula.

No attempt has been made to attach a variance to the estimate of seal numbers, even though seals may not be randomly distributed; for example, seals are known to gather in an area of upwelling 10 miles south-east of Cape Dorset, southern Baffin Island, where heavy concentrations of pelagic amphipods occur (McLaren, 1958*a*). Provided the counts are made over distances of only a few miles, such non-random patterns of distribution will be more easily detected and, as with any method that may be used, the more numerous the local areas surveyed the better will be the population estimates over wider areas. We have found that estimates based on shipboard censuses are low when compared with estimates based on other techniques, but they are useful in indicating relative abundance of seals.

The only other time of the year when ringed seals are amenable to counting is during the moulting period. Unfortunately the scattered distribution does not allow total counts to be made, but estimation of the population over a wide area is possible by making representative counts of seals on small well-defined areas of fast ice. The validity of this method depends on a sound knowledge of the ecology of the ringed seal; in particular its relation to the extent and stability of land-fast ice. There is ample evidence (McLaren, 1958*a*; 1962) that under-exploited ringed seal populations are not limited by food but by the amount of fast ice suitable for the construction of birth lairs.

The most important determinant of the quality and quantity of fast ice is coastal complexity, though weather conditions and large tidal ranges can be important modifying factors. The most stable fast ice with the greatest snow cover is found in bays and fiords, and in regions with numerous islands scattered offshore. Along straight coasts the ice is often unstable and there is usually only a narrow strip of fast ice. The best basis for determining the total population of ringed seals represented by a coastline would be a series of counts of birth lairs on ice of different conditions. These might be carried out in April and early May, in traditional Eskimo fashion, by using dogs to scent out the lairs; but lairs overlain by deeper snowdrifts would be missed by this method. If counts were left until later in the spring, when melting had caused the roofs of lairs to collapse, there would then be the danger of travelling on ice which might be liable to break. Aerial counts would be of little use, since it would not be possible to distinguish between ordinary breathing holes and those associated with breeding lairs. So far these practical limitations have prevented our being able to make useful assessments of this kind.

An alternative method of estimating populations is based on the assumption that almost the entire population of seals can be counted on the fast ice, which remains at the peak of the basking season in the late spring (McLaren, 1961). Counts made from a high point of land overlooking Ney Harbour in Frobisher Bay, south-eastern Baffin Island, best illustrate the seasonal progression of the moulting haul-out, and information from other localities

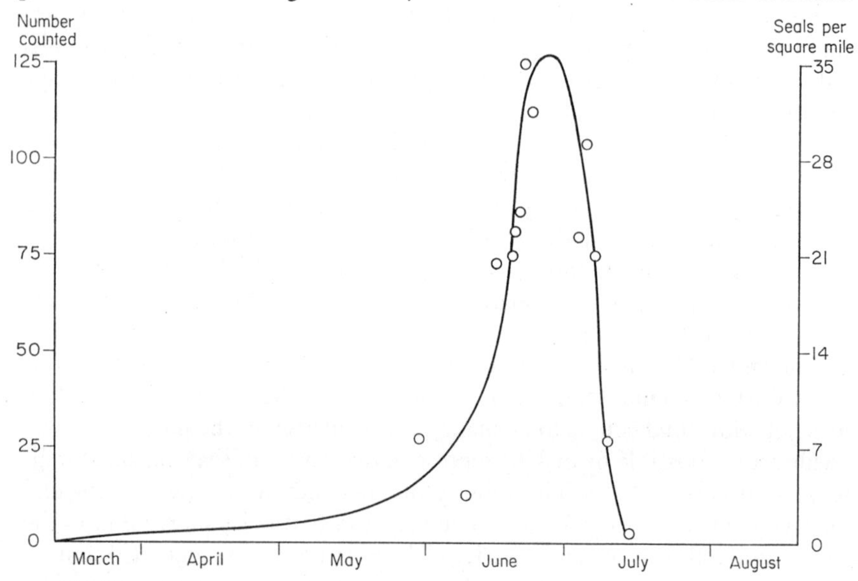

FIG. 5. Seasonal increase in the number of ringed seals hauled out on the fast ice of Ney Harbour, Frobisher Bay, south-east Baffin Island.

suggests that the time of peak haul-out varies directly with latitude (Fig. 5). The figure of thirty-five seals per square mile derived from the counts in Ney Harbour is presumed to apply to the best ice for breeding purposes; that is, ice within 1 mile of shore and over 1 mile from open water. On less suitable ice close to shore along straight coastlines or around the outlying islands of complex coasts (that is, ice within 1 mile of shore and within 1 mile of open water) the density of seals is presumed to be ten per square mile. For ice greater than 1 mile from shore, a figure of five seals per square mile is suggested. By applying these estimates of seal density to the areas of fast ice in each category, which one may calculate by planimeter from maps of suitable scale, population estimates have been derived for the eastern Canadian Arctic, south of Lancaster Sound (McLaren, 1958*b*). In the central Arctic, which is ice-locked in the winter and spring, there are complications caused by the migration of immature seals which have yet to be resolved.

More recently, aerial censuses of moulting ringed seals have been carried out in south-western Baffin Island (McLaren, 1966), but the results do not differ markedly from the earlier estimates.

VII. Sustainable Yield of Ringed Seals

Unlike the harp seal, the ringed seal does not lend itself to marking experiments, since the young are difficult to find when in their birth lairs, and they cannot be caught easily when basking on the ice. Since capture-recapture experiments cannot be performed, the only way of estimating the production of pups appears to lie in the construction of suitable life tables. Unfortunately this method is fraught with many difficulties, since random samples of age classes are hard to obtain. For example, in the hunting catch from south-west Baffin Island, there is considerable under-representation of the first-year seals, which are largely born in inaccessible areas; immature seals become more difficult to catch, since they tend to spend the winter under the fast ice as they get older; and adult seals become fewer as they withdraw progressively to more suitable, and therefore remote, breeding grounds. However, after about fifteen years, adult seals are probably equally accessible and easy to catch, and samples of them can be used to derive mortality curves. Similarly, older immature seals and young adults are probably adequately represented in samples taken in the open-water season.

The mortality rates derived from such samples, when used together with various assumptions about natural mortality in the first year and the proportionate effects of decreasing catchability and natural mortality in the years before maturity is attained, provide adequate data for the construction of realistic life tables. The results obtained by McLaren (1962) show that balanced populations can only vary in size within very narrow limits, in which the annual kill is between about 7% and 10% of the total population at the beginning of each seal year.

In 1958, when McLaren completed his economic analysis of seals in the eastern Canadian Arctic, there was no evidence of overexploitation of any local population. Up to 1962 a maximum of about 20,000 skins had been traded annually in the Arctic, representing perhaps half of the kill. In that year a marked increase in the price of sealskins on the world market led to a rise in the number of skins traded to about 70,000 representing most of the annual kill. This take was maintained until 1966, when greatly reduced prices caused it to drop to a level of about 50,000 seals.

It became apparent in the years of high catch that in some areas the maximum sustainable yield was being exceeded. For example, in Cumberland Sound, south-eastern Baffin Island, the number of skins traded in 1965 rose to 12,500, to which must be added another 10% or 1200 seals, to represent the approximate number lost by sinking (McLaren, 1961; Fig. 4). Even if we assume that immigration of seals from the adjacent undisturbed coastal areas occurred, the overall kill would still have exceeded the maximum sustainable yield given by McLaren (1958*b*) by nearly 2000 seals.

As a means of testing McLaren's estimates of seal abundance, we began a detailed study of ringed seal numbers in the heavily exploited area of Cumberland Sound, south-eastern Baffin Island, in 1966. In 1967 more intensive collections were made in Home Bay, eastern Baffin Island, an area of similar coastal complexity to Cumberland Sound, but relatively lightly exploited. A comparison of these two areas should reveal important information on survival in different age groups and changes in age-specific birth-rates under increased environmental pressure which, as we have seen, occurs in the harp seal.

In order to obtain accurate data on seasonal distribution of seals, we provided Eskimo hunters with maps of the area bearing a simple reference grid, suitable labels written in Eskimo, and containers for jaws and reproductive tracts. By paying an adequate price for accurately labelled specimens we were able to sample virtually the whole of the catch of about 5000 seals. The resulting data are now being prepared for computer analysis and much of the information will be printed out on maps of the area, in the correct position on the reference grids. One of the first things we hope to determine is the pup production in many of the areas of fast ice closer to the settlements where constant traffic probably results in a total kill of all pups born. Such information combined with refined mortality rates should enable us to construct more meaningful life tables and provide realistic quotas for those areas where exploitation levels are high.

VIII. Summary

Long-term studies of the highly migratory harp seal *Pagophilus groenlandicus* and the widely scattered, sedentary, ringed seal *Pusa hispida* show that population assessments can best be made by the collection of adequate biological data and the use of tagging techniques.

Counts of ringed seals basking on fast ice during the moulting period have been used in conjunction with estimation of areas of fast ice to determine absolute population size of this species throughout the eastern Canadian Arctic, but aerial surveys of harp seals during both the pupping and moulting periods have proved of limited value owing to lack of supporting behavioural observations.

References

Dorofeev, S. V. and Freimann, S. Y. (1928). An attempt at a numerical survey of the White Sea harp seal by the method of aerial photography. *Trud. nauch. ryb. Khoz. Moskva*, Ser. 4, 2.

Fisher, H. D. (1955). Utilization of Atlantic harp seal populations. *Trans. 20th N. Am. Wildl. Conf.* Pp. 507–18.

Khuzin, R. Sh. (1967). The variability of craniological characters of the harp seal. *Trud. poliar. nauch.-issled. Inst. morsk. ryb. Khoz.* 21, 27–50.

Laws, R. M. (1953). A new method of age determination in mammals with special reference to the elephant seal (*Mirounga leonina*, Linn.) *Falkland Islands Dependencies Sc. Rep.* 2, 11 pp.

McLaren, I. A. (1958*a*). The biology of the ringed seal (*Phoca hispida* Schreber) in the eastern Canadian Arctic. *Bull. Fish. Res. Bd. Can.* **118**, 97 pp.

McLaren, I. A. (1958*b*). The economics of seals in the eastern Canadian Arctic. *Fish Res. Bd. Can. Arctic Unit Circular* 1, 94 pp.

McLaren, I. A. (1961). Methods of determining the numbers and availability of ringed seals in the eastern Canadian Arctic. *Arctic* **14**, No. 3, 162–75.

McLaren, I. A. (1962). Population dynamics and exploitation of seals in the eastern Canadian Arctic. *In* "The Exploitation of Natural Animal Populations" (E. D. LeCren and M. W. Holdgate, eds), pp. 168–83. Blackwell Scientific Publications, Oxford.

McLaren, I. A. (1966). Analysis of an aerial census of ringed seals. *J. Fish. Res. Bd. Can.* **23**, No. 5, 769–73.

Naevdal, G. (1965). Protein polymorphism used for identification of harp seal populations. *Årbok Univ. Bergen, Mat.-Naturv.* No. 9, 20 pp.

Nazarenko, Y. I. and Yablokov, A. V. (1962). An evaluation of existing census methods for the White Sea harp seal and reflections on the state of the stock. *Zool. Zh.* **41**, 1875–1882. (Fish. Res. Bd. Canada, Translation Ser. 459.)

Popov, L. A. (1966). On an ice floe with the harp seals: Ice drift of biologists in the White Sea. *Priroda, Mosk.* 9, 93–101. (Fish. Res. Bd. Canada, Translation Ser. 814.)

Rasmussen, B. and Øritsland, T. (1964). Norwegian tagging of harp seals and hooded seals in North Atlantic waters. *Fisk. Dir. Skr.* **13**, No. 7, 43–55.

Sergeant, D. E. (1963). Harp seals and the sealing industry. *Can. Audubon* **25**, No. 2, 29–35.

Sergeant, D. E. (1964). Exploitation and conservation of harp and hood seals. *Polar Rec.* **12**, No. 80, 541–51.
Sergeant, D. E. (1965*a*). Capture-recapture marking of harp seals in the Gulf of St Lawrence. *Fish. Res. Bd. Can. Arctic Biol. Station Ann. Rep.* 35–37.
Sergeant, D. E. (1965*b*). Migrations of harp seals (*Pagophilus groenlandicus* Erxleben). *J. Fish. Res. Bd. Can*, **22**, No. 2, 433–64.
Sergeant, D. E. (1966*a*). On the population dynamics of the western harp seal stocks. *Int. Comm. Northw. Atlant. Fish.* **1749**, MS, 19 pp.
Sergeant, D. E. (1966*b*). Reproductive rates of harp seals (*Pagophilus groenlandicus* Erxleben). *J. Fish. Res. Bd Can.* **23**, No. 5, 757–66.
Sergeant, D. E. (1967). Canadian research on harp seals in 1967, with further results from 1966 and previous years. *Int. Comm. Northw. Atlant. Fish.* **1952**, MS, 22 pp.
Sergeant, D. E. (1968). Canadian research on harp seals in 1968. MS, 12 pp.
Yablokov, A. V. and Sergeant, D. E. (1963). Cranial variation in the harp seal (*Pagophilus groenlandicus* Erxleben, 1777). *Zool. Zh.* **42**, No. 12, 1857–65. (Fish. Res. Bd. Canada, Translation Ser. 485.)

Discussion

Biology of Seals

L. HARRISON MATTHEWS

These papers demonstrate that we need to learn more about the behaviour of seals under as well as above the ice. It is obvious, also, that more is known about the more accessible animals. Thus the Weddell seal is best known, the crabeater seal less well known, and the Ross and leopard seals comparatively little known.

COLOUR DIFFERENCES IN CRABEATER SEALS

A. W. MANSFIELD

In September 1952 several hundred crabeater seals entered inshore leads off the South Orkney Islands. They were in pairs, each pair appearing to consist of one silvery-coloured male and a darker, slightly mottled, female. Assuming that pelt colour changes at the moult, this dimorphism might suggest a different timing of moulting in the two sexes.

D. SINIFF

We were in the Weddell Sea throughout the moulting period, but our observations do not suggest sexual dimorphism. We felt that the older crabeater seals were the palest.

T. ØRITSLAND

I agree that there is a change in colour with age, but do not think there is a difference between the sexes. Every seal lightens considerably when it moults. In crabeaters the change is from fawn to a silvery hue. Ross seals probably change similarly: I showed a photograph of a darkish animal visibly shedding small patches of skin, while the Scott Polar Research Institute has a paler, probably post-moult, skin.

DIFFICULTIES IN SEAL-CENSUS WORK

R. W. VAUGHAN

Dr Ray mentioned misidentification of Ross seals and I can confirm this. When counting seals from a ship in the ice I twice took over watch and saw a Ross seal that the non-biologist I was relieving had logged as a Weddell or elephant.

There may be gross errors if the proportion of species among the seals seen is assumed to reflect the true ratio of species abundance. Dr Øritsland, for example, saw one Weddell only, but he worked during the time when the Weddells were inshore breeding, and his figures would have been different had he been in the ice after the Weddells had dispersed in November. Seasonal changes must be allowed for.

D. B. SINIFF

During our cruise we classified seals which we could not identify as "unknown" and then, for the density estimates, apportioned these on the basis of our identified samples. Certainly there are dangers in doing this. However, we again confirmed our census data during extensive blood-collecting operations on the ice floes, where we found the same general species composition. There are, incidentally, clear differences in blood-serum proteins between species.

M. S. R. SMITH

I must question the reliability of the method by which one can identify seals positively from 300 ft. It is important to take into account seasonal changes in dispersion, such as the dispersion of breeding Weddell seals, and other species would possibly complicate the picture. The proportion of seals in the water and lying on the ice at various seasons and times of day, and variable weather conditions must be assessed. These results may be forthcoming from Dr Carleton Ray's underwater studies on the Weddell seal. The time of day when the counts are taken will affect the numbers seen because the Weddell seal at least has a diurnal rhythm of lying on the ice. They feed in the evening hours.

In Smith (1965) I used four parameters of weather—temperature, wind velocity, solar radiation and cloud cover—to see what effect these have on the numbers of seals lying on the ice. Solar radiation was an accumulated result over the 24-hour period. It was seen that only wind velocity was significantly correlated with seal abundance in both years, but cross-correlation of this weather component suggested that its effect was augmented by the other factors.

But thermoregulation of polar pinnipedes presents two different situations: that in air where it is suggested that vasodilation and high skin temperatures are normal and in water where vasoconstriction and low skin temperatures are normal. In both it is suggested the animal seeks to maintain thermoneutrality.

References: Ray, C. and Smith, M. S. R. (1968). *Zoologica* 53, 1, pp. 33–46.
Smith, M. S. R. (1965). *Journ. Wild. Man.* 29 (3), pp. 446–7.

D. B. SINIFF

I agree identification from 300 ft can be difficult unless the animal moves, when behavioural characters are a great help.

C. RAY

This is not, in my experience, too bad a problem. A helicopter pilot can get most identifications right, after a little experience. On a sunny day with good visibility there is a marked colour difference between species and the aircraft generally disturbs the seals, making behaviour differences observable.

T. ØRITSLAND

A paper by Müller-Schwartze (1965)* on diurnal periodicity of hauling out in Weddell seal suggests a correlation between light intensity and the number hauled out.

M. S. R. SMITH

Cloud cover and incident radiation were not significantly correlated with hauling

* See p. 365.

out in my study. In December and January I looked to see whether seals had been feeding just before hauling out. Ten animals killed on emergence from their hole all had full stomachs, and I suggest they haul out to digest.

E. C. YOUNG

Ian Stirling has made a detailed study of population parameters in Weddell seal. One point is that this species is not confined to fast ice, but also found in the pack, and we must try to find the ratio between the numbers in these two situations.

C. RAY

Over 30% of the seals within 60 miles of shore in the Ross Sea were Weddells and half of these were in the pack. However, this may be a local phenomenon peculiar to the Ross Sea. Clearly some animals enter the pack elsewhere, but they seem less common there in the Weddell Sea and Peninsula regions. The Weddell seal is a bottom feeder, taking benthic Nototheniids especially, and it likes to stay in shallower water. Unquestionably the Weddell seal is more coastal than other species.

M. H. THURSTON

I can report Weddell seals in the Weddell Sea in two successive years: two out of a total of over 100 seals in January 1963 and three out of 200 in the following season. These Weddells were all in the same area, around 10°W and 200 miles offshore.

FUR SEALS

G. A. LLANO

In 1965–66 I flew to Elephant Island from USCGC *Eastwind* and along a mile or so of beach I counted fifty fur seals; ten of these had a light brown pelage. On the same cruise I observed two fur seals on the lee side of a large rock on Gibbs Island. Similarly, while in the vicinity of the South Orkney Islands about twelve elephant seals were observed on ice off Larsen Island. A large number of fur seals, estimated at 300, were seen in the water and on the beach in this area. These included five pups.

W. N. BONNER

Pale-coated fur seals were first reported in the South Orkney Islands by Dr Øritsland, and are also present at South Georgia. Since parallel appearance of this gene is unlikely, it suggests that the fur seals of the Scotia Ridge are derived from a single parent population, and this was possibly the South Georgia one.

POPULATION PARAMETERS OF ANTARCTIC SEALS

A. W. ERICKSON

Attention certainly needs to be given to the population parameters of Antarctic seals, and Dr Øritsland's report is a fine start in this direction. I am surprised, however, by the wide spread in the sexual maturity times he reports. I would rather suspect that the age-determination technique to which these reproductive data were related are in error. Confirmation of the tooth-sectioning age-determination technique needs to be obtained from known age marked animals, and I would urge that this be given early attention. I would also caution the back-calculation of sexual maturity on the basis of corpora albicantia, since it is likely that the life of corpora albicantia may be variously influenced by age, reproductive history, et cetera.

As an aside from Dr Øritsland's paper, I am also surprised to see such terms as "fertility" so widely misused in ecological studies. Fertility means "ability to reproduce". It does not mean "production of pups". Similarly ovulation incidence is the true reflection of potential pup production, not pup counts or pup: cow ratios. Such data are, in fact, seldom even a suitable indication of reproductive performance and are rather survival considerations. In view of this mixed jargon, I would propose that we adopt the terminology of the reproductive physiologist. Another point: the period when seals are ashore bearing young is surely the *whelping* and *rearing* period, not the *breeding* period unless actual breeding occurs at this time.

W. N. Bonner

Dr Øritsland *did* define what he meant and that is surely the essential point. Terminology has developed differently in different countries: if we all define our terms, confusion will not arise.

L. Harrison Matthews

In Europe "breeding" is used to refer to the whole reproductive period: the American Brer Rabbit was bawn an' bred in his briar patch!

In listening to Dr Mansfield I was impressed by the advantages to science that comes from the development of a sealing industry, with the consequent influx of material and knowledge. On this basis the development of a moderate Antarctic sealing industry might be the best way of advancing Antarctic seal research.

Part VIII

ADAPTATION IN SEALS

Adaptation in seals

The study of adaptation to polar conditions is one of the most readily justifiable fields of Antarctic research and the papers in this section demonstrate the range of research on marine mammals now going on. They demonstrate that adaptations of the heat-regulating system, summarized by L. Irving in the introductory review paper, involve not only the development of fatty insulating layers below the fur (which itself has little insulation value) but the adjustment of metabolic levels, and in some species the development of maternal behavioural adaptations to shelter a pup which could not withstand the environment unaided. N. A. Øritsland shows, further, that the hair and feather structures in polar homeotherms are adapted for efficient absorbtion of solar radiation.

These adaptations are paralleled by equally striking physiological adjustment in relation to diving, discussed by R. W. Elsner, C. Lenfant and their collaborators in the two following papers. Finally, A. C. Cuello and G. Wilson consider two quite different aspects of seal physiology, the relation between pineal function and annual cycle, and the visual adaptation in the Weddell seal. These papers, as a series, thus show the range of research topics for which Antarctic seals are now providing material.

Morpho-physiological Adaptations in Marine Mammals for Life in Polar Areas

LAURENCE IRVING
Institute of Arctic Biology, University of Alaska, College, Alaska, U.S.A.*

Exploration of waters near coasts of populated lands led to reduction of the population of seals and whales that reached its climax with the near extinction of many species in the nineteenth century. As the range of shipping increased and under pressure of increasing human demand for flesh and oils, sealers and whalers moved into Arctic and Antarctic waters. The selective influence of geographical accessibility brought about a great decline in many populations of warmer waters that accentuates the numerical predominance of the seals and whales now living in the Arctic and Antarctic.

The exploited whales are large among mammals, with long seasonal migrations commonly leading to extended periods in seas where they derive rich food supplies in oceanic conditions related to polar ice fronts. Narwhals (*Monodon*) dwell near and in Arctic ice; bow head whales (*Balaena*) and belugas (*Delphinapterus*) penetrate deeply into leads in Arctic ice where they are utilized by small Eskimo populations. A number of species of porpoises do not venture beyond warm waters, but one of the smaller kinds, the harbour porpoise (*Phocoena phocoena*) which weighs only 50 kg, shows adaptability to cold and even small whales show their versatility in thermoregulation by ranging between low latitudes and polar ice fronts.

The reproduction of whales occurs at sea, where it is not easy to locate their breeding areas. Seals and walrus, on the other hand, breed on firm bases of ice or shore, where their native localities can be determined, and the world populations of many species have been estimated by Scheffer (1958, pp. 3–5). The majority of species of seals and the most numerous populations breed on northern and southern ice. In fact, the only great population of shore-breeding seals is found in the northern but Subarctic shore rookeries of fur seals (*Callorhinus ursinus*). The near extinction of several easily accessible populations of shore-breeding seals may have selectively reduced the species now attached to shores, but it remains true that of thirty populations

* Publication No. 90.

of Phocidae (counting some subspecies) listed by Scheffer (1958), seventeen breed on ice. The habit was evidently anciently established in several species and only a few species show adaptability for both shore and ice breeding. Adding Scheffer's estimate of minimum numbers gives the sum of 11,000,000 individuals of ice breeders. The seals accordingly show a preference for polar conditions.

Utilization of icy waters demonstrates adaptability of those populations for life in cold water. In respect to diving and swimming the forms and physiology of marine mammals would not seem to require important adaptation to polar conditions except for the requirement of ability to preserve appropriate mammalian warmth in the cold polar waters. At the ice margins and in open sea leads within the ice, sea-water temperatures in superficial waters in which sea mammals feed are below −1°C. In view of the large heat capacity of water we may say that polar waters constitute the coldest environment occupied by mammalian life and that adaptation for heat conservation appears of special importance.

The heat generated by marine mammals has been measured by indirect calorimetry in small representatives of five species of seals on numerous occasions at rest, in air and in water (Fig. 1). All of these seals were of

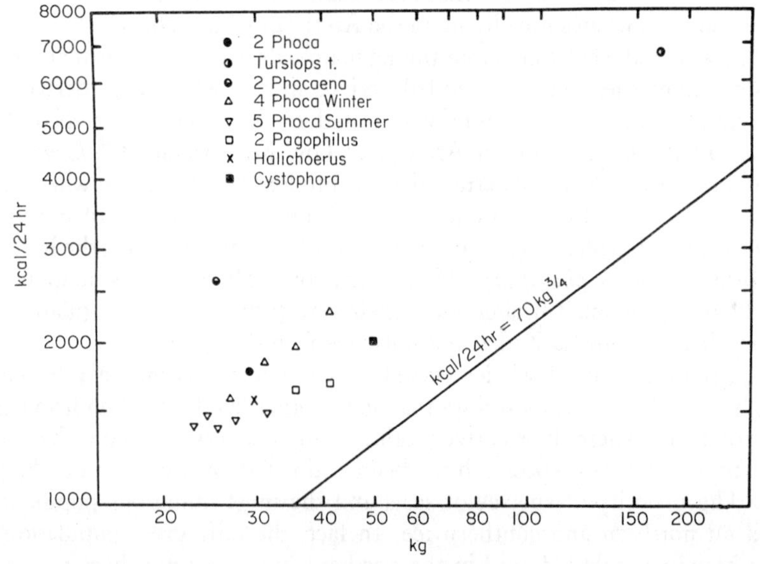

FIG. 1. Resting metabolic rates of seals and porpoise. Compiled from several authors.

northern range, but only harp (*Pagophilus*) and hooded (*Cystophora*) seals are of Arctic ice-breeding populations. There is a reasonable consistency in these measurements and common indication that their metabolic rates are from one and a half to over two times the rate commonly found in land mammals of corresponding size. It looks as if high metabolic rates are characteristic of seals, but we see no differentiation in the ice breeders.

I cannot forgo a comment upon the consistency of these measurements in several studies in which wild seals were more or less severely restrained. The experimenters remarked that the seals accepted the circumstances of restraint and breathing through a mask with apparent equanimity and remained metabolically undisturbed; going through experimental dives and changes in temperature with most agreeably regular reactions. This suitability for experimental treatment without disturbance makes the seals most satisfactory contributors to physiology. At the same time, the seals were neither phlegmatic nor intrinsically subdued, for they remained alert to bite accurately at a carelessly exposed hand.

Measurements of metabolism by indirect calorimetry in whales are confined to two species, *Tursiops* and *Phocoena*. In the warm water of Florida that is natural for them the metabolic rate of *Tursiops* was about double that of land mammals of their size (Irving *et al.*, 1941), and Kanwisher and Sundnes (1965) found similar elevated metabolism in a small (26 kg) *Phocoena* in cool (8°) water at Bergen. By measurements of heat flow from the skin of *Tursiops* and *Phocoena*, Kanwisher and Sundnes (1965) reckoned their heat production to be in accord with the respiratory measurements of metabolism. The amiable porpoises likewise appeared to accept experimental conditions without disturbance.

I would not care to extrapolate from porpoises to the metabolic heat production of large whales. Kanwisher remarked that, in producing more heat than land mammals of their size, since blubber is near half of their weight, the presumed active metabolizing fraction of the tissues of porpoises must be intensely active within their envelope of blubber.

Exposure of young harbour seals (*Phoca vitulina*) to cold air or water showed that their reactions differed in winter and summer by adaptation for more economical maintenance of bodily warmth during exposure to cold in winter (Fig. 2) (Hart and Irving, 1959). Harp seals (*Pagophilus*) did not increase metabolism in ice water (Irving and Hart, 1957). We can suspect that polar seals and whales can live in ice water without greater metabolic expenditure for maintenance of internal warmth than their relatives in milder climates. In respect to metabolic economy, polar mammals are not disadvantaged by cold nor is there any reason to suspect that they encounter metabolic stress. It is certainly a valuable physiological adaptation for polar life if the resident animals do not need to consume extra food in order to keep warm.

Among adult marine mammals fur seals are the only ones that utilize the insulation of fur in the economy of metabolic heat. The ice-breeding seals are sparsely covered with hair, which becomes wet through to their skin and has but little insulation in comparison with the thick fur covering of Arctic land mammals. Walrus and whales are hairless and their skin is in direct contact with ice water. For insulation the seals allow their skin to approach the temperature of the surrounding water. A gradient of temperature

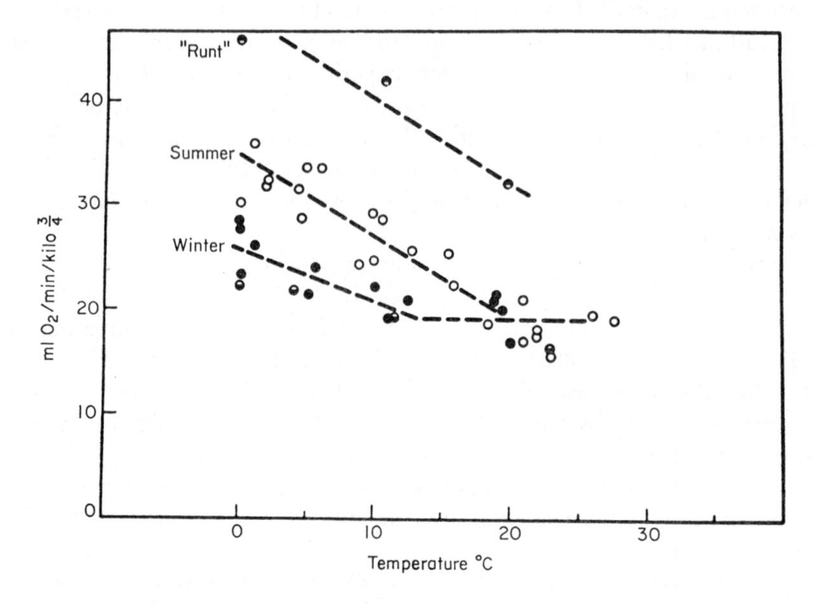

FIG. 2. Metabolism of harbour seals (*Phoca vitulina*) in winter and summer. From Hart and Irving (1959).

extends from skin to the interior, where warmth characteristic of mammals prevails (Fig. 3). In utilizing this gradient situation as an effective insulator in polar sea water a large mass of tissue may be over 30°C cooler than the warm interior of the body. In addition to this spatial variation in temperature the gradient must change from time to time, as the animal's metabolic heat production changes about tenfold in passing from rest to full activity, or as the seal emerges on to ice in the warm and strong sunshine of late spring.

That animals devoid of insulating fur utilize temperature gradients in their regulation of bodily heat is not novel; but the amounts of tissue involved and the rapidity of their large temperature changes is most impressive in polar marine mammals. This degree of heterothermous activity of their superficial tissues is essential for their metabolic economy. Although it has not been experimentally determined that the extent of this thermolability is peculiar to polar marine mammals, I believe that it is the adaptation that permits their successful existence.

More than is the case with us hairless humans, whose modest intrinsic insulation is provided by variability in superficial temperatures, the polar mammals bring forward the need for determining the ability of mammalian tissues to operate at low temperatures. As a suitable example, my colleague Keith Miller (1968*a*) has measured the characteristics of spinal nerve con-

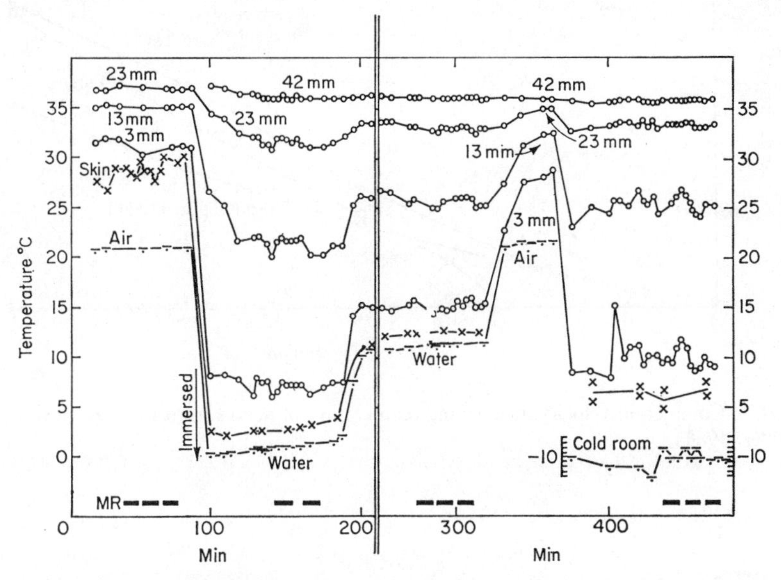

FIG. 3. Temperatures at various depths in a seal in air and water. From Hart and Irving (1959).

duction in four species of ice-dwelling seals on a recent cruise of Scripps R'V *Alpha Helix* through ice of Bering Sea in March 1968 (Fig. 4). An interesting summary is provided by the velocities of conduction shown by several nerves at various temperatures.

We can see that the excised peripheral nerves from the phalangeal region of the flippers, often naturally exposed to and approaching the −1·5°C to −1·8°C of the sea, continue to show normally operating action potentials down to −5°C, when they are some 4° supercooled below their measured freezing-point. The more central part of the nerve from the pelvic region showed a decrement in conduction below +5°C (ceasing at—3°C) and the phrenic nerve was blocked by cold at +7°C. The pelvic region is not exposed to temperature variations as large as the phalangeal tissues, and the phrenic nerve in its interior position operates under homoiothermous conditions.

Refractory periods of the nerves, which indicate capability for transmitting information by frequency modulation, show also marked decline in that capacity with cooling temperature (Fig. 5). Peripheral, deeper and internal

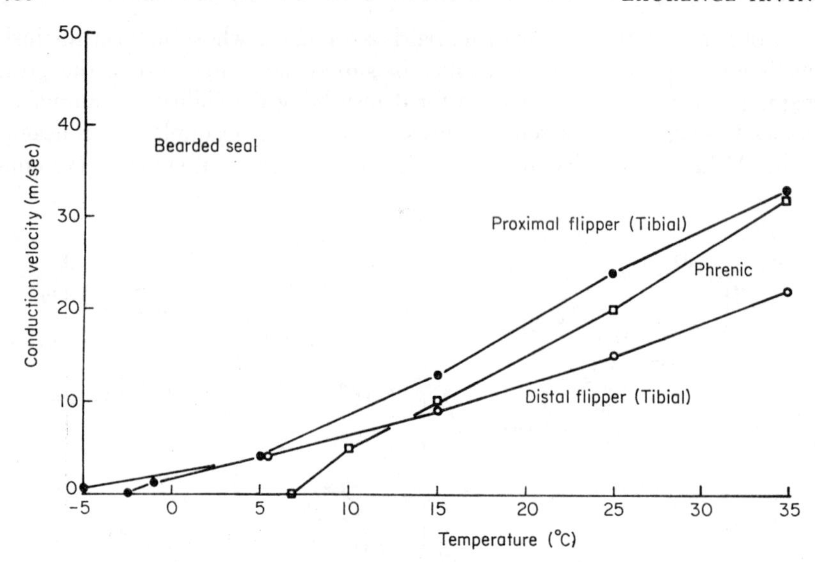

FIG. 4. Conduction velocity in warming temperature in nerves from Bearded Seal. From Miller (1968*a*).

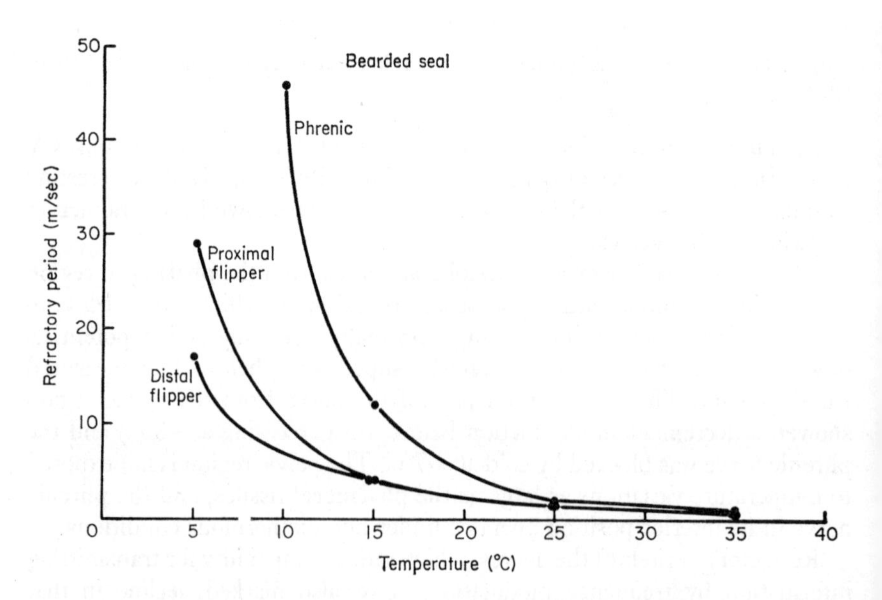

FIG. 5. Refractory periods of seal nerves at various temperatures. From Miller (1968*a*).

nerves increase refractory periods more in the order named. At the low temperatures that are often natural for phalangeal tissues the capability for frequency transmission in excised nerves is so reduced that it seems as if transfer of information would be quite limited.

Since Miller (1968*b*) has found the nerves from bare and thinly insulated tails of Arctic land aquatic mammals to exceed the nerves from well-furred and warm tails in capability for low-temperature operation, we must consider that the seal nerves illustrate the remarkable thermal adaptability of peripheral mammalian tissues to operate over a range of 40°C. Poikilothermous organisms and their tissues do not equal in thermal tolerance the range utilized by tissues of mammals and birds.

In spite of their tolerance of a wide thermal range, the mammalian nerves are similar in that cooling diminishes velocity of conduction by about one-half for each 10°C change. Although I have no useful speculation to present, I am puzzled how integration can be effected between the periphery and centre of a mammal through a communicating system in which velocity and rate functions are changing twentyfold to thirtyfold.

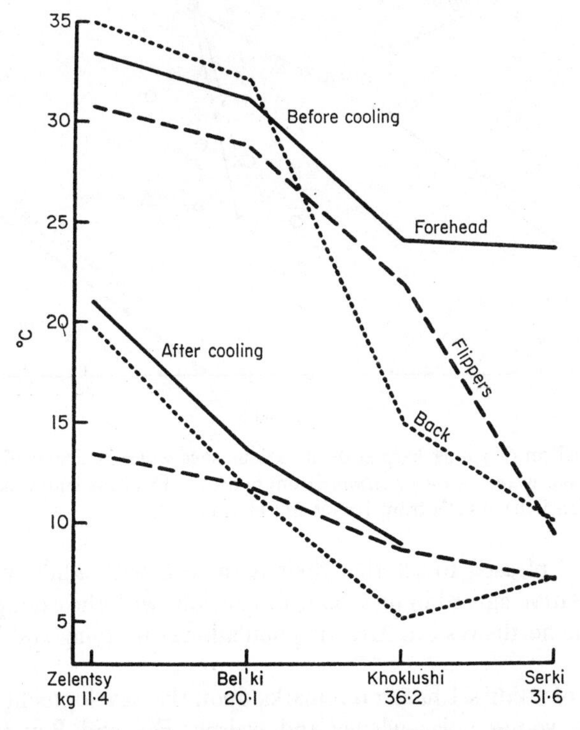

FIG. 6. Skin temperatures of young harp seals at various ages when dry in cool air and after immersion in cold water. From Davydov and Makarova (1964).

An interesting view of the development of thermoregulation is presented by the birth of the pups of ice-breeding seals with an insulating coat of fur comparable to that of Arctic land mammals. After a few weeks or months of rapid fattening in a non-aquatic air-dwelling life on ice the natal fur is moulted and replaced by the short adult hair cover. As infants their skin is kept warm by the covering fur; but gradually and quite rapidly with acquisition of an envelope of blubber the skin and superficial tissues gain the adult capability of tolerating cold and serving as an effective insulator in cold water, as is nicely shown by the demonstrations of Davydov and Makarova (1964) (Fig. 6). They showed that infant fur-covered harp seals (*Pagophilus*) from the White Sea population lost heat rapidly when immersed in cold water. After moulting and fattening the pups assumed the adult faculty of resisting ice water without special expenditure of metabolic heat (Fig. 7). I was

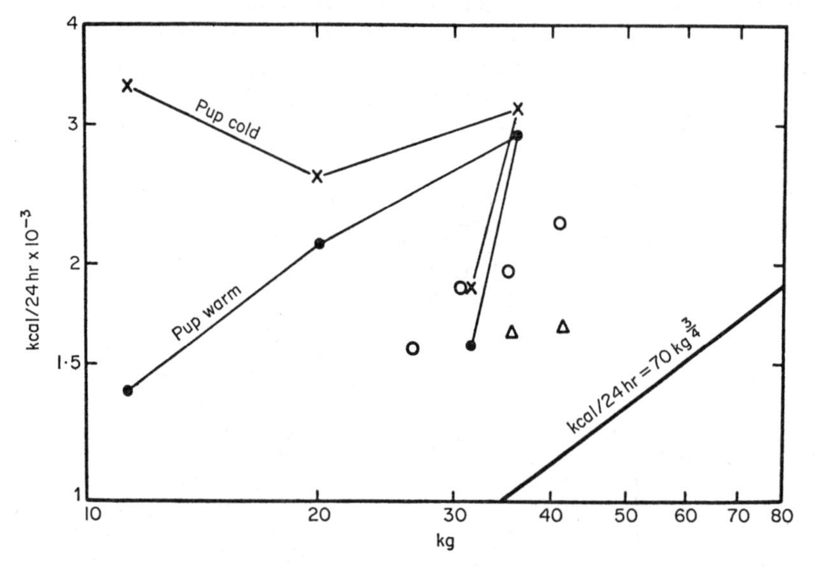

FIG. 7. Metabolism of young harp seals at various ages when in dry, cool air and after immersion in cold water. o, *Phoca vitulina* from figures of Davydov and Makarova (1964). Δ, western Atlantic harp seals from Irving and Hart (1957).

interested and pleased to see that their harp seals with adult type of bare-skinned insulation agreed in metabolic dimensions with the examples of harp seals from the north-western Atlantic population that Irving and Hart (1957) examined.

For want of studies I have no remarks upon the development of thermoregulation in young polar whales and walrus. Fay and Ray (1968) have shown, however, that walrus pups receive and require covering protection from their mothers in cold air, although tolerant of cold water at birth. This development of thermoregulation to tolerance of polar conditions shows combinations of morphological, physiological and behavioural adaptations and is of very great interest.

The adaptations of polar marine populations show the utilization of the versatile mammalian adaptability for which counterpart reactions are seen in land mammals. The severity of polar marine conditions demands exceptional exertion of what we may regard as common mammalian capabilities for thermoregulation. The evolution of these profound physiological developments is hard to understand when the time scale of evolution of modern polar environments is considered. Pleistocene and Post-Pleistocene climates and land environments have passed through enormous transitions at rates that seem too rapid for the progress of adaptive evolution. The capabilities of polar populations in accommodating to polar environmental changes is certainly impressive in extent and as we come to know better the stages in progress, the rate of adaptive changes will become a most illuminating subject for polar studies.

Acknowledgement

This work was supported in part by NIH Grant GM-10402.

References

Davydov, A. F. and Makarova, A. R. (1964). Changes in Heat Regulation and Circulation in New Born Seals. *Fedn Proc. Fedn Am. Socs exp. Biol.* Suppl. 24 (II), T 563–6.

Fay, F. H. and Ray, C. (1968). Influence of Climate on the Distribution of Walruses, *Odobenus rosmarus* (Linnaeus), 1. Evidence from Thermoregulatory Behavior. *Zoologica* 53, 1–18.

Hart, J. S. and Irving, L. (1959). The energetics of Harbor Seals in Air and in Water with Special Consideration of Seasonal Changes. *Can. J. Zool.* 37, 447–57.

Irving, L. and Hart, J. S. (1957). The Metabolism and Insulation of Seals as Bare-Skinned Mammals in Cold Water. *Can. J. Zool.* 35, 497–511.

Irving, L., Scholander, P. F. and Grinnell, S. W. (1941). The Respiration of the Porpoise, *Tursiops truncatus*. *J. cell. comp. Physiol.* 17, 145.

Kanwisher, J. and Sundnes, G. (1965). Thermal Regulation in Cetaceans. *In* "Whales, Dolphins and Porpoises" (K. S. Norris, ed) pp. 397–409. Univ. Calif. Press, Berkeley.

Miller, L. K. (1968*a*). Temperature Adaptation in Peripheral Nerve Tissue of Northern Hair Seals. (Unpublished).

Miller, L. K. (1968*b*). Metabolism and Temperature Regulation of Northern Beaver. (Unpublished).

Scheffer, V. B. (1958). "Seals, Sea Lions and Walrus: A Review of Pinnipedia." 179 pp. Stanford Univ. Press, Calif.

Energetic Significance of Absorption of Solar Radiation in Polar Homeotherms

NILS ARE ØRITSLAND
Institute of Zoophysiology, University of Oslo, Norway

I. Introduction

Temperature measurements on Arctic and Subarctic plants as well as poikilotherm animals, reported by Krog (1955), indicate special adaptations for utilization of solar radiation. Krog found that surface structures like transparent hairs function under a physical principle similar to the greenhouse window, i.e. bright hairs may transmit solar radiation to the underlying layers, but do not transmit long-wave radiation in an outward direction. Thus, the central temperature of structures such as *Salix* catkins or Arctiid (Lepidoptera) caterpillars "Woolly bears" may be 15°C warmer than the surrounding air when exposed to the sun.

Mammalian furs should be regarded as opaque to solar radiation and radiation with wavelengths up to 30μ when the skin surface is not visible through the fur and when the hair density is above 100–1000 hairs/cm^2 (Tregear, 1966). Examination of tropical merino sheep revealed that their wool gives significant protection against hyperthermia due to solar radiation (MacFarlane *et al.*, 1956).

Hamilton and Heppner (1967) studied the oxygen consumption of white zebra finches using an artificial sun in a cold environment and found a considerable decrease after the animals had been dyed black. These authors suggested that the colour of a homeothermic animal is of considerable importance for its energy budget in nature, reducing the metabolic cost of maintaining a constant body temperature.

Arctic and Antarctic homeotherms, living above the snow surface, are usually insulated effectively against conductive and convective heat loss to the surrounding air. However, solar radiation will always be a potential source of energy during the long summer days, is independent of air temperatures, and may be utilized. There is, therefore, special reason to investigate the role of solar radiation in the heat balance of Arctic and Antarctic homeotherms. The present investigations were performed on harp seals in order to analyze:

(1) the relationship between hair colour and the warming of seals by absorption of solar radiation;
(2) the relationship between the wavelength of the incident radiation and heat uptake by seals;
(3) the contribution of solar radiation to the heat balance of seals when lying ashore.

II. Methods

In order to examine the heating effect of solar radiation on skin covered with different-coloured hair; samples of dark-furred, bright-furred, and shaved skin were taken together with the adhering blubber and embedded in styrofoam. Subcutaneous temperatures were measured with thermocouple needles inserted from below through the blubber toward the skin (Fig. 1).

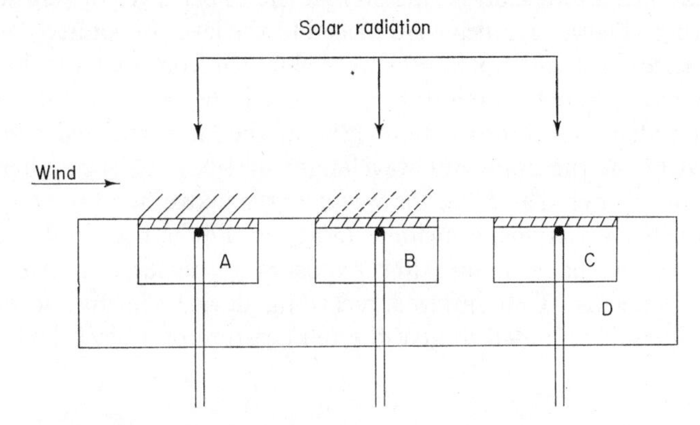

FIG. 1. Arrangement for recording skin temperatures of dark (A), bright (B) and shaved (C) pelts. The samples were embedded in a styrofoam block (D) and temperatures obtained subcutaneously by use of thermocouples.

The temperature of the air and stryrofoam were lower than those at the points of measurement in the skin, thus confirming that the heat flows were always directed outwards from the points of measurement to the immediate environment. Absorption of long-wave radiation from the surroundings was assumed to be close to 100% for all three samples, in accordance with the findings of Hammel (1956).

The first approach to an analysis of the radiation type which would produce an optimal differential heating effect was spectrophometric tests on normal hairs. The tests were performed with a Beckman DU and IR 8 and a Spectromaster I-R spectrophotometer. Filling the cell with an arbitrary number of hairs, transmission curves inevitably changed greatly when the hairs were repacked between series of measurements; but the general smooth slope of the curves was reproducible.

Examinations of transmittance in the 1·0–5μ band were accomplished by taping hairs to a paper with a rectangular aperture in such a way that the hairs lay across the opening and were penetrated by the light beam.

In order to perform reflectance measurements in the 350–1000 nm region, a reflectance attachment to the Beckman DU spectrophotometer was used, and diffuse reflectance of pelt samples was measured relative to the reflectance of magnesium carbonate, adjusting the instrument to read 100% reflectance for the standard material.

In a further attempt to determine the type of radiation having optimal heating effect on bright-furred versus black-furred skin, circular pieces of pelt 4·5 cm in diameter were fastened to the top of styrofoam cylinders with a liberal amount of dehydrated lanolin. The skin and adhering insulation were tightly fitted into a brass ring so that the upper layer of skin was level with the ring. Thermocouples were placed in the layer of connecting lanolin and differences in skin temperatures were obtained from a microvoltmeter.

A lamp radiating in the range 0·4–5μ was used as a source of radiation along with solar radiation. Approximately 72% of the lamp-radiated energy was distributed below the dominant wavelength of 1·4. A gelatine filter with a transmission greater than 90% for wavelengths above 890 nm was used to produce further variations in incident radiation. Differences in the radiating temperatures of the samples after exposure to incident radiation were obtained by means of an infrared recording device sensitive to radiation from 2·4–5μ and calibrated to give the temperature of a black body (Bjørk, 1967).

III. Results

The experiments to investigate the relationship between heat absorption and colouration clearly showed that pieces of bright pelt with adhering blubber were heated to higher skin temperatures than pieces with dark hair from the same animal when both were exposed simultaneously to solar radiation. The plotted skin temperatures from the bright-furred pieces gave curves with smoother slopes than those obtained from black-furred pieces (Fig. 2).

Examination of fresh harp seal cadavers on the hunting ground revealed skin temperatures ranging up to 50°C in body areas exposed to the sun, while the deep body temperatures were nearly 37°C. On a day with air temperatures ranging between −1 and −5°C, slight breeze and clear sky, a harp seal which had been shot in the neck and killed instantly was examined 10 min after death. Skin temperatures of 40°C were measured throughout the sun-exposed areas, while the rectal temperature was very stable at 37°C. Within 25 min the skin temperatures in one area exposed to the sun increased to 50°C; the rectal temperature remained at 37°C. Observations were disrupted by movement of the ice.

The first attempt to find the solar radiation type producing maximal differences in heating resulted in transmittance curves from 350 to 1000 nm,

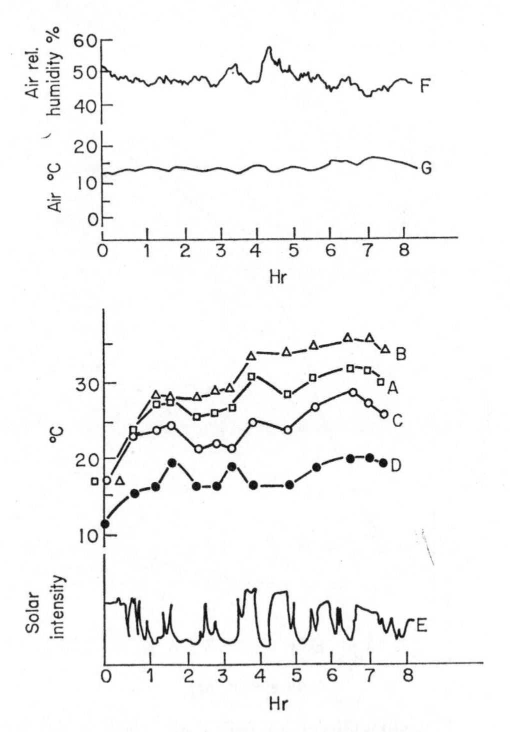

FIG. 2. Results of measurements at Oslo on 20 June 1965. Skin temperatures of dark pelt (A), bright pelt (B), shaved pelt (C) and styrofoam (D). Simultaneous recordings of solar intensity, air-relative humidity and air temperature are indicated in curves E, F, and G respectively.

showing a difference in slope between black and bright hairs in the 550–700 nm region. The quantitative differences could not, however, be considered significant, due to the questionable accuracy of the method. Curves covering transmittance above one indicated no significant difference in slope between the two hair types.

The reflectance measurements on bright-furred samples showed a large increase from 4–40% as the wavelength of the radiation increased from 350 to 1000 nm. The reflectance of dark-furred samples remained under 2% for wavelengths up to 800 nm and increased to 6% as the wavelength was increased to 1000 nm. The maximal plotted difference in reflectance between dark- and bright-furred samples was 30% at 850 nm (Fig. 3).

Further experiments showed that introducing an infrared lamp in addition to solar radiation produced higher skin temperature in bright-furred samples than in black-furred samples. The same effect was seen when an

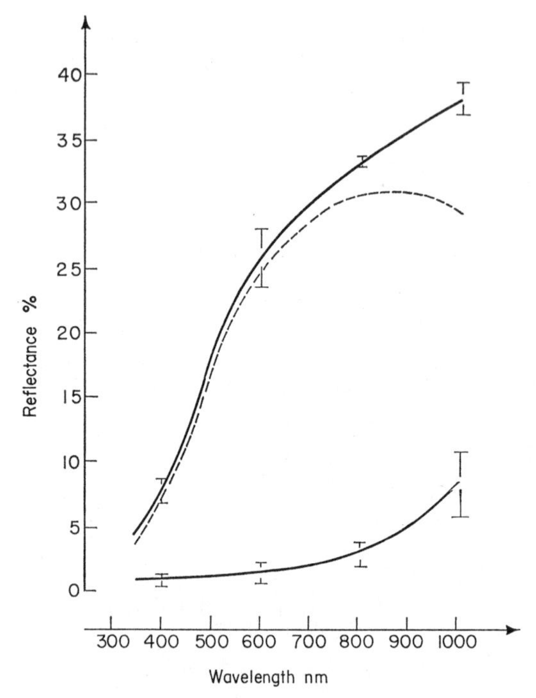

FIG. 3. Reflectance of bright pelt (upper curve) and dark pelt (lower solid curve). The difference in reflectance is indicated by the broken line. Each curve is the mean of five series of measurements on each type of pelt. Limits of accuracy are plotted for the mean reflectance values at 400, 600, 800, and 1000 nm.

infrared transmitting filter was introduced between the samples and the source of radiation. However, infrared recordings of radiation from samples, i.e. surface temperatures, showed that the black hairs were always heated to the highest temperatures.

IV. Discussion

The demonstration that light-coloured pelts attain higher skin temperature than dark pelts when both are simultaneously exposed to solar radiation is consistent with the findings of Krog (1955). The higher surface temperature of the dark pelts further confirms that differential skin heating is due to absorption of solar radiation in the peripheral layers of dark fur, while the radiation is absorbed in the deeper layers of the bright fur.

The difference in skin temperature between the two types of seal pelts is directly influenced by the type of heat transfer directed from the skin outward. The outflow of energy from the skin by conduction and convection in still air (Hammel, 1955) and in wind (Tregear, 1965) is proportional to skin temperatures and prevents a further increase in temperature in the bright-furred skin. Dark hairs, being warmer than the bright hairs, emit more energy by radiation, and this form of heat loss tends to increase the skin-temperature difference.

The incident radiation may penetrate the hairs (transmittance) or by-pass them through some type of scattering effect. The reflectance and the morphology of the hairs are significant in determining the degree of scattering of the incident radiation. The difference in slope of transmittance curves for black and bright hairs may reflect a quantitative difference in transmission for radiation between 550 and 700 nm. However, this could not be verified due to lack of filters and is not considered probable (Tregear, 1966).

Maximum quantitative difference in reflectance between the two types of pelts was approximately 30% in the 750–900 nm region (Fig. 2). This maximum correlates well with the facilitation of differential skin heating during exposure to the long-waved radiation obtained from an IR-lamp or to filtered solar radiation. Hence the reflectance of the hairs should be regarded as a significant factor affecting radiative heat flow in mammalian fur.

The findings of Hamilton and Heppner (1967) indicated that dark colouration enhanced the utilization of solar radiation. The discrepancy between their conclusions and those of the present investigation may, however, be due to the fact that absorption of radiation probably occurs in the peripheral layers of feathers covering the finches with which they worked, while scattering through the same layers may be relatively insignificant.

Seals utilizing solar radiation must be able, by circulatory adjustments, to transport the energy absorbed from the skin to the core. Simultaneously, they should be able to maintain a high insulation beneath the body areas which are not exposed to the sun. The rising skin temperatures of fresh seal cadavers indicate that the absorbed energy is transported away from the skin by means of the peripheral circulation. Variations in surface temperatures of an exercising harp seal (Øritsland, 1968) indicate that this animal does possess sufficient localized control of peripheral circulation to be able to perfuse the exposed areas and keep the remainder of the skin cooled. Thus, the harp seal may be able to absorb solar radiation and reduce its consumption of chemical energy proportionately.

Because of the influence of hair and feather morphology, as well as air movements, the solar heat load on homeotherms cannot be predicted simply by application of values for the incident radiation flux and the area exposed. The degree of utilization may further depend on the spectral energy distribution of the incident radiation, which again will depend on the sun's altitude and amount of moisture in the atmopshere.

Acknowledgements

This study was supported by grants from the Institute of Marine Research, Directorate of Fisheries, Bergen, Norway, and the Norwegian Sealing Council.

References

Bjørk, N. A. (1967). AGA Thermovision, a high speed infrared camera with instantaneous picture display. *J. Radiol.* 48, 30–33.

Hamilton, N. J. and Heppner, F. (1967). Radiant solar energy and the function of black homeotherm pigmentation: An hypothesis. *Science,N.Y.* **155**, 196–7.

Hammel, H. T. (1955). Thermal properties of fur. *Am. J. Physiol.* **182**, 369–76.

Hammel, H. T. (1956). Infrared emissivities of some Arctic fauna. *J. Mammal.* **37**, 375–8.

Krog, J. (1955). Notes on temperature measurements indicative of special organization in arctic and subarctic plants for utilization of radiated energy from the sun. *Physiologia Pl.* **8**, 836–9.

Macfarlane, W. V., Morris, R. J. and Howard, B. (1956). Water economy of tropical merino sheep.*Nature, Lond.* **178**, 304–5.

Øritsland, N. A. (1968). Variations in the body surface temperature of the harp seal. *Acta physiol. scand.* (In the press.)

Tregear, R. T. (1965). Hair density, wind speed and heat loss in mammals. *J. appl. Physiol.* **20**, 796–801.

Tregear, R. T. (1966). "Physical Functions of Skin". Academic Press, London, 185 pp.

Tolerance to Sustained Hypoxia in the Weddell Seal, *Leptonychotes Weddelli*

C. LENFANT, R. ELSNER, G. L. KOOYMAN
AND C. M. DRABEK
Department of Medicine, University of Washington, Seattle, Washington, Scripps Institution of Oceanography, University of California, La Jolla, California, and Department of Zoology, University of Arizona, Tucson, Arizona, U.S.A.

I. Introduction

Because it habitually remains in an area of solid fast ice the Weddell seal, *Leptonychotes weddelli*, appears to have developed an amazing ability to exploit and tolerate the under-ice environment.

Two behavioural characteristics seem to be extremely important in terms of physiological adaptation: one is an acute sense of orientation and the other is a diving ability which is outstanding in depth and in duration. Kooyman (1966) reported extreme values of 600 m for depth and 45 min for duration (Table 1). Most dives are shallower and shorter, but are still more remarkable than those reported for other species of pinnipeds.

TABLE 1
Maximum Dive (duration and depth) of the Weddell Seal, the Harbour Seal and Man

	Duration *min*	*Depth* *m*
Weddell Seal (Kooyman)	45	600
Harbour Seal (Harrison and Tomlinson, 1960)	28	91
Man (Craig, 1968)	2	65

Thus the question arises as to what mechanisms the Weddell seal has developed to perform so freely underwater. This study was undertaken to uncover and elucidate some of these mechanisms which are related to oxygen transport and supply.

II. Material and Methods

Blood samples from four pregnant females near delivery were used for this study. Blood was also obtained from their pups. All samples were collected on heparine and stored at 4°C when not used immediately. The haemoglobin concentration and the haematocrit were measured by spectrophotometry and by blood centrifugation in a Wintrobe tube, respectively. The method used to construct the 0_2-Hb dissociation curve has been described elsewhere (Lenfant and Johansen, 1965). Blood volumes were determined in two non-pregnant females using the isotope ^{51}Cr according to the procedure described by Sterling and Gray (1950).

III. Results and Discussion

Table 2 shows the mean values of haematocrit, haemoglobin and O_2 capacity in the adult and pup Weddell seal. For comparison, results from the common (harbour) seal *Phoca vitulina* and from adult and new-born humans

TABLE 2

Haematocrit, Haemoglobin and O_2 Capacity of the Weddell Seal

	Haematocrit %	*Haemoglobin* *gm/100 ml*	*O_2 Capacity* *Vol. %*
Weddell adult	61·5	23·7	31·6
Weddell pup	57·6	20·8	27·7
Harbour seal	51·0	20·2	26·4
Man adult	45·0	15·0	20·0
Man new-born	56·0	18·5	25·0

are also given. The haemoglobin concentration and O_2 capacity are among the highest in the mammals, being equalled only by a few other phocids such as the elephant seal (Lenfant, 1969) and the ribbon seal (Lenfant and Johansen, *unpublished*). Note that although the pups have a high O_2 capacity it is lower than that of the adults. This relationship is opposite to that existing in man residing at sea-level and in all other terrestrial mammals. It appears to be of adaptive value, as it limits the obligate blood flow to the uterus during diving in pregnancy. Were the O_2 capacity higher in the foetus than in the mother, she would then have to divert a higher blood flow to the uterus in order to secure sufficient oxygen to the foetus.

The amount of O_2 released into the tissue is greatly influenced by the haemoglobin concentration (which determines the quantity of O_2 present in the blood) and by the nature of the ties between O_2 and haemoglobin in relation to the pressure of oxygen in the blood. This latter factor depends in turn upon the shape and position of the oxygen haemoglobin dissociation curve.

Figure 1 shows the oxygen dissociation curve of adult and pup Weddell seals compared with humans. In adult seals the displacement of the curve to the right of that of humans, and of most other terrestrial species, constitutes an advantage, as it permits a greater unloading of oxygen into the tissues for any tension of O_2. The pup's curve does not, however, display a significant difference in position with that of the human new-born.

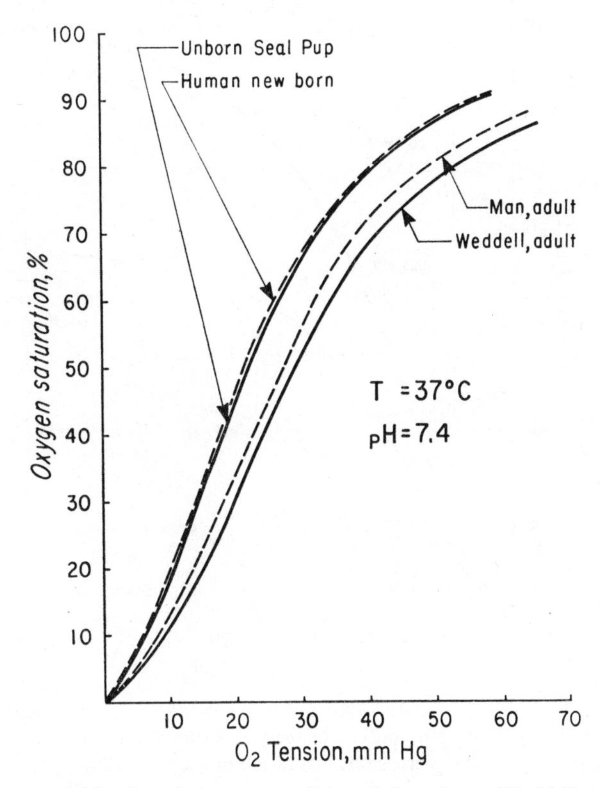

FIG. 1. Oxyhaemoglobin dissociation curve of the adult and pup Weddell seal compared with adult and new-born human. These curves are at pH = 7·4 and temperature = 37°C.

Figure 2 shows the magnitude of the additional oxygen available to the Weddell seal. Now the ordinate represents the absolute amount of O_2 contained in 100 ml of blood instead of the percentage of oxyhaemoglobin as in Fig. 1. When the animal is breathing regularly and has an arterial oxygen tension of about 100 mmHg its blood contains 30·5 vol. % of O_2 as compared to 19 vol. % in humans. If in both cases 5 vol. % are absorbed in the tissues, the oxygen tension in the venous blood and the tissues is much higher in the seal than in man. Again, this results from the high O_2 capacity and reveals a better ability to release O_2 into the tissues. The real benefit of these characteristics is, of course, during diving, when the animal must resort to using the oxygen stored in its blood. Consider, for instance, that both the Weddell seal and man can tolerate an hypoxia to 12 mmHg; it is then seen that the seal can utilize 25·8 vol % or 1·66 as much as a man would.

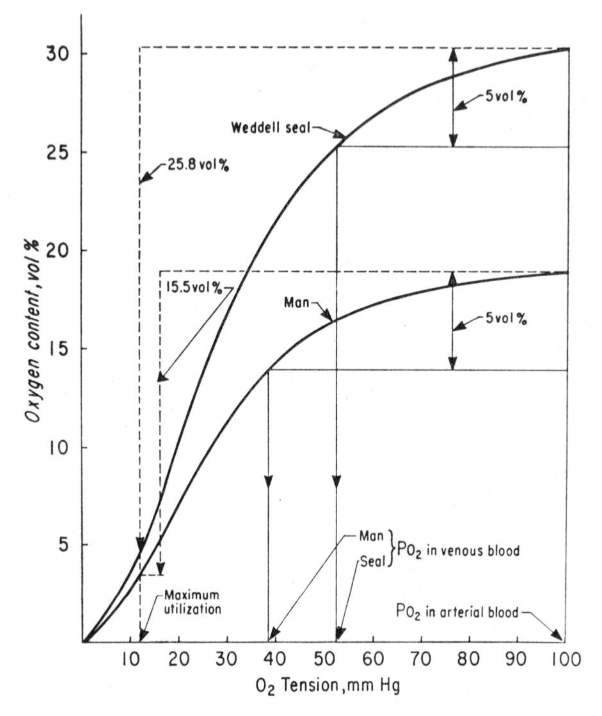

FIG. 2. Oxyhaemoglobin dissociation curve of adult Weddell seal and adult human. The ordinate is expressed in oxygen content instead of saturation as in Fig. 1. Content and saturation are related by the expression: saturation = (content/capacity) × 100.

So far, it has been established that in the Weddell seal the amount of oxygen contained in a volume of blood is greater and can be more completely utilized than in terrestrial species. The real question is, however, whether the total amount of available oxygen is greater in this species than in other species of pinniped in relation to the mass of active tissues. Figure 3, which shows the blood volume and O_2 capacity per kilogram of active tissues (skin and blubber subtracted), demonstrates that the Weddell seal has a blood-oxygen store approximately 1·7 times that of the harbour seal and 5·3 as large as in humans.

Recent data obtained from several species of pinnipeds indicate that this increase in relative O_2 store may be related to the diving performance of *L. weddelli* (Lenfant and Johansen, *unpublished data*). This factor alone, however, is not sufficient to prevent hypoxia during a dive, the consequences of which are limited only by means of the diving cardiovascular reflexes.

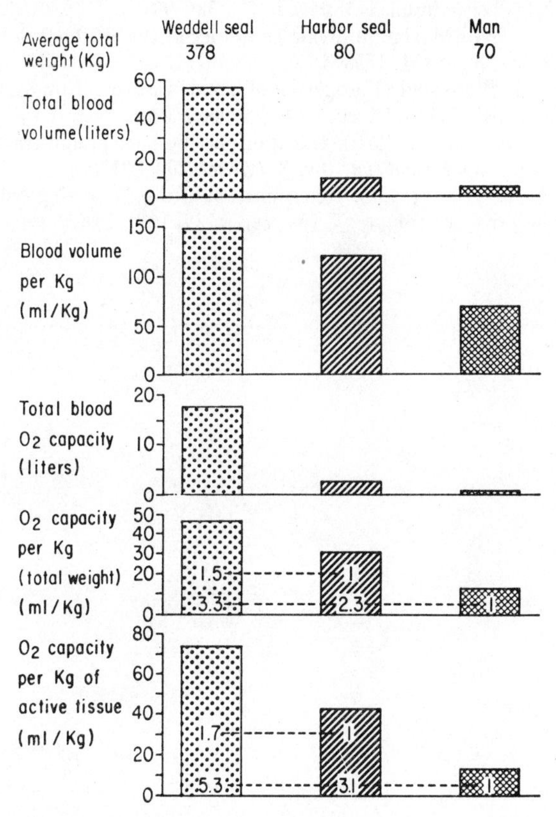

FIG. 3. Blood volume and total oxygen capacity of the blood of the adult Weddell seal, the Harbor seal and adult man.

Acknowledgements

This study was supported by grants GA1215 from the Office of Antarctic Program of the National Science Foundation and HE19174 from the National Institutes of Health.

References

Craig, A. B. (1968). Depth limits of breath hold diving. (An example of Fennology.) *Resp. Physiol.* **5**, 14–22.

Harrison, R. J. and Tomlinson, J. D. W. (1960). Normal and experimental diving in the common seal (Phoca vitulina). *Mammalia* **24**, 386–99.

Kooyman, G. L. (1966). Maximum diving capacities of the Weddell Seal, *Leptonychotes weddelli*. *Science*, N.Y. **151**, 1553–4.

Lenfant, C. (1969). Physiological properties of blood of marine mammals. *In* "Biology of Marine Mammals" (H. Andersen, ed.). Academic Press, New York.

Lenfant, C. and Johansen, K. (1965). Gas transport by hemocyanin-containing blood of the cephalopod, *Octopus dofleini*. *Am. J. Physiol.* **209**, 991–8.

Sterling, K. and Gray, S. J. (1950). Determination of the circulating red cell volume in man by radioactive chrominum. *J. clin. Invest.* **29**, 1614–19.

Diving Duration in Pregnant Weddell Seals

ROBERT ELSNER, GERALD L. KOOYMAN AND CHARLES M. DRABEK
Scripps Institution of Oceanography, University of California, La Jolla, California, U.S.A. and Department of Zoology, University of Arizona, Tucson, Arizona, U.S.A.

I. Introduction

Pregnancy imposes an extra metabolic load upon the maternal organism. It might be expected, therefore, that a pregnant marine mammal would be at a disadvantage in terms of diving duration and that the maximum time of submergence would be accordingly decreased with advancing pregnancy. In an attempt to describe the adjustments of a diving animal to pregnancy we have recorded duration and depths of submergence in gravid Weddell seals, *Leptonychotes weddelli*, near McMurdo Sound, Antarctica.

As a result of earlier studies by DeVries and Wohlschlag (1964) and Kooyman (1966) more information is available on the natural history of diving in *L. weddelli* than in any other aquatic mammal. These investigators attached depth recorders to free-swimming animals. In Kooyman's study seals were released at prepared holes in the sea ice. Instrument recovery was usually assured by locating the hole at a site remote from other holes or ice cracks and thus forcing the animal to return to the release location for breathing. Examination of thirty-one adult and subadult Weddell seals in this manner during 959 separate dives revealed a maximum diving time of 43 min 20 sec and a maximum depth of 600 m.

II. Methods

Adult female Weddell seals begin to appear in considerable numbers along sea-ice cracks near the shores of McMurdo Sound during late September or early October. The birth of pups starts a little later and reaches its peak rate about the end of October. Despite the large size of these animals (commonly 2½ m in length and 400 kg in weight), they are docile and are easily netted on the ice. Positive verification of pregnancy for our study was obtained by one or more of three methods: (1) drug immobilization and vaginal examination; (2) observation of foetal movements against the body wall, and (3) observation of a tagged animal after release until the appearance of her new-born pup was noted. Exchange of pups among mother seals occurs only very rarely (Ian Stirling, *personal communication*). Immobilization was safely produced by intramuscular injection of a mixture containing approximately 0·3 mg/kg phenylcyclidine (Sernylan, Parke Davis) and 0·2 mg/kg. propionyl phenothiazine hydrochloride (Tranvet, Diamond Labs.). At least 48 hrs was allowed for recovery from drug effects before experimental observations were begun.

A captured animal was transported by tractor-drawn sled to a site several miles out from shore on the sea ice and distant from other holes and cracks. Here a heated laboratory hut was placed over a hole opened through the 2 m thick ice by chain saw and blasting. A Bourdon tube recording depth indicator was attached to the seal before its release into the hole. Both the instrument and method of attachment to the animal have been described previously (Kooyman, 1965; Kooyman, 1968). Instruments were provided with clocks giving either one or two hours of continuous recording. The animals rapidly adjusted to the new situation without obvious signs of fear or discontent. They remained at the experimental site, freely diving, feeding and sleeping intermittently in the ice hole, some for several days, until they either discovered an under-ice route to a distant hole or were recaptured and released.

III. Results

Five pregnant seals were tested, and forty-one dives lasting longer than

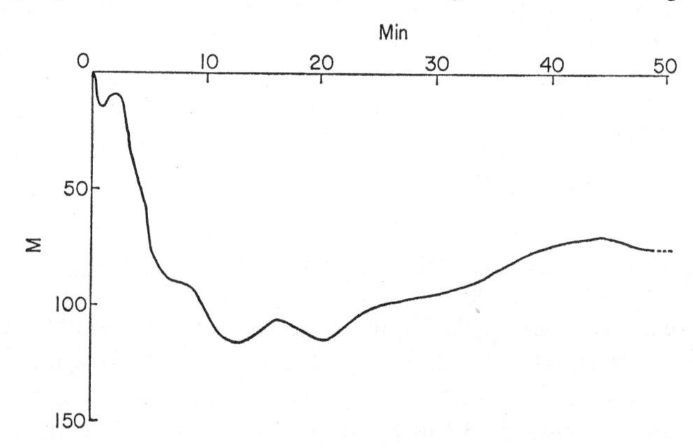

FIG. 1. Depth-time profile of a long dive of pregnant Weddell seal No. 1.

20 min were recorded. Complete depth-time data were not obtained for all dives. The maximum dive duration was 60 min, and the greatest depth recorded was 310 m. Depth-time profiles for some of these dives are plotted in Figs. 1, 2 and 3. All experimental data are summarized in Table 1. Three of the five seals were found after the tests, and were accompanied by apparently healthy new-born pups.

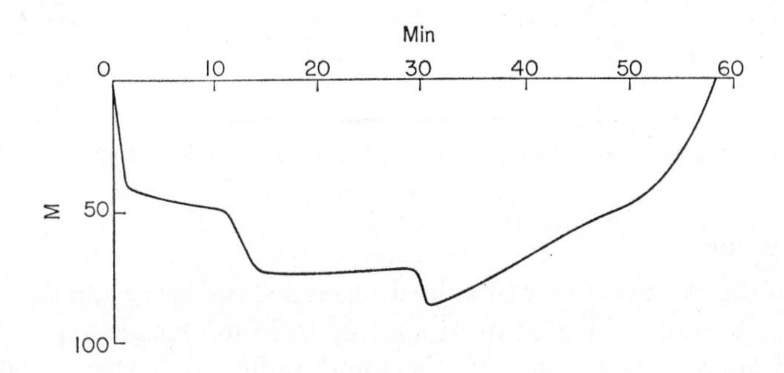

FIG. 2. Depth-time profile of the longest dive of a pregnant Weddell seal for which a complete record was obtained (seal No. 7).

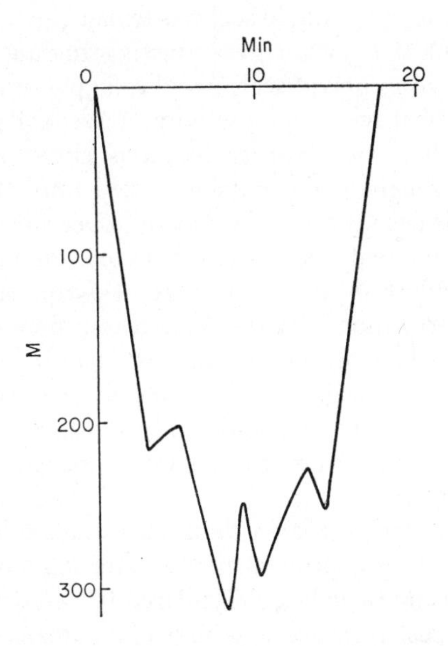

FIG. 3. Depth-time profile of the deepest dive recorded (seal No. 7).

TABLE 1

Pregnant Weddell Seals

No.	*Dives longer than 20 min*	*Max duration (min)*	*Max depth (m)*
1	1	49†	115
2	13	54	135
3	4	39†	180
6	12	60	150
7	11	58†	310

Summary of diving performance of pregnant Weddell seals. † Depth-time profiles obtained.

IV. Discussion

Four of the five experimental animals exceeded the maximum dive duration observed in the earlier study of a mixed male and female population of adult and subadult specimens in the same locality (Kooyman, 1966). It seems clear, therefore, that pregnancy did not restrict the diving capabilities of these *L. weddelli* individuals. An effort was made in the earlier investigation to obtain only non-pregnant animals. However, since six of the seals were adult females tested between October and December the possibility that some pregnant animals were used cannot be positively excluded. The longest diver of the study (43 min 20 sec) was female (Kooyman, 1968).

An explanation for our somewhat surprising finding that the longest recorded dives occurred in gravid seals may lie simply in the effect of near-term pregnancy on the behaviour of these animals. Weddell seals in McMurdo Sound characteristically choose sea-ice locations close to shore where the ice remains stable throughout the nursing period until the pups begin to swim and forage. This usually takes place by mid-December. Females in late pregnancy tested by us might have been expected, therefore, to seek with more than ordinary effort an under-ice route of escape as they sensed the impending time of parturition. For the same reason they may not have engaged in deep dives, which are usually associated with feeding (Kooyman, 1968). However, an explanation is still lacking for whatever special diving adaptations the pregnant seal may possess, if it is assumed that the recorded maximum diving durations for pregnant and non-pregnant animals are close to their limits of endurance.

It has been shown that pregnancy entails an increase in maternal metabolic rate approximately proportional to the extra mass of uterine content (Bohr, 1900; Ritzman and Benedict, 1931; Barcroft *et al.*, 1939). Accordingly, the foetus might be best regarded as a part of the maternal organism and subject to the same control mechanisms (Kleiber, 1965). Thus, the extra metabolic load carried by the pregnant seal is likely to be directly proportional to its increase in body weight.

It is well established that an important variable limiting duration of diving in seals is the total circulating blood oxygen (Scholander, 1940). A considerable body of evidence, obtained mostly from human studies, supports the finding of an increase in blood volume during pregnancy. Gemzell *et al.* (1957) for instance, using the carbon-monoxide dilution method in pregnant women on an adequate iron intake regime, noted average increases of blood volume from 62 ml/kg of body weight to 78 ml/kg and of haemoglobin from 7·7 gm/kgm to 9·1 gm/kg as pregnancy progressed. A similar or even smaller increase in the pregnant seal with the consequent elevation of total haemoglobin would provide additional oxygen storage for sustaining prolonged diving. It is known that the blood volume and oxygen capacity of non-pregnant *L. weddelli* is very high (Lenfant *et al.*, 1969), and the extent to which this could be elevated is questionable.

Evidence for the well-known circulatory redistribution during exposure to diving asphyxia has recently been reviewed (Elsner, 1969). Generally, the cardiac output is reduced and is directed through the most vital organs, thus effecting conservation of oxygen stored in the circulatory blood. The extent to which uterine blood supply takes part in the diving redistribution and its role in the maintenance of the foetus during a long dive is presently unknown. Recent findings of Lenfant *et al.* (1969) of both greater oxygen affinity in Weddell seal foetal than maternal blood and higher oxygen capacity in maternal than foetal blood suggest that effective gas exchange could take place at the placenta with minimum uterine artery blood flow.

Acknowledgements

This study was supported by National Science Foundation grant GA 1215 from the Office of Antarctic Programs, National Institutes of Health grant HEO8323 and NIH Research Career Development Award HE7469 to R. Elsner. U.S. Navy Operation Deepfreeze personnel and the U.S. Antarctic Research Program staff provided support and assistance.

References

Barcroft, J., Kennedy, J. A. and Mason, M. F. (1939). Direct determination of oxygen consumption of foetal sheep. *J. Physiol., Lond.* **95**, 269–75.

Bohr, C. (1900). Der respiratorische Stoffwechsel des Säugetierembryos. *Skand. Arch. Physiol.* **10**, 413–24.

DeVries, A. L. and Wohlschlag, D. E. (1964). Diving depths of the Weddell seal. *Science, N.Y.* **145**, 292.

Elsner, R. (1969). Cardiovascular adjustments to diving. *In* "The Biology of Marine Mammals" (H. T. Andersen, ed.), pp. 117–45. Academic Press, New York.

Gemzell, C. A., Robbe, H. and Ström, G. (1957). Total amount of haemoglobin and physical working capacity in normal pregnancy and puerperium (with iron medication). *Acta obs. gynec. scand* **36**, 93–136.

Kleiber, M. (1965). Respiratory exchange and metabolic rate. *In* "Handbook of Physiology" (W. O. Fenn and H. Rahn, eds), pp. 927–38, Section 3, Respiration, Vol. 2. Williams and Wilkins Co., Baltimore.

Kooyman, G. L. (1965). Techniques used in measuring diving capacities of Weddell seals. *Polar Rec.* **12**, 391–4.

Kooyman, G. L. (1966). Maximum diving capacities of the Weddell seal, *Leptonychotes weddelli*. *Science, N.Y.* **151**, 1553–4.

Kooyman, G. L. (1968). An analysis of some behavioral and physiological characteristics related to diving in the Weddell seal. "Biology of the Antarctic Seas", Vol. 2. Antarctic Research Series (W. L. Schmitt and G. A. Llano, eds). American Geophysical Union, Washington, 227–261.

Lenfant, C., Elsner, R., Kooyman, G. L. and Drabek, C. M. (1969). Respiratory function of the blood of the adult and fetal Weddell seal, *Leptonychotes weddelli*. *Am. J. Physiol.* (In the press.)

Ritzman, E. G. and Benedict, F. G. (1931). The heat production of sheep under varying conditions. *New Hampshire Agr. Exp. St. Tech. Bull.* **45**. (Cited in M. Kleiber, op. cit.)

Scholander, P. F. (1940). Experimental investigations of the respiratory function in diving mammals and birds. *Hvalradets Skifter, Norske Videnskaps—Akad. Oslo.* **22**.

The Glandular Pattern of the Epiphysis Cerebri of the Weddell Seal

AUGUSTO CLAUDIO CUELLO
Instituto de Neurobiologia and Instituto Antartico Argentino, Buenos Aires, Argentina

I. Introduction

Daily photoperiods influence the neurohumoral mechanisms which control cyclical activities, particularly reproduction. It has been demonstrated that light influences the hypophysis by way of retina and hypothalamus, bringing about an excitatory effect upon the reproductive system. This mechanism seems to govern the onset of the breeding season in mammals and birds (Hammond, 1954; Amoroso and Marshall, 1960; Wurtman, 1967).

It has been recently shown that the pineal-gland secretion has an inhibitory effect upon the reproductive system. The pineal-gland secretion is controlled by the environmental light conditions, this light acting by way of the retina, central nervous system and the superior cervical ganglia (Wurtman *et al.*, 1963; Wurtman *et al.*, 1964; Axelrod *et al.*, 1966; Moore *et al.*, 1966).

Experimental changes in environmental illumination produce variations in the morphology and physiology of the pineal gland of the rat (Fiske *et al.*, 1960; Quay, 1961; Wurtman *et al.*, 1963; Wurtman *et al.*, 1964; Miline, 1965; Reiter *et al.*, 1966). These findings stimulated the present study of the morphology of the pineal gland of an Antarctic seal, because these animals live in latitudes where light variations reach their extreme.

II. Material and Methods

Seventeen Weddell seals (*Leptonychotes weddelli*) belonging to both sexes were involved in this study. They were caught in the bay of Paradise Harbour, Antarctic Peninsula, during 1966. The bulk of the material was processed and studied at the Estación Cientifica "Almirante Brown", Antarctica, and the remainder at the Instituto de Neurobiologia, Buenos Aires.

III. Results

The pineal gland of the Weddell seal is a flattened body of romboidal shape, 20 to 30 mm long. The proximal end of the gland makes contact with the posterior and habenular commisures. It fits in the space between the splenium of the corpus callosum, the supracallosal girus and the superior colliculli and cerebellum.

Due to its unusually large size the gland makes an angle at the level of the superior colliculli and completely fills the space corresponding to the

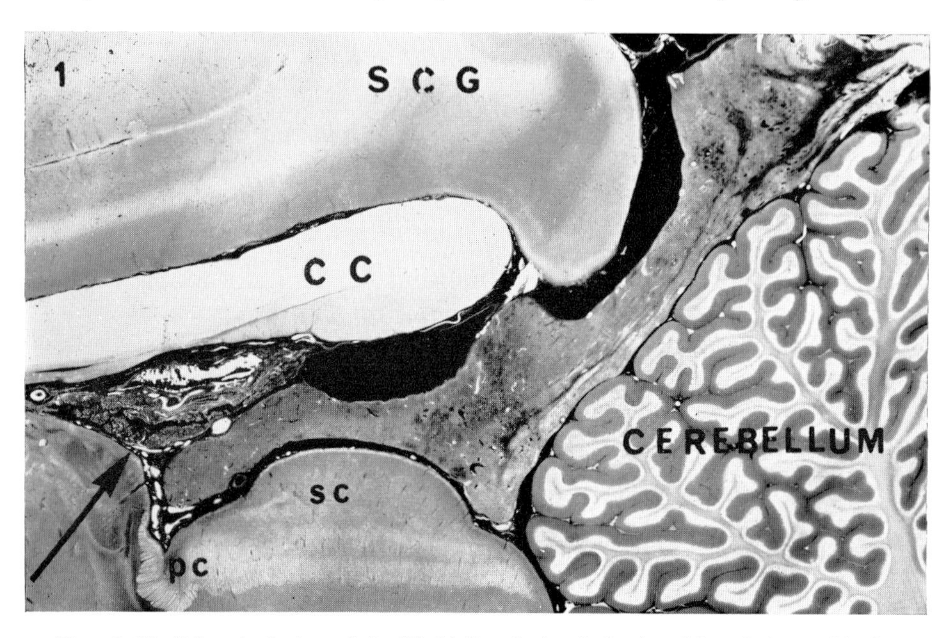

FIG. 1. Medial sagittal view of the Weddell seal pineal gland and its relations with the adjacent structures. CC: corpus callosum—SCG: supracallosal girus—sc: superior colliculm—pc: posterior commisure—arrow: chorioid plexuses of the third ventricle—(celloidin section—Gallocyanin stain).

superior cisterna. From the tentorium cerebelli there emerges a meningeal prolongation which becomes the capsule of the gland. In its proximal ends there exists an intimate relationship between the gland and the chorioid plexus of the third ventricle.

The gland is built up of a capsule, and cortical and medullar regions. The capsule shows regional differentiation: it is thick in the dorsal face and thin ventrally. Dorsally it has a pigmented layer on the distal part of the gland, and scattered mastocytes in the region near the chorioid plexus.

The cortical region contains the pinealocytes and glial cells. The pinealocytes are grouped in more or less well-defined islets surrounded by a rich capillary net. Among the pinealocytes there may be seen many glial cells whose processes are in relation with the pinealocytes as well as with the capillary blood vessels.

The medullar region consists of fibroblasts, ground substance, reticular and collagen fibres, blood vessels and nerve fibres. The fibroblasts and the capillary blood vessels are oriented parallel to the principal axis of the gland. A great number of nerve fibres end near these vessels.

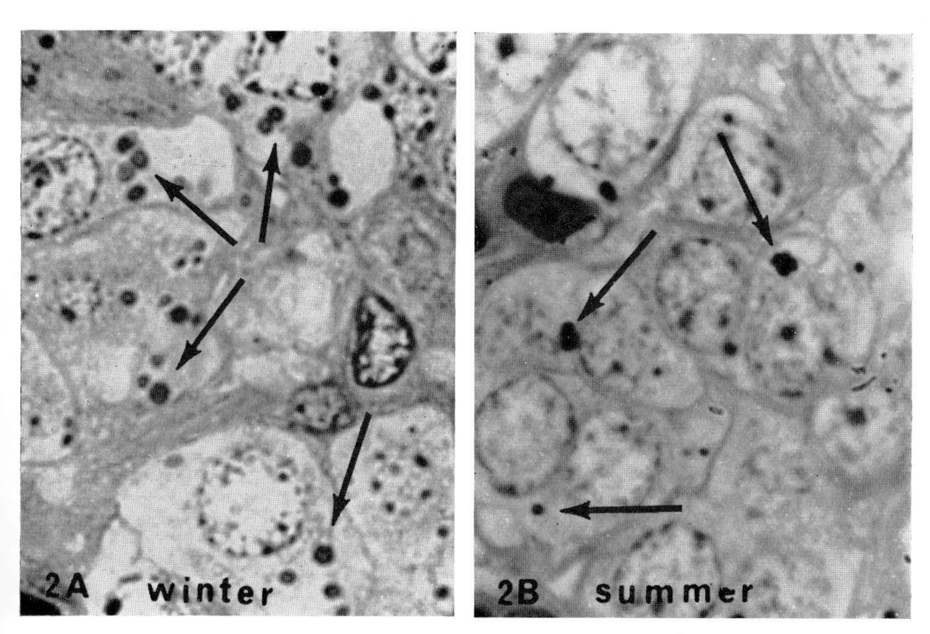

FIG. 2. A. Abundant lipidic droplets (arrows) in the cytoplasm of the parenchymal cells of the pineal gland of a seal caught in winter. B, Scarce lipidic droplets (arrows) in cells of the pineal gland of a seal caught in summer. (Ultra-thin section—Unna's polichorome blue stain.)

The parenchymal cell, the pinealocyte, has a big nucleus with one or two nucleoli. The cytoplasm does not show any basophilic material in animals caught either in winter or in summer. The cytoplasm of the pinealocytes of seals caught in winter contained a large number of lipid droplets,whereas hardly any were present in the animals caught in summer.

The big vessels enter the gland by its dorsal face, and the thin vessels by its ventral face. The blood vessels build up a network in the cortical layer surrounding the pinealocytes and the glial cells, and they change their direction in the medullar region.

A big nerve which has been recognized as the conarium nerve enters the gland by its dorsal and distal part. Upon entering the gland this nerve sends off axons which lie among the cells of the cortical region, while the main group of fibres ends in the medullar region. In this zone the axons covered by Schwann cells split and end in a "palisade-like" disposition. At this point many synaptic varicosities can be seen in the perivascular spaces. Each of these synaptic varicosities shows typical synaptic vesicles and dense-core synaptic vesicles.

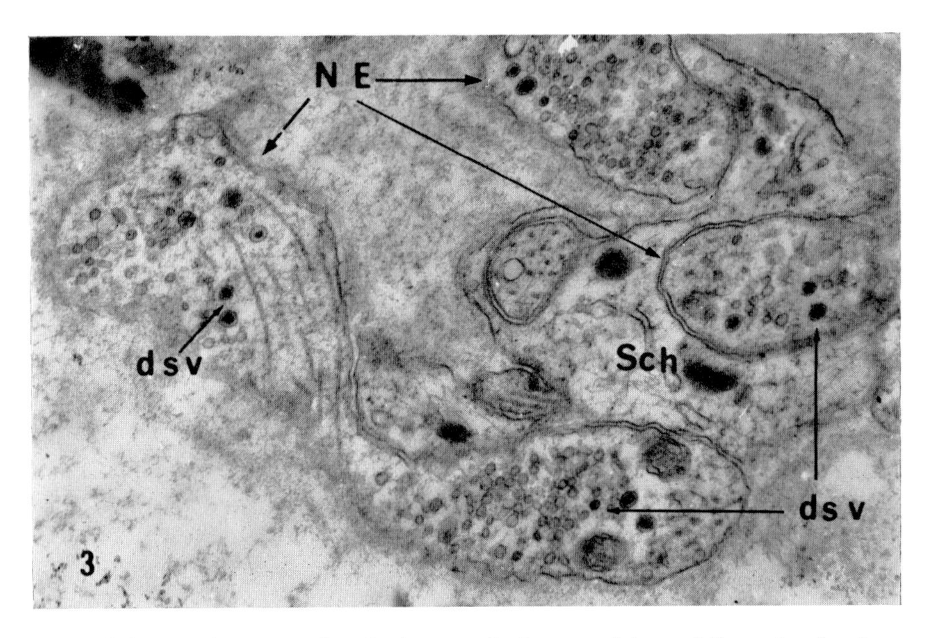

FIG. 3. Autonomic nerve endings in the ground substance of the medullar region showing the typical synaptic vesicles and two types of dense-core synaptic vesicles—NE: nerve endings—Sch: schwann cell cytoplasm—dsv: dense-core synaptic vesicles. (× 22·500.)

IV. Discussion

The localization and size of the pineal gland in some seals and in the walrus were described in 1888 by Turner. A brief description of the pineal gland in the Weddell seal is included in an anatomical monograph published by Hepburn in 1912. These works have been mentioned occasionally in reviews on the morphology of the mammalian pineal gland and, as far as we could find out, are the only papers published on the pineal gland of pinnipeds.

It is noteworthy that such large mammalian pineal glands have only been reported in polar pinnipedes (the walrus and the Weddell seal). This suggests that in these animals there may be an adaptative modification to the particular environmental light conditions of polar latitudes. This hypotheses could be tested by comparative studies on the morphology of the pineal gland in relation to habitat in a series of mammals.

An interesting finding of the present research is the distinctive and highly organized pineal structure in the Weddell Seal, which differs from that in all other known mammals. The gland has a cortical and medullary region: the parenchymal cells are confined within the outer region and the connective tissue is enclosed inside the medullar region where most of the nerves end around capillary vessels. This last formation replaces the "perivascular" or "septal connective tissue" in the pineal gland of other mammals. In fact, this part of the gland can be considered to be a "synaptic field".

As in other mammals the gland is innervated by autonomous nerves from orthosympathetic division which probably originate from the superior cervical ganglia (Ramon y Cajal, 1904; Ariëns Kappers, 1960, 1965; Rodriguez Perez, 1962). This may be the way by which the seal pineal gland receives information about environmental light. The ultrastructural appearance of the nerve endings is similar to that found in the pineal gland of other mammals. They contain the typical synaptic vesicles and two types of dense-core synaptic vesicles (De Robertis and Pellegrine de Iraldi, 1961; Pellegrino de Iraldi *et al.*, 1965; Wartenberg and Gusek, 1965; Wolfe, 1965; Anderson, 1965; Bondareff, 1965; Bondareff and Gordon, 1966; Duncan and Micheletti, 1966; Arstila, 1967; Wartenberg, 1968).

Lipid levels of the pineal gland of the rat show changes in relation to many physiological and experimental conditions (Ruggieri, 1914; Hungerfort and Panagiotis, 1962; Panagiotis and Hungerfort, 1962; Zweens, 1963; Ariëns Kappers *et al.*, 1964; Zweens, 1965). Environmental light produces changes in pineal activity (Wurtman *et al.*, 1963; Wurtman *et al.*, 1964; Reiter *et al.*, 1966) and a correlative variation in lipid content (Quay, 1961). As stated above, the pinealocytes of Weddell seals caught in the Antarctic summer when the photoperiods were very long contained few lipid droplets, while those caught in winter when the photoperiods were very short contained many such droplets. These findings suggest the existence of an annual rhythmic activity of the pineal gland which probably depends on the fluctuations in natural light conditions. As the Weddell seal is a monoestrous long-day breeding mammal, this rhythm may be related to the reproductive cycle.

V. Summary

(1) The largest pineal glands known occur in polar animals.

(2) The pineal gland of the Weddell seal has a structural pattern different from that known in other animals.

(3) The innervation of the Weddell seal pineal gland is supplied by orthosympathetic nerve fibres, probably coming from the superior cervical ganglia and ending mainly around the vessels in the medullar region.

(4) Annual variations in lipid content have been found in the pineal gland. These cytological changes could correspond to a functional cycle in the gland, and indicate that it participates in controlling seasonal activities.

Acknowledgement

I should like to acknowledge the kind assistance given to this work by Dr Bernardo A. Houssay and Dr Juan H. Tramezzani (of the Instituto de Biología y Medicina Experimental), as well as by Admiral Rodolfo Panzarini and Dr Otto Schneider (of Instituto Antártico Argentino).

References

Amoroso, E. C. and Marshall, F. H. A. (1960). External factors in sexual periodicity. *In* "Physiology of Reproduction", (F. H. A. Marshall ed.). Vol. 1—Part 2, pp. 707–831.

Anderson, E. (1965). The Anatomy of Bovine and Ovine Pineals. Light and Electron Microscopic Studies. *J. Ultrastruct. Res.* Suppl. 8, 1–80.

Ariëns Kappers, J. (1960). The Development, Topographical Relations and Innervation of the Epiphisis Cerebri in the Albino Rat. *Z. Zellforsch. mikrosk. Anat.* **52**, 163–215.

Ariëns Kappers, J. (1965). Survey or the innervation of the Epiphysis Cerebri and the Accessory Pineal Organs of Vertebrates. *In* "The Structure and Function of the Epiphysis Cerebri. Progress in Brain Research" (J. Ariëns Kappers and J. Schade, eds), **10**, pp. 87–151.

Ariëns Kappers, J., Prop, N. and Zweens, J. (1964). Qualitative Evaluation of Pineal Gland in the Albino Rat by Histochemical Methods and Paper Chromatography and the changes in the Pineal Rat Contents under physiological and Experimental Conditions. *In* "Lectures on the Diencephalon—Progress in Brain Research". (W. Bargmann and J. Schade, eds), Vol. 5; 190–9.

Arstila, A. U. (1967). Electron microscopic studies on the structure and histochemistry of the pineal gland of the rat. *Neuroendocrinology*, Supp. **2**, 1–101.

Axelrod, J., Snyder, S. H., Heller, A. and Moore, R. Y. (1966). Light induced changes in pineal hydroxyindole—0—Methyltransferase: abolition by lateral hyopthalamic lesions. *Science, N.Y.* **154**, 898–9.

Bondareff, W. (1965). Submicroscopic morphology of granular vesicles in sympathetic nerves of rat pineal body. *Z. Zellforsch Mikrosk. Anat.* **67**, 211–19.

Bondareff, W. and Gordon, B. (1966). Submicroscopic localization of norepinephrine in sympathetic nerves of rat pineal. *J. Pharmacol.* **153**, 42–47.

De Robertis, E. D. and Pellegrino de Iraldi, A. (1961). Pluvivesicular secretory processes and nerve endings in the pineal gland of rat. *J. biophys biocheml Cytol.* **10**, 361–72.

Duncan, D. and Micheletti, G. (1966). Notes on the fine structure of the pineal organ of cats. *Texas Rep. Biol. Med.* **24**, 576–87.

Fiske, V., Bryant, G. K. and Purman, J. (1960). Effect of light on the weight of the pineal gland in the rat. *Endocrinology* **66**, 489–91.

Hammond, J. Fr. (1954). Light regulation of Hormone secretion. Vitamins and Hormones. Vol. XII, pp. 156–206.

Hungerfort, G. F. and Panagiotis, N. (1962). Response of Pineal lipid to hormone imbalances. *Endocrinology* **71**, 936–42.

Miline, R. (1965). Contribution à l'etude du comportment corrélatif du complexe epithalamo-epiphysaire et de la zone glomérulaire des glandes surrénales sous l'influence de l'osbscurité. *In* "The Structure and Function of the Epiphysis Cerebri. Progress in Brain Research" (J. Ariëns Kappers and J. Schadé, eds), Vol. **10**, 612–26.

Moore, R. J., Heller, A., Wurtman, R. J. and Axelrod, J. (1966). Visual pathway mediating pineal response to environmental light. *Science, N.Y.* **155**, 220–3.

Panagiotis, N. and Hungerfort, G. (1962). Response of pineal gland to hypophysectomy, hormone administration and dietary sodium restriction. *Anat. Rec.* **142**, 264–5.

Pellegrino de Iraldi, A., Ziecher, L. M. and Robertis, E. De (1965). Ultrastructure and pharmacological studies of nerve endings in the pineal organ. *In* "The Structure and Function of the Epiphysis Cerebri. Progress in Brain Research" (J. Ariëns Kappers and J. Schadé, eds), Vol. **10**, 612–26.

Quay, W. B. (1961). Reduction of mammalian pineal weight and lipid during continuous light. *Gen. Comp. Endocrinol.* **1**, 211–17.

Ramon y Cajal, Santiago (1904). "Textura del Sistema Nervioso del Hombre y de los Vertebrados." Tomo II, segunda parte. Madrid.

Reiter, R. I., Hoffman, R.A. and Hester, R. J. (1966). "The Role of the Pineal Gland and of Environmental Lighting in the Regulation of the Endocrine and Reproductive System of Rodents." Edgewood Arsenal Technical Report 4032.

Rodriguez Pérez, A. P. (1962). Contribución al Concimiento de la Inervación de las Glándulas Endócrinas. IV Primeros Resultados Experimentales en Torno a la Inervacion de la Epifisis. *Trabajo del Instituto de Investigaciones Biológicas.* Tomo LIV: 1–12. Madrid.

Ruggieri, E. (1914). Modificazione del contenuto lipomitochondriale delle cellule della pineale dopo ablzaione completa degli organi genitali. *Rev. Nerv. Ment.* **19**, 649–59.

Wartenberg, H. and Gusek, W. (1965). Light und Elektronenmikroskopische Beobachtungen über die struktur der Epiphysis Cerebri des Kaninches. *In* "The Structure and Function of the Epiphysis Cerebri. Progress in Brain Research" (J. Ariëns Kappers and J. Schadé, eds), Vol. **10**, 296–316.

Wartenberg, H. (1968). The mammalian pineal organ: electron microscopic studies on the fine structure of pinealocytes glial cells and on the perivascular compartment. *Z. Zellforsch. Mikrosk. Anat.* **86**, 74–97.

Wolfe, D. E. (1965). The epiphyseal cell: an electron-microscopic study of its Intercellular relationships and Intracellular Morphology in the pineal body of the albino rat. *In* "The Structure and Function of the Epiphysis Cerebri. Progress in Brain Research" (J. Ariëns Kappers and J. Schadé, eds), Vol. **10**, 332–86.

Wurtman, R. J., Axelrod, J. and Chu, E. W. (1963). (b). Melatonin synthesis in the pineal gland: control by light. *Science N.Y.* **142**, 1071–3.

Wurtman, R. J., Axelrod, J. and Fisher, I. E. (1964). Melatonin synthesis in the pineal gland. Effect of light mediated by the simpathetic nervous system. *Science N.Y.* **143**, 1328–30.

Wurtman, R. J. (1967). Effects of Light and Visual Stimuli on Endocrine function. *In* "Neuroendocrinology", Vol. II, Chap. 18, pp. 19–59. (L. Martini and W. Ganong eds). Academic Press, London.

Zweens, J. (1963). Influence of the oestrous cycle and ovariectomy on the phospholipid content of the pineal gland in the rat. *Nature Lond.* **197**, 1114–15.

Zweens, J. (1965). Alterations of the pineal lipid content in the rat under hormonal influences. *In* "The Structure and function of the epiphysis cerebri. Progress in Brain Research" (J. Ariëns Kappers and J. Schadé, eds), Vol. **10**, 540–51.

Vision of the Weddell Seal (*Leptonychotes Weddelli*)

G. S. WILSON*
British Antarctic Survey Biological Unit, Monks Wood Experimental Station, Abbots Ripton, Huntingdon, England

I. Introduction

It is to be expected that the visual system of the seal will show some adaptation to its aquatic environment in keeping with changes in other parts of the body, and in some aspects this is immediately apparent. The naso-lacrimal canal which in a wholly terrestrial mammal would prevent tears from spilling over the lids, has disappeared. The similarity in refractive index of water and corneal tissue has occasioned the development of an almost spherical lens to compensate the optical loss of the cornea underwater. But perhaps the most interesting adaptation is that of astigmatism, first mentioned by Johnson (1893). As this discussion is concerned mainly with optics, it might be useful before summarizing the literature to say a few words about the factors which influence this aspect of the seal's eye.

Refractive index is a constant of a transparent material. If the refractive index and the radius of curvature of a regular surface are known, the optical power can be calculated, and this applies as much to the surface of a glass lens as it does to the cornea of the eye. However, as we know from our own difficulties in trying to see underwater, the power is influenced by another factor, and this is the refractive index of the medium in which the surface is immersed. The human eye is designed for clear vision in air, which has a refractive index of approximately zero; the refractive index of water is very close to that of corneal tissue, so that this structure loses its refracting ability almost completely when in water. The effect of this in man is that clear images are no longer formed on the retina, but somewhere behind it, and objects are seen blurred (Fig. 2).

Errors in the ability of the eye to focus light on the retina can be divided into two classes. In the first class, point objects form point images not on the retina where they should be but at some other position. If the image of a distant object is formed in front of the retina, the condition is called myopia (short-sightedness); if the image is formed behind the retina, the condition

* Present address: School of Optometry, University of California, Berkeley, California, U.S.A.

is one of hyperopia (Fig. 1). Myopia and hyperopia are normal variations of the focusing power of the human eye; however, it is also convenient in this discussion to think of the eye as hyperopic when immersed in water, because now the cornea has effectively lost its power.

The second class of refractive errors occurs when the refracting surfaces are not spherical, and here the point image is replaced by two lines; the condition is called astigmatism.

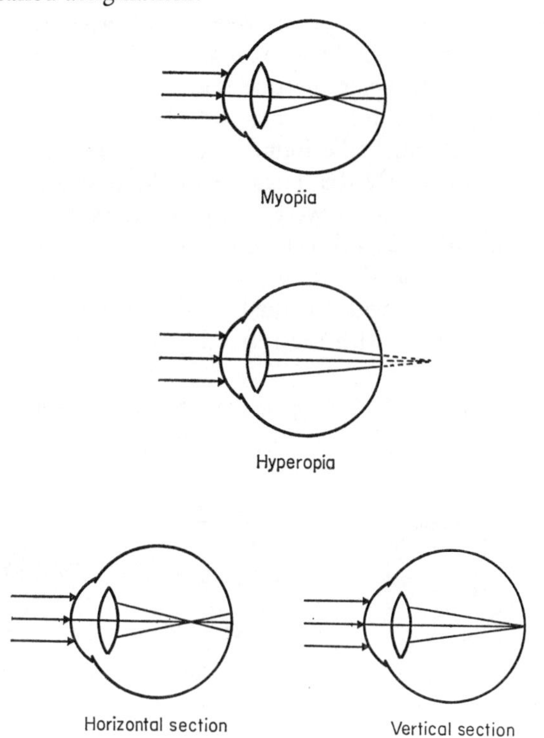

FIG. 1. Schematic sections of an eye to show how light from a distant object is focused in different kinds of refractive error. The Type of astigmatism illustrated corresponds to that found in the Weddell Seal.

II. Vision in Seals

The refracting system of the seal was first investigated by Johnson (1893). He found that the eye of the common seal (*Phoca vitulina*) had a refractive error in air of −4 diopters in the vertical meridian and −13 diopters in the horizontal meridian. This is a refractive condition of myopic astigmatism with the greatest error in the horizontal. With the seal immersed in water, the refractive error disappeared and it was reasoned that the cornea was responsible for the astigmatism. Later (1901) Johnson reported astigmatism of the same type in Steller's Sea Lion, and as Matthiesen (1893) had already found a lower degree in the whales he concluded that this must be a characteristic of marine mammals.

Walls (1942) enlarged on earlier interpretations of this refractive error, pointing out that the meridian in which it is lowest corresponds to the direction of the very narrow slit pupil. The optical properties of this pupil can be related to those of a pinhole or, more exactly, what is known as a stenopaic aperture. The stenopaic aperture is a thin slit sometimes used in the investigation of astigmatism in the human eye. If it is rotated while the eye looks through it, objects might be found to appear sharper at one position than any other, and obviously this position would represent the meridian in which the refractive error was lowest. In the seal the slit pupil corresponds to the stenopaic slit and its axis lies along the meridian of the eye where the refractive error is least, and therefore prevents rays from passing through which are likely to interfere with the quality of the retinal image (Fig. 2).

My work was concerned with the refractive mechanism of the Weddell

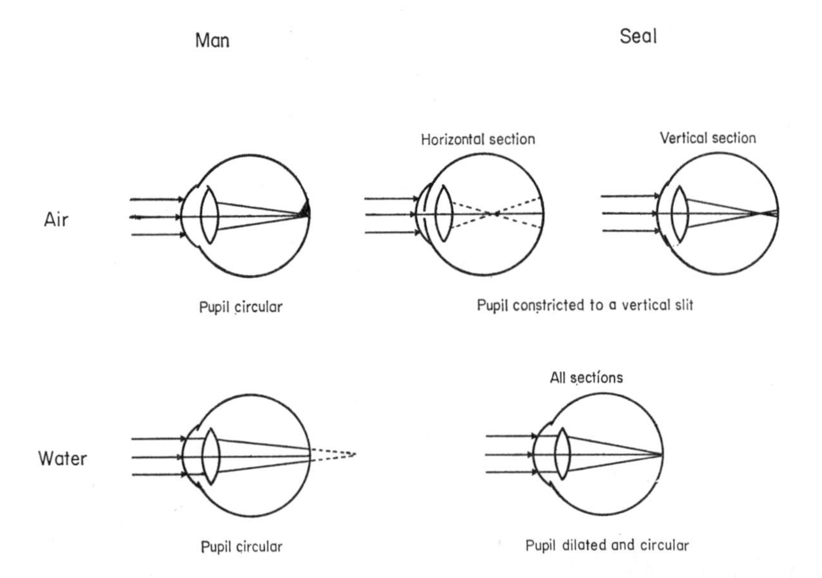

FIG. 2. Distant objects are focused on the retina in both the human eye in air, and the seal eye in water. The seal eye in air is myopic and astigmatic, the distortion in the retinal image that would be caused by this refractive error is reduced by the slit pupil, which prevents the passage of much light in the horizontal section. The section with the least refractive error (the vertical section) thus takes the greatest share in the forming of the retinal image.

seal (*Leptonychotes weddelli*), and it was found that in this species there was astigmatism like that previously described for non-Antarctic Pinnipedia. The astigmatism varied between 4·5 D and 12 D and the meridian with the lowest refractive error was the vertical. Immersed in water the eye showed low hyperopia or myopia, or low astigmatism, suggesting that in water the average condition is close to emmetropia. An extended account of this research will be published elsewhere (Wilson, 1969).

Successful measurements have also been recorded for other aquatic mammals. Cetacea have 3·9 to 4·5 D of astigmatism (Matthiesen, 1893), that is, less than in the Pinnipedia, and differ also in that the meridian of least power and the long axis of the slit pupil are in the horizontal. Both the seal and whale cornea when viewed from in front are elliptical, with the major diameter in the horizontal, though the difference between the horizontal and vertical diameters is more pronounced in the whale. Considering the form of the cornea, it is to be expected that where the cornea is broadest its radius of curvature will be large, and conversely where the cornea is narrow the radius of curvature will be less. This would result in the vertical meridian being the most steeply curved and hence the most powerful optically, which is the condition as it obtains in the whale. In the seal, as has been shown, the horizontal is the most powerful, and for this reversal to occur in a cornea which is horizontally elliptical must require local architectural adjustments to the curvature. The constant relation in seals and whales of the slit pupil to the flattest corneal meridian suggests that the interdependence of these two structures plays an important role in the optics of the eye. As the optical function of the cornea is negligible in water, it is tempting to consider these adaptations in terms of aerial vision, but caution must be observed in pronouncing any one characteristic as an adaptation to air when so many gross morphological and physiological changes are obviously referable to an aquatic environment.

If the sharpness of the retinal image influences visual acuity, it is not the only factor; the quality of the mechanism available for the interpretation of this image must also play a part. Observations have demonstrated that generally the two types of photoreceptor, rods and cones, are concerned with vision under different conditions. Cones are usually associated with colour vision and perception of detail in good illumination, whereas rods are associated with perception in low illumination, particularly of movement. The seal retina is believed to be rod-dominated (Walls, 1942), but there is scope for further verification of this, as the whale was held to be without cones until this belief was challenged (Mann, 1946). Certainly, consideration of the habits of the seal would not suggest a necessity for well-developed cone vision, and attempts to elicit colour awareness have been unsuccessful (Baldwin, 1966). A reflecting structure, called the tapetum, which increases sensitivity in low illumination is prominent in seals and must be particularly useful in the Weddell seal, which feeds in deep water and must spend much of the winter in the gloom beneath the Antarctic sea ice.

Except in some parts of the Arctic, seals are not exposed to land predators and the demands on vision in air are probably not great: the reconnaissance of possible landing places, the avoidance of obstacles between the sea and breeding sites, and perhaps some contribution to the organisation of breeding colonies. Probably social breeding demands recognition of some visual as well as auditory signals, though this varies widely throughout Otariids and Phocids, and in the grey seal, for example, successful mating, parturition and lactation has been observed in totally blind cows (E. A. Smith, *personal communication*). An adequate optical system is therefore provided by a slit pupil in connection with corneal flattening to reduce myopia. None the less the main function of the pupil must be the protection of the sensitive retina made doubly vulnerable to strong illumination by the addition of a tapetum.

Acknowledgement

The data for these experiments was collected while the author was a guest of the Instituto Antartico Argentino at Almirante Brown base on the Antarctic Peninsula.

References

Baldwin, H. A. (1966). Underwater Sensory Ability in the California Sea Lion. Proceedings of the Third Annual Conference on Biological Sonar and Diving Mammals, Stanford Research Institute, Menlo Park, California.

Johnson, L. (1893). Observations on the Refraction and Vision of the Seal's Eye. *Proc. zool. Soc. Lond.* 719–23.

Johnson, L. (1901). Contributions to the Comparative Anatomy of the Mammalian Eye, chiefly based on ophthalmoscopic examination. *Phil. Trans. R. Soc.* Ser. B. **194**, 1–82.

Mann, G. (1946). Ojo y Vision de las Ballenas. *Biologica* 4, 23–81.

Matthiesen, (1893). *Zeitschr. fur Vergl. AugenheilKunde* 7, 77–101.

Walls, G. L. (1942). "The Vertebrate Eye." Hafner Publishing Company, New York.

Wilson, G. S. (1969). Some Comments on the Optical System of Pinnipedia as a Result of Observations on the Weddell Seal (*Leptonychotes weddelli*). *British Antarctic Survey Bulletin.* (In the press.)

Discussion

Adaptation in Seals

THERMOREGULATION

C. Ray

Behavioural adaptations are important. The walrus calf is unable to withstand the most severe environmental conditions by physiological mechanisms alone. Maternal brooding is essential during the first weeks of life.

L. Irving

Such behaviour is an essential component of the heat regulatory mechanism. There is a dangerous tendency among physiologists to eliminate behaviour by anaesthesia and then to pretend it was never a factor!

R. L. Penney

Can we finally dispose of the idea that subcutaneous fat is present as an insulation rather than as a food reserve?

L. Irving

Subcutaneous fat in non-human populations is essentially a food reserve against an externally arising food lack. But it also, inevitably, provides insulation. Its effectiveness arises from quality and distribution. Back fat in the caribou under the thickest hair is probably of negligible insulation value. Conversely, seals and whales are enveloped in fat except for the snout and flippers, and there must be a calculable insulation effect. There are disadvantages in having thick subcutaneous fat layers, since once an animal is burdened with fat it is hard to get rid of it.

C. Ray

Weddell seals orientate themselves perpendicularly to the direction of the sun, and lie at random when the sun is hidden. But they do not usually stay hauled out in the evening despite the relative predominance of long-wave radiation at this time.

L. Irving

How hot does the real seal get inside its skin?

N. A. Øritsland

A newly killed seal has a temperature of 40°C; the temperature of a living animal is probably about 39°C.

My model was concerned with the qualities essential to the heat-trap properties of the pelt. Care must be used in speculating about pelts not specifically measured, and the reflectance properties must in particular be examined.

B. Stonehouse

The guard hair coat in seals and other mammals may be of particular significance, for these are longer and more refractory than the undercoat.

N. A. ØRITSLAND

I have done experiments on angles of radiation incidence. It does seem that the guard hairs are the most important and facilitate the inward reflection of radiation. The small hairs of the undercoat stop radiation above the skin and are less effective as radiation traps. In penguins feather morphology is also important. The black parts of the Adélie penguin may be the most efficient because of their feather structure. It would be interesting to look at chicks, whose down structure resembles a seal pelt.

C. RAY

In air, Weddell seals vasodilate and circulate blood through the skin. Under conditions of intense radiation the skin in the sunlight may be at 40–42°C, the subdermal tissue at 37°C and the skin on the underside in contact with the ice at 0°C. If you kill the seal the blubber quickly heats above 40°C. This demonstrates the role of blood in distributing heat from the exposed surface to the rest of the body.

ADAPTATIONS IN DIVING

N. A. ØRITSLAND

The electrocardiograms suggest that bradycardia develops more slowly in the foetus than in the adult. Is this because the nervous system is less fully developed?

R. W. ELSNER

In new-born elephant seals it develops faster than in the adult, during artificial dives. This is a consistent observation: none the less new-born elephant seals are not good divers and do not take to the water in their first month. Bradycardia in the foetus is probably related to other conditions, such as lowering oxygen tension.

C. KENYON

I have observed that the sea otter usually dives for about 1–1½ min, managing 4 min under stress, and this suggests the animal is far less adapted for an aquatic life than seals are. Have you any data?

R. W. ELSNER

No. We do plan to work on sea otters.

C. LENFANT

Certainly the animal seems to be a poor diver. Ten minutes is the maximum reported duration of a dive, and dives are always shallow.

R. J. HARRISON

Why would pregnancy reduce, rather than increase, diving performance (measured in terms of duration and depth)? In Harbour seal there is evidence pregnant females are the best divers. What is the stimulus to surface?

R. W. ELSNER

One might expect pregnant animals not to stay submerged as long as non-pregnant ones, because of the high oxygen demand of the foetus.

R. J. HARRISON

If both female and foetus exhibit bradycardia and the latter has a functional autonomic nervous system, it should be able to survive lengthy dives. I have removed a live foetus from a seal shot an hour earlier and that may be some indication of its survival capacity.

R. W. ELSNER

It is known that a foetus generally has a high anaerobic capacity, but this has not been proven in Pinnipedia. In general the capacity declines with age after birth.

L. IRVING

Isn't a new-born animal tolerant of asphyxia rather than endowed with an unusual capacity for anaerobic respiration?

R. W. ELSNER

Maybe. But Professor Harrison's information that he had removed a living foetus one hour after parental death is new to me and suggests more than just tolerance of asphyxia.

L. IRVING

Does the high concentration of haemoglobin in seal's blood make the blood viscous?

C. LENFANT

Yes. Similarly some men living at high altitudes have a 75% haematocrit level and it is very hard to work with their blood.

L. IRVING

With the additional problems posed by the low temperature of the peripheral tissues, this must create quite a viscosity difficulty for the circulation.

C. LENFANT

All pinnipedes and cetaceans have a higher concentration of plasma proteins than terrestrial mammals.

L. IRVING

Have you any information on how the circulation is adjusted in a non-pregnant uterus during diving?

R. W. ELSNER

In non-pregnant seals the uterus is a small organ. We have only a few measurements of blood flow, in sheep, which suggest that this behaves like that to gut or kidneys during asphyxia, with a low rate of flow.

DIVING CAPACITY

R. E. BENOIT

When seals are forced to dive, do they exhibit a behaviour pattern?

R. W. ELSNER

G. L. Kooyman showed that when first released into an ice hole a Weddell seal made short exploratory dives, and that these became longer and longer, probably as the animal searched for a new hole. Three types of dive were recognized—short exploratory ones, long deep dives, and long shallow dives during which the seals travelled to new places.

M. H. Thurston

What is the maximum distance a Weddell seal could cover during a dive?

R. W. Elsner

Marked animals have been seen a maximum distance of 2 miles from an ice hole following escape from experimental observation.

M. H. Thurston

How fast do they swim on a long shallow dive?

R. W. Elsner

I have no information. One interesting point: when working in our under-ice observation chamber G. L. Kooyman could watch the direction a seal disappeared in following release and often saw the animal appear again from the same direction: in other words they left the hole on a straight course and returned to the hole in the reverse direction.

C. Ray

I believe that seals often navigate by following the bottom topography. Admittedly this seems difficult when one is working in an area over deep water, but that was the impression I gained.

E. C. Young

We may not know how far Weddell Seals can travel under ice, but we do know something about the distance they *cannot* go. Around White Island, 10–12 miles south of McMurdo, there is an isolated population that has shown no interchange with that in the Sound during the last four years.

C. Ray

Weddell seals are slow swimmers, achieving an average 1–3 knots and a maximum of perhaps 6 to 8 over short distances.

L. Irving

To travel 10 miles they would need to keep up about 6 knots.

E. C. Young

What is the maximum depth of a dive?

R. W. Elsner

Kooyman's pressure recorders have given a maximum depth of 600 m, attained by one animal. Several animals have gone down to over 400 m.

FUNCTION OF PINEAL IN SEALS

W. N. Bonner

How did you kill the seals from which you extracted the pineal?

A. C. Cuello

By injection of phenobarbital and phencyclidine.

Question

Is there any abnormality in the structure or size relative to other parts of the brain of the pituitary body in seals?

A. C. CUELLO

The hypophysis is more or less of normal size in relation to the brain as a whole, but there are some differences from other mammals. The pars intermedia is invaded by fibres from the neurohypophysis, probably originating in the hypothalamus (cf. *Experientia* 24, 399, 1968).

A. W. ERICKSON

Dr Cuello related the cycle in pineal activity to the sexual cycle. But might it not be due to the annual variation in environmental illumination?

A. C. CUELLO

The pineal is undoubtedly affected by the duration of exposure to external light. The changes in the pineal gland of the Weddell seal are quite similar to those in rats exposed to similar photoperiods.

M. S. R. SMITH

Is there any similarity between the pineal gland in polar seals and that of seasonal breeders elsewhere, where the seasonal light differences are less extreme?

A. C. CUELLO

There are many papers on the relationship between environmental photoperiod and pineal activity. The pineal has a rhythmic activity in experimental animals. There is no proof of pineal control of sex cycles in these animals.

VISION IN SEALS

C. RAY

We should consider Mr Wilson's paper in an ecological context. Every time a seal dives it becomes a nocturnal animal with at least fourfold dimming of available light even at the surface—much more at depth or under ice. The capacity of the eye to vary pupil aperture quickly is significant. It must, to do this, have a slit pupil in air and a round pupil underwater. If the slit pupil is an adaptation to vision in air, astigmatism also could be an adaptive necessity.

G. WILSON

The slit pupil reduces the amount of light entering the eye and can do this more completely than a round one. I think none the less that it is curious that the slit lies along the axis in which the refractive error is least; and the same is true in whales, although in this case both slit pupil and astigmatism have been turned through 90°. Perhaps the flattening of the cornea might have something to do with fluid flow past the seal in water, but the constant relationship of astigmatism to slit pupil has its most obvious explanation as an adaptation to vision in air.

C. RAY

Does Hemmingsen allege that Weddell seals suffer from snow-blindness?

G. WILSON

It has also been described as blepharitis, but this is not established. Snow-blindness is essentially desquamation of the corneal epithelium induced by over exposure to ultraviolet light. On the face of it there is no reason for seals being any less susceptible to this condition than humans. It is certainly worth looking into.

S. Z. EL-SAYED

How far can a Weddell seal see in air?

G. WILSON

I can only infer this from eye structure. Emmetropia under water should allow good distance vision, but in air the retinal image is of a much poorer quality and consequently vision is worse, certainly not as good as in man. Experiments have been done to test discrimination between discs of different sizes; this has been done underwater, but not in air.

M. A. THURSTON

The shape of pupil contrasts with that in emperor penguins which have a cross-shaped aperture in bright light, a square pupil in medium conditions and a round pupil in dim light or under water.

G. WILSON

Pygoscelis antarctica is myopic and has a square pupil and no astigmatism. I have no explanation of the significance of this.

Part IX

ECOLOGY OF ANTARCTIC BIRDS

Ecology of Antarctic Birds

The Antarctic avifauna was one of the first subjects of biological research in the region, and is now better documented than any other animal group. The early research concentrated, as in other areas, on taxonomic and biogeographic studies and on details of breeding biology. The papers in this section are representative of recent programmes in which ecology, population dynamics, and behaviour have played an increasing part, even though some taxonomic problems remain to be solved. The review by R. Carrick and S. E. Ingham supplements their earlier paper (1967), and, read in conjunction with it, provides a comprehensive guide to the literature. It also summarizes important recent work on the regulation of numbers of breeding birds in Antarctic sea-bird species. Both Carrick and Ingham's paper and that by W. J. L. Sladen look ahead to the developments to be expected in Antarctic ornithology. Because of the great difficulties involved in following sea-birds during their pelagic life, there is some suggestion that research on the detailed mechanisms of their population regulation may not be productive, at least in the foreseeable future. It is also suggested that most of the Antarctic bird species that are suitable for quantitative population research are now being studied. Future work may thus concentrate more intensively on the physiology of Antarctic species (as research on seals is already doing).

References

Carrick, R. and Ingham, S. E. (1967). Antarctic sea birds as subjects for ecological research. *Proc. Symposium on Pacific-Antarctic Sciences, Tokyo*, 1966. *JARE Sci. Rep.*, Special Issue No. 1, pp. 151–84. Dept. of Polar Research, Tokyo.

Ecology and Population Dynamics of Antarctic Sea Birds

ROBERT CARRICK AND SUSAN E. INGHAM
Mawson Institute for Antarctic Research, University of Adelaide, South Australia

I. Introduction

At the First SCAR Symposium on Antarctic Biology in 1962 (Carrick *et al.*, 1964) there was no comprehensive ecological review of Antarctic birds. Falla, Murphy and Sladen reviewed the systematics and distribution of high-latitude birds, petrels and pygoscelid penguins respectively and Warham discussed breeding behaviour in Procellariiformes. Subsequently, Stonehouse (1964) and Voous (1965) have reviewed the distribution and ecological adaptations of Antarctic and Subantarctic birds, the former with special reference to climate, and the latter from a taxonomic viewpoint. Carrick and Ingham (1967) collated into comprehensive tabular form the available evidence on the breeding distribution, annual cycles, food and nest-site requirements of the thirty-six species of sea birds breeding in the Antarctic and Subantarctic, and discussed current and possible future lines of ecological research. Stonehouse (1967) discussed the distribution and ecological, morphological and physiological adaptations of penguins to sea temperature, land climate, distribution and numbers of food organisms, nest sites and predators. Since Carrick and Ingham's review results have been published of ecological studies on the Adélie penguin, *Pygoscelis adeliae* (Reid *et al.*, 1967; Emison, 1968; Penney, 1968; Yeates, 1968), wandering albatross, *Diomedea exulans* (Tickell, 1968), smaller albatrosses (Tickell and Pinder, 1967), the Atlantic and Antarctic fulmars, *Fulmarus glacialis* and *F. glacialoides* (Mougin, 1967), the white-headed petrel, *Pterodroma lessoni* (Warham, 1967), McCormick's skua, *Stercorarius skua maccormicki* (Le Morvan *et al.*, 1967) and the southern skua *Stercorarius skua lonnbergi* (Burton, 1968). The smaller, lesser-known and less accessible petrels continue to be underrepresented compared with the penguins and albatrosses. Tickell (1967), Tickell and Gibson (1968), Sladen, *et al.* (1968) report movements of banded birds. Preliminary ornithological results are available (Van Zinderen Bakker, in the press) of a survey of Marion and Prince Edward Islands that has filled the gaps in our knowledge of these islands. Surveys and studies of the birds of Iles Crozet by French ornithologists are now in progress.

The present paper aims to bring our previous review up to date, incorporating the above-mentioned publications as well as further results of our own work at Macquarie Island on the royal penguin, *Eudyptes chrysolophus schlegeli*, the wandering albatross and the giant petrels, *Macronectes giganteus* and *M. halli.*

II. Breeding Species

A. Systematic and Taxonomic Problems

Table 3 (see pages 518–522) brings up to date the similar table in Carrick and Ingham (1967).

By differentiation of the northern giant petrel, *Macronectes halli*, from *M. giganteus*, and by the discovery of the yellow-nosed albatross, *Diomedea chlororhynchus*, breeding at Prince Edward Island, the total number has been increased to thirty-seven Antarctic and Subantarctic species and another six whose main range lies to the north. The Marion-Prince Edward Islands' list has been revised, and the Iles Crozet included.

This table reveals several anomalous distributions, such as those of the black-browed and grey-headed albatrosses, *D. melanophris* and *D. chrysostoma*. In the Indian Ocean sector the black-brow is the more southern species, being present at Heard Island (south of the Antarctic Convergence) and absent from Marion (north of it), while the grey-head is absent from Heard, but present at Marion. In the New Zealand area the grey-head is more numerous than the black-brow at Macquarie Island (north of the Convergence) as might be expected, but a distinct race of the black-brow is very numerous at Campbell Island, farther north again, and present without the grey-head at Antipodes Island. In the Atlantic sector both are numerous at South Georgia (south of the Convergence), and the black-brow but not the grey-head extends north to the Falkland Islands. The two species have very similar nest sites and annual cycles, and at South Georgia show some differences in food preferences. There would appear to be ecological, physiological, or behavioural reasons for these geographical variations in distribution, which would merit investigation.

The discontinuous distribution of prions, especially the fulmar prion, *Pachyptila crassirostris*, and the thin-billed prion, *P. belcheri*, poses problems of ecology and systematics. The fulmar prion breeds in large numbers at Heard Island, in the Indian Ocean sector and south of the Convergence, and also at the Auckland, Antipodes, Bounty and Chatham Islands, in the New Zealand area and well north of the Convergence (Falla *et al.*, 1966). Is this, in fact, a single species (as it appears to be on morphological grounds) whose apparent absence at intermediate islands such as Kerguelen, Amsterdam and Macquarie may merely reflect inadequate knowledge? Or would further critical systematic study, employing modern techniques such as egg-albumen or blood-protein analysis, or detailed comparison of ecology and behaviour, demonstrate that two geographically isolated species have been included under one name? *P. belcheri*, known to breed only at Kerguelen and the Falklands, poses a similar problem.

The diving-petrels present a purely taxonomic problem to the ecologist. Systematists disagree whether the Kerguelen or Subantarctic diving-petrel, which breeds at Heard, Kerguelen, the Crozets, and Marion in the Indian Ocean, and at Auckland, Antipodes and Macquarie in the New Zealand region, should be given specific rank as *Pelecanoides exsul* or subspecific rank within the more northerly *P. urinatrix*. The only evidence so far available is morphological, and here again, use of biochemical techniques such as blood-protein composition, or an ethological approach through analysis of behaviour patterns, might help to solve the problem. The ecologist needs to know the true affinities of species, and especially how to differentiate similar species, in order to avoid the confusion of studying two as if they were one. Problem species require much more critical examination before they are available for ecological studies.

B. Systematics and Ecology of Giant Petrels

Recent work on giant petrels illustrates the point that has just been made. Formerly only one species, *M. giganteus*, was recognized, though field-workers were aware of wide variations in plumage and breeding ecology, even at a single location, e.g. Macquarie Island. Bourne and Warham (1966) separated *M. halli* as a distinct species, breeding only north of the Antarctic Convergence, on the basis of earlier breeding season, solitary nest site, absence of white-phase plumage, darker head in older birds, and pinkish rather than greenish bill. Although they could find very few skins of *M. halli* in existing collections, subsequent work has confirmed their general conclusions.

At Macquarie Island, young dark-phase *M. giganteus* are morphologically distinguishable from *M. halli* only by the greenish colour of the bill. In older *giganteus* the head, neck and breast can be much lighter-coloured than in any *halli*. Bill and tarsus length differ between the sexes, but not between the species. Blood-protein electrophoresis shows that the transferrins, albumen and haptoglobin of both white and dark-phase *giganteus* and *halli* are identical (Shaughnessy, in preparation); haemoglobins have not been tested.

Fledglings of *giganteus* disperse widely and have been recovered on the coasts of all the southern continents; the small number of *halli* banded at

Macquarie have so far been recovered from Australia, New Zealand and South America. Some older non-breeding *giganteus* go south in summer: two 6-year-olds from Macquarie have been recovered at Cape Crozier, as has one that was banded as a breeding adult nine years earlier and which had probably failed in breeding in the year of recovery.

The breeding cycle of *halli*, from laying to fledging, is about six weeks earlier than that of *giganteus*. There is a gap of about three weeks in September between cessation of laying in the one and its onset in the other. Differences in nest site are not so clear-cut as was first thought: although isolated nests in sheltered sites are typical of *halli*, it also forms small colonies or may nest with *giganteus*, but is always distinguishable by its more advanced breeding stage. These two species are both generalized predators and scavengers, and the ultimate factors to which their different annual time-tables are geared are not known. Nor are the proximate behavioural and physiological mechanisms which ensure their reproductive isolation.

During 1954–59 and 1961 over 7000 giant petrel chicks, mostly of *M. giganteus*, were banded at Macquarie. The oldest so far recovered were 13 years old, and at this age all had relatively dark heads and necks. This confirms that *giganteus* with light-coloured heads, necks and breasts, which are fairly common in breeding colonies, are much older birds. These recoveries also indicate that the onset of breeding in this species is a gradual process for any age group. No 6-year-olds have been recovered at Macquarie, even from a year when every chick on the island was banded. At 7 years old the few *giganteus* were of doubtful breeding status: one *halli* had an egg, but failed to incubate it successfully. Some 8- and 9-year-olds have chicks, but a much higher proportion of 11-year-olds, which suggests that by that time the age group is breeding successfully. Chicks tend to return to breed in the same part of the island as their birthplace. The earliest bird banded as a breeding adult had survived fifteen years when recovered, and was within a few hundred yards of its banding place.

C. Other Petrels and Penguins

The fulmars of the North Atlantic and the Antarctic are widely separated allopatric species. Mougin (1967) compared two small colonies and found that the chick's growth rate, onset of thermoregulation and age at departure are very similar, as is the adult mortality in the breeding season. The Antarctic fulmar, in a much less favourable climate, has a more sheltered nest site, and also a slightly shorter incubation period.

Warham (1967) has described breeding of the white-headed petrel at Macquarie Island, and indicated the effect of introduced predators, especially cats. Emison (1968), having developed a technique for removing food from the stomach of a live penguin, investigated it in breeding Adélies at Cape Crozier. He found that small shoaling fish were, by volume, a good second in importance to *Euphausia*, that all food is taken from the surface layers of the water, and that the penguins selected items over a minimum size.

Beck (1970: this Symposium) presents data on the annual cycle, breeding success, adult survival and onset of breeding in the snow petrel, *Pagodroma nivea*, Cape pigeon, *Daption capensis*, Wilson's storm-petrel, *Oceanites oceanicus*, and black-bellied storm-petrel, *Fregetta tropica*, at the South Orkney Islands. He suggests that differences between them in the timing of the breeding season may be related to the type of nest site and the probability of its being blocked by snow.

D. Seasonal Dispersal and Migration

Several nations band birds in the Antarctic, for study both of local populations and of migration and dispersal. Sladen *et al.* (1968) report on the numbers banded and list distant recoveries in the USARP Bird Banding Program from 1958 to 1965; the main species were the Adélie penguin, wandering, black-browed and grey-headed albatrosses, giant petrel and McCormick's skua; the Ross Sea area and South Georgia were the main centres of activity. The black-browed albatross and giant petrel provided the greatest number of distant recoveries: movements by Adélie penguins were few and local, and none is yet known to breed away from its birthplace. An international programme of banding McCormick's skuas, in which the other SCAR nations take part, is organized by R. C. Wood of USARP, and is giving information on both northward migration and coastwise movement round Antarctica (Wood *et al.*, 1967). Tickell (1967) further analyses the dispersal of black-browed and grey-headed albatrosses banded in South Georgia and the Falklands, and shows that the recoveries reflect a specific difference between the young birds. Black-brows seem to make for the coastal waters of the nearest continent: there are numerous recoveries, but they are localized, in South Africa for South Georgian and in eastern South America for Falkland Islands birds. Grey-heads disperse widely over the Southern Ocean, but rarely approach the continents: recoveries are few and scattered as far as New Zealand. Tickell and Gibson (1968) summarize results of ten years' banding of wandering albatrosses off the New South Wales coast in winter and at South Georgian breeding colonies in summer, and of recoveries at both places and elsewhere. It is clear that at least some birds, both breeding adults and non-breeders (subadults) commute regularly between these two areas; but probably it is individuals rather than island populations that patronize particular wintering areas, since birds banded off New South Wales have been found breeding at Kerguelen, Marion Island and Auckland Island as well as South Georgia.

III. Population Studies

A. Penguins

Some preliminary results of the long-term study of the royal penguin at Macquarie Island were given in Carrick and Ingham (1967). At a small colony of about 2000 breeding pairs, which fledges 500–1000 young each year, 16,755 chicks, 861 yearlings and 884 adults have been banded since 1955–56, and life histories recorded since 1962; the oldest are 13 years old in 1968–69. Samples of 10,000 chicks and 990 adults have been banded at three larger colonies.

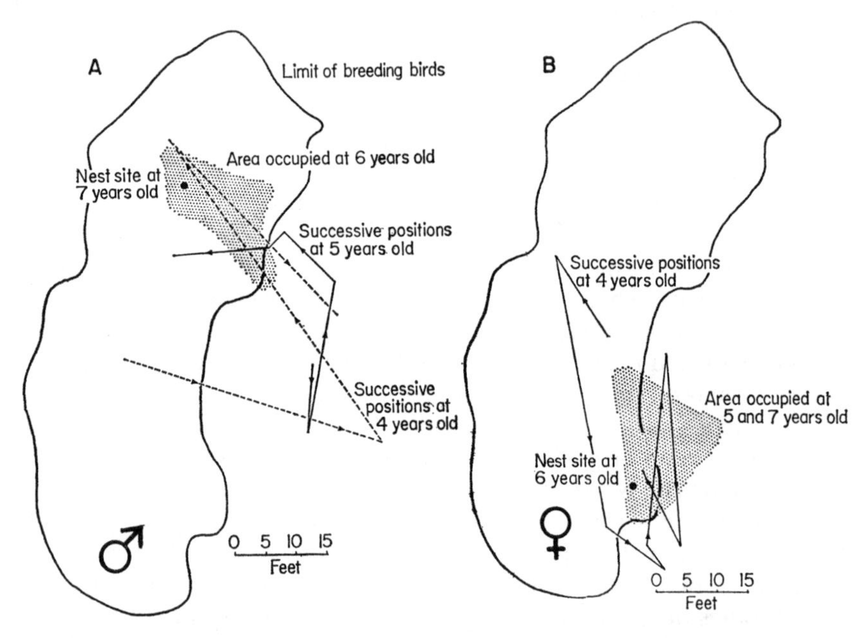

Fig. 1. Establishment of breeding site in Royal Penguins at Bauer Bay Sand colony; (*A*) Male, first breeding at 7 years old, ♂00849, single record without location at 3 years old; (*B*) Female, first breeding at 6 years old, ♀00784, on the beach at 3 years old.

Although most individuals are never recorded away from their birthplace, some 1-year-olds are found dispersed round the island; with increasing age they return to their natal colony, and very few settle to breed elsewhere. Only three of 2000 chicks are now breeding at the next colony, two miles from their birthplace. Interchange between "nurseries" only 200 yds apart, reached by common track from the beach, is nearly as rare. During its early pre-breeding years a bird when ashore moves at random round the edge of the colony, without settling at any one spot; later (at 4–7 years old) it becomes attached to a restricted area; in a subsequent season a male establishes a claim to a breeding site, and a female finds a mate among the site-holding unmated cocks, in this area (Fig. 1A, AB.) Some birds get permanent partners at the same time as or even before they get sites, and many pairs are recorded together during one or more seasons before they breed. The breeding bird, especially the older and successful one, usually remains constant to both site and mate. After loss of mate, the cock obtains another at the same site, but

TABLE 1

Breeding Success of Royal Penguin in relation to Age

Age in years	*% present at laying*		*% present with eggs*		*% of eggs that hatch*		*Number and % of chicks that fledge*	
	♂	♀	♂	♀	♂	♀	♂	♀
4	Very low		0	0	0	0	0	0
5	60	64	3·5	8·5	33	21	0	0
6	89	86	20	42·5	18·5	16	1=14%	1=9%
7	96	97	41	60	17	22	3=25%	1=5%
8	96	98	53	70	31	33	9=64%	7=35%
9	100	98	53	85	37·5	54	*(1=11%)	(2=11%)
10	100	100	60	85	(50)	(53)	(3=50%)	(2=22%)
11	100	100	100	100	(0)	(28·5)	(0)	(1=50%)
12	—	100	—	100	—	(50)	—	(0)

* These low figures are given in brackets because the oldest age groups are very small samples (40, 9 and 2 birds), and their hatching and fledging rates have been affected by trapping and weighing.

the hen attaches to an unmated cock within her restricted area. Such loss may interrupt breeding, and 43% of males and 17% of females that had lost their mates failed to breed the following season.

Minimum figures for survival during the first four years of life, from a sample of 4000 chicks banded in one year, are 67%, 43%, 34% and 20%. The minimum survival of known-age birds in the study colony is 12% at 5 years old, 10·4% at 6, 8·5% at 7 and 6·8% at 8. Although all banded survivors in these age groups are known, suspected loss of bands in earlier years introduces an error, and these figures are all minimal. In birds of breeding age the annual survival rate was 71% of 222 which returned in time to breed, whether they had eggs or not; it was 86% in a sample of 318 established breeders of unknown age.

With increasing age in the pre-breeding years, birds come ashore earlier in the season, stay longer, and improve their status at the colony. There is considerable variation within any age group; a few precocious birds breed, i.e. have eggs, for the first time at 5 years old, most do so between 7 and 9, a few not till 11 years old. Table 1 shows the proportion of each age group that arrives in time to breed, the proportion of these that actually have eggs, and the proportion of eggs that hatch. Although the sexes mature at the same rate (shown by the numbers present at laying) females are more precocious than males in both laying and successful incubation. At 10 years old 20% of males and 5% of females have never bred; the other non-breeders have lost their previous mates.

The breeding female royal penguin is ashore, fasting, for approximately five weeks through egg-laying and the first half of incubation. The male is ashore for the same length of time during the second half of incubation, hatching and brooding of the chick. Arrival weight, which indicates the amount of food reserves, is directly related to the arrival date, and profoundly affects breeding performance. On arrival in October the hen weighs from 4·2 to 6·3 kg, but hens lighter than 4·8 kg rarely lay, and most of these light birds are not settled and soon leave again. Hens over 4·8 kg usually lay, but incubation performance is related to age and previous experience as well as weight, so that 5- and 6-year-olds rarely incubate successfully, whatever their initial weight. At the end of her five weeks ashore the hen weighs about 3·5 kg, but some, whose mates are delayed, weigh as little as 3·0 kg before they eventually desert the egg. The cock returning to incubate is at least 5·0 kg, and those which rear chicks to the creche stage are almost all over 5·4 kg. During the chick-feeding period both parents maintain their weights about 4·0 kg. The initial weight of the hen in October is significantly related to the weight of her fledging chick in mid-January: this is taken to reflect the hen's feeding status at sea. High feeding status enables a royal penguin of either sex to come ashore early enough and with adequate food reserves to lay and hatch the egg and to provide enough food for the chick. Possession of a mate determines whether an individual breeds, while the age and experience of each bird of the pair affect the success of incubation and chick rearing, a better-than-average bird sometimes compensating for a poorer mate.

Recent papers on the Adélie penguin offer interesting comparisons with these results. At Cape Hallett, Reid *et al.* (1967) found that the proportion of surviving birds seen at their natal colony increased from 5–10% at 2 years old to 80% at 4, while the proportion of unsettled "wanderers" without nest sites decreased with age, to nothing at 5 and 6 years old. Older birds arrived earlier in the season than younger ones. Some hens bred at 4 and 5 years old, but laid only one egg; 6-year-olds laid the full clutch of two eggs. At Cape Crozier some birds have bred at 3 and 4 years old, but few of them do so successfully and even these rear only one chick (Sladen *et al.*, 1966). Only one of six 3-year-olds laid two eggs, compared with 70% of 4- and 5-year-olds; with age the interval between hatching of the two eggs decreases and the survival rate of the second chick increases, so that 4-year-olds rear an average of 0·81 chicks, 5-year-olds 1·11 chicks and controls of unknown age

1·63 chicks. The growth rate of chicks is related to their parents' feeding behaviour and to age (Wood *et al.*, 1967). At Cape Royds, Yeates (1968) found two of ten 3-year-olds present at egg-laying, but unmated; four of fourteen 4-year-olds bred, each laying a single small egg which was broken during incubation. He also related incubation behaviour and breeding success to the extent of fast ice in five seasons. The incubation shifts of an Adélie pair become shorter from laying to hatching, and both the number of shifts and their duration may vary. In a year when open water was never more than a mile from the colony the first (male) shift averaged 7·5 days; in three years when the ice broke out in December it was 9, 11 and 12·7 days; in a year of late-January breakout it was 13·75 days. The average second (female) shift varied from 8·0 to 12·5 days. This suggests that in a year when ice breaks out early the absent bird can feed nearer to the colony, with less intense competition, and can recover its weight more quickly than in a late year. Similarly, in the worst ice year chick mortality was high and only 26% of eggs gave rise to fledged chicks, compared with 50% and 67·5% in two years of December break-out.

Penney (1968) found that male Adélies are primarily attached to their nest sites, seldom change them, and the rare moves are only for short distances. Females return to surviving mates, or replace lost mates within the same colony of a few hundred birds. Pairs breeding together for the first time are less successful than established pairs. Only 11% of birds that had lost their previous mates did not breed again the next year. In the Ross Sea no Adélie penguin has yet been found breeding at a distance from its birthplace (Sladen *et al.*, 1968).

As suggested by Carrick and Ingham (1967), the Adélie penguin is able to reach breeding status several years earlier than the royal. The Adélie's fasting periods ashore during breeding are, except for the first one, shorter than in the royal. The young Adélie female can reduce the demands of breeding by laying one instead of two eggs, or by rearing one instead of two chicks, while the royal, with an effective clutch of one, must make the full effort if it breeds at all. Both species show wide variation in the age of first breeding, and in the status of birds in any age group during the pre- and early breeding years. Thus, 5-year-old royals include both breeding birds and some which do not come ashore until hatching is well under way; some 7-year-olds rear chicks, others breed but fail, others have a nest site or preferred area, but some remain completely unsettled throughout the season.

After the first year or two of life, age as such is much less important than experience and social status, which are expressed on land in the arrival date and weight and in breeding status and performance, but which primarily determine the capacity to obtain food. Subantarctic islands provide breeding areas which are small and concentrated relative to the extensive feeding areas of the Southern Ocean, so that intraspecific competition for feeding rights within foraging range of the colony must be severe. The coast of Antarctica provides the Adélie penguin with numerous breeding grounds spaced out relative to the feeding areas, which would reduce offshore competition and enable a higher proportion of the total population to breed. The contrast in the onset of breeding, and in the demands of incubation and provision of food for families so different in size, shown by the Subantarctic royal penguin and the Antarctic Adélie penguin, may also reflect differences in the logistics of feeding; the Adélie may need to travel relatively short distances, especially when the ice breaks out early, while the royal may have to face intense inshore competition or else travel further afield.

B. Wandering Albatross

As in the closely related royal albatross, *Diomedea epomophora*, it is now established at Macquarie Island (Carrick and Ingham, 1967) and Bird Island, South Georgia (Tickell, 1968), that the wandering albatross breeds every second year if successful, taking 11–13 months from egg-laying in late December to departure of the chick. Pairs which lose eggs or young chicks before July breed again the following year.

Tickell's (1968) comprehensive study of the large and stable population at Bird Island is complemented by the work at Macquarie Island on a small and recolonizing population. The existence of a large number of wanderers at Macquarie in the nineteenth century is attested by the recent discovery of over 100 skulls in caves inhabited by sealers or castaways. In 1911–13 there was only one known breeding pair. Adding the numbers present in two consecutive years, by 1950 and 1951 there were at least seventeen breeding pairs; in 1956 and 1957 at least twenty-four pairs; in 1960 and 1961 about thirty-five pairs and in 1967 and 1968 there were forty-four pairs, of which twenty-nine laid in each year, with an annual output of eleven and fifteen chicks respectively. Six other birds of breeding status are known, with about fifty others which are not known to have bred.

General observations have been made since 1949, some chicks banded during 1955–59 and all since 1960, and virtually all birds present in 1965–66 and 1966–67 and breeding in 1967–68 have been marked and recorded intensively. Forty known-age birds up to 13 years old have returned to the island; the majority were first seen at 5–7 years old but one at 3 and five at 4 years of age. Nine known-age birds have bred, i.e. reached the egg stage, five of them for the first time at 10 years old, the others between 8 and 13; all five surviving 13-year-olds have attained breeding status (Table 2). There is a marked tendency for birds to return to, and eventually breed in, the part of the island where they were born. Several years of attendance at the island in the breeding season, with increasing attachment and performance each year, are necessary before young birds breed. As birds which lose their mates take up to four years before they breed again, both at Macquarie and at Bird Island, it seems that the pair-bond is formed very slowly.

The youngest birds that have reared a chick successfully were 10 years old. However, known-age parents have reared only three chicks to fledging from thirteen eggs, and one of these chicks left the island so late (March) that its chance of survival seems low. For all one-egg clutches over the four years 1965–58, 61% of eggs hatched and 74% of chicks (45% of eggs) fledged. The corresponding figures from Bird Island are 72%, 81% and 59%

TABLE 2

Survival and Status of Known-age Wandering Albatross at Macquarie Island*

Age	*Number of chicks banded*	*Minimum number and % surviving*	*Number seen*	*Number that bred*
3	23	Not yet known	1	0
4	25	Not yet known	4	0
5	26	17=66%	10	0
6	27	15=55%	14	0
7	16	5=31%	4	0
8	8	3=37·5%	3	0(1)
9	8	4=50%	3	1
10	13	6=46%	6	4
11	21	8=38%	6	6
12	12	5=42%	5	4
(13)	(12)	(5=42%)	(5)	(5)

* Recovery data for 1966 and 1967, the years of intensive search, are given in full. Additional significant results from other years are shown in brackets.

(Tickell, 1968). It is clear that young birds breed less successfully than the population as a whole, and take several years to develop the breeding skill of older birds. The wanderer is so clumsy on land that even an old and experienced breeder has been seen to crack its egg as it climbed on to its nest, and young birds and newly established pairs often break their eggs within a few days of laying, quite independent of human or other disturbance. Newly hatched chicks are also vulnerable. If an egg survives the first few days, it has a good chance of hatching; if a chick survives the first week or so, it has a good change of flying. One pair at Macquarie Island has fledged a chick every alternate year from 1956 to 1968, and two (possibly three, as identification of a worn band-number is doubtful) of the four progeny old enough to have returned to the island by 1967 have done so.

The lower breeding success at Macquarie Island as compared with Bird Island suggests that the former population may include a higher proportion of young birds than the latter. As at Macquarie, young birds return to Bird Island at 4 years old or more (Tickell, 1968) but the onset of breeding there is not yet known. It will be of great interest to know whether it is the same as at Macquarie, or whether social pressures in this stable population retard it even further, and also reduce the proportion of young birds that survive to breed.

The survival rate after fledging is high. At Macquarie, 47% of seventy chicks have survived to five years or older, and 38% of twenty-nine chicks to 10 years old. Tickell (1968) recovered 38% of 656 chicks at 4–6 years old, and estimated the true figure at about 50%. Table 2 gives the numbers of known-age birds surviving, present and breeding in the two years of intensive observation at Macquarie. Although the samples are small, it is clear that there is considerable variation between year groups. The greatest contrast is between the chicks banded in two successive years, 1960 and 1961; two of eleven and thirteen of fifteen respectively reached 6 years old. It is not known whether differences in winter feeding of the chicks, or post-fledging conditions of weather and food, may have affected survival.

It is also clear from Table 2 that annual survival reaches a very high level by about 10 years old, i.e. as the young birds attain breeding status. Wanderers banded as breeding adults survive better than those banded as non-breeding adults (most of which are young): 59% of twenty-two breeders and 35% of twenty non-breeders survived for ten years from 1956 to 1957. The annual survival rate of breeding adults over four years at Macquarie Island was 94·6%, comparable to the figure of 95·7% at Bird Island. Tickell (1968) has also compiled a life table in which survival from the egg to a possible 80 years is calculated. His estimate of the world breeding population is 13,823+, but in this wide-ranging oceanic species there is as yet no evidence on how population size or breeding rate is regulated.

Two-egg clutches are very rare among Procellariiformes and have not previously been described in the great albatrosses. The single brood patch and frequent changeover between mates would surely prejudice the chance of either egg being properly incubated. At Macquarie Island eight two-egg clutches have been found over four seasons at three isolated nest sites. There is no evidence of more than one hen at any of these nests. All these eggs failed, with one surprising exception in which the two eggs lay apart in the nest and, apparently, only the successful one was continuously brooded until the other was lost after five weeks' incubation. It appears that these three hens are consistently two-egg layers, but the very low hatching success must tend to eliminate this character.

C. Skuas

The long-term population study of McCormick's skua, *Stercorarius skua maccormicki*, at Cape Crozier is yielding detailed and accurate results on survival and breeding that reveal processes comparable to those found in the penguins and albatross (Sladen *et al.*, 1966; Wood *et al.*, 1967). The high survival rate, about 94% of breeding adults, and evident longevity, with stability of the breeding population, indicate considerable social competition leading to deferment of maturity to at least 5 years old, and reduction of the first clutch to a single egg.

Le Morvan *et al.* (1967) found that skuas in Terre Adélie, whose numbers had been reduced by man, had a higher breeding success than those in the Ross Sea area; this is attributed to a better food supply and reduced intraspecific competition. Young (1970: this Symposium) has confirmed his earlier finding that in the Ross Sea area breeding skuas find most of their food at sea rather than in penguin colonies. Although some skuas occupy and defend breeding territories among Adélie penguins, they vary greatly in ability to prey on them, and the presence or absence of penguins in the territory does not affect breeding success.

At Signy Island and Macquarie Island the breeding southern skua, *S.s. lonnbergi*, feeds on land, taking penguin eggs and chicks, seal and penguin carrion, smaller petrels and, at Macquarie, the introduced rats and young rabbits. At Signy, skuas also feed on littoral organisms and some fish: at Macquarie their stomachs sometimes contain squid beaks.

Burton (1968) found that skuas at Signy Island are efficient breeders, rearing in three seasons an average of 59% of eggs to fledging, and losing few chicks after hatching. There is a reserve of adults without breeding territories, and three 7-year-old birds had not bred. Territories are large, and this probably reduces intraspecific predation of chicks in a terrain which provides little shelter. At Macquarie Island, Purchase (in preparation) made a two-year study of breeding success in relation to nesting terrain and food supply. He found that a breeding territory must include short grass or herbage for the nest site, and shelter (e.g. taller plants) for the chicks: the dense stands of high tussock grass on hill slopes and the barren wind desert at high altitudes are rarely used. Breeding birds feed as near their nests as possible, but some regularly travel several miles. Breeding success is influenced both by the distance of the territory from a reliable food supply, and by intraspecific competition, which is greater when the food supply and nesting terrain are good and close together, attracting potential breeders, than when either is inferior. The few pairs which were able to find nest sites in gaps in dense tussock round a very large penguin colony had little competition, and seventeen pairs reared an average of 1·35 chicks each; on good nest terrain near penguin colonies many pairs bred in small territories, competing for food and space, and twelve pairs reared 1·08 chicks each; on poor inland terrain more than a mile from good food sources pairs were scattered, had to travel and compete for food, and eleven pairs reared 0·90 chicks each.

TABLE 3

Breeding Sea Birds of Antarctica and Subantarctic Islands

Families and species	*Antarctic Continent*			*Peninsula and Subantarctic islands*								
				South of Convergence					*North of Convergence*			
	Coast and offshore islands, including											
	Balleny	and	Peter I.	Peninsula	S. Shetland Is. S. Orkney Is. S. Sandwich Is.	Bouvet I.	Heard I.	S. Georgia	Kerguelen	Iles Crozet	Marion I. Prince Edward I.	Macquarie I.
SPHENISCIDAE												
Emperor Penguin												
Aptenodytes forsteri		B		68°Sb]								
King Penguin					S.Sa.							
Apenodytes patagonica					[b	N.S.	b	B→	B	B	B	B
Adélie Penguin												
Pygoscelis adeliae	B	B	b	B	B	b]						
Chinstrap Penguin												
Pygoscelis antarctica	(b)		b	B	B	B	(b)]	B]				
Gentoo Penguin												
Pygoscelis papua				[B	B	p	B	B→	B	B	B	B]
Macaroni/Royal Penguin												Royal
Eudyptes chrysolophus				[b	b	b	B	B	B	b	B	B]
Rockhopper Penguin												
Eudyptes chrysocome							[B	?	B→	B→	B→	B→
DIOMEDEIDEA												
Wandering Albatross												
Diomedea exulans							?N.S.	[B→	B→	B→	B→	B→

Black-browed Albatross *Diomedea melanophris*							[b	B→	B	p	?	b→	Also Falklands, Cape Horn, Campbell, Antipodes.
Grey-headed Albatross *Diomedea chrysostoma*							?	[B	p	p	B	B→	Also Campbell, Cape Horn
Yellow-nosed Albatross *Diomedea chlororhynchus*									P		b, Prince Edward		
Light-mantled Albatross *Phoebetria palpebrata*							[b	[B	B	b]	b]	B→	
Sooty Albatross *Phoebetria fusca*											[B→		
PROCELLARIIDAE													
Giant Petrel *Macronectes giganteus*		b		b	B	p	B	B→	p	b	b	B	
Northern Giant Petrel *Macronectes halli*									B→	b	b	b→	
Cape Pigeon *Daption capensis*	B	B		B	B	B	B	b	b	b→		b→	
Antarctic Fulmar *Fulmarus glacialoides*	b	B	B	B	B	B		b]					
Snow Petrel *Pagodroma nivea*	B	→B	p	B	B	b		b]					
Antarctic Petrel *Thalassoica antarctica*	←B]												
Blue Petrel *Halobaena caerulea*					p				B	b	B	b	
Antarctic (Dove) Prion *Pachyptila desolata*		b		p	B	p	B	B	B	?	p	B→	
Fulmar Prion *Pachyptila crassirostris*							B						Also Auckland, Antipodes, Bounty, Chatham.

Families and species	Antarctic Continent	Peninsula and Subantarctic islands									
		South of Convergegence					North of Convergence				
	Coast and offshore islands, including Balleny and Peter I.	Peninsula	S. Shetland Is. S. Orkney Is. S. Sandwich Is.	Bouvet I.	Heard I.	S. Georgia	Kerguelen	Iles Crozet	Marion I. Prince Edward I.	Macquarie I.	
Fairy Prion *Pachyptila turtur*									b	b→	Also South Australia, New Zealand.
Thin-billed Prion *Pachyptila belcheri*							b				Also Falklands.
Medium-billed Prion *Pachyptila salvini*								B	B		
Sooty Shearwater *Puffinus griseus*										[b→	
White-chinned Petrel *Procellaria aequinoctialis*						[B→	B	b	B	?	
Grey Petrel *Procellaria cinerea*							[B		b→	b→	
Great-winged Petrel *Pterodroma macroptera*							[B	b	B		
White-headed Petrel *Pterodroma lessoni*							[B			B→	
Kerguelen Petrel *Pterodroma brevirostris*							[B	b	B		
Soft-plumaged Petrel *Pterodroma mollis*								[p	b→		

HYDROBATIDAE												
Wilson's Storm-petrel												
Oceanites oceanicus	p	←B	b	B	B	(b)	B	B→	b	b]		
Black-bellied Storm-petrel												
Fregetta tropica					[b	(b)		b	b	p	p	
Grey-backed Storm-petrel												
Garrodia nereis								[b→	b	b		b→
PELECANOIDIDAE												
South Georgian Diving-petrel												
Pelecanoides georgicus							[B	B	B	b	B]	
Kerguelen Diving-petrel												
Pelecanoides exsul							[B	→	B→	b	b	b→
PHALACROCORACIDAE												
Antarctic Shag												
Phalacrocorax atriceps				[b	(b)		b	B]				
Kerguelen Shag												
Phalacrocorax albiventer									[B	B	B	B
STERCORARIIDAE												
	S.s. maccormicki				S.s. lonnbergi							
Great Skua												
Stercorarius skua	b	←B	p	B	B	B	B	B→	B	B	B→	B→
LARIDAE												
Dominican Gull												
Larus dominicanus				[B	B		B	B→	B	B	B→	B
Antarctic Tern												
Sterna vittata			[b	b	b	b	b	B	B→	b→	p	b→
Kerguelen Tern												
Sterna virgata									[B	p	B]	

B, breeding—numerous; b, breeding—few; (b) breeding recorded; p, breeding possible, but not certain; N.S., not breeding because unsuitable terrain; ? not breeding, reason unknown; [southern limit;] northern limit; ←→ breeding also to north or south in this sector.

	Total	*Continent*	*South of Convergence*	*North of Convergence*
SPHENISCIDAE	7	2	6+1	4
DIOMEDEIDAE	4+2[a]	0	4	4+2[a]
PROCELLARIIDAE	15+4[b]	6	7	11+4[b]
HYDROBATIDAE	3	1	2+1[c]	1+2[d]
PELECANOIDIDAE	2	0	2	2
PHALACROCORACIDAE	2	0	1	1
STEROCRARIIDAE	1	1	1	1
LARIDAE	3	0	2	3
	37(+6)	10	25(+2)	27(+8)

a, *D. chlororhynchus*, *P. fusca*; b, *P. turtur*, *P. belcheri*, *P. griseus*, *P. mollis*; c, *G. nereis*; d, *F. tropica*, *O. oceanicus*.

D. Future Research

Ornithological literature teems with accounts of breeding biology, and there is an increasing number of quantitative population studies that demograph numerical fluctuations and provide survival data on which to base life tables. But those that offer direct evidence on how total population size is regulated are *rarae aves* indeed. Antarctic sea-bird studies, especially on the royal and Adélie penguins, make an important contribution to our knowledge of how breeding (as distinct from total) population size is limited, but even here the process of social competition for feeding status at sea has to be inferred from the resultant weights (stored reserves) of individuals of different social status and breeding success. The regulating mortality occurs during the winter dispersal, and the ultimate factor may well be availability of food, but even if logistic support for pelagic studies were available, it is more than doubtful whether specimens could be collected, and even more so whether information on their underwater activities could be obtained. Measurement of the plankton foods is more practicable, but correlation with bird feeding and mortality would be difficult.

The limits of the ocean environment must be admitted, and also the fact that few, if any, Antarctic sea birds other than those currently under study are suitable subjects for quantitative population research. The exception is the least marine of them all, the Dominican gull, *Larus dominicanus*, which is sedentary and a shallow-water, intertidal and terrestrial feeder. Plumage changes distinguish the first three years, and a short-term study of winter mortality was recently initiated at Macquarie Island.

Breeding ecology studies could be usefully extended by use of automatic or telemetric recorders to define foraging range and depth, and activity level, in relation to social status. Physiological studies, such as energy metabolism and endocrine balance in relation to breeding performance, naturally stem from these ecological results. Experimental manipulation of numbers, and of internal state, might be used to test empirical observations, but the criterion for future research should always be that the principle under investigation can only, or best, be studied on Antarctic species.

References

Beck, J. R. (1970). Comparative biology of smaller Antarctic petrels. (this symposium). 542–50.

Bourne, W. R. P. and Warham, J. (1966). Geographical variation in the Giant Petrels of the genus *Macronectes*. *Ardea* 54, No. 1/2, 45–67.

Burton, R. W. (1968). Breeding biology of the Brown Skua, *Catharacta skua lonnbergi* (Mathews), at Signy Island, South Orkney Islands. *Brit. Antarct. Surv. Bull.* 15, 9–28.

Carrick, R., Holdgate, M. and Prevost, J. (eds.), (1964). "Biologie Antarctique: Antarctic Biology", First SCAR Symposium on Antarctic Biology, Paris, 1962, 651 pp. Hermann, Paris.

Carrick, R. and Ingham, Susan E. (1967). Antarctic sea-birds as subjects for ecological research. Proc. Symposium on Pacific-Antarctic Sciences, Tokyo, 1966. *JARE Sci. Rep., Spec.* 1, 151–84. Department of Polar Research, Tokyo.

Emison, W. B. (1968). Feeding preferences of the Adélie Penguin at Cape Crozier, Ross Island. Antarctic Bird Studies, *Antarctic Res. Ser.* 12 (O. L. Austin, Jr., ed.), pp. 191–212. American Geophysical Union, Washington, D.C.

Falla, R. A., Sibson, R. B. and Turbott, E. G. (1966). *In* "A Field Guide to the Birds of New Zealand". Collins, London.

Le Morvan, P., Mougin, J. L. and Prévost, J. (1967). Ecologie du Skua antarctique (*Stercorarius skua maccormicki*) dans l'archipel de Pointe Géologie (Terre Adélie). *Oiseau, Paris* 37, 193–220.

Mougin, J-L. (1967). Etude écologique des deux espèces de Fulmars, le Fulmar atlantique (*Fulmarus glacialis*) et le Fulmar antarctique (*Fulmarus glacialoides*). *Oiseau, Paris* 37, Parts 1–2, 57–103.

Penney, R. L. (1968). Territorial and social behaviour in the Adélie Penguin. Antarctic Bird Studies, *Antarctic Res. Ser.* 12 (O. L. Austin, Jr., ed.), pp. 83–131. American Geophysical Union, Washington, D.C.

Reid, B. E., Kinsky, F. C., Cranfield, H. J. and Wood, R. C. (1967). Notes on recoveries and breeding behaviour of Adélie Penguins of known age at Cape Hallett. *Notornis* 14, No. 3, 140–3.

Sladen, W. J. L., Wood, R. C. and Emison, W. B. (1966). Antarctic avian population studies, 1965–1966. *Antarctic J., U.S.A.* 1, No. 4, 141–2.

Sladen, W. J. L., Wood, R. C. and Monaghan, E. P. (1968). The USARP Bird Banding Program, 1958–1965. Antarctic Bird Studies, *Antarctic Res. Ser.* 12 (O. L. Austin, Jr., ed.), pp. 213–62. American Geophysical Union, Washington, D.C.

Stonehouse, B. (1964). Bird Life. *In* "Antarctic Research" (Sir R. Priestley, R. J. Adie and G. de Q. Robin, eds) pp. 219–39. Butterworths, London.

Stonehouse, B. (1967). The general biology and thermal balances of penguins. *In* "Advances in Ecological Research" (J. B. Cragg, ed.), Vol. 4, pp. 131–96. Academic Press, London.

Tickell, W. L. N. (1967). Movements of Black-browed and Grey-headed Albatrosses in the South Atlantic. *Emu* 66, No. 4, 357–67.

Tickell, W. L. N. (1968). The biology of the great albatrosses, *Diomedea exulans* and *Diomeda epomophora*. Antarctic Bird Studies, *Antarctic Res. Ser.* 12 (O. L. Austin, Jr., ed.), pp. 1–55. American Geophysical Union, Washington, D.C.

Tickell, W. L. N. and Gibson, J. D. (1968). Movements of wandering albatrosses *Diomedea exulans. Emu* 68, No. 1, 7–20.

Tickell, W. L. N. and Pinder, R. (1967). Breeding frequencies in the albatrosses *Diomedea melanophris* and *D. chrysostoma*. *Nature, Lond.* 213, No. 5073, 315–16.

Van Zinderen Bakker, E. M., Jr. (1969). Comparative Avian Ecology of Marion and Prince Edward Islands. The Biological-Geological Expedition to Marion and Prince Edward Islands of 1965–1966.

Voous, K. H. (1965). Antarctic Birds. *In* "Biogeography and Ecology in Antarctica." Monographae Biologicae, No. 15 (J. van Mieghem and P. Van Oye, eds), pp. 649–89. Junk, The Hague.

Warham, J. (1967). The White-headed Petrel *Pterodroma lessoni* at Macquarie Island. *Emu* 67, No. 1, 1–22.

Wood, R. C., LeResche, R. E. and Sladen, W. J. L. (1967). Antarctic avian population studies, 1966–1967. *Antarctic J., U.S.A.* 2, 101–3.

Yeates, G. W. (1968). Studies on the Adélie Penguin at Cape Royds 1964–65 and 1965–66. *N.Z. Jl mar. fw. Res.* 2, No. 3, 472–96.

Young, E. C. (this symposium). The relation between the Adélie Penguin and McCormick's Skua.

Young, E. C. (1970). The techniques of a skua-penguin study. This symposium, 568–84.

Adaptation in Polar and Subpolar Penguins (Spheniscidae)

B. STONEHOUSE
Department of Zoology, University of British Columbia, Vancouver, Canada

I. Introduction

Penguins are widely distributed throughout the Southern Hemisphere, and especially prominent in cool temperate subpolar and polar regions; for a recent review of their ecology and full bibliography see Stonehouse (1967*a*). Table 1 lists the eighteen species currently recognized and indicates their breeding ranges, and Fig. 1 shows the latitudinal distribution of breeding areas, emphasizing the concentration of species in latitudes 45° to 58°S. This paper deals especially with three species (emperor, chinstrap, Adélie) which breed entirely south of the Antarctic Convergence, and four (king, gentoo,

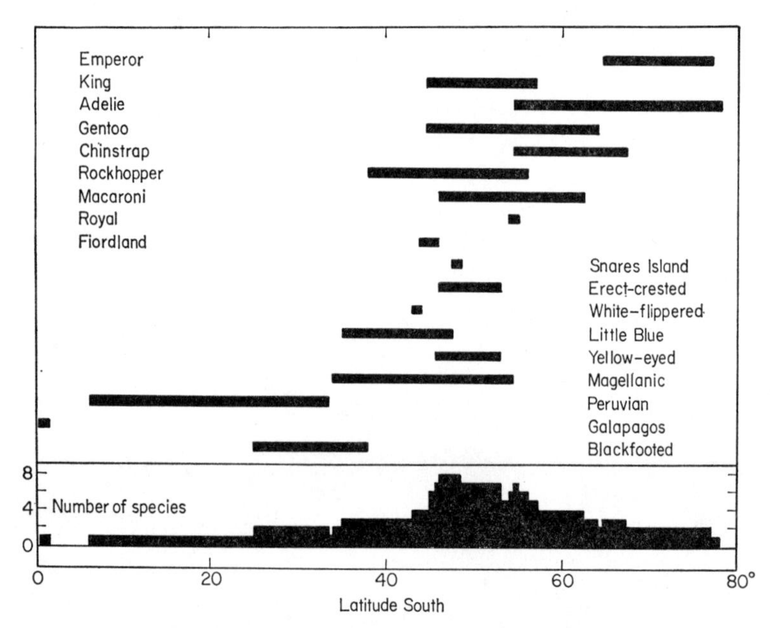

FIG. 1. Latitudinal spread of penguin breeding areas. After Stonehouse (1967*a*).

TABLE 1
Distribution of Penguins

Species	*Antarctic* Continental	*Antarctic* maritime	*Antarctic* peripheral	*Subantarctic* Cold temperate	*Subantarctic* Warm temperate	*Subtropical and tropical*
Emperor *Aptenodytes forsteri*	+	−	−	−	−	−
King *Aptenodytes patagonica*	−	−	+	+	−	−
Adélie *Pygoscelis adeliae*	+	+	−	−	−	−
Chinstrap *Pygoscelis antarctica*	−	+	+	−	−	−
Gentoo *Pygoscelis papua*	−	+	+	+	−	−
Macaroni *Eudyptes chrysolophus*	−	+	+	+	−	−
Rockhopper *Eudyptes crestatus*	−	−	+	+	+	−
Royal *Eudyptes schlegeli*	−	−	−	+	−	−
Erect-crested *Eudyptes atratus*	−	−	−	+	−	−
Fiordland *Eudyptes pachyrhynchus*	−	−	−	−	+	−
Snares Island *Eudyptes robustus*	−	−	−	+	−	−
Yellow-eyed *Megadyptes antipodes*	−	−	−	+	+	−
Galapagos *Spheniscus mendiculus*	−	−	−	−	−	+
Peruvian *Spheniscus humboldti*	−	−	−	−	−	+
Magellanic *Spheniscus magellanicus*	−	−	−	+	+	−
Blackfooted *Spheniscus demersus*	−	−	−	−	−	+
Little Blue *Eudyptula minor*	−	−	−	−	+	+
White-flippered *Eudyptula albosignata*	−	−	−	−	+	−

Breeding zones defined as follows:

Continental Antarctica: all continental shores except Antarctic Peninsula north of 65°S, also Peter I Øy, Charcot, Scott and Balleny Islands.

Maritime Antarctica: Antarctic Peninsula south to 65°S, South Orkney and South Shetland Islands, Bouvetøya, and South Sandwich Islands south of the northern limit of pack ice.

Peripheral Antarctic islands: South Georgia, Heard, and Macdonald Islands and Archipel de Kerguelen and northern South Sandwich Islands.

Cold temperate: Macquarie, Marion, Prince Edward, Falkland, Snares, Bounty, Antipodes, Auckland and Campbell Islands, Iles Crozet and the South American and New Zealand coasts south of the 10°C mean annual isotherms for air.
Warm temperate Subantarctic islands and coasts: islands of the Tristan da Cunha group, Iles St Paul and Amsterdam, Chatham Islands and South American and New Zealand coasts lying between the 10°C and 14°C mean annual isotherms for air.
Subtropical and tropical: penguin breeding areas north of the 14°C mean annual isotherm for air.

---

macaroni and rockhopper) which breed on either side of the Convergence in Antarctic and cool temperate Subantarctic regions. Of the remaining species, three (Peruvian, blackfooted, Galapagos) breed entirely north of the subtropical convergence, two (little blue or fairy, and Magellanic) breed on either side of the subtropical convergence, and six species breed only in warm or cool temperate New Zealand and neighbouring islands.

The seven Antarctic species, including two complete genera and representatives of a third, penetrate southward to varying degrees. Of the genus *Aptenodytes*, emperors (largest of all living penguins) breed entirely on the shore, offlying islets and fast ice of continental Antarctica; kings breed on most Subantarctic islands, but in the Antarctic region penetrate only to the peripheral islands—Heard, Macdonald, South Georgia, and possibly the northern islands of the South Sandwich chain. Of the genus *Pygoscelis*, chinstraps breed only in the maritime sector and South Georgia, and Adélies have the southernmost distribution in maritime and continental Antarctica. Gentoos are plentiful in the Subantarctic, and extend southward to peripheral and maritime Antarctic regions; this species alone shows geographical diversity, with a distinct southern race and marked variation between northern island populations (Murphy, 1947; Stonehouse, 1970; and see below). The genus *Eudyptes* is represented by rockhoppers, widely distributed in the Subantarctic and penetrating south to Macdonald and Heard Islands, and macaroni penguins, which in the Subantarctic are plentiful on Marion Island, but rare on the Falklands, Archipel de Kerguelen and Iles Crozet, and in Antarctic waters breed on Heard Island, South Georgia, Bouvetøya and the South Sandwich and South Shetland Islands. Royal penguins of Macquarie Island are closely akin to macaronis, sufficiently so for some authors to judge them allopatric subspecies, although no formal assessment has been made. Thus each Antarctic genus is well represented in the Subantarctic, providing closely related species and subspecies for comparison.

Of the three non-Antarctic genera, *Eudyptula* includes only small penguins of burrowing or cryptic habit, restricted to the Australasian region and reaching a southern limit at the southern tip of Stewart Island. *Megadyptes* is a monospecific genus of southern New Zealand, Auckland and Campbell Islands, unknown on neighbouring Macquarie Island. *Spheniscus* includes equatorial, tropical and subtropical species of burrowing penguins, with one representative reaching the Subantarctic in Tierra del Fuego and the Falkland Islands. *Eudyptula* may be excluded from cold water by its small size, involving an unfavourable surface-to-volume ratio (see below). Yellow-eyed and Magellanic penguins are larger birds which would not suffer this disadvantage. However, both breed under vegetation or in cavities, and Magellanic penguins burrow, so that neither would be suited by conditions immediately to the south of its present range.

II. Climate and Environment

Figure 2 shows seasonal temperature frequency curves for four weather stations close to breeding areas in temperate and polar regions. Penguins live in the coldest and in all but the very warmest seas, but are restricted to situations where annual range of sea temperature is small. At most breeding stations the annual range of offshore waters is 5°C or less. Populations breeding where the range is wider avoid extremes by migrating annually with the isotherms (Stonehouse, 1967*a*).

Penguins also seek the most constant temperature regimes available on land, generally nesting close to the sea in micro-climates controlled by sea surface temperatures. Tropical, subtropical and warm temperate species nest in caverns or burrows, or under dense vegetation, usually in solitary pairs or small scattered communities. Though shortage of breeding space may lead to high-density nesting, e.g. on the guano islands of the Benguela and Falklands currents, social colonies on open ground are rare in areas of intense solar radiation. On land the birds are most active at night, thereby avoiding both wide temperature fluctuations due to insolation, and also the direct warming effect of solar radiation on the temperature gradient within their plumage (see below). Sea temperatures experienced by tropical and subtropical species vary from about 23°C in the southern Galapagos archipelago to 13–16°C off southern Africa and Australia. Air temperatures rise higher inland, but generally remain close to this range on the coast. Species of warm temperate regions experience sea temperatures between 10°C and 15°C off South America, the Tristan da Cunha group, Iles Amsterdam and St Paul, and northern New Zealand. Small islands are especially dominated by seasonal shifts of sea temperature, modal air temperatures remaining close to marine surface values throughout the year. Insolation is strong, and most penguins of warm temperate areas incubate in caves or under vegetation.

Cold temperate and polar species breed in dense social colonies on open ground, where hazards of snowdrift formation are reduced, the warming effects of solar radiation are generally welcome, and the presence of many companions helps to generate a favourable microclimate. The change from solitary, cryptic nesting to large open colonies occurs between latitudes 40° and 50°S. North of 47°S social breeding above ground is known only among

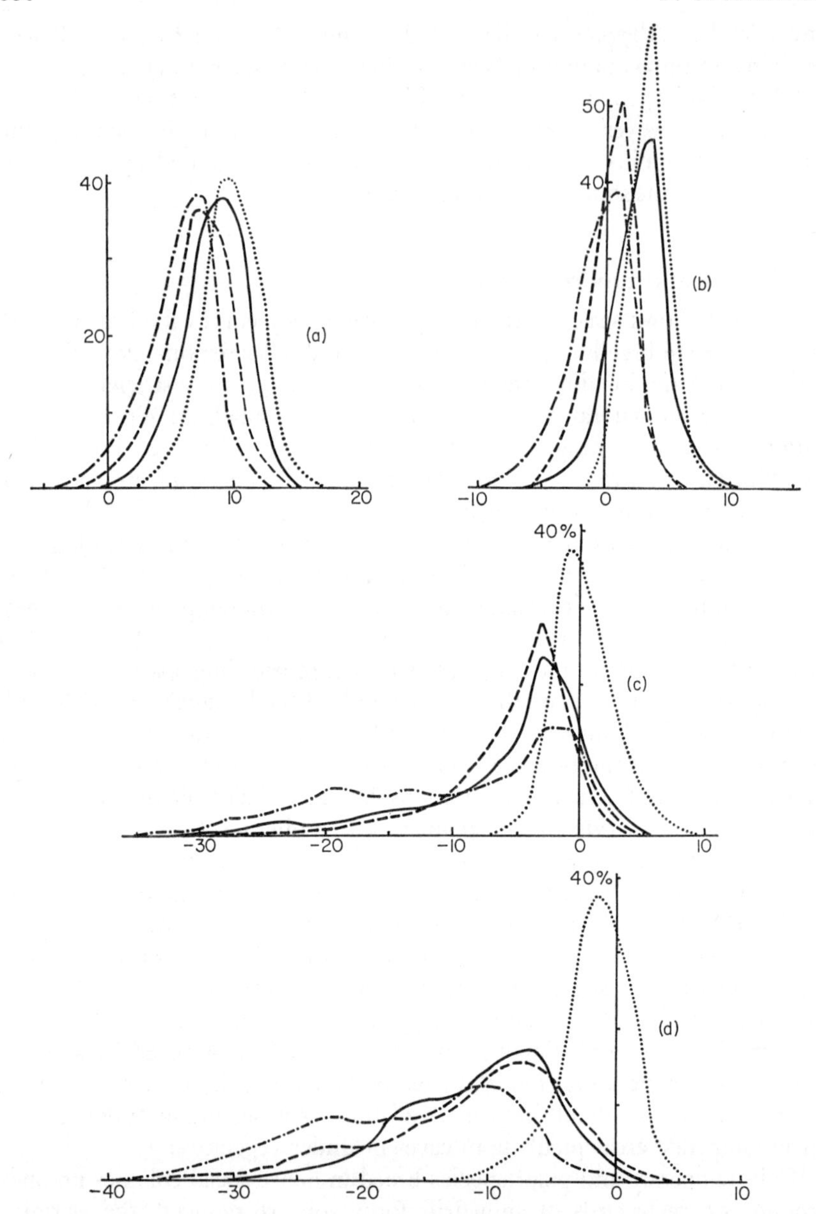

FIG. 2. Seasonal temperature frequency curves for Subantarctic and Antarctic stations. Temperatures in °C. After Stonehouse (1967*a*). (*a*) Campbell Island, (*b*) Heard Island, (*c*) Signy Island, South Orkney Islands, (*d*) Wilkes Station, Antarctic continent.
. . . . . December, January, February; ——— March, April, May; – – – – June, July, August; — · — · — · September, October, November.

Snares Islands penguins in open forest colonies, erect-crested penguins on the bare Bounty Islands, and rockhoppers in the Tristan da Cunha-Gough Island group which breed among tussock grass. South of 50°S cryptic breeding by solitary pairs is restricted to local populations of Magellanic penguins in South America and the Falkland Islands, and yellow-eyed penguins on Auckland and Campbell Islands. Westerly winds predominate in the cold temperate regions, bringing maritime temperatures to shore breeding stations with little seasonal variation (Fig. 2*a*). Insolation is strong but generally diffuse from persistently overcast skies. Nesting penguins tend to settle in exposed rocky sites which catch the sun (rockhoppers, macaronis), or on sheltered sunny flats (kings, macaronis, royals), or in tussock-grass bowers exposed to full sunlight (gentoos).

Polar penguins characteristically breed in extensive colonies of several thousands of pairs, with nests usually less than 1 m apart and often at densities of 2–3 per sq m. King and emperor penguins, which rear young in winter, dispense with nests and hold the single egg or small chick on their feet; incubating emperors, and both king and emperor chicks, huddle together and reduce heat losses. The smaller polar species breed only in late spring and summer, when sea ice is dispersing, minimum air temperatures are moderated by the presence of open water, and maximum temperatures are held close to 0°C by the thermal demands of melting snow. In autumn and winter they move out to the pack ice and open sea, where temperatures are both higher and more constant than in coastal Antarctica. Direct insolation is strong on the continental shore, providing an important source of local heating which is not disclosed by climatic records. Temperatures immediately above ground in a sunny penguin colony, either on a shingle beach or on well-trodden, guano-covered sea ice, are consistently higher than in a meteorological screen near by. Strong sunlight on the dark dorsal plumage of a penguin provides it with a personal micro-environment closer to subtropical than to polar conditions (see below).

The similarity of summer air temperatures in continental, maritime and peripheral Antarctica (Fig. 2*b–d*) reflects a remarkable constancy of summer conditions over a wide latitudinal range. Winter differences over the same range are determined mainly by the presence or absence of sea ice. Peripheral islands north of the northern limit of pack ice are warmed in winter by the proximity of open water, a factor affecting both the abundance and luxuriance of their vegetation (e.g. the presence of tussock grasses) and their suitability as breeding grounds for king penguins, which rear chicks throughout winter. The peninsula and islands of the maritime Antarctic region are in contrast invested by pack ice for nine months or more each year; insulated from the sea's warmth, they are dominated by the proximity of the polar continent and suffer long, cold winters. Thus pack ice and fast ice extend the influence of

Antarctica far beyond its own boundaries. Extensive areas of open water (polynyas), kept free of ice throughout winter by strong currents and dry offshore winds, are important local sources of heat in winter and of food in early spring (Ledenev, 1963; Stonehouse, 1967*b*), on which both emperor and Adélie penguins rely when breeding in high latitudes close to the continental shore.

III. Morphology

Penguins are among the smallest marine homeotherms; the largest living species is 15–20% shorter than the smallest adult seal and less than half its weight. The smallest penguin weighs 1 kg, about one-thirtieth of the weight of the largest (for weights of all species see Stonehouse, 1967*a*). Taking the surface-to-volume ratio of a small seal as unity, the ratio for emperor penguins is about 1·5, for Adélies and gentoos (5–6 kg) 2·8, for rockhoppers (2·5 kg, smallest of species breeding in the Antarctic region) 3·4, and for little blue penguins about 4·5. The high surface-to-volume ratio of small species implies greater losses of heat through the surface, which in cold environments would need to be countered by higher, possibly disgenic, levels of metabolism or insulation. This may help to explain the absence of *Eudyptula* from Antarctic waters, but within the family as a whole there is no clear correlation between body size and ambient temperature. In the genus *Aptenodytes* emperors of the far south are larger than kings of the polar-subpolar fringe, and macaronis are both the largest and the most southerly of *Eudyptes* species. But Adélies are smaller than gentoos, and among geographical races of gentoos the largest are most northerly, the smallest most southerly in distribution (Stonehouse, 1970). Large species of penguins may suffer little disadvantage in warm water; the very large Tertiary fossil penguins of New Zealand, Patagonia and Seymour Island (Simpson, 1946) were birds of temperate to tropical seas (Stonehouse, 1969), which may have required only thin insulation and adequate auxiliary radiating surfaces (see below) to fit them for their environment. Size in penguins is more likely to be related to diving ability than to environmental temperature, the largest being most efficient at deep diving. The current absence of large species from warm waters is more probably due to the evolution of predators in Tertiary and recent times than to environmental thermal problems (Stonehouse, 1969).

Most penguins spend at least half their time at sea, and all breed and moult on land or fast ice. Thus they are required to maintain a high and constant body temperature for prolonged periods in two media of differing thermal capacity, under varying conditions of metabolic heat production. Tropical species may be exposed to water 18° cooler than body temperature and to air well above body temperature; polar species experience water at freezing-point and still or moving air as much as 50°C lower, i.e. 90°C below body temperature. Subdermal fat and feathers are their main defences against heat loss; both are thicker in polar than in tropical species, but the differences are slight. This may be because both tropical and polar species are insulated primarily against heat losses in water, which over their whole geographical range varies only from −1·8°C to 23°C; tropical species require considerable thermal insulation, polar species only a little more. Both give evidence of being overinsulated for their life on land (see below).

The subdermal fat used as insulation forms a layer some 2 cm thick over back and abdomen in emperors at the start of breeding, 1–2 cm in Adélies and about 1 cm in Gentoos; the degree to which tropical species store fat before breeding is unknown. Fat has a thermal conductivity coefficient of 0·0003–0·00049 cal/cm/sec/°C (Lipkin and Hardy, 1954), and provides an efficient heat barrier when the blood vessels permeating it are constricted. Vasodilation under the control of the autonomic nervous system allows the free passage of warm blood through the subdermal fat and skin. All penguins acquire a store of visceral and subdermal fat, amounting to 45–50% of normal body weight in a range of temperate and polar species, in preparation for the starvation period of three to five weeks which accompanies their moult. Polar penguins acquire a similar weight at the start of their breeding season, and retain a proportion of it throughout the year. Thus the amount of fat amassed by polar penguins is not exceptional, but their ability to acquire it other than in preparation for moult, and to retain a high level of fat throughout life, is possibly a polar adaptation. Metabolic rates during courtship and incubation have been calculated from daily weight losses (Stonehouse, 1967*a*). Both Adélie and emperor penguins use up most of their stored fat during these activities, and appear to maintain a very delicate balance with the thermal demands of their environment.

Penguin plumage depends for its efficiency on air trapped between the overlapping feathers. The number of feathers per unit area is roughly the same for tropical and polar species, large and small 11–12 per cm^2. Each flattened rachis curves caudally, the tips forming diagonal overlapping rows which are both windproof and watertight. The feather tips can be raised by muscular action at the feather bases, allowing disturbance of the air layer underneath and reduction of insulating properties. Aftershafts form a filamentous undershirt around the feather bases, which is denser in polar than in tropical species, but cannot be varied *in situ*. This layer prevents water and cold air from penetrating to the skin, and forms a barrier against sudden shedding of heat through the plumage.

Feather shafts on the dorsal surface vary in mean length from about 2 cm (all tropical and subtropical species, and little blue penguins) to 4 cm or more (emperors) (Stonehouse, 1967*a*, Table 1). Actual thickness of plumage is less, about 0·5 cm in small and tropical species, 1·0–1·5 cm in emperors.

Though feather length and body size are related, feathers of emperors, Adélies, rockhoppers and southern stocks of gentoo penguins are significantly longer than would be expected from their size. Conversely, many warm-water species (including all of the genus *Spheniscus*) have feathers significantly short for their size. Feathers of macaroni, chinstrap and northern stocks of gentoo penguins are not especially long. King penguins have remarkably short plumage, suggesting that their heat losses are adequately controlled by fat reserves, possibly aided by their small surface-to-volume ratio. Conductivity coefficients for fur and feathers are difficult to measure accurately, but Neild (1968) obtained the following comparable values (in Cal/secm^2°C) from sections of dried and salted skins: emperor 0·00072, yellow-eyed 0·00079, little blue 0·00106.

Adélie penguins incubating or resting on calm, overcast days, with air temperature 7–8°C below freezing-point, lose little heat through their surface; the entire temperature gradient between body wall and environment is accommodated within the subdermal fat and plumage, allowing the outer tips of the feathers to take up or remain close to ambient temperature. In these conditions winds which fail to disturb the feather arrangement have little effect on heat losses. Reduced ambient temperatures allow greater losses through the surface, but can be countered by lowering body temperature; Guillard and colleagues (in Prévost and Sapin-Jaloustre, 1964) recorded rectal temperatures down to 33°C in incubating emperors and 36°C in Adélies, respectively 7° and 4–5° lower than normal resting temperatures. Heat losses can also be reduced by huddling, which in adult emperors is estimated to reduce exposed surfaces by five-sixths. Weight losses of individual emperors kept in isolation under winter conditions suggest that fat reserves would be insufficient to sustain non-huddling birds through their two months of incubation.

Incident radiation from the sun reaches high daily levels in coastal Antarctica during late spring and summer, when daylight is continuous and cloud sparse. Under strong direct insolation the outer layer of dorsal feathertips is warmed 20–25°C above ambient temperature, reducing or even reversing the flow of heat between core and environment. The intense but diffuse light of maritime and peripheral Antarctic regions yields slightly lower dorsal-plumage temperatures. Pale ventral plumage is also warmed by direct or diffuse solar radiation. The lemon-yellow plumage of emperors, unique among penguins, yields higher temperatures than dark plumage in hazy, early-morning sunlight, suggesting a greenhouse effect; under strong direct insolation dark plumage warms more quickly and reaches higher temperatures (Stonehouse; research in progress). In still air at or below freezing-point incubating Adélie penguins and resting emperors gape and respire rapidly under strong insolation, ridding themselves of metabolic heat which cannot be shed through the irradiated plumage. Lustick (1969) has demonstrated reduced metabolic rate in small birds under experimental irradiation.

The efficiency of penguin insulation and the presence of the non-adjustable down undershirt necessitate the provision of uninsulated areas from which heat can disperse rapidly. In every species the greatest need to shed heat is probably felt during swimming, when the relatively large pectoral muscles (accounting for 14% of body weight in small species, up to 27% in emperors) are in continuous use, and evaporative cooling through respiration is inhibited. Heat stress must also arise on land during courtship, fighting and other activities, even among polar and subpolar species whose insulation is thickest.

As in other birds, the head and bill are poorly insulated. Tropical penguins (Peruvian, Galapagos) have a notably large head and heavy, unfeathered bill, with bare facial patches; polar species have a relatively small head and short bill, with feathered skin covering proximal surfaces. Feet and flippers are radiating surfaces subject to vasodilation, flushing visibly with blood during exercise and returning to normal colour during rest. Temperatures of Adélie and emperor penguin feet and flippers have been recorded under Antarctic field conditions (Prévost and Sapin-Jaloustre, 1965) and temperate species have been shown to use a similar cooling mechanism (Stonehouse, unpublished); further experimental investigation throughout the family is needed. Early dissection accounts (Watson, 1883; Filhol, 1883) suggest a possible anatomical basis, but it is not clear whether polar and tropical species differ in their capacity for shedding heat by this route. Emperor penguins have proportionately smaller feet and flippers than other species; though 10% taller than kings and weighing twice as much, emperors have flippers only marginally longer than kings, and slightly shorter feet.

Body, culmen, foot and flipper lengths of three stocks of gentoo penguins have been compared (Stonehouse, 1969*a*). Gentoos of maritime Antarctica are 13% shorter in body length and 11% lighter in weight than those of South Georgia, and their extremities are respectively 14%, 9% and 9% shorter. Though the difference in length of extremities is in each case significant ($p < 0{\cdot}01$), the foot and flipper of southern gentoos are longer in proportion to body size than those of their northern neighbours. Thus the southern subspecies appears to defy both Bergmann's and Allen's rules simultaneously. However, the bill of southern birds is proportionately more slender (Murphy, 1947); the flipper is narrower as well as shorter, with a resulting reduction in surface area of 14·0%. Their dorsal plumage tends also to be longer than that of other stocks. Thus the southern birds seem adapted for a harsher environment both in the relative reduction of potential radiating surfaces and in a slight thickening of plumage. Gentoos of the Falkland Islands, probably the largest of all local variants (though precise weights and measurements are lacking), have significantly longer feet ($p < 0{\cdot}01$) and culmen ($p < 0{\cdot}05$), and tend to have longer flippers, than gentoos of South Georgia; in all respects under discussion they are significantly larger than the southern subspecies, and they appear to have the shortest plumage (Stonehouse, 1970).

IV. Breeding Adaptation

Adaptation for polar and subpolar life appears in the breeding behaviour of southern species, and in the growth and development of their chicks. As in all other birds, the time of breeding is likely to be determined primarily by seasonal availability of food; selection favours chicks which reach independence in healthy condition, at a time when food is readily available for them. In Antarctic and Subantarctic waters this is the period between November and April, when surface production of plankton is high and food species of penguins (notably larval fish, euphausids and other small crustaceans, and squid) are plentiful in surface waters. Food demands of parents both before and after the chicks are released, and the necessity for young birds to continue growth and fatten before winter, restrict the optimum time of release to the middle of summer (for an account of feeding in Adélie penguins see Emison, 1968). In high Antarctic latitudes both the beginning and the end of the effective breeding period are determined by sea-ice dispersion and formation; although laying at different times of the year, Adélie and emperor penguins have short laying periods of three to four weeks, while most other species extend their laying over longer periods.

Five of the seven polar species are small penguins with weights ranging between 3 kg and 6 kg. These contain their courtship, incubation and chick rearing within a period of three to four months. Typically, they return to traditional breeding colonies in late October or early November, begin laying within two to three weeks, and liberate their chicks between late January and March. This programme leaves time both for the maturation and fattening of the chicks after release from the colony, and for the parents' own post-nuptial moult, before the onset of winter. For Adélie penguins in maritime and continental regions the schedule is tight, requiring their return to the breeding grounds before the start of the summer thaw, often over many miles of inshore sea ice. Courtship is rapid, and based on territory held in previous seasons. Both partners fast during courtship, and males continue their fast during the first incubation watch; those at the southernmost breeding stations use up most of their available energy reserves during this prolonged starvation period, which may total four to five weeks in subzero temperatures. Two eggs are laid, and relaying is rare and restricted to replacement of the first egg only. Gentoo and chinstrap penguins in maritime Antarctica breed to a similar routine, but gentoos on South Georgia and

Subantarctic islands have a more leisurely time-table, with a wider spread of breeding dates, less rigorously determinate territorial behaviour, and the possibility of clutch replacement (Sladen, 1958; Sapin-Jaloustre, 1960; Taylor, 1962*a*; Stonehouse, 1963; Penney, 1968).

The two large species of Antarctic penguins take longer to incubate and rear their chicks, and cannot fit their breeding cycles within the few months of a single polar summer. Emperor penguins fatten during the final flush of plankton production in April and lay their single egg in late May or June, usually in large colonies on recently formed sea ice. Males hold the single eggs for most of all of the two months' incubation period, continuing a fast which began four to eight weeks before laying. The chicks are fed initially by the males on a crop secretion, later on triturated fish and squid brought firstly by returning females and subsequently by both parents. Laying, incubation and early weeks of feeding occur during the coldest months of winter. Growth is extremely slow at first (see below), but more rapid during early summer; the chicks leave for the sea in December and January. Parents moult between January and March, and are probably ready to breed again in the following May. King penguins in lower latitudes fatten and start their pre-nuptial moult with the first flush of plankton in September and October, and begin laying during October and November. Incubation of seven and a half weeks is shared by both parents, the chicks growing rapidly to reach 75–80% of adult weight by March and April. Laying continues until April, but eggs laid after January are unlikely to be reared successfully. During the autumn and winter dearth chicks are maintained at starvation level and lose weight; after October they fatten again, and achieve independence in November. Adults laying early in one season have time to lay again after moult in December or January and rear a chick in the following season, but the late maturation of the second chick does not leave time for breeding in the third successive summer. Breeding cycles of emperor and king penguins, and their relation to annual cycles of food species in surface waters, are discussed fully in Stonehouse (1960) and Prévost (1961).

Incubation periods and growth rates of penguins have been reviewed by Lack (1968); data for six polar and subpolar species are given in Table 2, and two aspects of growth are graphed in Fig. 3. The two largest species produce a single egg, small in relation to body size, and incubate longest. Emperor penguins are on average twice the weight of kings, but their eggs are only 30% larger and incubation takes only 16% longer; this may suggest evolutionary pressure toward short incubation, though the emperor's incubation period of sixty-two days is among the longest recorded for birds and exceeded only by some of the larger albatrosses. Adélie penguins give clearer evidence of a comparatively short incubation period; similar in weight to yellow-eyed penguins, and with eggs of comparable size, their incubation of thirty-three to thirty-four days is 21% shorter—similar in length to that of smaller species of Subantarctic breeding ranges.

Growth after hatching is most rapid in cold temperate species and slowest in emperors. During the first week yellow-eyed and little blue penguins maintain the highest daily increments (Fig. 3), while kings, Adélies and rockhoppers grow at more moderate rates; from the second to the fourth week their curves of daily increment run almost parallel, converging toward the level of 4–6%. In contrast emperor penguins grow very slowly during their first week and more rapidly during their second and third, daily percentage increments remaining consistently below those of other species throughout

TABLE 2

Incubation Periods, Hatching Weights and Initial Growth of Penguin Chicks

Species	*Incubation (days)*	*Weight at hatching (gm)*	*% adult*	*Time (days) to multiply hatching weight by— Two*	*Five*	*Ten*
Emperor	62	320	1·1	17	40–45	75
King	55	220	1·5	7	15	21
Adélie	34	90	2·2	3–4	8–9	14–15
Rockhopper	34	75	2·9	5	9–10	19
Yellow-eyed	43	85	1·6	3–4	9–10	16
Little Blue	38	42	3·8	2–3	9–10	16

Data from Kinsky, 1960; Taylor, 1962; Richdale, 1957; Stonehouse, 1953, 1960; Prévost, 1961; Warham, 1963.

the first month. While the five smaller species take only two to three weeks to reach ten times their hatching weight, emperors in the same time barely double their hatching weight, and take nearly eleven weeks to achieve a tenfold increase. During the first three to four weeks after hatching emperor chicks are fed initially by crop secretion from the male parents, later from a single cropful of food (perhaps enhanced by secretion) provided by returned females. The harsh environment hereafter demands persistent brooding at least until the end of the second month, so that only one parent can forage at a time.

Thus the smaller species appear to have reached similar levels of rapid growth, perhaps the greatest growth rates attainable in their circumstances of thermoneutral environment and abundant food. Emperors in contrast have evolved a slow rate of growth consistent with food shortage in an environment of unusual severity.

Total growth of the six species is compared in Fig. 3 (inset), where times taken to achieve independence are reduced to a common percentage scale and weights are expressed as percentages of adult weights. Curves representing growth of Adélie, yellow-eyed, rockhopper and little blue penguins are basically similar for the first 70% of the fledging period. During later growth differences between northern and southern species develop. Chicks of yellow-eyed penguins grow steadily toward independence, which they achieve in fourteen weeks from hatching at weights slightly above mean weight for the species. Rockhopper and little blue penguins take less time to

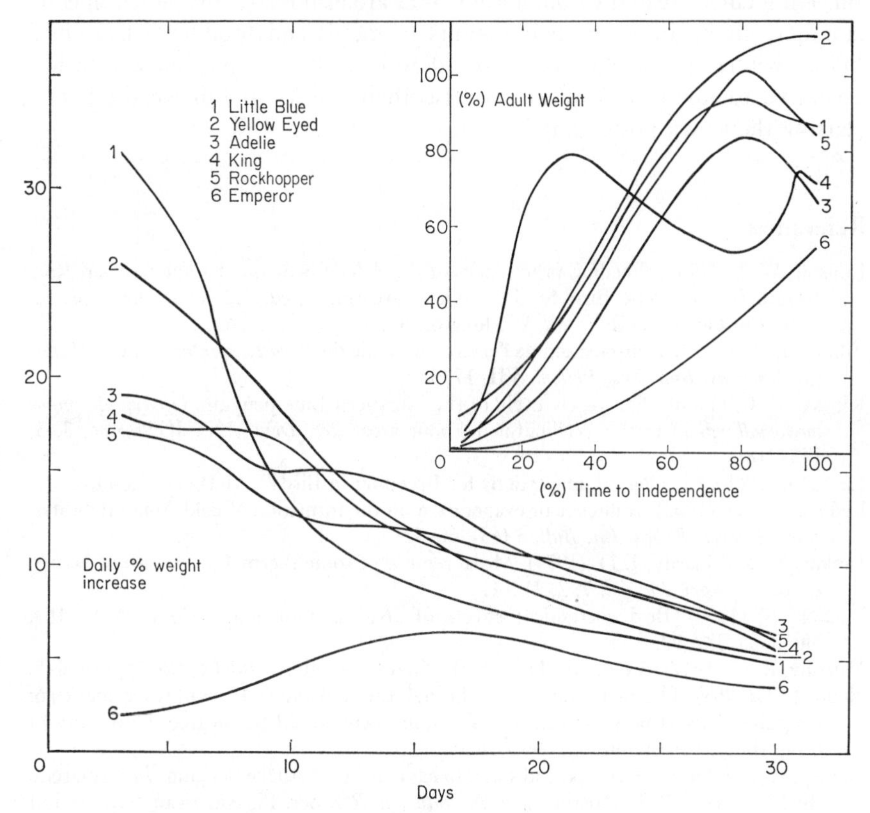

FIG. 3. Growth of six species of penguins. Data from Kinsky (1960), Richdale (1957), Stonehouse (1953, 1960), Taylor (1962*b*) and Warham (1963).

fledge, but are reared to adult weight and released (after losses associated with moult and reduced parental attention) at about 85% of adult weight. Adélie penguins, similar in size to yellow-eyed penguins, achieve independence in eight weeks from hatching, without reaching adult weight; their moult begins during the sixth or seventh week at about 85% of body weight, and they leave for the sea at 50–80% of adult weight. King penguin chicks achieve 80% of adult weight during their first fattening, fall to 50–60% in winter, and fatten to 70–80% or more before leaving in spring. Emperor chicks grow slowly through spring and summer, reaching only about 55% of adult weight when they leave for the sea in January.

Thus chicks of the two high Antarctic species moult precociously, continuing to grow and develop independently in late summer, and allowing their parents time to complete a post-nuptial moult while food is still plentiful. King chicks reared through the winter are also ready for the sea in early summer, giving time for their parents to moult and produce a late chick before winter. Little blue, yellow-eyed and rockhopper penguins, with less incentive to hurry, can afford to raise their chicks to full weight before starting their own post-nuptial moult.

References

Emison, W. B. (1968). Feeding preferences of the Adélie penguin at Cape Crozier, Ross Island. *In* "Antarctic Bird Studies" (O. L. Austin, Jr, ed.). *Antarctic Res. Ser.* **12**, American Geophysical Union, Washington, D.C.

Filhol, H. (1883). De la disposition de l'artere humerale du *Pygoscelis antarctica* et *Spheniscus demersus*. *Bull. Soc. Philom.* **VII**, 17, 92.

Kinsky, F. C. (1960). The yearly cycle of the Northern Blue penguin. (*Eudyptula minor novaehollandiae*) in the Wellington harbour area. *Rec. Dom. Mus. Wellington*, **3**, 3, 145–218.

Lack, D. (1968). "Ecological adaptations for Breeding in Birds". Methuen, London.

Ledenev, V. G. (1963). Influence of evaporation on the formation of cold Antarctic water. *Sov. Antarct. Exped. Inf. Bull.* **5** (43), 50–52.

Lipkin, M. and Hardy, J. D. (1954). Measurement of some thermal properties of human tissues. *J. appl. Physiol.* **7**, 2, 212–17.

Lustick, S. (1969). Bird energetics; effects of artificial radiation. *Science, N.Y.* **163**, No. 3865, 387–90.

Murphy, R. C. (1947). A new zonal race of the Gentoo penguin. *Auk* **64**, No. 3, pp. 454–5.

Neild, J. A. (1968). Thermal conductance through the skin and feathers of three species of penguins. Thesis presented in partial requirement for M.Sc. degree, University of Canterbury, Christchurch, New Zealand.

Penney, R. L. (1968). Territorial and social behaviour in the Adélie penguin. *In* "Antarctic Bird Studies" (O. L. Austin, Jr, ed.). *Antarctic Res. Ser.* **12**, American Geophysical Union, Washington, D.C.

Prévost, J. (1961). "Ecologie du Manchot Empereur". Hermann, Paris.

Prevost, J. and Sapin-Jaloustre, J. (1965). Ecologie des manchots antarctiques. *In* "Biogeography and Ecology in Antarctica" (J. van Mieghem, P. van Oye, and J. Schell, eds). Monographae Biologicae No. 15, Junk, The Hague.

Richdale, L. E. (1957). "A Population Study of Penguins". Oxford Univ. Press, London.

Sapin-Jaloustre, J. (1960). "Ecologie du Manchot Adéliae". Hermann, Paris.

Simpson, G. G. (1946). Fossil penguins. *Bull. Am. Mus. nat. Hist.* **87**, 5–99.

Sladen, W. J. L. (1958). The Pygoscelid penguins, Parts 1 and 2. *Scient. Rep. Falkd Isl. Depend. Surv.* **17**, 1–97.

Stonehouse, B. (1953). The Emperor penguin *Aptenodytes forsteri*. 1. Breeding behaviour and development. *Scient. Rep. Falkld Isl. Depend. Surv.* **6**, 1–33.

Stonehouse, B. (1960). The King penguin *Aptenodytes patagonica* of South Georgia. *Scient. Rep. Falkld Isl. Depend. Surv.* 23, 1–81.

Stonehouse, B. (1963). Observations on Adélie penguins (*Pygoscelis adeliae*) at Cape Royds, Antarctica. *Proc. 13th Internat. Orn. Congr., Ithaca 1962*, 766–79.

Stonehouse, B. (1967*a*). The general biology and thermal balance of penguins. *In* "Advances in Ecological Research" (J. B. Cragg, ed.). Vol. 4. Academic Press, London.

Stonehouse, B. (1967*b*). Occurrence and effects of open water in McMurdo Sound, Antarctica, during winter and early spring. *Polar Rec.* 13 (87), 775–78.

Stonehouse, B. (1969). Environmental temperatures of Tertiary penguins. *Science, N.Y.* **163** (3868), 673–75.

Stonehouse, B. (1970). Geographic variation in Gentoo penguins *Pygoscelis papua*. *Ibis* **112** (1).

Taylor, R. H. (1962*a*). The Adélie penguin at Cape Royds. *Ibis* **104**, No. 2, 176–204.

Taylor, R. H. (1962*b*). Growth of Adélie penguin (*Pygoscelis adeliae*) chicks. *N.Z.JSci.* 5, No. 2, 191–7.

Warham, J. (1963). The Rockhopper penguin *Eudyptes chrysocome* at Macquarie Island. *Auk* **80**, No. 3, 229–56.

Watson, M. (1883). Report on the anatomy of the Spheniscidae collected during the voyage of HMS Challenger. *Challenger Reports, Zoology*, **VII**, pp. 1–243.

Breeding Seasons and Moult in some Smaller Antarctic Petrels

J. R. BECK
British Antarctic Survey Biological Unit, Monks Wood Experimental Station, Huntingdon, England

I. Introduction

The breeding ecology of petrels has received considerable attention in recent years at Signy Island, South Orkney Islands. The largest of the six species breeding on the island, the southern giant petrel *Macronectes giganteus*, is the subject of a current study and is not considered here. Of the remaining five breeding species, the medium-sized fulmarine petrels, the snow petrel *Pagodroma nivea* and cape pigeon *Daption capensis* belong to monotypic genera with a breeding distribution confined to the Antarctic and Subantarctic, while the smaller dove prion *Pachyptila desolata*, Wilson's storm-petrel *Oceanites oceanicus* and black-bellied storm-petrel *Fregetta tropica* are cold-water representatives of genera widely distributed in the Southern Hemisphere from the Subantarctic to the tropical zone. All these species except *Fregetta tropica*, which has a breeding population of probably less than a hundred pairs, breed in large numbers near the British Antarctic Survey base. Marked populations of the larger species have been maintained since 1955. Signy Island thus provides excellent facilities for long-term studies of a group of petrels of widely diverse size, breeding habit and distribution.

Sufficient information is now available for all five species to allow some preliminary comparisons to be made. This paper aims to assess the adaptive significance of interspecific differences in the timing of breeding and moult. Information for *Pachyptila* and *Daption* is taken from the detailed studies by Tickell (1962) and Pinder (1966) respectively, supplemented by some personal observations on moult and food. The data for *Pagodroma* and *Oceanites*/*Fregetta* are from recent studies by D. W. Brown and myself which will be more fully discussed elsewhere.

II. Breeding Seasons and their Timing

Figure 1 summarizes the main features of the breeding cycles of the five petrels in relation to seasonal abundance of marine zooplankton in the 0–50 m depth layer of Antarctic surface water (data from Table 3 in Foxton, 1956). The species are arranged in descending order of size from the top of the figure. The "kites" give the percentage of eggs laid and chicks hatched and fledged plotted in two-day class intervals against date. Numbers in brackets below each "kite" are the number of observations in the sample. It

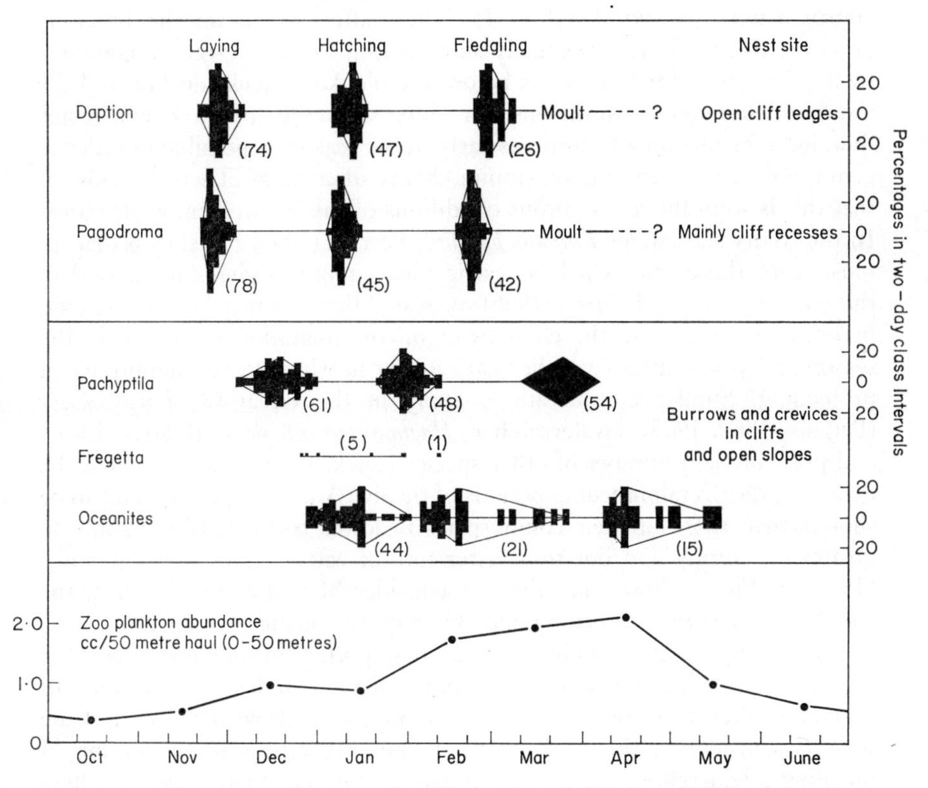

FIG. 1. Breeding seasons of five petrels at Signy Island in relation to plankton abundance.

should be noted that these totals are aggregates over several seasons involving both complete and incomplete nest-histories and do not represent breeding success. Information for *Fregetta*, with five egg-laying dates and one hatching date, is meagre but sufficient to indicate that the breeding cycle resembles that of *Oceanites*. Since annual variations in laying period are small in these petrels, the figure gives a fairly accurate picture of the breeding regimes in any single season.

A feature of particular interest is the tendency for the five species to form two distinct groups. The first group, containing *Daption* and *Pagodroma*, is characterized by early laying, an extreme degree of breeding synchrony and exposed or semi-exposed nest sites. In the second group, comprising *Pachyptila*, *Oceanites* and *Fregetta*, laying begins later, there is a much lower degree of synchrony and the nest is hidden in a deep rock-crevice or burrow.

The milder summer weather at Signy Island normally lasts for about four months, while the zooplankton standing crop remains at a high level for approximately six months (Fig. 1). Thus, after arrival on the breeding grounds, there is only a relatively short period for the petrels to complete their protracted breeding cycles before the plankton stocks decline and the weather deteriorates with the onset of winter. It would appear advantageous, therefore, for breeding to begin as early in the season as possible in order to give the fledged young the maximum chance of survival. There is evidence that this is so in the less rigorous conditions of the North Temperate Zone. In the Manx shearwater *Puffinus puffinus*, Perrins (1966) has shown that, in most years, those pairs which lay earliest leave more surviving progeny than those laying later, and Harris (1966) suggested that this may be because food becomes scarce around the colonies or on the migration route late in the season and young fledging earlier have longer in which to become proficient in feeding. Similar considerations apply in the Great tit, *Parus major* (Perrins, 1963, 1965), Oystercatcher, *Haematopus ostralegus* (Harris, 1967), and probably in a number of other species (Lack, 1966, 1968). As might be expected, the overall breeding periods of the five Antarctic petrels tend to be shorter than those of their counterparts in lower latitudes (due mainly to greater synchrony and not to a faster rate of egg or chick development). However, Fig. 1 shows that there is considerable variability between the species in the start of breeding and this requires further examination.

Two factors are likely to be particularly important in timing the breeding seasons of Antarctic birds; the availability of food, and the accessibility of nest sites in terms of freedom from snow and ice blockage at the start of the season. Considering the food situation first, differences in the timing of breeding might reflect adaptations to exploit different food supplies. Alternatively, on theoretical grounds (such as Gause's principle, discussed by Lack, 1954), these differences might indicate that the five species share a common prey, but avoid competition by staggering their breeding cycles so that the heaviest demands on the prey, i.e. by birds feeding young, do not occur simultaneously.

The wide range of body size and bill structure in these petrels might appear to support the former view. It is known, however, that at Signy Island the krill *Euphausia superba* forms the staple diet of at least three species—*Pagodroma*, *Daption* and *Oceanites*. *Pagodroma* also feeds fish to the young and amphipods and cephalopods are taken occasionally by *Daption* and

Pachyptila respectively, but the proportion of these other organisms is thought to be small. Thus, although further information is needed, particularly for *Pachyptila* and *Fregetta*, it seems unlikely that differences in food preference are sufficiently marked to account for the differences in laying season.

Since *Euphausia superba* is important in the diet of several species, the possibility that breeding is staggered as an adaptation reducing competition for food needs consideration. Three points suggest that this explanation is incorrect. First, it is necessary to assume that the stocks of *E. superba* are so low that depletion is great enough to impair the survival of adults and young. Strong selection pressure would then favour mechanisms which would lessen the effects of competition. It is well established, however, that stocks of *E. superba* must be immense during the summer months (see, for example, Moiseev (1970; this symposium) and Makarov *et al.* (1970; this symposium)). Second, if competition were important, its effects might be shown in extreme form by the abundant and similarly sized *Pagodroma* and *Daption*, yet their breeding seasons closely coincide. Further, even if competition were largely avoided by differential timing of breeding, the shortness of the Antarctic summer allows so little divergence in this respect that some signs of periodic food shortage might still be expected, especially in the young. As yet, there is no evidence that the young of these petrels either die of starvation or that they often fledge seriously underweight. These facts suggest that food supplies are probably superabundant, at least during the latter part of the season, so that differences in laying season are not due to competition for food.

The chief effect of food availability will thus be simply to determine the broad limits of the breeding season in relation to the needs of the young. Figure 1 shows that, despite differences in laying season, the chick-feeding and fledging periods of all five species coincide approximately with the period of maximum plankton abundance from February to April. Another important effect will be food availability during the pre-laying period when the female is forming the proportionately large egg. Egg weight as a percentage of female weight varies inversely with body weight, ranging from 15% in *Daption*, 21% in *Pagodroma* and *Pachyptila*, 26% in *Fregetta* to 28% in *Oceanites*. Although the percentages are lower in *Daption* and *Pagodroma*, food availability probably sets the limit to the start of their laying season if the female cannot find enough food to form the egg earlier and if other factors do not intervene.

Whereas annual variation in the seasonal cycle of available food will be small in the uniform marine environment, the accessibility of nest sites at the start of the summer is a much more variable factor, depending on the accumulation of snow and ice from the preceding winter and the degree and duration of the spring melt. In some years sites at Signy Island may be clear of snow and ice by early November, but when a late melt follows a "hard" winter sites often remain blocked into late December. The robust fulmarine petrels arrive from late October onward. Possessing powerful bills and claws, they are quickly able to clear their exposed sites, a process assisted by solar radiation. The more delicate, crevice-nesting species, arriving in mid-November, are capable of clearing small amounts of loose snow, but are unable to deal with ice and hard-packed snow blocking their sheltered sites. It is probably significant that *Pachyptila*, which has a strong bill and claws for its size, begins laying earlier than the two storm-petrels.

To summarize, if food supplies are superabundant for much of the summer, then the breeding seasons may be fixed only approximately by the food requirements of the young and other factors must account for the precise timing of laying in the different species. In the petrels of the first group, while they are relatively unaffected by snow conditions by virtue of their size and strong build, laying cannot begin until November, when the first increase in available zooplankton allows the female to find enough food to form the egg. In contrast, food availability during the pre-laying period is less important for petrels in the second group. Here, egg laying appears to be determined by the average date at which melt of accumulated snow and ice allows access to the nest holes, since the slighter build of these species does not allow them to take an active part in hastening the process to any great extent. Breeding thus cannot begin until late December, by which time plankton production is well advanced and the females presumably have little difficulty in finding food. Hence, each species begins laying as early as the different environmental timing factors permit.

III. Significance of Breeding Synchrony

Figure 1 shows that there is a marked difference between the two groups in the degree of synchrony of breeding activity. The fulmarine petrels have remarkably constant and restricted laying periods—the snow petrel completes laying in eleven days and the cape pigeon in fifteen days. Comparable restricted laying seasons occur in the migratory shearwaters *Puffinus tenuirostris*, *P. gravis* and *P. griseus* (but not in *P. puffinus*), while the young of all four species lay down large fat stores which enable them to survive the period of desertion by the parents shortly before fledging (Serventy, 1963; Marshall and Serventy, 1956; Rowan, 1952; Richdale, 1963). These features may serve an important function in allowing the adult shearwaters to depart on migration early, implying that food becomes scarce late in the season, either near the colony or on the migration route (Harris, 1966; Lack, 1968). As discussed earlier, it seems probable that food is superabundant in the latter part of the Antarctic summer. The restricted laying seasons in *Pagodroma* and *Daption* mean that all the young fledge by the end of the first week in March, although there is no reason to suppose that later layings would prove unsuccessful. The most probable explanation for compression of breeding into the early part of the season is to allow time for completion of the post-breeding moult (discussed below) near the breeding grounds while food remains plentiful.

The spread of laying of the petrels in the second group is twice as long—twenty-eight days in *Pachyptila*, thirty-six days in *Fregetta* and thirty-five days in *Oceanites*. The extended spread in the two latter species, together with the late start in laying, means that some young do not fledge until May. As mentioned earlier, these petrels are vulnerable to snow blockage of their nest sites, although the dove prion is a partial exception. It can be seen from Fig. 1 that if there were a heavy snowfall on, for example, 20 February, persisting for several days, *Oceanites* chicks hatching on that day would almost certainly die because the adults would be unable to feed them. But, even more important, the chicks would have no fat reserves to draw upon while the nest holes remained blocked. By 20 February, however, other chicks hatched earlier could be up to fifteen days old. These would have laid down fat stores and many would survive. Thus, if laying by *Oceanites* were as compressed as in the fulmarine petrels, heavy snowfalls could kill virtually the entire season's output of young. By laying over an extended period, the chances of at least a proportion of young surviving are greatly increased. It is significant that the dove prion, which has better digging capabilities, has the least extended spread in laying. Similarly, Nelson (1966) has suggested that the spread in laying in the gannet *Sula bassana* might allow more young to survive bad-weather conditions at the breeding colony or in the post-fledging period.

Although it is clear that extended laying could have considerable survival value, quantitative evidence to support this is limited at present. However, some observations on *Oceanites* during the 1967–8 season demonstrate the degree of vulnerability of this species. Between 4 and 17 January twenty-one eggs were laid in marked nests, but an exceptionally heavy snowfall on the night of 17–18 blocked the holes for four days and prevented many other birds from laying. Nineteen eggs did not hatch, either through excessive chilling or waterlogging, and the two chicks which did hatch succumbed to a further snowfall soon afterwards. These observations indicate that the mechanism suggested above would apply only in normal seasons—exceptionally severe snowfalls nullify any advantages of extended laying.

IV. Moult

Breeding and moult make the heaviest energy demands in the annual cycle and it is therefore of considerable interest to establish the timing, sequence and duration of moult in Antarctic species, since adaptations comparable to those in the breeding cycle may be expected. Recent work at Signy Island shows that body moult in both fulmarine petrels begins during incubation (see also Maher (1962) and Brown (1966) for *Pagodroma*). In successful breeders moult of the primary feathers does not commence until the young are near fledging, whereas in failed breeders primary moult may begin within a week of egg or chick loss. This is similar to the situation found earlier in the northern fulmar *Fulmarus glacialis* (Carrick and Dunnet, 1954), and the selective advantage of delayed primary moult in successful breeders is clearly to retain maximum wing efficiency while feeding young. There is a general exodus of failed and pre-breeding snow petrels and cape pigeons from about early January until they return with the successful breeders at the end of March and reoccupy their nests for a short time before final departure. It is believed that snow petrels renew their primaries during this period and this has been confirmed for the cape pigeon; birds captured on return have almost full-grown outermost primaries and have begun to replace the rectrices. Body moult continues through the absence period and is still heavy on return. Thus the fulmarine petrels have undergone a complete moult by the time zooplankton levels begin to decline as winter approaches (Fig. 1).

The situation in the small crevice-nesting petrels is quite different. No birds handled showed any sign of primary moult, although limited body-feather renewal occurred in failed breeders prior to the autumn migration. All three species replace the flight feathers in winter quarters, presumably because their late and protracted breeding cycles allow no time and because food is too sparse at the end of the season for moult to begin on the breeding grounds.

V. Conclusion

It is suggested that the adaptations outlined in this paper may stem basically from the differences in size and structure between the two groups of petrels. On the one hand, the large strongly built fulmarine petrels, which possess well-developed powers of oil ejection, are almost immune both to snow conditions and to predation by skuas, *Catharacta skua lonnbergi*. These features allow them to breed early in the summer in exposed situations, thus leaving time for a complete moult near the breeding grounds. On the other hand, the smaller and more delicate prion and storm-petrels may have had to become nocturnal and to breed in deep crevices in order to survive skua predation. Their limited digging capabilities inevitably make them vulnerable to snow conditions, necessitating late and extended breeding periods, which then in turn force them to moult in winter quarters.

VI. Summary

The five small petrels breeding at Signy Island can be separated into two groups according to breeding season and nest site. In *Daption* and *Pagodroma*, breeding is early and extremely synchronized and nests are relatively exposed; in *Pachyptila*, *Fregetta* and *Oceanites*, breeding begins later, there is less synchronization and nests are hidden in crevices. Differences in timing of breeding seasons are discussed. Laying in the fulmarine petrels is probably determined by availability of food, but in *Pachyptila*, *Fregetta* and *Oceanites* may be related to snow melt and accessibility of nest holes.

Early synchronized breeding in *Daption* and *Pagodroma* allows time for a complete moult in the breeding area before food becomes scarce in autumn. Wing moult in unsuccessful breeders begins before that of successful breeders.

It is suggested that the spread in laying in the crevice-nesting species may reduce mortality from bad weather acting against small young of similar age. Moult takes place on the wintering grounds, presumably because, after breeding, time is too short and food insufficient at or near the breeding colonies.

Differences between the two groups in breeding season and moult may be indirectly related to differences in body size and structure.

Acknowledgements

It is a pleasure to thank all my companions on Signy Island for their assistance in so many ways. I am especially grateful to D. W. Brown and J. W. H. Conroy for much valuable discussion and for help with the field-work. D. W. Brown also allowed me to incorporate some preliminary results from our joint study of the two storm-petrels which is still in progress. Dr M. P. Harris, E. A. Smith, P. J. Tilbrook and my wife kindly read the manuscript and offered many helpful suggestions.

References

Brown, D. A. (1966). Breeding biology of the Snow petrel *Pagodroma nivea* (Forster). *ANARE Sci. Rep.* Ser. B. (1) *Zool. Publ.* 89, 1–63.

Carrick, R. and Dunnet, G. M. (1954). Breeding of the Fulmar *Fulmarus glacialis*. *Ibis* **96**, No. 3, 356–70.

Foxton, P. (1956). The distribution of the standing crop of zooplankton in the Southern Ocean. "*Discovery*" *Rep.* 28, 191–236.

Harris, M. P. (1966). Breeding biology of the Manx shearwater *Puffinus puffinus*. *Ibis* **108**, No. 1, 17–33.

Harris, M. P. (1967). The biology of Oystercatchers *Haematopus ostralegus* on Skokholm Island, S. Wales. *Ibis* **109**, No. 2, 180–93.

Lack, D. (1954). "The Natural Regulation of Animal Numbers". Clarendon Press, Oxford.

Lack, D. (1966). "Population Studies of Birds". Clarendon Press, Oxford.

Lack, D. (1968). "Ecological Adaptations for Breeding in Birds". Methuen, London.

Maher, W. J. (1962). Breeding biology of the Snow petrel near Cape Hallett, Antarctica. *Condor* **64**, No. 6, 488–99.

Makarov, R. R. ,Naumov, A. G. and Shevtsov, V. V. (1970). The biology and the distribution of the Antarctic krill. This symposium, 173–76.

Marshall, A. J. and Serventy, D. L. (1956). The breeding cycle of the Short-tailed shearwater *Puffinus tenuirostris* (Temminck), in relation to trans-equatorial migration and its environment. *Proc. zool. Soc. Lond.* **127**, No. 4, 489–510.

Moiseev, P. A. (1970). Some aspects of the commercial use of the krill resources of the Antarctic seas. This symposium, 213–16.

Nelson, J. B. (1966). The breeding biology of the Gannet *Sula bassana* on the Bass Rock, Scotland. *Ibis* **108**, No. 4, 584–626.

Perrins, C. M. (1963). Survival in the Great tit *Parus major*. *Proc. Int. orn. Congr.* **13**, 717–28.

Perrins, C. M. (1965). Population fluctuations and clutch-size in the Great tit *Parus major* L. *J. Anim. Ecol.* 34, No. 3, 601–47.

Perrins, C. M. (1966). Survival of young Manx shearwaters *Puffinus puffinus* in relation to their presumed date of hatching. *Ibis* **108**, No. 1, 132–5.

Pinder, R. (1966). The Cape pigeon, *Daption capensis* Linnaeus, at Signy Island, South Orkney Islands. *Bull. Br. Antarc. Surv.* 8, 19–47.

Richdale, L. E. (1963). Biology of the Sooty shearwater. *Proc. zool. Soc. Lond.* **141**, No. 1, 1–117.

Rowan, M. K. (1952). The Greater shearwater at its breeding grounds. *Ibis* **94**, No. 1, 97–121.

Serventy, D. L. (1963). Egg-laying timetable of the Slender-billed shearwater *Puffinus tenuirostris*. *Proc. Int. orn. Congr.* **13**, 338–43.

Tickell, W. L. N. (1962). The Dove prion, *Pachyptila desolata* Gmelin. *Scient. Rep. Falkld Isl. Depend. Surv.* 33, 1–55.

Biennial Breeding in Albatrosses

W. L. N. TICKELL
The Nature Conservancy, Hope Terrace, Edinburgh, Scotland*

I. Introduction

Most procellariiform species lay a single egg which, if lost, is not replaced in the same season. Two egg clutches and replacement eggs have been reported, but they are very infrequent. The great albatrosses are notable in that fertility has been reduced even further by decreasing the breeding frequency. Biennial breeding implies that a pair nests only once every two years and spends the intervening season elsewhere. In this paper I shall describe the unusual features of the biennial cycle and point out their relevance to the ecology of albatrosses.

The literature relating to biennial breeding in the royal albatross, *Diomedea epomophora*, and wandering albatross, *Diomedea exulans*, has been reviewed by Carrick *et al.* (1960). It is necessary here only to acknowledge that Matthews (1929) first suggested it for wanderers at South Georgia and that Richdale (1950, 1952) demonstrated it clearly in his studies of the royals at Taiaroa Heads, New Zealand.

II. The Biennial Cycle

Ten years ago at Bird Island, South Georgia (54°00′S. 38°02′W.), studies were begun on a large stable population of wandering albatrosses (Tickell and Cordall, 1960). The island is 5 km long and about 1 km wide. Approximately two-thirds of it offer suitable nesting ground for wanderers and support a breeding population of 3194 pairs. Between 1958 and 1964 when field-work ceased, over 6000 wanderers were banded and several hundred also marked individually with coloured plastic spirals and coloured spots of cellulose paint. Studies of these marked birds have yielded new information about the biennial cycle.

At South Georgia wanderer eggs are laid from 10 December to 8 January and hatching occurs from 27 February to 30 March. Chicks do not leave the

* Present address: Department of Zoology, Makerere University College, Kampala, Uganda.

nest until the following summer between 17 November and 8 January. The mean overall length of the breeding cycle (i.e. between first arrival of parents and their departure after rearing their chick) is 383 days. At the time parents are delivering final feeds to their chicks other wanderers are arriving to begin the following season's breeding. The gonads of the newly arrived birds are fully developed and copulation takes place soon after arrival. In marked contrast those birds feeding young at the same time have gonads that show complete post-nuptial collapse.

Breeding records over six years at Bird Island indicate that about two-thirds of pairs laid three times, i.e. only in alternate years. The other one-third laid four or five times and there are many instances of pairs laying eggs in two consecutive seasons. All pairs that lost eggs immediately after laying and that remained alive returned to the nesting grounds and bred the following season. One marked pair in my study area produced an egg each season for six years running, but never reared a chick, a dramatic demonstration that the wandering albatross has the capacity to come into breeding condition annually. It is only when incubation and care of the young progresses that the capacity to return and breed again the following year declines. By April, when all eggs are hatched and parents brooding young chicks, this decline is already noticeable, for only seven out of ten pairs that lost chicks that month returned the following season. During the next two months it is more obvious; one out of three pairs that lost chicks in May and two out of four pairs that lost them in June returned and laid again the following December. In contrast none of the sixteen pairs that lost chicks between July and October bred the following season; but the males of them were caught and killed in December near their old nests. The testes of both were undergoing spermatogenesis. One, whose chick had been killed in July had testes on 11 December that would have allowed it to breed successfully almost immediately. The other, whose chick had been killed in August had a new interstitium and could perhaps have maturated if external conditions had been propitious. I am indebted to the late Professor A. J. Marshall, who generously examined and interpreted the histological material.

It is apparent therefore that the reproductive organs of the wandering albatross cycle annually, presumably under the same extrinsic factors as annual breeders (Marshall and Serventy, 1956), but once the bird is involved with incubation or care of young there is presumably some neuro-endocrine feedback associated with this behaviour that inhibits gametogenesis. Variation in the response of individuals is to be expected; females perhaps require more time for maturation of the ovaries, while age and experience probably account for other differences.

In undisturbed areas of South Georgia approximately half the population breeds each year. The mechanism that maintains this balance depends upon the fact that the physiological cycle is an annual one when not inhibited by care-giving behaviour. Twenty per cent of pairs laying at Bird Island in one season do so again the following year; in other words 55% of the total breeding population nest each year. As we have seen, the overlap is due to loss of eggs or young. If no eggs or young were lost, none of the pairs breeding in year x would do so again in year $x + 1$, and the annual proportion of the total breeding population nesting would be exactly 50%. At the other extreme, if all eggs were lost in year x, then the total breeding population would nest in year $x + 1$ and this would continue for as long as 100% loss persisted. But as soon as this population or colony was left undisturbed the numbers of pairs subsequently breeding each year would oscillate until restored to balance. The time taken to accomplish this would be slow if the natural egg/chick mortality were low and rapid if it were high.

There are thus two fundamental tenets of biennial breeding that have relevance to ecological studies of great albatrosses. First, the fraction of the population breeding in any one year is directly proportional to the egg/chick mortality, and second, the rate at which a breeding population is restored to balance after catastrophic loss of eggs, chicks or adults is proportional to the egg/chick mortality.

In the summer of 1962–63, 266 eggs were removed from nests in one area of Bird Island. The above hypothesis predicts that when 20% of birds breeding in year x do so again in year $x + 1$ balance between the proportion of the breeding population nesting each year will be achieved in twelve years (Fig. 1). A hypothetical population of the same size, but with higher egg/chick mortality such that 50% of pairs breeding in year x do so again in year $x + 1$, would achieve balance in five years (Fig. 2). Balance is arbitrarily defined here as a state when the difference in the numbers of pairs nesting each year is less than 10% of the total breeding population.

III. Ecological Considerations

Although biennial breeding reduces fertility, the special mechanism that maintains balance between the proportions of the breeding population nesting each year also enhances fecundity. If the two-year cycle of the great albatrosses were strictly equivalent to that of annual breeding petrels and albatrosses, a pair would lay an egg once every two years and always spend the intervening year at sea irrespective of whether or not a chick had been successfully reared. In practice we see unsuccessful breeders laying replacement clutches and colonies exploited for eggs laying almost twice the number they would produce if undisturbed, a most unusual phenomenon within the procellariiformes.

Young wanderers begin to return to the breeding grounds at South

Georgia at 4 years of age, and by the age of 6 approximately half those that fledged have returned. Similarly 55% of royal albatrosses were seen back at Taiaroa Heads (Richdale, 1952) between their fourth and eighth years. None of the 6-year-old wanderers had mated at the time I left South Georgia, but at Macquarie Island a marked wanderer has nested at the age of 9 (Carrick, *personal communication*), the same age at which Richdale's royals bred. Young

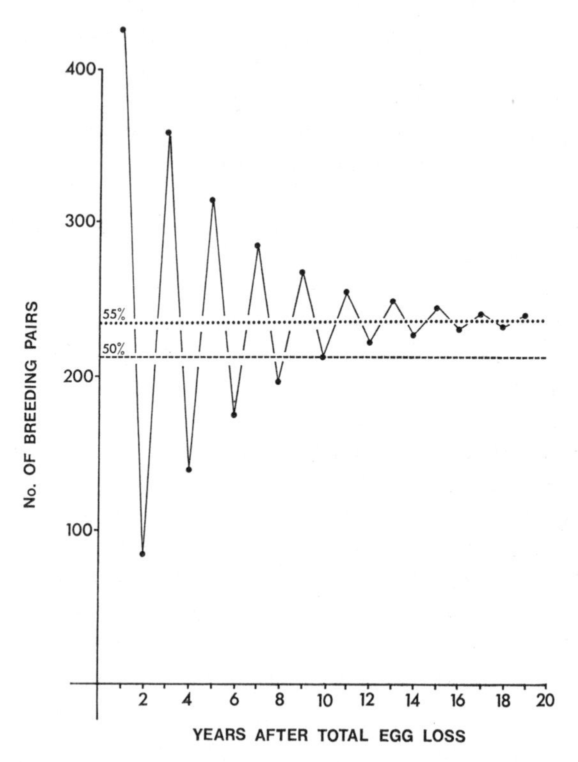

FIG. 1. Predicted fluctuations in the numbers of pairs breeding each year in a study area at Bird Island, South Georgia, following the removal of all eggs in 1962–63. 55% of the total breeding population nest each year.

of both species visit the breeding grounds for a number of years before they mate, and the significance of the biennial mechanism is manifest in that such young birds, prospecting for mates, return each year. The same is true of older adults that have lost mates and are establishing new pair bonds. The opportunity to breed in any approaching season is bypassed only when there is a high probability of a successful conclusion to the current breeding.

The mechanism of the biennial cycle also has relevance to recent discussions of population regulation (Wynne-Edwards, 1962; Ashmole, 1963;

Lack, 1966). In great albatrosses the breeding population is always greater than the number of nests occupied at any one time except in years following catastrophic loss. Thus although the nesting grounds and the surrounding seas normally support approximately half the breeding pairs, there may at any time be up to twice that number. If there is a density-dependent mechanism delicately attuned to the balance between the numbers of birds and the

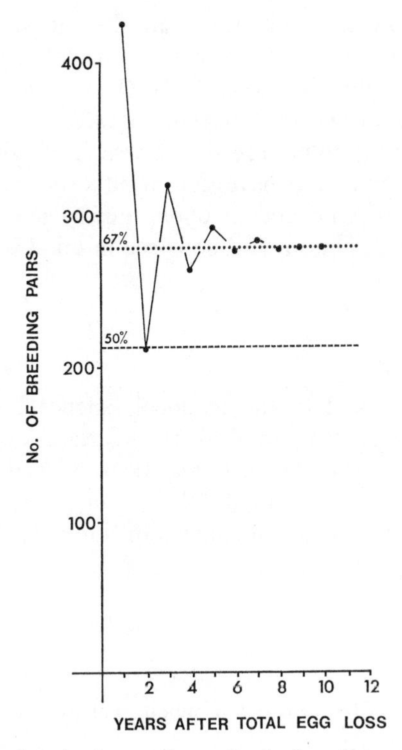

FIG. 2. Predicted fluctuations in the numbers of pairs breeding each year following the removal of all eggs from a hypothetical population equivalent in size to that of Fig. 1, but where 67% of the total breeding population nest each year.

productivity of the surrounding seas, is it related to the numbers that actually nest at any one time or to the theoretical numbers that might nest? It could be that the ability to adjust the size of albatross breeding colonies gives us unique facilities for investigating experimentally the relationship between sea-bird numbers and ocean productivity.

Extended fledging confers one notable advantage upon the wandering albatross at South Georgia; it escapes the dangers of early laying. The three other species of albatross that breed at South Georgia, *Diomedea melanophris*,

D. chrysostoma and *Phoebetria palpebrata*, all rear their chicks within a single summer and are therefore obliged to return to the island and lay in October. At this time it is not unusual for the ground to be frozen (Tickell and Richards, 1967) and completely snow covered, with the result that nests cannot be properly constructed and massive egg loss results. Laying in midsummer, wanderers invariably have conditions suitable for nest construction and egg loss is therefore consistently low.

At present the two great albatrosses are the only species proven to breed biennially, but there are indications that some of the smaller albatrosses, *D. immutabilis* (Rice and Kenyon, 1962), *D. chrysostoma* (Tickell and Pinder, 1967), *D. irrorata* (Nelson, 1968) and *D. chlororhynchos* (C. C. H. Elliott, *personal communication*) do not breed each year. Ecological studies invariably call for census work and, as we have seen, accurate determination of biennially breeding populations is dependent upon knowledge of breeding frequency and breeding success. This should be borne in mind in all future studies of albatrosses.

Acknowledgements

I am deeply indebted to the National Science Foundation for grants (G19590 and G23943) in support of albatross research at South Georgia and to Dr W. J. L. Sladen, M.B.E., for encouragement and facilities at Johns Hopkins University. I am also grateful to W. N. Bonner, P. A. Cordall, H. Dollman and R. Pinder for their help and companionship in the field.

References

Ashmole, N. P. (1963). The regulation of numbers of tropical oceanic birds. *Ibis* **103B** 458–73.

Carrick, R., Keith, K. and Gwynn, A. M. (1960). Fact and fiction on the breeding of the Wandering Albatross. *Nature, Lond.* **188**, 112–14.

Lack, D. (1966). "Population Studies of Birds". Clarendon Press, Oxford.

Marshall, A. J. and Serventy, D. L. (1956). The breeding cycle of the short-tailed shearwater, *Puffinus tenuirostris* (Temminck), in relation to trans-equatorial migration and its environment. *Proc. zool. Soc. Lond.* **127**, 489–510.

Matthews, L. H. (1929). The birds of South Georgia. *"Discovery" Rep.* **1**, 561–92.

Nelson, B. (1968). "Galapagos, Island of Birds". Longmans, London.

Rice, D. W. and Kenyon, K. W. (1962). Breeding cycles and behaviour of Laysan and Black-footed Albatrosses *Auk*, **79**, 517–67.

Richdale, L. E. (1950). "The Pre-egg Stage in the Albatross Family". Dunedin.

Richdale, L. E. (1952). "The Post-egg Period in Albatrosses". Dunedin.

Tickell, W. L. N. and Cordall, P. A. (1960). South Georgia Biological Expedition 1958–59. *Polar Rec.* **10**, 145–6.

Tickell, W. L. N. and Pinder, R. (1967). Breeding frequencies in the albatrosses *Diomedea melanophris* and *D. chrysostoma*. *Nature, Lond.* 213 126–9.

Tickell, W. L. N. and Richards, P. A. (1967). Earth temperatures at Bird Island, South Georgia. *Br. Antarct. Surv. Bull.* 14, 89–91.

Wynne-Edwards, V. C. (1962). "Animal Dispersion in Relation to Social Behaviour". Oliver and Boyd, Edinburgh.

The Role of the Little Auk, *Plautus alle* (L.), in Arctic Ecosystems

MAGNAR NORDERHAUG
Norsk Polarinstitutt, Oslo, Norway

I. Introduction

This paper briefly outlines a recent study of the ecology of the little auk and discusses its relationship to other organisms in the Arctic. Field-work was carried out in Spitsbergen, Svalbard, in 1962–65, and was supported by the University of Oslo and Norsk Polarinstitutt. No direct comparisons are made with Antarctic ecosystems, but there are fairly evident parallels between the ecology of sea birds in both polar regions and for this reason the present study may be of interest to Southern Hemisphere workers.

II. Breeding Biology

The little auk [*Plautus alle* (L.)] is one of the smallest members of the family Alcidae. It is a high-Arctic species, breeding in the Atlantic part of the Arctic Basin from Severnaya Zemlya and Franz Josef Land to the eastern parts of the Canadian archipelago. It is probably the most numerous of all alcids, breeding along the Arctic coasts in colonies numbering hundreds of thousands of pairs. Like the small plankton-feeding alcids of the North Pacific, its diet consists mainly (95% or more) of planktonic crustaceans.

The importance of the little auk in Arctic ecosystems arises from its abundance, restricted breeding area, and marine diet. Information on the breeding biology and general ecology of the species has, however, been relatively restricted, probably due to the climatic conditions in the breeding area and practical difficulties of field-work in these localities.

In Spitsbergen there are colonies of many hundred thousand breeding pairs of little auks. Density of nests varies with the composition and structure of the talus, but more than one nest per square metre has been observed in some colonies. The egg (normally one in each clutch) is laid on a layer of pebbles, half a metre or more from the surface of the slope and is incubated by both parents. In Svalbard hatching takes place in the last half of July.

The young ones leave the nest after a period of 26–29 days (average 27·1 days), and in Svalbard most have left the colony (by active flight) before the end of August. During the whole nesting period the nestling is fed on plankton, mainly *Calanus*, brought in by the parents in their well-developed mouth cavity.

III. Consumption of Plankton

Preliminary studies of plankton consumption by little auk nestlings, from hatching up to the time of departure, were carried out in 1962–64. The following main results were obtained:

1. One hundred and sixteen complete food samples were collected from adult birds caught on the way to their nests to feed their chicks, and these permitted a fairly representative analysis of the bird's food. The volume of plankton varied from 0·7 to 7·0 ml. Average weight (wet weight) was 0·97 gm/ml.
2. The average volume of plankton delivered per feed increased with the age of the nestling from 2·4 ml in the first week after hatching to 3·6 ml in the last week before the nest was abandoned.
3. Direct observation of selected nests (the observer being concealed) indicated a normal frequency of 8–9 feeds (average 8·5) per 24 hrs (based on 320 observed feeds in 880 hrs of nest observation).

During the 27 days spent in the nest, each nestling was estimated to consume an average of 710·7 ml of plankton. Studies of weight development in 111 little auk nestlings in 1963–64 showed an average increase in net weight of 92·8 gm in the same period. One-day-old chicks weighed 21·5 gm on average, while chicks 27 days old averaged 114·3 gm. The average adult weight is 160 gm. Hence a plankton consumption of 710·7 ml (689·6 gm) was converted into a little auk biomass of 92·8 gm. This indicates a yield of 13·5% in the production of little auk from plankton in this ecosystem.

IV. Enrichment of the Terrestrial Ecosystem

A considerable amount of plankton is in this way transported from the marine environment to little auk colonies. In a colony of 100,000 pairs, approximately 70 tons of plankton must be brought in for consumption by the nestlings during only four summer weeks. Because of their abundance, and the consequent large influx of organic matter of marine origin to little auk colonies, these have a marked influence on the ecosystem of adjacent land areas. Colonies are often located some hundred metres or more from the sea on mountain slopes behind a coastal plain. These coastal plains accumulate organic deposits more effectively than do Arctic bird cliffs located close to the sea (where a high proportion of the organic deposits are returned to the sea after a relatively short period of time). Deposits on coastal plains below little auk colonies support a rich vegetation: the vegetation furthermore conserves water during the summer and forms biotopes inhabited by a varied fauna of Arctic insects. These vegetated areas are also attractive to different bird species, like pink-footed goose (*Anser fabalis brachyrhynchus*), purple sandpiper (*Calidris maritima*) and snow bunting (*Plectrophenax nivalis*).

V. Predators

A more direct relationship to little auk colonies is observed among predatory birds, particularly the Arctic skua (*Stercorarius parasiticus*) and the glaucous gull (*Larus hyperboreus*). Both are euryphagous species with marked predatory habits during the summer months. Both species breed near to little auk colonies and take food from them. Eggs and nestlings are included in their diet, and glaucous gulls also kill adult birds. Juveniles are furthermore frequently taken when leaving the nest in the second half of August.

Glaucous gulls specialized as predators of little auk mainly breed in colonies close to the prey. Arctic skuas breed in scattered pairs on the coastal plains. One mammal, the polar fox (*Alopex lagopus*) has also a close connection with little auk colonies. Dens of one or more polar fox families are normally found close to big colonies of little auks, and in these localities the diet of the foxes consists mainly of little auks during the summer, with a consequent local reduction in predation on other breeding birds. When the little auks leave their colonies in the second half of August, a switch to less attractive species like Arctic terns (*Sterna macrura*) may be observed.

The little auk is also valuable to man in some parts of the Arctic. In Greenland, eggs, nestlings and adults are taken for food during the summer, and birds are stored for the winter. Little auks are furthermore taken in numbers during the extensive winter hunting of sea birds in south-west Greenland. It is worth mentioning that most of the birds taken in this area are probably produced in other parts of the Arctic. Of 11,000 adult birds ringed in Svalbard, twelve were recovered abroad, all in south-west Greenland. Of these, eleven were taken by man during the winter.

VI. Conclusions

The little auk is thus a highly specialized bird, and its restriction to high Arctic breeding grounds, its abundance in these areas and its marine feeding habits puts this small alcid in a rather central position in Arctic ecosystems.

A more detailed account of this investigation will be published elsewhere.

Biology of the Great Skua

R. W. BURTON
British Antarctic Survey Biological Unit, Monks Wood Experimental Station, Huntingdon, England

I. Introduction

The biology of the great skua, *Catharacta Skua*, including breeding, feeding and agonistic behaviour, has been studied in several parts of the world, sometimes in great detail. It is now possible to make some comparisons between populations, which are of particular interest in the great skua because of its unusual bipolar breeding distribution. Comparisons will have to be sketchy, as some programmes are still in progress and, in any case, it is often difficult to compare the results of different workers. Moreover, one has to be on guard for generalizations from observations based on a few animals over a short space of time. Unfortunately, such observations are often the only ones available. However, differences are becoming apparent, although explanation of them is often not possible.

II. Feeding Habits

In examining the results of work on breeding biology it is obvious that no conclusions based on any one study can be said to be representative of all great skuas. Breeding success varies greatly, as do the factors that influence breeding success. Diet and feeding behaviours also vary. In general the great skua is an opportunist feeder using a great many sources of food, but sometimes one population will ignore a source of food that another will exploit. For instance, at the Argentine Islands (lat. 65° 15′S, long. 64°16′W), the blue-eyed shags (*Phalacrocorax atriceps*) are the target of thieving by great skuas, but at Signy Island (lat. 64°43′S, long. 43°38′W), where the shag is common, no such thieving has been recorded (Burton, 1968*a*). M. W. Holdgate (*personal communication*) informs me that he has similarly seen great skuas forcing shags to regurgitate off the south of Isla Navarino in southern Chile, but has never seen this behaviour in the Antarctic or Subantarctic or directed against other sea birds at Tristan da Cunha (where there are no shags).

Young (1969) has described the relationships between great skuas and Adélie penguins (*Pygoscelis adeliae*) at Cape Bird. Despite the apparent simplicity of the system involving skuas, penguins and fish, he has shown that the predatory behaviour of the skuas is complex. At Signy Island skuas have a far greater range of prey. There are three species of penguin, Adélie, chinstrap (*P. antarctica*) and gentoo (*P. papua*), and all are preyed on by skuas. Because there is approximately one month's difference between the breeding dates of the Adélies and the chinstraps, the skuas breeding near colonies where both species are abundant have penguin broods available to them for most of their own breeding period. At Cape Bird, on the other hand, Young found that penguin broods were only available at limited times during the season, and that this profoundly affected the skuas' lives.

At Signy Island the skuas also prey on petrels such as cape pigeon (*Daption capensis*), dove prion (*Pachyptila desolata*), snow petrel (*Pagadroma nivea*), and Wilson's storm-petrel (*Oceanites oceanicus*). Except for cape pigeons, these are taken throughout the summer. It seems that the cape pigeon's cliff-nesting habit confers some immunity on it. It is able to fly on or off the open nest, whereas the other petrels, which nest in burrows or crevices, have to walk to and from the entrance, during which time they fall an easy prey to waiting skuas. Petrels were not a major source of food at Signy Island during the two years of the present study, but counts of corpses around certain skua nests during two seasons showed that in the first year they took many more petrels than they did in the second year.

I found a more marked variation in the year-to-year exploitation of food sources in the Shetland Islands. Before visiting the island of Foula in 1967 I was told that great skuas feed on puffins, *Fratercula arctica*, and on any sheep that dies or is weakened, and I would find the tops of the cliffs liberally littered with the remains of puffins stripped of all flesh and that sheep carcasses would be reduced to skeletons. This is how petrel remains and seal carcasses are found at Signy Island. However, during my summer stay on Foula I found no more than half a dozen puffin carcasses and these were merely disembowelled, and sheep carcasses were barely touched.

The conclusion to be drawn from this is that some other food preferred by skuas to puffins and sheep was varying in abundance from year to year. It is to be presumed that this was obtained at sea.

III. Breeding Success and Nest Density

In gulls it has been shown that the distance between nests is governed by the resultant of factors tending to space them out and those tending to bring them together (Tinbergen, 1953). Skua colonies are by no means as dense as gull colonies. This may result from evolutionary or environmental causes.

If environmental, an examination of the skuas' environment should reveal whether there is any good reason for the nests being spaced. In the far south of their range, e.g. at Cape Royds, it seems that skuas nest on sheltered ground, or on available snow-free ground (Young, 1963), which would favour aggregation, but this does not hold for the dense colonies in the Shetland Islands, in warmer latitudes. On the other hand, predation of skua chicks by other skuas, as described by Young (1963), would favour a spacing of nests to reduce the possibilities of such predation. If so, the degree of spacing should be correlated with breeding success, and this is shown by Table 1. Although data are not very good in many cases it does seem that breeding success is higher when nests are well spaced.

TABLE 1

Breeding Success and Nest Density of Great Skua at Different Localities*

Location	*Date*	*Number of pairs*	*% Breeding success*	*Nest density*	*Authority*
Cape Hallett	?	?	21	High	Reid quoted by Young (1963)
Cape Royds	1959	67	23	High	Young (1963)
Windmill Islands	1957	40	47	High	Eklund (1961)
Shetland Islands†	1946	149	51	High	Perry (1948)
Heard Island	1951	30	58	Low	Downes *et al.* (1959)
Signy Island	1958–65	50–80	average 61	Low	Burton (1968*a*)
Fair Isle†	1952–56	8–17	average 66	Low	Williamson (1957)

* M. B. Tollu tells me that at Kerguelen Island they have a breeding success of *c*. 60% and have a low nest density.

† Northern Hemisphere.

High breeding success could also be due to an abundance of food, so that chicks do not starve and the adults are not forced to become cannibals, rather than due to widely spaced nests preventing cannibalism. At Signy Island there was never any shortage of food to encourage cannibalism, so that it was not possible to test the hypothesis that wide spacing of nests would have reduced the chick predation that Young found at Cape Royds during times of shortage. (Low success in high-density populations could be induced by disturbance while studying the birds, but in this case relatively easily invaded small territories should be more affected than large territories.)

The reactions of skuas to other skuas coming into their territories also seem to suggest that widely spaced nesting has reduced the threat of intra-specific predation. At Cape Royds, where nests are close together, skuas react to other skuas only when they circle over the territory, that is, when they show hunting behaviour (Young, 1963). The same reaction has been noted in black-headed gulls, *Larus ridibundus*, when intruding herring gulls, *Larus argentatus*, start to stall (Kruuk, 1964). At Signy Island, skuas did not react in this way.

Table 2 shows the reaction of skuas to intruding skuas, whose behaviour was classed as "fast flight" if they were flying rapidly in a straight line, or "slow flight" if meandering and circling. The responses by the defending skuas, which consist of displays and flying after the intruders, show that they are not specially reacting to hunting behaviour on the part of the intruders. So at Signy Island the intruders are merely regarded as violators of the territory rather than as predators of the brood.

TABLE 2

The Response of Three Breeding Pairs to Intruding Skuas Flying over the Territory

	Behaviour of intruder	
	Fast flight	*Slow flight*
Response	58	71
No response	30	35
Total	88	106
% response	66	67

IV. Agonistic Displays

Four accounts of the displays of the great skua have now been published, and combining these with unpublished observations it is possible to make some comparisons between populations.

One display that shows variations is the upright. There are two types of upright, the aggressive and the intimidated, the names describing, roughly, their motivation. These types are found in all populations of great skua so far studied, except at Signy Island (Table 3), where only the aggressive upright is seen. One of the features of the upright is that the carpal joints are held out from the body, but, again, this has never been seen at Signy Island.

TABLE 3

Variation in Upright Displays of Great Skuas

Location	*Carpal joints out*	*Intimidated upright*	*Authority*
Shetland Islands	X	X	
Patagonia	X	X	Moynihan (1962)
South Georgia	X	X	Stonehouse (1956)
Signy Island			Burton (1968*b*)
Cape Royds	X	X	I. F. Spellerberg (*pers. comm.*)

Another behaviour pattern not seen at Signy Island, but reported from other populations, is grass pulling, which occurs in high-intensity territorial disputes. The absence of grass pulling at Signy Island may be due to the

TABLE 4

Displays and Nest Densities of Skuas and some Gulls

Species	*Displays*					*Nest density*	*Authority*
	Upright	*Oblique*	*Choking*	*Head tossing*	*Head flagging*		
SKUAS							
Great skua (*Catharacta skua*)	X	X				Low	
Arctic skua (*Stercorarius parasiticus*)	X	X				Low	Perdeck (1963)
Long-tailed skua (*S. longicaudus*)	X	X			X	Low	Drury (1960)
Pomarine skua (*S. pomarinus*)		X				Low	Pitelka *et al.* (1955)
GULLS							
Hemprich's gull (*Larus hemprichi*)	X	X	X	X	X	Low	Fogden (1964)
Sabine's gull (*Xema sabini*)	X	X	X	X	X	Low	Brown *et al.* (1967)
Black-headed gull (*L. ridibundus*)	X	X	X	X	X	High	Moynihan (1955)
Grey gull (*L. modestus*)	X	X	X	X	X	High	Moynihan (1962)
Herring gull (*L. argentatus*)	X	X	X	X	X	High	Tinbergen (1953)
Common gull (*L. canus*)	X	X	X	X	X	High	Weidmann (1955)
Laughing gull (*L. atricilla*)	X	X	X	X	X	High	Noble and Wurm (1943)
Dolphin gull (*L. scoresbii*)	X	X		X	X	High	Moynihan (1962)
Ivory gull (*L. eburneus*)	?	X	X	X	X	High	Bateson and Plowright (1959)
Hartlaub's gull (*L. novae-hollandiae*)	X	X	X		X	High	Tinbergen and Broekhuysen (1954)
Little gull (*L. minutus*)	X	X		X	X*	High	Moynihan (1955)

* The little gull has the equivalent tilting.

widely spaced nests and consequent rarity of territorial disputes, but it is impossible to give reasons for the absence of the intimidated upright and the raising of the carpal joints.

V. Comparison of the Displays of Gulls and Skuas

Skuas (Stercorariinae) have fewer displays than gulls (Larinae) (Table 4) and this is correlated with a greater incidence of overt fighting. The difference could be taxonomic, in that the skuas diverged from the gull stock before all the displays had been evolved, but this only explains differences in the display repertoire and not the lack of displays. Skuas have no equivalent, for instance, to the gulls' choking, which conveys the meaning "Don't attack; if attacked will fight back", and they have no equivalent to the appeasing head tossing. Therefore, there must have been a difference in the environments of skuas and gulls which reduced the need for skuas to evolve displays. Such a difference could be the nesting density. Most gulls nest in relatively dense colonies, whereas skuas have large territories. In these territories there is less chance of conflict between neighbours, so there has not been the same pressure to reduce fighting by substituting displays as there has been in the tightly packed gull colonies. Table 4, which is based on scanty data for nest density, shows that there is a correlation between few displays and low nest density in skuas and many displays and high nest density in gulls. If it can be accepted that the two exceptions, Hemprich's gull, *Larus hemprichi*, and Sabine's gull, *Xena sabini*, developed widely spaced nesting after the displays had evolved, then it is possible to conclude that the skuas became widely spaced nesters early in their evolution from the gull-like ancestor and that they were not subject to the same pressure to form displays as the gulls.

References

Bateson, P. P. G. and Plowright, R. C. (1959). Some aspects of the reproductive behaviour of the ivory gull. *Ardea* 47, Afl. 1–2, 157–76.

Brown, R. G. B., Jones, N. G. B. and Hussell, D. J. T. (1967). The breeding behaviour of Sabine's gull *Xema sabini*. *Behaviour* 28, Parts 1–2, 110–40.

Burton, R. W. (1968*a*). Breeding biology of the brown skua, *Catharacta skua lönnbergi* (Mathews), at Signy Island, South Orkney Islands. *Br. Antarct. Surv. Bull.* **15**, 9–28.

Burton, R. W. (1968*b*). Agonistic behaviour of the brown skua, *Catharacta skua lönnbergi*. *Br. Antarct. Surv. Bull.* **16**, 15–39.

Downes, M. C., Ealey, E. H. M., Gwynn, A. M. and Young, P. S. (1959). The birds of Heard Island. *Interim. Rep. Aust. natn. Antarct. Res. Exped.* Ser. B, **1**, 1–135.

Drury, W. H. (1960). Breeding activities of the long-tailed jaeger, herring gull, and Arctic tern on Bylot Island, Northwest Territories, Canada. *Bird-banding* **31**, No. 2, 63–79.

Eklund, C. R. (1961). Distribution and life history studies of the South Polar skua. *Bird-Banding* 32, No. 4, 187–223.
Fogden, M. P. L. (1964). The reproductive behaviour and taxonomy of Hemprich's gull *Larus hemprichi. Ibis* **106**, No. 3, 299–320.
Kruuk, H. (1964). Predators and anti-predator behaviour of the black-headed gull (*Larus ridibundus L.*). *Behaviour*, Suppl. **11**, 129 pp.
Moynihan, M. (1955). Some aspects of the reproductive behaviour in the black-headed gull (*Larus ridibundus ridibundus* L.) and related species. *Behaviour*, Suppl. 4, 201 pp.
Moynihan, M. (1962). Hostile and sexual behaviour patterns of South American and Pacific Laridae. *Behaviour*, Supplement 8, 1–365.
Noble, G. K. and Wurm, M. (1943). The social behaviour of the laughing gull. *Ann. N.Y. Acad. Sci.* 45, Part 5, 179–220.
Perdeck, A. C. (1960). Observations on the reproductive behaviour of the great skua or bonxie *Stercorarius skua skua* (Brünn) in Shetland. *Ardea* 48, Afl. 3–4, 111–36.
Perdeck, A. C. (1963). The early reproductive behaviour of the Arctic Skua *Stercorarius parasiticus* (L). *Ardea*, 51, Afl. 1. 1–15.
Perry, R. (1948). "Shetland Sanctuary". Faber and Faber, London.
Pitelka, F. A., Tomich, P. Q. and Treichel, G. W. (1955). Breeding behaviour of jaegers and owls near Barrow, Alaska. *Condor* 57, No. 1, 3–18.
Stonehouse, B. (1956). The brown skua *Catharacta skua lönnbergi* (Mathews) of South Georgia. *Scient. Rep. Falkld Isl. Depend. Surv.* **14**, 25 pp.
Tinbergen, N. (1953). "The Herring Gull's World". Collins, London.
Tinbergen, N. and Broekhuysen, G. J. (1954). On the threat and courtship behaviour of Hartlaub's gull *Hydrocoloeus novae-hollandiae hartlaubi. Ostrich* 25, No. 2, 50–61.
Weidmann, U. (1955). Some reproductive activities of the common gull *Larus canus* (L.). *Ardea* 43, Afl. 1–3, 85–132.
Williamson, K. (1957). The bonxies of Fair Isle. *Bird Notes News* 27, No. 6, 164–9.
Young, E. C. (1963). The breeding behaviour of the South Polar skua *Catharacta maccormicki. Ibis* **105**, No. 2, 203–33.
Young, E. C. (1970). The techniques of a skua-penguin study. This symposium, 568–84.

The Techniques of a Skua—Penguin Study

E. C. YOUNG
University of Canterbury, Christchurch, New Zealand

I. Introduction

During four seasons a study has been made of the relation between McCormick's skua (*Catharacta maccormicki*) and the Adélie penguin (*Pygoscelis adeliae*) in colonies on Ross Island in McMurdo Sound. During this period a great deal has been learned of methods of study; of which techniques give good results and which provide misleading ones, and of the reactions of the birds to the different approaches. The present study is the first one since the realization that skuas are sea-feeding gulls able to breed successfully independently of penguins and not specially adapted for preying on penguins. The evidence backing this conclusion appeared in two papers by Young (1963*a* and *b*), and a further three years' study at the larger, more typical colony at Cape Bird has confirmed these original conclusions. This appreciation of the niche of the skua has necessarily changed the overall view of its relation to the penguin.

The purpose of this paper is to give from this experience recommendations for other studies of the two birds, partly as an aid to establishing uniform methods throughout the bird's range and so make it easier to interpret results obtained by different workers, and partly to show that even now, in an age of intense instrumentation, there is no substitute for direct observation.

There have been other recent studies touching on the feeding habits of the skua (Maher, 1966; Reid, 1964; Spellerberg, 1966). Points from these, especially where they relate to techniques of study, will be considered later.

II. General Recommendations

The aim in any complete study of the two birds should be an assessment of the relation between them, of the effect of the association on breeding behaviour and success of both predator and prey, both in the short term during the seasons under study and in the long term on the evolutionary history of the populations.

Ideally the study is best done in an isolated undisturbed area in which the habit of life of the two birds seems to be typical for the species in Antarctica. Good numbers of both birds are needed to provide a wide range of different relationships between them and to allow for some experimentation. There are disadvantages also in overwhelming numbers, so that possibly between 10,000 and 40,000 breeding pairs of penguins and 100 to 300 breeding pairs of skuas would be fair numbers to aim for. The problem of what is to be considered a "typical" relative dispersion of the two birds is not yet resolved. In the smaller colonies, and those with well-separated breeding groups in broken terrain or in country suitable for skua nesting, it is probable that most of the colony area and all penguin breeding groups will fall within defended breeding territories of skuas. This is so for the three colonies at Cape Bird and the smaller ones at Cape Royds and in at least parts of the colony area at Cape Crozier. At Cape Hallett, it is clear, however, that the vast majority of breeding skuas nest at some distance from the penguin colony and that most of the colony proper is undefended or little defended. Information on this aspect of the relation of the two birds in other penguin colonies is desperately needed and because of its overriding effect on the behaviour of the individual skuas (determining whether or not they have free range over the entire colony) and because of the different penguin breeding mortalities expected under the different conditions, this aspect should be the first to be examined. Parallel studies are envisaged if it can be substantiated that in some areas of an otherwise defended colony skuas do indeed have free access to penguins: one in the part where breeding skuas defend penguin breeding groups and the other in the undefended part. This sort of situation, if discovered, would allow intensely interesting comparisons.

An important prerequisite to the study is that the skuas should be individually recognizable through banding and the sexes of the pairs known. It is still fair to assume that where the two birds of the pair are differently coloured the darker one is the male, even though exceptions are now known. Their territories must also be mapped and the boundaries indicated on the ground, and the division of the penguins among the individual territories ascertained. It would be desirable also for the hierarchy among the pairs of skuas to be known; to know, for instance, which birds can penetrate into other territories for feeding or scavenging with fair impunity, while knowledge of the history of the pairs would aid in assessing the effects of experience on ability to prey upon penguins, as this behaviour has a major learned element. Finally, knowledge of the flight paths about the colony area, and to and from the feeding grounds at sea, and of the bathing areas in the sea or in pools along the coast, would quickly allow interpretation of flights seen.

In any study of this sort relying heavily on direct observation of a natural situation it is essential to be able to recognize symptoms of disturbance, and know when the birds are being affected by the observer's presence.

The observations on penguins are less likely to be misleading because of disturbance than those on skuas, unless the overall effect of people moving about the rookery is enough, as Stonehouse (1967) suggests, to deter prospective recruits.

It is difficult to determine whether skuas are, in fact, being disturbed when they are aware of the observer, yet seem to be behaving normally. Light, and at first undetectable disturbance, may not show clearly in their behaviour for a day or two. The first symptom is generally nervousness in the brooding bird at the nest, and its failure to settle into the normal long periods of incubation. At the same time the male bird often appears reluctant to return directly to the territory after feeding. Once these patterns emerge one can be sure that the birds have all along been affected by the observer. Moving among skuas nesting close together invites disruption and the strong chance of egg predation as other birds exploit the territorial defence flights of a pair by stealing their eggs.

Skuas are also very sensitive to movement within hides close to the nest and there is no clear indication yet, from two seasons' photography of nests, how serious this disturbance is in the long term. There is, however, no assurance in these observations that encasement in canvas provides a cloak of invisibility.

Because of the preoccupation with working with the natural situation large areas of the Cape Bird penguin colony are out of bounds to all scientists and visitors. Fortunately access to the main colony areas is easily gained without passing through nesting concentrations of skuas.

The Northern Rookery at Cape Bird, site of the present study, is on these criteria almost ideal. There are some 24,000 breeding pairs of penguins here and about 250 pairs of skuas in the immediate area. The penguin breeding groups vary in size from some with fewer than twenty nests to two with more than 1000 nests and the skuas nest both about the periphery of the colony and among the penguins, so that almost all situations of association between the two birds can be easily discovered, especially the critical ratios of prey to predator numbers and of penguin nest number to perimeter in a breeding group. The colony has the added advantages of being relatively undisturbed, of being over 40 miles from the food and waste dumps at the southern end of Ross Island and in having close at hand two almost undisturbed companion colonies to act as controls. The value of having control areas like these, containing birds of the same overwintering group which can be expected to have had to meet the same difficulties in coming into the breeding grounds in the spring, was well brought out in 1967/68. In this season the occupation of nests in spring in the Northern Rookery was well below that of the preceding two years. Mindful of the possibility that even the small disturbance of this scientific study may affect recruitment into breeding groups (Stonehouse, 1967), it was very reassuring to find comparable reductions in the other two colonies.

III. The Prey

Away from the scientific stations and the shipping lines sources of food for skuas through the breeding season are severely restricted. Fish, crustacea and cephalopods from the sea and penguin eggs and chicks from the colonies are the only major sources. In some areas birds may feed at petrel colonies and in early summer at Weddell seal pupping areas, but for the most part the birds either feed wholly at sea or supplement this food by feeding at the penguin colonies.

A. Sea Food

Some assessment of the place of sea food, for the Ross Island colonies of skuas mainly the fish *Pleurogramma antarcticum*, in the skua economy and the ease with which it can be taken can be achieved simply by timing the birds as they fly to and from the feeding areas at sea and recording the number and weights of the fish given up at the end of the flight to the mate in courtship feeding or to the chicks during chick feeding. Such records made through the season show the seasonal changes in the demand for sea food, important in showing up shortages in the supply from penguin colonies, and variability in fishing success, as measured by time away from the territory. It is important that the birds are undisturbed, since otherwise no feeding occurs on return to territory—accounting for the fact that students on weigh-and-measure-walk-rounds of the nests of breeding skuas seldom see feeding behaviour. This, no doubt, in the absence of alternative observations, led to exaggeration of the place of the penguin in the food ecology of the skua.

The sea feeding areas may be restricted, as in McMurdo Sound, and this makes observations of flights away from the territory easier to interpret. For example, flights to the specific foraging area at sea that end without food transfer to a hungry mate can be interpreted as being unsuccessful, indicating that food is difficult to obtain at that moment.

Throughout summer notes should be kept of the sea-ice cover as it ebbs and flows with the changing wind pattern. In the Ross Sea area ice cover, because of its effect on sea feeding, is a major factor affecting skua breeding success and except for prolonged high winds the only factor causing total nesting disruption in the Cape Bird colonies. More recently the U.S. Naval Oceanographic Office has carried out systematic surveys on sea-ice cover in some areas and have made these particularly valuable maps generally available.

B. FOOD FROM PENGUIN COLONIES

It seems easier to keep records of the prey available to the skuas at the colony. At Cape Bird this is done at two levels. Counts made in the second week in December of all penguin nests with eggs at all three colonies give an indication of the gross changes in the number of breeding pairs with eggs at this date from season to season. These figures are the base line for determining both the number of eggs and chicks present in the colonies by extrapolation from the study colonies and the number of breeding pairs in each skua territory. In a more detailed study some 10% of nests in about thirty breeding groups are followed closely through each season to give data on egg production and egg and chick mortality in all nest situations in the groups and for groups variously positioned in the colony, especially in relation to skua breeding concentrations. Through these two series of observations a fair estimate can be reached of the amount of food available at any time and the number of eggs and chicks actually lost from the colonies, most of which will be gained by the skuas. As the results from the study groups are extrapolated to give estimates for the colony as a whole it is most important that they give a fair picture of the changes occurring among undisturbed birds. To reduce observer-effect the nest positions in all of these breeding groups are mapped at the start of the season and these maps are used to locate pairs whose breeding success is observed from outside the colony. The study groups are examined every fourth or fifth day and there has been little difficulty in interpreting the small changes in nest position, pair number, or nest content occurring over this interval. This technique, although very time consuming, ensures that neither the birds nor chicks are put off the nests and allows a more meaningful interpretation of the nest desertions noted.

On occasions, especially within the large breeding groups or to mark eggs, it becomes necessary to lift birds from the nest. Disturbance is reduced by bending over the penguin from in front and lifting it by the tail, so that it immediately drops the bill, digging it into the ground. A pair of gloves dangling from a neck trace distracts the penguin while its tail is grasped. This new method of lifting a bird at the nest is so much better than bodily pushing it off with the foot while it is protesting vigorously and raucously that the earlier technique should be given up.

None of these penguins is banded, because of the vast upheaval that would have taken place initially, so that each year begins anew. It would certainly be advantageous to work with banded groups and studies able to exploit these situations would be priceless.

The problems of counting penguins, or for that matter any colonial grouping of sea birds, have not been fully solved (for a discussion of the difficulties see Morton Boyd, 1961). In the present study the nests were counted at a time when a minimum number of adult birds were in the colonies, and virtually all were incubating. Counts made at this time are more accurate than at any other and, as the real aim of this study is to determine the numbers of eggs present, provide the most directly useful figure. A series of simple factors converting this nest count to estimates of total eggs laid and eggs lost in the colony are found from the study groups and are applied to similar groups throughout the colony. The nest count is used in the same way to obtain estimates of peak adult and nesting numbers and the changing number of occupied nests in the colony through the year. Counts made from technically outstanding photographs of the colony at this time of year would also provide a base line for these calculations. Photographs taken at other times are more difficult to interpret and in the absence of simultaneous ground counts of a part of the area are of limited value. In one test made at Cape Bird photographs taken from a slope overlooking three breeding groups totalling nearly 700 nests gave figures on interpretation over 8% above the true numbers, largely through the separation of the two birds of a pair at the nest. These were superb prints in which each bird stood out clearly; the errors are, of course, magnified increasingly as the quality of definition falls off.

IV. The Effect of the Association on the Penguins

The study falls clearly into two parts; there is on the one hand the work among the penguins and about the skua territories to assess the food resources through the season and to record the amount lost from the colonies or found as prey remains, and on the other the recording by direct observation from a distance the natural, undisturbed behaviour of the two birds where they come into contact about the colony. The first part requires movement among the birds and little of the association behaviour is ever seen, but it gives the necessary data on prey resources. The other provides details of behaviour and the effect of skuas on the penguin, but by itself cannot give precise data on resources or even the weight and size of prey taken. The dilemma in setting up a programme with restricted labour is in striking a balance between the two parts, and here the individualities of the observers must play a major role.

The breeding season of the penguin can be conveniently broken up into five partly overlapping sections. The most useful and appropriate methods for studying the effect of skuas in each of these are considered below.

A. Prior to Penguin Egg Laying

The skuas arrive after the penguins and show little interest in them during the period before the eggs are laid. No food has been left in the colonies at Cape Bird from one season to the next, as suggested at Cape Hallett (Reid, 1964). The possibility always exists, however, that this could occur following heavy mortality of penguin chicks in a late summer blizzard.

B. The Penguin Incubation Period

There are several ways of determining loss of eggs from the colonies, and subsequent gain to the skuas, during this period.

1. *Counting Egg Shells on the Skua Territories—a Search-and-destroy Technique*

This is a commonly used technique, but gives minimal information and is subject to considerable error. Errors arise in three ways. First, territory boundaries do not mark the foraging range of individual birds at this time and because skuas can pick up and carry eggs easily in flight many are lost from the colony to birds from outside the immediate area and are consequently not counted. Second, egg shells are lost through being blown or carried about, through being buried in the snow or finely broken or eaten. Third, towards the end of the incubation period it is difficult to tell the shells of hatched eggs from those eaten by skuas. The method gives no information on the origin of the eggs, nor even the basic information of whether they were taken from covered or deserted nests. Nor can it indicate how the egg was taken by the skua or whether it was living or dead, except that eggs with live embryos late in incubation become smeared with blood when punctured.

2. *The Change in Egg Numbers Recorded from the Regular Examination of the Study Groups*

This method provides figures for the number of eggs lost through the incubation period within these breeding groups and, if the study groups are selected judiciously, may give a very accurate estimate for the colony as a whole. It also shows the position of the nests losing eggs in the group and often, by reconstruction and hindsight, some indication of the cause of the loss. It suffers, however, from a number of shortcomings; it is not infallible at the start of the season, when newly laid eggs may be lost from a nest before being recorded in the nest checks, and it often cannot distinguish between loss of eggs and loss of chicks over the hatching period. Finally, when the main consideration may be food actually reaching the skuas, it assumes that all eggs lost from the nests are ultimately eaten by skuas.

3. *Direct Observation of the Penguin Colonies*

In this method the birds are watched for as long as possible, in the present study for 8–12 hrs through two days in every five, and all losses and all behaviour relevant to egg predation recorded. It gives information on which skuas actively prey on penguins, on where the eggs were taken, whether from covered or deserted nests, the methods used and any factors contributing to the success of the skuas such as fighting among the penguins. It also provides information on the extent of predation by outside birds within the territories of the breeding skuas and the limitations of territorial defence.

Even with the present duration of observation some assessment of total loss of eggs from the colony over the season can be made and precision could be increased markedly by extending the watching period.

This is the only method that satisfactorily examines predation at the start and close of the incubation period and the only one giving information on the behaviour of the two species. For these reasons it is the preferred method of the present study and, when backed by basic information on the prey stock, is capable by itself of providing a detailed account of egg predation.

The practice of counting egg shells taken by skuas and left in their territories, although seemingly direct and straightforward, can give rise to vast errors and should be used warily. Some of its shortcomings show in the following comparison. Maher (1966) counted shells in this way at the Cape Hallett colony at the same time that Reid (1964) was keeping a detailed record of the number of eggs and chicks actually lost from the penguin breeding groups. Maher estimated that skuas took 1889 eggs from the colony, and as few eggs lie exposed without being taken by skuas, this estimate is probably that also for the total loss from the colony. Reid, however, calculated that 23,775 eggs were lost, a figure far in excess of that determined by Maher.

C. Early Chick Rearing

This is the most difficult period in which to obtain accurate figures of egg and chick predation, as the chicks are so small they can be eaten quickly, leaving no trace and, as noted before, it is often impossible to be certain from the nest checks whether the loss recorded was of an egg or recently hatched chick. There are only two techniques applicable at this stage. The first is the recording of losses from the study groups. If these checks are made often enough and the laying dates of pairs known, then many of the problems of interpretation can probably be resolved. Because of the heavy selection against young chicks at this time, however, figures of hatching success determined by this method alone must still be regarded as doubtful. Direct observation of skuas working about the colonies gives a far more complete record not only of the total numbers of eggs and chicks taken but of the methods and site of attack as well. The marked selection against the first chicks to hatch in the colonies and against the first chick of a pair at a nest before the second hatches is evident, arising because chicks are far easier to grab than eggs. To demonstrate the degree of selection it is necessary to know the egg:chick ratios in the breeding groups at the time, especially in the peripheral nests that are most often attacked, and to be able to see the contents of an attacked nest or to locate the nest on a map for checking later. Most observation is through 16 × 60 binoculars, which have high enough power to check nests yet are convenient enough to follow the fast movement of the skuas. These observations allow estimation also of the proportions of dead to live eggs and chicks taken.

D. Late Chick Rearing: Late Guard Stage and the Crèche Stage

During this period the chicks are able to offer some resistance to the skuas, and many indeed escape from an attack. They are also large enough to satisfy a pair of skuas for some time and for part of the body to be left after feeding as an indication of predation. At the beginning of this stage there is abundant food for skuas, but this declines through early January, until by the middle of the month most chicks are too large for skuas to prey on them. In general it seems easier to get precise information about the weight of prey taken at this stage than at any other. A number of techniques, which if used together can give a wide understanding of the effect of predation, are available.

1. *Direct Counting of Chicks*

Counting heads becomes increasingly easier, quicker and more accurate as the chicks grow and stand away from the adult birds, and the earlier counting schedules can be usefully expanded. It becomes possible to determine losses over short intervals late in the season, but because of chick movement blocks of breeding groups rather than individual groups need to be counted.

2. *Recording of Penguin Chick Remains in the Skua Territories*

From about the last week in December the chicks are so large that at least the feet, leg skeletons and pelvic girdle remain. Skeletons may be trafficked about the territories, but knowledge of the territory boundaries in relation to the breeding groups, of which skuas attempt to scavenge in other territories and of the weight skuas can lift or drag under different wind conditions coupled with the advantage to the observer at this stage of the long period needed to take, kill and eat large chicks, means that in practice few are missed and precise information on the number, size and nutritive condition of the prey can be gathered. Two areas at Cape Bird are watched closely to collect this information. Chicks seen taken are weighed entire, without the stomach, and after complete evisceration and the foot length and weight and flipper length and width are measured. Such measurements of a wide range of killed chicks and the regular measurement of live chicks in the colonies have provided indices to calculate live weights from carcasses already partly eaten. Even the weights of carcasses already cleaned down to the feet and pelvic girdle when found can be evaluated from a series of regression equations relating total live weight to foot length, determined separately for each set of measurements made at five-day intervals throughout the growth period. The separate equations minimize the effect of the slowing down of growth of the foot well before the full weight of the chick is achieved. It is not possible to develop useful regression equations relating weight to foot length using pooled data taken through the season. The ratio of foot weight to foot length is a sensitive index of body condition of penguin chicks: undernourished chicks have feet lighter than average. Chicks that are dead before being dragged out of the colonies by skuas are usually only partly eaten and are easily recognizable from chicks taken alive.

These collections give only one side of the predation situation—the number, age and condition of the prey actually taken. The other side, the condition of the prey resource, is found at Cape Bird by weighing and measuring all the chicks in a series of breeding groups at about five-day intervals, together with others taken as randomly as possible from the very large groups in nets. Comparisons of the two series of animals—those taken and those available to be taken—through the season provide information about selection by skuas and the relative importance of scavenging as distinct from predation. They show a clear and not unexpected relationship between predator : prey ratio and the nature of the food taken. The relative level of scavenging declines and the average size of the chicks taken increases as the number of penguins per skua decreases. Skuas thus have to work much harder as true predators when they have fewer penguins in their territories.

There have been few injured or starving penguin chicks, as distinct from simply hungry ones, in the colony in any year of the study so far and predation has been almost entirely of healthy, fed chicks.

3. *Direct Observation of Skuas*

As in the earlier stages, this is the most productive technique. It gives information about the efficiency and intensity of predation effort (measured as time searching per chick taken), the method and position of attack, whether the chick was protected or not, how the birds select and capture a very mobile prey and the response of the chicks to threat of skua attack. The development of confidence in the face of skua attack as the chicks age and mature provides a fascinating series of observations each year. During a sustained watch it is not possible to disturb the area by retrieving the prey taken for measurement, but size, condition, especially stomach size, and activity are noted, and this aids in the assessment of the weight of the chick when the parts left are later examined and measured. How quickly a carcass can be stripped, how much can be taken from it at a single feeding, and its movement around the territories as each pair become satiated in turn, are all discovered by direct observation. The important conclusion that some few birds may be killing for whole groups of skuas followed from this approach and it is difficult to imagine how else this might have been determined.

E. Late in Season

After mid-January few chicks can be taken by skuas at Cape Bird and more and more birds turn exclusively to feeding at sea. The penguin chicks remain until early February and Crustacea and fish spilt in feeding provide valuable food for scavengers. A few skuas have learned to fly close to regurgitating penguins and disturb them so that food is spilled. It is only through meticulous observation and recording that the great importance of this spilt food as a resource can be appreciated.

V. Experimental Work

The following section describes some experiments that can aid in the study of the two birds.

A. Penguin-breeding Success Without Skua Interference

The figures for success found during the standard observations are typical for the colony to the extent that the relation between the two birds is left undisturbed and that a wide range of nesting conditions are examined. A study of breeding success in penguins without predators requires a different approach. At Cape Bird four or five breeding groups have been fenced off from the skuas each year by overhead and peripheral wiring and breeding success determined, as described earlier, by mapping followed by observations from the colony margin. These penguins are scarcely touched by the skuas, which seem afraid to go beneath the wires even though they are set high enough to let the penguins pass beneath.

Fencing also provides a check on egg losses soon after laying, as any displaced or deserted by inexperienced birds in these groups are not taken by skuas and are found later.

B. Experiments to Determine the Effect on Skua Predation Effort of Alterations to their Demand for Food

From observation it is found that skuas may feed more intensely in the penguin colony when supporting chicks. Indeed, they may change spectacularly and very quickly from casual scavengers to aggressive predators if their chicks persistently demand food. As skuas seem to adjust their efforts to meet the immediate requirements of their chicks, there is scope for experimental investigation of how the predation effort may be altered by changing the demand. This may be done, for example, by adding chicks to the nest, by removing the catch before any is eaten or by providing supplementary food in the territory.

C. The Effect of Nest Position in the Colony and Breeding Experience on Predation Mortality in Penguins

The few studies so far of penguins of known age seem to indicate that on average the nests of older, more experienced pairs are more centrally located in the colony, with the younger less experienced ones about the margin. This is confirmed by maps of egg clutch numbers, which show that most single-clutch nests are peripherally located, and by watching the growth of the breeding groups, especially during the reoccupation period, when most, although by no means all, new nests are placed near the margins.

Skuas spend most time about the margins of the breeding groups, and can only attack the larger chicks there. It seems important to discover whether their concentration and greater success at the margins is simply because they have more freedom to attack there or whether the nesting birds on the margins are less able, through inexperience, to cope with skua attack. In a study area containing birds of known age there is no difficulty in resolving this problem, for age and experience can be plotted against position in the colony to arrive at a result. For other places not so endowed, including the Cape Bird colony, the problem can also be tackled, but by experimental methods. On the one hand, supposing that the birds are older towards the centre, stripping off the outer two rows of nests* from established breeding groups, by lifting the eggs and causing the parents to desert, exposes a different group of penguins to the skuas on the margin. On the other hand, the marginal nests may be fenced off from the skuas to determine how well these birds can breed in the absence of predators. Comparison of the success of these groups of birds with those in control areas gives a fair idea of the relative importance of age and position in the colony for breeding success in the face of skua predation, especially if the areas are set up within single skua territories. Ultimately, long-term banding programmes, such as that a Cape Crozier, will, of course, give results of far greater certainty.

D. The Removal of Established Pairs of Skuas Holding Territories in Penguin Colonies

These experiments examine the forces operating in the selection of breeding territories and the importance of learned behaviour in predation.

Once the territories and the identity of the pairs of skuas holding them have been fully determined a great deal can be learned about the selection of territories by removing blocks of established breeders early in the season and allowing their places to be taken up by birds from the "club". Blocks of several pairs need to be removed, as little change in the territory boundaries has been found when a new pair becomes established following the loss of one or both of a single pair.

If the establishment of new pairs were followed in a range of areas with different kinds of penguin group, some conclusions should be reached on the

* In this study, and by coincidence that at Cape Crozier (LeResche, *personal communication*), the outer two rows of nests with eggs are considered to be peripheral nests. All other nests are then termed central nests.

vexed question of the extent to which breeding penguins are attractive to skuas. This question is not otherwise easily resolved, because the strong nest-site fidelity of established skua pairs normally precludes movement of birds from the peripheral and supposedly marginally suitable areas to the centres of the penguin breeding groups.

Most of the new skua pairs would as "club" birds have had only limited experience of attempting to prey on penguins, and could therefore be expected to perform very poorly as predators compared to the birds they have replaced on the territory. To be really useful this sort of study requires that most skuas in the immediate area, both "club" and territory-holding birds, have a known history and are banded. The territories must also be well known and the behaviour of the established breeders in relation to the penguins must be sufficiently catalogued for valid comparisons to be made with the new birds in the next season.

At Cape Bird the skuas taken from territories will be kept in captivity during the summer and released again in the late autumn, when skuas again show reproductive territorial behaviour. It is expected that most will regain their original territories.

E. Food Requirements of Skua Chicks and Adult Birds

There are no detailed records yet of the food requirements either of the chicks through their growth period or the parents during the stages of the breeding cycle. These figures have been roughly estimated from direct observation through a full day of the food supplied by wild birds, but the uneven level of feeding during such a period makes conclusive figures difficult to obtain.

Caged chicks thrive well (Maher, 1966) and there seems little difficulty in determining the amount of food (either penguin or fish) they require in order to make comparable growth to wild chicks. Similar figures for adults are more difficult to obtain because caged adults do not settle down quickly and because of the different energy requirements of free and caged birds. Birds in open cages attract others and it is necessary to cover the cages.

VI. Aspects of Skua Aggressive Behaviour

A study confined to straightforward, mathematical analysis of breeding success and mortality would give little real insight into how the two species are, in fact, associated, and would cover only part of a desirable programme. It seems almost trite to state that a study of the behaviour of the two birds, especially where they are in contact, is an integral part of an examination of the association, yet it is in the area of behaviour that least has been accomplished; perhaps because results from this sort of work do not so readily form into reassuring columns and tables.

In the first years of the present study the activity of the skuas about the colony was described during the long watches as fully and completely as time allowed, but this long-hand, non-systematic recording has obvious drawbacks when making comparisons between birds at one time or the same pair from season to season. In the last years the behaviour of skuas in contact with penguins has been catalogued so that the behaviour of any bird could be recorded quickly and precisely and, once the system was organized, fairly objectively. Separate values on a scale from one to ten are assigned to each category, according to the degree of interest in the penguins, the intensity of aggressive behaviour, the risk to the attacking skua and the probability of the attack being successful. These indices allow very precise comparisons of levels of activity. The categories of activity, arranged in increasing order of aggressiveness in each series, are set out in Table 1.

The scheme breaks up the behaviour into two main groups: that during the incubation and guard stage of the penguin and that during the crèche stage. The first group contains series for three different forms of attack: attacks by birds standing at the margin of the colonies, by birds in flight over the colonies and by birds part flying part running from the margin into the colony. The second group contains two series: the first including feeding on food spilt by regurgitating adult penguins and attacks on chicks within the colony or crèche, and the second attacks on chicks outside the colony, often during a feeding chase. The division of the categories into groups for the different parts of the season makes it easy to keep track of the coding, for at any one time seldom more than half the categories are in use. The code is used by recording the highest level of interest attained for each bird during set short intervals at Cape Bird during each $2\frac{1}{2}$-min period. It is rare for all pairs in an area to be working simultaneously and there has been little difficulty in following six to ten pairs at a time with this system.

A general summary of attacks witnessed and of the activity of all birds in the area during the watch is recorded on tape to supplement the rather terse account produced from the coded records.

VII. Penguin Behaviour in Response to Skua Attack

It has proved more difficult to catalogue penguin behaviour in a way similar to that used for the skuas, but this must be done if only to be able to predict, as skuas seem able to do, which nesting penguins are most likely to be a useful food source. It is more awkward to examine for two reasons: the subtle differences in flipper, eye and crest movements are scarcely visible from the normal viewing position high above the colonies, and the response to the rapid and spectacular behaviour of the skuas is limited in range and, on the surface, appears somewhat stereotyped.

TABLE 1

Code of Skua aggressive behaviour towards penguins

GROUP 1. ATTACKS DURING INCUBATION AND GUARD STAGE

Ground attacks

0. Skua away from the territory and colony area.
1. On the territory, but without obvious interest in the penguins.
2. Standing or sitting close to the penguins, alert and watchful.
3. Standing or sitting close enough to the penguins for them to show nervousness.
4. Walking along the margin of the colonies, not aggressively, and apparently scavenging.
5. Walking along colony margins more aggressively and occasionally stabbing beneath nesting penguins, but attack not sustained.
6. Active attack by one bird from in front of penguin.
7. Active attack by one bird from front and sides of penguin.
8. Active attack by one bird running and flying about penguin.
9. Attack by two birds from in front of penguin.
10. Attack by two birds one from each side.
11. Attack by two birds from in front and behind the penguin, the one behind distracting by tail pulling.
12. Single bird pulling penguin off the nest by the tail.

Flight attacks

13. Territory defence flight.
14. Mainly territorial, but with some observation on flight back to nest area.
15. Wheeling flight above the penguins, whether in or out of the territory.
16. Aggressive flight over the penguins, swooping low and hovering.
17. Stooping into a deserted nest with eggs, dead or moribund chicks.
18. Flight over the colony away from the territory with return with eggs or chicks.
19. Stooping into defended nest.
20. Stooping from low, hard flight into defended nest on colony margin.
21. Crash flight into defended nest on colony margin in attempt to knock out eggs or chicks, adult buffeted.

Jump attacks

22. Jump from margin into deserted nest or free egg or chick near margin.
23. Running flight from at least five yards into defended margin nest.
24. Jump flight hitting penguins at nest with feet and attempt to grab egg or chick.
25. Flight jump into middle of colony and attempt to drag large chick out through the nests to the margin.

GROUP II. ATTACKS DURING CRÈCHE STAGE

Attacks on chicks out of colony

26. Feeding on crustacea or fish lost in penguin chick feeding.
27. Flying about feeding penguins to cause food to be spilled.
28. Tentative attack from flight (without contact) on chick out of the colony.
29. Severe attack from flight on chick out of the colony, catching by the head, but release forced by adults immediately.
30. Severe attack from ground or flight on chicks notwithstanding adult defence.

Attacks on chicks within Colony

31. Flight at chicks standing at margin of crèche or colony, no contact.
32. Chick knocked out of crèche or colony by flight attack.
33. Run into sleeping chick in the colony, without contact.
34. Run into sleeping chick in colony and at least jabbing at it.
35. Attack on alert chick on the colony or crèche edge.
36. Attack on alert chick within the colony.
37. Crèche chicks actively worked by skuas to reach those small enough to be attacked.

Mr E. B. Spurr, of Canterbury University, is at present studying the intraspecific behaviour of Adélie penguins and as soon as this is well documented and understood an attempt will be made to apply the findings to their behaviour in response to skua attack. Much of this study will need to be done from the analysis of film.

VIII. The Effect of Penguins on Skua Breeding Behaviour and Success

The converse problems of the effect of the penguins upon skua breeding also falls within the scope of a study of the relation between the two birds. Direct observation of the natural population can certainly show some aspects of this side of the relationship, including important phenomena such as aggression by wandering penguins towards nesting skuas and the loss of skua eggs or young to other skuas by pairs too concerned with preying on penguins. However, the degree to which the dispersion of breeding skuas and the onset of breeding is determined by the penguins in accordance with a prey-predator relationship cannot be fully examined in this way. What is also required is some measure of the attractiveness of the penguin colonies to skuas. This assessment is aided by plotting skua breeding densities in relation to topography and climate factors as well as to the penguins, all the time bearing in mind the fact that the two birds are similarly restricted by requiring snow-free, dry, sheltered nesting areas close to open water. Recording the dates in which territories are claimed at the start of the season may yet prove useful, although up to now little difference has been found for pairs nesting in and away from the colonies. From earlier experience it appears that radical modification of the breeding territories, as outlined earlier, is more likely to provide an understanding of the basis for selection of territories than the records of occupancy collected season after season. However, the long-term studies of banded, known-age birds being undertaken by R. C. Wood (Johns Hopkins University) at Cape Crozier, with the opportunity to follow movement of individual birds, will in the end provide the definitive answer.

Comparisons of the breeding success of skuas holding territories containing penguins with those without penguins seems also on the face of it a perfectly simple and direct method of examining the place of the penguin in the breeding ecology of the predator. It is not, however, enough simply to add up and compare the numbers of young fledging in each group. This sort of comparison would only be valid provided it was known certainly that the history and experience of the pairs in each group were on average similar, that those with penguins were, in fact, utilizing this source of food to a significant extent, and that losses occurring were in the one group in some way connected with the penguins and in the other with the absence of penguins and not due to other reasons. If this was known; if the losses could be grouped under specific headings separating out different causes and only those seemingly related to the different relation to the penguin retained; and if, because of the very low breeding success of the skuas, these differences were consistent over several years, then there might, after all, be some value in these comparisons. All the levels of significance in the world cannot give meaning to data collected and arranged without scientific insight. The study of natural history has been unfashionable for too long, for it is largely through direct observation of the birds going about their day-to-day activities that the understanding required to make analysis reasonable and relevant is developed.

References

Maher, W. J. (1966). Predations impact on penguins. *Nat. Hist., N.Y.* 75. pp. 42–51.

Morton Boyd, J. (1961). The gannetry of St. Kilda. *Ibis* **30**, pp. 117–36.

Reid, B. E. (1964). The Cape Hallett Adélie Penguin Rookery. *Rec. Dom. Mus., Wellington* 5, pp. 11–37.

Spellerberg, I. F. (1966). Ecology of the McCormick Skua, *Catharacta maccormicki* (Saunders) in Southern McMurdo Sound, Antarctica. Thesis, University of Canterbury.

Stonehouse, B. (1967). Penguins in high latitudes. *Tuatra* **15**, pp. 129–32.

Young, E. C. (1963*a*). The breeding behaviour of the South Polar Skua, *Catharacta maccormicki. Ibis* **105**, pp. 203–33.

Young, E. C. (1963*b*). Feeding habits of the South Polar Skua *Catharacta maccormicki. Ibis* **105**, pp. 301–18.

New and Developing Techniques in Antarctic Ornithology

WILLIAM J. L. SLADEN AND ROBERT E. LERESCHE
Department of Pathobiology, Johns Hopkins University, Baltimore, Maryland, U.S.A.

I. Introduction

Especially in long-term population and behaviour studies of birds, old methods of collecting, temporary marking and sometimes disruptive counting must be supplanted by more permanent, more sophisticated and less traumatic techniques. Antarctica, which provides some of the finest populations for such studies, has been a proving ground for new approaches. This paper reviews some of the advances in bird-study techniques developed in Antarctica and emphasizes the need for further progress.

II. Methods of Capture

Eklund (1961) perfected two methods of capturing adult-plumaged south polar skuas, *Catharacta maccormicki*; one by net, as territorial birds dived to defend their nests; the other by pole, line and noose. There are very few individuals that cannot be caught by one of these methods, and thus it is feasible to mark almost an entire adult skua population, as well as the chicks, which are easily caught when they are fledging at the end of the season.

Penguins are easier to catch than skuas, but capturing large numbers of adults in crowded colonies is extremely disruptive to breeding birds. The USARP* Bird Banding Program has concentrated on banding large numbers of full-grown Adélie penguin, *Pygoscelis adeliae*, chicks before they depart to sea at the end of their first season. Only in this manner can a large population of banded known-age birds be created over the years for long-term population studies (Sladen *et al.*, 1968*b*). At Cape Crozier, Ross Island, an efficient method has been developed for corralling Adélie chicks using portable pens made of light aluminium alloy tubing. By this method as many as 5000 chicks have been banded in four days in their hatching areas with minimum disturbance.

* United States Antarctic Research Program.

Penguins and skuas are rarely seen away from the breeding areas where they are being studied. The procellariiformes, however, are frequently seen at sea during their circumpolar (Sladen *et al.*, 1968*a*) or north-south migrations (Roberts, 1940), and it has been of some importance to develop techniques for catching these birds unharmed for further banding and for studies of oceanic distribution and feeding preferences. Gibson and Sefton (1959) have used a hand-thrown net to capture the wandering albatross, *Diomedea exulans*, at sea and this method has been modified by Gill *et al.* (*in press*) for Wilson's petrels, *Oceanites oceanicus*, and greater shearwaters, *Puffinus gravis*. Excellent data have been collected by Tickell and Gibson (1968) from the breeding grounds and at sea to show that the wandering albatross breeding on South Georgia have winter feeding areas 7000 miles away off the coast of New South Wales, Australia.

III. Methods of Marking

The ideal band is one that will outlive the bird and has reference numbers easily read from a distance without disturbance.

The first bands were placed on Antarctic birds over sixty years ago by Gain (1914) and the first organized banding programme with addressed bands was started by the British (Falkland Islands Dependencies Survey) forty years later. A review of Antarctic bird banding, 1909 to 1965, is given by Sladen *et al.* (1968*a*) with particular reference to the USARP Bird Banding Program and International co-operation through SCAR. Band designs have been developed to aid in immediately identifying the age of the bird and the location where it was hatched and/or found breeding.

Penguin flipper bands (Fig. 1) have replaced the tarsus bands (Richdale, 1951) used in earlier studies. These flipper bands, first tried in 1948 (Sladen, 1952), have now become standard in penguin studies by Australian (Gwynn, 1955; Carrick and Ingham, 1970, British (Sladen, 1958; Stonehouse, 1960), French (Sapin-Jaloustre, 1960; Prévost, 1961), New Zealand (Kinsky, 1960; Taylor, 1962; Reid, 1968), and U.S.A. (Penney, 1968, Sladen *et al.*, 1968*b*) biologists. They can be made of aluminium, monel, or plastic. A durable plastic, teflon* has been used for emperor penguins, *Aptenodytes forsteri*, at Cape Crozier (Penney and Sladen, 1966). These bands have remained almost as new after four years of wear on the birds under some of the most arduous environmental conditions known to vertebrates.

Other band designs developed by Antarctic ornithologists include one-inch tall bands for skuas (Fig. 1) with duplicated reference numerals that read vertically (instead of the conventional method of reading around); double inscription bands for albatrosses (Tickell, 1968*a*) and large petrels, or over-

* Trade name for product made by Dupont, Wilmington, Delaware.

lapping monel bands for small petrels, to counteract abrasion on rocks; and types of plastic and tape (scotch-lite or scotch tape) for colour bands or for applying to metal bands as indicators of age groups or local populations. Other marking methods also conventionally used elsewhere include: web-punching (for age-groups and as an indication of band-loss); dyes (special inks, nyanzol, picric acid and rhodamine-B (Tickell, 1968*b*)); quick-drying celluloid paint; coloured plastic streamers, etc.

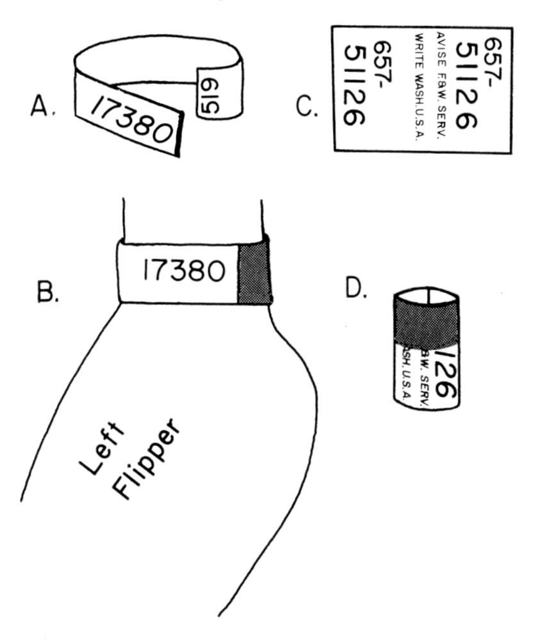

FIG. 1. Bands used by the USARP Bird Banding Program. *A*. Open Adélie penguin flipper-band. *B*. Flipper band in position; stippled area is tape of various colors, indicating age group. *C*. Flattened south polar skua leg-band. *D*. Shaped skua band, showing colour-coded tape.

IV. Identification of Sex

For behavioural, ecological and physiological investigations, it is necessary to identify the sex of the study subjects. Most Antarctic bird species are monomorphic, differences in sex being manifest partly in behavioural and partly in slight but often overlapping size differences. For example, the nine possible ways of sexing Adélie penguins (Sladen, 1958) are not infallible and are dependent on marking and subsequent observation of breeding birds. It has not hitherto been possible to sex an Adélie penguin, or other monomorphic species, away from its nest other than by dissection. A new technique for examining the cloaca by a simple instrument, the "cloacascope" (Sladen and LeResche, in press), has been perfected at Cape Crozier. This method is almost 100% reliable with experience, and does not harm the bird. Using the cloacascope it was found during the 1967–8 season that the small percentage of Adélies breeding at 3 years of age (4%) were all females and that 83% breeding at 4 years were females, as were 64% breeding at 6 years (Sladen *et al.*, 1968*b*). It is now also possible to analyse the sex composition of another important social component of a penguin rookery, the wandering non-breeders.

V. Feeding Preferences

Studies of the feeding preferences of Antarctic birds are important in understanding food chains and ecosystems. Conventional methods of killing many birds for stomach analysis are both wasteful and restricting in scope, particularly when dealing with the less numerous species and when studying individual birds that need to be followed throughout a breeding season. Some birds, particularly the petrels and albatrosses, regurgitate their stomach contents when handled for banding. This habit was exploited by Tickell (1964) for his analysis of the feeding habits of two closely related species, the black-browed albatross, *Diomedea melanophris*, and the grey-headed albatross, *D. chrysostoma*.

A promising technique was developed by Emison (1968) for his studies of the feeding preferences of the Adélie penguin. By inserting a plastic tube gently into their stomachs and sucking up a portion of the contents, Emison analysed 170 samples without harm to the birds.

Several species of marine organisms, hitherto rarely described by biologists, have been recorded as a result of these studies. For example, the southern lamprey, *Geotria australis*, was found to be present in 23% and 20% of samples taken in 1959 and 1961 respectively from grey-headed albatrosses breeding in South Georgia, and fourteen species of amphipods, some rare records for the Ross Sea, were present in the stomach samples of Adélie penguins at Cape Crozier. The birds are thus proving, at times, to be more specialized collectors of organisms than the marine biologists.

VI. Population Analysis from Photography

The value of photography for studies of population dynamics, particularly of penguins, has been emphasized by Sapin-Jaloustre and Cendron (1953), Sladen (1958), Caughley (1960), and Bauer (1967). Air photos of the Adélie colony at Cape Crozier have now been taken at times of peak population in November for eight consecutive years. By counting birds on these photographs, numbers and distribution of nesting birds can be determined, and a permanent precise record is provided of locations of nests of marked birds.

Three major but easily solved problems of this method are: (1) avoiding disturbance of nesting birds, (2) taking photographs at the proper time of season to give the most accurate estimate of the desired population parameter (e.g. breeding pairs, total birds), and (3) estimating numbers in large (over 50,000) colonies by sampling rather than total counting.

Bauer (1967) reports photography of king, *Aptenodytes patagonica*, and macaroni, *Eudyptes chrysolophus*, penguin colonies from altitudes of 100 m (328 ft). Our experiments show these to be dangerously low altitudes in terms of disturbance to Adélie colonies. Before egg laying in 1967, we conducted tests in co-operation with U.S. Navy VX-6 to determine levels of disturbance created by a helicopter flying at various altitudes over Adélie colonies. The results (Table 1) stress that 2000 ft (610 m) is the minimum altitude a helicopter should fly when taking aerial pictures of Adélies. Even at this altitude some disturbance is evident, and all flights directly over birds

TABLE 1

Responses of Adélie Penguins to Helicopter Flights during Early-season Occupation Period (LH-34 helicopter: ground speed approximately 40 knots: 1 November 1967: East Rookery, Cape Crozier, Ross Island)

Altitude		*Response*
ft	m	
3000	914	*Slight:* cessation of ecstatic displays, sneezing, shaking of heads. No movement from territories.
2500	767	*Slight:* a few birds stand, and quiet mutual displays increase. Fewer than 1% move from territories.
2000	610	*Slight:* about 5% birds stand, 5% quiet mutual displays. Fewer than 5% leave territories.
1500	457	*Moderate:* quiet mutual displays in half the pairs. Fifteen to 20% leave territories, causing squabbles when they return. Were eggs present some would certainly be lost in the fights or to skuas.
1000 (two passes)	305	*Moderate—Great:* quiet mutual displays remain at about the same level. 20–30% leave territories. Eggs would be lost.
Landing 600 ft away	183	*Great:* 50–80% of birds flee territories, depending upon proximity to landing area. All return once aircraft is on the ground. Eggs or chicks would be lost in initial flight and in territorial fights on return.

at any altitudes should be discouraged except for specific and important scientific purposes, or at times of emergency.

In addition to those from the LH-34 helicopters, pictures have been obtained using LC-121J Super Constellations and a De Havilland Otter.

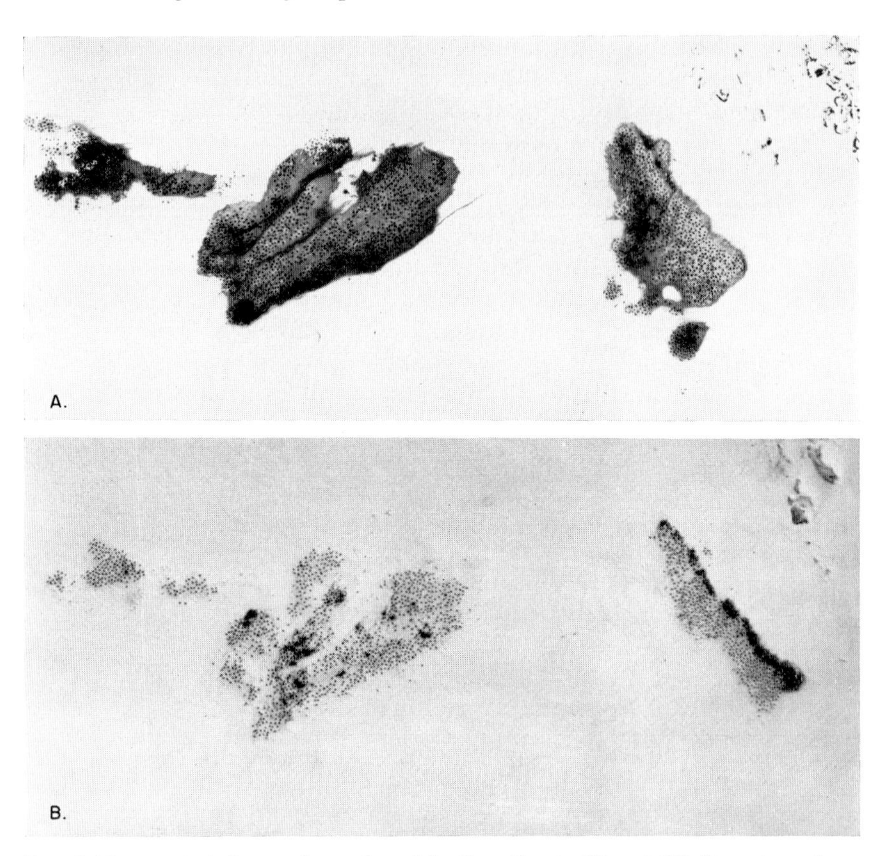

FIG. 2. Two vertical photos of a portion of the Cape Crozier West Adélie Penguin rookery. *A*. Taken 16 November 1963; 2000 ft; 305 mm lens. *B*. Taken 12 November 1966; 2500 ft; 12 in lens. Note the change in the colony on the right (B4.0), which has been partially drifted over during the intervening three years, and the disappearance of a small associated subcolony.

These fixed-wing aircraft have proved superior to helicopters because they are less noisy. The ideal aircraft and altitude for photography is an Otter, flying at 2000–2500 ft (610–762 m) with 305 mm lens. The use of large lenses (see Fig. 2) at these altitudes produces photos of equal or better quality than those taken with smaller (e.g. 125 mm) lenses at lower (100 m) altitudes (Bauer, 1967). At high altitudes the one brief disturbance of the colony has less effect than the prolonged presence of ground observers making a count.

If an assessment of breeding population is required, the peak time of egg laying for the colony concerned must be determined and the photographic flights arranged as near to this date as possible—when few eggs have been lost and almost all nests are occupied by only one bird of a pair. Phenology varies slightly from year to year, but we have found that a standard date of 14 November $\pm$ 2 days is sufficiently accurate for photographing Adélies at Cape Crozier. Lighting is best at 1200 $\pm$ 2 hrs local time, when shadows are minimal.

When accurate counts of large areas are required and are not feasible from the ground (or when total counts on the ground would disturb birds excessively), sample breeding groups are counted on the ground on the day of the photography. Number of nests, birds present, and nests with eggs are recorded then and periodically until egg laying is complete. The total count from the photos is then altered by a factor derived from these data.

For example, on the day air photographs were taken at Cape Crozier in 1968 seven intensively studied groups contained a total of 3114 birds. Many pairs had not completed their clutches and were both present at the nest (i.e. the photos were too early). Eleven days later 1991 birds were present in these colonies, almost all lone birds on eggs. Midway between these dates the peak of laying (as determined from a smaller group of very closely followed birds) had occurred, and since then 28% of nests in this group had been deserted. Thus, 1991 $=$ 0·72X, and the true breeding population (pairs) is X (or 2765) for the sample group and 2765/3114 (or 0·888) times the count for the entire colony. If the count for the colony from air photos was 175,000, for example, the corrected number of breeding pairs would be 0·888 $\times$ 175,000, or 155,400 pairs.

In practice, such precise estimation is necessary only in intensively studied colonies, and simple counting, if photography is within several days of peak egg laying (or peak population or reoccupation if estimating total numbers rather than breeders), is sufficient for periodic surveys of many colonies.

Similarly, precise counting of dots (penguins) on photographs of large colonies is often unnecessary, and sampling of photographs by randomly dropped frames is a valuable short cut. This method is especially valid in penguins, which are very uniformly distributed during nesting (Bauer, 1967; Penney, 1968). In Adélie colonies such as the ones at Cape Crozier care must be taken to sample areas filled with birds (many breeding groups are long and narrow), but elimination of sparse areas is not difficult and results are accurate enough for most purposes. In large uniform colonies of some species (e.g. Macaroni/Royals), sampling is probably as accurate as total counting.

VII. Biotelemetry

Biotelemetry was used for the first time in Antarctica in 1957 when Eklund and Charlton (1959) measured the incubation temperatures of Adélie penguin and south polar skua eggs. Since then an enormous amount of work has been done in this field in all parts of the world (cf. Slater, 1962). Biotelemetry is proving to be one of the best technical aids for the study of movements and physiology of unrestricted animals.

Penney (1965) used transmitters attached to harnesses on the backs of Adélie penguins for orientation experiments. At Cape Crozier small transmitters, weighing less than 20 g, were implanted into the abdominal cavity of Adélie and emperor penguins for studies of body temperature (Sladen *et al.*, 1966; Boyd *et al.*, 1967). However, research using this technique has been on a small scale and, with birds, has been confined to the United States programme.

VIII. Discussion and Future Work

Significant data on the ecology and population dynamics of Antarctic sea birds is accumulating (Carrick and Ingham, 1967 and 1970) from land-based studies, but these cover only about 40% of the annual life cycle of the species; perhaps much less when we consider that at any time a large portion of the population of any one breeding area is away at sea collecting food, or does not return to land for several years after hatching.

Antarctic ornithologists should now be planning to spend more time with their study subjects at sea and to further develop methods for capturing birds unharmed following the examples of Gibson and Gill *et al.* Only by well-organized teamwork with the marine biologists can we hope to improve our poor knowledge of food chains and begin to estimate the biomass and the productivity of the southern oceans. This task should be no more arduous for the ornithologist than for the marine biologist or marine mammalogist. The pioneer studies of Tickell and Emison have shown that research on feeding preferences may hold a key to more sophisticated studies of the smaller marine organisms, especially the ones that shoal or live in the euphotic zone. In fact, similar techniques are now being used (e.g. Ashmole and Ashmole, 1968) to study seasonal variation in surface fauna in the tropics. This work does not require elaborate or expensive equipment, but it does require special training, for a euphausid or fish looks somewhat different when pulled from a bird's stomach than when emptied from a trawl net.

We are still not satisfied that band designs have evolved sufficiently to outlive the bird. Some of the new plastics, such as teflon, show promise and need to be further exploited. These have an advantage over metal, as there is no danger of metal fatigue or icing.

The technique for determining sex by cloacascope now being used for Adélie penguins could be applied to other penguins and other monomorphic species such as the albatrosses, petrels, gulls, skuas and cormorants in Antarctica and elsewhere. The cloacascope may even prove less traumatic for waterfowl than the conventional technique of manually everting the cloaca (Taber, 1963).

Biotelemetry studies are still in their infancy. Both Eklund and our Johns Hopkins University group originally planned to use our equipment to study emperor penguins, but on each occasion the more readily accessible and territorial Adélie penguin became the study subject, for the dangers of camping alongside emperors on unstable sea ice, and their habit of breeding during the winter and of carrying eggs and young chicks on their feet, made it imperative to have implanted transmitters with a range of several miles. Only then could data be safely received in a hut on firm ground. To date no transmitters capable of such performance from inside a bird have been available, but these new electronic techniques are the only way to add to our knowledge of emperor behaviour and physiology in winter within the requirements of undisturbed birds and human safety.

Future advances in telemetry, most especially the use of satellites for tracking purposes (Warner, 1963), promise the ultimate in movement and migration studies of wide-ranging polar sea birds. Giant petrels, the albatrosses and perhaps the migratory pygoscelids could be tracked during winter this way.

We should be constantly reassessing our techniques for handling, marking and studying Antarctic birds in light of sound conservation principles. Murphy (1962, 1967) has eloquently stated the importance of following such principles and has stressed that scientific research, not carefully planned and thoughtfully pursued, is potentially as damaging to Antarctic biota as out-and-out exploitation.

Perhaps more than anything else, the helicopter has opened Antarctica to research. With carefully tested guidelines (cf. above) it can continue to be the biologist's indispensable ally.

As ornithologists turn more to the sea, methods of capturing and marking birds, collecting their food, and monitoring their physiology *without killing* the birds must be constantly sought and improved. To date, Antarctic ornithology has progressed well along these lines, and hopefully techniques will be expanded to meet future needs.

Acknowledgements

The Johns Hopkins University work has been supported by grants for Antarctic avian population studies from the Office of Antarctic Programs,

National Science Foundation. We are grateful for help and good counsel from NSF, especially from George Llano, and for logistic support from the U.S. Navy. E. P. Monaghan kindly drew Fig. 1.

Annex: Cine-photography as a Record of a Field Programme

A colour motion picture, running for 55 min, has been made by W. J. L. Sladen to display the social behaviour of adult and juvenile Adélie penguins at Cape Crozier. It illustrates the methods of study (banding, web-punching, corralling, etc.) described in this paper and provides a pictorial progress report of the long-term study of *Pygoscelis adeliae*, in a colony of 300,000 birds, and of the predator-prey relations with the south polar skua, *Catharacta maccormicki*, and the leopard seal, *Hydrurga leptonyx*.

During the past seven consecutive seasons over 30,000 Adélie chicks have been flipper-banded and web-punched at Cape Crozier (Sladen *et al.*, 1968*a* and 1968*b*), thus creating each year an increasing population of marked birds of known age. The fledglings depart to sea, returning to land in later seasons, first as non-breeding juveniles, then as inexperienced breeders and finally as established breeders (Sladen, 1958). No marked birds have been recovered during their first year. Thereafter small numbers (less than 10% of the original cohort) of 2-, 3-, 4-, 5- and 6-year-old birds return to the rookery each year, often to the precise colony of their birth. This is in marked contrast to the more than 90% return of birds marked when already breeding, and demonstrates a high mortality inflicted on yearlings in the pack ice. No 2-year-olds have yet bred and the few 3- and 4-year-olds that have bred are almost all unsuccessful in rearing their chicks to the fledgling stage. Probably Adélies do not become established breeders until 6 or even 7 years old.

The film compares juvenile non-breeding (mostly 2- and 3-year-olds) and first-time breeding behaviour (mostly 4-year-olds) with the behaviour of inexperienced and experienced breeders. The older age groups arrive first, the younger later. The non-breeders are seen attempting to establish territory on the edge of the colonies or wandering around the rookery individually or in small groups. If they build nests (usually males), their stones are often removed by older birds (often females as illustrated). The social interactions of these young birds, and of the unsuccessful breeders, is often detrimental to the stability of the community, and is illustrated by three examples:

(*a*) when an incubating bird is disturbed on its egg during a snowstorm; (*b*) when an incubating female is beaten up and driven off her nest with loss of the eggs; (*c*) when a chick gets separated from the crèche and is subsequently killed by a pair of skuas.

Five hunting methods of the leopard seal are illustrated: in slush ice at the beginning of the season, when Adélies are returning to the colony; below the ice foot; in brash ice; along the beach in the surf; and in deeper waters. The predation of eggs and chicks by the skua is also illustrated.

Its location at the edge of the Ross Ice Shelf and its exposure to the swell of the Ross Sea and the violent storms that blow from the south make the Cape Crozier rookery especially vulnerable to ice and weather conditions. Massive chunks of ice are hurled against the beaches. Parents making dramatic landings in bad weather must avoid these, and the leopard seals, if they are to rear their chicks.

References

Ashmole, N. J. and Ashmole, N. P. (1968). The use of food samples from sea birds in the study of seasonal variation in the surface fauna of tropical oceanic areas. *Pacif. Sci.* 22, (1), 1–10.

Bauer, Albert (1967). Dénombrement des manchotières de l'Archipel Crozet et des îles Kerguelen à l'aide de photographies aériennes verticales. *T.A.A.F.* No. 41, 3–21.

Boyd, J. C., Sladen, W. J. L. and Baldwin, H. A. (1967). Biotelemetry of penguin body temperatures, 1966–1967. *Antarctic J. U.S.A.* 2, 97–99.

Carrick, R. and Ingham, S. E. (1967). Antarctic sea-birds as subjects for ecological research. Proc. Symposium on Pacific-Antarctic Sciences, Tokyo, 1966. *JARE Sci. Rep., Special Issue* No. 1, pp. 151–84. Dept. of Polar Research, Tokyo.

Carrick, R. and Ingham, S. E. (1970). Ecology and population dynamics of Antarctic sea birds. This symposium, 505–25.

Caughley, G. (1960). The Cape Crozier Emperor Penguin rookery. *Rec. Dom. Mus., Wellington* 3, 251–62.

Eklund, C. R. and Charlton, F. E. (1959). Measuring the temperatures of incubating penguin eggs. *Am. Scient.* 47, 80–86.

Eklund, C. R. (1961). Distribution and life history studies of the South Polar Skua. *Bird-Banding* 32, 4, 187–223.

Emison, W. B. (1968). Food Preferences of the Adélie Penguin at Cape Crozier, Ross Island. "Antarctic Research Series, Vol. 12, Antarctic Bird Studies", 191–212, (O. L. Austin, Jr, ed.). American Geophysical Union, Washington, D.C.

Gain, L. (1914). Oiseaux antarctiques, "Deuxieme Expedition Antarctique Francaise", 1908–10, 200 pp. Paris.

Gibson, J. D. and Sefton, A. R. (1959). First report of the New South Wales Albatross Study Group. *Emu* 59, 73–82.

Gill, D. E., Sladen, W. J. L., and Huntington, C. E. (In press.) A technique for capturing petrels and shearwaters at sea. *Bird-Banding.*

Gwynn, A. M. (1955). Penguin marking at Heard Island, 1953. *Interim Rep. Aust. Natn. Antarct. Res. Exped.* 8, 8–12. Melbourne.

Kinsky, F. C. (1960). The yearly cycle of the Northern Blue Penguin (*Eudyptula minor Nov Aehollandiae*) in the Wellington Harbour Area. *Rec. Dom. Mus., Wellington* 3, 145–218.

Murphy, R. C. (1962). Antarctic Conservation. *Science, N.Y.* 135, No. 3499, 194–7.

Murphy, R. C. (1967). The urgency of protecting life on and around the great southerly continent. *Nat. Hist., N.Y.*, June/July, 18–31.

Penney, R. L. (1965). Some practical aspects of penguin navigation-orientation studies. *BioScience* **15**, 4, 268–70.

Penney, R. L. and Sladen, W. J. L. (1966). The use of Teflon for banding penguins. *J. Wildl. Mgmt* **30**, 847–9.

Penney, R. L. (1968). Territorial and social behavior in the Adélie Penguin. *In* "Antarctic Research Series, Vol. 12, Antarctic Bird Studies" (O. L. Austin, Jr., ed.) American Geophysical Union, Washington, D.C. 83–131.

Prevost, J. (1961). "Ecologie du Manchot Empereur". Expeditions Polaires Francaises—Actualities Scientifiques et Industrielles. Hermann, Paris. pp. 204.

Reid, B. (1968). An interpretation of the age structure and breeding status of an Adélie Penguin population. *Notornis* **15**, 3, 193–7.

Richdale, L. E. (1951). Banding and marking penguins. *Bird-Banding* **22**, 47.

Roberts, B. B. (1940). The life cycle of Wilson's petrel (*Oceanites oceanicus*). *Scient. Rep. Brt. Graham Ld Exped.* **1**, 141–94.

Sapin-Jaloustre, J. and J. Cendron (1953). Une technique de dénombrement et d'étude d'une rookerie de Manchots Adélie par la photographie systématique. *La Terre et la Vie* **1**, 1–27.

Sapin-Jaloustre, J. (1960). Ecologie du manchot Adélie. *Expeditions Polaires Francaises* **208**, 211 pp.

Sladen, W. J. L. (1952). Notes on methods of marking penguins. *Ibis* **94**, 541–3.

Sladen, W. J. L. (1958). The Pygoscelid Penguins. I—Methods of Study. II—The Adélie Penguin. *Scient. Rep. Falkld Isl. Depend. Surv.* **17**, 97, Plates I–XII.

Sladen, W. J. L., Boyd, J. C. and Pedersen, J. M. (1966). Biotelemetry studies on penguin body temperatures. *Antarctic J. U.S.A.* **1**, 142–3.

Sladen, W. J. L., Wood, R. C. and Monaghan, E. P. (1968*a*). The USARP bird banding program, 1958–1965. *In* "Antarctic Research Series, Vol. 12, Antarctic Bird Studies" (O. L. Austin, ed.). American Geophysical Union, Washington, D.C. 213–62.

Sladen, W. J. L., LeResche, R. E. and Wood, R. C. (1968*b*). Antarctic Avian Population Studies, 1967–1968. *Antarctic J. U.S.A.* **3**, 6, 247–9.

Sladen, W. J. L. and LeResche, R. (In press.) Sexing Adelie penguins by behavior and cloacascope.

Slater, L. E. (ed.) (1962). "Interdisciplinary Conference on the Use of Telemetry in Animal Behavior and Physiology in Relation to Ecological Problems". McMillan, New York.

Stonehouse, B. (1960). The King Penguin *Aptenodytes patagonica* of South Georgia, I. Breeding Behaviour and Development. *Scient. Rep. Falkl. Isl. Depend. Surv.* 23.

Taber, R. D. (1963). Criteria of sex and age. *In* "Wildlife Investigational Techniques" (H. S. Mosby, ed.). 119–89. The Wildlife Society, Edward Brothers Inc., Ann Arbor, Michigan.

Taylor, R. H. (1962). The Adélie Penguin (*Pygoscelis Adeliae*) at Cape Royds. *Ibis.* **104** 2, 176–204.

Tickell, W. L. N. (1964). Feeding preferences of the albatrosses *Diomedea melanophris* and *D. chrysostoma* at S. Georgia. *In* "Biologie Antarctique: Antarctic Biology" (R. Carrick, M. W. Holdgate and J. Prévost, eds.). 383–7. Hermann, Paris.

Tickell, W. L. N. (1968*a*). The biology of the great albatrosses, *Diomedea exulans* and *D. epomophora*. *In* "Antarctic Research Series, Vol. 12, Antarctic Bird Studies" (O. L. Austin, ed.). American Geophysical Union, Washington, D.C. 1–55.

Tickell, W. L. N. (1968*b*). Color dyeing albatrosses. *Bird-Banding* **39**, 36–40.

Tickell, W. L. N. and Gibson, J. D. (1968). Movements of Wandering Albatrosses. *Emu* **68**, 7–20.

Warner, D. W. (1963). Space tracks. *Nat. Hist.* N.Y. **72**, 8–15.

Discussion

HISTORY OF PENGUINS

N. M. WACE

Although I appreciate that Bergmann's rule is now not wholly upheld, it has often been alleged that penguins fit it very well. How do fossils fit in with the ideas that Dr Stonehouse has advanced? Do they show a comparable gradation of size with latitude?

B. STONEHOUSE

This can best be demonstrated if I show two slides. (Dr Stonehouse showed a slide of a series of penguins including fossil forms in comparison with a human figure, and a second showing Australasian fossil occurrences with a late Cretaceous and Tertiary paleotemperature curve.) Fossil dimensions have been calculated from the size of the tarsus and metatarsus; there is good evidence that some forms stood up to 5 ft high. Ambient temperatures of Australasian Tertiary penguins are now known, from recent oxygen isotope paleotemperature determinations. The Cretaceous showed a climatic cooling to approximately the present level; at about this time penguin stocks diverged from petrels. By the mid-Eocene, the first fossil penguins existed in sea temperatures about 20°C, as in the Galapagos today. In the early Miocene of New Zealand, Patagonia and Seymour Island (Antarctica) four different size ranges of penguins were in existence, from 5 ft high super emperors, through emperor size to two smaller forms. In the three areas birds of all four sizes seem to have lived side by side. Thus there is no evidence at present of a correlation between size and latitude or temperature at this period. A sharp drop in temperature in the Oligocene may well have been due to the local influence of cold westerly circulation in the New Zealand area, and it is by no means certain how widespread its influence was. Modern subspecies of penguins do not obey the ecological size rules. The largest species lives in the coldest place and the smallest species in the warmest, but size and temperature are not correlated in intermediate form.

R. W. MORRIS

Surely the relationship between the species and the food is likely to have been more important than the relationship between the species and the temperature cline.

K. G. MCKENZIE

I have looked similarly at a relationship between palaeo-latitudes, palaeo-climates and size, and it was suggested to me that it would be more precise to analyse size variation with latitude in a single species rather than compare sizes of the different species in a single genus. I took the point, but still believe that a trend exists when the subject is studied in this more general way.

TEMPERATURE RELATIONSHIPS OF PENGUINS

C. R. GOLDMAN

Is there any correlation between the posture adopted by penguins and the position of the sun? For example, do they sit with the white or alternatively the dark side exposed to incoming radiation?

B. STONEHOUSE

I looked for this in an emperor penguin colony in Marguerite Bay in the winter on the first days after the sun returned. When the huddle in the morning broke up as the sun appeared, all the birds turned to face the sun, as indeed we did. However, there was a good deal of radiation from the sky anyway at that time, and the sun was so low that there was probably relatively little direct radiation. On warm days incubating Adélie penguins adjust themselves to the temperature problems posed by excessive radiation; they sit up, spread their flippers, open their beaks and feathers and generally arrange themselves to lose the maximum amount of heat.

R. W. MORRIS

It may well be that wind is a more important factor than radiation in determining behaviour.

M. H. THURSTON

Emperor penguins certainly turn their backs to the wind when the wind velocity is quite low, particularly in cold weather.

R. L. PENNEY

I have also observed an orientation with regard to wind among Adélie penguins at Wilkes Station. Before hatching the birds turn into the wind, but after hatching they turn the other way.

E. C. YOUNG

This is probably because of the difficulty of covering the chicks and protecting them, hence the adults have to position themselves to shield the chicks from the wind once hatching has taken place.

N. A. ØRITSLAND

If a penguin is indeed setting out to absorb solar radiation, I suggest that it should face the sun in the morning, avoid it at midday, and turn its back on the sun in the evening. If there is any significant utilization of solar radiation by penguins, it should be possible to measure this effect directly.

W. J. L. SLADEN

I think one must be careful in interpreting observations such as that incubating penguins face into the wind. If you look at the pattern of guano splashes on the snow, you will find that this is arranged in a regular manner around the nest. As most people know, when penguins defecate they expel the guano in a considerable jet, and it seems likely that the birds rotate on the nest when they turn the egg, and that this is responsible for this rather uniform pattern. In storms birds can be seen in positions in which the drift becomes intermingled with the feathers.

J. C. Boyd

The structure of the feathers can be more important than the colouration, and it seems that the shiny covering of the adult penguin is important. Young chicks in contrast have no shiny reflecting surface and consequently receive more radiation and become heated up very much more.

B. Stonehouse

The chick is also metabolizing faster and more erratically; this will affect its heat balance and often give it a tendency to overheat. Radiation from penguins certainly does not depend on colour, but uptake of solar and sky radiation may well do so. I have done some unpublished preliminary studies on this effect.

M. C. Lewis

Do we have any figures for the thermal emissivity of penguins?

N. A. Øritsland

The emissivity of most mammals and birds is approximately equal to unity. This is true even for human skins whether they be black or white.

R. Carrick

Is there any evidence for the creation of a significant microclimate among colonies of king or Adélie penguins which are after all spaced out at distances of between 1 ft and 1 m.

B. Stonehouse

The influence of the colony in breaking up wind is significant, even in quite open colonies.

DIVING AND FOOD OF PENGUINS

S. Z. El-Sayed

Is there any information about the depth to which an emperor penguin dives?

B. Stonehouse

None published. However, both kings and emperors feed on squids and large nototheniid fishes and must dive to a significant depth to obtain them.

S. Z. El-Sayed

Certainly oceanic squids are unlikely to be found at the surface, hence the birds must dive to considerable depths.

B. Stonehouse

This may well help to explain the emperor penguin's large size. Larger birds are likely to be more efficient at deeper diving. There is some information to this effect from shags and auks.

R. Elsner

Dives up to 60 m in depth and 18 min duration have been recorded by G. L. Kooyman for emperor penguins on four or five test occasions.

G. A. Knox

In considering the importance of squids as indicators of diving in penguins, one must remember that these animals frequently come to the surface by night, even in Antarctic waters.

B. Stonehouse

Would this apply in really high Antarctic latitudes with twenty-four hours illumination in summer?

T. J. Hart

This period only lasts for a few weeks at midsummer, and the "apparent length of day" is further reduced by the low altitude of the sun, at depth.

W. J. L. Sladen

Did not Scholander say that penguins were less efficient in diving than ducks?

L. Irving

I don't think there is any firm proof of this. I would like to ask a further question. How deep do tropical penguins dive? What is likely to be the effect of the temperature profile in the sea?

B. Stonehouse

The penguins in the Galapagos Islands and on the Peruvian and South African coasts feed on the same fish as cormorants and other shallow divers, presumably in similar surface layers. In the Galapagos Islands the penguins breed only in the south-west corner where the cool Humboldt current is strongest. They are seldom reported further north in warmer waters. It is possible that in diving they do not pass out of the surface layers.

R. Carrick

The little blue penguin in the shallow waters of Australia appears to forage in the same range of depths as is explored by divers with scuba apparatus.

T. J. Hart

Euphausia crystallorophius was said to be the diet of Adélie penguins at McMurdo, but this crustacean has a very limited range in the extreme south, and the Adélies must take *E. superba* further north.

W. J. L. Sladen

W. Emison found that the Cape Crozier Adélies took *E. crystallorophius*, while F. C. Kinsky showed *E. superba* was the dominant food of Adélies at Cape Hallett.

BREEDING BIOLOGY OF PENGUINS

R. Carrick

I would emphasize the high survival of the breeding population in winter, when the birds are dispersed over a wide area. Competition for feeding space is a problem only in the breeding season. If there were more islands within the range of royal penguins, it is almost certain that more would be able to breed. In this context it is interesting to note that around the Antarctic Continent, where there is a continuous belt of feeding grounds, and the Adélie colonies are spread out along it, the Adélie penguins breed at 3 years old as compared with 7 or 8 years for the onset of breeding in the royal penguin. The importance of feeding to breeding success is well shown by the correlation between the weight of the chick at the end of fledging period and the weight of the female at the beginning of the breeding season. The heaviest females in October are those which produce the heaviest chicks at fledging. It seems most important that female penguins reach a certain basic adequate weight if they are to lay eggs and raise broods successfully.

S. Z. El-Sayed

Has the homing intensity been estimated for emperor penguins from banding returns?

B. Stonehouse

Banded birds do come back to a colony in which they have bred previously. The site of the colony may shift, but the birds seem to come back to their original assemblage.

E. C. Young

Can one determine the ages of penguins not banded as chicks?

W. J. L. Sladen

The first-year plumage is distinctive, and the second-year bird may be distinguished by having a residual *bursa fabricialis*, but for older groups there are no established methods.

SENSITIVITY OF BREEDING PENGUINS AND SKUAS TO DISTURBANCE

B. Stonehouse

The effects of disturbance on a penguin colony may be more subtle than has been appreciated. Its greatest impact may be on the recruitment of young birds. Very dense, noisy, boisterous colonies seem to deter prospective new members, and the effect of visiting helicopters and congressmen may likewise be not on the breeding birds but on the peripheral prospective recruits. During the years of greatest disturbance the Cape Royds colony declined at a rate of 6% per year, suggesting that recruitment was not keeping pace with natural mortality.

In Antarctic penguins the metabolic rate is reduced during incubation. Those spending long periods on the nest depend critically on the amount of their food reserves and must be allowed to consume this at the lowest possible rate if they are to last out their full stint. Disturbance can keep the metabolic rate high and so cause reserves to be consumed more quickly. Thus even the casual wandering of observers in colonies can do real damage.

W. J. L. Sladen

There are species differences in sensitivity to disturbance. Skuas seem less affected than Adélie penguins. Near the hut and helicopter landing site at Cape Crozier there were initially seventy-one pairs of skuas. Five years later, after 200 helicopter landings and 2400 man/days of field work, there are sixty-seven pairs.

One former territory was occupied by the hut, another by the helicopter port. The skuas sit tightly even when the draught from the helicopter ruffles their feathers.

E. C. YOUNG

There is always movement in an Adélie colony. Some birds move every 5 sec or so, and at no stage is the whole colony quiescent. Probably these birds are alert all the time. In contrast to the Crozier situation, the species at Cape Royds have suffered badly since human visits began, even after the early period when many birds were killed by ignorant people with an "anti-predator" bias.

SKUAS AND PENGUINS

E. D. RUDOLPH

To what extent is predation from immature skuas a factor in penguin colonies that Dr Young has studied?

E. C. YOUNG

The immature birds form a club which totals some 250 birds and is located in the northern end of the penguin colony area. They do take a few penguins, although they are very inefficient at killing penguin chicks. The remainder of the colony is fully taken up by the territories of breeding birds, and therefore is not available to the non-breeders. When next year we remove the breeding skua adults one of the first consequences we anticipate is that some of these immature birds will take up territories in their place.

B. TOLLU

I have seen the raised carpal joints in upright displays and have also seen intimidated upright displays among skuas at Kerguelen, in contrast to Mr Burton's record of their absence at Signy Island.

M. H. THURSTON

I would like to ask Mr Burton about the taxonomic state of northern and southern skuas. I myself have seen large dark skuas, presumably *lonnbergi*, associating with typical *maccormicki* at Halley Bay.

R. W. BURTON

I would prefer not to get involved in this subject, especially as I have not myself been further south than the South Orkney Islands.

R. CARRICK

I have discussed the matter with Vouus at Amsterdam. His general conclusion is that this is simply a super-species, if it is not just a single species. We need far more data on hybridization and variations in breeding behaviour. For the time being, however, Vouus is inclined to call the whole complex *Stercorarius skua* and regard all the forms as subspecies.

G. A. KNOX

Are there examples in the Antarctic where skuas do not nest in association with penguin colonies?

E. C. YOUNG

Certainly there are many such cases. There are some 1000 pairs of skuas in the general McMurdo Sound area and many of these are further south than Cape Royds and outside the range of distribution of the Adélie penguin.

A. W. ERICKSON

I was interested in Mr Burton's account of the response of an incubating skua to a bird passing by. Could this not be related to the time rather than the speed involved? A bird passing over on a straight flight might not have been observed by the time it had passed out of the territory, whereas a bird moving slowly and with irregular flight has a much greater chance of being noticed and responded to.

R. W. BURTON

The territories with which I was working were very large and the skuas habitually stood on raised places where they could overlook the territory and there was little chance of an intruding skua not being detected. Also, my hide was situated close to the birds. I could therefore see them and noted that they were showing awareness of intruders. The response was very much an individual matter and different birds behaved differently.

A. W. ERICKSON

Surely a skua that hovered in a territory is far more likely to attract a response than one that is passing rapidly?

R. W. BURTON

There is not all that difference in the time normally spent by a skua thus crossing a territory. In the one case we are dealing with direct flight, but the period of passage is of comparable duration.

BREEDING BIOLOGY OF ALBATROSSES

R. L. PENNEY

When Dr. Tickell removed 260-odd albatross eggs from the colony, was there then competition the following year when the dispossessed birds would be competing for breeding sites with those that would normally return to breed in that season?

W. L. N. TICKELL

We had this very much in mind when we did the experiment, and collected our eggs from the densest part of the colony. All the birds came back and all found sufficient room.

A. W. ERICKSON

Dr. Tickell's account of the breeding biology of the wandering albatross suggests that there is a similarity between this bird and certain mammals with altricial young where there is also inhibition of breeding while an immature animal is receiving care. Does this indicate that under steady-state conditions only 50% of the population would, in fact, be breeding.

W. L. N. TICKELL

Only 50% of the adults would be breeding if there was no loss of eggs or chicks.

A. W. ERICKSON

How are new breeding birds recruited to the population?

W. L. N. TICKELL

The reproductive cycle starts off on an annual basis. The first birds to return to the colony come back at 4 years old and they endeavour to breed in each year from that age onwards. Success is not usual before the age of 10. Adults who lose a mate also return each year and do not postpone their breeding unless there are offspring of the current mating.

R. CARRICK

There is an interesting population of wandering albatross at Macquarie, where the original birds were eaten out by sealers and castaways. In 1912 there was only one pair on the island. Now there are forty-four pairs and in each year additional birds return. Some 240–50 individuals have now been banded and the young birds that are returning to nest are slowly increasing the numbers. We find that breeding does not succeed before the age of 10 or even 11 or 12.

W. L. N. TICKELL

The youngest chick seen returning to the breeding ground on Bird Island was 4 years old. The oldest bird of known age to have returned when we left the island was 6 years old. By that time we had recovered 50% of the sample banded in our first year, but no chick up to 6 years old had succeeded in breeding. If albatrosses were strictly comparable with other birds, they would nest one year, miss the next, and so forth. In fact, the principle of regulation appears to be that they will lay a repeat clutch one year after an initial clutch has been destroyed. If the population is exploited therefore by the collection of eggs, it should be possible to maintain productivity at almost double that in an undisturbed population.

R. CARRICK

Three females on Macquarie Island regularly each lay two eggs, and yet since the brood patch is so small that only one egg can be brooded, they regularly lose these double clutches because both eggs get cold.